Thinking and
Problem Solving

Handbook of Perception and Cognition
2nd Edition

Series Editors
Edward C. Carterette
and **Morton P. Friedman**

Thinking and Problem Solving

Edited by
Robert J. Sternberg

Department of Psychology
Yale University
New Haven, Connecticut

Academic Press

San Diego   New York   Boston
London   Sydney   Tokyo   Toronto

This book is printed on acid-free paper. ∞

Academic Press
a division of Harcourt Brace & Company
525 B Street, Suite 1900, San Diego, California 92101-4495, USA
http://www.apnet.com

Academic Press Limited
24-28 Oval Road, London NW1 7DX, UK
http://www.hbuk.co.uk/ap/

Library of Congress Catalog Card Number: 94-4844
International Standard Book Number: 0-12-667260-1

PRINTED IN THE UNITED STATES OF AMERICA
98 99 00 01 02 03 BB 9 8 7 6 5 4 3 2 1

Contents

2 Contemporary Approaches to the Study of Thinking and Problem Solving

K. Anders Ericsson and Reid Hastie

3 Knowledge Representation

Timothy P. McNamara

4 *Concepts and Categories*
Brian H. Ross and Thomas L. Spalding

5 *Deduction and Its Cognitive Basis*
Lance J. Rips

6   *Inductive Reasoning*
Jeffery Bisanz, Gay L. Bisanz,
and Connie A. Korpan

7   *Problem Solving*
Earl Hunt

8 *Language and Thought*
Richard J. Gerrig and Mahzarin R. Banaji

9 *Intelligence*
Robert J. Sternberg

10 *Creativity*
Todd I. Lubart

11 *Development of Problem Solving*
Shari Ellis and Robert S. Siegler

12 *Cultural Dimensions of Cognition: A Multiplex, Dynamic System of Constraints and Possibilities*
Robert Serpell and A. Wade Boykin

13 *The Teaching of Thinking and Problem Solving*
Raymond S. Nickerson

Contributors

Numbers in parentheses indicate the pages on which the authors' contributions begin.

Mahzarin R. Banaji (233)
Psychology Department
Yale University
New Haven, Connecticut 06520

Gay L. Bisanz (179)
Department of Psychology
University of Alberta
Edmonton, Alberta, Canada T6G 2EP

Jeffrey Bisanz (179)
Department of Psychology
University of Alberta
Edmonton, Alberta, Canada T6G 2EP

Lyle E. Bourne, Jr. (1)
Department of Psychology
University of Colorado
Boulder, Colorado 80309

A. Wade Boykin (369)
Department of Psychology
Howard University
Washington, D.C. 20059

Roger L. Dominowski (1)
Department of Psychology
University of Illinois at Chicago
Chicago, Illinois 60607

S. Ellis (333)
Department of Psychology
Carnegie-Mellon University
Pittsburgh, Pennsylvania 15213

K. Anders Ericsson (37)
Department of Psychology
Florida State University
Tallahassee, Florida 32306

Richard J. Gerrig (233)[1]
Department of Psychology
Yale University
New Haven, Connecticut 06511

Reid Hastie (37)
Center for Research on Judgement
and Policy
University of Colorado at Boulder
Boulder, Colorado 80309

Earl Hunt (215)
Department of Psychology
University of Washington
Seattle, Washington 98195

Connie A. Korpan (179)
Department of Psychology
University of Alberta
Edmonton, Alberta, Canada T6G 2EP

Todd I. Lubart (289)
Department of Psychology
Yale University
New Haven, Connecticut 06520

Timothy P. McNamara (81)
Department of Psychology
Vanderbilt University
Nashville, Tennessee 37240

Raymond S. Nickerson (409)
Bedford, Massachusetts 01730

Lance J. Rips (149)
Department of Psychology
Northwestern University
Evanston, Illinois 60208

Brian H. Ross (119)
Beckman Institute
University of Illinois
Urbana, Illinois 61801

Robert Serpell (369)
Department of Psychology
University of Maryland
Baltimore, Maryland 21228

Robert S. Siegler (333)
Psychology Department
Carnegie-Mellon University
Pittsburgh, Pennsylvania 15213

Thomas L. Spalding (119)
Beckman Institute
University of Illinois
Urbana, Illinois 61801

Robert J. Sternberg (263)
Department of Psychology
Yale University
New Haven, Connecticut 06520

[1] *Present address:*Department of Psychology, State University of New York at Stony Brook, Stony Brook, New York 11794.

Foreword

The problem of perception and cognition is understanding how the organism transforms, organizes, stores, and uses information arising from the world in sense data or memory. With this definition of perception and cognition in mind, this handbook is designed to bring together the essential aspects of this very large, diverse, and scattered literature and to give a precis of the state of knowledge in every area of perception and cognition. The work is aimed at the psychologist, the cognitive scientist in particular, and at the natural scientist in general. Topics are covered in comprehensive surveys in which fundamental facts and concepts are presented, and important leads to journals and monographs of the specialized literature are provided. Perception and cognition are considered in the widest sense. Therefore, the work will treat a wide range of experimental and theoretical work.

The *Handbook of Perception and Cognition* should serve as a basic source and reference work for those in the arts or sciences, indeed for all who are interested in human perception, action, and cognition.

Edward C. Carterette and Morton P. Friedman

Preface

How do people predict the future on the basis of past events? How do they solve complex problems, whether in mathematics or in everyday life? How do they come up with new ideas that seemingly differ from all of the ideas to which they have been exposed? These are the kinds of questions addressed in this volume, whose goal is to provide an up-to-date yet historically grounded review of the psychological literature on thinking and problem solving.

This volume covers most of the topics that historically form the foundation of the field; however, it does not, of course, cover every topic that might conceivably be included. For example, topics such as expertise and mental models are covered in the context of several chapters, but these topics are not addressed in individual chapters because they are not viewed as playing the same key, long-term roles historically as the other topics that were chosen. For example, decision making has a key, long-term historical presence, but it is covered in other volumes.

Chapter 1, entitled "History of Research on Thinking and Problem Solving," is an overview. In their review, Dominowski and Bourne trace the origins of thinking about thinking to its philosophical roots in ancient Greece and show how this thinking evolved through various psychological schools of thought, such as associationism, structuralism, and functionalism. The major part of their review ends with coverage of ideas until 1960, when the modern cognitive revolution began. Chapter 2 and the remainder of this book are based on the modern cognitive revolution.

In Chapter 2, "Contemporary Approaches to the Study of Thinking and Problem Solving," Ericsson and Hastie briefly review the earlier history of the field, and then they concentrate on major contemporary topics, such as the information-processing account of thinking, the relation between thinking in the laboratory and thinking in everyday life, and the acquisition of complex knowledge and skills, especially with regard to how novices become experts. The general overview of the field sets the stage for the other, more narrowly focused, chapters of the book.

Chapter 3, "Knowledge Representation," describes the major models in cognitive psychology and how information is represented. In this chapter, McNamara considers topics such as the nature of knowledge representations, analogical representations, symbolic representations, and procedural representations (such as production systems). McNamara reviews the fundamental research supporting, and in some cases, tending to undermine, the validity of each type of representation.

Chapter 4, "Concepts and Categories," reviews the literature on how people classify and categorize the concepts, objects, and experiences they encounter in their lives. Ross and Spalding compare alternative views of classification—including classical, probabilistic, exemplar, and mixed models—and discuss the evidence for and against each position. The authors also discuss the notion of theory-based conceptual knowledge and consider current directions in which the field of concepts and categories is moving.

In Chapter 5, "Deduction and Its Cognitive Basis," Rips opens with a consideration of just what is deductive reasoning. He continues by showing how deductive reasoning can be understood psychologically. Reviewed in some detail are alternative accounts that might be described as pattern-processing theories, including diagrammatic and connectionist accounts. In this chapter, Rips essentially bypasses the traditional accounts such as atmosphere and conversion, which describe effects rather than provide models of how people reason deductively.

In Chapter 6, "Inductive Reasoning," Bisanz, Bisanz, and Korpan review the literature, consider what inductive reasoning is, and consider the two main approaches of study, which the authors refer to as the cognitive-components approach and the pragmatic approach. The former approach attempts to isolate components of information processing in inductive reasoning, whereas the latter approach concentrates more on the roles of knowledge, content, and context. The authors suggest how the two approaches can be seen as complementary to each other rather than being seen in opposition.

Chapter 7, "Problem Solving," reviews the literature and considers the relation of problem solving to reasoning. In his chapter, Hunt traces some of the early history of research in this area and then considers modern research on topics such as problem-solving heuristics (including means–

ends analysis, backward problem solving, and forward problem solving), schematic thinking, and domain-specific problem solving.

Chapter 8, "Language and Thought," by Gerrig and Banaji, revisits the Sapir-Whorf hypothesis (that language determines or at least strongly influences thought) and reviews research relevant to these claims, including research on color, memory, and on counterfactual reasoning. The authors consider various other topics as well, such as conceptual metaphors, language acquisition, and bilingualism.

Chapter 9, "Intelligence," by Sternberg reviews four main approaches to studying intelligence: biological, cognitive, contextual, and systematic. The relation of each of these approaches both to thinking in general and to each other is considered, and it is argued that each approach deals with a somewhat distinctive set of questions about intelligence. Thus, the argument rejects reductionistic notions, which suggest that all theory and research about intelligence ultimately ought to be reduced to a biological level.

Chapter 10, "Creativity," by Lubart, considers how creativity is defined and moves on to a discussion of topics such as the distribution of creativity and the extent to which creativity is domain specific. Part of the chapter is devoted to presenting alternative approaches to creativity, such as the cognitive approach, the social-psychological approach, and the confluence approach. The chapter also examines the various components of creativity as well as alternative means for measuring creativity.

Chapter 11, "Development of Problem Solving," reviews the literature on early-problem solving and then moves on to consider later-problem solving. Ellis and Siegler consider a number of topics, such as representational development, self-regulation, and the role of schooling.

In Chapter 12, "Cultural Dimensions of Cognition: A Multiplex, Dynamic System of Constraints and Possibilities," Serpell and Boykin consider the dimensions of cognition that are susceptible to cultural influence, aspects of cultural context, processes of bicultural mediation, and educational implications of the role of culture. They also review some specific studies that help shed light on the relation of culture to cognition.

In Chapter 13, "The Teaching of Thinking and Problem Solving," Nickerson discusses why we need to teach thinking and problem solving, and why people have been interested in the teaching of these constructs; it then continues with a consideration of methods and programs for teaching thinking and problem solving. The chapter is a fitting end to the volume because it shows that interventions can work, so that virtually anyone can increase the facility with which they think and solve problems.

CHAPTER 1

History of Research on Thinking and Problem Solving

Roger L. Dominowski
Lyle E. Bourne, Jr.

It is difficult to decide where to begin any history, because no matter where you start there are always obvious antecedents. This is no less true of the field of psychological inquiry known as thinking than it is of any other area or issue. We choose to start in the relatively recent past, two to three hundred years ago, where we find most of the important immediate precursors of a formal and independent experimental approach to human thought.

I. MAJOR ANTECEDENTS OF THE SCIENCE OF PSYCHOLOGY

The two problems that characterize the modern psychology of thinking are *mental representation* and *mental computation*. The general idea is that thinking is something internal or cognitive rather than behavioral. This means that thinking goes on more or less invisibly and that we have no direct observational access to it. That idea is debatable (see Bourne, Ekstrand, & Dominowski, 1971), but we will accept it as a given in light of its current popularity. As an invisible something that goes on internally, then, psychologists have to worry about both the structure and the function of thinking, the problems of representation and computation. Thinking is performed on versions of the external world called representations existing somewhere (most presume within the brain) within the organism. Thinking also entails operations or processes that work to change or to augment these representations, the functional or computational aspect of thought. Even the earliest efforts to understand human thought, in philosophy and other domains of inquiry, spoke to either or both of these issues of representation and computation (Dellarosa, 1988).

A. Associationism

Associationism was perhaps the first movement within science and philosophy to capture in a formal sense the problems of representation and computation. According to Associationism, the world is represented within us by ideas and our behavior is guided by associations formed among these ideas. But this is getting a little ahead of the game. We begin by noting that Associationism is by far the most important precursor of the scientific psychology of thinking. It is a tradition that extends as far back as Aristotle. But we are more concerned with the associationistic doctrine developed by the empiricist moral philosophers of Great Britain in the seventeenth and eighteenth century. We will pick up the tradition first in the writings of the English philosopher John Locke, who characterized psychology as the study of the mind or mental life. The mind represents the world as a network of ideas, connected to one another through experience. The idea is the irreducible representational unit of human thought. It represents meaning, knowledge, and abstraction. Anything that the human mind can comprehend is represented by a complex of ideas. This complex, in turn, can be analyzable into its component elemental ideas. This empiricism in Locke's position comes from his insistence that ideas are not innate, but rather arise through experience (Boring, 1950). Indeed, like Aristotle, Locke viewed the human mind without experience as a blank slate (from Aristotle, a Tabula Rasa). Experience inscribes its message on this slate. Experience leaves traces of itself as ideas. Simple ideas bind together, by association, into more complex ones. The level of complexity and interrelatedness among ideas grows from childhood through adulthood, again by experience. Simple ideas are elemental and unanalyzable, the irreducible units of the mind. The process of association, a simple computational process, allows the same simple idea to enter into a variety of relationships with other ideas to form more complex entities.

According to Locke there are two experiential sources of simple ideas. First, ideas arise from our senses as they detect energy changes in the world. A second source of ideas is the mind itself, through reflection upon its own activity. Thus, the mind is capable of being conscious of its own content and processes, an assumption that stands at the basis of a soon-to-be-developed experimental method known as *introspection*. Because the mind is essentially independent of overt behavior, the only way its activity could be known is through an individual's ability to describe it, and this presumes some degree of awareness of mental representation and/or computation.

Associations are formed between or among ideas according to certain principles. These principles were implicit in the writings of Locke, but later philosophers like George Berkeley, David Hume, and David Hartley further developed and widely publicized them, turning Associationism into a formal philosophical doctrine (Hothersall, 1990). Among the many principles that were assumed to govern the association of ideas, several have stood the test of time and data, continuing to service interpretations of mental phenomena even today. These principles include (1) *contiguity*, two ideas that occur together in time or in space tend to be associated or linked; (2) *similarity*, the more similar two ideas are, the greater their chance of being associated; and (3) *repetition*, the more often two ideas occur together, the greater the strength of their association. Associationists attempted to capture the entirety of mental life. That is, the development of the mind follows a course established in the experience of an organism, proceeding from idea to idea according to how these ideas have been associated in the past. Thought processes, then, were characterized by a train or sequence of ideas, progressing from those stimulated by a sensory experience through those that produce some sort of activity by the organism.

The development of philosophical Associationism reached its apex in the mid-nineteenth century. James Mill, and his son John Stuart Mill, both British philosophers, brought associationism to the brink of an experimental psychology. The senior Mill distinguished between sensations and ideas as fundamental classes of elements in the mind. Sensations, he proposed, are the primary elements of consciousness from which ideas, which are pure abstractions, are derived. The processes of association pertain to ideas, with contiguity being the basic principle. Possibly the most relevant point to the soon-to-be established science of psychology was Mill's discussion of the strength of associations between or among ideas and his suggestion of possible measures of strength. Although not a scientific researcher himself, Mill provided some important leads for later scientists interested in mental processes. Mill's criteria of strength are not unfamiliar to the modern researcher: (1) *permanence*, the more persistent an association over time, the greater its initial strength; (2) *certainty*, the more confident the individual of an association, the greater the strength; and (3) *facility*, the greater the speed and effortlessness with which an association arises, the greater its strength. Modern researchers interested in long-term memory, recognition confidence and the feeling of knowing, and fluency will recognize Mill's criteria.

In addition to methodological issues, however, Mill addressed certain theoretical matters. One need only elaborate slightly on Mill's definition of an idea to produce the modern concept of a mediator, a symbol, or a symbolic process. Today we recognize that sensation or stimulus input triggers internal symbolic or mediating processes. Mill called these ideas. For the modern theorist, the mediator intervenes between input and eventual action. There is nothing in Mill's proposal that directly links the idea with resultant behavior, although the step is rather obvious. Second, Mill's conception of a complex idea, as an additive compounding of simpler ones through association, is the essence of many modern hierarchical conceptions of meaning and of the structure of memory.

John Stuart Mill differed from earlier associationists in his insistence that complex ideas can actually be different from an additive mixture of simpler elements. He suggested that simple ideas lose their identity when they enter into a compound and can produce a molar thought that, as the Gestalt psychologists were later to argue, is different from the sum of its individual parts. The argument is not unlike mental representations of well-integrated sets or series of individual stimuli or responses in modern cognitive psychology [see, e.g., the compilation process of Anderson (1990, 1987) in ACT*]. For Mill, this possibility necessitated something more than analysis into parts if one is to understand the mind fully. The researcher, according to J. S. Mill, ought to study complex ideas in and of themselves as well as simpler constituent elements.

B. Faculties of the Mind

British Associationism takes us, in time, to the very beginnings of experimental psychology. But before we describe this work, we return briefly to the seventeenth century to pick up a philosophical position on mental activity that was nonassociational in nature. A major source of competition for Associationism, within philosophy, was provided by a group of intellectuals who became known collectively as the Scottish School of philosophy (Boring, 1950). Members of the Scottish School conceptualized the mind not as a set of ideas or representations of the world but as a set of faculties, powers, or computational capacities that operate on incoming sensations. Their major objection to Associationism was its emphasis on elementary elements, which among other things appeared to violate the orthodox religious notions of the unity of mind and soul prominent at the time. Thomas Reid was the earliest important representative of the Scottish tradition, his most relevant writings appearing in the last half of the seventeenth century. He describes some thirty powers of the mind, such as self-preservation, pity, imagination, judgment, and memory, which are said to form the computational basis of all mental activity.

As time passed, faculty psychology drew closer to Associationism. Thomas Brown, writing in the eighteenth century, thought it necessary to invoke the principle of association or representation, along with faculties, to account for the succession of thoughts that seem to be typical of mental life. Brown is commonly given credit for being the first philosopher to treat explicitly and rigorously the secondary or specific laws of association. He was concerned primarily with questions about why one idea occurs in consciousness when several seem possible. He proposed a series of laws that guided associational processes and accounted for the finer differentiations among ideas. Among these were relative frequency, recency, and vividness; within a set of alternative ideas, the one that stands highest on these scales will tend to occur. We should note that all of these concepts are familiar in the modern study of human thought. By the time of Brown and John Stuart Mill, all the basic theoretical ideas that characterize the modern psychology of thought were reasonably well known and written about within philosophy. The time had come to find a way to examine these ideas scientifically.

II. AN EXPERIMENTAL PSYCHOLOGY OF THINKING

A. Thinking According to Wundt

In any historical account of psychology, no matter what the area of interest, it is difficult to avoid discussing the work of Wilhelm Wundt. Wundt is generally credited with founding the "new science" of psychology, partly because his was the first laboratory devoted explicitly to the study of psychological phenomena and partly because he was the first to develop and publicize a systematic, concerted program of research (Wundt, 1912). Wundt was tireless, prolific, and deeply committed to his work. While his laboratory at Leipzig, Germany was not formally established until 1879, his writing about psychology began to appear as early as the 1860s. The philosophy that guided Wundt and most of his students from 1880 on had been fairly well formulated prior to that time by the associationists and other philosophers.

1. Dualism

Wundt was a dualist. He argued for the separation of mind and body. The mental world, for Wundt, is the world of experience, that is, the world as we know it, represent it, and are consciously aware of it. Although events in the physical world might parallel those in the mental world, they do not interact or exert any mutual causal influence. Wundt took it to be the task of scientific psychology to understand the structure and the processes of the mind, employing very much the same explanatory models and methods as the natural sciences. He adopted as the proper approach to this study the method of trained *introspection*. Because of its emphasis on the structure of mental representation, the name Structuralism, coined by Titchener, one of Wundt's most prominent students, is often used in reference to work in this tradition.

Research emanating from Wundt's laboratory had three distinct phases: first, an attempt to analyze conscious experience, as reported by trained introspectionists, into its building-block elements; second, an exploration of the attributes of those elements in an effort to determine their function and their role in associational processes; third, the intense introspective study of associations in hopes of uncovering fundamental principles about how they are formed and how they function. Only one kind of psychological explanation was acceptable to Wundt. Complex events and processes are to be understood in terms of simpler ones of which they are composed. Obviously, Wundt was strongly influenced by the empiricist–associationist movement in England.

2. Structuralism versus Associationism

Despite certain similarities, there were basic differences between Structuralism and Associationism. Wundt brought to psychology the techniques of science. He was convinced of the need for and of the adequacy of introspective experimentation as a means of understanding the human mind. He sought to find the true irreducible elements of the mind through this technique, beginning with the study of sensory processes. He thought this work revealed a variety of mental elements including *sensations,* the primary data of consciousness, *images,* the purely mental counterparts of sense data, and *feelings,* a kind of affective constituent of the mind. Although the emphasis was on structure, Wundt described the mind as an active computational mechanism. He accepted the laws of associations, as formulated by the British associationists, as descriptive of this activity.

3. The Nature of Thinking

The bulk of research in Wundt's laboratory dealt with sensory and perceptual processes. There was, in addition, some research on related problems like the span of attention and response times to various forms of stimulation. Little emphasis was placed on more complex mental processes, including memory and thinking. Wundt himself ruled out higher mental processes in his laboratory because he considered them inaccessible to introspection. To study the mind, the observer must know what to watch for and focus on. Thought processes, according to Wundt, are too complex and irregular. They lack stability, and, for that reason, cannot be introspected. Thoughts are considered sufficiently regular only when they can be eternalized and agreed to by consensus, as in a society. Thinking, according to Wundt, is a kind of social psychological problem best studied naturalistically.

   Wundt seemed to be saying that one must approach thought through the investigation of social and cultural processes, involving naturalistic and historical investigation. Introspective laboratory studies are simply incapable of yielding anything meaningful about thought. While such an argument is unjustified in the modern view, still Structuralism continued to represent an important force in psychology through the first decade or two of the twentieth century, until the rise of Behaviorism in America. Fortunately, some of Wundt's students and contemporaries did not rigidly adhere to his pronouncements on the nature of higher mental processes. The scientific study of thinking began elsewhere only shortly after the establishment of Wundt's laboratory.

B. Thinking According to Ebbinghaus

On the empirical side prior to 1900, one need be concerned with the efforts of only one researcher, Hermann Ebbinghaus. Ebbinghaus was not unaware of Wundt's dictum declaring the inaccessibility of higher mental processes to experimentation. Still, he undertook a prodigious program of research on memory, using the most rigorous of experimental techniques. His work was motivated more by the writings of a psychophysicist, Gustav Theodor Fechner, than by those of Wundt.

Ebbinghaus was an innovator. There was no precedent for his kind of experiment. He set for himself the task of studying how associations are formed between words and wordlike elements. In the process, he developed measurement techniques, experimental procedures, and learning materials that not only were original but continued to be used widely well after his death. Indeed, we can see evidence of these techniques in modern cognitive psychology. Bothered by the strong possibility that any meaningful verbal material would already be highly associated with other material in the mind through past experience, he invented a verbal unit known as the nonsense syllable, typically three letters in consonant–vowel–consonant order, which constitute neither prefix, suffix, nor word. Learning associations between or among these items, Ebbinghaus reasoned, would be less affected or contaminated by past experience than would those between series of meaningful words.

Ebbinghaus developed several methods of presenting materials and testing for the strength of learned associations and their retention through time. With these techniques, he was able to demonstrate several important principles of memory still recognized today. For example, he showed the effectiveness of repetition or frequency of items as a determinant both of association strength and of retention. He studied variables such as number of items to be learned for their influence on time to learn. He demonstrated the apparent existence not only of direct associations between successive items in a list to be learned but also of remote associations between nonadjacent items and backward association between items and their predecessors in a list. Perhaps his most famous finding was the classical "forgetting curve" showing the decline of association strength over a time interval devoid of practice. Ebbinghaus's program of research was presented in a monograph, *On Memory*, which first appeared in 1885, only six years after the founding of Wundt's Leipzig laboratory. What is perhaps even more remarkable is that Ebbinghaus's efforts were accomplished without the benefit of a laboratory and with the services of only a single subject, Ebbinghaus himself.

Although he is no doubt best known in psychology for his study of memory and for the path he opened to rigorous investigation of higher mental processes, Ebbinghaus had extensive other interests. Among his related contributions was the development of a test of verbal intelligence, only slightly after the pioneer work of Binet and Simon.

III. LATER DEVELOPMENTS

A. Act Psychology

Structuralism was not the only scientific approach to psychology, even before the turn of the century. Possibly the most influential of other approaches, in historical perspective, was Act Psychology. Act psychologists questioned the structuralists' emphasis on elements and on the static structure of the conscious mind, that is, their emphasis on representation. They argue that psychologists might more profitably study mental function, that is, the directed, ongoing activities of the mind, which we have called computation and which are not always conscious. In contrast to Wundt, act psychologists de-emphasized associationistic principles, supplementing them with more complex organizational processes. They attempted to change the focus of research from "thought" to "thinking," from representation to computation.

1. The Würzburg School of Act Psychology

Act Psychologists were unwilling to exclude thought from laboratory study. Oswald Külpe (see e.g., Külpe, 1893) was a pioneer in this tradition. In the early years of the twentieth century, Külpe and his students at Würzburg reported a series of introspective studies on the mental activity accompanying controlled association and judgment. Subjects were asked to describe any and all mental events interceding, for example, between the presentation of a stimulus word, say, "black," and a response required by the task, which might be to say its opposite, "white," or its category, "color." Responses to even these simple problems were not automatic but rather required intervening mediational or computational activity. The initial experiments in this series raised questions about whether all important components of thought are conscious and fit neatly into the traditional structuralist categories of elements. Introspective and retrospective descriptions by subjects of the content of consciousness during the time between problem presentation and response often revealed a richness of sensations and images far greater than a structuralist would expect. Rather than being rationally composed and a simple sum total of elemental sensations, the mind's content appeared to be clearly directed in an organized way toward the solution. This "determining tendency" or "set" eventually generated a solution to the problem posed.

2. Logic, Reasoning, and Imageless Thought

Külpe's evidence seemed to contradict the commonly accepted notion that human thinking and reasoning can be fully described in terms of rationally or logically associated constituent elements. It also questioned the notion that fundamentals of thinking are conscious and associatively connected. Although critics argued that not all mental content was reported by subjects in these experiments, the repeatability of the Würzburg findings strongly implied that thinking is at least in part unconscious and imageless, yet goal directed and processlike.

Wundt never accepted the evidence from Würzburg, claiming that introspection as a technique is useless for studying unpredictable mental processes. The subject, no matter how well trained, is simply unable to focus attention in advance, as required by introspection, on the significant phenomena of thought involved in consciousness. E. B. Titchener, a Wundt-trained experimental psychologist who dominated psychology in the United States in the early part of this century, was willing to accept some of these findings, but argued that the imageless and unconscious aspects of thought reported by subjects in the Würzburg laboratory are in reality the associated context or meanings of sensory or imaginal events. Titchener championed a context theory, which held that the meaning of any idea derives from a background or context of associated ideas, some conscious, some unconscious. The results of Külpe's experiments, then, were not able to settle the issue of consciousness in thought, but they did show the inadequacy of introspection and of Structuralism to account for certain important psychological phenomena.

3. Determining Tendencies

The more positive contribution of these studies was to point up the important role of motivation in thought and in behavior in general (Boring, 1950). H. P. Watt, one of Külpe's students, noted that the time needed to complete even the simplest thought problems might be long enough to introduce contamination into introspection. That is, it is possible that a subject will not report all conscious experience because some of it passes from short-term memory before it can be described. To minimize these effects, Watt devised a divided problem methodology. Problems were separated into four periods: (1) *preparation,* during which the subject is given instruction as to the type of response required, for example, "give an association which is subordinate to the stimulus word"; (2) *presentation* of the stimulus word, for example, "animal"; (3) the subject's *search* for a proper response; and (4) the *response* itself, for example, "horse." The subject was asked to introspect on only one of these periods in successive problems. With this technique, Watt discovered that period 3 was often devoid of conscious representational content, the response occurring in an automatic or direct retrieval fashion. By far the greatest amount of representational content was reported in period 1. Thus, conscious thinking, according to these data, takes place in advance of the actual problem, which begins with the presentation of the stimulus. The purpose, task, or *Aufgabe* in German, is established during period 1, allowing the remainder of the thought process to proceed uninterrupted and largely on an unconscious level. In a continuation of this line of research, Narziss Ach, another student of Külpe, argued that the *Aufgabe* gives rise to unconscious *determining tendencies* or a priming effect that governs the course of thought and behavior. Ach set the stage for what is accepted almost universally in modern cognitive psychology, the unity of thinking and acting. According to Ach, the determining tendency or priming supplied during the preparation period potentiates a certain set of associations, so that when a stimulus actually arrives, the subject's response is constrained to a certain subset of associations that are allowable under the *Aufgabe*.

4. Timing Mental Events

The mid-nineteenth century had seen the development of precise techniques for measuring the speed of human reaction to environmental events. From the notion of a personal equation employed by astronomers to correct for individual human differences in the recording to celestial events came a mental chronometry (Boring, 1950), or a system for measuring the time characteristics of the mind. F. C. Donders, a Dutch psychologist, constructed the system on the assumption that the duration of mental events can be computed from the difference between simple reaction time and speed of reactions in situations that require some intervening mental process (see also Wundt, 1912). For example, to measure the time to make a mental discrimination, an experimenter would determine both the speed of reaction to a single stimulus, such as light onset, and the speed of reaction in a task requiring the subject to respond to only one of two or more distinct stimuli. In the second task, the subject must discriminate between or among the stimuli before responding. If one further assumes that the second task involves the compounding in an additive fashion of two events, discrimination plus simple reaction, then it follows that time for discrimination is the difference between the response times in the two tasks. By similar reasoning, procedures were developed for measuring other mental events such as choice, association, judgment, and the like.

Mental chronometry is based on plausible assumptions. In practice, how-ever, experimenters had to contend with a great deal of variability in their reaction-time data, variability not only between subjects but also within the same subjects from time to time. Moreover, it became clear that reaction times of any sort are subject to influence by practice, fatigue, attention, distraction, and other factors. In addition, Külpe pointed out that adding components to the simple reaction time situation does more than introduce another step in the chain of mental events intervening between stimulus and response. The effect of these additional components is to change the task in substantive ways. More specifically, the nature of the task, as described for the subject in preliminary instructions, establishes a preparatory set. Each task produces a different set or a predisposition to respond. The important differences between simple and other reactions were not found in the num-ber of separable mental components but rather in the events preceding the stimulus. Furthermore, Külpe was unable to find any counterpart of dis-crimination, choice, and the like in the introspective reports of subjects serving in these tasks. It is important to keep in mind that Külpe's criticism does not bear directly on the procedures or measurement of reaction time, but rather on the interpretation of the effects of certain variables on these times. As a matter of fact, the results of early experiments hold up excep-tionally well, and even today, reaction-time methodology is an important tool in the repertoire of experimental psychologists who study cognition.

B. Early British Psychology

American experimental psychology was shaped largely by events in Ger-many, many researchers having received their formal training in Wundt's laboratory. To understand American psychology fully, however, it is im-portant to recognize some of the early work going on in Great Britain.

1. Darwin and Evolution

One key idea for psychology, which derives directly from Darwin (1909) and the theory of evolution, is the denial of a separate creation for each of the various species of animals and the acceptance of phylogenetic develop-ment and continuity. The idea is that human beings, like other complex species, evolved from simpler organisms and that human anatomy, physiol-ogy, and behavior are in many ways a product of an evolutionary process that produces increasing complexity and differentiation in animal form. One can, therefore, expect to find structural and functional similarities among the species. This notion was instrumental in focusing attention on and developing a comparative psychology. Indeed, the study of thinking and behavior in lower animals has helped significantly to define the general nature of human symbolic processes.

The second important notion from evolutionary theory is that organisms are, to a degree, able to adapt to environmental requirements. That organism which is best equipped to change or to fit into a wide variety of conditions is best able to survive and to perpetuate its form and species. This principle helped to bring into focus the important relationship between biological structure and psychological function.

2. Individual Differences

Francis Galton (1874), the great British naturalist, spent many years studying the capacities of human beings to adapt. Of his many contributions, three seem particularly significant for American psychology. First, Galton created a variety of tests of human mental capacity, focusing on human performance rather than intangible mental events. Second, his results underlined the importance of individual variations and differences among human beings, moving psychology away from its formerly exclusive focus on the "generalized mind." Third, Galton developed some genuinely original quantitative techniques for the description and the analysis of behavior. Each of these contributions had a significant legacy in the development of modern cognitive psychology.

IV. THE PSYCHOLOGY OF THINKING IN AMERICA

Despite their hard-line training in the German tradition, early American psychologists quickly picked up on the leads of Darwin and Galton. Except for Titchener's group, early American psychology was more functional or process oriented than it was structural or representation oriented. What this means, in brief, is that early American psychologists were more concerned with the whys and hows of consciousness and behavior than with the whats. Emphasis was placed on the functional significance of the mind, on its role in the adaptation of the organism to the environment, and on its properties as a mechanism that encompasses or controls behavior.

A. William James

Although most of his significant writing in psychology was published before the turn of the century, William James's ideas are remarkably contemporary. James was not really an experimental psychologist and conducted no experiments of significance. Rather he was a theorist and a systematizer. His fundamental position on psychology was set forth in a classic book entitled *Principles of Psychology* (1890). In this work, James described the mind as an array of functions and consciousness as a dynamic stream of interacting events (with no rigid structure). He characterized psychology, in general, as the study of adaptive processes before the advent of functionalism as an American school of psychology. James was a pragmatist. He attempted to explain both behavior and consciousness through the concept of mind as a quasi-biological organ whose function(s) can be used for environmental adaptation. Other than its greater intricacy, abstractness, and complexity, the mind is no different from any other bodily structure such as the heart or the lungs, all of which play vital roles in organismic functioning. The mind, according to James, has evolved in human beings to a point where its functions are more versatile and pervasive than those of any other single organ. While it was often said that James contributed primarily to the establishment of a functionalistic tradition in American psychology, it is easy to detect his influence in Behaviorism, Gestalt psychology, and modern information-processing theories of cognition.

B. Functionalism

Functionalism was never a cohesive system, in the same way that Structuralism was under Titchener. Rather it represented a kind of protest against Structuralism and its insistence on the exclusive study of consciousness and elementism. Functionalism was led mainly by William James and John Dewey (of the University of Chicago). James's principles were the foundation of Functionalism, but these were embellished by the insights and observations of Dewey and others who quickly picked up the theme.

1. The Significance of Consciousness

Obvious as it might be to the modern student of psychology that learning, memory, motivation, problem solving, and the like are basic processes in human behavior, these were simply not widely recognized as important topics of investigation before 1900. Relying largely on common sense, functionalists argued for the study of more real-life-like and less highly structured psychological tasks. They promoted behavior in these tasks to equal status with consciousness as the focus of psychological investigation. They opened up areas of research in comparative psychology, child psychology, and individual differences and showed the important possibilities of applying psychological principles to education and other practical problems.

The importance of consciousness was not disputed by functionalists, but its position as the primary problem for psychology was. Consciousness was treated by the functionalists much as mediators and symbolic processes are treated in modern psychological theory. That is, the role of consciousness is as a set of events and processes intervening between environment and reaction. This principle, coupled with the general idea that the function and purpose of mind and behavior are matters to be explained, diminished the importance of dualism, the separation of mind and body.

2. Dewey's Theory of Thinking

According to Dewey (1910), thinking is a multistaged, goal-oriented process with the following characteristics: (1) recognition of a problem, or a "felt difficulty"; (2) location and definition of the problem and the isolation of its relevant features; (3) formulation of possible alternative solutions; (4) mulling over or reasoning through the various possibilities to determine the most likely candidate solution; and (5) testing the selected solution possibility. One clearly recognizes in this analysis many of the stages and processes that are the focus of research on problem solving even today, including categorization, coding, decision making, judgment, and the like. Inherent in this description is a stagelike analysis of thought, which was later refined by Graham Wallas, based on a survey of anecdotal evidence on the symbolic processes of creative scientists. According to Wallas (1926), the four stages of creative acts are: (1) *preparation,* or the collection and assembly of problem-relevant information; (2) *incubation,* a mulling over period; (3) *illumination* or insight, the conception of a solution; and (4) *verification* that the solution actually works.

C. Later Functionalism

While functionalism might have gained its initial notoriety in the work of researchers at the University of Chicago, focus moved in the early years of this century to Columbia University where Cattell, Woodworth, and Thorndike came together.

E. L. Thorndike pioneered the experimental study of animal behavior and intelligence (1911). His studies of cats in puzzle boxes will be described in more detail later. These studies and other observations with human beings and animals led Thorndike to formulate a mechanistic theory of learning, some principles of which are central even to modern behavior theory. For example, he concluded that learning and problem solving are, in general, gradual processes based on the increasing strength of the connection between the stimulus situation and certain response possibilities. The connection between stimulus and response strengthens according to two basic laws, namely, the law of repetition or *exercise* and the law of *effect*. The latter principle bears a strong resemblance to the modern-day principle of reinforcement. It states, in brief, that an act or response that is followed by a pleasurable state of affairs tends to become associated with the stimulus situation effective at the time of its occurrence. Conversely, the connection between a response that is followed by an annoying state of affairs and the stimulus to which it occurs tends to be weakened.

Thorndike wrote as if he were convinced that animal behavior is not mediated by ideas or symbolic processes. Responses are linked directly to the stimulus situation as it is sensed by the subject. Because the data of experiments with human subjects often appeared similar in form to those of animals, Thorndike was led to believe that essentially the same learning principles are fundamental among all species. His simplifying assumption has been questioned by most researchers of human thinking in later years.

D. Behaviorism

John B. Watson (1924) was trained as a functionalist but rejected the functionalist assumption that consciousness is essential to the interpretation of human behavior. For the functionalist, behavior is an indicator of the underlying state or representation and process or computation of the organism's mind. Watson's system, called Behaviorism, placed behavior or performance at the focus of attention, and made it the primary or sole datum of psychology. Behaviorists claimed that there is no point in trying to understand the inaccessible and possibly nonexistent consciousness when the real data of psychology are open, observable, and available to direct measurement. Inferred conscious states and processes are excess baggage, according to Watson. Knowledge of the regularities of performance is all that a psychologist really needs to be concerned with.

It is difficult to resolve the extreme Watsonian position with the intuitively obvious fact that much of animal and human behavior is symbolic and unaccompanied by gross motor movement. In fairness, it should be said that Watson did not deny either the existence or the importance of symbolic events. He merely refused to conceive or to speak of them as mentalistic entities, such as images or feelings. Watson even balked at Thorndike's early law of effect because it attributed feelings of satisfaction or annoyance to an organism. Rather, Watson attempted to translate states of consciousness into behaviors. Feelings, images, thoughts and the like are units of covert behavior, which, if we knew when, where, and how to look, would be found to be just as recordable and reliable as grosser forms of movement.

According to Watson, we should eventually find out that much of what is considered mentalistic is in reality implicit or miniaturized motor activity, largely in the voice mechanism. Words are responses we have learned to apply to objects and events in the environment. They can be called symbols, in the sense that they represent things that they themselves are not. We can, then, think of these objects or events in terms of their verbal counterparts. When we "think to ourselves" about them, we are merely suppressing the overt verbal response of naming to a point where it becomes difficult or impossible for others to detect. But with appropriately sensitive recording and measuring equipment, we should find evidence of them in tiny laryngeal movements. Thus, according to Watson, much of what we call thinking is subaudible speech. This idea is sometimes called the motor theory of thinking, which places the accent on muscular or glandular changes rather than on central or ideational changes.

Throughout the period of the 1920s and 30s, a series of experiments was conducted on muscular activity in the vocal apparatus and elsewhere to test Watson's idea that these activities are present during tasks that normally require thought (see Woodworth & Schlosberg, 1954). For example, Jacobson (1930) reported that, when relaxed subjects were instructed to imagine certain events or actions, their thoughts were almost invariably accompanied by patterns of electrical activity recorded from particular muscular loci associated with the imaging process. When a subject was instructed to think of flexing the right forearm, electrical signals of muscular activity were picked up from that arm but not from the left. When asked to imagine the Eiffel Tower, electrodes on the subject's brow gave evidence of incipient up–down scanning movements of the eyes. Jacobson's results seem to indicate clearly that specific patterns of muscular activity accompany and correlate with the content of thought processes. Freeman (1931) reported other experiments that indicated that elementary mental activities such as adding numbers mentally or completing a jigsaw puzzle could be facilitated by inducing an increase in generalized muscular tone in the subject.

Thus it appears that there are muscular (especially vocal) correlates of thinking. It might be that mental activity is in some sense dependent on some specific muscular tonus. But the evidence has not been sufficient to convince all psychologists that thought and action are identical or that thought can be represented completely by patterns of peripheral activity. In fact, the muscular activity recorded in many of the behaviorist experiments might be merely an epiphenomenon. That is, as thinking occurs, its neurological or central correlates send out weak signals to the muscles and glands. These peripheral organs are thereby activated during thinking, but comprise no essential part of the thought process. This description represents the antithesis of Behaviorism. The issue is far from resolved. Some intermediate position might be closer to the truth, such as one that allows for facilitative support of thinking provided by some (optimal) level of muscular tonus, but that also admits to the primary role of central, neurological events in the ongoing process.

E. Gestalt Psychology

The notions of Gestalt psychology originated in Germany and were brought to the United States when its three founders, Max Wertheimer, Kurt Koffka, and Wolfgang Köhler immigrated. Like Behaviorism, Gestalt psychology was a protest against Structuralism. The name, *Gestalt,* is a

German word with no precise English equivalent, but it is usually translated as "organized whole" or as "configuration." The name captures the essence of the Gestalt protest against Structuralism. Gestalt psychologists (see Koffka, 1935) argued that psychological experience is not compounded of static, discrete representational elements, but rather consists of an organized, dynamic field of events that interact or mutually affect one another. When an organism experiences its environment, it reacts to the whole configuration of environmental forces. Properties of the whole psychological field are different from the sum of its individual parts, and thus no analysis into parts can be entirely successful. Gestalt psychology can be characterized as anti-elementaristic. Sensations, perceptions, images, associations, reflexes, and the like are not accepted as meaningful elemental psychological units. To understand psychological phenomena, one must consider a system of stimulation in which the alteration of any part can affect all the other parts.

In historical perspective, Gestalt psychology deals primarily with perception. Actually, Gestalt psychology was self-consciously general, attempting to treat the whole range of psychological phenomena, including learning, thinking, motivation, and others. Its emphasis on perception was more than anything else a result of its attack on and rejection of Wundt and Structuralism, which also focused on sensation and perception.

1. Gestalt Description of Thinking

From a Gestalt point of view, a problem is said to exist when there are unresolved tensions or stresses in the psychological field, resulting from some interaction of perceptual and/or memory factors. The word stress is used in Gestalt theory as a hypothetical construct involving a competition of forces, as in physical stress. Thinking occurs as the stresses work themselves out, which in turn compels the thinking organism to action. The emphasis is on computational processes, which follow, in general, the principles of field theory from physics. Past experience with related problems is no guarantee of solution. Solutions arise from the problem as it is perceived, just as apparent movement arises from a series of still pictures in a movie. Thinking is a process of resolving field stresses. But problem solution does not always occur, of course, at least not on the first attempt. The problem solver might have to restructure the immediate environment, that is, look at it from several different angles, before the interaction of events forces a clear picture of the solution. Further, external direction acting to readjust a system under tension might be required. But when the proper way of looking at the problem is achieved, solution appears almost automatically, in a moment of insight. In the Gestalt theory, there is a clear and strong relation between thinking and perception. Both are governed by essentially the same principles of field theory, the major difference being that thinking goes on at a more symbolic level and is less under control of external events.

2. Evaluation

The insistence of Gestalt psychologists on the fundamental and basic importance of insight as a principle of learning has embroiled them in a long-standing controversy with those who conceptualize learning as a gradual process. But, whether learning and problem solving are based on trial and error or insight is far too simple a way of looking at the issue. One might observe either type of behavior depending on a number of factors, such as whether or not the relationship between a problem solution and the response to produce it are clear and comprehensible.

Reasons for such controversies are not always clear at the time they take place. In retrospect, we realize that when Gestalt psychology arrived in the United States, experimentalism was firmly in the grip of Behaviorism, which viewed the organism much as a machine, subject to the various sources of external stimulation and reacting to them in an essentially automatic fashion. The doctrine of Behaviorism had, in effect, stripped animal and human being alike of any "higher mental processes." Behaviorism viewed insight as an unfortunate return to mentalism. Yet insightful learning is a common experience that is verifiable in and outside the laboratory without much difficulty. Gestalt theory, although its principles were sometimes rather vague, helped psychology to achieve a more balanced and realistic view of complex human behavior than would have been possible on the basis of Behaviorism alone.

V. THINKING RESEARCH TO 1960

Beginning around 1910, Behaviorism imposed its theoretical and methodological agenda on much of psychology, particularly in the United States. For the next fifty years, research on thinking existed but was not dominant. In reviewing research on thinking during this period, we have tried not just to describe the research of that era, but to highlight research and ideas that anticipated and are relevant to modern cognitive psychology. Our review will focus on research in the areas of concept learning, problem solving, and reasoning.

Perhaps nothing is more humbling to a modern researcher than to peruse the literature from decades ago, even nearly a century ago, and to discover a rich collection of ideas that seem so current. Some of these ideas have been reborn in modern form; others, perhaps unfortunately, have been forgotten.

A. Research on Concepts

Prior to the 1950s, research on concept formation was sporadic. Nonetheless, important issues began to be addressed. In the attempt to understand human conceptual behavior, two central questions are: (1) How are concepts defined? (2) How are concepts acquired? We will discuss several different approaches to these questions.

1. Common-Element Concepts

The attempt to determine "the common nature" of things belonging to a set can be traced back to Socrates. Within psychology, the definition of concepts in terms of common elements was advocated strongly by Hull (1920). He described concept formation as the abstraction of elements common to a class of stimuli and the attachment of a single response to those elements. New stimuli sharing those elements would elicit the same response, producing a phenomenon called *stimulus generalization*.

Hull studied concept learning by having people learn which nonsense syllable was paired with each of twelve Chinese characters. Each character has its own unique element embedded within it. The basic task was one of paired-associate learning. The distinctive feature of the study was that six consecutive lists were learned; the Chinese characters changed from list to list, but the unique elements and their associated syllables remained constant. Across lists, learning was faster, such that responses to the very first presentation of the characters on the sixth list were 60% correct. Hull interpreted this result as indicating that the unique elements had been abstracted, with responses based on these elements. Because most subjects were unable to explain the basis for their responses to new characters, Hull concluded that the learning process was relatively unconscious and automatic.

These two ideas, that concepts are defined by common elements, and that concept learning is a gradual, automatic associative process, remained popular for a long time. For example, Bourne and Restle (1959) developed a formal, mathematical model based on these ideas, to which they added an adaptation process: that stimulus elements having inconsistent associations with category responses will be adapted out, and thus ignored. Although there were data consistent with a common-elements approach, challenges to these ideas arose. Osgood (1953) maintained that the common-elements approach was too restrictive and really did not capture the meaning of concept formation. Osgood argued that there were many concepts that are not based on common elements, and that requiring the learner to exhibit only a consistent response did not distinguish between simple labeling and more complete understanding of a concept.

2. Mediational Processes and Hypotheses

There were several types of contrasts to the common-elements approach. Smoke (1932) studied the learning of concepts based not on common physical elements but on common perceptual relations. For example, all the "daxes" might be triangles (of different sizes, orientation, and angular composition) with a line extending at a right angle from their shortest side. The category would be characterized by a distinct perceptual relation rather than a unique physical element. Osgood (1953) remarked that even common perceptual relations were inadequate to describe many concepts: "What perceptual commonness exists among mittens, hats, and neckties (. . . all 'clothing')? . . . Among France, Japan, and Russia (they are all 'nations')?" (p. 668). For Osgood, the key notion was that concepts reflect not external factors, but the mediational processes generated by the concept learner.

The idea that concepts can be based on different kinds of criteria was nicely illustrated in research by Heidbreder (e.g., 1946). The experimental task she used was, on the surface, similar to that used by Hull (1920)—learning which nonsense syllable is associated with each collection of pictorial stimuli. However, none of the concepts she employed was based on common physical elements; rather, the categories were based on either concrete objects (e.g., trees), spatial forms (e.g., anything circular—clock, wreath, etc.), or numbers (e.g., three objects). Heidbreder found that concrete-object concepts were learned most quickly, with spatial concepts learned faster than number concepts. She believed that this ordering of the concept types reflected natural tendencies in human cognition; dealing with objects was considered primary (compared to attending to nonobject spatial form), with abstract concepts requiring more than perception being least dominant. In Heidbreder's studies, members of a concept always had "something in common," but that "something" might be complex and abstract. To Osgood, making a common symbolic response to physically dissimilar stimuli was crucially different from responding to common physical elements—only the former warranted being called *conceptual behavior* in his view.

Heidbreder (e.g., 1924) also reported findings that challenged Hull's (1920) view of the concept-learning process. In Hull's approach, learning was passive—stimulus elements get conditioned to responses (or not) in an automatic fashion. Heidbreder reported two kinds of behavior by her concept-learning subjects: *participant* and *spectator* behavior. Participants formulated and actively tested hypotheses about what the basis might be of concepts they were learning. Spectators, typically after a series of wrong responses, responded "randomly" in categorizing stimuli, waiting for a new hypothesis to suggest itself. There are two important aspects to these results: (1) That concept learners (sometimes) actively pursue their ideas about what a particular concept might be, and (2) that a concept-learning task might be approached in more than one way. In the 1950s, these themes would be pursued with greater vigor.

3. Strategies and Kinds of Concepts

In 1956, Bruner, Goodnow, and Austin published *A Study of Thinking,* in which they reported some thirty experiments. This volume presaged the cognitive revolution of the sixties and influenced research on concept attainment for fully two decades. Whereas other researchers at that time restricted their studies to concepts defined by common elements and analyzed only trials or errors to solution, Bruner et al. expanded their research in a variety of ways.

They considered not only conjunctive (common-element) concepts but also disjunctive ("or") and probabilistic concepts. They distinguished between the typical *reception* concept-learning task for which the sequence of instances was controlled by the experimenter and a *selection* format in which the learner chose the stimuli about which category information would be given. To study the selection task they created what came to be known as a "Bruner board," a large array of cards, each containing a different combination of stimulus attributes. In the selection task, the learner would point to a card to receive information about its category placement. This procedural innovation called attention to issues concerning memory; once a card had been selected, it could be marked to show its category membership, left unmarked, or removed, thus creating quite different memory requirements (such manipulations were investigated a decade later).

Major emphasis was placed on the use of strategies for acquiring concepts. A variety of strategies was described, with each strategy considered in terms of its logical, information-gaining properties as well as its *cognitive strain.* By cognitive strain, Bruner et al. meant the load on memory and inference (what would later be called *working memory*); they noted that there could be conflict between maximizing information gain and minimizing cognitive strain, so that a concept learner might employ a less-than-optimal strategy in order to keep cognitive strain to an acceptable level.

One strategy, which subsequently received considerable attention from researchers, was called *conservative focusing.* This strategy, applicable to learning common-element (conjunctive) concepts under the selection procedure, both maximizes information gain and holds cognitive strain to a low level. It begins with a positive instance of the target concept (i.e., an instance that belongs to the concept to be learned). The strategy consists of selecting (for category feedback) instances that differ in one and only one feature from the initial positive instance, and noting whether the chosen instance is positive or negative. For example, having learned that a card with *one, small, red triangle* belongs to the target concept, the learner might select a card with *two, small, red triangles.* The inference rules for interpreting category feedback are straightforward: If this card also belongs to the concept, then the *number* of figures is not important. If, however, this card does *not* belong to the concept, then *one figure* is a critical feature of the target concept. By continuing in this way to test each of the features of the initial positive instance, the learner will determine which are critical and which are irrelevant to category membership.

Conservative focusing is an excellent way to identify a conjunctive concept. As it depends on working from a positive instance, initially presenting negative instances should not (and did not) yield progress toward acquiring the target concept. Applied to identifying a concept that is, in fact, disjunctive (having no common elements), the strategy can lead to disaster. As an example of a different type of strategy, consider what Bruner et al. called *successive scanning*. This strategy consists of making a guess about what the target concept might be and simply sticking with it until it proves wrong, then making another guess, and so on. This approach yields low information gain (a great deal of potential information is ignored) but also involves low cognitive strain. One facet of Bruner et al.'s research was to study how strategy usage was affected by changes in task characteristics. A generalization from their findings is that, as the concept-learning task becomes more "stressful," the likelihood increases that learners will use simpler (and less effective) strategies.

Bruner et al. focused on processes and were willing to ask for and analyze learners' reports of hypotheses they were considering (if any). This approach led them not only to discuss overall learning strategies but also to study the processing that takes place on a single trial. With a procedure in which the learner must predict the category membership of an instance before receiving category feedback, any prediction can be right or wrong. Building on work by Hovland (e.g., Hovland & Weiss, 1953), Bruner et al. also attended to whether the instance itself was a member or nonmember of the target concept (positive vs. negative instance). The combination of these two binary classification yields four kinds of trials, and Bruner et al. investigated whether the type of trial affects the likelihood of subjects' drawing correct inferences from the trial information. Logically, correct predictions should lead to maintaining hypotheses, whereas wrong predictions should be followed by adopting new hypotheses that are consistent with the information presented. The type of instance (positive or negative) does not matter logically but can be expected to affect performance because of the greater processing demands typically associated with negative instances. Bruner et al. found that both trial characteristics affected performance, with learners least likely to draw correct inferences from trials involving wrong predictions about (what turned out to be) negative instances. They went further to point out that different strategies have unequal chances of encountering the several types of trials, thus providing a trial-by-trial processing explanation of overall differences in strategy success rates.

Bruner et al. presented a systematic exploration of a broad range of concept-learning situations. Their focus on strategies and cognitive strain enabled them to discuss coherently a variety of experimental results. Their procedural innovations allowed them to show how learners' reported hypotheses could be meaningfully related to task parameters and to standard measures of concept-learning efficiency. Their book is today a rich source of ideas and data about human thinking. Two final comments: First, only some of their findings and ideas received a high level of attention from subsequent researchers. For example, they not only described multiple strategies that could be used for concept learning but also found subjects using different strategies for any particular conceptual task. The idea of multiple strategies, the analytic procedure of sorting learners by strategy type, did not receive much attention in the subsequent literature. Second, while recognizing the artificiality of the concepts used in their studies, they nonetheless believed that their findings were relevant to "real-life" conceptual behavior. This belief was rejected, perhaps erroneously, by researchers advocating the study of "natural concepts" some two decades later.

B. Research on Problem Solving

Throughout the history of psychology there has been reasonable agreement that the essential features of a problem are that an organism has a goal but lacks a clear or well-learned route to the goal. Thus the emphasis in research on problem solving has been on response discovery—how the organism arrives at effective, goal-attaining behavior. On this topic there often has been controversy, usually over the role of learning or past experience in problem solving. Our review of trial and error, insight, set, and transfer effects will illustrate the conflict between emphases on learning and emphases on perception as central components of problem solving.

1. Trial and Error

Because a problem solver must find a solution, it might seem inevitable that an essential activity is trying different approaches and making errors until the right approach is found. At a purely descriptive level, this is so. But early in problem-solving research, trial and error became associated with the view that acquiring a solution is a gradual, undirected process that does not involve perception or comprehension of problem requirements or structure.

An emphasis on trial and error is well illustrated by Thorndike's (1898) studies of animals' behavior in puzzle boxes. Cats were most often the subjects in these experiments. The essential features of the experimental situation were: A hungry cat was placed in a cage with food located outside the cage; the food could not be reached from inside the cage. Rather, the door to the cage could be opened by triggering some mechanism, for example, pulling a string or pushing against a pole somewhere in the cage. The cats' typical behavior was to make direct and futile attempts to get the food, clawing, biting, or trying to squeeze through the bars of the cage. In general, there was considerable, agitated activity. At some point, the cat would trigger the door-opening mechanism and gain the food. When placed in the cage a second time, the animal's behavior resembled that seen in the first encounter, with noticeable clawing, biting, and thrashing about, as well as the eventual release of the door and attainment of the food. Over repeated trials in this situation, the cats' behavior gradually changed, becoming more localized in the area of the triggering mechanism; after many trials, the animals would make relatively direct efforts to activate the door-opening mechanism. Thorndike saw in this behavior pattern no evidence of "seeing through" the problem; rather, problem solving was viewed as a process in which unsuccessful responses were gradually "stamped out" and successful responses "stamped in."

A key feature of the puzzle-box problems was that the solution mechanism was hidden; the critical elements of the situation were not readily available for inspection. Woodworth and Schlosberg (1954) summarize a number of investigations using less opaque situations in which simpler solution methods were required and critical objects were in plain view. With various animal species as subjects, some trial and error typically occurred prior to a solution. Harlow and Settlage (1934) presented multiple-string problems to monkeys; one string was attached to the reward—what varied was the number of distractor strings and the complexity of the string arrangement. With greater complexity there were more erroneous responses; there was little trial and error for moderately complex arrangements. For example, with two strings arranged in an X pattern, only 9% of responses were erroneous.

Woodworth and Schlosberg (1954) remarked that overt trial and error can sometimes be necessary, as a means of exploring the environment and gaining information about, say, the physical properties of objects. Even hypothesis testing could be viewed as a form of trial and error. But an important shift in emphasis seemed to occur when researchers employed non-puzzle-box problems, a shift away from sheer activity and toward problems of attention. Thus, a cat might be described as failing to notice a string that could be used to retrieve a piece of food, but as responding quickly and appropriately once the string "caught her eye." This description is remarkably similar to those used to characterize insightful problem solving.

2. Insight

The gradual process of solution acquisition seen in cats led Thorndike to conclude that no perception of critical relations was involved. In contrast, Yerkes (1916) observed sudden transitions from trial and error to solution in chimpanzees, who also showed good retention of solutions and some transfer to new situations. Comparable observations were made by Kohler (1925/1976) in his extensive studies of problem solving in apes. The animals were typically given the task of obtaining a desired piece of food (e.g., banana, orange), which was located out of reach either inside or outside the cage. The fruit might be hung from the ceiling, too high to reach by jumping but attainable by moving a box under the goal object and climbing to box to retrieve the fruit. Alternatively, the fruit might lie outside the cage, too far away to be grasped directly or even with a short stick, but retrievable with a long stick (also outside the cage), which could be obtained by using the short stick.

When first presented with such a problem, the apes typically made direct attempts to obtain the fruit by reaching, stretching, or jumping, perhaps even trying to use the short stick, always in vain. There would also be considerable attacking of the cage and bashing about of any objects that were handy. At some point, a period of relative quiescence would occur, with the animal perhaps pacing and most often gazing at the objective. Then, with a sudden and deliberate movement, the ape would use the critical object(s) to obtain the fruit. Kohler pointed out that the apes handled objects differently when solving the problem than they might have while thrashing about unsuccessfully; the deliberate nature of the solution was most impressive to him. It must be emphasized that there was substantial variation in the time required to arrive at a solution; some animals succeeded within 5 or 15 minutes, but others were unsuccessful for hours before finding a solution.

When a problem was repeated, the apes almost always solved with dispatch. There appeared to be at least one instance in which an ape forgot the solution for a while. In addition to showing good retention of solutions, the apes also exhibited some flexibility. For example, if the stick previously used to obtain fruit were not available, a different but suitable object (e.g., a branch) might be used. Kohler noted that the apes spent considerable time playing with and manipulating objects, through which they might acquire object knowledge relevant to later problem solving. Birch (1945) found that a few days' experience playing with sticks (in ways other than reaching) substantially helped young chimpanzees succeed in using sticks to retrieve food. Note that this experience was general, rather than specific to the problem-solving behavior; the finding shows an influence of past experience but does not establish experience as the explanation of the patterns of behavior seen in the problem situation.

Kohler also noted that the placement of the objective and the implement in the animal's visual field was important. If the fruit were placed at the opposite end of the cage from the critical implement (e.g., a stick), so that the ape could not look at them simultaneously, attainment of a solution was severely retarded. This effect of visual separation was particularly important on the first exposure to a problem situation, a finding that is consistent with the idea that solving a problem involves a change in perception of the situation.

3. Problem-Solving Set

The phenomenon of *set* occurs in many situations, reflecting a state of preparation for a particular input and response. In many circumstances where a speedy but accurate reaction is desired, sets serve positive purposes. To be prepared is to detect and react more quickly than would otherwise be the case. Contrast the reactions of runners who are given a "ready" signal to what would happen if the starting gun were fired unannounced. In a variety of experimental situations, warning signals have been found to facilitate responding. It is therefore somewhat curious that sets have been discussed largely in terms of negative effects in the context of problem solving.

The positive effects of set mentioned above are best understood in terms of general preparedness. A different aspect of set is to prepare the organism for a particular type of input or response, in effect, to bias the organism. For example, advance information that the next word to be presented is a flower name would speed reactions to *rose* but retard reactions to nonflower names. In the usual problem situation, initial perceptions or expectations are wrong, hence sets would be seen as impairing discovery of the correct response.

According to Woodworth and Schlosberg (1954), what Maier (1930) called "direction" was a kind of set. Maier (1940) distinguished between *habitual directions* and *new directions;* habitual directions would correspond to sets. Along with others, Maier believed that problem-solving efforts were guided by a direction or orientation that was not itself a habit but reflected (also) the influence of the problem situation. That is, the structure of the problem situation was held to affect the direction that would be followed. When problem solving requires doing something new, habitual directions must be overcome and new directions created. Indeed, Ruger (1910) had noted that some subjects stubbornly adhered to a particular line of attack despite repeated failure. From this perspective, any instance of insightful problem solving can be seen as breaking or disrupting a set. The usual meaning of problem-solving set as a predisposition or bias that exists when a problem is initially presented corresponds to Maier's concept of habitual direction. Most research on sets focused on negative transfer from prior experience to a problem situation.

One example of a negative set is *functional fixedness,* a term coined by Duncker (1945) to refer to the fact that an object with a strong customary function will not easily be seen as serving a different function. More specifically, problem presentations or prior experiences that emphasize the usual function were predicted to inhibit the use of an object in a more novel fashion.

For example, in the box–candle problem, the solution requires using a small box as a platform for a candle. In the solution, the box must be tacked to a wall, with the candle then mounted on the box. The critical manipulation concerned the function exhibited by the box when the problem materials were presented. Compared to presenting an empty box with tacks spread out on a table, presenting the box filled with tacks significantly impaired solution (Adamson, 1952). The essential idea was that the filled box emphasized the usual function of a box, thus blocking the idea of using the box as a platform. Although later research led to a subtle modification of the explanation, this version of functional fixedness has proven to be a reliable phenomenon.

Another variation of functional fixedness employed a transfer design. In a first phase, some subjects would employ an object in its usual fashion, for example, using a switch to complete a small electrical circuit. When subsequently given a problem requiring a novel use of an object, and having two suitable objects available, those subjects who had just used a switch in its usual, electrical function would avoid using it in the new, more novel function (e.g., Birch & Rabinowitz, 1951). The test problem was the two-string problem, arranged to require that a small object of suitable size and weight be tied to the end of one string. Doing this would allow that string to be swung back and forth (the "pendulum solution") so that the problem solver, grasping the second string, could catch the swinging string and tie the two strings together. Two suitable objects were made available, a small electrical switch, and a small electrical relay. If people had just used the switch to complete an electrical circuit, they almost always used the relay to solve the two-string problem (and vice versa). The essential point was that using an object in its ordinary function blocked an unusual use of the object. An important additional finding was that the impairment was unidirectional, that is, unusual use of an object had no effect on its likelihood of being used for its ordinary function (e.g., van de Geer, 1957).

Research on functional fixedness focused on uses for particular objects. A quite different approach to problem-solving set concerned the dominance of a particular type of response to situations with a high degree of surface similarity. The typical procedure was to give subjects experience with solving a series of similar problems in "the same way," then to test them with apparently similar problems that could (or must) be solved in a different way. The research thus focused on the acquisition of problem-solving sets and their subsequent (usually negative) effects on later problem solving.

Luchins's (1942) work provides an excellent example (later research showed his essential findings to be quite replicable). The basic procedure was to give people a series of "water jar" problems to solve. These problems involve giving subjects three jars with specified capacities (and, important, no gradations), and requiring them to indicate how they would measure (obtain) a specified amount of water. For example, given jars holding 21, 127, and 3 quarts, respectively, the subject would be asked to indicate how to measure out exactly 100 quarts. The solution was to fill the largest jar (B), and then to fill the second largest jar (A) once from B, then to fill the smallest jar (C) twice from B, which would leave the desired amount (100 quarts) in B. The "shorthand" description of the solution was thus B − A − 2C.

The basic procedure was to give subjects a number of "set-inducing problems," all of which could be solved (only) by the B − A − 2C method. Following this experience, one or more test problems would be presented; these could be solved by either the B − A − 2C method or by a simpler procedure. For example, given "A = 14, B = 36, C = 8, obtain 6," one solution is "36 − 14 − 8 − 8 = 6," whereas a new and simpler solution is "14 − 6 = 8." The basic finding was that people who had been exposed to the set-inducing series of problems were far more likely to use the (unnecessarily) long solution method. In other research, the test problems included "extinction problems" that could not be solved by the "set" method, in which case it was found that set-inducing experience delayed finding a solution (e.g., Gardner & Runquist, 1958).

Problem-solving sets, up to a point, were amenable to study from an associative-learning (behavioristic) perspective. That is, sets could be conceived (and experimentally investigated) as the product of a variable number of learning (conditioning) trials, as subject to extinction (from counter-set problems) and "spontaneous recovery." A number of results fit this scenario, but there were also discordant findings that may well have contributed to the emergence of the "cognitive revolution" of the 1960s. The attempt to extend associative-learning principles (à la Hull, and Spence, primarily) to "higher processes," required adherence to certain conditioning principles. Therefore, Kendler, Greenberg, and Richman's (1952) finding that problem-solving sets were stronger after massed training, compared to distributed training, posed a problem because the typical learning result was that distributed practice was superior. Partial reinforcement (of set solutions) should have produced greater resistance to extinction, but contradictory findings were obtained (e.g., Mayzner & Tresselt, 1956). To maintain the distinction between habit strength and drive, Maltzman (e.g., 1955) argued that sets established by instructions (akin to drive) should be more transient than those established by training (habit strength), but results were at best inconclusive (e.g., Maltzman & Morrisett, 1953). The difficulties encountered in attempts to extend associative ideas to more complex behavior might have smoothed the way for a new theoretical orientation.

4. Transfer of Principles

Research on problem-solving sets tended to emphasize the negative effects of prior experience. There also was research focusing on attempts to aid problem solving by some kind of prior training. One basic question to ask is whether problem solvers improve as they gain experience with a particular type of problem. One would expect the answer to be "yes," and there were some reports over time that supported this expectation. Thorndike (1898) noted that cats who had learned the solution to one puzzle-box problem sometimes mastered rather quickly a modified version of the problem. Good transfer to appropriate novel situations was assumed to be a hallmark of insightful problem solving; Kohler (1925/1976) indicated that apes who had used a box as a platform from which to capture hanging fruit would employ tables, stones, coils of wire, even the animal keeper as a springboard—seemingly, whatever was available that would fulfill the desired function. Harlow (1949) demonstrated that extensive practice with multiple examples of object-discrimination problems led monkeys to become quite efficient at solving them. Studies of human problem solvers' learning to solve simply by practice were relatively scarce; improvement was observed (e.g., Taylor & Faust, 1952). There were also some reports of no improvement with practice, but small and probably inadequate amounts of practice were provided (see Duncan, 1959).

A more popular approach to the study of problem-solving transfer involved providing some form of training prior to presenting test problems. One theoretically driven question concerned whether training that emphasized understanding of solution principles would yield better transfer than training that stressed "rote memorization" of solutions. Theorists who argued for the importance of understanding of solution principles predicted that principle training would be superior (Bartlett, 1951; Katona, 1940). Katona employed a variety of tasks and techniques in his studies; here is one example.

The card-arrangement task requires the problem solver to arrange a deck of playing cards so that, when one alternates between placing the top card on the table and moving the top card to the bottom of the deck, a specified order of cards will be placed on the table. For example, suppose one must arrange the cards Ace through 8 so that, following the alternation scheme described above, the cards are placed on the table in the order *A 1 2 3 4 5 6 7 8*. The way to accomplish this is to arrange the deck in the order *A 5 2 7 3 6 4 8*. Memorization training would have the subject rehearse the correct order until it could be produced reliably. Training stressing understanding would include a diagram of the deck to be filled in by the subject, encouraging the subject to realize that, for example, the first four cards placed on the table must be in the 1st, 3rd, 5th, and 7th positions in the deck, and so on.

Transfer tasks would pose different card-arrangement problems, for example, arranging four red and four black cards so that, when alternated as above, the order produced would be *RBRBRBRB* (the solution is *RRBR-RBBB*).

Katona's results favored training via understanding. Across time and researchers, quite heterogeneous studies were conducted. There was variation in the kinds of problems used, the methods labeled training via principles or understanding, and the amount of training provided. Results were also variable, although there was a tendency for training by understanding of solution principles to show better transfer to similar but slightly more difficult transfer problems. Nonetheless, there were many unsettled issues (Duncan, 1959; Woodworth & Schlosberg, 1954). Empirical and procedural ambiguities, coupled with the importance of the basic question, made the role of understanding of principles in problem-solving transfer a central topic for research for many years—indeed, to the present day.

C. Research on Reasoning

Reasoning—drawing inferences and evaluating given information—is a part of most cognitive tasks. For example, one can ask whether a person derives appropriate inferences from a trial in a concept-learning experiment, or whether one is using a logically efficient strategy to solve a troubleshooting problem. Attention is directed toward reasoning processes by using tasks that emphasize the use of information, especially relational information. Reasoning was not a major research focus during the period being reviewed, but several important findings were obtained.

As a general influence, it was psychologists' data that pointed to the discrepancies between "ordinary" human reasoning and the dictates of formal logic. Such findings challenged the view that logic was "the way the mind worked." More specifically, early researchers showed that people would fail to make use of all relevant information provided them, that people might fail to extract all the information logically available to them, and that people were inclined to *convert* propositions, for example, accepting "All *X* are *Y*" to also mean "All *Y* are *X*" (see Woodworth & Schlosberg, 1954). All of these findings anticipate later proposals in cognitive psychology.

1. Atmosphere Effect

The syllogism is a classic means of training and testing reasoning. Two premises and a conclusion are presented; each statement concerns two terms, with a total of three terms involved. The conclusion links two terms that have not appeared together in the premises, and the essential question is whether the conclusion follows logically from the premises. For example, given (premises) *All X is M* and *Some M is Y,* does the conclusion *Some X is Y* follow logically? The answer is "no" (in brief, because the *X*'s need not be among the *M*'s that are *Y*). Syllogisms for which the conclusion does not logically follow from the premises are called *invalid;* research quickly showed that people often accepted invalid conclusions.

Woodworth and Sells (1935) proposed that the atmosphere established by the premises was an important determinant of these errors. Atmosphere reflected the modifiers found in the premises (*All, some, no*), with the idea being that negative premises created a negative atmosphere, and so on. The effects of negative and particular ("some") premises were held to be strongest, so that having just one premise of these types would determine the atmosphere, and thus determine the kind of invalid conclusion people would accept. For example, given *Some X is M* and *No M is Y* as premises, the atmosphere hypothesis predicted that people would accept the invalid conclusion *Some Y is not X.* Sells (1936) obtained data supporting atmosphere effects—invalid conclusions were more often accepted if favored by atmosphere. Research done in the modern era has raised questions about the adequacy of the atmosphere hypothesis as an explanation of syllogistic reasoning. Nonetheless, the principle underlying atmosphere—that people's responses in a reasoning task can result from quickly established, shallow encoding of problem information—is a component of some current theories of reasoning (e.g., Evans, 1989).

2. Content Effects

From the perspective of logic, the particular kind of content found in a reasoning task is not important. That is, regardless of what *X, Y,* and *M* might be, the validity (or lack thereof) of the conclusion to a syllogism remains the same. Abstract symbols are used to describe syllogisms precisely because the type of content has no logical consequence. Yet early on, researchers wondered whether people's reasoning might be affected by problem content. The following two syllogisms illustrate the contrast between abstract and concrete content:

Syllogism A:	Syllogism B:
Given: All *A*'s are *B*'s	Given: All dogs are mammals.
Given: All *C*'s are *B*'s	Given: All cats are mammals.
Therefore: All *A*'s are *C*'s	Therefore: All dogs are cats.

A substantial percentage of college students will accept the invalid conclusion to the abstract syllogism, but none will accept that "All dogs are cats." The central point is that the two syllogisms are logically identical. Wilkins (1928) compared abstract syllogisms with syllogisms containing familiar, concrete material, and found a slight advantage in performance with the concrete syllogisms.

It is not the case, however, that people simply reason better with familiar, concrete materials. Introducing meaningful content raises the possibility that people's responses reflect their biases for or against certain conclusions, perhaps with little or no reasoning involved. In an early study of biases in reasoning, Morgan and Morton (1944) presented "emotional" syllogisms that dealt with hopes and fears concerning World War II. The basic idea was that people might have difficulty accepting a valid conclusion that contradicted their hopes or rejecting an invalid conclusion that expressed one of their beliefs. Morgan and Morton found that people more often followed biases than either atmosphere or logic. Subsequent researchers found bias effects of varying strengths; interest in content effects broadened to other reasoning tasks, and the complexity of the issues unfolded over time. The determination and explanation of content effects on human reasoning remains a central issue in reasoning research. For example, researchers currently seek a precise account of how biases affect thinking (e.g., Oakhill, Garnham, & Johnson-Laird, 1990).

VI. TRANSITION TO THE NEW COGNITIVE ERA

The year of 1960 is a convenient if approximate marker of a transition in research on thinking. By the mid-1960s, research on thinking was showing considerable vigor, especially regarding concept learning and problem solving. Discussions of these topics employed cognitive concepts such as *hypothesis, strategy, heuristic, encoding,* and *retrieval.* The situation was quite different from a decade earlier, even though there was movement away from Behaviorism, toward Cognitivism, during the 1950s.

A number of immediate precursors of the new cognitivism can be identified. As mentioned earlier, attempts were made to extend conditioning principles to human problem solving and concept learning, but predictions were not consistently upheld by the results. In addition, conditioning analyses of complex behavior seemed cumbersome and vague. Alternative approaches were becoming available. The development of information theory (Shannon & Weaver, 1949) led psychological researchers to examine tasks in terms of information load and to be concerned with how information is processed. Linguists, particularly Noam Chomsky (e.g., 1957), attacked behaviorist accounts of language by focusing on the creative aspects of language—producing and comprehending novel sentences. Chomsky and others proposed an alternative account based on distinguishing between competence (knowledge) and performance (action), describing linguistic competence in terms of abstract rules, and arguing that the facts of language development required the postulation of a biologically given language-acquisition device. The linguists' theories were radically different from behaviorist accounts, and their arguments were persuasive.

Finally, the emergence of computer technology had a profound effect on the psychology of thinking. Computers were seen as systems for processing symbols, for operating on information. In a most influential article, Newell, Shaw, and Simon (1958) outlined a theory of human thinking that was based on the idea that human beings were information-processing systems and that drew heavily on analogies between human processing and computer processing. The introduction of the computer metaphor supported the postulation of "unseen" cognitive processes, encouraged the study of more complex activities, and offered a new type of mechanism as an account of human behavior. All of the above-mentioned developments encouraged researchers to investigate new topics and to consider new modes of explanation. The transition to a period of cognitive dominance had begun.

References

Adamson, R. E. (1952). Functional fixedness as related to problem solving: A repetition of three experiments. *Journal of Experimental Psychology, 44*, 288–291.

Anderson, J. R. (1987). Skill acquisition: Compilation of weak-method problem solutions. *Psychological Review, 94*, 192–210.

Anderson, J. R. (1990). *The adaptive character of thought.* Hillsdale, NJ: Erlbaum.

Bartlett, F. C. (1951). *The mind at work and play.* London: Allen.

Birch, H. G. (1945). The relation of previous experience to insightful problem solving. *Journal of Comparative Psychology, 38*, 367–383.

Birch, H. G., & Rabinowitz, H. S. (1951). The negative effect of previous experience on productive thinking. *Journal of Experimental Psychology, 41*, 121–125.

Boring, E. G. (1950). *A history of experimental psychology.* New York: Appleton-Century-Crofts.

Bourne, L. E., Jr., Ekstrand, B. R., & Dominowski, R. L. (1971). *The psychology of thinking.* Englewood Cliffs, NJ: Prentice-Hall.

Bourne, L. E., Jr., & Restle, F. (1959). A mathematical theory of concept identification. *Psychological Review, 66*, 278–296.

Bruner, J. S., Goodnow, J. J., & Austin, G. A. (1956). *A study of thinking.* New York: Wiley.

Chomsky, N. (1957). *Syntactic structures.* The Hague: Mouton.

Darwin, C. (1909). *Origin of species* (2nd ed.) London: Collier.

Dellarosa, D. (1988). A history of thinking. In R. J. Sternberg & E. E. Smith (Eds.), *The psychology of human thought.* Cambridge: Cambridge University Press.

Dewey, J. (1910). *How we think.* Boston: Heath.

Duncan, C. P. (1959). Recent research on human problem solving. *Psychological Bulletin, 56*, 397–429.

Duncker, K. (1945). On problem-solving. *Psychological Monographs, 58* (5, Whole No. 270).

Ebbinghaus, H. (1913). *Uber das Gedachtnis* [On memory] (H. A. Ruger & C. E. Bussenius, Trans.). New York: Teachers College, Columbia University. (Original work published 1885)

Evans, J. St. B. (1989). *Bias in human reasoning: Causes and consequences.* Hove, UK: Erlbaum.

Freeman, G. L. (1931). Mental activity and the muscular process. *Psychological Review, 38*, 428–447.

Galton, F. (1874). *English men of science: Their nature and nurture.* London: Macmillan.

Gardner, R. A., & Runquist, W. N. (1958). Acquisition and extinction of problem solving set. *Journal of Experimental Psychology, 55,* 274–277.

Harlow, H. F. (1949). The formation of learning sets. *Psychological Review, 56,* 51–65.

Harlow, H. F., & Settlage, P. H. (1934). Comparative behavior of primates. VII. Capacity of monkeys to solve patterned string tests. *Journal of Comparative Psychology, 18,* 423–435.

Heidbreder, E. (1924). An experimental study of thinking. *Archives of Psychology of New York,* No. 73.

Heidbreder, E. (1946). The attainment of concepts: II. The problem. *Journal of General Psychology, 35,* 191–223.

Hothersall, D. (1990). *History of psychology* (2nd ed.). New York: McGraw-Hill.

Hovland, C. I., & Weiss, W. (1953). Transmission of information concerning concepts through positive and negative instances. *Journal of Experimental Psychology, 45,* 175–182.

Hull, C. L. (1920). Quantitative aspects of the evolution of concepts. *Psychological Monographs* (Whole No. 123).

Jacobson, E. (1930). Electrical measurements of neuro-muscular states during mental activities: IV. Evidence of contraction of specific muscles during imagination. *American Journal of Physiology, 95,* 703–712.

James, W. (1890). *The principles of psychology.* New York: Holt.

Katona, G. (1940). *Organizing and memorizing.* New York: Columbia University Press.

Kendler, H. H., Greenberg, A., & Richman, H. (1952). The influence of massed and distributed practice on the development of mental set. *Journal of Experimental Psychology, 43,* 21–25.

Koffka, K. (1935). *Principles of Gestalt psychology.* New York: Harcourt, Brace.

Kohler, W. (1976). *The mentality of apes.* New York: Liveright. (Original work published 1925)

Külpe, O. (1893). *Outlines of psychology* (E. B. Titchener, Trans.). New York: Macmillan.

Luchins, A. S. (1942). Mechanization in problem solving: The effect of Einstellung. *Psychological Monographs, 54* (Whole No. 248).

Maier, N.R.F. (1930). Reasoning in humans: I. On direction. *Journal of Comparative Psychology, 10,* 115–143.

Maier, N.R.F. (1940). The behavior mechanisms concerned with problem solving. *Psychological Review, 47,* 43–58.

Maltzman, I. (1955). Thinking: From a behavioristic point of view. *Psychological Review, 62,* 275–286.

Maltzman, I., & Morrisett, L., Jr. (1953). The effects of simple and compound classes of anagrams in set solutions. *Journal of Experimental Psychology, 45,* 345–350.

Mayzner, M. S., & Tresselt, M. E. (1956). The effect of the competition and generalization of sets with respect to manifest anxiety. *Journal of General Psychology, 55,* 241–247.

Morgan, J. J. B., & Morton, J. T. (1944). The distortion of syllogistic reasoning produced by personal convictions. *Journal of Social Psychology, 20,* 39–59.

Newell, A., Shaw, J. C., & Simon, H. A. (1958). Elements of a theory of human problem solving. *Psychological Review, 65,* 151–16.

Oakhill, J., Garnham, A., & Johnson-Laird, P. N. (1990). Belief bias effects in syllogistic reasoning. In K. J. Gilhooly, M. T. G. Keane, R. H. Logie, & G. Erdos (Eds.), *Lines of thinking: Reflections on the psychology of thought* (Vol. 1). Chichester, England: Wiley.

Osgood, C. E. (1953). *Method and theory in experimental psychology.* New York: Oxford University Press.

Ruger, H. (1910). The psychology of efficiency. *Archives of Psychology of New York,* No. 15.

Sells, S. B. (1936). The atmosphere effect: An experimental study of reasoning. *Archives of Psychology of New York,* No. 200.

Shannon, C. E., & Weaver, W. (1949). *The mathematical theory of communication.* Urbana: University of Illinois Press.

Smoke, K. L. (1932). An objective study of concept formation. *Psychological Monographs, 42* (Whole No. 191).

Taylor, D. W., & Faust, W. L. (1952). Twenty questions: Efficiency in problem solving as a function of size of group. *Journal of Experimental Psychology, 44,* 360–368.

Thorndike, E. L. (1898). Animal intelligence: An experimental study of the associative processes in animals. *Psychological Monographs,* No. 8.

Thorndike, E. L. (1911). *Animal intelligence.* New York: Macmillan.

van de Geer, J. P. (1957). *A psychological study of problem solving.* Haarlem: Uitgeverij De Toorts.

Wallas, G. (1926). *The art of thought.* New York: Harcourt, Brace.

Watson, J. B. (1924). *Behaviorism.* New York: People's Institute.

Wertheimer, M. (1945). *Productive thinking.* New York: Harper.

Wilkins, M. C. (1928). The effect of changed material on ability to do formal syllogistic reasoning. *Archives of Psychology of New York,* No. 102.

Woodworth, R. S., & Schlosberg, H. (1954). *Experimental psychology* (rev. ed.). New York: Holt.

Woodworth, R. S., & Sells, S. B. (1935). An atmosphere effect in formal syllogistic reasoning. *Journal of Experimental Psychology, 18,* 451–460.

Wundt, W. (1912). *An introduction to psychology* (2nd ed.). New York: Macmillan.

Yerkes, R. M. (1916). The mental life of monkeys and apes, a study of ideational behavior. *Behavior Monographs,* No. 12.

CHAPTER 2

Contemporary Approaches to the Study of Thinking and Problem Solving

K. Anders Ericsson
Reid Hastie

I. INTRODUCTION

Recent reviews of thinking (Holyoak & Spellman, 1993; Oden, 1987) distinguish between a general definition of thinking that includes all intelligent cognitive activities and a more specific definition that includes only the most "complex" forms of cognitive activities, such as reasoning, decision making, and problem solving. Most reviewers, then, restrict their discussion to findings from empirical studies examining performance on laboratory tasks designed to induce particular forms of complex thinking, usually under conditions where the subject is motivated to achieve a clearly specified goal. This amounts to focusing on extensional aspects of the meaning of the term "thinking," and especially on experimental tasks designed by researchers to capture empirically analyzable aspects of thinking. In fact, the table of contents from the present volume could probably serve as an exemplar-based definition of an academic psychologist's concept of thinking: representation and categorization, deduction, induction, problem solving, creativity, wisdom (we might add one or two categories such as decision making and scientific discovery).

Most nonpsychologists would probably endorse the more general conception of thinking. For example, a typical dictionary definition would begin: "Think . . . To have or formulate in the mind . . . To reason about, to reflect on, to ponder . . ." (American Heritage Dictionary, Second College Edition, 1982). But, linguistic analysis and ratings of word meanings reveal a culturally shared collection of everyday concepts with thinking, very much like the professional psychologist's, as the superordinate for activities such as problem solving, reasoning, conceptualizing, and deciding, and with coordinate, contrasting categories such as perceiving, feeling, dreaming, wishing, remembering, and willing (D'Andrade, 1987; Rips & Conrad, 1989). The interesting (and perhaps sobering) conclusion is that technical and everyday definitions of thinking are not very discrepant and there is probably as much systematic structure within the layperson's system of related concepts as there is in the professional psychologist's.

If we attempted to piece together a more intentional definition from various dictionary and encyclopedia entries, we would conclude with something like: *A sequence of internal symbolic activities that leads to novel, productive ideas or conclusions.* We could supplement this definition with a suggestion that the symbolic activities represent events external to the thinker and that the sequence is not simply the reflection of externally driven perceptual experiences or the reproduction of long-term memories. We suspect that the major difference between the layperson's and the psychologist's intentional definitions would involve the psychologists' focus on tasks in which thinking is motivated to achieve a clearly specified goal; while a layperson would be likelier to include various types of spontaneous reflection and reverie in the category.

One reason we are so concerned with the relationship between the layperson's and the researcher's definitions of thinking is because a fundamental goal of research on thinking is to elucidate phenomena that occur in everyday situations. Researchers have tended to focus on important phenomena such as exceptional achievement in intellectual tasks (for example, mathematical reasoning, engineering problem solving, and predictive and diagnostic judgment). However, more mundane achievements (for example, daily planning and navigation, arithmetic calculation, mechanical troubleshooting) are also important. The layperson's conceptions of thinking are also of interest because, in a nascent science like Psychology, there is considerable interest in simply changing "folk models of the mind" or at least in conducting research that demonstrably goes beyond everyday conceptions.

Where the layperson's intuitions and the researcher's assumptions about thinking differ sharply is in notions about how the systematic study of thought processes should be carried out. Many people today view thinking and conscious experience as reflecting ineffable spiritual aspects of our existence, in contrast to the mechanistic and material aspects of our physical environment. A more sophisticated version of this anti-empirical orientation is seen in the writings of many philosophers, who have concluded that the nature and structure of thought could never be studied with objective methods or described by general laws and mechanisms. When confronted by the expanding corpus of empirical results from the behavioral sciences, most people respond that "thinking" studied in the laboratory (or by other systematic methods) is artificial and doesn't capture the more interesting forms of thinking in everyday life. They are also likely to endorse techniques for studying thinking, such as self-observation and introspection, without considering serious deficiencies of these methods.

To fully account for thinking we need to consider the complexity and diversity of adult thinking in the context of accumulated knowledge and skills acquired over a lengthy developmental experience. We are far from approaching these goals and some argue that the current research methods are insufficient to ever attain them. In preparation for our discussion of the contemporary approaches to thinking, we will outline the history of the study of thinking with its major approaches. Most modern themes, now represented in approaches to empirical research, can be found in historical precedents. But, causal interpretations are dubious, as there is a fundamental problem with historical hindsight: A multitude of historical themes are not reflected in any contemporary trends.

II. A BRIEF HISTORY OF THE STUDY OF THINKING

A. Prescientific and Philosophical Accounts of Thinking

Around the time civilization emerged, it appears that thinking was not differentiated from experience in general. It was only when philosophers found that some experiences did not simply reflect the outside world that thinking was distinguished from perception. If thinking included experience that was not directly related to perception or divinely transmitted, where did the ideas and thoughts in our heads come from? Could they all be explained in terms of transformations of our sensory inputs and through a study of developmental experience?

Aristotle is generally credited with the first systematic analyses of his own thinking. Aristotle's method of introspection consisted of extensive self-observation, with observation leading to general hypotheses, which were then evaluated by further self-observation. His goal was to induce the general laws describing thought from these instances of self-observation. Anticipating later specialized definitions of thinking, Aristotle excluded perceptions (experiences reflecting the current external world) and reproductive memories of specific past experiences from the category of thinking. He also distinguished between contemplation, thought directed at the attainment of new knowledge, and deliberation, thought directed toward practical action (cf. Sternberg, Conway, Ketron, & Bernstein, 1981, for a similar distinction between kinds of intelligence).

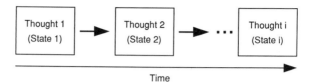

FIGURE 1   A schematic diagram of the sequence of thoughts postulated by Aristotle.

Aristotle concluded that thinking, in particular recall, corresponded to a sequence of thoughts, as illustrated in Figure 1. This led to further reflections on the relations between consecutive thoughts and the discovery that these relations could be described by a small number of associations, such as similarity, contiguity, and contrast. Hence Aristotle went beyond a recording of recalled sequences of thoughts primarily by his extraction of the relations between thoughts.

Aristotle's findings and methods were elaborated until the eighteenth century, but then new issues concerning the origin and elements of thoughts started to be approached by more systematic theoretical analysis, with less emphasis on naive observation of one's naturally occurring flow of thinking. Philosophers would relax, let the mind wander, and focus on a particular thought. This thought state was then carefully analyzed into its *sensory* components. Locke argued that complex ideas and experiences were made up of previously experienced simpler ideas. Many efforts were made to identify the previous experiences corresponding to a given idea. Following Aristotle, there was general agreement that thinking was a sequence of thoughts. However, the nature of the transition between two thoughts was controversial. To find the mechanism linking one thought to the next, the relations between consecutive thoughts were analyzed to discover general principles of association. As a result of these new efforts, introspective "observations" of mental processes became intertwined with the philosophical analyses. Thus, even more than in Aristotle's approach, this increasingly analytical approach blurred the distinction between theory and observation.

In the latter half of the nineteenth century, psychologically inclined philosophers began to challenge whether detailed introspective analysis of thoughts was even possible. The most general criticisms originated from the common assumption that no mental states were ever alike (James, 1890/1950). If the same thoughts could not be reliably reproduced, the scientific study (with its requirement for reproducible empirical results) of thinking and subjective experience would seem to be impossible. One significant response to these philosophical doubts was empirical research programs that sought linkages between thinking and its underlying neural substrates.

B. Early Laboratory Studies on Sensation and Thinking

Progress toward a laboratory-based science of psychology was attained by explicit efforts to avoid the complexities of thinking and everyday experience. For unstructured reveries, the preferred material of early introspectionists, it would be especially difficult to detect reliable patterns in the thought states. Doubts concerning the ability of the introspective method to analyze stable mental states into their elementary components led to proposals for refinements of the method, to focus on perceptual experiences. For example, Hamilton (1870) conducted experiments in which he threw marbles on the ground, opened his eyes for a brief glance, and then tried to recall what he saw. His estimate was that only four or five marbles or familiar configurations of marbles could be apprehended, anticipating modern research on the limited capacity of short-term memory.

Following Weber and Fechner (and the example of philosophers like Hamilton), Wilhelm Wundt set out to study the sensory experience of simple physical stimuli. With sophisticated equipment, it was possible to present the same simple physical stimulus to an observer many times. The highly practiced observer was given the task of focusing on the sensory activation due only to the presented stimulus. This research was concerned with *immediate* experience, which was believed to reflect neural activation prior to any contact with stored memories of earlier meaningful experience. Based on studies of reaction time, investigators found evidence for the immediate availability of sensory information reflecting the output of sensory processing.

Given that primarily peripheral neurophysiological structures were involved, problems of the effects of experience of prior tests should be minimal, especially with sufficiently long intertrial intervals. Highly reproducible results concerning the "psychophysical" relations between physical stimulus dimensions and experience were uncovered in a wide range of perceptual domains and modalities. These first successful applications of experimental methods in psychology have often been misrepresented as efforts to study the structure of normal experience with introspective methods; in fact, these studies were aimed at uncovering the structure of the sensory *nervous system* by examining the output of this system in response to systematically varied physical stimuli.

The distinction between introspective analysis of normal thinking and introspection as a method in psychophysics is best documented by a brief review of the controversy over "imageless thought." Külpe at Würzburg and a number of other investigators started to study complex conceptual thinking using methods like those developed in the psychophysical tradition (see a review by Humphrey, 1951, for more details). Trained observers gave retrospective reports on their thought processes while performing simple tasks, such as generating an experimenter-specified association to a presented word, for example, the superordinate concept of the word "chair." Later studies by Bühler used tasks that required more complex inferences. For example, subjects were timed as they responded to Yes/No questions, such as, "Do you know where the stop watch is?," instructed to respond as fast as possible, and then asked to report their introspective analysis of their thinking in terms of sensory components. Taxonomies for different types of images and other thoughts were constructed.

These reports often included references to thoughts that lacked any associated sensory imagery. Bühler took the reports that no concurrent imagery was experienced to imply that no sensory neural activity was associated with these imageless thought states. This violated Wundt's central premise that each mental state had a correspondence in neural activity. Wundt replied that the act of engaging in thinking made subjects unable simultaneously to monitor neural activity everywhere in the central nervous system. Furthermore, Wundt suggested that it would be impossible to induce a specific thought state repeatedly in these complex experimental tasks, where the observers would be able to direct their attention to any concurrent neural activity. The conclusion of this controversy was that analysis of complex thoughts into their sensory components was not possible, but that retrospective accounts of the sequence of recalled thoughts were possible (Ericsson & Crutcher, 1991) and were potentially a valid source of data on thinking.

Bühler's conclusion that thought and neural activity are not integrally linked represents an answer to one of the oldest questions raised by philosophers, the mind–body problem. The answer that the two systems are not integral, or that the linkage between them is obscure, leads to a continuing vigorous debate concerning the proper level of theorizing in research on thinking. For many, the answer is that there is an appropriate "symbolic" or "cognitive" level, which cannot (at least in the near future) be linked to neural structures and events, at which theorizing should proceed (cf. Anderson, 1987; Newell, 1990). This level is frequently associated with conscious experience; with optional control by the thinker's deliberate "will"; and with a limited capacity of mental resources. However, partly because it is not linked to the physical, neural level, disagreements among theorists about exactly where this level is located, how many levels are needed, and what is its "language," are epidemic in research on thinking (Anderson, 1987; Fodor, 1985; Marr, 1982; Pylyshyn, 1984; Smolensky, 1988).

Although Wundt rejected the possibility of studying the fluid and complex structure of individual thinking directly, he suggested that the stable products of thinking reflected in shared cultural artifacts (*Völkerpsychologie*) such as language and systematic culturally transmitted knowledge, should be studied in a historical perspective to give insights into the structure of thought. Wundt's suggestion that people study the cultural context and artifacts of thinking is reflected in the current interest in "situated cognition," a movement within the field of cognitive psychology toward use of methods and theories that include everyday context to a greater extent than the traditional laboratory-based analyses of thinking.

C. From Conscious Experience to Performance

Reported experience was not only difficult to systematically reproduce but, since the experiences of subjects could never be directly observed, inconsistencies between different observers could not be empirically resolved. In virtually all aspects of everyday life, individuals differ in the accuracy and the speed by which they complete tasks. The abilities of individuals to complete athletic events and to take tests of knowledge on almost any subject are remarkably stable and can be reliably measured on repeated occasions. When individuals are given well-defined tasks and are motivated to do their best, we refer to the observable behavior as *performance*. Under those conditions, the observed performance is a valid indicator of subjects' abilities and, ideally, it is impossible for subjects to fake or by other means attain a performance that is higher than their true capabilities. Furthermore, measures of performance, such as accuracy of response and total time to complete a task, provide simple numeric indices that summarize the characteristics of the mediating cognitive processes. By restricting the analysis to performance measures, investigators were able to avoid the theoretical issues concerning the detailed structure of thought processes.

Many previously used paradigms to study memory and perception could easily be converted from studies of reported experience to studies of performance. For example, many of the early introspective analyses of memory simply accepted the subjects' judgments of familiarity as evidence for the retrieval of information about a prior experienced event. This type of procedure is obviously susceptible to bias, and subjects who wanted to attain a high level of memory performance could incorrectly report recognition of stimuli or confabulate recall reports without risk of detection (e.g., McCloskey, Wible, & Cohen, 1988; Neisser & Harsch, 1991). In contrast, procedures measuring memory *performance* could include an equal mix of presented stimuli and other, not previously presented stimuli. Accurate memory performance, identifying presented stimuli while correctly rejecting the nonpresented stimuli, cannot be "faked" and provides a more valid picture of memory. More generally, the "performance" approach attempts to set up controlled situations, where subjects are presented with stimuli and instructed to make an observable response meeting some specified criteria. The careful design of experimental situations sharply constrains subjects' strategies for generating correct responses, and successful performance implies the execution of the particular type of processes under study.

It was generally recognized that individuals' ability to perform on tasks was primarily determined by their prior experience and relevant knowledge. Given that experience and knowledge had to have been acquired previously, the search for general laws was focused on the basic processes that regulate the acquisition of new experiences and knowledge. By creating experimental situations that were virtually unrelated to everyday life, the experimenters hoped to study these basic processes in a relatively pure form. When the applicability of subjects' specific and idiosyncratic knowledge had been eliminated, only the effects of the basic processes would remain. Experimental situations were designed to be simple and use abstract and independent cues to facilitate the evaluation of the impact of variation of specific variables on the target performance. This approach, which had been used to study sensory perception, was extended to higher cognitive processes such as memory. In his classic study of memory, Ebbinghaus (1885/1913) showed how he, being his own subject, could study memory for nonsense syllables, which were designed to induce basic memory associations and to minimize memory encodings facilitated by pre-existing knowledge. To further decrease the likelihood of complex encodings, Ebbinghaus used a fast presentation rate. Subsequent studies using groups of naive subjects have consistently replicated Ebbinghaus's initial results and extended them to a wide range of materials, such as lists of unrelated words, digits, and even to selections of prose and poetry.

This type of experimental approach clearly limits the degree to which more complex phenomena, such as deduction or problem solving, can be effectively studied. Within the behaviorist movement, there was even a bias against theoretical constructs that could not be explicitly defined in terms of directly observable entities, such as prior history of experiences. The key promise of the reductionistic approach, studying basic mechanisms in learning and memory, was that once the general laws and principles had been identified, more complex learning could be readily described as a straightforward extrapolation. However, a number of phenomena involving thought, even some that could be demonstrated in clearly controlled experimental situations, were not easily accounted for without the introduction of additional mechanisms. The emerging critics of Behaviorism focused on empirical evidence that could not be accounted for by previous experience and implicated nonobservable states and entities, such as sensory memory (Sperling, 1960), short-term memory (Miller, 1956), abstract concepts in concept formation (Levine, 1966), and logical reasoning (Woodworth & Sells, 1935).

Contemporary with the behavioristic research on basic learning, less formal analyses of thinking continued, relying primarily on accounts of naturally occurring thought. Rather than focusing on mundane everyday thinking, interest was directed toward the highest forms of thinking, such as scientific discovery (Poincaré, 1952) and artistic creation (Wallas, 1926), and to phenomena such as insight, where accounts in terms of retrieval of past experiences (reproductive thought) and incremental trial-and-error conditioning processes seemed least convincing. Most of the empirical evidence was in the form of anecdotal reports, many of them written down years after the actual event (Gruber, 1981b; Holmes, 1989). These reports suggested the sudden emergence of the critical ideas (insight), without any relevant thoughts preceding them. Hence, the emergence of these ideas was proposed to reflect the extended operation of unconscious processes initiated by deliberate unsuccessful attempts to solve some particular problem.

A first step toward studying these complex thought processes was taken in successful efforts to design laboratory tasks that frequently induced such experiences. Durkin (1937) monitored the subjects' thought processes by retrospective reports and compared the thoughts occurring prior to the insight experience to those occurring afterward. Later, Duncker (1945) designed experimental problems that could not be solved based on subjects' prior experience with related problems (reproductive thought) and, hence, required the production of new combinations of ideas (productive thought). However, the careful study of think-aloud protocols of subjects solving these types of problems allowed Duncker (1945) to identify a number of intermediate thoughts and goals that directed the subjects to their eventual solutions, even for this type of productive problem solving.

A pioneering effort in studying thought processes of experts in the laboratory was made by de Groot (1946/1978). Expert chess players display their superior performance in chess games, where every game differs from every other, making any simple "reproductive" interpretation of skilled performance implausible. However, de Groot proposed that expert performance in many different domains was mediated by a large number of stored patterns that would directly elicit the appropriate actions thus allowing for smooth and efficient performance.

III. THE INFORMATION-PROCESSING ACCOUNT OF THINKING

Newell, Simon, and Shaw (Newell & Simon, 1961) were the first theorists to show that a machine (computer) could be programmed to simulate the generation of productive thought for tasks involving the generation of proofs in propositional logic. Provided with a problem similar to those presented to human subjects, the program would generate goals and subgoals in a manner similar to thinking-aloud subjects confronted with the same tasks. This model was later generalized into the General Problem Solver, which could solve several different types of problems relying on the general method of Means–Ends Analysis (Ernst & Newell, 1969). Further research on thinking in cryptarithmatic, logic, and chess allowed Newell and Simon (1972) to specify a model of the human information-processing system, where a small number of elementary information processes could successfully reproduce human performance in several tasks, when programmed with only a small amount knowledge about the domain and the specific task. The "architecture" of the human information-processing system was designed to be consistent with the retrieval and storage characteristics of the sensory, short-term, and long-term memory systems identified in contemporary research on attention and memory (Atkinson & Shiffrin, 1968; Simon, 1974).

The central claim of the human information-processing theory is that cognitive processes and thinking can be described as a sequence of states each defined by a limited amount of information active in attention (short-term memory). Each state provides the necessary input for the access or generation of information in the following state. Although the kind of information hypothesized to be available in attention was richer and included goals and directive information that constrain associative retrieval, the overall structure was consistent with the sequential nature of thinking accepted since Aristotle.

The key issue in this theory is to explicate the background knowledge and relevant information heeded by subjects in the process of generating solutions. Typically, the investigator performs a task analysis identifying the relevant knowledge available to subjects based on the information presented in the problem and as prior knowledge already stored in long-term memory (learned from pre-experimental experience). Then the investigator explicates the logically possible sequences of steps that could generate the correct solution. This type of task analysis can be easily performed on well-defined tasks of low to moderate complexity, where the subjects' relevant knowledge can be identified or inferred from shared experience, such as instructional materials.

The human information-processing theory makes predictions about observable behavior (e.g., eye movements and verbal reports of the contents of attention) that provide indicators of thought processes and states. With an additional assumption about immediacy of processing, it is possible to infer when subjects process a specific piece of information (Just & Carpenter, 1980). According to Ericsson and Simon's (1993) model of the verbalization of thoughts, subjects verbalize their thoughts as these thoughts enter attention under a concurrent verbalization ("think aloud") instruction. These verbal reports provide "dense" records of the thoughts mediating the generation of the solution. Verbal reports are the only type of data that allow investigators to monitor the contents of information accessed from long-term memory, which would not correspond to perceptually available information. The correspondence between sequences of intermediate steps identified by the task analysis and the inferred steps based on verbal reports and eye fixations has been remarkably good, and these converging analyses support detailed claims about the structure and contents of sequences of thoughts for a broad range of tasks.

The process data, especially the verbal reports, offer a rich description of the thought processes even for a single subject's solution to a particular problem. Hence it is possible to compare thought sequences of two subjects solving the same problem. These comparisons often reveal a large diversity of solutions by different subjects. Although each of the different solution sequences may be consistent with one of the logically possible sequences of steps identified by the task analysis, it is usually impossible to find a single sequence of steps and a corresponding deterministic process model that could account for the generated solutions of all individuals. This evidence has direct implications for theories and associated statistical analysis of performance data, arguing against the summary of performance data, across subjects, as a single "average" sequence of processes with only strictly random error variance.

Perhaps the most important conclusion of Newell and Simon's (1972) effort to show the sufficiency of the human information-processing theory as an account of problem solving and thinking was the central importance of relevant knowledge, especially for skilled performance in domains such as chess. In a classic study, Chase and Simon (1973) outlined how an increase in *only* organized knowledge (familiar configurations of chess pieces associated with appropriate chess moves) could explain the superior ability of chess experts to select the best move for chess positions as well as their superior immediate memory for briefly presented chess boards. Based on computer simulations, Simon and Chase (1973) estimated that chess masters must have acquired approximately 50,000 different configurations of chess pieces ("chunks") during a period of at least ten years of intensive study of chess. These estimates of the massive amounts of expert knowledge make any effort to fully specify the background knowledge of an expert virtually impossible, even disregarding the methodological problems of identifying and explicating that knowledge.

Subsequent research on the solution of algebra word problems (Berger & Wilde, 1987; Hinsley, Hayes, & Simon, 1977) and physics problems (Chi, Glaser, & Rees, 1983; Larkin, McDermott, Simon, & Simon, 1980) has shown that, with experience, individuals acquire abstract schemas and concrete patterns allowing rapid access to correct solutions and procedures as part of the comprehension of the text of the problems. Studies of practice and skill acquisition (Anderson, 1982; Fitts & Posner, 1967; Shiffrin &

Schneider, 1977) have shown that after large amounts of practice the speed of sequential processing is increased and finally transformed into direct access of the corresponding correct responses. The acquired direct access of responses has been found to be surprisingly specific to the practiced procedures and repeatedly shows a lack of transfer to different tasks and domains (Singley & Anderson, 1989).

Consistent with human information-processing theory the attainment of skill and expertise appears to entail only the acquisition of domain-specific knowledge and pattern–action connections without changing basic processes and information-processing capacity limits. Furthermore, the nature of the direct, "automatic" access implies that little useful information about the cognitive processes of experts can be obtained from verbal reports of the mediating cognitive processes. We will later discuss this common assumption in light of more recent empirical evidence.

Some Issues in Research on Information Processing

In the last two decades, the information-processing approach has become the modal approach in the study of thinking. Most empirical research projects are conducted in accordance with its theoretical and methodological assumptions, and alternative approaches can usually be described in terms of variations on some of its assumptions. The three fundamental assumptions of the information-processing approach were present in many of its historical precursors. First, thinking can be described as a sequence of identifiable knowledge states or thoughts separated by some processing activity that determines the transition from one state to its successor. Second, each state can be described by a limited number of activated Working Memory structures and thoughts that represent the primary input to the processes that produce the next state. Third, except in rare conditions, the basic processes operating to transform one knowledge state into another and the basic processing capacity limits (e.g., working memory or attentional capacity) are fixed and constant across healthy adult individuals.

These assumptions lead to the image of the thought process as movement from location to location, tracing a unique path through a "problem space" of potential knowledge states (Newell, 1981; cf. Figure 1 above). These same assumptions underlie the ubiquitous tendency by investigators to summarize complex thinking strategies in terms of a model series of substages in flow charts. Thus, if we survey empirical research on almost any of the traditional "thinking-and-problem-solving" tasks, we find alternate theories expressed with reference to competing claims about the substage structure of the modal strategies, and in terms of disagreements about the details of processing within stages. But the background assumptions concerning serial knowledge states and state-to-state transformation processes are implicitly or explicitly accepted almost universally. Furthermore, the assumption of elementary process and capacity constancy leads to the search for explanations of individual differences in terms of (1) the amount, structure, and accessibility of task-relevant background knowledge, and (2) learned strategies or algorithms for utilizing "internal" (from long-term memory) and "external" (sensory inputs from the task environment) information to generate new states from current states.

The importance of these assumptions becomes apparent if one considers the logical possibilities in terms of the problem-space metaphor. For even the simplest problems, there are an enormous number of knowledge states that are never visited by individual problem solvers, even in the space of *relevant* knowledge; and the set of *non*activated knowledge becomes inconceivably large if we consider the vast amounts of merely associated knowledge in the head of any adult problem solver. If a theoretical account of thinking required a realistic description of even one individual's idiosyncratic accumulated knowledge and associated activations, the study of thinking would be virtually impossible. Fortunately, study after study supports the assumption that knowledge activation is limited and specific and the utility of the analysis of thinking processes in terms of the "route" through the knowledge "space." However, there is a caveat; the studies that provide the strongest support for seriality and knowledge specificity have come from a tradition of homogeneous, highly controlled laboratory experiments.

The problem of controlling for the availability and accessibility of task-relevant knowledge and strategies has been frequently confronted by the methodological means of intentionally selecting experimental tasks, for which the subjects have little, if any, relevant pre-experimental knowledge. These well-defined tasks with explicit goals and measurable performance provide subjects with strong cues that constrain the retrieval of relevant information for a successful solution. Furthermore, subjects typically show little memory of previously encountered puzzle and stimulus configurations for the types of stimulus events they encounter as they perform these laboratory tasks (Coltheart, 1971; Karat, 1982; Reed, Ernst, & Banerji, 1974). The absence of retrievable memory of past experience within the experimental problem-solving session further simplifies the description of the thought process in terms of states of information in attention.

These limiting conditions have produced many demonstrations that it is possible to describe individual thinking as paths through problem spaces, and even that the likely paths can be predicted by a priori task analyses of the corresponding tasks. Note that these theoretical descriptions of thinking are not complete accounts of all individual subjects' verbalized information throughout the solution efforts, but they provide a convincing account of those aspects of thinking that are most relevant to the solution of the problem. Thus, all of the major models that are sufficient to generate solutions to traditional complex thinking tasks involving deductive reasoning (Braine, 1978; Johnson-Laird, 1983; Newell, 1981; Rips, 1983; Sternberg, 1980), analogical reasoning (Anderson & Thompson, 1989; Gentner, 1983; Holyoak, 1984; Sternberg, 1977), problem solving (Newell & Simon, 1972; Reed, 1987), choice (Payne, 1982), and induction (Bourne & Restle, 1959; Gregg & Simon, 1967; Levine, 1975) yield hypotheses about subjects' behavior that can be expressed easily in terms of the problem–space metaphor. [Of course, as critics have noted, the explanatory generality of the problem-space metaphor means that it lacks predictive power (Rips, 1988).]

A complete process model, based on these sequential descriptions of the solution paths for a problem type, would require the specification of processes connecting the sequence of states. This turns out to be an especially challenging problem for empirical research because even the most informative measures of behavior, concurrent and retrospective verbal reports, provide information only on the sequences of thoughts and not on the processes that bring these thoughts into attention (Ericsson & Simon, 1993). Hence, the generality and structure of these processes cannot be directly inferred from the subjects' reports of thought sequences. This problem confronted philosophers who attempted to infer general laws of thought, such as processes of association, from experienced thought sequences during daydreaming. One, far from universal solution to this problem is to assume that the processes that produce state-to-state transitions can be reduced to procedures composed of only a few elementary information processes (Newell & Simon, 1972; Posner & McLeod, 1982). When the set of permissible elementary information processes is limited, conclusions can be often drawn about an intervening process given information about only the bordering states.

In the context of traditional laboratory "thinking" tasks, which were selected to minimize the availability of relevant experiences and knowledge, it is reasonable to assume that the processes will be general and independent of the specific knowledge. When information consistent with the same or similar processes is observed for other unfamiliar tasks and materials, the general nature of these processes is empirically supported. Thus, we see means–ends "distance-from-the goal"-based evaluation processes appearing in many different studies of problem solving (Greeno & Simon, 1988); the same "vary-one-element-of-the-most-recent-unsuccessful-hypothesis" abduction strategies are common across many studies of concept attainment (Bruner, Goodnow, & Austin, 1956; Johnson, 1978; Levine, 1975); and the same natural inference rules appear in many studies of formal and informal reasoning with a variety of contents and syntactic forms (Rips, 1990; Smith, Langston, & Nisbett, 1992).

Many of the recent criticisms of the information-processing approach can be traced back to specific disagreements with individual authors' claims about these unreportable general processes. For example, research on rule learning in artificial grammar acquisition tasks has been interpreted as inconsistent with the process of deliberate hypothesis testing observed in traditional laboratory studies of concept formation. According to the traditional information-processing hypothesis, the subject moves through a problem space of rulelike hypotheses, and the current hypothesis is active in Working Memory and verbally reportable. But, research on the acquisition of artificial grammars has demonstrated that information about rules can be acquired, while the subjects are unable to verbally describe the rules they are following when questioned retrospectively at the end of the experiment. Reber (1976) concluded that learning in the absence of being able to verbally describe the rule must reflect unconscious learning processes, different in kind from the deliberate hypothesis-testing strategies proposed by information-processing researchers.

However, more recent research shows that the grammar acquisition process may be consistent with an information-processing analysis after all. *At the time of testing,* subjects can verbally describe and communicate the information used to make the category judgment for specific test items. These reports show that the subjects store information about presented exemplars in long-term memory and that test items serve as cues to retrieve relevant information about previously stored exemplars (Dienes, Broadbent, & Berry, 1991; Mathews et al., 1989; Reber, 1989). Given that subjects need the cue support of specific test items to retrieve the relevant information, they cannot report on their knowledge retrospectively at the end of the experiment. Similar findings have been observed in other related learning environments (Berry & Broadbent, 1984, 1988; Sanderson, 1989; Stanley, Mathews, Buss, & Kotler-Cope, 1989). Thus, it would be inappropriate to refer to this process as unconscious because it involves attention at encoding as well as at retrieval, when the grammaticality judgment is made (Ericsson & Simon, 1993). Furthermore, although these studies show that memory of specific instances can in some situations circumvent the use of standard hypothesis testing strategies, these exemplar retrieval processes are completely compatible with the information-processing approach (Chase & Simon, 1973).

In problem solving in new domains several investigators (Anderson, Farrell, & Sauers, 1984; Pirolli & Anderson, 1985; Ross, 1984) have shown that when encountering new problems subjects recall solutions to previously solved similar problems. However, when new problems do not share surface features with analogous problems encountered earlier, access is quite low (Holyoak, 1985).

We find substantial support for a description of state-to-state transitions with a limited set of general information processes; but, again, the supportive results are obtained primarily from a set of methodologically homogeneous studies. The basic problem is that these studies establish the existence of general processes under conditions where problem solvers' background knowledge is sharply limited; but one cannot infer that these same processes will be important and general in tasks where substantial amounts of task-relevant knowledge and experience are available.

Doubts about the representativeness of highly controlled, limited pre-experimental knowledge laboratory tasks are the basis for the most common criticisms of the information-processing approach: Is the approach relevant to cognition in everyday life (Lave, 1988; Neisser, 1976)? Much of this criticism is not specific to the theoretical assumptions of the information-processing approach, but implicates the methodological tactic of beginning research by studying subjects' performance in unnatural, controlled laboratory tasks. We are in agreement with the critics, that one must be cautious in generalizing from theories based only on laboratory tasks to everyday situations where much greater amounts of experience and knowledge are available to the thinker. Given the centrality of this issue we will discuss it in the next section prior to returning to the other issues raised above.

IV. THE RELATION BETWEEN THE STUDY OF THINKING IN THE LABORATORY AND IN EVERYDAY LIFE

We found that modern theories of thinking originated in observations of spontaneous thinking in everyday life. However, the philosophers who initiated the quest for a comprehensive theory of thinking did not attempt to systematically sample all aspects of thinking. Preference was given to observations of thinking that occurred under quiet and relaxed conditions, which we refer to as reverie or daydreaming. Given that this type of thinking is not highly constrained by external tasks and stimuli it was essentially impossible to arrange experimental conditions that could reliably reproduce the content and structure of such thinking. Hence investigators turned to goal-directed thinking, where the task and externally presented stimuli provided direction and constraints on the thought processes studied. Similar concerns led the behaviorists to study the performance of motivated subjects in well-defined tasks.

In our historical review we have emphasized one important dimension related to the generalizability of laboratory research to everyday life, namely the complexity of task-relevant knowledge. In Figure 2 we have located three types of phenomena on this hypothetical dimension of knowledge complexity.

We have placed laboratory research on basic processes at the lower end, as this research attempts to minimize the influence of relevant experience and complex knowledge. At the other extreme we have placed expert perfor-

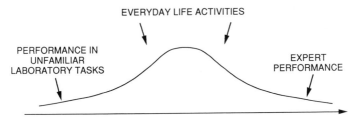

FIGURE 2 A hypothetical task dimension of relevant knowledge complexity.

mance in specific domains of expertise, which exemplifies the highest degree of complexity of knowledge as well as the largest amounts of relevant experience within a constrained set of objects and activities. In the middle we have placed the diverse category of everyday thinking, corresponding to an intermediate level of complexity of experience and knowledge.

The ultimate goal of the scientific study of thinking is to provide an understanding of the nature and structure of all types of thinking, preferably in terms of general laws. A coordinate goal is to understand the most frequent and important types of thinking that occur in everyday life. Therefore, it would be tempting to attain those goals by observing thinking in everyday life as it spontaneously occurs. Although we will review some interesting efforts to observe thinking in its natural context, most researchers believe that observation and analysis alone are unlikely to allow us to determine the important, general factors in the complex context of everyday life. Some type of systematic study, usually controlled experiments, is necessary.

We can distinguish between two experimental routes to the discovery of general laws of thought. The first begins in the laboratory, with attempts to design experimental tasks, however artificial, that capture the most general and fundamental thought processes. The assumption is that once the basics are established, everyday phenomena can be explained by a method of reduction. The second starts in the "field," attempts to identify informative, naturally occurring phenomena, and then moves into the laboratory to create experimental analogs that reproduce the phenomena from the "field" under controlled conditions that permit analysis and eventually support extrapolation back to the "field."

A. The Quest for General Processes

The most popular approach to the study of thinking has been focused on uncovering general laws of thinking and cognitive processes. Drawing on the successful natural sciences, such as physics and chemistry, this approach involves identifying the most simple and best controlled situations, where reproducible phenomena obeying the general laws can be found. According to this approach, there is no benefit to be gained from studying more complex phenomena than is absolutely necessary. The general laws, if they are truly general, should operate in the same manner in all cases. According to this approach one should first identify the general laws under ideal conditions and only then turn to analyses of more complex phenomena, where other factors will contribute additional influences. A key assumption of this approach is that the general laws regulating basic phenomena can be readily applied and easily extended to more complex phenomena. Both the behaviorist S–R theory and the information-processing theory propose that the same basic processes determine simple and complex phenomena. The primary difference lies in the complexity of the units of knowledge and experience. Hence, according to this approach, complex phenomena can be understood merely by describing the complexity of the corresponding knowledge.

An illustration of this approach is seen in the many studies we have cited in which think-aloud, move times, and solution rates were used to identify the strategies subjects used to solve simple, knowledge-barren, toy problems. Note that these problems were selected for study primarily because they allowed the careful dissection of solution processes; not because they were clearly relevant to important everyday intellectual achievements.

Another research tactic, popular with researchers who focus on the quest for fundamental processes, is illustrated by the use of experimental methods to assess the information-processing capacity for the execution of cognitive activities. For example, Gilhooly, Logie, Wetherick, and Wynn (1993) found some selective interference with performance of abstract deductive reasoning tasks, when subjects retained information concurrently in short-term memory. Similar interference has been observed in other laboratory tasks of reasoning and problem solving (Baddeley, 1986), where the task is unfamiliar and the amount of supporting relevant knowledge is minimal.

However, some results from research on interference paradigms seem to be problematic for the research strategy that attempts to identify basic processes through studies of the performance of unpracticed tasks. For example, Baddeley (1986) showed that performance of highly familiar, text comprehension tasks is surprisingly unaffected by a concurrent short-term memory task, suggesting that the mechanism of Working Memory in text comprehension is qualitatively different from that relevant to digit-span and Short-Term Memory. Furthermore, experts show vastly superior memory performance for briefly presented information from their domains of expertise. This superior memory performance, acquired through extended training, is almost unaffected by experimental procedures interfering with storage in traditional short-term memory during the presentation or retention phases of a memory task (Charness, 1976; Chase & Ericsson, 1981; Ericsson & Polson, 1988a, 1988b; Ericsson & Staszewski, 1989). These memory skills allow individuals to circumvent the limits of short-term memory, which subjects in laboratory experiments are forced to use because the experimenter has designed the tasks to minimize the relevance of prior knowledge and acquired skills.

There are also some methodological habits that are associated with the tactic of seeking basic processes in simple, highly controlled situations that have been criticized as counterproductive. First, although many reviewers exhort their colleagues to collect process data, such as eye movements and verbal reports, the collection of such data is still the exception rather than the rule. Furthermore, when such data is collected and analyzed, subjects are found to rely on not one but several different strategies as revealed by their verbal reports and confirmed by consistent differences in accuracy and reaction times for trials with different strategy reports (Marquer & Pereira, 1990; Siegler, 1987). Perhaps most problematic of all, the effect sizes of the manipulated variables in most studies are small compared to the differences in performance of individual subjects. The most popular solution to the problem of low power (and the desire to achieve some generality across subjects) involves aggregation of subjects' data into averages, which are difficult to interpret if the assumptions of general processes and of uniform process sequences are not met.

Another conundrum for theories based on studies of performance of unfamiliar laboratory tasks concerns the correlation between individual differences in basic capacities and complex performance. Contrary to expectation, the search for measures of basic capacity that correlate with performance in complex tasks of everyday life has been mostly unsuccessful. A long time ago, Binet (Varon, 1935) sought to design a test of general intelligence, but after considerable effort he gave up on measuring basic processes and capacities and turned to measures of complex comprehension and retrieval of knowledge. Binet found that with a moderate amount of practice on the tasks measuring basic capacities, substantial improvement resulted, which decreased differences between subjects of low and high intelligence. The only test of basic information-processing capacity that is normally included in contemporary intelligence tests is the digit-span test, which is viewed as a measure of the capacity of short-term memory. However, research with extended practice on the digit-span test has shown that performance can be improved from around 7 digits to over 80 digits (Chase & Ericsson, 1982; Ericsson, 1985). With practice, normal subjects acquire a memory skill allowing them to rapidly encode and store even abstract digit information in highly retrievable form in long-term memory.

The more stable and extreme performance of experts is even more poorly predicted by measures of basic processes and capacities than the performance of typical subjects (for a review, see Ericsson, Krampe, & Tesch-Römer, 1993). Even tests of general intelligence appear limited to predict performance during and immediately after job-related training with correlations in the 0.2 to 0.3 range (Baird, 1985; Ghiselli, 1966). Furthermore, after extended amounts of experience in the job the correlations are reduced to such low values that the tests are rendered useless for practical selection purposes (Hulin, Henry, & Noon, 1990).

The advantages of precision and control, available in the laboratory, coupled with the emphasis on "significant" (i.e., reliable, but often small) differences between average response measures, may actually direct researchers' attention away from larger, more important phenomena. Furthermore, we observe a common pattern in many areas of research: A neat experimental task is introduced that appears to have relevance to some important everyday situations. Research proceeds for a decade or so, and the average behavior of inexperienced subjects in the laboratory is well established. A collection of competing theories emerge and competitive tests, based on directional hypotheses about average data, are conducted and some of the theories are eliminated. Then, after a considerable amount of understanding has accumulated, researchers (and observers from outside the "experimental paradigm") conclude that the phenomena captured by the controlled task (now fairly well understood) appear to have relatively little bearing on the pertinent everyday phenomena. The relevance and generalizability of research on concept acquisition, problem solving in "toy" tasks, short-term memory, and iconic memory for artificial materials have been repeatedly questioned (Crowder, 1982; Haber, 1983; Neisser, 1976). New and different tasks continue to be introduced in laboratory research often because their structure is viewed as more similar to tasks in everyday life (Berry & Broadbent, 1988; Reber, 1989).

B. Capturing Everyday Phenomena in Laboratory Tasks

If the modal research tactic can be described as moving from the simple to the complex, relying on synthesis and extrapolation, there are other approaches drawing inspiration from natural sciences, such as biology and meteorology, that advocate an alternative relationship to naturally occurring phenomena. These approaches identify phenomena in everyday life and then try to reproduce the phenomena for systematic study under controlled conditions in the laboratory. Examples of this approach are found in the successful isolation of the mechanisms underlying different types of diseases and studies of imprinting and other types of behavior originally identified "in the field" by ethologists (Eibl-Eibesfeldt, 1970). An illustration of this approach to capturing cognitive phenomena from everyday life is offered by

Brown and McNeill's (1966) studies evoking tip-of-the-tongue memory states in the laboratory by requiring subjects to retrieve low-frequency words in response to dictionary definitions. A wide range of tasks and goal-directed activities, such as reading, text comprehension, and solving "real" problems in mathematics and physics, which occur naturally, especially in school settings, have been transferred successfully into controlled laboratory settings.

The phenomena-based approach ideally requires that highly reproducible results are identified, often in the form of large differences between two conditions or two groups of subjects. Furthermore, the differences must be stable so they can be repeatedly reproduced and, ideally, they would be unaffected by efforts to measure and study them. One "source" of large, robust differences in performance is found in comparisons between experts and less accomplished individuals in a fixed domain of performance. In many domains of activity, most notably individual performance in sports, performance is "tested" under standardized conditions that can be easily transferred into the laboratory. Performance in other domains is more interactive and extends over long periods of time; however, even in these more complex situations, controlled research is possible.

One such difficult-to-study domain is chess, where ability in chess playing is determined by competition in chess games between the different opponents. Almost every chess game is different. In his pioneering study of chess expertise, de Groot (1946/1978) decided that the critical chess ability is captured in the selection of the next move for a given chess position. De Groot identified several chess positions from unfamiliar games and instructed the chess experts to select the best move for each game while thinking aloud. In a comparison of the think-aloud protocols of chess expert versus international chess masters, de Groot found evidence for extensive mental exploration and evaluation of different potential sequences of chess moves, although the depth and the amount of search did not differ dramatically between the two groups of chess players. However, the move sequences considered by the international chess masters differed from those considered by the chess experts and the best moves identified by the international chess masters were often not even considered by the chess experts. According to de Groot the international chess masters would encode the board position differently, during the initial phase of presentation, which in turn led to focusing on the best moves for sequential exploration.

Numerous subsequent studies have used a similar approach to study the highest levels of thinking in accepted experts in various domains of expertise (Chi, Glaser, & Farr, 1988; Ericsson & Smith, 1991a). Capturing expert performance by a collection of tasks in the laboratory is far from trivial and requires careful observation and analysis of the expert performance as it naturally occurs, before laboratory analogue tasks are designed. It is also important to focus on the essence of the expert performance, that aspect that discriminates individuals at different levels of performance, and hence the part of expert performance that is the most difficult to attain. One should then seek a collection of similar well-defined tasks for which performance can be measured. How similar these situations have to be to the real-life situations is an empirical question. In general, one should strive for the simplest situation in which the superior performance of the experts can still be reliably reproduced.

Once the superiority of experts' performance has been repeatedly reproduced in the laboratory with the designed tasks, it becomes possible to analyze the mediating mechanisms by various types of process tracing and the systematic variation of factors in the experimental situation. It is important to recognize that this approach requires that the nature of the relevant expertise be well enough understood to identify a stable performance advantage of recognized experts (cf. Camerer & Johnson, 1991, for an example of a domain in which expert–novice differences in achievement have been difficult to identify). This approach starts with a robust, complex phenomenon and then through systematic analysis isolates the mechanisms responsible for its specific characteristics (Ericsson & Smith, 1991b).

We are obviously enthusiastic about the research tactic of beginning with a large, stable, naturally occurring phenomenon (and our prime example is expert–novice differences in performance) and then moving into the laboratory for empirical analysis, but there are some drawbacks to this approach to cognitive skill. First, the ground rules for the approach and successful examples of its application are less available than for the more popular laboratory-based alternative. Although there are some examples of the careful analysis of thinking phenomena outside the laboratory with subsequent return to study under controlled conditions, there is still no clear set of guidelines for the analysis of everyday thinking. Second, one inevitable consequence of the move outside the laboratory is that we must be prepared to identify, describe, and possibly model the large amounts of task-relevant knowledge that have been acquired over a lifetime of experience by ordinary people. This is a daunting challenge. Again, we can cite some examples of attempts to deal with these issues, but there are no well-defined guidelines for either descriptive of modeling work.

C. Differences in Knowledge and Skill

We have highlighted the differences between the two most popular general approaches to study thinking, but both assume that acquired knowledge and skill is the major variable that accounts for the largest individual differences in performance among normal adults. The traditional approach tries to minimize the influence of previously acquired knowledge and skills in order to study the basic processes more effectively, whereas the study of expert performance emphasizes the results of maximal influence of experience and acquired knowledge and skills. Both approaches are consistent with specificity of performance and the commonly observed lack of transfer of acquired skills. Both approaches would attribute the limited scope of cognitive skills to the specificity of the knowledge required for high performance in a particular task. When the goal is to produce a general theory of thinking encompassing all phenomena involving activities with low to high complexity of knowledge, one would expect that approaches moving from simple to complex and complex to simple will converge on the same general description. The key assumption necessary for convergence is that the general basic processes remain the same even as the complexity of the knowledge increases and expert performance is eventually attained.

The fundamental obstacle to "scaling up" from basic processes, such as those studied in traditional laboratory tasks, to complex processes, such as those occurring in major cognitive achievements outside the laboratory, is the dependence of performance on background knowledge and learned algorithmic strategies. Many of the "basic" strategies (e.g., Means–Ends Analysis) that have been identified in "toy" tasks are default responses that occur in the absence of more effective methods, but more effective strategies will be adopted if opportunities to acquire relevant knowledge and skills are available. This critique of the quest for basic processes in unpracticed laboratory tasks yields two research imperatives: (a) studies of the contents and structure of complex task–relevant knowledge bases; and (2) studies of the acquisition processes for complex knowledge bases and thinking strategies.

The most predictable difference between novice and expert performance is the increase in the amount of domain-specific knowledge. Even when we disregard the academic subjects (e.g., history, biology, physics) where the increased knowledge is virtually synonymous with expertise, there is evidence that higher levels of performance are correlated with standard tests of amount of domain-specific knowledge, for example, in chess (Pfau & Murphy, 1988), mathematics (Webb, 1975), and sports (French & Thomas, 1987).

The amount of knowledge necessary for expert performance can be roughly estimated from books and encyclopedias describing the state of art in the respective domains. The estimated amount of necessary knowledge is vast (Charness, 1991), and a further complication is that the knowledge and experiences of individual experts may differ considerably. Recent efforts to elicit experts' knowledge and procedures have shown that knowledge extraction is difficult even for restricted tasks in the domain (Hoffman, 1987; Olson & Biolsi, 1991; Olson & Reuter, 1987).

A simple index of the complexity of the knowledge and acquired skills that are necessary to attain expert performance is given by the shortest time that even the most able individuals can attain that level. International levels of performance in a domain of expertise require around ten years of intense, full-time practice to be attained (Ericsson et al., 1993; Simon & Chase, 1973). Once the duration of learning corresponds to months and years, it is impossible to monitor all relevant activity. Maybe even more important, the extended duration forces investigators to address issues of sustained motivation and effort.

Given that a detailed description of the individual experts' knowledge in terms of content and organization is out of the question in any realistically complex domain of achievement, a methodological solution to this problem is offered by the use of well-defined tasks that dramatically restrict the *relevant* knowledge. For a specific task, even in a domain with large amounts of knowledge, only a small fraction of that knowledge will be relevant to "solve" a particular problem.

When the thought processes of individuals at different levels of expertise are compared for specific problems, the most consistent and striking differences concern the representation of the presented task. An expert quickly attains an integrated representation of the task situation. After one reading, a competent physicist has fully represented a typical "textbook" problem and, for "easy" problems, a plan is generated within seconds that allows the expert to calculate the solution in a manner called forward reasoning (Larkin et al., 1980). In contrast, an undergraduate physics student, working on the same problem, retrieves knowledge and formulas in a time-consuming piecemeal fashion using means–ends analysis. The rapid formation of a problem representation that integrates presented information with relevant background knowledge also appears to be a general characteristic of experts in domains, such as chess, medicine, and sports (Patel & Groen, 1991).

Due to the rapid formation of the expert's representation of the task it has been difficult to study intermediate stages in its generation. Consequently, research has focused on studying the structure and content of the problem representation after the initial exposure and processing involving planning, reasoning, and evaluation. The most common methodology has involved presenting representative stimuli from the domain and then comparing recall among individuals differing in expertise. There are two assumptions underlying this method: (1) recall and other memory measures will provide clues about the manner in which task-relevant information has been comprehended and transformed in the problem-solving process; and (2) novice versus expert comparisons will identify the crucial, functionally significant aspects of the representations. The most general result is that experts recall more information for meaningful stimuli, but the advantage of the experts disappears when randomly arranged versions of the same stimuli are presented in chess (see Charness, 1991, for a review), bridge (Charness, 1979; Engle & Bukstel, 1978), go (Reitman, 1976), music (Sloboda, 1976), electronics (Egan & Schwartz, 1979), computer programming (McKeithen, Reitman, Rueter, & Hirtle, 1981), dance, basketball, and field hockey (Allard & Starkes, 1991), and figure skating (Deakin & Allard, 1991). Other research has shown that short film sequences of athletic performances are far better recalled by experts than novices (Pinheiro & Simon, 1992) and that the memory superiority is restricted to those aspects that are relevant to the particular event (Ste-Marie & Lee, 1991). In domains with an emphasis on speed and rapid reactions experts acquire representations that allow them to prepare actions in advance in typewriting (Salthouse, 1991), in sight reading of music (Sloboda, 1985), and in predicting events in sports (Abernethy, 1991).

In some cases the experts' superior memory for relevant information is attained at the expense of memory for irrelevant information. Expert radiologists have superior memory for relevant abnormalities in x-ray images, but exhibit inferior memory for normal variations compared to novices (Myles-Worsley, Johnston, & Simons, 1988). Expert computer programmers tend to recall the structure of programs better at the expense of details, whereas novice computer programmers show the reverse pattern (Adelson, 1984).

The most detailed analyses of the structure of these representations have been made in studies of physics, chess, and memory experts. Novices in physics tend to group problems based on the mention of objects in the text (surface features), whereas experts encode the abstract physical principles involved, which are more directly related to the solution procedures (Chi et al., 1982). After brief exposures of chess positions experts are able to encode and recall the global structure and the relations between chess configurations (Chi, 1978; de Groot, 1946/1978). In one study a chess master was able to retrieve information about the briefly presented chess board with an accuracy and speed comparable to perception of the same information when the board remained visible (Ericsson & Staszewski, 1989).

Research on a wide range of memory experts shows that these individuals are able to use their pre-existing, domain-specific knowledge to store the presented information in long-term memory in the context of predetermined retrieval plans. When recall is required, these individuals can activate the corresponding retrieval plan, which leads to rapid retrieval of the desired information; incidentally these memory skills greatly increase effective working memory capacity (Chase & Ericsson, 1982). Recent research has shown how the superior memory of experts in many practical domains can be accounted for by similar mechanisms of "Skilled Memory," that rely on retrievable storage in long-term memory (Ericsson & Staszewski, 1989). Skilled Memory Theory predicts increases in the amount of information in working memory *for a specific domain,* without violating the assumption that thinking is a sequence of states, where each state can be characterized by a severely limited number of active knowledge structures in attention. The "extended working memory capacity" is attributed to the fact that more information can be directly retrieved from long-term memory using specific retrieval cues.

The generation of the initial representation of the task is rarely sufficient to access a plan or an answer, except for familiar simple problems. When confronted with a more complex task, experts are found to engage in a substantial amount of reasoning about alternative solutions and procedures prior to giving their answers. Naturally, a key empirical question concerns the skills employed by experts, during this systematic exploration, that enable them to, for example, discover better chess moves than those suggested by the initial representation, to recover from initially incorrect assumptions and biases, and to generate explanations consistent with the relevant evidence (de Groot, 1946/1978; Lesgold et al., 1985; Patel & Groen, 1991). In chess, much of this exploration consists of planning and evaluating sequences of potential chess moves for the current board position. Consistent with the acquisition of memory skill to support storage of the information for planning, the depth of search of move sequences has been found to increase with levels of skill up to the level of chess experts (Charness, 1981, 1989; de Groot, 1946/1978). Charness (1989) showed that expertise in the game of bridge was closely linked with the ability to generate successful plans for playing the cards in the best order. In other domains, such as physics, experts adopt representations that incorporate the relevant information and facilitate further inferential processing often in the form of two-dimensional diagrams (Anzai, 1991; Larkin & Simon, 1987).

It is also important to recognize the advantage to the expert of having learned a vast "library" of past situations and cases. Chess masters' achievements such as playing "blindfold" games at a level comparable to their normal chess ability (Ericsson & Staszewski, 1989; Holding, 1985), are explicable with reference to the concepts of Skilled Memory and the assumption of a large, orderly, long-term memory store of chess board configurations. With increasing expertise in medicine, basic medical knowledge becomes organized around the experts' clinical knowledge about specific diseases and their symptoms (Boshuizen & Schmidt, 1992). And, in many fields such as medicine (Brooks, Norman, & Allen, 1991), law (Burton, 1985; Hastie & Pennington, 1991), and business (Wagner, 1991), both educational curricula and the knowledge bases acquired by practicing experts are organized around specific situations and cases (cf. Kolodner, 1992; Slade, 1991).

Expert performance reflects an adaptation to a specific domain to attain a high performance on tasks within that domain. However, expert performance is not a faster, "automatized" version of the sequential processes of the novices, nor is it simply increased amounts of accumulated knowledge (Ericsson & Smith, 1991b; Salthouse, 1991). Expert performance also involves qualitative changes in the mediating problem representations that allow the expert to encode new and different information, plus memory skills to hold more information accessible to Working Memory to support reasoning, planning, and evaluation. Only by identifying the naturally occurring performance conditions and by using representative tasks from the domain can performance be captured under more controlled conditions in the laboratory and the specific cognitive mechanisms isolated and systematically studied. The emphasis on complex skills and knowledge also demands research on the conditions that promote the acquisition of these abilities.

V. THE ACQUISITION OF COMPLEX KNOWLEDGE AND SKILLS

The general question of how a given skill or competency has been acquired requires a consideration of the skilled individuals' past activities and experiences. This conclusion has been reached by many of the major theorists in cognitive psychology; and it is no accident that the most comprehensive theories ("architectures") of cognitive processes have been developed with an emphasis on learning and skill acquisition as it occurs in designed instructional settings (e.g., Anderson, 1981, 1983, 1993; Klahr, Langley, & Neches, 1987; Newell, 1990; Rumelhart, McClelland, & the PDP Research Group, 1986; Van Lehn, 1990).

The most commonly recognized predictor of competency in a specific type of activity is the amount of experience of that particular activity (N.B.: there are some domains in which expertise seems to be illusory and in which the amount of experience does not predict competency or accuracy; Camerer & Johnson, 1991; Dawes, 1989). This introduces further "motivational" complexities, because, in everyday life outside the laboratory, individuals have a fair amount of control over how their time is allocated and, thus, motivational factors determine the nature and amount of experience and attained performance.

It is also apparent that most of the relevant skills in everyday life are attained as a result of normal interaction without any need for specially designed educational activities. In response to difficulties and problems in our traditional school system, scientists are becoming increasingly interested in how learning occurs so smoothly in many everyday settings. Many interesting examples of the acquisition of complex skills in everyday life have been documented and the broader social context or situations in which the skill is acquired are emphasized in empirical and theoretical analyses (Greeno, 1989; Lave, 1988; Saxe, 1991). Thus, as anticipated by many historical precursors, motivation emerges as a central issue in any theory of complex thinking that is likely to be useful outside the laboratory. However, as we noted in our review of current approaches to the study of thinking, most research has focused on circumstances (e.g., 50-minute experimental sessions in which undergraduates perform novel thinking tasks) that avoid problems of motivation. Once we consider learning activities extended over months and years, attention and motivation cannot be taken for granted, as any school teacher will agree.

A. Learning of Different Types of Performance

Advances in the efforts to measure socially significant performance competencies provide us with a useful tool to study the learning and acquisition of some forms of performance. The collections of tasks designed to measure the essence of the desired performance can be used as a well-defined reference point for measurement of the learning. Our schema for characterizing the complexity of knowledge and skills in different types of thinking (see Figure 2) is also applicable to the task of attaining those types of thinking and the corresponding mastery of the relevant activities. Let us briefly comment on some of the differences between the three types of skills, requiring low, medium, and high levels of background knowledge, and how they have been studied.

1. Laboratory Studies of Skill Acquisition

Many laboratory studies select tasks that require a minimum of necessary background knowledge and skills. The tasks are designed to allow subjects to reach accurate performance after a brief period of instruction and familiarization. Subjects are explicitly instructed to try to increase their performance and, with further practice, it is primarily the speed of generating answers that improves (Anderson, 1982; Fitts & Posner, 1967). The focus of these studies is to measure the quantitative effect of practice on performance in controlled tasks. Active efforts are made to keep subjects motivated to give their best performance by keeping practice sessions short (around an hour) and by rewarding subjects for their participation. The total duration of practice in these studies is rarely greater than five hours. Given the simple and explicit structure of these tasks, the primary relevance to the study of thinking concerns the disappearance of mediating thoughts and the emergence of direct access and automated responses.

Using a similar methodology, the effects of practice have been examined on memory and perceptual-motor tasks, where accuracy is the primary variable of interest. Concurrent observations of strategies and representations show qualitative changes in the processes with further practice (see Ericsson et al., 1993, for a review), suggesting that active problem solving is required to attain more effective strategies. In these studies, the duration of practice was still typically less than ten hours, but a few studies have extended practice to several hundred hours (Chase & Ericsson, 1982; Staszewski, 1988). The tasks used for practice are identical or similar to the tasks measuring the attained-skill performance, allowing investigators to continuously measure the relevant performance during the practice period.

To assure uniform improvement on such tasks it is not efficient to wait for subjects to be successful in their problem-solving efforts, rather it is more effective to provide instruction on the best strategies. Several large-scale research programs have focused on the acquisition of complex cognitive skills, when deliberate instruction is provided, such as arithmetic computation, natural language grammar acquisition, logic and geometry theorem proving, and computer programming. This area of research is subject to rapid changes and is populated by sharply discrepant theoretical approaches. One general approach emphasizes the production of system models for skilled processing and has proposed a number of plausible learning mechanisms based on the composition or chunking of small productions into more task-appropriate units (e.g., Anderson, 1993; Newell, 1990; Van Lehn, 1990), and has focused on explaining the shapes of learning curves, understanding the common finding of task specificity and little positive transfer (across even very similar tasks), and the invention of useful computer tutors. Other approaches, emphasizing neurally inspired processes and incremental learning algorithms, have focused on demonstrations of the abilities of uniform and simple learning processes to acquire complex, discontinuous-appearing habits (e.g., arithmetic and grammar processing capacities; Hinton, 1989; Rumelhart et al., 1986; Seidenberg, 1992; cf. Mc-Closkey & Cohen, 1989; Pinker & Prince, 1988).

2. Skill Acquisition in Everyday Life and Expert Performance

Activities in everyday life are organized around goals that seldom explicitly include learning. We will distinguish two general categories of activities with different goals. First, there is work, where individuals generate products and services that are rewarded socially and monetarily. Second, there is leisure and other types of activities that are inherently enjoyable and thus provide their own intrinsic rewards. In both work and leisure activities any participant needs to understand the relevant activity and to acquire necessary skills. These skills can often be attained through observation and some limited amount of explicit instruction. In general, there appears to be little time in leisure and work set aside for training and improvement of performance. It is generally believed that with more experience performance will increase. The scant amounts of data on productivity in new job situations show that performance increases at least during the first few years "on the job" (Hofmann, Jacobs, & Gerras, 1992). However, we are remarkably ignorant about skill acquisition in everyday work and leisure situations. To some extent this is due to the fact that performance under standard conditions in which motivation to perform at the highest levels achievable is rarely measured or reported in everyday tasks.

In several of the domains of leisure and work, expert performance is observed. However, expert performers are rarely "regular participants"; their careers are different from the beginning. In most domains there is a system of organized education to allow promising young individuals to efficiently attain their highest levels of performance. Recent studies of international-level performers (Bloom, 1985a) find that these individuals, after an initial short period of playful interaction in the domains, are provided individual instruction by special teachers from an early age.

B. Activities Relevant to Everyday Skill Acquisition

In order to understand the mechanisms of learning and skill acquisition in everyday life we need to go beyond the notion of simple accumulation of all kinds of experience and differentiate specific activities that effectively mediate improved performance. A direct approach would describe the nature and amount of different categories of activities for specific individuals and then relate these durations to observed improvements in a specific aspect of performance. When the relevant time period of work and leisure spans months and years, such an inductive approach will be time consuming and difficult to successfully complete. However, there is a substantial amount of knowledge from laboratory research about necessary conditions for learning, and we can thus rely on this knowledge to selectively identify everyday activities plausibly related to skill acquisition.

A century of research on learning has identified conditions for skill acquisition. Motivated subjects are typically given well-defined tasks and many trials with immediate feedback about their performance. In absence of feedback even motivated subjects do not improve their performance, except in some special cases. Furthermore, errors and "impasses" appear to be necessary to lead subjects to change their cognitive processes and representations (Van Lehn, 1991). Depending on the particular skill to be acquired it is possible to design training activities that incorporate the necessary conditions for efficient skill acquisition; these activities we will refer to as deliberate practice (Ericsson et al., 1993).

When we review everyday activities in leisure and work, we find little evidence for spontaneous engagement in deliberate practice or other related learning activities. In leisure activities, such as tennis and golf, individuals spend most of their time playing, under conditions in which new and different situations are constantly generated. There is no chance to interrupt the game to correct errors and mistakes, and there might be weeks until another similar situation emerges naturally. In fact, continuous playful interaction appears critical to produce the inherent enjoyment of the leisure activity. Based on interviews of individuals participating in many activities, Cszikszentmihalyi (1990) identified the existence of inherently enjoyable states called "flow." The desirable flow states are experienced as a seemingly effortless engagement in the activity occurring under conditions in which there is a close match between the individual's ability and the demands of the current situation. States corresponding to flow and "highs" occur under circumstances that are quite different from the goal-directed efforts to improve and refine performance in deliberate practice (Ericsson et al., 1993). Hence, expert performers and other individuals find inherent enjoyment in many activities in a domain, but these activities are not those that are most instrumental in improving performance.

The other broad category of activities in everyday life we refer to as work. The goal of work is to deliver some service or generate some product efficiently. Once individuals have acquired a sufficient set of proven methods to perform their job reliably they tend to continue to employ those methods (Ashworth, 1992). When errors and mistakes unexpectedly occur the focus is typically on dealing with the consequences of those errors rather than their causes. The real-time constraints of reliable production discourages individuals to explore new and alternative methods with unknown reliability. Hence neither of the two broad categories of everyday-life activities provides individuals with situations with effective opportunities for learning and improvement of performance.

In many of the same domains, where most participants simply engage in the main activities, knowledge on how to train and improve performance has been accumulated and educational settings with full-time teachers have been developed. Although most adult participants are aware of these educational opportunities they rarely seek them out due to the associated costs in money and time and the effortful nature of the required training. Most individuals that enroll in these educational activities are young and viewed as having special promise for attaining expert-level performance as adults.

The lives of individuals who ultimately attain the highest levels of performance differ dramatically from the lives of other individuals (Bloom, 1985a; Chambliss, 1988). The typical biography of an expert begins in early childhood (at about age 4 in many domains that have been studied), when the individual is exposed to activities of the given domain in a playful and enjoyable manner. When interest and promise for high performance in the domain is discovered, parents arrange for individualized instruction by a qualified teacher, who designs practice activities suited for that particular individual. This type of instruction has all the features of effective learning identified during a century of research on learning and skill acquisition (Ericsson et al., 1993). Recent developments in education that stress the importance of individualized instruction are consistent with the instructional practices of coaches and expert performers. Computerized tutoring systems provide opportunities for individualized instruction of students and the attained performance of such students surpasses that of students receiving traditional education (Anderson, Boyle, Corbett, & Lewis, 1990; Wenger, 1987).

Occasionally individuals, especially children, reveal an exceptional ability in some activity without prior instruction. Careful analyses of these individuals' performance under laboratory conditions have revealed mediating thought processes and strategies similar to those in individuals attaining the corresponding skills deliberately. Systematic interviews on the developmental history of these individuals show these abilities to have been acquired by self-generated practice activities (Ericsson & Faivre, 1988; Howe, 1990).

Given that deliberate practice is not intrinsically motivating as an activity, parents and teachers actively support and encourage the children's practice activities and help children recognize the improvements resulting from practice (Bloom, 1985b). To establish a steady pattern, practice is scheduled at regular times and for relatively constant durations every day. As these children grow older and their performance levels increase, the daily amount of practice increases and their lives become centered around their training. At some point during adolescence, the individuals make a commitment to a full-time life as a performer and reach a maximum amount of practice of around four or five hours per day. Based on analyses of detailed diaries of expert performers and a review of the literature, Ericsson et al. (1993) concluded that this amount of practice is the highest that can be sustained indefinitely without leading to exhaustion and "burn out." The total amount of deliberate practice over the course of individual performers' development was directly related to their adult levels of performance, even when the analysis was restricted to only expert performers.

Deliberate practice is effective in attaining the highest levels of skill and knowledge only in a specific domain in which teachers and coaches know how to communicate and transmit their knowledge to their students. The ultimate contribution to a domain involves the generation of new knowledge and techniques that goes beyond the available knowledge in a domain and changes the domain. These rare contributions are not directly instructable and their occurrence is not predictable, hence, it is virtually impossible to study them as they originally occur. However, it has been possible in several cases to examine the records and diaries of eminent scientists making such contributions to uncover the extended processes of discovery (Gruber, 1981a; Tweney, 1989).

In sum, high levels of performance are not a natural consequence of extensive experience in a domain. The highest levels of performance are observed only after a decade of deliberate efforts to improve one's skill. Typically these deliberate efforts correspond to individualized instruction by teachers along with large amounts of practice on designed training tasks. Deliberate practice is sometimes incorrectly equated with mechanical repetition similar to rote memorization. Although it may often be difficult to distinguish those two forms of activities by mere observation, verbal reports and other indicators of cognitive processes reveal fundamental differences. Some of our knowledge about the cognitive processes of deliberate practice comes from the descriptions of master teachers and coaches (Ericsson et al., 1993). Other evidence is found in the earlier reviewed studies of cognitive processes of experts encountering representative problems and process-tracing studies of skill acquisition. Some interesting new data show differences in the cognitive processes during studying by students at different ability levels (Chi, Lewis, Reimann, & Glaser, 1989). We believe that systematic study of the thought processes during deliberate practice will become a key to study of skill acquisition in everyday life and expert performance. Of particular interest are the conditions under which individuals spontaneously initiate such deliberate learning efforts.

A full understanding of learning and thinking cannot be attained without an account of the factors influencing the prerequisite motivation to engage in goal-directed focused efforts, namely motivation to practice. A fundamental, perhaps even counterintuitive, precept that has emerged from our review is that performance and the conditions of effective acquisition of a skill (practice) are not one and the same (cf. Brehmer, 1980). We believe that the study of learning, thinking, and skill acquisition as it occurs in everyday life is necessary to identify the important factors, both social and motivational, that induce and promote deliberate learning activities. Only then can laboratory studies be designed to capture the full context of thinking and learning. As the duration of experience and the complexity of the associated skill increase and activities relevant to acquisition become a significant part of individuals' lives, we need to consider the functional role of activities beyond those directly relevant to acquisition. Many seemingly unrelated activities, including patterns of *non*practice or resting, may be critical motivational prerequisites that are necessary to sustain the skill acquisition process over extended time periods.

VI. SUMMARY AND CONCLUSIONS

In this chapter we have adopted a broad view of the study of thinking in order to discuss a wide range of approaches with their respective strengths and limitations. Given the enormous complexity of thinking and its acquisition, all approaches must make some explicit or implicit theoretical assumptions to identify those phenomena that can be successfully studied and that are most likely to provide important insights into thinking. Fundamental preliminary assumptions also dictate which types of observations to collect and the level at which the data should be analyzed and interpreted. Our goal, as reviewers, was to discuss approaches in terms of their assumptions and methods and to strive for an accumulation of findings and insights about thinking across approaches.

The first efforts to study thinking were based on self-observation of thinking in relaxed states, such as daydreaming. Thinking was defined as a sequence of thoughts, where the transitions between mental states were sudden and impossible to observe. Efforts to study the processes determining the transitions were based on theoretical inferences about associative processes. Early systematic empirical methods involved efforts to introspect on a given thought and image for an extended time. However, the introspective method was challenged on the grounds that it altered the original thought state and produced results of uncertain reliability and validity. Nonetheless, in spite of repeated failures to find independent empirical evidence to resolve theoretical disputes, it was generally assumed that spontaneous reports of the sequence of thoughts were useful descriptions of the general structure of thinking.

With the introduction of experimental methods into psychology, the emphasis changed toward the design of conditions that would produce stable and reproducible performance. Well-defined tasks were given to highly motivated subjects. Studies of thinking now had to meet an additional test; successful performance on the research tasks must be shown to imply the mediation of productive thinking, which could not be reduced to simple retrieval of relevant past experience. For this and other reasons, investigators studied behavior in controlled, artificial tasks and used arbitrary stimulus materials, which would minimize the influence of relevant pre-experimental experience. A number of different tasks were identified that virtually defined (at least in academic circles) various types of thinking, such as concept formation, reasoning (logic proof problems), and problem solving ("brain teaser" problems).

The human information-processing approach, based on early electronic computers, offered a significant advance in its proposals for explicit mechanisms for different forms of thinking in a general theoretical framework that emphasized limits in the capacities of different memory stores. Based on an extensive data base that included process data (concurrent and retrospective reports, eye fixations and latencies) and task analyses, thinking was represented as a sequence of states, where each state corresponded to a limited amount of active information in attention or short-term memory. Furthermore, to construct fully specified theoretical models that could be implemented as computer programs, it was necessary to infer processes generating the sequence of states. Given that the studied tasks were designed to minimize the influence of prior knowledge, general processes underlying the main types of thinking were proposed.

It is important to acknowledge the great importance of this achievement of providing sufficient theoretical accounts of thinking in well-defined tasks. Among other contributions, these theoretical achievements overcame many of the objections raised by behaviorists concerning the arbitrariness of cognitive theories, giving a new generation of researchers license to return to principled mentalistic theories. However, once a specific account for these thinking processes in a well-defined task is developed, its generalizability can be questioned. In our review we found that current controversies center around a couple of general issues. First, several alternative theoretical accounts for the processes have been proposed and are still competing for the "theoretical championship," even for the most popular laboratory tasks. For example, the competition between models based on general inference rules versus accounts in terms of the retrieval of specific exemplars is ongoing in the analysis of subjects' performance of several popular laboratory tasks. Second, the general issue of how these theories can be extended to thinking in nonlaboratory environments, where subjects have extensive knowledge and experience, is unresolved.

The modal approach to create a comprehensive theory of thinking strives to identify simple conditions under which a given type of thinking can be reliably reproduced. Following the successful example of experimenters in many of the natural sciences, the goal of this approach is to discover general laws and invariant constraints (e.g., on attentional capacity) in well-defined tasks that do not require access to complex knowledge and experience. Once these general laws and processing limits are identified, it is assumed that these theories can be easily extended to tasks requiring more complex knowledge and experience. However, many theoreticians question the degree to which general methods and information-processing limits generalize to thinking in more complex tasks domains.

The most popular alternative approach to the study of thinking starts by examining performance in everyday life, to identify stable and reproducible phenomena. Of particular interest is expert performance, because it offers the highest levels of performance and also the largest stable individual differences in performance, when compared against that of beginners. The next step, following the identification of an important phenomenon outside the laboratory, is the design of tasks that allow this performance to be reproduced under standard conditions. Once the superior performance is captured, process-tracing methodology and experimental variation can be applied to identify the thought processes and mechanisms mediating that performance. An important conclusion from this approach is that the thinking of expert performers is not merely an accumulation of more knowledge about appropriate actions that can be directly accessed by perceptual patterns. Instead, expert performance reflects acquired domain-specific representations and working-memory skills that support specialized planning, reasoning, and evaluation, which are essential for the high levels of performance. The performance and thinking of experts can be viewed as an extreme adaptation to the specific demands in a particular domain. Studies of the acquired cognitive mechanisms of experts reveal novel alternatives and possibilities for the structure of thinking in familiar activities of everyday life (Ericsson & Kintsch, 1994).

An understanding of thinking will be incomplete unless it provides an account of how the elements of adult thought, such as concepts, representations, and skills, are acquired. Research on learning and skill acquisition, on the whole range of activities ranging from performance on simple laboratory tasks to complex life-long efforts to attain expert performance, shows that effective learning is not an automatic consequence of extended experience. Sustained improvements in performance, both in laboratory studies and in training of expert performers, require that subjects engage in special training activities, which involve thinking and are effortful and not inherently motivating. Any theory of skill acquisition will have to include an analysis of the social context of learning, which accounts for how the motivation to improve performance and to engage in deliberate practice is generated and maintained over extended time periods.

The criticism that laboratory research lacks relevance for the understanding of everyday activities does not appear to be directed to the methodology of laboratory research, per se. Rather, the tasks commonly studied in laboratory research do not capture the situational characteristics and background knowledge of everyday life. Based on current and future descriptions of the structure of everyday life activities that successfully promote some desired goal, it should be possible to capture these situations and phenomena under controlled laboratory conditions. The ultimate goal, to fully understand thinking and its acquisition, is far from being reached; but a clearer articulation of what would be required will allow a wide range of different approaches to jointly contribute to this end.

Acknowledgments

The authors thank Mary Luhring for her assistance with the preparation of the manuscript. Support for R. Hastie was provided by NSF Grant SES-9122154.

References

Abernethy, B. (1991). Visual search strategies and decision-making in sport. *International Journal of Sport Psychology, 22,* 189–210.

Adelson, B. (1984). When novices surpass experts: The difficulty of the task may increase with expertise. *Journal of Experimental Psychology: Learning, Memory, and Cognition, 10,* 484–495.

Allard, F., & Starkes, J. L. (1991). Motor-skill experts in sports, dance and other domains. In

K. A. Ericsson & J. Smith (Eds.), *Toward a general theory of expertise: Prospects and limits* (pp. 126–152). Cambridge: Cambridge University Press.

Anderson, J. R. (1981). *Cognitive skills and their acquisition.* Hillsdale, NJ: Erlbaum.

Anderson, J. R. (1982). Acquisition of cognitive skill. *Psychological Review, 89,* 369–406.

Anderson, J. R. (1983). *The architecture of cognition.* Cambridge, MA: Harvard University Press.

Anderson, J. R. (1987). Methodologies for studying human knowledge. *Behavioral and Brain Sciences, 10,* 467–505.

Anderson, J. R. (1993). *Rules of the mind.* Hillsdale, NJ: Erlbaum.

Anderson, J. R., Boyle, C. F., Corbett, A., & Lewis, M. W. (1990). Cognitive modeling and intelligent tutoring. *Artificial Intelligence, 42,* 7–49.

Anderson, J. R., Farrell, R., & Sauers, R. (1984). Learning to program in LISP. *Cognitive Science, 8,* 87–129.

Anderson, J. R., & Thompson, R. (1989). Use of analogy in a production system architecture. In S. Vosniadou & A. Ortony (Eds.), *Similarity and analogical reasoning* (pp. 267–297). New York: Cambridge University Press.

Anzai, Y. (1991). Learning and use of representations for physics expertise. In K. A. Ericsson & J. Smith (Eds.), *Toward a general theory of expertise: Prospects and limits* (pp. 64–92). Cambridge: Cambridge University Press.

Ashworth, C. A. (1992). Skill as the fit between performer resources and task demands. In *Proceedings of the Fourteenth Annual Cognitive Science Meeting* (pp. 444–449). Hillsdale, NJ: Erlbaum.

Atkinson, R. C., & Shiffrin, R. (1968). Human memory: A proposed system and its control processes. In K. Spence & J. Spence (Eds.), *The psychology of learning and motivation* (Vol. 2, pp. 89–195). New York: Academic Press.

Baddeley, A. (1986). *Working memory.* New York: Oxford University Press.

Baird, L. L. (1985). Do grades and tests predict adult accomplishment? *Research in Higher Education, 23,* 3–85.

Berger, D. E., & Wilde, J. M. (1987). A task analysis of algebra word problems. In D. E. Berger, K. Pezdek, & W. P. Banks (Eds.), *Applications of cognitive psychology: Problem solving, education and computing* (pp. 123–137). Hillsdale, NJ: Erlbaum.

Berry, D. C., & Broadbent, D. E. (1984). On the relationship between task performance and associated verbalizable knowledge. *Quarterly Journal of Experimental Psychology, 36A,* 209–231.

Berry, D. C., & Broadbent, D. E. (1988). Interactive tasks and the implicit-explicit distinction. *British Journal of Psychology, 79,* 251–272.

Bloom, B. S. (Ed.). (1985a). *Developing talent in young people.* New York: Ballantine Books.

Bloom, B. S. (1985b). Generalizations about talent development. In B. S. Bloom (Ed.), *Developing talent in young people* (pp. 507–549). New York: Ballantine Books.

Boshuizen, H. P. A., & Schmidt, H. G. (1992). On the role of biomedical knowledge in clinical reasoning by experts, intermediates and novices. *Cognitive Science, 16,* 153–184.

Bourne, L. E., Jr., & Restle, F. (1959). A mathematical theory of concept identification. *Psychological Bulletin, 66,* 278–296.

Braine, M. D. S. (1978). On the relation between the natural logic of reasoning and standard logic. *Psychological Review, 85,* 1–21.

Brehmer, B. (1980). In one word: Not from experience. *Acta Psychologica, 45,* 223–241.

Brooks, L. R., Norman, G. R., & Allen, S. W. (1991). Role of specific similarity in a medical diagnostic task. *Journal of Experimental Psychology: General, 120,* 278–287.

Brown, R., & McNeill, D. (1966). The "tip of the tongue" phenomenon. *Journal of Verbal Learning and Verbal Behavior, 5,* 325–337.

Bruner, J. S., Goodnow, J. J., & Austin, G. (1956). *A study of thinking.* New York: Wiley.

Burton, S. J. (1985). *An introduction to law and legal reasoning.* Boston: Little, Brown.

Camerer, C. F., & Johnson, E. J. (1991). The process-performance paradox in expert judgment: How can the experts know so much and predict so badly? In K. A. Ericsson & J. Smith (Eds.), *Towards a general theory of expertise: Prospects and limits* (pp. 195–217). Cambridge: Cambridge University Press.

Chambliss, D. F. (1988). *Champions: The making of Olympic swimmers.* New York: Wm. Morrow.

Charness, N. (1976). Memory for chess positions: Resistance to interference. *Journal of Experimental Psychology: Human Learning and Memory, 2,* 641–653.

Charness, N. (1979). Components of skill in bridge. *Canadian Journal of Psychology, 33,* 1–6.

Charness, N. (1981). Search in chess: Age and skill differences. *Journal of Experimental Psychology: Human Perception and Performance, 7,* 476.

Charness, N. (1989). Expertise in chess and bridge. In D. Klahr & K. Kotovsky (Eds.), *Complex information processing: The impact of Herbert A. Simon* (pp. 183–208). Hillsdale, NJ: Erlbaum.

Charness, N. (1991). Expertise in chess: The balance between knowledge and search. In K. A. Ericsson & J. Smith (Eds.), *Towards a general theory of expertise: Prospects and limits* (pp. 39–63). Cambridge: Cambridge University Press.

Chase, W. G., & Ericsson, K. A. (1981). Skilled memory. In J. R. Anderson (Ed.), *Cognitive skills and their acquisition* (pp. 141–189). Hillsdale, NJ: Erlbaum.

Chase, W. G., & Ericsson, K. A. (1982). Skill and working memory. In G. H. Bower (Ed.), *The Psychology of learning and motivation* (Vol. 16, pp. 1–58). New York: Academic Press.

Chase, W. G., & Simon, H. A. (1973). The mind's eye in chess. In W. G. Chase (Ed.), *Visual information processing* (pp. 215–281). New York: Academic Press.

Chi, M. T. H. (1978). Knowledge structures and memory development. In R. S. Siegler (Ed.), *Children's thinking: What develops?* (pp. 73–96). Hillsdale, NJ: Erlbaum.

Chi, M. T. H., Glaser, R., & Farr, M. J. (Eds.). (1988). *The nature of expertise.* Hillsdale, NJ: Erlbaum.

Chi, M. T. H., Glaser, R., & Rees, E. (1982). Expertise in problem solving. In R. S. Sternberg (Ed.), *Advances in the psychology of human intelligence* (Vol. 1, pp. 1–75). Hillsdale, NJ: Erlbaum

Chi, M. T. H., Lewis, M. W., Reimann, P., & Glaser, R. (1989). Self-explanations: How students study and use examples in learning to solve problems. *Cognitive Science, 13,* 145–182.

Coltheart, V. (1971). Memory for stimuli and memory for hypotheses in concept identification. *Journal of Experimental Psychology, 89,* 102–108.

Crowder, R. G. (1982). The demise of short-term memory. *Acta Psychologica, 50,* 291–323.

Csikszentmihalyi, M. (1990). *Flow: The psychology of optimal experience.* New York: Harper & Row.

D'Andrade, R. G. (1987). A folk model of the mind. In D. Holland & N. Quinn (Eds.), *Cultural models in language and thought* (pp. 112–148). New York: Cambridge University Press.

Dawes, R. M. (1989). Experience and the validity of clinical judgment. *Behavioral Sciences and the Law, 7,* 457–467.

Deakin, J. M., & Allard, F. (1991). Skilled memory in expert figure skaters. *Memory & Cognition, 19,* 79–86.

de Groot, A. (1978). *Thought and choice and chess.* The Hague: Mouton. (Original work published 1946).

Dienes, A., Broadbent, D., & Berry, D. (1991). Implicit and explicit knowledge bases in artificial grammar learning. *Journal of Experimental Psychology: Learning, Memory, and Cognition, 17,* 875–887.

Duncker, K. (1945). On problem solving. *Psychological Monographs, 58*(5, Whole No. 270).

Durkin, H. E. (1937). Trial-and-error, gradual analysis and sudden reorganization: An experimental study of problem solving. *Archives of Psychology,* p. 210.

Ebbinghaus, H. (1913). *Über das Gedächtnis* (On memory). (H. A. Ruger and C. E. Bussenius, Trans.). New York: Teachers College, Columbia University. (Original work published 1885).

Egan, D. E., & Schwartz, B. J. (1979). Chunking in recall of symbolic drawings. *Memory & Cognition, 7,* 149–158.

Eibl-Eibesfeldt, I. (1970). *Ethology: The biology of behavior.* New York: Holt, Rinehart & Winston.

Engle, R. W., & Bukstel, L. H. (1978). Memory processes among bridge players of differing expertise. *American Journal of Psychology, 91,* 673–689.

Ericsson, K. A. (1985). Memory skill. *Canadian Journal of Psychology, 39,* 188–231.

Ericsson, K. A., & Crutcher, R. J. (1991). Introspection and verbal reports on cognitive processes—two approaches to the study of thought processes: A response to Howe. *New Ideas in Psychology, 9,* 57–71.

Ericsson, K. A., & Faivre, I. (1988). What's exceptional about exceptional abilities? In L. K. Obler & D. Fein (Eds.), *The exceptional brain: Neuropsychology of talent and special abilities* (pp. 436–473). New York: Guilford Press.

Ericsson, K. A., & Kintsch, W. (1994). *Long-term working memory* (Tech. Rep. No. 94-01). Boulder: University of Colorado, Institute of Cognitive Science.

Ericsson, K. A., Krampe, R. Th., & Tesch-Römer, C. (1993). The role of deliberate practice in the acquisition of expert performance. *Psychological Review, 100,* 363–406.

Ericsson, K. A., & Polson, P. G. (1988a). An experimental analysis of a memory skill for dinner-orders. *Journal of Experimental Psychology: Learning, Memory, and Cognition, 14,* 305–316.

Ericsson, K. A., & Polson, P. G. (1988b). Memory for restaurant orders. In M. Chi, R. Glaser, & M. Farr (Eds.), *The nature of expertise* (pp. 23–70). Hillsdale, NJ: Erlbaum.

Ericsson, K. A., & Simon, H. A. (1993). *Protocol analysis: Verbal reports as data* (2nd ed.). Cambridge, MA: Bradford Books/MIT Press.

Ericsson, K. A., & Smith, J. (Eds.). (1991a). *Toward a general theory of expertise: Prospects and limits.* Cambridge: Cambridge University Press.

Ericsson, K. A., & Smith, J. (1991b). Prospects and limits in the empirical study of expertise: An introduction. In K. A. Ericsson & J. Smith (Eds.), *Toward a general theory of expertise: Prospects and limits* (pp. 1–38). Cambridge: Cambridge University Press.

Ericsson, K. A., & Staszewski, J. J. (1989). Skilled memory and expertise: Mechanisms of exceptional performance. In D. Klahr & K. Kotovsky (Eds.), *Complex information processing: The impact of Herbert A. Simon* (pp. 235–267). Hillsdale, NJ: Erlbaum.

Ernst, G. W., & Newell, A. (1969). *GPS: A case study in generality and problem solving.* New York: Academic Press.

Fitts, P. M., & Posner, M. I. (1967). *Human performance.* Belmont, CA: Brooks-Cole.

Fodor, J. A. (1985). Fodor's guide to mental representation. *Mind, 94,* 55–97.

French, K. E., & Thomas, J. R. (1987). The relation of knowledge development to children's basketball performance. *Journal of Sport Psychology, 9,* 15–32.

Gentner, D. (1983). Structure mapping: A theoretical framework for analogy. *Cognitive Science, 10,* 155–170.

Ghiselli, E. (1966). *The validity of occupational aptitude tests.* New York: Wiley.

Gilhooly, K. J., Logie, R. H., Wetherick, N. E., & Wynn, V. (1993). Working memory and strategies in syllogistic-reasoning tasks. *Memory & Cognition, 21,* 115–124.

Greeno, J. G. (1989). Situations, mental models, and generative knowledge. In D. Klahr & K. Kotovsky (Eds.), *Complex information processing: The impact of Herbert A. Simon* (pp. 285–318). Hillsdale, NJ: Erlbaum.

Greeno, J. G., & Simon, H. A. (1988). Problem solving and reasoning. In R. C. Atkinson, R. J. Herrnstein, G. Lindzey, & R. D. Luce (Eds.), *Stevens' handbook of experimental psychology* (2nd ed., Vol. 2, pp. 589–672). New York: Wiley.

Gregg, L. W., & Simon, H. A. (1967). Process models and stochastic theories of simple concept formation. *Journal of Mathematical Psychology, 4*, 246–276.

Gruber, H. E. (1981a). *Darwin on man* (2nd ed.). Chicago: University of Chicago Press.

Gruber, H. E. (1981b). On the relation between "aha experiences" and the construction of ideas. *History of Science, 19*, 41–59.

Haber, R. N. (1983). The impending demise of the icon: A critique of the concept of iconic storage in visual information processing. *Behavioral and Brain Sciences, 6*, 1–11.

Hamilton, W. (1870). *Lectures on metaphysics and logic* (Vol. 1). Edinburgh: Blackwood.

Hastie, R., & Pennington, N. (1991). Cognitive and social processes in decision making. In L. B. Resnick, J. M. Levine, & S. D. Teasley (Eds.), *Perspectives on socially shared cognition* (pp. 308–330). Washington, DC: American Psychological Association.

Hinsley, D. A., Hayes, J. R., & Simon, H. A. (1977). From words to equations: Meaning and representation in algebra word problem. In M. A. Just & P. A. Carpenter (Eds.), *Cognitive processes in comprehension* (pp. 62–68). Hillsdale, NJ: Erlbaum.

Hinton, G. (1989). Connectionist learning systems. *Artificial Intelligence, 40*, 185–234.

Hoffman, R. R. (1987). The problem of extracting the knowledge of experts from the perspective of experimental psychology. *AI Magazine, 8*(2), 53–67.

Hofmann, D. A., Jacobs, R., & Gerras, S. J. (1992). Mapping individual performance over time. *Journal of Applied Psychology, 77*, 185–195.

Holding, D. H. (1985). *The psychology of chess skill*. Hillsdale, NJ: Erlbaum.

Holmes, F. L. (1989). Antoine Lavoisier and Hans Krebs: Two styles of scientific creativity. In D. B. Wallace & H. E. Gruber (Eds.), *Creative people at work: Twelve cognitive case studies* (pp. 44–68). New York: Oxford University Press.

Holyoak, K. J. (1984). Analogical thinking and human intelligence. In R. J. Sternberg (Ed.), *Advances in the psychology of human intelligence* (Vol. 2, pp. 199–230). Hillsdale, NJ: Erlbaum.

Holyoak, K. J. (1985). The pragmatics of analogical transfer. In G. H. Bower (Ed.), *The Psychology of Learning and Motivation* (Vol. 19, pp 59–87). New York: Academic Press.

Holyoak, K. J., & Spellman, B. A. (1993). Thinking. *Annual Review of Psychology, 44*, 265–315.

Howe, M. J. A. (1990). *The origins of exceptional abilities*. Oxford: Basil/Blackwell.

Hulin, C. L., Henry, R. A., & Noon, S. L. (1990). Adding a dimension: Time as a factor in the generalizability of predictive relationships. *Psychological Bulletin, 107*, 328–340.

Humphry, G. (1951). *Thinking: An introduction to its experimental psychology*. London: Methuen.

James, W. (1950). *The principles of psychology* (Vol. 1). New York: Dover. (Original work published 1890)

Johnson, E. S. (1978). The validation of concept-learning strategies. *Journal of Experimental Psychology: General, 107*, 237–266.

Johnson-Laird, P. N. (1983). *Mental models*. Cambridge, MA: Harvard University Press.

Just, M. A., & Carpenter, P. A. (1980). A theory of reading: From eye fixations to comprehension. *Psychological Review, 87*, 329–354.

Karat, J. (1982). A model of problem solving with incomplete constraint knowledge. *Cognitive Psychology, 14*, 538–559.

Klahr, D., Langley, P., & Neches, R. (Eds.). (1987). *Production system models of learning and development*. Cambridge, MA: MIT Press.

Kolodner, J. L. (1992). An introduction to case-based reasoning. *Artificial Intelligence Review, 6*, 3–34.

Larkin, J. H., McDermott, J., Simon, D. P., & Simon, H. A. (1980). Models of competence in solving physics problems. *Cognitive Science, 4*, 317–345.

Larkin, J. H., & Simon, H. A. (1987). Why a diagram is (sometimes) worth ten thousands words. *Cognitive Science, 11,* 65–99.

Lave, J. (1988). *Cognition in practice.* New York: Cambridge University Press.

Lesgold, A., Rubinson, H., Feltovich, P., Glaser, R., Klopfer, D., & Wang, Y. (1985). *Expertise in a complex skill: Diagnosing X-ray pictures* (Tech. Rep.) Pittsburgh: University of Pittsburgh, Learning Research and Development Center.

Levine, M. (1966). Hypothesis behavior by humans during discrimination learning. *Journal of Experimental Psychology, 71,* 331–338.

Levine, M. (Ed.). (1975). *A cognitive theory of learning: Research on hypothesis testing.* Hillsdale, NJ: Erlbaum.

Marquer, J., & Pereira, M. (1990). Reaction times in the study of strategies in sentence-picture verification: A reconsideration. *Quarterly Journal of Experimental Psychology, 42A,* 147–168.

Marr, D. (1982). *Vision: A computational investigation into the human representation and processing of visual information.* New York: Freeman.

Mathews, R. C., Buss, R. R., Stanley, W. B., Blanchard-Fields, F., Cho, J. R., & Druhan, B. (1989). Role of implicit and explicit processes in learning from examples: A synergistic effect. *Journal of Experimental Psychology: Learning, Memory, and Cognition, 15,* 1083–1100.

McCloskey, M., & Cohen, N. J. (1989). Catastrophic interference in connectionist networks: The sequential learning problem. In G. H. Bower (Ed.), *The psychology of learning and motivation* (Vol. 24, pp. 109–165). San Diego: Academic Press.

McCloskey, M., Wible, C. G., & Cohen, N. J. (1988). Is there a special flashbulb-memory mechanism? *Journal of Experimental Psychology: General, 117,* 171–181.

McKeithen, K. B., Reitman, J. S., Rueter, H. H., & Hirtle, S. C. (1981). Knowledge organization and skill differences in computer programmers. *Cognitive Psychology, 13,* 307–325.

Miller, G. A. (1956). The magical number seven, plus or minus two: Some limits on our capacity for processing information. *Psychological Review, 63,* 81–97.

Myles-Worsley, M., Johnston, W. A., & Simons, M. A. (1988). The influence of expertise on X-ray image processing. *Journal of Experimental Psychology: Learning, Memory, and Cognition, 14,* 553–557.

Neisser, U. (1976). *Cognition and reality: Principles and implications of cognitive psychology.* San Francisco: Freeman.

Neisser, U., & Harsch, N. (1991). Phantom flashbulbs: False recollections of hearing the news about *Challenger.* In U. Neisser & E. Winograd (Eds.), *Flashbulb memories: Recalling the "Challenger" explosion and other disasters.* New York: Cambridge University Press.

Newell. A. (1981). Reasoning, problem solving, and decision processes: The problem space as a fundamental category. In R. Nickerson (Ed.), *Attention and performance VIII* (pp. 693–718). Hillsdale, NJ: Erlbaum.

Newell, A. (1990). *Unified theories of cognition.* Cambridge, MA: Harvard University Press.

Newell, A., & Simon, H. A. (1961). Computer simulation of human thinking. *Science, 134,* 2011–2017.

Newell, A., & Simon, H. A. (1972). *Human problem solving.* Englewood Cliffs, NJ: Prentice-Hall.

Oden, G. (1987). Concept, knowledge, and thought. *Annual Review of Psychology, 38,* 203–237.

Olson, J. R., & Biolsi, K. J. (1991). Techniques for representing expert knowledge. In K. A. Ericsson & J. Smith (Eds.), *Toward a general theory of expertise: Prospects and limits* (pp. 240–285). Cambridge: Cambridge University Press.

Olson, J. R., & Rueter, H. H. (1987). Extracting expertise from experts: Methods for knowledge acquisition. *Expert Systems, 4,* 152–168.

Patel, V. L., & Groen, G. J. (1991). The general and specific nature of medical expertise: A critical look. In K. A. Ericsson & J. Smith (Eds.), *Toward a general theory of expertise: Prospects and limits* (pp. 93–125). Cambridge: Cambridge University Press.

Payne, J. W. (1982). Contingent decision behavior. *Psychological Bulletin, 92*, 382–402.

Pfau, H. D., & Murphy, M. D. (1988). Role of verbal knowledge in chess skill. *American Journal of Psychology, 101*, 73–86.

Pinheiro, V. E. D., & Simon, H. A. (1992). An operational model of motor skill diagnosis. *Journal of Teaching in Physical Education, 11*, 288–302.

Pinker, S., & Prince, A. (1988). On language and connectionism: Analysis of a parallel distributed processing model of language acquisition. *Cognition, 28*, 73–193.

Pirolli, P. L., & Anderson, J. R. (1985). The role of learning from examples in the acquisition of recursive programming skills. *Canadian Journal of Psychology, 39*, 240–272.

Poincaré, H. (1952). Mathematical creation. In B. Ghiselin (Ed.), *The creative process* (pp. 33–42). Berkeley: University of California Press.

Posner, M. I., & McLeod, P. (1982). Information processing models: In search of elementary operations. *Annual Review of Psychology, 33*, 477–514.

Pylyshyn, Z. (1984). *Computation and cognition: Toward a foundation for cognitive science.* Cambridge, MA: MIT Press.

Reber, A. S. (1976). Implicit learning of synthetic languages: The role of instructional set. *Journal of Experimental Psychology: Human Learning and Memory, 2*, 88–94.

Reber, A. S. (1989). Implicit learning and tacit knowledge. *Journal of Experimental Psychology: General, 118*, 219–235.

Reed, S. K. (1987). A structure mapping model for word problems. *Journal of Experimental Psychology: Learning, Memory, and Cognition, 13*, 124–139.

Reed, S. K., Ernst, G. W., & Banerji, R. (1974). The role of analogy in transfer between similar problem states. *Cognitive Psychology, 6*, 436–450.

Reitman, J. (1976). Skilled perception in go: Deducing memory structures from inter-response times. *Cognitive Psychology, 8*, 336–356.

Rips, L. J. (1983). Cognitive processes in propositional reasoning. *Psychological Review, 90*, 38–71.

Rips, L. J. (1988). Deduction. In R. J. Sternberg & E. E. Smith (Eds.), *The psychology of human thought* (pp. 116–152). New York: Cambridge University Press.

Rips, L. J. (1990). Reasoning. *Annual Review of Psychology, 41*, 321–353.

Rips, L. J., & Conrad, R. (1989). Folk psychology of mental activities. *Psychological Review, 96*, 187–207.

Ross, B. H. (1984). Remindings and their effects in learning a cognitive skill. *Cognitive Psychology, 16*, 371–416.

Rumelhart, D. E., McClelland, J. L., & the PDP Research Group. (1986). *Parallel distributed processing: Explorations in the microstructure of cognition* (2 vols.). Cambridge, MA: MIT Press.

Salthouse, T. A. (1991). Expertise as the circumvention of human information processing limits. In K. A. Ericsson & J. Smith (Eds.), *Toward a general theory of expertise: Prospects and limits* (pp. 286–300). Cambridge: Cambridge University Press.

Sanderson, P. M. (1989). Verbalizable knowledge and skilled task performance: Association, dissociation and mental models. *Journal of Experimental Psychology: Learning, Memory, and Cognition, 15*, 729–747.

Saxe, G. B. (1991). *Culture and cognitive development: Studies in mathematical understanding.* Hillsdale, NJ: Erlbaum.

Seidenberg, M. S. (1992). Connectionism without tears. In S. Davis (Ed.), *Connectionism: Theory and practice* (pp. 84–122). New York: Oxford University Press.

Shiffrin, R. M., & Schneider, W. (1977). Controlled and automatic human information processing: II. Perceptual learning, automatic attending and a general theory. *Psychological Review, 84*, 127–189.

Siegler, R. S. (1987). The perils of averaging data over strategies: An example from children's addition. *Journal of Experimental Psychology: General, 116*, 250–264.

Simon, H. A. (1974). How big is a chunk? *Science, 183,* 482–488.

Simon, H. A., & Chase, W. G. (1973). Skill in chess. *American Scientist, 61,* 394–403.

Singley, M. K., & Anderson, J. R. (1989). *The transfer of cognitive skill.* Cambridge, MA: Harvard University Press.

Slade, S. (1991). Case-based reasoning: A research paradigm. *AI Magazine, 12*(1), 42–55.

Sloboda, J. A. (1976). Visual perception of musical notation: Registering pitch symbols in memory. *Quarterly Journal of Experimental Psychology, 28,* 1–16.

Sloboda, J. A. (1985). *The musical mind: The cognitive psychology of music.* Oxford: Oxford University Press.

Smith, E. E., Langston, C., & Nisbett, R. E. (1992). The case for rules in reasoning. *Cognitive Psychology, 16,* 1–40.

Smolensky, P. (1988). On the proper treatment of connectionism. *Behavioral and Brain Sciences, 11,* 1–23.

Sperling, G. A. (1960). The information available in a brief visual presentation. *Psychological Monographs, 74*(Whole No. 498).

Stanley, W. B., Mathews, R. C., Buss, R. R., & Kotler-Cope, S. (1989). Insight without awareness: On the interaction of verbalization, instruction and practice in a simulated process control task. *Quarterly Journal of Experimental Psychology, 41A,* 553–577.

Staszewski, J. J. (1988). Skilled memory and expert mental calculation. In M. T. H. Chi, R. Glaser, & M. J. Farr (Eds.), *The nature of expertise* (pp. 71–128). Hillsdale, NJ: Erlbaum.

Ste-Marie, D. M., & Lee, T. D. (1991). Prior processing effects on gymnastics judging. *Journal of Experimental Psychology: Learning, Memory and Cognition, 17,* 126–136.

Sternberg, R. J. (1977). Component processes in analogical reasoning. *Psychological Review, 84,* 353–378.

Sternberg, R. J. (1980). Representation and process in linear syllogistic reasoning. *Journal of Experimental Psychology: General, 109,* 119–159.

Sternberg, R. J., Conway, B. E., Ketron, J. L., & Bernstein, M. (1981). People's conceptions of intelligence. *Journal of Personality and Social Psychology, 41,* 37–55.

Tweney, R. D. (1989). Fields of enterprise: on Michael Faraday's thought. In D. B. Wallace & H. E. Gruber (Eds.), *Creative people at work: Twelve cognitive case studies* (pp. 91–106). New York: Oxford University Press.

Van Lehn, K. (1990). *Mind bugs: The origins of procedural misconceptions.* Cambridge, MA: MIT Press.

Van Lehn, K. (1991). Rule acquisition events in the discovery of problem-solving strategies. *Cognitive Science, 15,* 1–47.

Varon, E. J. (1935). The development of Alfred Binet's psychology. *Psychological Monographs, 46*(Whole No. 207).

Wagner, R. K. (1991). Managerial problem-solving. In R. J. Sternberg & P. Frensch (Eds.), *Complex problem solving: Principles and mechanisms* (pp. 159–183). Hillsdale, NJ: Erlbaum.

Wallas, G. (1926). *The art of thought.* New York: Harcourt.

Webb, N. L. (1975). An exploration of mathematical problem-solving processes (Doctoral dissertation, Stanford University, 1975). *Dissertation Abstracts International, 36,* 2689A. (University Microfilms No. 75-25625)

Wenger, E. (1987). *Artificial intelligence and tutoring systems: Computational and cognitive approaches to the communication of knowledge.* Los Altos, CA: Morgan-Kaufmann.

Woodworth, R. S., & Sells, S. B. (1935). An atmosphere effect in formal syllogistic reasoning. *Journal of Experimental Psychology, 18,* 451–460.

CHAPTER 3

Knowledge Representation

Timothy P. McNamara

Each of the three houses I have owned has been at least 15 years older than its predecessor, and the one I own now was built in 1910. Old houses have many charming features, but the plumbing is typically not one of them. On one of my recent forays in search of plumbing parts, I found myself headed north on the bypass, rapidly approaching a major interstate highway, needing to decide quickly whether to enter the highway headed in a westerly or an easterly direction. I knew that Fessler's Lane, the street I was looking for, intersected the highway, but I couldn't recall whether it did so on the western or the eastern side of the bypass. To solve this problem, I imagined traveling out of town on the interstate highway headed in an easterly direction, and tried to visualize whether the Fessler's Lane exit came before or after the intersection with the bypass. I decided that the exit came before the bypass, and quickly took the west exit off of the bypass. My decision was correct, but I didn't know that Fessler's Lane was one of those streets that can be accessed in one direction but not the other, and I was headed in the wrong direction.

This anecdote illustrates a number of important aspects of knowledge representations. First, it underscores a point that will be made in other chapters of this volume, namely, that knowledge representations play an essential and sometimes surprising role in reasoning, problem solving, and thinking. As it turned out, fixing my sink depended on my knowledge of

Thinking and Problem Solving

obscure spatial relations among the roads of Nashville. Second, the anecdote is revealing about the complex ways information can be organized in memory. Consider the following:

- My knowledge of the layout of places and roads in Nashville was not organized in such a way that I could retrieve the relative locations of the Fessler's Lane exit and the bypass;
- Access to this information depended on the relatively laborious procedure of mentally traversing the highway in a particular direction;
- My knowledge was inaccurate, or at least incomplete: I didn't know that Fessler's Lane was inaccessible for westbound traffic on the highway.

My goal in this chapter is to provide a tutorial review of the fundamental building blocks of knowledge. The questions I hope to answer are these: How is our knowledge of the world represented in memory? In what forms do knowledge representations come and how are they used?

One's first impression may be that these questions are intractable. After all, people have knowledge of the visual appearance and the feel of objects; sounds, odors, and tastes; as well as knowledge that is abstract and amodal. Moreover, people know skills that are extremely difficult, if not impossible, to convey to others in any way but showing them. It would be a Herculean task indeed to catalog all that people can know, let alone all of the ways that this knowledge is mentally represented.

We will see, however, that knowledge representations can be classified into a small number of categories. As illustrations of this point, answer each of the following questions (without looking or otherwise cheating):

On which side of a standard desk telephone is the receiver cord attached?
How far is it in your home from the refrigerator to the nearest sink?
Which is higher in pitch, the trumpeting of an elephant or the neigh of a horse?
In two or three sentences, explain why President Bush lost the election in 1992.
Describe the mental processes that occurred as you comprehended the sentences above.

The experiences I have while answering these questions differ dramatically but can be sorted into three categories. The first three questions evoke visual, spatial, or auditory imagery; the knowledge I use to answer the question seems to represent in a direct way properties of the object being represented. For example, to answer the elephant–horse question, I imagine an elephant's trumpeting sound and a horse's neigh, and then compare their imagined pitch. When I answer the fourth question, there is no correspond-

Implicit procedural Memory - Sadomasichistic
- experience +
- perception

ing experience, but I am nevertheless able to answer the question. The fifth question, however, produces a blank stare: I have no experience of the mental processes that occur when I understand or produce language; ideas just pop into my head.

These demonstrations provide informal illustrations of the differences between three qualitatively different types of knowledge representation. One type of knowledge representation seems to preserve perceptual properties of objects in a direct manner. A second type of knowledge representation is abstract, amodal, and does not preserve perceptual properties of objects, but is of the same genus as the first. The third type of knowledge representation is fundamentally different from the first two, and seems to underlie perceptual and cognitive skills. In this chapter, I explore the properties of these modes of mental representation.

The plan of the chapter is as follows. I begin by discussing the nature of mental representation. In this section of the chapter, I examine whether or not the study of knowledge representation is a reasonable scientific endeavor, and briefly discuss three forms of representation: analogical, symbolic, and procedural. The second section investigates the properties of each of these forms of representation. The third section of the chapter examines complex representations, such as schemata and cognitive maps, and the fourth considers the role of connectionist models in the study of knowledge representation. The chapter concludes with a few speculations on where this field should be headed.

I. THE NATURE OF KNOWLEDGE REPRESENTATIONS

A. What Are Mental Representations and Why Are They Necessary?

The concept of mental representation is as fundamental to cognitive psychology as force is to physics. It is true that there are schools of psychology, both old (e.g., Skinner, 1957) and new (e.g., Gibson, 1979), that eschew the concept of mental representation, but the cognitive sciences are predicated on the existence in the mind of representations of the world. I will not explore in detail the problem of mental representation because excellent discussions can be found elsewhere, including those by Fodor (1975), Pylyshyn (1984), and Shepard (1975, 1981, 1984). However, I will define briefly the concept and attempt to demonstrate why mental representations are posited.

For current purposes, the most important properties of mental representations are (1) that they preserve information about and interpretations of objects and events in the world, and (2) that they exist in a representational system that includes mental processes defined on the representations. For example, one's mental representation of the spatial layout of one's kitchen should preserve (at least) the relative locations of objects in the space. This mental representation supports a number of abilities, including imagining the kitchen from different viewpoints, estimating distances from memory, navigating in the dark, and so on, all of which depend on mental processes that operate on the spatial representation. One of the major points of this chapter is that mental representations differ in the types of information they naturally preserve and in the processes that are naturally defined over them.

There are many reasons to posit the existence of mental representations, but the most important one is that the behavior of organisms cannot be explained without specifying how the organism represents the world to itself. The contemporary history of this idea can be traced to Chomsky's (1959) critique of behaviorist accounts of language acquisition (Skinner, 1957). As an example, consider the introductory anecdote. My action of taking the west exit off the bypass cannot be explained without appealing to ideas of the following kind: "McNamara believed that Fessler's Lane was west of the intersection of the bypass and the highway," "McNamara thought that he could exit the highway onto Fessler's Lane," and so on. In short, one must know how I interpreted the world and represented it to understand why I did what I did. My belief that I could get to Fessler's Lane from the highway is especially enlightening because my action makes no sense at all when viewed from the perspective of an accurate description of the physical environment; it is sensible only if one knows that I *mis*represented crucial information about the roads of Nashville. Likewise, a description of my behavior in terms of the behavior of neurons will never count as an explanation of my behavior, because the latter exists only in the cognitive vocabulary of *interpretation, belief, desire,* and so on, and to the best of our knowledge, neurons do not have interpretations, beliefs, and desires.

This brief discussion should raise many more questions than it answers. A thicket of thorny issues surrounds any discussion of mental representation, including the relationship between an organism and its mental representations, the role of neuroscience in explaining cognition, the nature of consciousness, and even the mind–body problem. Conceptual analyses of these problems have helped to elucidate the basal assumptions of cognitive psychology and to delineate its proper goals, but they will take us too far from the important issues at hand.

B. Can Knowledge Representations Be Distinguished?

Any discussion of knowledge representation, especially one in which forms of representation are distinguished, raises concerns about whether knowledge representations can be studied experimentally. In the 1970s and the early 1980s, a debate raged in psychology over the nature of mental representation (a few of the key papers are Anderson, 1978; Kosslyn & Pomerantz, 1977; Pylyshyn, 1973, 1981). The question was whether various kinds of stimuli were mentally represented in an "analog" or a "propositional" format. The definition of analog representation varied from advocate to advocate, but the essential characteristic seemed to be that these representations preserved the structure of stimuli in a direct quasi-pictorial manner (the debate centered almost exclusively on visual imagery). Propositions, on the other hand, were abstract amodal representations of ideas. It is hard to imagine a contrast more intuitively clear or more amenable to experimental investigation. Despite these appealing attributes, analogical and propositional explanations of psychological phenomena, such as mental imagery, turned out to be quite difficult to distinguish empirically. Anderson (1978) went so far as to conclude that behavioral data could not distinguish between alternative theories of mental representation, let alone whether something was represented analogically or propositionally. Even though Anderson's argument is severely limited in generality and probably is not valid in psychologically realistic cases (Pylyshyn, 1979), many cognitive psychologists still hold this belief. Indeed, in recent correspondence with me, a well-known and respected psychologist cited the analog–propositional debate as evidence that research on mental representation was a waste of time. The point was that if we could not answer a question as basic as whether a particular stimulus was represented in an analog or a propositional format, how could we hope to answer any of the more subtle questions that must arise in developing theories of memory and knowledge representation?

It is axiomatic that behavior in cognitive tasks is a function of how things are represented in memory and how they are processed. This fact implies that tests of theories of knowledge representation are really tests of representation–process pairs (Anderson, 1978). It is well known, for instance, that judgments about the spatial relations among geographical landmarks can be amazingly inaccurate (e.g., Stevens & Coupe, 1978; Tversky, 1981). For example, many people think that San Diego, California is west of Reno, Nevada, when in fact the reverse is true (Stevens & Coupe, 1978). This phenomenon can be explained by appealing to distortions in an analogical spatial representation or to inferential processes that operate on incomplete but accurate propositional representations (e.g. San Diego is in California, Reno is in Nevada, and California is west of Nevada, so San Diego must be west of Reno) or to some other representation–process combination. In other words, we cannot learn about underlying representation unless the processes are specified, and vice versa. This theoretical Catch 22 has engendered in many psychologists a profound sense of doubt about the ability of behavioral data to distinguish between alternative theories of mental representation (e.g., Anderson, 1978; Palmer, 1978). In fact, formal analyses (Pylyshyn, 1979, 1984) and a retrospective appraisal of progress in the field indicate that this pessimism is unwarranted.

The solution to this conundrum exists in the simultaneous employment of two methodological strategies. First, the sedulous application of converging operations is essential (e.g., Garner, Hake, & Eriksen, 1956). Converging operations can be used in many ways. One effective method is to examine properties of memory with two or more tasks in a single experiment. The logic is this: If performance in several tasks is affected by a variable in the same way, then the likelihood is low that these effects are caused by unique features of the tasks, and if the only common feature of the tasks is the presumed mental representation that supports performance, then one can conclude with some confidence that the variable affects how information is mentally represented. As we shall see below, this strategy is made even more effective by combining results from cognitive tasks with data from neuroscience and clinical neuropsychology.

The second strategy is to strive to use methods that satisfy what I call the *automaticity criterion*. These methods minimize performance demands, and are associated with performance that is fast, relatively effortless, and not consciously controlled (e.g., Posner & Snyder, 1975). Methods that satisfy this criterion are particularly useful in reducing the degrees of freedom afforded by the contributions of strategic or elaborative processing. Examples of tasks that meet the automaticity criterion include associative priming in recognition (e.g., Ratcliff & McKoon, 1981a), naming (e.g., Seidenberg, Waters, Sanders, & Langer, 1984), and—in the proper circumstances— lexical decisions (e.g., McNamara & Altarriba, 1988), as well as various forms of repetition priming (e.g., Cave & Squire, 1992; Jacoby & Dallas, 1981; Schacter, 1987). It is notable that all of these tasks are forms of priming. In the proper circumstances, priming seems to be directly informative about properties of memory divorced from retrieval strategies. A task that satisfies automaticity will not be affected by subjects' beliefs, and hence, is cognitively impenetrable (Pylyshyn, 1984). Of course, failure to satisfy the automaticity criterion does not render a task useless for investigating knowledge representation; the point is that inferences about structure and content are facilitated when the cognitive demands of the task are minimized.

C. A Taxonomy

The upcoming discussion will be facilitated if we begin by considering a taxonomy of knowledge representations (for similar taxonomies, see Anderson, 1983; Paivio, 1983; Squire, 1987). Figure 1 summarizes the conceptual framework around which this chapter is organized.

There are at least two senses in which a person can be said to know. One kind of knowledge can be verbalized, visualized, declared in some manner, and for these reasons has been called *declarative knowledge*. A second type of

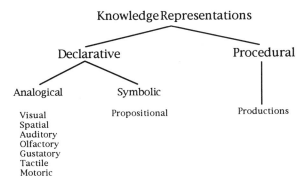

FIGURE 1   A taxonomy of knowledge representations.

knowledge consists of skills, cognitive operations, knowledge of how to do things, and has been called *procedural knowledge*. For example, if I ask when you were born, what you had for breakfast this morning, or what the Eiffel Tower looks like, you will be able to respond in a way that allows you to communicate an answer, even if this response may require drawing a picture. In contrast, if I ask how you are able to ride a bicycle or how you are able to understand what I write in this passage, you will not be able to give a satisfactory answer, and certainly another person could not learn from the answer how to perform the activity.

This distinction is not everywhere precise and its popularity has waxed and waned over the years (e.g., Anderson, 1976; Norman, Rumelhart, & the LNR Research Group, 1975; Ryle, 1949; Squire, 1987), but there are good reasons to sanction it. A separation of the cognitive operations involved in memory storage from other cognitive processes has proven to be useful in theories of cognition (e.g., Anderson, 1983). The distinction also has turned out to be fundamental in the literature on amnesia. Damage to the hippocampus, for example, can cause a total inability to learn new facts but preserve the ability to learn cognitive skills (as well as a heterogeneous collection of other abilities; Squire, 1992).

In the present taxonomy, declarative knowledge can be represented in two ways:

Analogical representations preserve properties of objects and events in an intrinsic manner. Intrinsic representations are those in which the representational system has the same inherent constraints as the system being represented (Palmer, 1978). Examples may help to clarify this point. In The Audubon Society Encyclopedia of North American Birds (Terres, 1980), shapes of birds are represented by schematic silhouettes, similar to the one in Figure 2. These representations preserve visually salient and distinctive properties of birds in a concrete way. In fact, spatial properties of the birds

FIGURE 2   A depiction of a bird. Reprinted from Terres, J. K. (1980). *The Audubon Society encyclopedia of North American birds.* New York: Knopf. With permission of Chanticleer Press, Inc., NY.

are preserved in the same spatial properties of the representation. For example, birds with long, thin tails will have representations with long, thin tails. Intrinsic representation need not be so concrete, however. If the relative weights of objects on a pan scale are represented by the relative sizes of real numbers, then relations between the weights of objects, such as transitivity (if A is heavier than B and B is heavier than C then A is heavier than C), are preserved by inherent properties of the numbers. It is an empirical question whether analogical representations in human memory are as concrete as the silhouettes or as abstract as measurement.

The second type of representation is *symbolic.* These representations preserve structure extrinsically. In such representations, the inherent structure of the representational system is arbitrary but that of the represented system is not. The system to be represented is modeled by a relational system that has no inherent structure; all of the necessary structure is built into the system explicitly (Palmer, 1978). As an example, consider a representation of relative weight in which the symbols "heavier (A, B)" stand for the empirical observation that object A outweighs object B on a pan scale. Through suitable comparisons of the objects, one could construct a set of statements, for example, "heavier (A, B), heavier (B, C), heavier (C, D)," modeling the observations that A outweighed B, B outweighed C, and so on. Note that there is nothing in this representational system that guarantees preservation of transitivity of relative weight. Transitivity can be preserved in the representation only by adding structure to the representation [e.g., heavier (A, B) and heavier (B, C) implies heavier (A, C)] or by imposing extrinsic constraints (e.g., that the representation model the world accurately). If this example is not clear, substitute an arbitrary set of symbols, such as "A*B" for "heavier (A, B)" and work through the example a second time. These representations are examples of propositional representations, which will be examined closely later in this chapter.

It is instructive to compare the numerical and the propositional representations of relative weights in more detail. In the numerical representation, an object is represented by a number. All there is to know about the relative weights of the objects on the pan scale can be gleaned directly from the relative sizes of the numbers. I should emphasize that the objects are represented by numbers, not by the conventional symbols used to represent numbers (the numerals, 1, 2, etc.). In contrast, in the propositional representation, the objects are represented by arbitrary names, A, B, C, and so on. Nothing can be learned about the objects by inspecting their representations. The only way to learn something about relative weight is to consult the representation of relative weight, which is captured in the relational elements, "heavier (X, Y)." These systems also differ markedly in their internal structure. The properties of numbers allow us to say that 1 is less than 2 but not that 2 is less than 1. This constraint exists independently of the role of the numbers in representing relative weight, or anything else for that matter. However, either "heavier (A, B)" or "heavier (B, A)" is admissible in the propositional representation; the constraint on admissible orderings exists in the represented world, not in the system of representation.

The gap between declarative knowledge and behavior is bridged by *productions* (e.g., Anderson, 1976; Newell, 1973; Post, 1943). Production systems provide a general and powerful formalism for modeling the procedural knowledge that supports cognitive skills, such as reasoning, problem solving, and language comprehension. Production systems will be explored in depth later in the chapter. At this point, I want to discuss briefly their important properties.

A production is a condition–action rule: If the condition is satisfied, the action is performed. The condition of a production specifies a pattern of information that must hold in working or long-term memory. If the pattern exists, the production applies and the action is performed. An action could consist of adding information to working memory, executing an external behavior, or both. For example, accomplished drivers have available a production of the form:

IF *the traffic light turns green* THEN *resume driving*.

In this production, *the traffic light turns green* is the condition of the production and *resume driving* is the action. A moment's consideration will reveal that the productions that underlie even a simple activity can be quite complex. A more detailed (but far from complete) "driving" production might be,

IF *the goal is to resume driving*
and one is stopped at a red traffic light
and the traffic light turns green
and the intersection is not obstructed
and no emergency vehicles are approaching
THEN *resume driving.*

This example illustrates the detail with which cognitive operations must be specified to be modeled in production systems.

It is tempting to view productions as just another example of stimulus–response (S–R) bonds. This interpretation is incorrect, however. The stimulus in an S–R bond must be observable or potentially observable, but the conditions of productions can be observable stimuli (as represented in working memory), unobservable cognitive states (e.g., a thought), or even abstract entities (e.g., variables). S–R bonds are also difficult to define over patterns of elements, whereas the conditions of productions can specify that a particular configuration of elements be present (see also Anderson, 1976).

A characteristic of productions, and procedural knowledge in general, that distinguishes them from declarative knowledge is flexibility. The conditions of productions must be specific to preclude their application in the wrong circumstances. The cost of this specificity is that productions do not generalize to new situations. In contrast, a mental image or a fact can be used in innumerable situations and contexts.

II. SIMPLE KNOWLEDGE REPRESENTATIONS

In this section of this chapter, each form of representation—analogical, symbolic, and procedural—will be explored in detail. These representations are "simple" in the sense that they are the components of more complex representations, such as concepts, schemata, and cognitive maps.

A. Analogical Knowledge Representations

Analogical representations probably exist for all of the sensory modalities. This chapter, however, will focus primarily on visual–spatial representations. Remarkably little research has been conducted on analogical representations in other modalities, with the exception of audition (e.g., Reisberg, 1992) and the motor system (e.g., Smyth & Pendleton, 1989), and the work that has been conducted seems to tell the same story as the research on visual and spatial imagery. The structure of visual analogical representations is revealed by a number of mental transformations that occur on them (e.g., Kosslyn, 1980; Shepard & Cooper, 1982). Two of these transformations are particularly relevant for the current discussion, mental rotation and image scanning.

1. Properties of Analogical Representations

Many cognitive psychologists have contributed to our understanding of mental images, but the earliest and some of the most influential work was conducted by Roger Shepard and his colleagues (Shepard & Cooper, 1982). One of Shepard's first findings concerned the imagined rotation of three-dimensional shapes (Shepard & Metzler, 1971). These experiments are legendary and probably discussed in every introductory psychology text, but are worth reviewing here because they illustrate perfectly the phenomenon of interest.

Subjects in Shepard and Metzler's (1971) experiments were shown displays of pairs of block figures like those in Figure 3. On each trial of the experiment, a subject would see two block figures side by side. The subject's task was to decide whether the two figures were the same (Figure 3A and B) or different (Figure 3C). Shepard and Metzler manipulated two variables: Whether objects had to be rotated in the plane (3A) or in depth (3B), and the angular disparity between the figures. The results of Shepard and Metzler's experiment are summarized in Figure 4, which contains average response times plotted as a function of the angular deviation between the test figures. Figure 4A contains the results for planar rotations and Figure 4B contains the results for depth rotations.

There were two important discoveries in these experiments: First, the relationship between response time and angular disparity was almost perfectly linear, and second, the slopes of the linear relationships were about the same for planar rotations (19 ms/deg) and for depth rotations (17 ms/deg). Shepard and Metzler concluded from these data that mental rotation is "analogical"; they meant by this that the mental events occurring during imagined rotation were very similar to the mental events occurring during the perception of actual rotation. Subsequent experiments by Cooper and Shepard strongly supported this conjecture, because they showed that the process of imagined mental rotation actually passes through intermediate states that correspond to the intermediate states of actual rotation (see Shepard & Cooper, 1982).

Additional properties of analogical representations have been evinced in a series of studies on "mental scanning." In an experiment by Kosslyn, Ball, and Reiser (1978), subjects studied a map of a fictitious island (see Figure 5). After subjects had memorized the island and were able to visualize it with their eyes closed, they took part in a task in which they had to scan from one location to another. The experimenter named a starting location (e.g., the grass hut), and then named a destination (e.g., the tree). The subjects' task

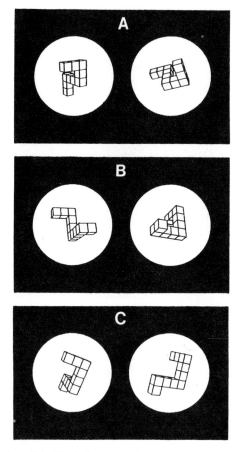

FIGURE 3 Examples of the block figures used by Shepard and Metzler (1971) in their experiments on mental rotation. Reprinted from Shepard, R. N., & Metzler, J. (1971). *Mental rotation of three-dimensional objects, Science, 171,* 701–703.

was to imagine a black dot moving from the starting location to the destination, and to press a response button as soon as the dot arrived at the destination. Of course, the map was not visible during this test phase; subjects imagined the dot moving on a mental image of the map.

The major finding was that response, or scan, time increased as a linear function of distance (see Figure 6). This result points to another correspondence between the representations and the processes used in imagery and those used in perception. Scanning a mental image seems to require the same or similar mental processes as those required in scanning an actual object, map, or scene. One criticism of this experiment is that the performance of subjects might have been determined by the peculiar demands of the task (Pylyshyn, 1981). After all, should we be surprised that scan times

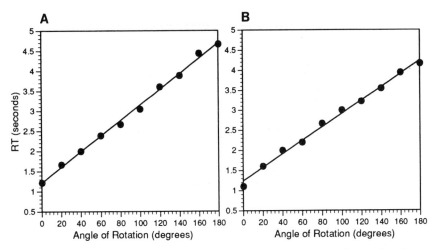

FIGURE 4 Response latency in Shepard and Metzler's (1971) experiment plotted as a function of angular disparity. (Figure 4A contains the results for planar rotations; Figure 4B contains the results for depth rotations.)

FIGURE 5 A replica of the map used by Kosslyn, Ball, and Reiser (1978) in the experiment on image scanning. Reprinted from Kosslyn, S. M., Ball, T. M., & Reiser, B. J. (1978). Visual images preserve metric spatial information: Evidence from studies of image scanning. *Journal of Experimental Psychology: Human Perception and Performance, 4,* 47–60. Copyright 1978 by the American Psychological Association. Reprinted by permission.

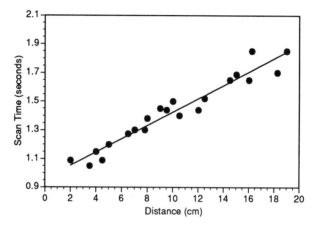

FIGURE 6   Image scanning time plotted as a function of Euclidean distance.

and distance were strongly correlated given that subjects were told to imagine a dot moving from one place to another on their mental image? As it turns out, similar results are obtained even when subjects are not explicitly instructed to scan an image (e.g., Finke & Pinker, 1983).

2. Neuroanatomy and Neurophysiology of Imagination

Experimental investigations of mental rotation, image scanning, and other operations on mental images have revealed many parallels between imagination and perception (Finke, 1985). These similarities suggest that visual imagery may rely on some of the same structures of the brain as those supporting vision (Farah, 1988), and in fact, recent studies support this conjecture.

Kosslyn and his colleagues (Kosslyn et al., 1993) measured cerebral blood flow with positron emission tomography (PET) while subjects were engaged in imagery and perceptual tasks. The assumption in research of this kind is that regional blood flow is an index of processing activity in the brain. Although the results differed somewhat from experiment to experiment, one general finding emerged: Visual imagery activated areas of the visual cortex that are known (or are likely) to be topographically organized. In Experiment 3, for example, subjects closed their eyes and imagined letters at very small or large sizes, and then made one of four possible judgments about the letters (e.g., whether or not the letters were symmetrical about the vertical axis). The PET scans showed that topographically organized areas of visual cortex (Area 17) were activated by the task; in particular, posterior regions of visual cortex were activated more when imagining small letters than when imagining large letters, and anterior regions were activated more when imagining large letters than when imagining small letters. This activation was specific to the right hemisphere. Similar results occur when people perceive stimuli of varying sizes (e.g., Fox et al., 1986).

The analogical nature of imaginal processes was revealed in experiments conducted by Georgopoulos, Lurito, Petrides, Schwartz, and Massey (1989). In previous studies, Georgopoulos and his colleagues (e.g., Georgopoulos, Schwartz, & Kettner, 1986) showed that actual and intended directions of arm movements by trained monkeys could be predicted by the collective activity of populations of neurons in motor cortex. Individual neurons respond maximally to a particular direction of movement but also respond to a wide range of directions, producing bell-shaped tuning curves. A linear combination of the vectors defined by individual neurons' preferred directions produces a population vector, which points in the direction of movement. This relationship was exploited by Georgopoulos et al. (1989), who trained monkeys to move a handle in the direction of a stimulus (direct task) or in the direction 90° to the left of the stimulus (rotation task). The crucial finding was that prior to the initiation of movement in the rotation task, the population vector—which summarized the directional tendency of the population of neurons—"rotated" continuously from pointing in the direction of the stimulus to pointing in the direction of movement.

These studies are important for at least two reasons. First, they illustrate dramatically the yield of converging operations. The experimental work in cognitive psychology defined the problems and provided compelling evidence on the underlying mechanisms. The subsequent research in cognitive neuroscience demonstrated similar results in animals and provided plausible neuroanatomical and neurophysiological models of those mechanisms. Second, the experiments show how an analogical representation and process might be implemented neurally. At the level of an individual neuron, direction in space is represented as firing rate, such that continuous changes in activity are associated with continuous departures from a preferred direction; at the level of a cell ensemble, direction is represented by a function defined over individual neurons' firing rates. This representation is analogical but abstract. The population vector is not a physical entity; it exists only at the level of a formal analysis of the activity of a population of neurons.

3. The Structure of Analogical Representations

One of the hot issues in the analog–propositional debate concerned whether visual images should be thought of as "pictures in the head." Georgopoulos's investigations of the motor system suggest that this would be a poor conception, and the same conclusion was reached earlier by way of conceptual analysis and behavioral experimentation. For example, analogical representations are conceptually interpreted, not "raw" sensory data (Anderson & Bower, 1973); when visual memories are forgotten, meaningful parts are lost, they don't fade away like the decaying image on a television tube (Pylyshyn, 1973); analogical representations can be horribly inaccurate (Nickerson & Adams, 1979); and, notably, analogical representations have internal structure. The internal structure of images has been demonstrated in several lines of research. Reed (1974), for instance, showed that some parts of an imagined figure could be recognized more quickly than other parts, which indicated that the internal representation of the figure had hierarchical structure. More recent studies have shown that mental images of letters and letterlike patterns are generated part-by-part in sequences that correspond to how the patterns are drawn (Kosslyn, Cave, Provost, & von Gierke, 1988).

4. Functions of Analogical Representations

It would be impossible to catalog all of the situations in which analogical representations are used. They include everyday problem solving (e.g., the introductory anecdote), mental practice of physical skills (e.g., Grouios, 1992), and vocabulary learning (e.g., Atkinson & Raugh, 1975). An especially important function of visual analogical representations may be their role in visual object recognition. Several theories of object recognition posit that visual input is matched against depictive representations in memory (e.g., Lowe, 1987; Ullman, 1989). In Ullman's model, for example, visual object recognition consists of two stages. In the *alignment* stage, a viewed object is aligned with models of objects in memory using simple low-level properties, such as inflections and cusps on the object's boundary, salient points, or the dominant orientation. The *matching* stage then selects the object model that best matches the viewed object. The object models are quasi-pictorial replicas of objects, and the matching process is pictorial in that it consists of comparing properties at corresponding locations in the object model and the aligned image of the viewed object.

Another function of analogical representations may be to preserve information that may not be recognized as important at the time of an experience. For example, I never recognized the potential importance of the spatial relation between Fessler's Lane and the bypass, and consequently, did not encode that information propositionally (e.g., "The Fessler's Lane exit is west of the bypass on I-40"). However, my experiences traveling in Nashville have produced a sufficiently rich spatial representation to enable me to access the spatial relation when I needed it. But the only way I could access this information was by imaging myself traveling on the highway, passing the various exits and intersections along the way. In short, analogical representations may comprise the mind's attempt to recreate the world as it was previously experienced.

B. Symbolic Knowledge Representations

Although much of our conscious experience may be filled with images, we clearly have the capacity for "imageless thought." Consider for a moment your memory of what you have read so far. Can you remember which of the following sentences was actually in the text?

1. Many parallels between imagination and perception have been revealed in experimental investigations of mental rotation, image scanning, and other operations on mental images.
2. Experimental investigations of mental rotation, image scanning, and other operations on mental images have revealed many parallels between imagination and perception.
3. Research on mental rotation, image scanning, and other operations on mental images has revealed few parallels between imagination and perception.

If there is one consistent finding in thirty years of research on memory for written and spoken language, it is that people remember the gist of a passage much better than the properties of the language used to express it (e.g., Anderson, 1976; Bransford, Barclay, & Franks, 1972; Sachs, 1967). For example, in the demonstration above, you should have found sentence 3 easy to reject because it violates the basic message of the text. On the other hand, sentences 1 and 2 differ only in form and might have been difficult to choose between (the correct answer is 2). Of course, we know that people can memorize the exact wording of a passage; the point is that in normal comprehension memory for structure is poor. This observation is important because it suggests that whatever representational form is used to encode meaning, it must be different from analogical representations, which seem to preserve perceptual properties of the stimulus.

This section of the chapter is organized differently from the previous one. For reasons that are not entirely clear, the existence of symbolic representations has never been as controversial as the existence of analogical representations. This is surprising because none of the logical arguments in favor of symbolic representations is compelling when examined closely (Anderson, 1978). Theories of symbolic representation also have been developed much more systematically (e.g., Anderson, 1976; Kintsch, 1974; Norman et al., 1975). For these (and I am sure other) reasons, the history of research and theoretical development is quite different in the two domains. In this section of the chapter, I begin by discussing the formal structure of propositional representations, which are the dominant symbolic representation in the cognitive sciences. I then turn to the empirical evidence.

1. The Structure of Propositional Representations

Our good memory for gist but poor memory for form is easy to understand if meaning is represented in propositions. A proposition is the smallest unit of knowledge that can stand as an assertion; the smallest unit that can be true or false. For example, consider the sentence, "Bush declared war against the oil-rich country of Iraq, which was led by Saddam Hussein." This sentence contains three propositions:

1. Bush declared war against Iraq.
2. Iraq has an abundance of oil.
3. Saddam Hussein was the leader of Iraq.

Propositions are not the same as words; they are best thought of as ideas that can be expressed in words. For example, the proposition that there is a particular book on a particular table can be conveyed in the English sentence, "The book is on the table," in the Spanish sentence, "El libro está sobre la mesa," or even with a picture of the book on the table. The words in the two sentences are different, and the picture doesn't use words at all. In order to divorce propositions from the words used to express them, it is customary to use special notation to designate propositions. For example, using a variant of Kintsch's (1974) notation, the three propositions in the Bush sentence can be written as follows:

1. (DECLARE-WAR, Bush, Iraq)
2. (OIL-RICH, Iraq)
3. (LEADER-OF, Saddam Hussein, Iraq)

The first word in each proposition expresses the *relation,* and the next one or two words are called *arguments* of the proposition.

Propositional representations are often depicted in networks, and there are many schemes for doing so (e.g., Anderson, 1976; Norman et al., 1975). The example in Figure 7 represents a combination of several of these methods. In this network, the circles represent the propositions, the ellipses represent relations and arguments, and the lines represent the associations between them. The circles and ellipses are commonly called *nodes,* and the lines are called *links.* The only spatial relation of importance in the network is the topological relation of connectedness.

There are many retrieval schemes associated with propositional networks, but most are based on a concept of spreading activation (e.g., Anderson, 1976, 1983; Collins & Loftus, 1975; Quillian, 1967). The spreading activation process that seems best to account for retrieval dynamics (McNamara, 1992a; Ratcliff & McKoon, 1981b) follows from the formal

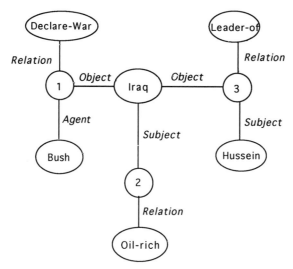

FIGURE 7 A propositional network representation of the sentence, "Bush declared war against the oil-rich country of Iraq, which was led by Saddam Hussein."

development of ACT, a general model of cognition proposed by Anderson (1983). According to this model of spreading activation, retrieving an item from memory consists of activating its internal representation. The activation of a node passes through the links to other nodes in the network, and the rate of spread is extremely rapid (1 or 2 milliseconds per link). A node is a source of activation as long as it is the focus of attention, but when attention is shifted, activation decays rapidly. Activation also decays exponentially with distance in the network. Finally, the time required to retrieve a memory trace is inversely related to its activation level; that is, more active traces are retrieved faster than are less active ones.

2. Evidence for Propositional Representations

These representational and processing assumptions may seem abstract and arbitrary. What evidence is there for any of them? Actually, the evidence is strong, and we turn to it here.

An early but important piece of evidence comes from experiments conducted by Kintsch and Keenan (1973). Subjects in this experiment read sentences that had the same number of words but differing numbers of propositions. The results showed that reading time increased linearly with the number of propositions.

Another line of evidence consistent with propositional representations comes from experiments conducted by Ratcliff and McKoon (1978). In one of their experiments, subjects studied a series of sentences, such as these:

The host mixed a cocktail but the guest wanted coffee.
The driver bruised a hip and the passenger strained a knee.
A gust crushed the umbrella and rain soaked the man.

After reading a set of sentences, subjects received a recognition test in which they saw a series of words on a computer display and had to decide whether or not each had been in the set of sentences. Ratcliff and McKoon were interested in the speed of responding on a particular item (e.g., passenger), depending on what item had appeared on the previous trial (e.g., hip vs. knee).

Figure 8 contains a network representation of the propositional structure of one of the sentences listed above. This network represents the major conceptual relations in the sentence but omits details to keep the diagram simple. The proposition attached to "&" corresponds to the proposition defined by the conjunction of the simple propositions in the sentence. Note that distances in this network between concepts in the same proposition are less than distances between concepts in different propositions. For example, "knee" and "passenger" are closer in the network than are "hip" and "passenger." According to the retrieval assumptions outlined above, more activation will accumulate at "passenger" when it is preceded, or primed, by "knee" than when it is primed by "hip." Thus, if sentences are mentally represented in terms of propositions, then responses to a target word should be faster when it is primed by a word in the same proposition than when it is primed by a word in a different proposition. This facilitation is called "associative priming."

The experiments showed clearly that priming was determined by propositional relations. Mean response times were 550 ms when a word was primed by a word from the same proposition, but 595 ms when it was primed by a word from a different proposition. Crucially, same and different proposition pairs were separated in the sentences by the same number of

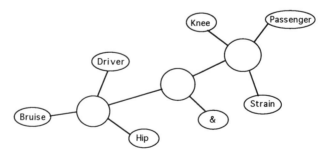

FIGURE 8   A propositional network representation of the sentence, "The driver bruised a hip and the passenger strained a knee."

— Can do one for essay question and literature Review.

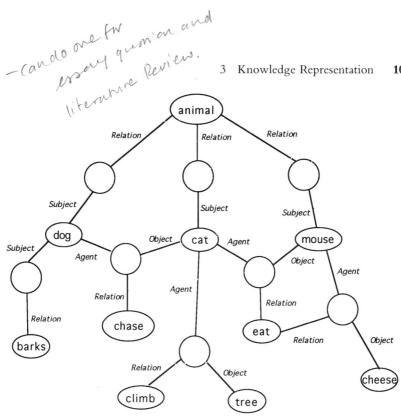

FIGURE 9   A propositional network representation of generic knowledge.

words. Another important finding in these experiments was that distance in the surface form of the sentence had no effects on priming. For example, no more priming occurred between "hip" and "passenger" than between "hip" and "knee." These results argue strongly that mental representations of even simple sentences preserve propositional relations but not perceptual properties of the stimulus.

This example illustrated an application of propositional representations to "episodic" memory, or memory for information acquired at a particular place and time. Propositional representations, however, were originally applied to "semantic" memories, or memories for general knowledge about the world (e.g., Collins & Loftus, 1975; Quillian, 1967). An example of such a propositional network is presented in Figure 9. This network depicts a small part of a person's general knowledge about dogs, cats, and mice, and represents ideas such as "dogs are animals," "cats climb trees," and "mice eat cheese."

A crucial prediction of a propositional model of this kind is that priming should vary systematically with network distance. Activation of a concept will spread throughout the network, and the amount of activation that accumulate at other concepts will depend on how far they are from the source of activation. These processes imply that concepts that occur in the same proposition (e.g., mouse–cheese) should prime each other more than concepts separated by two propositions (e.g., cat–cheese), and concepts separated by two propositions should prime each other more than concepts separated by three propositions (e.g., dog–cheese), and so on. The original tests of this prediction yielded ambiguous results (Balota & Lorch, 1986; de Groot, 1983); more recent studies, however, have confirmed it (McKoon & Ratcliff, 1992; McNamara, 1992c; McNamara & Altarriba, 1988; but see McKoon & Ratcliff, 1992, for an alternative interpretation of these results).

The first step in these experiments was to estimate the associative relations between concepts in memory. This was done with a free-association task. Large numbers of college students were given single words, such as *dog,* and asked to list the first words that came to mind. These lists of associates were used to construct associative chains, such as *dog–cat–mouse–cheese,* in which successive pairs were associated in memory but nonsuccessive pairs were not associated. For example, *cat* appeared frequently as an associate of *dog,* but *mouse* and *cheese* did not; similarly, *mouse* was listed as an associate of *cat,* but *cheese* was not. The assumption was that if two words did not appear as mutual associates in large samples of free-association responses, then they probably were not directly associated in memory.

The second step in these experiments was to give other subjects a lexical decision task. In this task, words and "nonwords" (e.g., blit) appeared one at a time at a fixed position on a computer terminal; the subjects' task was to decide whether or not each item was a word in English. In these experiments, the primes and the targets could be separated in memory by a single proposition (e.g., mouse–cheese), two propositions (e.g., cat–cheese), three propositions (e.g., dog–cheese), or an unknown but large number of propositions (e.g., window–cheese). The latter condition was treated as a control condition against which the others were compared.

As in Ratcliff and McKoon's (1987) recognition experiment, the dependent variable was response time. The graph in Figure 10 contains average priming effects as a function of the propositional distance between the primes and the targets (data from McNamara, 1992c, and McNamara & Altarriba, 1988). Priming was defined as the mean response time in the control condition minus the mean in the appropriate experimental condition. All of these effects are reliably different from zero, and, as predicted by the theory, they decline roughly exponentially with propositional distance. In principle, it might be possible to look for 4- or 5-step priming (e.g., barks–cheese). There are two practical problems, however. First, 3-step priming in these experiments was only 10 ms, which means that 4- or 5-step priming would be extremely small. The second problem is that as concepts get farther apart, it becomes more and more difficult to rule out the possibility that shorter pathways exist.

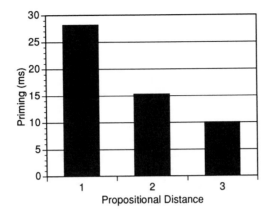

FIGURE 10   Priming effects as a function of the propositional distance between primes and targets.

In summary, there is strong evidence that meaning is represented in a propositional format. Propositions are discrete representations of elemental pieces of knowledge, and they seem to be interconnected in memory based on their shared arguments. This representational form contrasts sharply with analogical representations, which represent information continuously and intrinsically rather than discretely and extrinsically.

3. Functions of Propositional Representations

The functions of propositional representations have been documented by a number of researchers; especially thoughtful treatments have been published by Anderson (1976) and by Pylyshyn (1984). Three of the more important ones are these:

First, it is commonly accepted that propositions can represent any well-specified set of information, which implies that propositional representation is a general formalism for representing human knowledge. The power of propositional representations is so great that some analysts have doubted whether analogical representations are even necessary (e.g., Anderson & Bower, 1973). On the other hand, others have argued that this power is a weakness of the formalism (Kosslyn & Pomerantz, 1977; Shepard, 1981). The crux of the latter argument, recast in terms of the analysis of representation presented at the beginning of this chapter, is that symbolic representations in general, and propositional representations in particular, have no intrinsic constraints; the constraints are all external to the representational system. One of the consequences of this absence of intrinsic constraints is that propositional models are difficult to falsify; a given set of data can almost always be explained by an appropriately constructed model. The goal of converging operations is to impose constraints by forcing theoretical commitments in one domain of investigation that must be honored in other domains.

A second function of propositional representations is to preserve meaning but not surface form. There is no way to recover, for example, from a propositional representation whether an idea was expressed in an active or in a passive sentence. This feature is attractive given what is known about memory for language.

Taken together, these functions of propositional representations lead to a third, which is that propositions support in a natural way the making of inferences. Propositional representations are powerful, and, when combined with appropriate inferential machinery, almost certainly have sufficient computational power to explain human cognition (Anderson, 1976). The inferential rules are simplified because propositions preserve meaning but do not preserve details that may interfere with the ability to make an inference. For example, in a propositional representation, there is no need to handle inferences from active and passive sentences differently because both are represented identically.

C. Procedural Knowledge Representations

Inference is a crucial link between thought and action, and is an important function of procedural knowledge. Consider, again, the introductory anecdote. My mental traversal of the highway allowed me to conclude that the intersection of Fessler's Lane and the highway was west of the intersection of the highway and the bypass. This conclusion in turn supported the inference that I should take the west exit off of the bypass onto the highway. These inferences could be captured in productions of the following forms:

IF *one is headed in an easterly direction*
and location 1 is encountered before location 2
THEN *location 1 is west of location 2.*

IF *the goal is to be at location 1*
and location 1 is west of location 2
and one is located at or near location 2
THEN *travel in a westerly direction will get one closer*
to location 1.

The formal representation of procedural knowledge has a long history, but has often been studied under different guises. For example, stimulus-sampling theory (Estes, 1959) and TOTE hierarchies ("test–operate–test–exit"; Miller, Galanter, & Pribram, 1960) can be considered models of procedural knowledge. The dominant formalism in contemporary cognitive psychology for modeling procedural knowledge is the production (Anderson, 1976, 1983, 1993; Newell, 1973; Newell & Simon, 1972). Production systems have two attractive features: They are precise, which means that cognition can be modeled at a level of detail unmatched by most other formalisms, and they are computationally powerful, which guarantees that they can explain the complexity of human cognition. Anderson's ACT model (1976, 1983, 1993), for example, includes in its purview basic memory functions, such as recognition and recall; language comprehension, production, and acquisition; as well as reasoning and problem solving. Anderson (1976) has shown that ACT has the computational power of a Turing machine, and hence is capable of any well-specified behavior. In practice, however, ACT will produce resource-limited performance, as do humans.

1. An Example of a Simple Production System

The best way to gain an understanding of how production systems work is to examine a production-system model of a simple task, such as the Sternberg (1969) memory search task. On each trial of this task, a set of items is presented, which the subject must hold in memory. Next, a probe is presented; the subject's task is to decide whether or not the probe is in the memory set. The typical results are that decision time increases roughly linearly with memory set size, and that the slopes of the functions are about the same for positive and negative decisions. This task can be accomplished in ACT with two productions (Anderson, 1983):

> P1: IF *the goal is to decide whether or not the probe is in the memory set*
> *and the probe is present*
> *and the probe is in the memory set*
> THEN *respond yes.*
> P2: IF *the goal is to decide whether or not the probe is in the memory set*
> *and the probe is present*
> *and the probe is not in the memory set*
> THEN *respond no.*

The simplicity of these productions belies the complexity of the model. Figure 11 contains a schematic illustration of the pattern-matching network for the productions and the possible contents of working memory on a particular trial.

In this example, the probe is the digit 5 and the memory set contains the digits, 3, 5, and 9. The probe is represented as the proposition, "the probe is 5." The memory set is represented as three propositions (e.g., "the set contains 3"). The memory set could be represented as a unit, and either the probe or the memory set could be represented analogically. These representations would require different productions, but the overall model would be

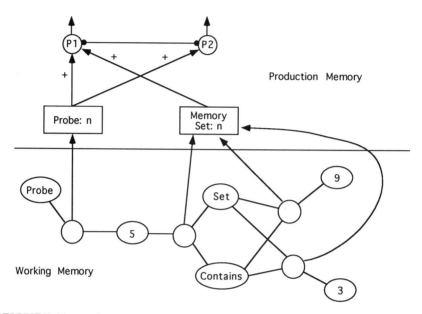

FIGURE 11   A schematic illustration of procedural and declarative memory on a trial of a memory scanning experiment.

similar. Connections between these propositions in working memory and other propositions in long-term memory (e.g., 3, 5, and 9 are odd numbers; 9 is a multiple of 3; etc.) have been omitted to simplify the figure.

The upper half of Figure 11 illustrates production memory, which contains the productions responsible for accomplishing the task and the network that matches the conditions of the productions against the contents of declarative memory. The pattern-matching networks in ACT are similar to the interactive nets used by McClelland and Rumelhart (1981; Rumelhart & McClelland, 1982) in their model of word recognition. Each condition of the productions (except for the goal condition, which has been omitted for simplicity) has a corresponding element at the bottom of the network. These terminal nodes perform tests to find elements of declarative memory that match them. For example, the node "Memory Set: n" looks for the digit "n" in the memory set. These nodes feed their outputs to the pattern nodes above, which test whether or not the variables in the terminal nodes have the same values. P1 receives input from both terminal nodes, and responds if the probe is in the memory set. P2, however, only receives input from the probe, and responds if the probe is absent in the memory set. This test for the absence of the probe is implemented by making the connection between P1 and P2 mutually inhibitory and increasing the gain on the connection between the probe node and P2. When the probe is in the memory set, activation flows from both terminal nodes to P1 but from only the probe node to P2. The two positive inputs to P1 more than offset the increased gain from the probe to P2, and P1 suppresses P2. When the probe is absent in the memory set, the probe node alone sends activation to P1 and P2, but because the gain on P2 is greater, it tends to accumulate more activation and suppress P1.

This model predicts both of the major results obtained in the Sternberg (1969) task. The rate of application of the productions is a function of the level of activation of the pattern-matching nodes, which in turn is a function of the level of activation of the elements in declarative memory. As the size of the memory set increases, less activation will accumulate at each element of the memory set, producing a "fan" effect (e.g., Anderson, 1976). The linear relation between response latency and set size is produced because the spreading activation system is linear when activation levels have stabilized (see Anderson, 1983, for details).

2. Evidence for Production Systems

The principal support for production systems comes from their success at modeling human cognition (e.g., Anderson, 1976, 1983, 1993; Kintsch, 1988; Newell & Simon, 1972). There have been a few experimental tests of production systems, but these tests have tested properties of the models that are shared with other models rather than properties specific to productions. For example, Anderson (1976) reported the results of two studies that were consistent with parallel application of productions, strengthening of productions with practice, and the separation of procedural and declarative knowledge. But as Anderson acknowledged, these results could be accounted for by a number of alternative models. Another line of evidence consistent with production system models can be found in research such as that by Brown and Van Lehn (1980), who showed that children's subtraction errors can be explained by the absence of necessary productions.

III. COMPLEX KNOWLEDGE REPRESENTATIONS

Images, propositions, and productions all can be considered simple representations in that they are the elements of more complex representations and representational systems, such as concepts, schemata, cognitive maps, and mental models. I do not have the space to review each of these domains in detail, but I will say a few words about the latter three because they are not covered elsewhere in this volume.

A. Schemata

The concept of a schema is usually traced to the work of Bartlett (1932), although modern conceptions are quite different from his (e.g., Bobrow & Winograd, 1977; Minsky, 1975; Schank & Abelson, 1977). A schema is a knowledge structure that captures regularities of objects and events. In most theories, schemata have a "slot" structure in which object properties, typical sequences of events, agents, and so on, can be specified. For example, a partial schema for a living room might contain the following information:

Schema:	Living room.
Category:	Room in a house.
Parts:	Walls, floor, ceiling.
Contents:	Furniture, houseplants.
Function:	Room for gathering; often for formal occasions.
Shape:	Rectilinear.
Size:	100–1000 ft².
Appearance:	[Images of living rooms.]

The slots in a schema specify typical properties of an object or event, and can contain default values. Default values are particularly useful in event schemas, or scripts (e.g., Schank & Abelson, 1977). For example, a schema for a visit to a restaurant will specify that customers typically pay for their meals. This knowledge would be useful in reading a story, such as the following,

> Gwen went to McDonalds, quizzed the clerk about the content of the salads, and left with a milkshake.

Given the default assumption that people pay for their meals, one is not inclined to conclude that Gwen is a thief.

There is a host of data consistent with the existence of schemata or schematalike knowledge representations in memory (e.g., Alba & Hasher, 1983). Bower, Black, and Turner (1979), for example, showed that after reading stories about common events (e.g., going to a doctor's office), people tended to recall events that were part of the schema but had not actually been mentioned in the story. In other experiments, they showed that people tended to recall actions in an event schema according to a standard temporal sequence (e.g., paying for a meal after eating it), even when the events were described as occurring in a different, atypical order (e.g., paying for a meal before receiving it). Brewer and Treyens (1981) demonstrated similar results. In their experiment, subjects sat in an office for 35 seconds, and then were taken to a different room, where they were asked to recall the contents of the office. Virtually all of the subjects recalled typical objects in the office (e.g., the desk), many fewer recalled atypical objects (e.g., a skull), and subjects often recalled typical objects that were not actually present (e.g., books).

B. Cognitive Maps

The term "cognitive map" refers to memories of interobject spatial relations. Models of spatial memory have ranged from maplike Euclidean models (e.g., Thorndyke, 1981) to abstract conceptual models (e.g., Stevens & Coupe, 1978). Recent models, however, have emphasized both analogical and symbolic components (e.g., Huttenlocher, Hedges, & Duncan, 1991; McNamara, 1992b; McNamara, Halpin, & Hardy, 1992).

The analogical component of spatial memories may be the easiest to appreciate. People often report that they solve spatial problems by conjuring an image of a scene. For example, your answer to the distance-estimation problem in the introduction might have depended on your ability to imagine the relative locations of objects in your home. This anecdotal evidence is buttressed by the similarities between studies of mental imagery and studies of spatial memory. Rieser (1989; Rieser, Guth, & Hill, 1986), for example, has documented mental-rotation-like effects in judgments of relative direction, and Kosslyn (1980) has shown that images of objects and of collections of objects are scanned in similar ways.

Spatial memories also have a hierarchical component. Hierarchical effects have been documented in judgments of relative direction (as in the Reno–San Diego example; e.g., McNamara, 1986; Stevens & Coupe, 1978; Tversky, 1981). People also overestimate distances between objects separated by boundaries, even if the boundaries are only perceptual (e.g., McNamara, 1986). Spatial priming is also greater for objects in the same region of a spatial layout than for objects in different regions (e.g., McNamara, 1986). These effects in distance estimation and spatial priming are present when normative or explicit boundaries are absent (e.g., Hirtle & Jonides, 1985; McNamara, Hardy, & Hirtle, 1989).

These and other results suggest that when people learn a spatial layout, they form two mental representations: A metric structure that encodes interpoint distances and a hierarchical nonmetric structure that encodes categorical spatial relations, such as adjacency and containment. The results of experiments conducted by McNamara et al. (1992) support this dichotomy, and suggest further that temporal-order information is encoded in the metric representation (see also Kosslyn et al., 1988). Although the latter result may seem surprising, it makes sense when one considers that spatial memories must encode when an object was in a particular place (because the same place may be occupied by different objects at different times), and that routes through an environment can be defined as temporally ordered sequences of scenes.

C. Mental Models

According to several theories of reading comprehension, understanding a narrative produces, and is supported by, mental representations of the events or the situations described in the text. These representations have been called *mental models* or *situation models*. According to Kintsch's theory (e.g., Kintsch, 1988; van Dijk & Kintsch, 1983), mental models are complex propositional representations. In other theories, however, there is an implicit suggestion, if not explicit claim, that mental models contain both analogical and symbolic components (e.g., Bower & Morrow, 1990; Johnson-Laird, 1983; Tversky, 1991).

There is a large body of evidence consistent with the mental model framework (for a review, see McNamara, Miller, & Bransford, 1991). In an experiment by Glenberg, Meyer, and Lindem (1987), for example, subjects read texts that described characters and objects as spatially associated (e.g., "John put the last flower in his buttonhole, then left the house to go shopping for groceries") or spatially dissociated (e.g., "John put the last flower in the vase, then left the house to go shopping for groceries"). Later in the narrative, subjects were given a recognition test. Responses to target objects (e.g., flower) were faster in the associated than in the dissociated versions of the texts, suggesting that representations of these objects were maintained in subjects' mental models. A simple propositional representation of the text would predict equivalent response times in the associated and the dissociated conditions because in both cases, the protagonist and the object are arguments of a common proposition (e.g., "John put the flower in the buttonhole" vs. "John put the flower in the vase").

Glenberg, Kruley, and Langston (in press) have proposed a computational model that can simulate these and related findings. In this simulation, text is first represented as propositions. These propositions are used to construct a mental model in a three-dimensional spatial medium corresponding to Baddeley's (1990) visual/spatial sketchpad. The dimensions of this medium are normally spatial, but can also correspond to nonspatial dimensions, such as time, mass, and so on. Objects in the spatial medium are pointers to nodes in the propositional representation. The simulation learns from the mental model using a process called "noticing." Noticing occurs when the mental model has been changed or manipulated in some way. The system searches for pointers close to the one just manipulated, and generates propositions describing relations between the pointers. These propositions are stored in memory. The noticing process allows the simulation to learn information that is not stated explicitly in a text. For example, if a text described object A as close to B, and B as close to C, then A would be at least moderately close to C in the spatial mental model. In the appropriate circumstances, the noticing process could recognize this spatial relation, and deposit the proposition "A is close to C" in memory. Glenberg et al. (in press) have shown that the simulation can account for a number of results on the use of mental models in text comprehension.

IV. CONNECTIONIST MODELS

The perspective taken in this chapter is based on the assumption that human cognition consists of the interpretation, manipulation, and transformation of mental representations. Computational theories of mind have many instantiations, ranging from those grounded firmly on the computer metaphor of the mind (e.g., Pylyshyn, 1984) to those more biological in orientation (e.g., Shepard, 1984). Recently, a number of cognitive scientists have begun to doubt whether the computer metaphor, in particular, is a fruitful heuristic for cognitive science. These researchers have offered instead a "brain metaphor" in which human cognition is viewed as the product of the interactions among many simple neuronlike elements. Many of these so-called "connectionist" models exist (e.g., Grossberg, 1980; McClelland & Rumelhart, 1986; Rumelhart & McClelland, 1986), but they share the following features: (1) a large collection of simple, neuronlike elements or units; (2) the units are densely interconnected with excitatory and inhibitory associations; (3) learning is accomplished by adjusting the strengths, or weights, of these interconnections; and (4) knowledge is distributed throughout the system; in particular, the pattern of weights comprises what the network "knows."

The appeal of connectionist models is multifaceted: Connectionist models appear to be structurally and functionally similar to neural systems in the brain, and are often called "neural networks"; they exhibit many of the features of human learning, such as the ability to learn from examples and to extract prototypical features; they are robust; and they tend to be relatively easy to program. The problems with connectionist models are also multifaceted: The similarity between most connectionist models and neural systems is specious (e.g., the most common learning algorithm, back propagation, does not occur in real neural systems); it remains to be seen whether the level of analysis occupied by connectionist models—in between neural systems and information-processing models—will be a fruitful one to explore; and many of the models are subject to catastrophic retroactive interference (i.e., material learned recently can completely obliterate prior memories; e.g., Ratcliff, 1990).

One should not be surprised to learn that there has been considerable debate about whether connectionist models constitute a revolutionary development that will supplant traditional models of knowledge representation (e.g., Rumelhart & McClelland, 1986) or are charlatans (e.g., Fodor & Pylyshyn, 1988). Even a cursory examination of the history of psychology indicates that the wise investor should avoid both of these extremes. Progress in understanding human cognition will be driven by the development of neurally inspired models, more traditional information-processing models, and above all, by systematic experimentation. Even now we are beginning to see a proliferation of models that combine information-processing and connectionist components (e.g., Holyoak & Thagard, 1989). Moreover, in cases where cognitive and neurophysiological investigations have focused on the same problem, the results have been encouraging. Georgopoulos and his colleagues (1989), for example, showed how the cognitive process of mental rotation might be implemented in the activity of neurons in motor cortex. One cannot find a neural network more plausible than the brain itself, and yet the cognitive and the neurophysiological data coexist in perfect harmony.

V. SUMMARY AND PROSPECTUS

I set out in this chapter to answer two questions: How is our knowledge of the world represented in memory? In what forms do knowledge representations come and how are they used? At least partial answers were obtained to both questions.

Our knowledge of the world can be divided into two broad categories, declarative knowledge, or knowledge of facts, and procedural knowledge, or knowledge of skills. Declarative knowledge is communicable, it can be acquired quickly, and is flexible. Declarative knowledge representations can be further divided into analogical representations and symbolic representations. Analogical representations preserve information intrinsically, are tied to a particular sensory modality, and play a crucial role in many tasks, but especially those whose solution requires the reenactment of previous experiences. Symbolic representations preserve information extrinsically, are abstract and amodal, and form the principal basis of logical inference. In contrast to declarative knowledge, procedural knowledge is difficult or impossible to communicate, it tends to be learned gradually and to require extensive practice, and is used in narrow, well-defined situations. The procedural knowledge employed in cognitive skills can be represented formally as productions. These condition–action rules comprise the connection between thought and action. Together, these representational forms are the bricks and the mortar out of which our knowledge of ourselves and our environment is built.

Although our knowledge about knowledge representations has increased dramatically over the past two decades, there is still much to learn. Opinions will differ on what the important outstanding issues are, but the following three should be strong candidates on anyone's list:

First, there is an obvious need for compelling tests of production system models and for investigations of alternative models of procedural knowledge. Production systems have proven themselves to be a powerful means of modeling cognitive skills, but there has been so little systematic study of alternatives that the success of production systems is difficult to evaluate.

Second, we need to explore further the neural implementation of knowledge representations and of the mental processes that operate on them. Cognitive theories are difficult to falsify because they are ad hoc: They are designed to explain existing bodies of evidence, and are not grounded in natural law or in known biological mechanisms. Embarrassing data can usually be accommodated by adding mechanisms to the theory or by altering an axiom or two. The cost of these modifications can be measured in metrics of simplicity, elegance, and heuristic value, but rarely if ever against established principles of nature. The use of converging operations at a given level of analysis helps to reduce the degrees of freedom available to a theory, and its use across levels of analysis will restrict even further the inherent lability of cognitive models.

Third, and finally, the molecular view afforded by an understanding of the neural foundations of mental representations must be accompanied by a molar view of the roles played by these representations in intelligent behavior. In reflecting on the development of his own ideas about knowledge representations, Anderson (1983, p. 45) commented: "When I observed what was good or bad about a representation, I found it was not its form or notation that was important . . . rather, the important issue was what could or could not be done easily with a representation." Anderson continued by noting that different aspects of a single problem, such as a proof in geometry, beg to be represented in different ways because they have different functions in the solution. At the same time, however, representations are defined by what can be done with them. The links between concepts in a propositional representation, for example, carry information about associative relations only if processes exist to use that information. This deep complementarity between representation and process implies that a taxonomy of the functions of knowledge representations in language, problem solving, and reasoning will further constrain models of their content and structure, completing a continuum of understanding from action potential to action.

Acknowledgments

Preparation of this chapter was supported in part by National Science Foundation Grants BNS 8820224 and SBR 9222002. I am grateful to Carolyn Cave, Kyle Cave, and Robert Sternberg for their comments on preliminary versions of this chapter.

References

Alba, J. W., & Hasher, L. (1983). Is memory schematic? *Psychological Bulletin, 93,* 203–231.

Anderson, J. R. (1976). *Language, memory, and thought.* Hillsdale, NJ: Erlbaum.

Anderson, J. R. (1978). Arguments concerning representations for mental imagery. *Psychological Review, 85,* 249–277.

Anderson, J. R. (1983). *The architecture of cognition.* Cambridge, MA: Harvard University Press.

Anderson, J. R. (1993). *Rules of the mind.* Hillsdale, NJ: Erlbaum.

Anderson, J. R., & Bower, G. H. (1973). *Human associative memory.* Washington, DC: Winston.

Atkinson, R. C., & Raugh, M. R. (1975). An application of the mnemonic keyword method to the acquisition of Russian vocabulary. *Journal of Experimental Psychology: Human Learning and Memory, 1,* 126–133.

Baddeley, A. (1990). *Human memory*. Boston: Allyn & Bacon.

Balota, D. A., & Lorch, R. F. (1986). Depth of automatic spreading activation: Mediated priming effects in pronunciation but not in lexical decisions. *Journal of Experimental Psychology: Learning, Memory, and Cognition, 12,* 336–345.

Bartlett, F. C. (1932). *Remembering: A study in experimental and social psychology*. New York & London: Cambridge University Press.

Bobrow, D. G., & Winograd, T. (1977). An overview of KRL, a knowledge representation language. *Cognitive Science, 1,* 3–46.

Bower, G. H., Black, J. B., & Turner, T. J. (1979). Scripts in memory for text. *Cognitive Psychology, 11,* 177–220.

Bower, G. H., & Morrow, D. G. (1990). Mental models in narrative comprehension. *Science, 247,* 44–48.

Bransford, J. D., Barclay, J. R., & Franks, J. J. (1972). Sentence memory: A constructive versus interpretive approach. *Cognitive Psychology, 3,* 193–209.

Brewer, W. F., & Treyens, J. C. (1981). Role of schemata in memory for places. *Cognitive Psychology, 13,* 207–230.

Brown, J. S., & Van Lehn, K. (1980). Repair theory: A generative theory of bugs in procedural skills. *Cognitive Science, 4,* 397–426.

Cave, C., & Squire, L. R. (1992). Intact and long-lasting repetition priming in amnesia. *Journal of Experimental Psychology: Learning, Memory, and Cognition, 18,* 509–520.

Chomsky, N. (1959). Review of Skinner's "Verbal Behavior." *Language, 35,* 26–58.

Collins, A. M., & Loftus, E. F. (1975). A spreading-activation theory of semantic processing. *Psychological Review, 82,* 407–428.

de Groot, A.M.B. (1983). The range of automatic spreading activation in word priming. *Journal of Verbal Learning and Verbal Behavior, 22,* 417–436.

Estes, W. K. (1959). The statistical approach to learning theory. In S. Koch (Ed.), *Psychology: A study of a science* (Vol. 2). New York: McGraw-Hill.

Farah, M. J. (1988). Is visual imagery really visual? Overlooked evidence from neuropsychology. *Psychological Review, 95,* 307–317.

Finke, R. A. (1985). Theories relating mental imagery to perception. *Psychological Bulletin, 98,* 236–259.

Finke, R. A., & Pinker, S. (1983). Directional scanning of remembered visual patterns. *Journal of Experimental Psychology: Learning, Memory, and Cognition, 9,* 398–410.

Fodor, J. A. (1975). *The language of thought*. New York: Crowell.

Fodor, J. A., & Pylyshyn, Z. W. (1988). Connectionism and cognitive architecture. In S. Pinker & J. Mehler (Eds.), *Connections and symbols*. Cambridge, MA: MIT Press.

Fox, P. T., Mintun, M. A., Raichle, M. E., Miezen, F. M., Allman, J. M., & Van Essen, D. C. (1986). Mapping human visual cortex with positron emission tomography. *Nature (London), 323,* 806–809.

Garner, W. R., Hake, H. W., & Eriksen, C. W. (1956). Operationism and the concept of perception. *Psychological Review, 63,* 149–159.

Georgopoulos, A. P., Lurito, J. T., Petrides, M., Schwartz, A. B., & Massey, J. T. (1989). Mental rotation of the neuronal population vector. *Science, 243,* 234–236.

Georgopoulos, A. P., Schwartz, A. B., & Kettner, R. E. (1986). Neuronal population coding of movement direction. *Science, 233,* 1416–1419.

Gibson, J. J. (1979). *The ecological approach to visual perception*. Boston: Houghton Mifflin.

Glenberg, A. M., Kruley, P., & Langston, W. E. (in press). Analogical processes in comprehension: Simulation of a mental model. In M. A. Gernsbacher (Ed.), *Handbook of psycholinguistics*.

Glenberg, A. M., Meyer, M., & Lindem, K. (1987). Mental models contribute to foregrounding during text comprehension. *Journal of Memory and Language, 26,* 69–83.

Grossberg, S. (1980). How does the brain build a cognitive code. *Psychological Review, 87,* 1–51.

Grouios, G. (1992). Mental practice: A review. *Journal of Sport Behavior, 15,* 42–59.

Hirtle, S. C., & Jonides, J. (1985). Evidence of hierarchies in cognitive maps. *Memory & Cognition, 13,* 208–217.

Holyoak, K. J., & Thagard, P. (1989). Analogical mapping by constraint satisfaction. *Cognitive Science, 13,* 295–355.

Huttenlocher, J., Hedges, L. V., & Duncan, S. (1991). Categories and particulars: Prototype effects in estimating spatial location. *Psychological Review, 98,* 352–376.

Jacoby, L. L., & Dallas, M. (1981). On the relationship between autobiographical memory and perceptual learning. *Journal of Experimental Psychology: General, 3,* 306–340.

Johnson-Laird, P. N . (1983). *Mental models.* Cambridge, MA: Harvard University Press.

Kintsch, W. (1974). *The representation of meaning in memory.* Hillsdale, NJ: Erlbaum.

Kintsch, W. (1988). The role of knowledge in discourse comprehension: A construction-integration model. *Psychological Review, 95,* 163–182.

Kintsch, W., & Keenan, J. (1973). Reading rate and retention as a function of the number of propositions in the base structure of sentences. *Cognitive Psychology, 5,* 257–274.

Kosslyn, S. M. (1980). *Image and mind.* Cambridge, MA: Harvard University Press.

Kosslyn, S. M., Alper, N. M., Thompson, W. L., Maljkovic, V., Weise, S. B., Chabris, C. F., Hamilton, S. E., Rauch, S. L., & Buonanno, F. S. (1993). Visual mental imagery activates topographically organized visual cortex: PET investigations. *Journal of Cognitive Neuroscience, 5,* 263–287.

Kosslyn, S. M., Ball, T. M., & Reiser, B. J. (1978). Visual images preserve metric spatial information: Evidence from studies of image scanning. *Journal of Experimental Psychology: Human Perception and Performance, 4,* 47–60.

Kosslyn, S. M., Cave, C. B., Provost, D. A., & von Gierke, S. M. (1988). Sequential processes in image generation. *Cognitive Psychology, 20,* 319–343.

Kosslyn, S. M., & Pomerantz, J. R. (1977). Imagery, propositions, and the form of internal representations. *Cognitive Psychology, 9,* 52–76.

Lowe, D. G. (1987). Three-dimensional object recognition from single two-dimensional images. *Artificial Intelligence, 31,* 355–395.

McClelland, J. L., & Rumelhart, D. E. (1981). An interactive model of context effects in letter perception: I. An account of basic findings. *Psychological Review, 88,* 375–407.

McClelland, J. L., & Rumelhart, D. E. (1986). *Parallel distributed processing* (Vol. 2). Cambridge, MA: MIT Press.

McKoon, G., & Ratcliff, R. (1992). Spreading activation versus compound cue accounts of priming: Mediated priming revisited. *Journal of Experimental Psychology: Learning, Memory, and Cognition, 18,* 1155–1172.

McNamara, T. P. (1986). Mental representations of spatial relations. *Cognitive Psychology, 18,* 87–121.

McNamara, T. P. (1992a). Priming and constraints it places on theories of memory and retrieval. *Psychological Review, 99,* 650–662.

McNamara, T. P. (1992b). Spatial representation. *Geoforum, 23,* 139–150.

McNamara, T. P. (1992c). Theories of priming: I. Associative distance and lag. *Journal of Experimental Psychology: Learning, Memory, and Cognition, 18,* 1173–1190.

McNamara, T. P., & Altarriba, J. (1988). Depth of spreading activation revisited: Semantic mediated priming occurs in lexical decisions. *Journal of Memory and Language, 27,* 545–559.

McNamara, T. P., Halpin, J. A., & Hardy, J. K. (1992). Spatial and temporal contributions to the structure of spatial memory. *Journal of Experimental Psychology: Learning, Memory, and Cognition, 18,* 555–564.

McNamara, T. P., Hardy, J. K., & Hirtle, S. C. (1989). Subjective hierarchies in spatial memory. *Journal of Experimental Psychology: Learning, Memory, and Cognition, 15,* 211–227.

McNamara, T. P., Miller, D. L., & Bransford, J. D. (1991). Mental models and reading comprehension. In R. Barr, M. L. Kamil, P. B., Mosenthal, & P. D. Pearson (Eds.), *Handbook of reading research* (Vol. 2). White Plains, NY: Longman.

Miller, G. A., Galanter, E., & Pribram, K. H. (1960). *Plans and the structure of behavior.* New York: Holt, Rinehart, & Winston.

Minsky, M. L. (1975). A framework for representing knowledge. In P. H. Winston (Ed.), *The psychology of computer vision.* New York: McGraw-Hill.

Newell, A. (1973). Production systems: Models of control structures. In W. G. Chase (Ed.), *Visual information processing.* New York: Academic Press.

Newell, A., & Simon, H. (1972). *Human problem solving.* Englewood Cliffs, NJ: Prentice-Hall.

Nickerson, R. S., & Adams, M. J. (1979). Long-term memory for a common object. *Cognitive Psychology, 11,* 287–307.

Norman, D. A., Rumelhart, D. E., & the LNR Research Group. (1975). *Explorations in cognition.* San Francisco: Freeman.

Paivio, A. (1983). *Mental representations.* New York: Oxford University Press.

Palmer, S. E. (1978). Fundamental aspects of cognitive representation. In E. Rosch & B. Lloyd (Eds.), *Cognition and categorization.* Hillsdale, NJ: Erlbaum.

Posner, M. I., & Snyder, C. R. R. (1975). Attention and cognitive control. In R. L. Solso (Ed.), *Information processing and cognition.* Hillsdale, NJ: Erlbaum.

Post, E. L. (1943). Formal reductions of the general combinatorial decision problem. *American Journal of Mathematics, 65,* 197–268.

Pylyshyn, Z. W. (1973). What the mind's eye tells the mind's brain: A critique of mental imagery. *Psychological Bulletin, 80,* 1–24.

Pylyshyn, Z. W., (1979). Validating computational models: A critique of Anderson's indeterminacy of representation claim. *Psychological Review, 86,* 383–394.

Pylyshyn, Z. W. (1981). The imagery debate: Analogue media versus tacit knowledge. *Psychological Review, 88,* 16–44.

Pylyshyn, Z. W. (1984). *Computation and cognition.* Cambridge, MA: MIT Press.

Quillian, M. R. (1967). Word concepts: A theory and simulation of some basic semantic capabilities. *Behavioral Science, 12,* 410–430.

Ratcliff, R. (1990). Connectionist models of recognition memory: Constraints imposed by learning and forgetting functions. *Psychological Review, 97,* 285–308.

Ratcliff, R., & McKoon, G. (1978). Priming in item recognition: Evidence for the propositional structure of sentences. *Journal of Verbal Learning and Verbal Behavior, 17,* 403–417.

Ratcliff, R., & McKoon, G. (1981a). Automatic and strategic priming in recognition. *Journal of Verbal Learning and Verbal Behavior, 20,* 204–215.

Ratcliff, R., & McKoon, G. (1981b). Does activation really spread? *Psychological Review, 88,* 454–462.

Reed, S. K. (1974). Structural descriptions and the limitations of visual images. *Memory & Cognition, 2,* 329–336.

Reisberg, D. (1992). *Auditory imagery.* Hillsdale, NJ: Erlbaum.

Rieser, J. J. (1989). Access to knowledge of spatial structure at novel points of observation. *Journal of Experimental Psychology: Learning, Memory, and Cognition, 15,* 1157–1165.

Rieser, J. J., Guth, D. A., & Hill, E. W. (1986). Sensitivity to perspective structure while walking without vision. *Perception, 15,* 173–188.

Rumelhart, D. E., & McClelland, J. L. (1982). An interactive activation model of context effects in letter perception: II. The contextual enhancement effect and some tests and extensions of the model. *Psychological Review, 89,* 60–94.

Rumelhart, D. E., & McClelland, J. L. (1986). *Parallel distributed processing* (Vol. 1). Cambridge, MA: MIT Press.

Ryle, G. (1949). *The concept of mind*. London: Hutchinson.

Sachs, J. (1967). Recognition memory for syntactic and semantic aspects of connected discourse. *Perception & Psychophysics, 2,* 437–442.

Schacter, D. L. (1987). Implicit memory: History and current status. *Journal of Experimental Psychology: Learning, Memory, and Cognition, 13,* 501–518.

Schank, R. C., & Abelson, R. P. (1977). *Scripts, plans, goals, and understanding: An inquiry into human knowledge structures*. Hillsdale, NJ: Erlbaum.

Seidenberg, M. S., Waters, G. S., Sanders, M., & Langer, P. (1984). Pre- and postlexical loci of contextual effects on word recognition. *Memory & Cognition, 12,* 315–328.

Shepard, R. N. (1975). Form, formation, and transformation of internal representations. In R. L. Solso (Ed.), *Information processing and cognition*. Hillsdale, NJ: Erlbaum.

Shepard, R. N. (1981). Psychophysical complementarity. In M. Kubovy & J. Pomerantz (Eds.), *Perceptual organization*. Hillsdale, NJ: Erlbaum.

Shepard, R. N. (1984). Ecological constraints on internal representation: Resonant kinematics of perceiving, imagining, thinking, and dreaming. *Psychological Review, 91,* 417–447.

Shepard, R. N., & Cooper, L. A. (1982). *Mental images and their transformations*. Cambridge, MA: MIT Press.

Shepard, R. N., & Metzler, J. (1971). Mental rotation of three-dimensional objects. *Science, 171,* 701–703.

Skinner, B. F. (1957). *Verbal behavior*. New York: Appleton.

Smyth, M. M., & Pendleton, L. R. (1989). Working memory for movements. *Quarterly Journal of Experimental Psychology, 41A,* 235–250.

Squire, L. R. (1987). *Memory and brain*. New York: Oxford University Press.

Squire, L. R. (1992). Memory and the hippocampus: A synthesis from findings with rats, monkeys, and humans. *Psychological Review, 99,* 195–231.

Sternberg, S. (1969). Memory scanning: Mental processes revealed by reaction time experiments. *Acta Psychologica, 30,* 276–315.

Stevens, A., & Coupe. P. (1978). Distortions in judged spatial relations. *Cognitive Psychology, 10,* 422–437.

Terres, J. K. (1980). *The Audubon Society encyclopedia of North American birds*. New York: Knopf.

Thorndyke, P. W. (1981). Distance estimation from cognitive maps. *Cognitive Psychology, 13,* 526–550.

Tversky, B. (1981). Distortions in memory for maps. *Cognitive Psychology, 13,* 407–433.

Tversky, B. (1991). Spatial mental models. In G. H. Bower (Ed.), *The psychology of learning and motivation: Advances in research and theory* (Vol. 27, pp. 109–145). San Diego: Academic Press.

Ullman, S. (1989). Aligning pictorial descriptions: An approach to object recognition. *Cognition, 32,* 193–254.

van Dijk, T. A., & Kintsch, W. (1983). *Strategies of discourse comprehension*. New York: Academic Press.

CHAPTER 4

Concepts and Categories

Brian H. Ross
Thomas L. Spalding

I. INTRODUCTION

People have an amazing number of concepts that allow easy classification of new objects and inferences about those objects. For example, our concepts of various animals provide us with a probable classification of a briefly seen animal. From this classification, we make predictions about the animal's behavior, which, in turn, influence our behavior. An approaching animal classified as a dog leads to different actions than those generated by an animal classified as a skunk.

The importance of concepts and categories extends beyond simple objects. For example, two physicians may note the same history and symptoms of a patient but end up with differing diagnoses (disease categories). These different categorizations may lead to greatly different treatments and long-term consequences for the patient. As another example, your categorization of a political figure as a liberal, conservative, or fascist may determine your vote and influence other political actions such as volunteer work or contributions.

We simply could not get by without categories. What are categories, how do we categorize new things, and how do we make use of these categorizations? In this chapter we will address these questions. We will begin by examining how models of classification account for the way in which people classify new instances. We will then consider a number of problems with these models of classification. Next, we outline a recent development that makes use of people's naive theories and discuss the advantages and disadvantages of such an approach. Finally, we will provide a brief glimpse of some important new directions of research. Before getting to the classification models, we begin by defining concepts and categories and briefly examining some of their uses.

A. Definition of Concepts and Categories

A **concept** is a mental representation of a class (e.g., skunks, liberals), which includes what we know about such things. A **category** is the set of examples picked out by a concept. In the literature, these two terms are often used synonymously to refer to both the mental representation and any examples it picks out.

B. Functions of Categories

We appear to have concepts and categories for most objects and situations we face. Why? What are the functions of concepts and categories? An important distinction is between the classification function of concepts and the use made from these classifications. Going back to the approaching animal example, classification would be the decision that it is a skunk. However, deciding it is a skunk is not helpful by itself; one still needs to decide what to do. This distinction between classification and use is, we believe, a central one for understanding concepts. Concepts and categories are used in many ways. For ease of exposition, after examining the classification function, we consider three broad uses: inference, combinations, and communication.

1. Classification

As we have already stated, a central function of concepts is **classification.** Classification is important for two reasons. First, it provides access to all the knowledge one has about such entities. Classifying an animal as a skunk allows one to access the other knowledge you have about skunks in order to decide what to do. Second, it can be viewed as a decision about the relevant equivalent class. That is, by classifying an animal as a skunk, there is a tentative decision that the differences between this skunk and other skunks are irrelevant, but that the differences between this skunk and other small mammals are relevant. Clearly, such classifications depend on the goal of the classifier (as we will address later); if one has a pet skunk, then distinguishing it from other skunks is not only relevant, but crucial.

2. Inference

A main function of concepts is to allow inference; for understanding, explanation, and prediction. Having made a classification, one can access the relevant knowledge and bring it to bear on interpreting the situation. If one sees a person running from a small animal, classifying the animal as a skunk provides knowledge that allows one to understand and explain the person's seemingly strange behavior. In addition, because one understands how the concepts of *skunk* and *animal* are related, one can infer properties of skunks that one may not know directly, such as that they must sleep and eat. The same accessed body of relevant knowledge allows one to make predictions concerning the classified item and to act accordingly. If one encounters a skunk, one may predict how it will react to being scared and thus plan on making a quick, but nonthreatening, retreat. Clearly, it is not the classification of the animal as a skunk per se that causes a quick but nonthreatening retreat. It is our knowledge of skunks and their spray that gives rise to the behavior. If a person has been taught to recognize skunks but has not been told anything else about skunks, that person would likely have a very different response to the animal.

3. Combination

Concepts can also be combined to create new concepts. Concepts can be seen as building blocks from which we can construct new, more complex concepts. Thus, one can understand what "pet skunk" means (or "escaped pet skunk" or even "rabid escaped pet skunk") without ever having encountered such entities.

4. Communication

The final important use for concepts that we will discuss is in communication. Although people may not have exactly the same knowledge about each concept, in many cases we use words to refer to approximately the same classes and ideas. Because of this common knowledge, we can use the words for concepts to communicate without having to go into endless descriptions (which would have problems as well if the descriptive terms did not refer to common knowledge). This communication function allows us to learn from others' experience without having to directly experience the event ourselves. Thus, the passed-down knowledge of how to avoid being sprayed by skunks allows many of us to miss out on this memorable experience.

II. HOW DO PEOPLE CLASSIFY?

How do people classify new instances? E. E. Smith and Medin (1981) have provided an influential overview of classification models, dividing them into three main types: classical, probabilistic, and exemplar. Because most of the work in this area has concerned object categories, we will mainly consider object categories in our discussions.

A. The Classical View

The classical view assumes each concept has a set of properties that are singly necessary and jointly sufficient to categorize an instance. For example, a triangle may be defined as a closed, two-dimensional figure with three sides, and angles that sum to 180 degrees. Any triangle must have every one of these properties and any figure with all these properties is a triangle. The classical view, then, assumes that we have something like definitions or strict rules for determining class membership. This way of thinking about classification has a long history, dating back at least to Aristotle, and has been held by psychologists as diverse as Hull and Piaget.

Problems for the Classical View

Although this classical view works well with triangles, it runs into a number of problems in providing an account of many other concepts. We concentrate here on two major problems with this view: the specification of defining properties and typicality effects (see E. E. Smith & Medin, 1981, for other problems with this view). Although one can specify defining properties for triangles, what are the necessary and sufficient properties for classifying something as a dog? Any set of defining properties needs to exclude all nondogs (e.g., wolves, cats, foxes), while also capturing the properties used in classifying all dogs. No one has been able to derive such properties. As another, perhaps more compelling example, think about what would define the concept of furniture.

A second problem with this classical view is that instances of a category vary in how typical they are of the category. For instance, *robin* is viewed as a much more typical bird than is *penguin*. Typicality differences occur not only in typicality ratings (e.g., Rosch & Mervis, 1975), but in a variety of measures. People are faster to verify the statement that "A robin is a bird" than "A penguin is a bird" (Rips, Shoben, & Smith, 1973) and to verify a picture of a robin as a bird than a picture of a penguin as a bird (Murphy & Brownell, 1985). If a set of defining properties is being matched, why do instances consistently vary in how typical a member of the category they are considered to be?

B. The Probabilistic View

An alternative view is that instances are classified more loosely, using a probabilistic account of likely features, rather than the necessary and sufficient defining features. The common assumption is that there is a prototype, an abstraction for the category, consisting of characteristic features (e.g., Posner & Keele, 1970; Rosch, 1978). Classification is determined by the match of the features of the instance to the various prototypes. For instance, the characteristic features of birds might be "winged, lays eggs, feathered, flies, chirps, builds nests in trees," and so on. To be classified as a bird, an object would have to have some threshold number of these features. Usually, one assumes that these features vary in how important they are to the category, so the threshold is some weighted sum of the different properties. Thus, although an ostrich does not fly, chirp, or build nests in trees, it may be classified as a bird because it has many of the highly weighted characteristic properties, such as winged, lays eggs, and feathered. A bat may not be classified as a bird because it lacks these last two properties.

This view provides answers to both criticisms mentioned for the classical view. First, the failure to specify the defining features is addressed by the claim that there are no defining features, only ones that tend to be true of a concept. Second, it provides a direct account of the typicality effects mentioned earlier. More typical instances have more of these characteristic properties that are associated with the category. Thus a robin is typical because it is winged, lays eggs, is feathered, flies, chirps, and builds nests in tress. An ostrich is less typical because it does not have these last three properties. Because more typical instances have more of the characteristic features, they would presumably lead to faster meeting of a threshold (explaining the faster verification) and higher final matches (explaining the higher typicality ratings).

What does this view say about category structure? It draws heavily on the idea of family resemblance (Rosch & Mervis, 1975). Imagine a picture of an extended family, say three generations with a grandmother, grandfather, children, spouses of children, and grandchildren. If you look at such a picture, you often notice that there is a family resemblance. What does this mean? Some features tend to occur often, though no single feature may occur in all of the family members. For instance, this family might tend to have dark hair, small noses, and pointed chins, though the grandmother may have a large nose and some of the children and grandchildren may have only some (or none) of these features. The spouses of children will tend to not look like most members of the family. However, their children will tend to have some of their features. Thus, looking at the whole picture, one can easily see that some of the family members look more like they "belong" to this family than others, even though the less typical members may look like they do belong.

This way of thinking about concepts suggests that concepts "carve the world at its joints." That is, concepts that have high family resemblance will tend to maximize the similarity within categories, while also minimizing the similarity between categories. In other words, members of a category will tend to be similar to each other, and will tend to be dissimilar from members of other categories (Rosch, 1978).

Problems for the Probabilistic View

The simple idea of a prototype is that there are a number of separate (independent) features, each with some weight. The features of a new instance are compared to the features of the various prototypes. The best match (in terms of the weighted sum of matching features) determines the classification. The idea that we classify by similarity to a prototype may seem intuitively correct, but it does have problems. (More complex versions of prototypes are possible, for example; see Barsalou, 1990, but we will deal with such complications under the heading of Mixed Models.) We mention here three problems with this view.

First, it appears that people use knowledge that goes beyond the prototype for classification. For example, two instances that are equally similar to the prototype may be classified at different speeds and accuracy, depending on the similarity of the new instances to the particular instances used to form the prototype (e.g., Whittlesea, 1987). In particular, if one of the instances is very similar to an instance presented during learning, it will often be classified more easily than another instance of equivalent similarity to the prototype. Thus, classification appears to make use of knowledge that goes beyond the prototype.

Second, people appear to have knowledge beyond the central values of each feature that is used in categorization. For example, people often know the range of values that a property might have and make use of this in classifying a new instance (e.g., Rips, 1989; Walker, 1975). In addition, rather than treating each property as independent, people know that some properties go together and use this information in classifying objects (Malt & Smith, 1984; Medin, Altom, Edelson, & Freko, 1982). For example, birds tend to be small and tend to sing, but large birds tend not to sing. One can extend the prototype view to allow the features to be distributions and the relation of features to vary as well, but unless one has prior constraints on what feature relations are considered, the scheme becomes quite complicated.

Third, prototype views have difficulty accounting for the flexible classification of instances as a function of context (e.g., Roth & Shoben, 1983). For example, in the usual context, *robin* is much more typical than *turkey*. However, in the context of "The holiday bird looked delicious," *turkey* is much more typical than *robin*. The prototype view provides little insight into these changes.

What underlies these problems for the prototype view? One way of thinking about the difficulty is that the prototype is not flexible enough. The idea that we always use the same summary representation to classify instances of a concept is appealing, but may be too limiting an application of our knowledge. How can our classifications be sensitive to particular instances, various statistical properties (range, correlations), and context effects?

C. The Exemplar View

A third view of classification is the exemplar view. Unlike the classical and probabilistic views, the exemplar view does not assume that the same representation is used to classify all members of a category. Rather, it assumes that a concept consists of multiple representations and that any one (or several or even many) of them may be used to classify a new instance (e.g., Brooks, 1978, 1987).

For example, consider the category *bird*. The prototype view is that there exists a single summary representation for classifying all birds. While people have an idea what the characteristic features of birds are, they also have memories of particular birds. Exemplar models incorporate the idea that these memories of birds can be useful in classification. Rather than assuming that the same representation would be used to classify all new members of a category, exemplar theories assume that various exemplars are used, with the choice a function of the similarity between the instance and the various stored exemplars. Thus, an eagle might be matched to other eagles (or other birds of prey), while a swan would be classified as a bird by a match to some waterfowl (or swan) representation.

The examples oversimplify the idea, because most exemplar theories allow multiple representations to play a role in classification, with the influence of each weighted by its similarity to the instance (e.g., Hintzman, 1986; Medin & Schaffer, 1978). Thus, an eagle might be classified by using representations of eagles, birds of prey, and other birds, presumably weighted in that order.

How does this view help in dealing with the classification results? There are two parts to the question: does it account for the results that prototype theories account for and does it account for additional results? There are many varieties of exemplar theories, so it is difficult to make a blanket statement about all of them. However, two ideas, the context model (Medin & Schaffer, 1978; and its generalization by Nosofsky, 1986) and MINERVA (Hintzman, 1986), have been developed in much detail and will be used to answer these questions.

Exemplar theories can account for many of the same results as the prototype views. Although this ability may seem counterintuitive, the exemplar theories are able to do so because they are retaining the information from which the prototype was formed (i.e., the exemplars). Thus, when faced with a new instance to categorize, the exemplar theories may bring to bear all their relevant knowledge, though it will generally be weighted by its similarity match to the instance (e.g., Hintzman, 1986). Although this relevant knowledge is not equivalent to the prototype, it is greatly influenced by the central tendency of the category. For example, consider the typicality results, which prototype models assume is a consequence of the family resemblance structure. A robin, a typical exemplar for the category *bird*, will have many high-frequency properties of birds and thus will tend to be similar to many other exemplars (e.g., other robins, as well as sparrows, thrushes, and blackbirds). However, an atypical exemplar, such as a swan, will be highly similar to only a few other exemplars. Thus, the exemplar view accounts for the typicality results because the family resemblance is represented in the stored exemplars. In other words, robins are typical because they are similar to many other birds, while swans are atypical because they are similar to relatively few other birds. (The frequency of the different birds also plays a role in typicality).

In addition to accounting for many prototype-like effects, the exemplar theories can account for the three findings that were problematic for prototype views. First, exemplars that are highly similar to stored exemplars are classified faster and more accurately than other exemplars with equivalent similarity to the prototype. Given that exemplar models assume classification is done by similarity to exemplars, such a result is directly predicted by the exemplar view.

Second, people know about the statistics of the features (e.g., range) and some of the correlations among properties. The exemplar theories allow for such knowledge to be available implicitly across the stored exemplars. For example, the size of birds may not be a property you have given much thought to, but you can compute a rough estimate of it using knowledge you have about different birds. Similarly, the correlation between bird size and noise (song or squawk) can be computed over the different birds.

Third, instance classification may be affected by the context. Although exemplar theories have not fully developed an account for this result, they do allow for different representations to differentially influence classification. If the context tended to activate exemplars that are associated to the context, these exemplars may tend to be more influential during classification. Thus, to return to our earlier example, memories of previous holiday dinners may activate exemplars of turkeys from previous meals. In this way, turkey can be more typical than robin in the context of a holiday dinner.

Problems for the Exemplar View

Although the exemplar theories do a good job accounting for many results (see Medin & Ross, 1989, for a review), they also have problems. In particular, sometimes people appear to be using abstractions (e.g., Medin, Dewey, & Murphy, 1983; Ross, Perkins, & Tenpenny, 1990; Spalding & Ross, in press). Malt (1989) found that people seemed to be able to use either exemplars or prototypes, depending on study instructions. In addition, there is a more general issue that seems problematic. What makes these exemplars "go together"? Why are dissimilar birds like penguins, eagles, and robins together in one category, while similar sea animals like sharks and porpoises are in separate categories?

D. Mixed Models

We consider here two types of mixed models: a mixture of classical and probabilistic and a mixture of probabilistic and exemplar. Each brings some of the advantages of their components to the mixture.

1. Classical and Probabilistic

The mixture of classical and probabilistic is sometimes referred to as core plus prototype. The idea is that the concept consists of a set of easily perceived properties that provide a good initial guess at identification or classification (the prototype), as well as a set of less visible defining features (the core). The prototype would usually be used for classification, but the core could be used to determine unclear cases or provide justification. In such a case, the typicality effects would arise from the prototype, though category membership could be determined by the core if necessary (E. E. Smith & Medin, 1981). We should note that we are including only strict mixtures of classical and probabilistic models. Models that include relationships between defining features and characteristic features will be discussed later.

Such a mixture brings the important constraints from the classical view (so that it is clear what makes an instance a member of a category), but still allows classification to be sensitive to typicality. It helps to explain why even "well-defined" concepts, like *grandfather,* may show typicality effects (see, e.g., Armstrong, Gleitman, & Gleitman, 1983). Although one could unambiguously classify someone as a grandfather or nongrandfather if enough information about children and their children could be obtained, classification ease may depend on more visible features. For instance, one can easily imagine that men fitting the definition who are tightrope walkers might be classified less easily than gray-haired chair rockers.

Despite the advantages of such a position, the core idea runs into the same problem that the classical view did in terms of being unable to specify the defining features. In addition, the core may be outweighed by physical features in determining category membership even for unspeeded judgments and well-known concepts (Malt, 1993; Malt & Johnson, 1992).

2. Probabilistic and Exemplar

A second mixture view combines the probabilistic and exemplar views. In particular, it retains the multiple representations of the exemplar view, but allows that these representations may also be abstractions. Some exemplar views do have more abstract representations (e.g., Medin & Schaffer, 1978), but the difference of the more recent views is that they provide some means by which these abstractions may arise. Two examples may be helpful in understanding the power of such views.

First, if some features are selectively attended to during learning, then the values of the other features may not be represented. This selective attention has the consequence of encoding abstractions. Early exemplar models posited such selective attention (Medin & Schaffer, 1978), while later modifications provided detailed explanations of how such selective attention may be tuned during learning (Nosofsky, 1986). In addition, a recent trend has been the use of Parallel Distributed Processing (PDP) models to provide an even more detailed exploration of how this learning may come about (Kruschke, 1992).

Second, the encoding of abstractions may occur as a function of initial classifications (e.g., Medin & Edelson, 1988; Ross et al., 1990; Spalding & Ross, in press). By this account, using old exemplars to classify new exemplars has important consequences that go beyond storing a new exemplar. In particular, the features of the new and old exemplars may be compared and their commonalities may be used in helping to classify later instances. Thus, if an instance with features {a b c} was used to classify a new instance with features {a b d}, the common features {a b} might be additionally highlighted (either stored again or weighted more in the representation), resulting in an abstraction. This learning account provides a mechanism for having multiple representations that include abstractions.

We have discussed several different classification models. Classical models make clear how category membership is determined, but are limited and inflexible. Exemplar models have great flexibility, but are not clear about why category members go together. Other models seem to fall somewhere in between the classical and exemplar views. In short, we have seen that each of these classification models has certain strengths and weaknesses. We now wish to consider some general difficulties of all of these models.

III. PROBLEMS FOR ALL MODELS OF CLASSIFICATION

These classification models provide a good account of much of the classification data. However, other work suggests they may be missing important aspects of conceptual knowledge. In this section, we discuss three ways in which the classification models are incomplete. First, these models deal mainly with the issues of organization within concepts at a particular level of abstraction (e.g., how is *chair* represented?). They provide little insight into relations between concepts or why instances are classified at one level and not another. Second, these classification models do not tell us much about the many other ways in which our conceptual knowledge is used. Finally, we will discuss some shortcomings of these models as models of classification.

A. Between-Concept Relations: Basic Levels

Classification models are mainly concerned with the representation of features within a single concept. However, we do not simply have a collection of concepts, rather we have an interrelated system of concepts. The relations among concepts provide some additional complexities to the study of classification.

An important aspect of the relations among concepts has to do with the level of abstraction at which a particular entity might be classified. For example, suppose you see a kitchen chair. This particular object might be (correctly) classified as "kitchen chair" or "chair" or "furniture" or even "thing." As you might guess, "chair" is the usual classification.

Rosch and her colleagues (Rosch, Mervis, Gray, Johnson, & Boyes-Braem, 1976) demonstrated that one level (which they call the **basic level**) is psychologically privileged. This basic level is neither the most abstract nor the most specific level, but rather is an intermediate level of abstraction (e.g., "chair" in the example above).

Much of our knowledge of object classes can be characterized as a taxonomy, a hierarchy in which lower levels become increasingly more specific. So, for example, consider a simple partial taxonomy of objects relating to furniture. At the top level, often referred to as the **superordinate level,** is *furniture.* At the next lower level, the basic level, are different types of furniture, such as *chair, table,* and *bed.* At the next lower level, the **subordinate level,** are the different types of chairs, tables, and beds. For instance, the subordinate level under *chair* would include *recliner, rocking chair, desk chair,* and the like. To give another example, for the category fruit, *fruit* would be the superordinate and *apple, orange, banana,* and so on would be the basic level. Then, for *apple, Granny Smith,* and *Macintosh,* for example, would be the subordinate level.

1. Evidence for Basic Levels

As we mentioned, there is a great deal of evidence to suggest that the basic level is psychologically privileged. Rosch et al. (1976) demonstrated that the basic level is privileged in many ways. When presented with an object and asked to name it, the basic level is the overwhelming choice. If given a category name (e.g., furniture, chair, or rocking chair) and then shown an object (rocking chair), people are fastest to verify the match between name and object for the basic level term (chair). In addition to these performance measures, a wide variety of observations support the privileged status of basic levels. Basic level concepts are learned earlier than concepts at other levels. In language, basic level concepts are often referred to by shorter and more frequent words than are subordinates and, in American Sign Language, basic level concepts often have a single sign. Finally, basic level concepts are the highest level at which instances share many features. Rosch et al. (1976) had subjects list features that were true of most objects in the category. The instances of superordinate categories (e.g., different types of furniture) have few common features. The basic level instances (e.g., different types of chairs) have far more features in common, while the subordinate instances (e.g., different kitchen chairs) have only a few more than the basic level. This same pattern, of a large increase in common features when one moves from subordinate to basic, with only a small increase when moving from basic to superordinate, is found with a variety of measures: overlap in shape, actions used in interacting with objects in the category, and number of parts (Tversky & Hemenway, 1984).

The idea that there is a basic level concept appears to extend beyond object categories. Similar results have also been found with personality categories (Cantor & Mischel, 1979), locations (Tversky & Hemenway, 1983), and events (Morris & Murphy, 1990).

2. Theories about Basic Levels

What makes the basic level so "basic"? Several theories have been proposed to explain basic level effects (e.g., Murphy & Brownwell, 1985; Rosch, 1978), but we focus here on the idea that the basic level is a compromise between two opposing goals of the categorizer: the desire to have the most informative categorization possible and the desire to have these categories be as discriminable (or distinctive) as possible. The informativeness desire pushes toward more and more specific categories while the discriminability often leads to higher categories. The informativeness relates directly to one of the primary functions of categories—allowing useful inferences. The usefulness of the inferences increases greatly as one moves down from superordinate (*furniture, fruit*) to basic level (*chair, apple*), but, again, does not increase by much when going further down to subordinates (*kitchen chair, Macintosh apple*). In addition, distinguishing basic level categories is often quite easy even for close contrast categories (e.g., *chair* from *table; apple* from *orange* or *pear*), while distinguishing subordinate level categories is difficult because they differ on only a few features (*kitchen chair* vs. *desk chair; Macintosh apple* vs. *Delicious apple*). The basic level may allow for useful inferences without requiring detailed analysis.

The distinctiveness idea predicts some exceptions to this general picture of basic levels. First, people are fastest to verify a picture as a member of the basic level category. However, Murphy and Brownell (1985) found that pictures of atypical subordinates (e.g., a beach chair) are verified fastest at the subordinate level (*beach chair*), not at the basic level (*chair*). This result is important in that it suggests that the basic level is basic only for some (though most) members of the category. The exceptions appear to be just those cases that the distinctiveness explanation would predict. That is, atypical instances are often ones that have high distinctiveness from other instances in their basic level category. For example, *bird* is a basic level category, and penguins (an atypical subordinate) have many features that distinguish them from most birds (such as robins, sparrows, eagles). Similarly, beach chairs are distinguished from other chairs (e.g., desk chairs, rockers, kitchen chairs) on many features such as location, material, and height. Thus, atypical subordinates are informative and distinctive, like basic level categories. Although these results complicate the idea of basic levels, they provide some converging evidence about the inference use of categories. If one is trying to make useful inferences from the category to which a new instance is assigned, atypical instances may be sufficiently different (remember that they usually have low family resemblance relative to other instances) that one would not want to make an inference based on the basic level, but a more specific, subordinate-based inference.

Second, the level of the hierarchy that is basic changes with expertise. Experts often categorize at a subordinate level. For example, Tanaka and Taylor (1991) tested bird and dog experts on the category name–picture verification task. In their area of expertise, experts were as fast on the subordinate terms (e.g., oriole, collie) as they were on the basic level terms (bird, dog). Again, distinctiveness provides a reasonable way of viewing these results. If one spends much time with particular objects (e.g., a breed of dogs), they begin to look more different from one another. After some time, distinctions that initially seemed difficult come effortlessly. It appears that experts have learned to identify more features that distinguish subordinate categories, making those categories both informative and distinctive.

3. Classification Models and Basic Levels

Classification models have generally focused on how objects of a particular level are classified. We have just reviewed work showing that the level of abstraction has strong effects on classification. What are the implications for the classification models? We break this question into two different questions. First, do these classification models provide accounts of the basic level effects? Second, might concepts at different levels of abstraction be classified in different ways?

First, what do classification models have to tell us about the nature of these basic level effects? Simply put, they generally have not dealt with classification at different levels. We are not claiming that the models are inconsistent with basic levels (e.g., Rosch, 1978, has a chapter presenting an overall probabilistic framework for both prototypes and basic levels), but such extensions have not been made (though see Anderson, 1991, and Corter & Gluck, 1992, for a different approach trying to incorporate basic levels). These classification models address how a new instance is classified into one of a set of mutually exclusive categories and provide little insight into choosing among levels.

Second, might different levels be represented in different ways? That is, when we considered the mixed models earlier, we were asking whether the classification of a single concept may require more than one of the three simple models. Here, we are asking whether different simple models may be useful for different levels. This brief section is largely intuitive and speculative, but we think it is worth pursuing.

The superordinate level may be a prime candidate for exemplar representation, if one allows the exemplars to be abstractions as well as individual exemplars. For example, an object may be classified as *furniture* if it is a chair or a table or a bed or a dresser, and so on. In American Sign Language, superordinates are sometimes signed by conjoining basic level terms (Newport & Bellugi, 1978). For example, fruit may be designated by signing "apples and oranges and bananas and etc." Recently, some single signs have been introduced for many superordinate terms, but the existence of these combined terms is at least suggestive of an exemplar representation.

Subordinate level concepts may be well represented by prototypes. For instance, consider rocking chairs. There is a strong similarity among the different rocking chairs one may have experienced. The central tendency is close to most of the instances, making it an excellent summary representation for classifying new instances.

What about the basic level? Our guess is that the basic level may be some mixture of prototype and exemplar representations. For instance, chair may be represented by a prototype, for example, a straight, four-legged, straight-backed, wood chair. However, this representation may be augmented by atypical category members (e.g., bean bag chair, beach chair). In addition, it is possible that instead of a single prototype, there may be multiple prototypes (desk chair, easy chair, rocking chair).

In summary, we have seen that there is a default level for classification, the basic level, which may be a compromise between informativeness and distinctiveness. Current models of classification generally provide no insight into the basic level phenomena. Finally, it may be that different levels of abstractions are represented in different ways.

B. Classification Disconnected from Other Uses of Concepts

A second major shortcoming of these models is that they seem disconnected from other uses of concepts. As discussed earlier, classification is not useful in and of itself. Classification is useful in that it accesses knowledge about a concept that we are then able to use in various ways. However, classification models rarely tell us much about how concepts are used (though see Anderson, 1991; Heit, 1992). (For the purposes of the rest of this chapter, we refer to the classification models discussed above as **similarity-based models**.)

We believe that this dissociation between classification and use leads to some serious problems with these similarity-based views of classification. To explain these problems, we break them down into two parts. First, the representations used in current classification models are simply not rich enough to capture what we know about concepts. Second, if richer representations are used, then the models' accounts of classification may change greatly.

Researchers interested in how knowledge is used recognize the need for highly structured representations. Knowledge structures such as schemata, scripts, frames, and mental models have been proposed as ways of capturing relations among features of concepts and among concepts as well (see Gentner & Stevens, 1983; Minsky, 1975; Rumelhart, 1980; Schank & Abelson, 1977). For example, a person's concept of a room should include not only features such as walls, floor, and ceiling, but also relations among the features (walls connected to floor and ceiling in particular ways, etc).

These relations provide a coherence to the concept that is crucial for how the concept is used. For example, the representations need to include an understanding of how the various features are interrelated in order to be useful for inference. Suppose one sees a bird with a broken wing. This injury will greatly affect what predictions are made about its behavior. One understands how the broken wing affects flying, which affects nesting and the ability to get food and avoid predators.

One might think that these richer representations are important for concept use but may not be needed for classification. However, their use is so integral to classification that we often just do not even think about how important the relations among features are. For instance, one can describe a skunk as a small, four-legged, black animal with a white stripe, but the representation used to classify skunks must also include much structured knowledge (not even arguing for now about what "animal" must be represented as). A small black animal with four legs in one row and a white stripe on its belly is not a skunk. The point is that the relations among features are part of the representation of the concept and are used for classifying as well as the other functions. As another example, imagine seeing a new type of chair. Depending on the imaginativeness of the designer, the chair may be quite different from other chairs you have seen (i.e., it may have a few features common to other chairs), but the relations among the features may allow you to see that the object could be used for sitting.

What are the implications for classification? Well, at the very least, the models will be quite a bit more complicated, because the matching of structured representations is more complex. For example, even if two concepts shared certain features, those shared features might not "count" as similarities between the concepts unless the features were related in the same way in the two concepts (Goldstone, Medin, & Gentner, 1991). As we shall see later, recognizing the importance of including relations in categories allows for the possibility of a qualitatively different type of classification view.

In short, our knowledge of concepts is much more than just arbitrary lists of features. The classification models lack the structure necessary to provide an account of concept use, and to provide a full account of classification. Our concepts must be connected to the underlying knowledge of relations among features and concepts in order to be useful in the variety of tasks in which concepts play a role.

C. Difficulties for Classification: Features and Similarity

We have been focusing on aspects of classification and concept use that go beyond the data for which these classification models were originally constructed. In this section, we address some basic assumptions of the classification models. In particular, the models assume that the instances are represented as features and that these feature sets are compared to stored representations, with the classification made to the most similar representation. We have already argued the need for a more structured representation. However, even ignoring that, there are fundamental problems with the assumptions of features and similarity.

The feature assumption is problematic because what can count as a feature is unconstrained. It may seem reasonable to represent a cat using features like "furry, carnivorous, whiskers," and so on, but the models provide no basis for deciding what aspects should be considered features. Why not include "number of whiskers, oxygen breathing, nonexplosive"? The unconstrained nature of features is a serious problem, because the classifications depend on feature overlap. The indeterminacy of features means that any two entities can be arbitrarily similar or dissimilar, depending on what things are included as features. For example, both pears and house cats weigh less than 100 tons (and 101 tons), grow, are found in homes, and so on. In other words, pears and house cats share an infinite number of features. By the same token, by choosing other features (e.g., has feet, is green), pears and house cats can be made arbitrarily dissimilar. In short, though these formal systems for classifying may be correct when operating over the appropriate features, there is nothing in the models to identify which features are appropriate (see Medin & Wattenmaker, 1987; Murphy, 1993; Murphy & Medin, 1985).

One might wish to argue that the relevant features are "hardwired" into our perceptual systems. That is, one could argue that our perceptual systems are tuned (presumably by evolution) to parse the world into relevant features. However, many of the features that are important for our concepts are not perceptible (e.g., the edible feature of pears). In addition, many sensory inputs are ambiguous so that rather than simply encoding perceptible features of the object, we use our knowledge to interpret the object (Wisniewski & Medin, 1991). For feature comparisons between objects (e.g., similarity judgments), the difficulty is greater. The features of an object depend on what it is being compared to. For example, an ambiguous physical feature of an object can be interpreted in different ways, depending on the other object in the similarity comparison (e.g., Medin, Goldstone, & Gentner, 1993).

D. Summary

The classification models that we presented earlier have a common set of general assumptions. The new instance is represented as a set of features, the person's knowledge is probed for the most similar category representation, and the new instance is classified as being a member of that category. In this section we have pointed to problems with the assumptions concerning the representation, similarity, and the sufficiency of focusing on single concept representations. The representations of these models run into difficulties both because the features are unconstrained and because of the need for more structured representations. The similarity computation is of dubious explanatory power both because it relies on the features (which are unconstrained) and because similarity is far more complex than the feature overlap considered by these models. Finally, the work on basic levels points to the need to consider the concept as part of a system, not simply in terms of a single concept representation.

IV. THEORY-BASED CONCEPTUAL KNOWLEDGE

We have seen a number of problems with models that classify new instances by the similarity between the instance and some knowledge representation. In this section, we review a recent proposal that represents a dramatic shift from these similarity-based views of classification. By this view, concepts are seen as being based on theories we have about the world (e.g., Carey, 1985; Keil, 1989; Murphy & Medin, 1985). As we will see, this view provides for a closer link between classification and how the concept is used. Before we examine the theory-based view in more detail and consider some of its potential problems, let us first see why such a view might be useful.

To begin this discussion, let's address a basic question: Why do we have the categories we do? Although it is clearly partially due to the world, it is also due to ourselves. It is unlikely that we categorize the world in the same way as other organisms such as bees, birds, or beagles.

We begin by focusing on the inference function of concepts and asking how classification allows for useful inferences. The different similarity-based views of classification would all claim the same point: because the important features of instances in a category are similar, it is likely that inferences based on the category are going to be useful for the test instance. Thus, if one sees a new bird that is much like a robin, it would be useful to predict that such a bird will fly, eat worms, and make a nest. Such a claim seems reasonable much of the time, but does not provide a sufficient answer, because there are times when similarity is not sufficient for explaining why we have the categories we do. Three examples may make this point more clearly.

First, some categories contain instances that are rather dissimilar. For example, although sharks, guppies, and manta rays are quite dissimilar, all of them are fish. In addition, porpoises seem rather similar to sharks, but are not fish.

Second, we appear to be able to spontaneously classify highly dissimilar items into new categories. For example, we can form the concept of *things to take from your home in case of a fire* and quickly decide that children, money, photographs, and important papers are members of the category, while wall safes, newspapers, and antique beds are not. Barsalou (1983) shows that these "ad hoc" categories have many of the characteristics of common categories (e.g., graded membership), but are certainly not based on a simple similarity metric.

Third, classification and similarity judgments may lead to different patterns of responses. For example, Rips (1989) reports a study in which subjects had to compare a test instance to the categories of quarter and pizza, knowing only its size. Although they were willing to say that its small size made it more similar to a quarter, they were unwilling to classify it as a quarter unless it was exactly the same size as a quarter. Their knowledge of quarters (such as their production and purpose) did not allow for any variation in size.

These results remind us that the functions of categories go beyond what may be accounted for by similarity. We have the categories we do, presumably, because they allow us to act and think in intelligent, goal-directed ways. Common categories (birds, chairs, etc.) are often useful for our goals, but perhaps not always. Our classifications need to allow for more flexible uses of our knowledge.

What do these results show? One interpretation is that similarity is really a heuristic for classification, not the ultimate basis. For example, a new dog usually looks like old dogs, but even a dog that looked much like a cat might well be classified as a dog IF we had some other evidence of its dogginess. Gelman and Markman (1987) show that even young children will use their knowledge of category membership to override strong perceptual similarities in making inferences.

A slightly weaker interpretation is that similarity is still being used, but it is not the simple perceptual features that are being used. Rather, the features include those deeper features concerning what we know about the concept. For instance, for *things to take from your home in case of a fire,* we may decide that the important features are "valuable" and "easily transportable" and use this pair of features to classify new instances and provide typicality ratings. We believe that this is part of the answer, but does not go far enough. In particular, what is missing is an explanation of how we know what deeper features are relevant for particular goals. Let us begin our discussion by explaining the current view of how concepts may be based on theories.

A. The Theory-Based View

This view is still under development, but we can characterize its present state in the following way. The representation of a concept is assumed to be embedded within a larger structure that includes some explanatory relations among the features of the instances, as well as information about how the concept relates to other concepts. Explanatory relation is used loosely to mean any knowledge that relates instances to concepts, features to instances, features to concepts, or features to features, as well as relating concepts to other concepts. These theories, then, are assumed to be the knowledge of interrelations among instances, features, and concepts. Note that such relations do not imply that there are features common to all exemplars, just that the exemplars are related through some explanation.

Consider the following example (Murphy, 1993): A physician looks at the results of two types of medical tests that both indicate a particular disease. The physician sees these results as similar, though the particular results (e.g., a blood test and a CAT scan) would be quite different in form. The results are similar in that both relate to the doctor's knowledge of the disease.

The same idea applies to concepts. One may have a theory of what it means to be a bird, which allows one to decide if new instances are birds and also what inferences to make about concept members. In this case, the theory may be rather vague, perhaps that there is some genetic structure that decides the issue. Such a belief can increase one's confidence in various inferences, to the extent that these inferences can be seen as being generated from the theory. Thus, for a new robinlike bird, we might feel comfortable inferring it has hollow bones, flies, and eats worms (or at least something like worms), because we see these properties as closely related to the central properties of *songbird*. We would feel less confident about predicting it would have blue eggs (as do robins), unless we had knowledge relating robinlike features to the color of eggs.

We should examine more closely what we assume by this view. First, we have some theory about the concept, structured knowledge that we believe is central to its being. From our example, our theory might include the vague idea of genetic structure, among other things. Second, we have knowledge about the properties that would usually be true of category members, such as the fact that birds have (at least usually) wings and hollow bones. Third, we understand something about how these properties are related to the theory. For example, our rather vague intuitive theories about genetics tell us that birds are usually going to be born with wings, partly because of the evolutionary role of flight. In addition, our theories represent what we know about the role of wings and hollow bones in allowing flight.

Let us go back and see how this helps with the ad hoc categories. For *things to take from your home in case of a fire,* our theory would include knowledge that the fire could destroy contents not taken, that taking objects must be done quickly and without much help, and that some objects are more valuable to us than others. This theory or knowledge is what allows us to decide that the features of "valuable" and "easily transportable" are the ones we want to use for classifying objects. Given these properties and an understanding of how they relate to the theory, we can classify new members. The relation of properties and theory is crucial for any unclear case. What about an extremely valuable item that is hard to transport (e.g., an invalid relative) or an item of moderate value that is easy to transport (such as a $50 bill)?

Similarity

Although we argue that similarity is not sufficient in characterizing classification and concept use, this does not mean that similarity is not useful. Part of the reason the similarity-based models may do well in predicting results is that similar instances will often be covered by the same theory or explanatory principle. Perceptual similarity can be useful to the extent that the observable features are correlated with more important, but less observable, features. For example, Medin and Ortony (1989; Medin, 1989) point out that one may have a theory that gender is genetically determined. However, genetic analysis is rarely done to determine whether someone is male or female. Rather, we use more observable features, though these features may differ in their relation to the underlying theory. Some of these features, such as hair length, are empirically correlated with the category. Other features, however, such as facial hair, are not only empirically correlated, but are seen as biologically connected to the underlying genetic differences. Although these latter features may allow more confident categorization (at least of bearded individuals), any known empirical correlation may allow similarity to be used as a heuristic. However, it is a heuristic, not the underlying principle for classification.

B. What Do We Gain?

What is the advantage of the theory view, given its current vagueness? Proponents argue that the difficulties of similarity-based views are so basic that an alternative approach is crucial. Does this theory view at least provide the potential for addressing the difficulties encountered by the similarity-based views?

First, because of its reliance on world knowledge and representing structured knowledge, it provides a natural way to describe the relation *between* concepts. As Murphy and Medin (1985) point out, in order to be coherent, a concept must have internal structure *and* must fit into the complete knowledge base in the domain. Concepts that have a strong internal structure but no relation to other knowledge of the world would not be helpful concepts for daily use.

In terms of the idea of basic levels, again the theory view provides a richer structure that may be beneficial. To the extent that the appropriate explanation for basic level superiority is due to some idea of distinctiveness, theories are important in that they provide some idea of what is the relevant set of distinctive and shared features. The role of theories in determining relevant features is discussed more fully below.

Second, the theory view overcomes a major difficulty of the similarity view of having simple feature lists. We argued earlier that structured representations are crucial for reasonably representing the knowledge that can be used for classifying instances. These theories would directly represent the relations that underlie structured representations.

Third, the theory view provides at least a beginning to understanding how similarity might be constrained. Because there is some explanatory principle providing coherence to a concept, the theory-based view allows a rough determination of what features might potentially be relevant.

Imagine walking by a car dealership and seeing two new cars, both labeled "snarp." Now what do you know about other snarps? For example, if both cars you saw were green, would you predict that all snarps are green? Imagine that you had seen two birds at a zoo. Both birds were called "prans" and both were green. Now would you predict that all prans are green? What if you were told that one of the prans was male and one female? Now would you predict that all prans are green?

Theories about cars and birds (or biology more generally, perhaps) give information about which features are relevant and which are not. Thus, it seems unlikely that all of the cars called snarps will be green, due to what we know about cars, marketing, and so on. In the case of the birds, we know that male and female birds are often different colors, so we might not wish to generalize from two birds without knowing the sex of those two birds. In all cases, our theories of the domain of interest help to direct us to what is relevant.

One final point should be made about theory-based concepts. Such a representation has the potential to bring together classification and concept use. As we argued earlier, it is the knowledge associated with concepts that make the concepts so useful in inference, combination, and communication. The theory view explicitly recognizes the need to include such knowledge for classification, as well as for other uses. So, although this view is still in its infancy, we believe it has great potential to provide a unified perspective on classification and concept use.

C. Problems with the Theory View

Although this theory view of concepts seems to us to hold much promise for pulling together in a coherent way many of the issues in concepts and categories, we certainly do not wish to give the impression that all is understood. This view has not been developed in any great detail. There is little in the way of constraints on what a theory is, how an instance is classified as a member of a category, or any formal model that allows prediction in the experimental paradigms used to test the different classification models.

In addition, this view leads to some further issues that need to be addressed. Perhaps most importantly, how can we integrate this theory view with the observation that we also learn about concepts from experience with many instances? That is, how can this more "top-down," knowledge-based approach be integrated with a "bottom-up," similarity-based approach?

Similarity and knowledge may interact in many ways. As one example, we may notice by chance that two creatures have a couple of features in common, combine this with other knowledge to propose a tentative explanation, and then use this explanation to selectively examine additional creatures. Wisniewski and Medin (1991) provide evidence that the interaction can be even more complex than this. They found that theories can lead to people considering abstract features and treating particular instances of those abstract features as equivalent. Evidently, theory and empirical experience interact in many complicated ways. We believe that such interactions necessitate an integration of theory-based and similarity-based learning.

In summary, the theory view seems to have great potential, and deals with some important issues that are not dealt with by the similarity-based classification models. However, it needs to be developed in much greater detail and needs to find a way to integrate effects of experience with instances.

V. CURRENT DIRECTIONS

When giving an overview, it is important to also consider where the field is going. In this section, we point to some recent research that we think has important potential for improving our understanding of concepts. We first consider some work on three functions of concepts—classification, inference, and combination. We then briefly review some work on applying these ideas to other research domains.

A. Classification

The work on classification appears to be thriving, but the focus is changing. The modal study used to have people learn some new set of arbitrary, but simple, concepts and examine their performance. Current work extends this paradigm by investigating learning and knowledge effects.

1. Learning

An important current direction is to incorporate learning. That is, these views need to account not only for final performance, but performance throughout the learning. As we develop models that allow for greater flexibility, the models may well be more complicated. A focus on learning will help to provide some additional constraints. In recent work on classification models, investigation of learning has increased substantially (Estes, 1986; Gluck & Bower, 1988; Kruschke, 1992).

2. Knowledge Effects

A second interesting direction involves investigating the use of a theory or background knowledge in classification. A number of studies have shown how knowledge may influence classification. For example, usually a conjunctive rule ("and") is easier to learn than a disjunctive rule ("or"). However, Pazzani (1991) shows that which type of rule is easier to learn depends on the content of the particular material to be learned. Most of the performance and learning models have concentrated on more bottom-up classification, using the features to induce the appropriate classifications. Now, research often focuses on how to integrate this empirical, experience-based learning with more knowledge-based learning (e.g., Wisniewski & Medin, 1991).

B. Inference

Although most work on concepts has examined classification, the inference function has been gaining more prominence lately. An important type of inference is how one can go from knowing the features of a category to making predictions about new members of the category. To the extent that the categories are good ones for the task, such inductions should be made confidently. Some work has followed in the general tradition of classification models, but in addition to being able to classify new instances, such models are also able to make predictions about other features. That is, given some partial description of a new instance, two interesting questions that could be asked of a learner are: what category is this instance in and what is the value of some particular feature(s)? This research examines how the classification and prediction functions might be related. For example, Heit (1992) has extended an exemplar model (Medin & Schaffer, 1978) and Anderson (1991) has developed a new model that is capable of making both classifications and feature predictions using the same basic procedure.

Other work in this area has shown how prior knowledge of categories may be used to make feature predictions, even in young children. For example, Gelman and Markman (1987) showed 4-year-olds a picture of a flamingo and a bat. They told the children that the flamingo feeds its baby mashed-up food and the bat feeds its baby milk. They then showed the children a picture of a blackbird (which was similar in appearance to the bat picture) and asked how the blackbird feeds its baby. The children often made the inferences not on the basis of the perceptual similarity, but on the basis of the category membership.

Category-Based Induction

In addition to this work on feature prediction of new instances, some recent research examines how categories may be used in reasoning about other categories. That is, not only do we have knowledge about each concept, but we also know its relation to other concepts. This knowledge is what allows us to make inferences, such as that robins must have hearts because birds have hearts. However, often the inferences are not definite, but rather an induction based on other categories. For example, if one knows that robins have property X (the premise), how confident is one that sparrows do (the conclusion)? How about penguins? How about all birds?

Osherson, Smith, Wilkie, Lopez, and Shafir (1990) have been exploring what factors influence the perceived strength of such category-based inductions (i.e., how good an induction it appears to be). They find that the strength of the induction depends on two factors. First, the more similar the premise and target categories, the stronger the inference. Hence, *robin* to *sparrow* leads to a stronger inference than *robin* to *penguin*. Second, if there are multiple premise categories, the better they "cover" the combined category, the stronger the inference. The coverage is a type of overall similarity measure. Suppose there is some category containing both premise and target categories. For example, if *robin* and *eagle* are the premise categories and *penguin* the target, then the simplest category containing all of these would be *bird*. Coverage refers to how well the premise categories are "spread out" across this combined category. If they are well spread out (e.g., *robin, eagle, swan*), then they will lead to a strong inference to most birds, because one of the premise categories is likely to be somewhat similar to the target (i.e., the premise categories "cover" the space). If they are not well spread out (e.g., *robin, sparrow, cardinal*), then they will lead to strong inferences only to similar birds. Such work is a good example of the many interesting properties of how we reason about concepts that remain to be examined.

C. Conceptual Combinations

A third function of concepts is to provide building blocks. Many new concepts come about because two (or more) old concepts are put together, conceptual combination. We can easily understand combinations of concepts that we have not heard before, such as "mountain coat." How are we able to understand all these new combinations of concepts?

One simple idea is that new concepts are represented as some intersection of old concepts, such as a pet fish is a fish that is a pet (i.e., it is both a pet and a fish). The problem is that when trying to understand how such a concept is related to its constituents, one quickly finds the relation is highly variable. For instance, a guppy is a typical pet fish, but is neither a typical pet nor a typical fish (E. E. Smith & Osherson, 1984). In addition, many combinations are not intersections at all (e.g., dog race).

Perhaps the combination requires some modification of the existing concepts. E. E. Smith and Osherson (1984; E. E. Smith, Osherson, Rips, & Keane, 1988) propose a modification model for adjective–noun pairs. They assume nouns are represented as attributes and values. For instance, a spoon would have the attributes material, size, and so on, with a distribution of values for each attribute, reflecting the proportion of spoons made of different materials (metal, wooden, plastic) and spoons of various sizes (small, medium, large). For wooden spoon, one would modify the material value (of the spoon representation) to be wooden and weight this attribute heavily, so that only spoons that are wooden would be similar to it. The problem with this view is that a change in one attribute often means a change in another attribute. For instance, wooden spoons tend to be larger than spoons in general, so the size value needs to change as well in order to account for people's judgments (Medin & Shoben, 1988). Thus, these combinations make use of some world knowledge, at least in terms of empirical correlations.

In fact, the case becomes even more complicated, because people use their background knowledge in more complex ways as well. For instance, Medin and Shoben (1988) had people rate the similarity of adjective–noun pairs and showed that the effect of the adjectives depended on the particular noun. So, when the colors white, gray, and black were added to the noun "clouds," gray and black were viewed as more similar. However, when added to the noun "hair," white and gray were judged as more similar. People appear to make use of their theories of storm clouds (gray clouds and black clouds) and aging (white hair and gray hair) in these judgments. As another example, properties can emerge as prominent from these combinations even though they are rare in the constituents. Pet birds are often kept in cages, though this is not generally true of birds or of pets (Murphy, 1988).

This review of conceptual combinations may seem to raise more questions than it answers, but we think it shows a field in progress. It may turn out that various strategies are used in understanding conceptual combinations, and progress here may depend on a better understanding of how world knowledge is used in understanding.

D. More Radical Extensions

To this point, we have mainly discussed object concepts, but it is clear that people have and use many concepts that do not concern objects. For example, many concepts concern social aspects of the world (see E R. Smith & Zarate, 1992; Wattenmaker, in press). Such concepts are extremely important in understanding the (social) world. In addition, people don't usually encounter objects in isolation. Rather, people encounter objects in a situation; they experience episodes or events. How are such events represented, classified, and used? Social concepts, event concepts, and object concepts, as well as other types of concepts, all need to be understood in order to provide a complete picture of the conceptual system.

We have been examining different ways in which concepts might be used, but so far we have emphasized concept tasks. How might this work on categories affect our understanding of other complex tasks in which categories play a central role? We mentioned earlier the example of diagnoses and the implications they have for treatments.

In problem solving, categories are coming to play an increasingly important role. Many researchers believe that good problem solving requires people to develop problem categories and associated procedures for identifying problems of that type (e.g., Chi, Feltovich, & Glaser, 1981). Experts are often thought to have clear problem categories, organized around the deep principles necessary for solution, to which they can quickly assign new instances. An interesting issue raised by these examples is the clear relation between the importance of classification and the use of the knowledge accessed.

VI. CONCLUDING REMARKS

Research on concepts and categories is progressing rapidly in many directions. In this chapter, we have tried not only to present some of the interesting recent work, but also to provide the reader with a sense of the issues that have driven the changing research in the field.

Given the great amount of work in the field, any review of concepts and categories has to select (and not select) from many issues, areas, and results. An interesting question to ask about any selection is what it contributes to our understanding of how concepts help us to act intelligently. From this perspective, we want to conclude with a reminder about the functions of concepts. Throughout this chapter, we have emphasized the distinction between classification and other uses of concepts. A consideration of intelligent behavior requires a better understanding of classification, but also of how the classification might be used. Although much of the work has focused on classification, we see a trend toward examining other functions of concepts. In addition, this distinction forces us to consider if and how the knowledge underlying classification might be related to the knowledge used for these other functions.

Although this distinction may make the enterprise seem even more difficult, our view is that it simply makes more evident the complexities that underlie concepts and categories. Further progress will come as we begin to understand the different functions of concepts and how they relate to each other, as well as how the different functions relate to more general knowledge of the world.

Acknowledgments

Preparation of this chapter was supported by Air Force Office of Scientific Research Grant 89-0447 to B. H. Ross. We thank Barbara Malt and Gregory Murphy for their helpful comments on an earlier version of this paper.

References

Anderson, J. R. (1991). The adaptive nature of human categorization. *Psychological Review, 98,* 409–429.

Armstrong, S. L., Gleitman, L. R., & Gleitman, H. (1983). What some concepts might not be. *Cognition, 13,* 263–308.

Barsalou, L. W. (1983). Ad hoc categories. *Memory & Cognition, 11,* 211–227.

Barsalou, L. W. (1990). On the indistinguishability of exemplar memory and abstraction in category representation. In T. K. Srull & R. W. Wyer, Jr. (Eds.), *Advances in social cognition* (Vol. 3 pp. 61–88). Hillsdale NJ: Erlbaum.

Brooks, L. (1978). Nonanalytic concept formation and memory for instances. In E. Rosch & B. B. Lloyd (Eds.), *Cognition and categorization* (pp. 169–211). Hillsdale, NJ: Erlbaum.

Brooks, L. (1987). Decentralized control of categorization: The role of prior processing episodes. In U. Neisser (Ed.), *Concepts and conceptual development: Ecological and intellectual factors in categorization* (pp. 141–174). New York: Cambridge University Press.

Cantor, N., & Mischel, W. (1979). Prototypes in person perception. In L. Berkowitz (Ed.), *Advances in experimental social psychology* (Vol. 12, pp. 3–52). New York: Academic Press.

Carey, S. (1985). *Conceptual change in childhood*, Cambridge, MA: MIT Press.

Chi, M. T., Feltovich, P. J., & Glaser, R. (1981). Categorization and representation of physics problems by experts and novices. *Cognitive Science, 5,* 121–152.

Corter, J. E., & Gluck, M. A. (1992). Explaining basic categories: Feature predictability and information. *Psychological Bulletin, 111,* 291–303.

Estes, W. K. (1986). Array models for category learning. *Cognitive Psychology, 18,* 500–549.

Gelman, S. A., & Markman, E. M. (1987). Young children's inductions from natural kinds: The role of categories and appearance. *Child Development, 58,* 1532–1541.

Gentner, D., & Stevens, A. L. (Eds.). (1983). *Mental models*. Hillsdale, NJ: Erlbaum.

Gluck, M. A., & Bower, G. H. (1988). From conditioning to category learning: An adaptive network model. *Journal of Experimental Psychology: General, 117,* 227–247.

Goldstone, R. L., Medin, D. L., & Gentner, D. (1991). Relational similarity and the nonindependence of features in similarity judgments. *Cognitive Psychology, 23,* 222–262.

Heit, E. (1992). Categorization using chains of examples. *Cognitive Psychology, 24,* 341–380.

Hintzman, D. L. (1986). "Schema abstraction" in a multiple-trace model. *Psychological Review, 93,* 411–428.

Keil, F. C. (1989). *Concepts, kinds, and cognitive development*. Cambridge, MA: MIT Press.

Kruschke, J. (1992). ALCOVE: An exemplar-based connectionist model of category learning. *Psychological Review, 99,* 22–44.

Malt, B. C. (1989). An on-line investigation of prototype and exemplar strategies in classification. *Journal of Experimental Psychology: Learning, Memory, and Cognition, 15,* 539–555.

Malt, B. C. (1994). Water is not H_2O. *Cognitive Psychology, 26.*

Malt, B. C., & Johnson, E. C. (1992). Do artifact concepts have cores? *Journal of Memory and Language, 31,* 195–217.

Malt, B. C., & Smith, E. E. (1984). Correlated properties in natural categories. *Journal of Verbal Learning and Verbal Behavior, 23,* 250–269.

Medin, D. L. (1989). Concepts and conceptual structure. *American Psychologist, 44,* 1469–1481.

Medin, D. L., Altom, M. W., Edelson, S. M., & Freko, D. (1982). Correlated symptoms and simulated medical classification. *Journal of Experimental Psychology: Human Learning and Memory, 8,* 37–50.

Medin, D. L., Dewey, G. I., & Murphy, T. D. (1983). Relationships between item and category learning: Evidence that abstraction is not automatic. *Journal of Experimental Psychology: Learning, Memory, and Cognition, 9,* 607–625.

Medin, D. L., & Edelson, S. (1988). Problem structure and the use of base rate information from experience. *Journal of Experimental Psychology: General, 117,* 68–85.

Medin, D. L., Goldstone, R. L., & Gentner, D. (1993). Respects for similarity. *Psychological Review, 100,* 254–278.

Medin, D. L., & Ortony, A. (1989). Psychological essentialism. In S. Vosniadou & A. Ortony (Eds.), *Similarity and analogical reasoning* (pp. 179–195). New York: Cambridge University Press.

Medin, D. L., & Ross, B. H. (1989). The specific character of abstract thought: Categorization, problem-solving, and induction. In R. J. Sternberg (Ed.), *Advances in the psychology of human intelligence* (Vol. 5, pp. 189–223). Hillsdale, NJ: Erlbaum.

Medin, D. L., & Schaffer, M. M. (1978). Context theory of classification learning. *Psychological Review, 85,* 207–238.

Medin, D. L., & Shoben, E. J. (1988). Context and structure in conceptual combination. *Cognitive Psychology, 20,* 158–190.

Medin, D. L., & Wattenmaker, W. D. (1987). Category cohesiveness, theories, and cognitive archaeology. In U. Neisser (Ed.), *Concepts and conceptual development: Ecological and intellectual factors in categorization* (pp. 25–62). New York: Cambridge University Press.

Minsky, M. (1975). A framework for representing knowledge. In P. H. Winston (Ed.), *The psychology of computer vision* (pp. 211–277). New York: McGraw-Hill.

Morris, M. W., & Murphy, G. L. (1990). Converging operations on a basic level in event taxonomies. *Memory & Cognition, 18,* 407–418.

Murphy, G. L. (1988). Comprehending complex concepts. *Cognitive Science, 12,* 529–562.

Murphy, G. L. (1993). Theories and concept formation. In I. Van Mechelen, J. Hampton, R. Michalski, & P. Theuns (Eds.), *Categories and concepts: Theoretical views and inductive data analysis* (pp. 173–200). London: Academic Press.

Murphy, G. L., & Brownell, H. H. (1985). Category differentiation in object recognition: Typicality constraints on the basic category advantage. *Journal of Experimental Psychology: Learning, Memory, and Cognition, 11,* 70–84.

Murphy, G. L., & Medin, D. L. (1985). The role of theories in conceptual coherence. *Psychological Review, 92,* 289–316.

Newport, E. L., & Bellugi, U. (1978). Linguistic expression of category levels in a visual-gestural language: A flower is a flower is a flower. In E. Rosch & B. Lloyd (Eds.), *Cognition and categorization* (pp. 49–71). Hillsdale, NJ: Erlbaum.

Nosofsky, R. (1986). Attention, similarity, and the identification-categorization relationship. *Journal of Experimental Psychology: General, 115,* 39–57.

Osherson, D. N., Smith, E. E., Wilkie, O., Lopez, A., & Shafir, E. (1990). Category-based induction. *Psychological Review, 97,* 185–200.

Pazzani, M. J. (1991). Influence of prior knowledge on concept acquisition: Experimental and computational results. *Journal of Experimental Psychology: Learning, Memory, and Cognition, 17,* 416–432.

Posner, M. I., & Keele, S. W. (1970). Retention of abstract ideas. *Journal of Experimental Psychology, 83,* 304–308.

Rips, L. J. (1989). Similarity, typicality, and categorization. In S. Vosniadou & A. Ortony (Eds.), *Similarity and analogical reasoning* (pp. 179–195). New York: Cambridge University Press.

Rips, L. J., Shoben, E. J., & Smith, E. E. (1973). Semantic distance and the verification of semantic relations. *Journal of Verbal Learning and Verbal Behavior, 12,* 1–20.

Rosch, E. (1978). Principles of categorization. In E. Rosch & B. Lloyd (Eds.), *Cognition and categorization* (pp. 27–48). Hillsdale, NJ: Erlbaum.

Rosch, E., & Mervis, C. (1975). Family resemblances: Studies in the internal structure of categories. *Cognitive Psychology, 7,* 573–605.

Rosch, E., Mervis, C., Gray, W. D., Johnson, D. M., & Boyes-Braem, P. (1976). Basic objects in natural categories. *Cognitive Psychology, 8,* 382–439.

Ross, B. H., Perkins, S. J., & Tenpenny, P. L. (1990). Reminding-based category learning. *Cognitive Psychology, 22,* 460–492.

Roth, E. M., & Shoben, E. J. (1983). The effect of context on the structure of categories. *Cognitive Psychology, 15,* 346–378.

Rumelhart, D. E. (1980). Schemata: The building blocks of cognition. In R. J. Spiro, B. C. Bruce, & W. F. Brewer (Eds.), *Theoretical issues in reading comprehension* (pp. 33–58). Hillsdale, NJ: Erlbaum.

Schank, R. C., & Abelson, R. P. (1977). *Scripts, plans, goals, and understanding.* Hillsdale, NJ: Erlbaum.

Smith, E. E., & Medin, D. L. (1981). *Categories and concepts.* Cambridge, MA: Harvard University Press.

Smith, E. E., & Osherson, D. N. (1984). Conceptual combination with prototype concepts. *Cognitive Science, 8,* 337–361.

Smith, E. E., Osherson D. N., Rips, L. J., & Keane, M. (1988). Combining prototypes: A selective modification model. *Cognitive Science, 12,* 485–527.

Smith, E. R., & Zarate, M. A. (1992). Exemplar-based model of social judgment. *Psychological Review, 99,* 3–21.

Spalding, T. L., & Ross, B. H. (in press). Comparison-based learning: Effects of comparing instances during category learning. *Journal of Experimental Psychology: Learning, Memory, and Cognition.*

Tanaka, J. W., & Taylor, M. (1991). Object categories and expertise: Is the basic level in the eye of the beholder? *Cognitive Psychology, 23,* 457–482.

Tversky, B., & Hemenway, K. (1983). Categories of environmental scenes. *Cognitive Psychology, 15,* 121–149.

Tversky, B., & Hemenway, K. (1984). Objects, parts, and categories. *Journal of Experimental Psychology: General, 113,* 169–193.

Walker, J. H. (1975). Real-world variability, reasonableness judgments, and memory representations for concepts. *Journal of Verbal Learning and Verbal Behavior, 14,* 241–252.

Wattenmaker, W. D. (in press). Knowledge structures and linear separability: Integrating information in object and social categorization. *Cognitive Psychology.*

Whittlesea, B. W. A. (1987). Preservation of specific experiences in the representation of general knowledge. *Journal of Experimental Psychology: Learning, Memory, and Cognition, 13,* 3–17.

Wisniewski, E., & Medin, D. L. (1991). Harpoons and long sticks: The interaction of theory and similarity in rule induction. In D. H. Fisher, Jr., M. J. Pazzani, & P. Langley (Eds.), *Concept formation: Knowledge and experience in unsupervised learning* (pp. 237–278). San Mateo, CA: Morgan Kaufmann.

CHAPTER 5

Deduction and Its Cognitive Basis

Lance J. Rips

The psychological study of deduction is the study of people's apprehension of a special sort of relation that holds among sentences. Consider, for example, the pairs of sentences in (1) and (2):

(1) a. Clare brought a salad and Allan brought a torte.
     b. Clare brought a salad.
(2) a. Everybody brought an appetizer.
     b. Karen brought an appetizer.

In reading these pairs, we seem to feel that the (a) sentences fully warrant the (b) sentences, in that no evidence we could have for the (b) sentences could be stronger than what the (a) sentences provide. Indeed, the warrant that (a) gives to (b) in each pair appears to be equal in strength to what (b) gives itself. In contrast, this relationship of one sentence fully warranting another does not seem to hold in the following pairs:

(3) a. Clare brought a salad or Allan brought a torte.
     b. Clare brought a salad.
(4) a. Somebody brought an appetizer.
     b. Karen brought an appetizer.

The (a) sentences in (3) and (4) may provide some warrant for the corresponding (b) sentences, but they clearly are not conclusive in the manner of (1) and (2). If Clare brought a salad *or* Allan brought a torte, then it might be that Clare did not bring a salad at all: maybe Allan brought the torte and

Clare brought an entrée. Similarly, it is consistent with (4a) that someone other than Karen brought the appetizer. Let us call the full-warrant relationship that (1a) bears to (1b) and (2a) to (2b) the *entailment* relation. So, the (a) sentences in (1) and (2) entail their (b) sentences, whereas (3a) does not entail (3b) nor does (4a) entail (4b).

We immediately perceive the relationship between the sentences in (1) and (2), but it is not always a simple matter to tell whether sentences entail one another. The hypotheses of a mathematical theorem entail its conclusion, though we may have to trace painfully through the steps of a proof to convince ourselves that this is so. The research literature in psychology, as we will see, is also full of examples in which most people's judgments about entailment deviate from what appears on reflection to be the correct answer. In experiments of this sort, investigators usually give their subjects a short list of sentences (the *premises*) that they are supposed to assume to be true. The subject's job is then to determine whether a further sentence (the *conclusion*) is entailed by the premises (i.e., to determine whether the conclusion "must be true whenever the premises are true" or whether the conclusion "logically follows from the premises"). The premises and conclusion, taken together, constitute an *argument,* in the sense of the term that is common in logic. In other types of deduction experiments, subjects must complete an argument by selecting from a set of alternative conclusions the one that follows logically, or they must produce for themselves a conclusion that follows logically from the premises. It is obvious that (1b) follows logically from (1a), and that (3b) *does not* follow logically from (3a). But we can complicate the problems in these tasks so as to undermine subjects' judgments. As one example, ask yourself whether Sentences (5a) and (5b) entail (5c):

(5) a. For any three people x, y, and z: if x admires y then z admires x.
    b. Clare admires Allan.
    c. Everybody admires everyone.

How could you tell? One possibility is to consider two arbitrary individuals, say *a* and *b,* and to check whether *a* admires *b*. To see that this is so, notice first that since Clare admires Allan, then *b* must admire Clare, according to (5a). Second, since *b* admires Clare, *a* must admire *b* by the same reasoning. So it follows that everybody admires everyone, because we chose *a* and *b* arbitrarily. Our perception of this relationship is not immediate, however, and only 60% of Stanford undergraduates affirmed that (5c) logically follows from (5a) and (5b) when this problem was presented to them (Rips, 1994, Table 7.4).

I. WHAT ACCOUNTS FOR ELEMENTARY INFERENCE?

The explanation I gave for why (5a) and (5b) entail (5c) proceeded in a series of steps, each of which was supposed to be intuitively correct. It seems to be an important fact about human cognition that we can sometimes employ this type of chaining to apprehend nonobvious entailments such as (5) on the basis of simpler entailments. As the difficulty of the example makes clear, however, it is not always easy to find the right inferential chain. One source of trouble in this example is that with Allan, Clare, *a*, and *b* all in play, there are many ways of substituting these instances for the variables *x*, *y*, and *z* in (5a), and not all of these substitutions will advance the proof. Second, we had to go through the substitution step twice—once with Clare for *x*, Allan for *y*, and *b* for *z*, and the second time with *b* for *x*, Clare for *y*, and *a* for *z*. It seems likely, given the usual resource limits on human information processing, that the more required steps in the inference sequence, the more likely we are to forget some of the necessary facts or to blunder in carrying out a step. There is controversy in the research literature about whether people who are untutored in logic ever do produce proofs of the type we just glimpsed. Most theories of deduction agree, however, that people sometimes decide about complex problems such as (5) by breaking them down into a set of steps.

Our ability to deal with deduction problems in this analytic way presupposes that we can immediately recognize the individual steps as correct. The inference chain would not be convincing if the component steps were not themselves convincing. It seems reasonable to think that these components are entailments such as those in (1) and (2) that seem correct as stated and recognizable without further proof. [Indeed, it would be difficult to see how we could explain the correctness of (1) and (2) to someone who was not already convinced of them.] But then how do we appreciate—what psychological mechanism is responsible for our appreciation of—these simple examples? This chapter looks at several approaches to this problem that appear in the psychological literature. The following section (Section II) briefly examines approaches that posit individual mental rules for elementary entailments based on logical operators, such as *and*, *or*, *not*, *if*, *for all*, and *for some*. Section III looks at *instrumental* theories, which claim that people learn rules based on concepts such as causality or obligation that help them accomplish their goals. Section IV turns to accounts in which recognizing entailments is supposed to be a matter of perceiving patterns rather than of applying rules. These pattern-perception theories include connectionist accounts and accounts that posit explicit mental diagrams.

II. INFERENCE RULES AND LOGICAL FORM

Perhaps the simplest approach to explaining elementary entailments is to suppose that people possess mental rules that carry out the corresponding inferences. For example, imagine a rule that monitors the contents of working memory for sentences of the form *P and Q* and responds to such sentences by placing in memory the separate sentences *P* and *Q*. When this rule encounters Sentence (1a), for instance, it will add to working memory Sentence (1b) and, separately, the other half of the conjunction, *Allan brought a torte*. Mental rules of this sort are quite similar to rules in formal natural-deduction systems in logic, which were invented in the 1930s by Gerhard Gentzen and Stanisław Jaśkowski. (Many introductory logic textbooks—for example, Bergmann, Moor, and Nelson, 1980—contain descriptions of these systems). Of course, not all entailments will correspond to individual inference rules; in some cases people will have to apply several mental rules in order to determine whether one sentence entails another. Thus, we would expect that multiple-rule entailments will be more difficult to recognize than single-rule entailments, in the way that (5) is more difficult than (1).

The most important feature of these rules, for present purposes, is that they respond to the logical form of the sentences that trigger them. The rule just described, for example, will operate in the same way for all sentences whose main connective is *and,* no matter which sentences the *and* connects. In particular, the connected sentences could themselves be conjunctions, so that the rule could apply iteratively to its own output. For example, the rule would derive from (*P and Q*) *and* (*R and S*) the two sentences (*P and Q*) and (*R and S*); from these sentences, in turn, the rule would produce *P, Q, R,* and *S* as separate items. Exactly which aspects of a sentence are parts of its logical form, however, depend on what the correct logical analysis happens to be. Formal logic systems differ in which features of a language count as logical operators. Most systems of logic take as logical constants the standard sentence connectives (*and, or, not,* and *if*) and quantifiers (*for all* and *for some*), but there are also formal logics for tenses and for core concepts such as knowledge and belief, necessity and possibility, obligation and permission, causality, and others.

Deduction rules in psychology differ from rules in logic, however, in incorporating strategic information. In their usual formulations, logical rules will generate an infinite number of new sentences from a fixed set of premises, whether or not these sentences are relevant to the task at hand. A realistic psychological system obviously cannot afford to spin out these irrelevant sentences; hence, the rules must be carefully specified in order to keep the system on track. For example, consider a rule that takes as input sentences of the form *Every x F's* and produces as output the sentence *a F's,* where *F* is a predicate (e.g., *. . .brings an appetizer, . . . is red, . . . walks,* etc.) and *a* is a proper name (e.g., *Madonna, Endel Tulving, Julius Caesar*). This rule would account for the entailment in (2), and in contexts such as this where the domain of *every x* is implicitly restricted, it may do no harm to draw all of the possible inferences (*Karen brought an appetizer, Fred brought an appetizer,* etc.). But in most situations, drawing all inferences from a sentence with *every x* will be psychologically out of the question. If we learn that everyone has 23 pairs of chromosomes, we do not want to conclude automatically that Madonna has 23 pairs of chromosomes, Endel Tulving has 23 pairs of chromosomes, Julius Caesar has 23 pairs of chromosomes, and so on, for all proper names. A solution to this difficulty is to revise the rule in such a way that the conclusion *a F's* is drawn only when it is needed as a direct answer to a query or when it serves as a subgoal for a direct answer. Psychological rule systems with restrictions of this strategic type were proposed originally by Newell, Shaw, and Simon (1957), and more recently by Braine, Reiser, and Rumain (1984), Osherson (1975, 1976), and Rips (1983, 1994).

Inference rules provide one way of explaining how people recognize elementary entailments and why some entailments are more difficult than others. Nevertheless, the explanation they furnish may seen incomplete. Although it may be true that people know that (1a) entails (1b) because they possess a mental rule that produces *P* from *P and Q,* this provokes questions about where these mental rules come from and why people have rules for certain entailments but not others, such as (5). There is an argument (Fodor, 1975; Macnamara, 1986) that some basic set of logical principles must be innate, since it is unlikely for there to be a model of learning that does not presuppose such principles. This argument may well be correct and may even help motivate the idea of mental inference rules; however, it still leaves some uneasiness about why people possess one subset of rules and not others. This uncertainty has led some researchers to try to relate or to reduce inference principles to more basic psychological mechanisms in an effort to make them more comprehensible from an empirical point of view. As we are about to see, one such effort relates inference rules to methods for making correct predictions and satisfying human goals; another effort reduces inference rules to pattern perception or constraint satisfaction. Both of these frameworks lead away from the traditional concept of inference rules as operations on the logical form of sentences.

III. INSTRUMENTAL THEORIES

A traditional (psychological) answer to the question of how we appreciate elementary entailments is that these supply predictions that help us get what we want. People try to predict what will happen on the basis of current evidence in an effort to achieve their goals. For example, on the basis of Sentence (1a) you might come to believe (1b) as a way of predicting what Clare will bring to the dinner party. Some inferences might be more successful than others, however, in their predictive powers. An inference from (3a) to (3b), for instance, may be much less successful than that from (1a) to (1b). Predictive success will strengthen inferences responsible for those successes, and predictive failure will weaken inferences responsible for those failures (Holland, Holyoak, Nisbett, & Thagard, 1986). The greater an inference's strength, the more likely people will employ that inference again and the more convincing it will seem. Hence, during a child's development, inferences such as (1) will dominate those such as (3). And, perhaps, over evolutionary time, inferences like (1) will tend to be built into human cognition, whereas inferences like (3) will not. Of course, on an evolutionary scale, the inferences that matter will presumably be about topics more essential than who brings what to a dinner party. But change the example: Imagine that we learn either that *Plants with spiky leaves are edible and plants with rounded leaves are edible* or alternatively that *Plants with spiky leaves are edible or plants with rounded leaves are edible*. Then drawing the inference *Plants with spiky leaves are edible* from these sentences may produce the sort of difference that has consequences for selection.

This type of explanation might be a start in understanding how we learn to trust (1) and (2) and how we learn not to trust (3) and (4). What needs to be accounted for, however, are not these particular examples, but the more general classes they represent. You probably never encountered (1)–(4) prior to reading this chapter; yet you had no trouble recognizing that (1) and (2) possess the entailment relationship and that (3) and (4) do not. One way to account for this recognition in the case of (1) and (2) is to assume that you've learned something more abstract in your prior experience, perhaps along the lines of the rules mentioned earlier, which we can write in the form of (6) and (7).

(6) a. p and q.
    b. p.
(7) a. Everybody F's.
    b. a F's.

An unlimited number of entailments can be derived from (6) by replacing p q with sentences, and from (7) by replacing F with predicates and a with expressions that refer to an individual. If this is correct, we need to add to the account of the previous paragraph some generalization mechanism that can abstract these schemas from specific instances such as (1) and (2).[1]

A. Two Qualifications

Predictive success (and generalization) may help explain our faith in (1) and (2), but they do not tell us why the first sentences of these pairs—and others that share the form of (6) and (7)—entail the second. To answer the latter question we have to appeal to some further facts about the relationship between the (a) and (b) sentences, since the presence or absence of entailment does not seem to depend on the contingencies of prediction. In the right circumstances, the predictive track record for (3) could equal that for

(1); yet this would not change the face that (3a) does not entail (3b), at least in the view of many philosophers (e.g., Frege, 1884/1974). Predictive successes do not necessarily guarantee entailment, even when the predictions are quite accurate. To take another example, suppose that eating nothing but French fries for 200 days predicts death by malnutrition in all previous cases. But the sentence *Fred eats nothing but French fries for 200 days* does not entail the conclusion *Fred dies by malnutrition*. It is perfectly possible, albeit unlikely, that Fred has discovered a serum that permits him to eat unlimited fries with no ill effects. Or perhaps there is something unusual about Fred's metabolism or about the nutritional content of his new brand of fries. Certainly, the sentence about eating fries ought to increase our confidence in the sentence about death by malnutrition. The conclusion is much more likely to be true given the premise than it is on base-rate information alone; so the inference might be said to be *inductively strong* (Skyrms, 1966). But this relation differs from the entailment relation in (1) and (2), since there are *no* possible circumstances in which the (a) sentences are true and the (b) sentences false.

Conversely, the entailment relationship by itself does not guarantee correct prediction (Harman, 1986). Suppose you believe (1a) and on this basis predict (1b). You then find, when you arrive at the potluck, that Clare brought an entrée. Since this is impossible if (1a) were true, what you have discovered is that you must have been mistaken about (1a). In other words, entailment guarantees that (1b) is true if (1a) *is true;* but it doesn't guarantee (1b) merely because (1a) is something you *believe*. However, the instrumental theory about how we appreciate the entailment in (1) is a theory about people's beliefs. Successful prediction in the context of instrumental theories means correctly projecting what will happen on the basis of what you believe is the case. Since entailment doesn't guarantee correct prediction, the entailment relation may be of less help in this regard than might have first appeared.

These qualifications suggest that the relation between entailment and predictive success may be indirect, but is it too indirect to explain how we appreciate the entailment relation? A satisfactory answer to the question of how we *recognize* entailments ought not require that prediction should *constitute* or *determine* entailment. The theory would be adequate as long as success in prediction explains the psychological facts that lead us to recognize the elementary entailments that we do. For this purpose an indirect relation between the two might work, and if so the first qualification above is not fatal. What does cause difficulty for the theory is that we seem able to grasp entailment relations even in circumstances where they lead to incorrect predictions. This suggests there must be more to our appreciation of entailment than predictive success. Let us suppose for the moment, however, that successful prediction is at least one factor in determining how we recognize entailment in pairs such as (1) or (2). What further consequences does this have about people's inference abilities?

B. Experimental Implications

Investigators who have taken this instrumental approach toward reasoning have not focused on cases such as (6) or (7) but instead on reasoning within the *Selection task,* a well-known experimental paradigm invented by Peter Wason (1968; Wason & Johnson-Laird, 1972). In the standard version of this task, subjects see four cards and learn that each card contains a letter on one side and a numeral on the other. The face-up sides of the cards might display the symbols E, K, 4, and 7. The experimenter also informs the subjects about a conditional "rule" that refers to these cards, such as: *If a card has a vowel on one side, then it has an even number on the other side.* The subjects' task is to name the cards (without first inspecting the underside) "which need to be turned over to determine whether the rule is true or false" (Wason & Johnson-Laird, 1972, p. 173). In this example, the E card would conform to the rule if it had an even number on its flip side, but would violate the rule if it had an odd number. Similarly, the 7 card would conform to the rule if it had a consonant on its flip side and would violate it if it had a vowel. Since neither of the remaining cards could do other than conform to the rule, the correct response would seen to be E and 7. In fact, most subjects choose either E alone or E and 4.

Variations in the experimental set up, however, can produce large improvements in performance on the Selection task. Griggs and Cox (1982) told subjects to

> imagine that you are a police officer on duty. It is your job to ensure that people conform to certain rules. The cards in front of you have information about four people sitting at a table. On one side of a card is a person's age and on the other side of the card is what the person is drinking. Here is a rule: IF A PERSON IS DRINKING BEER, THEN THE PERSON MUST BE OVER 19 YEARS OF AGE. Select the card or cards that you definitely need to turn over to determine whether or not the people are violating the rule. (p. 415).

The cards in this version had the labels *drinking a beer, drinking a coke, 16 years of age,* and *22 years of age.* With these instructions 72% of subjects produced correct responses (beer and 16), whereas none of these subjects chose the correct response for the letters–and–numbers version. (See Evans, 1989, chap. 4, and Rips, 1994, chap. 9 for reviews of facilitation effects in the Selection task).

Instrumentalists take these findings as evidence that people reason more effectively when they are dealing with relationships, such as permissions and obligations, that are related to useful goals. Since people do not ordinarily deal with situations involving arbitrary conditional relations between letters and numerals, they do not have the mental procedures they need to obtain the correct response in the original Selection task. The drinking regulation, however, invokes circumstances that are related to the subjects' goals and for which they have abstracted the correct procedures for testing whether the regulation is obeyed or violated. Instrumentalists deny that this is merely a matter of subjects' familiarity with drinking laws per se. Experience with similar situations is supposed to lead people to routines that generalize over broad domains, such as permissions and obligations (Cheng & Holyoak, 1985) or social contracts (Cosmides, 1989). In support of this interpretation, instrumentalists have found improved performance even for unfamiliar or abstract Selection rules if those rules mention permissions or contracts. Cheng and Holyoak (1985), for example, instructed subjects:

> Suppose you are an authority checking whether or not people are obeying certain regulations. The regulations all have the general form, "If one is to take action 'A,' then one must first satisfy precondition 'P.'" In other words, in order to be permitted to do 'A,' one must first have fulfilled prerequisite 'P.' The cards below contain information on four people: one side of the card indicates whether or not a person has taken action 'A,' the other indicates whether or not the same individual has fulfilled precondition 'P.' In order to check that a certain regulation is being followed, which of the cards below would you turn over? Turn over only those that you need to check to be sure. (p. 403).

With these instructions 61% of subjects made the correct response, versus 19% of subjects who picked the right answer for the original version of the task.[2]

Instrumentalists conclude from studies like these that "people typically reason using abstract knowledge structures organized pragmatically, rather than in terms of purely syntactic rules of the sort that comprise standard logic" (Cheng, Holyoak, Nisbett, & Oliver, 1986, p. 314); that "inferential rules of the sort beloved by the logician, that is, the rules of formal logic, are not an important part of the layperson's repertoire and cannot readily by taught by purely abstract means" (Holland et al., 1986, p. 255); and that "people lack a 'mental logic'" (Cosmides, 1989, p. 235). Instead, people employ rules that are keyed to useful situations and that do not necessarily embody the entailment relation (Cheng & Holyoak, 1985, p. 397). Cheng and Holyoak call these rules *pragmatic reasoning schemas*. An example would be a rule that produced from a sentence of the form *If the action is to be taken, then the precondition must be satisfied* the further sentence *If the precondition is not satisfied, then the action must not be taken.* Versions of the Selection task that mention regulations or permissions activate such rules, which are then responsible for the improved performance. By contrast, the standard versions of the Selection task do not make contact with these goal-oriented rules and, hence, do not promote correct responding. The type of "syntactic" or "formal" rules that instrumentalists downgrade are especially the rules associated with the material conditional in classical logic (see, e.g., Bergmann et al., 1980, for an introduction to the material conditional and to classical logic). An example of such a rule would be one that produced from a sentence of the form *If p then q* one of the form *If not q then not p.* The latter rule might help subjects solve the letters-and-numerals version of the Selection task. However, it does not capture information that is useful in achieving everyday goals, according to instrumentalists, and is therefore not normally accessible to subjects in their reasoning.[3]

Although the Selection experiments provide some support for instrumental theories, other evidence creates difficulties for this view. A prediction from these theories would seem to be that people's performance should be relatively poor on other reasoning problems that are phrased in arbitrary terms. For example, suppose we tell subjects that the sentences in Argument (8) are about the arrangement of letters on an imaginary blackboard and that they should decide whether the second sentence must be true whenever the first sentence is true.

(8)   There is an O and there is a Z.
        _____
        There is an O.

This problem seems fully as arbitrary and as free of goal-related information as the letters-and-numerals version of the Selection task. Yet adult subjects made no mistakes in identifying this argument as correct in one experiment (Braine et al., 1984), and only 8% of 7th- and 8th-grade subjects made mistakes on this argument in another (Osherson, 1975, Experiment 3).

Some instrumental theories grant that people might have abstract logic rules, which they can use as backup procedures when goal-oriented rules do not apply (Cheng et al., 1986). On this account, subjects may be using a mental inference rule, along the lines of the entailment in (6), to obtain the correct answer for (8). In order to explain the data, however, these abstract rules (i.e., ones that have no special relation to goals) must be fairly easy for subjects to reason with. This raises the question of why the same is not true for the letters-and-numerals Selection task. Perhaps the abstract rules that subjects need to solve the Selection problem are absent or are harder for them to use than the rules needed for (8). Alternatively, the special demands of the Selection task may divert subjects from recognizing the need to apply these rules. The general point is that when we look beyond the Selection task there appears to be no evidence that goal-related information (e.g., mention of permissions or regulations or social contracts) is necessary for good reasoning performance.

IV. PATTERN PROCESSING THEORIES: DIAGRAMMATIC AND CONNECTIONIST ACCOUNTS

Another idea about how we recognize elementary entailments relies on an analogy to perceptual recognition. We can immediately recognize a visually presented object (say, a particular oak leaf) as an instance of a familiar category (leaves), despite the fact that we have never seen an instance with its exact shape and size. In assessing an argument such as (8), we immediately sense that it is an entailment, despite the fact that this argument is not one we have seen before. Perhaps our ability to classify (8) as logically correct rests on a pattern-recognition skill that is revealingly similar to that responsible for object recognition. Of course, there is a trivial way in which any theory about entailments has to include a recognition component: We have to recognize the component sentences as belonging to the category of entailments or nonentailments. However, our skill in dealing with elementary examples such as (8) may be perceptionlike in a way that goes beyond the necessities of classification itself. This notion seems especially appealing to those who believe that people try to simplify reasoning by recruiting cognitive processes that are accurate and relatively effortless. Because pattern recognition is often accurate and easy in this way, it offers a method to reduce what might otherwise be lengthy calculations (Rumelhart, 1989). The reasoning-as-pattern-perception idea also appeals to those who believe, along with Gestalt psychologists (e.g., Wertheimer, 1945), that reasoning entails global insight emerging from many local constraints (Greeno, 1977).

Investigators who are tempted by the idea that recognizing entailments is like perceiving patterns generally contrast their position with rule-based approaches. As we have noted, a mental rule for dealing with an argument such as (8) might stipulate that if a sentence has the form p *and* q, then the separate sentences p and q follow (for formulations of this *AND Elimination* rule see Braine et al., 1984; Osherson, 1975; Rips, 1994). Since the premise of (8), *There is an O and there is a Z*, matches this rule's condition, the rule will proceed to verify the sentence *There is an O*, which is (8)'s conclusion. Notice that a simple form of pattern recognition takes place in rule theories because the conditions on the rules have to match specific elements in the premise and conclusion. For example, the AND Elimination rule has to assign *There is an O* to p and *There is a Z* to q. What is distinctive about rule theories, however, is that the rules apply to a structured set of symbols and manipulate the symbols (in virtue of their structure) to produce output (Rips, 1990b; Smith, Langston, & Nisbett, 1992). Pattern-processing theories claim, by contrast, either that no structured symbols are involved in reasoning or that the symbols are tied to concrete diagrammatic entities. The idea that recognizing entailments is perceiving patterns is a metaphor, and there are several ways to develop it.

A. Diagrammatic Theories

One way of thinking about reasoning as pattern perception emphasizes the role of mental diagrams. Hard-copy diagrams have, of course, a long history as teaching tools in logic (Gardner, 1958). Devices like Venn diagrams and Euler circles enable students to represent set relations on paper in a way that brings out the constraints among the sets. This makes these methods especially appropriate for dealing with Aristotelian syllogisms (e.g., *All y are z; some x are y; therefore, some x are z*) and similar problems, although there are some theoretical upper limits on the complexity of the set relations they can deal with (Quine, 1972). Erickson (1974) and Yule and Stenning (1992) have proposed that people determine which conclusions follow from syllogistic premises by constructing mental versions of Euler circles, and other theories have attempted to generalize this method to handle a wider variety of deduction problems (Guyote & Sternberg, 1981; Johnson-Laird & Byrne, 1991).

Let us consider how one such method deals with arguments such as (8). According to this theory (Johnson-Laird & Byrne, 1991), people represent a simple sentence such as *There is a Z* or *Clare brought a salad* as a single symbol token, say p. The negation of a simple sentence, such as *There is not a Z* or *Clare did not bring a salad,* appears as an explicit negation sign (i.e., "¬") preceding the token: ¬p. This is similar to the representation in rule systems and in formal logic, as we will discuss momentarily, and we can borrow the term *literal* from these systems to refer to simple tokens and their negations. If two or more literals are true in a particular state of affairs, the literals are aligned in a single row. Thus, the sentences *There is an O and there is a Z* and *Clare brought a salad and Allan brought a torte* each appear as in (9a), and the sentences *There is an O and there is not a Z* and *Clare brought a salad and Allan did not bring a torte* appear as in (9b).

(9) a.   p   q

 b.   p   ¬q

Johnson-Laird and Byrne refer to each row in such a diagram as a *mental model.*

In order to represent sentences that contain the connective *or,* Johnson-Laird and Byrne's method requires more than one row or model. For example, the full representation for *Clare brought a salad or Allan brought a torte* contains two or three models, depending on whether the *or* is exclusive (Clare brought a salad or Allan brought a torte, but not both) or inclusive (Clare brought a salad or Allan brought a torte or both). The representation for exclusive *or,* for instance, has one model consisting of a token indicating

Clare brought a salad and a negated token for *Allan did not bring a torte;* the second model consists of a negated token for *Clare did not bring a salad* and another token for *Allan brought a torte* [see (10c), below]. According to Johnson-Laird and Byrne, however, the initial representation of a disjunctive sentence (one whose main connective is *or*) can be neutral with respect to whether the sentence is exclusive or inclusive. These *implicit* mental models are noncommittal, but they can be "fleshed out," if need be, to *explicit* models that distinguish the inclusive and the exclusive interpretations. Johnson-Laird and Byrne (1991, Table 3.1) give (10a) as the implicit models for a disjunction, (10b) as the explicit models for an inclusive disjunction, and (10c) as the explicit models for an exclusive disjunction.

(10) a.   p

                     q

    b.   [p]   [¬q]

         [¬p]   [q]

         [p]   [q]

    c.   [p]   [¬q]

         [¬p]   [q]

Here, the brackets mean that no further tokens of the indicated type can occur in the representation. The explicit model for the conjunction *Clare brought a salad and Allan brought a torte* would be the same as (9a) above, except that brackets would enclose both the *p* and the *q*.

We recognize entailments, according to Johnson-Laird and Byrne's theory, by noticing that the entailed sentence is true in all mental models of the entailing sentence. The simplest entailments are those for which there is only a single model of the entailing sentence (or, more accurately, for which no more than one model is needed to rule out certain nonentailed sentences). Consider once again Argument (8) or the comparable argument from (1a) to (1b): *Clare brought a salad and Allan brought a torte; therefore, Clare brought a salad.* The representation of the premise is (9a), and the representation of the conclusion is the single token *p*. Since there is only one model (i.e., row) in the premise representation and since the conclusion is part of this model, the premise entails the conclusion. Consider, however, the invalid argument from (3a) to (3b): *Clare brought a salad or Allan brought a torte; therefore, Clare brought a salad.* The implicit representation of the premise is the two models in (10a), and the explicit representation is either (10b) or (10c). Since each representation contains a model in which the conclusion (*p* = *Clare brought a salad*) is absent, the premise does not entail the conclusion.

1. Entailment via Mental Models

Let us consider in more detail this proposed solution to the entailment problem. I have called the mental-models approach a diagrammatic method, rather than a perceptual or imaginal one, because the models are not necessarily perceptual depictions. As Johnson-Laird and Byrne (1991, p. 39) acknowledge, a mental model often "transcends the perceptible." For example, in a situation in which the sentence *Clare brought a salad and Allan did not bring a torte* is true, there is nothing in the perceptual environment that corresponds to the "¬" of the model for this sentence in (9b). The abstract nature of this notation is also evident from the fact that the representations in (9) and (10) are isomorphic to expressions for the same sentences in *disjunctive normal form* in formal logic (Johnson-Laird, Byrne, & Schaeken, 1992). Sentences in disjunctive normal form have the structure of (11), in which the *P*'s, *Q*'s, and *R*'s are literals.

(11) (P_1 and P_2 and. . . and P_i) or (Q_1 and Q_2 and . . . and Q_j) or . . .or (R_1 and R_2 and . . .and R_k)

To get from mental models to disjunctive normal form, you simply connect the tokens within a row (model) with *and*'s, and then you connect the rows with *or*'s. For example, the representation in (9a) is equivalent to the disjunctive normal sentence in (9a′), (9b) to (9b′), (10b) to (10b′), and (10c) to (10c′).

(9)   a′.   p and q

(9)   b′.   p and ¬q

(10)   b′.   (p and ¬q) or (¬p and q) or (p and q)

(10)   c′.   (p and ¬q) or (¬p and q).

It's also possible to construct a test for entailment using disjunctive normal form that parallels the model's procedure.[4] Johnson-Laird et al. mention that the computer program that simulates their theory uses a similar test.

After noting the isomorphism between the mental models' procedure and the one based on disjunctive normal form, Johnson-Laird et al. (1992, p. 436) go on to deny that this implies that mental models are equivalent to rule theories: "What is crucial for the present argument, however, is that human beings can understand the meaning of connectives and that this process cannot consist of transforming a premise into disjunctive normal form. DNF is merely another linguistic expression, which in turn would need a semantic interpretation. The model theory assumes that human beings are conceptually equipped to envisage alternative situations—to construct alternative models—and that they learn how the semantics of connectives relates to sets of these envisaged alternatives." Johnson-Laird et al. believe that the ability to form such a model is beyond existing computer programs since they have no "real grasp of meaning" but might be possible for robots since they can "represent the world." Interacting with the world apparently endows a robot's or a human's representations with semantics, and this allows the representations to initiate inferences.

These remarks of Johnson-Laird et al. (1992) are interesting because they pull in two seemingly opposite directions. On one hand, the emphasis on connections to the environment and on representing the world implies that what licenses entailments in mental-model theory is the relation between the mental models and the world. This is consistent with semantics in formal logic, where the validity of an argument is defined in terms of the truth of its premises and conclusion. An argument is valid if and only if the conclusion of the argument is true in all states of affairs in which the premises are true. (See Bergmann et al., 1980, for an introduction to logical semantics, and van Fraassen, 1971, for a more advanced treatment.) According to the mental-model theory, the reason that (1a) entails (1b) is that whenever the model for (1a) stands in a certain relation to the world so does the model for (1b). This seems to suggest that the internal nature of the representation is of less importance than this external relation. But then any representation that has the same structure [in the way, e.g., that (9a′) has the same structure as (9a)] ought to be able to bear the same relation to the environment and, thus, ought to be able to mediate entailments. On the other hand, Johnson-Laird et al.'s description of sentences such as (9a′) as "merely another linguistic expression, which in turn would need a semantic interpretation" implies that there is something that allows (9a) but not (9a′) to have a semantic interpretation (i.e., an external relation to the environment). The difficulty for Johnson-Laird et al.'s approach lies in determining what this added something could be. It clearly will not work to say that these mental models are closer to one's perceptual experience of the environment than are disjunctive normal forms, since on all accounts both representations "transcend the perceptible" by including elements such as negation signs.

One reasonable way to eliminate this dilemma is to hold onto the notion that what ultimately sanctions entailments are relations to external referents, while letting go of the idea that there is some principled difference between mental models such as (9a) and mental sentences such as (9a′). From this vantage, it might be tempting to go further: Perhaps these external relations are causally responsible for people's ability to draw correct inferences or recognize entailments. As before, (1a) entails (1b) because whenever (1a) stands in the proper relation to the world, so does (1b). But, in addition, something about these external relations *causes* us to deduce (1b) from (1a) or to notice that the entailment holds. This viewpoint is a tempting one for those who believe that cognition is a strongly "situated" activity (e.g., Barwise, 1987). There would be less need for such a theory to posit special internal processes that transform mental representations (models or sentences) in order to decide which sentences entail others. It is not immediately clear, however, how such an account could explain why certain entailments are so much more easily recognized than others, and for this reason diagrammatic theories in psychology have not adopted this type of direct account. All diagrammatic theories include mental procedures that operate on the diagrams or models in order to determine whether an entailment holds. In Johnson-Laird and Byrne's (1991) theory, for example, computational procedures search for new models that provide counterexamples to tentative inferences. So although external relations may explain what it means for one sentence or mental representation to entail another, it is the computational procedures that explain how people recognize these entailments. In this respect, too, model theories resemble rule theories, though the details of the internal procedures may vary.

The entailments that we have been examining are based on connectives such as *and* and *or*. For inference tasks involving spatial relations, Johnson-Laird and Byrne (1991) have proposed mental models with internal spatial arrangements that are similar to those in the situation they denote. For example, to represent the fact that a plate is to the left of a spoon, Johnson-Laird and Byrne propose a mental model in which a token representing the plate (e.g., p) is to the left of a token representing the spoon (s):

$$p \qquad s$$

These spatial models have a better claim to mirroring perceptual data than the mental models discussed above, although many of the same issues about whether mental models have a privileged semantic status arise for these spatial mental models, too (Pylyshyn, 1984; Rips, 1986). The present point, however, is that we need to be cautious in interpreting claims about diagrammatic methods. Especially outside the realm of explicit spatial reasoning, these methods do not simply piggyback on existing perceptual mechanisms; they require specialized procedures for dealing with negation signs, the row and column organization of the representations, and so on, that are crucial in determining when an entailment holds.

2. Empirical Implications

As we noticed earlier, Johnson-Laird and Byrne (1991) base their empirical predictions on the number of mental models that people need to solve a problem. The larger the number of required models, the greater the demands on working memory, and the larger the number of errors that subjects should commit. For example, in one experiment, Johnson-Laird et al.

(1992) asked subjects to formulate conclusions for the premises in (12) and in (13).

    (12)   June is in Wales, or Charles is in Scotland, but not both.
                Charles is in Scotland, or Kate is in Ireland, but not both.

?

    (13)   June is in Wales, or Charles is in Scotland, or both.
                Charles is in Scotland, or Kate is in Ireland, or both.

?

Each premise in (12) contains an exclusive *or*, which subjects should represent using the two models in (10c). Combining these premise models into a representation for the entire problem produces the two models in (12′), where *j* denotes *June is in Wales*, *c* denotes *Charles is in Scotland*, and *k* denotes *Kate is in Ireland*.

    (12′)   [j]   [¬c]   [k]
             [¬j]   [c]   [¬k]

Problem (13), however, contains inclusive *or*'s, which require three models for each premise, as in (10b). Combining these representations yields the five models in (13′).

    (13′)   [j]   [c]   [k]
             [j]   [c]   [¬k]
             [j]   [¬c]   [k]
             [¬j]   [c]   [k]
             [¬j]   [c]   [¬k]

In accord with the predictions of the model theory, 21% of subjects were able to produce a correct conclusion for Problem (12), but only 6% of subjects were able to produce a correct conclusion for (13).

The data, however, have not always flattered predictions based on number of mental models. Consider arguments (14) and (15), which differ only in their first premise.

    (14)   Fred is in Minnesota and Lola is in Pennsylvania.
                 If Fred is in Minnesota, then Earl is in Florida.
                 If Lola is in Pennsylvania, then Earl is in Florida.

                 Earl is in Florida.

    (15)   Fred is in Minnesota or Lola is in Pennsylvania.
                 If Fred is in Minnesota, then Earl is in Florida.
                 If Lola is in Pennsylvania, then Earl is in Florida.

                 Earl is in Florida.

The premises of both of these arguments entail their conclusion, but Argument (15) requires more models. The first premise of (15) is a disjunction, so its representation has two or three models, as in (10b) or (10c), depending on whether it is understood as exclusive or inclusive. The first premise of (14), however, is a conjunction, so its representation is the single model in (9a). The remaining premises are the same in the two arguments and do not change the disparity in number of models. Thus, Johnson-Laird et al.'s theory predicts that subjects should have more difficulty determining the logical correctness of (15) than of (14). However, exactly the same percentage of subjects (89.2%) affirmed each of the two arguments in a test of this prediction (Rips, 1990a).

The same experiment also demonstrated that subjects' performance can vary greatly even when the number of models is held constant. For example, Argument (16) has the same number of models as (14) and is also logically valid.

(16)   It is not true that: Fred is in Minnesota or Lola is in Pennsylvania.
       If Fred is not in Minnesota, then Earl is in Florida.
       If Lola is not in Pennsylvania, then Earl is in Florida.

       _____

       Earl is in Florida.

However, only 64.9% of subjects identified this argument as correct, compared to 89.2% for Argument (14).

These results should not be taken to mean that people never use mental diagrams to aid reasoning. People are no doubt able to learn diagrammatic methods (e.g., Euler circles) and to employ them mentally in organizing and solving certain problems. However, there is no evidence to suggest that diagrams are essential for drawing deductive inferences. This may be because the entailment relationship is not an intrinsically perceptual one, at least for cases involving connectives and quantifiers. There is a tendency for psychologists to reason along the following lines: (1) the entailment relation can be defined in terms of the truth of the relevant sentences (i.e., S_1 entails S_2 if and only if S_2 is true in all states of affairs in which S_1 is true); (2) people often judge the truth of sentences on perceptual evidence; hence, (3) judgments of entailment must often be perceptual. This tendency should be resisted. Although the entailment relation can be defined in terms of truth, we can easily judge that one sentence entails another even when we have no inkling about the truth of the component sentences, as in many of the examples we have considered so far. (Recall the discussion of Argument [8] in the preceding section.) Moreover, entailment requires that the relation between sentences hold in all states of affairs, not just the current state. Should we then say that judging entailments is a matter of *imagining* what it is like for the entailed and entailing sentences to be true? This seems to be the underlying motivation for mental models and similar theories. (Cf. Johnson-Laird et al.'s, [1992] comment, cited earlier: "human beings are conceptually equipped to envisage alternative situations—to construct alternative models—and . . . they learn how the semantics of connectives relates to sets of these envisaged alternatives.") However, as soon as we try to give an account of envisioning what it is like for negative sentences to be true (*Allan did not bring a torte*) or for universally quantified sentences to be true (*All even numbers are divisible by two*), we seem to be thrown back on devices (e.g., negation signs) that are just as abstract as the original sentences.

B. Connectionist Theories

Another way of thinking about deduction as pattern recognition places more emphasis on satisfying constraints than on processing internal diagrams or pictures. It is common to view object recognition as the result of many facilitory and inhibitory forces, deriving both from perceptual input and from previous experience. The final category to which we assign the object is a compromise among these forces. This suggests that recognition of entailments also depends on integrating forces, not directly from perceptual input, but from the roles that the component terms play in language. From this point of view, what makes an entailment convincing is that it provides a good fit to previous uses of its key operators (e.g., *or, and, all,* or *some*). The role that the connectives and quantifiers play in natural language ensures that we will recognize the correctness of elementary entailments that preserve these roles. For example, the use of *and* in everyday contexts implicitly restricts how it can function, including what follows from sentences containing it (Dummett, 1975). Since connectionist networks are designed to integrate multiple constraints, they might provide one way to account for the simple entailments we have looked at.

A connectionist network consists of a set of nodes and links between them. Excitation or inhibition travels from each node across the links to other nodes. Each link mediates the amount of activation that travels across it, weighting the activation by some modifiable quantity. Changes to these weights determine the global behavior of the network. To deal with entailments, networks must represent the entailing and entailed sentences, usually by encoding the former as a pattern of activation in a first set of nodes and the latter as a pattern of activation in a second set. The network could be said to recognize an entailment between two sentences if the entailing sentence's pattern produces the entailed sentence's pattern. Alternatively, the network could contain a specially designated node representing whether an entailment exists between two sentences; the network recognizes that the first sentence entails the second if this node is active.

1. A Connectionist Network for Logic

As an illustration of how this sort of system works, we can consider a sample network from Bechtel and Abrahamsen (1991) that attempts to learn whether certain arguments are valid or invalid. A schematic picture of this network appears in Figure 1. The bottom row of nodes in this network encodes a two-premise argument: The first premise is *If p then q, p or q,* or *Not both p and q;* and the second premise is *p, q, Not p,* or *Not q.* The conclusion is *p* or *Not p* if the second premise if *q* or *Not q,* or else *q* or *Not q* if the second premise is *p* or *Not p.* (The *p*'s and *q*'s could themselves be positive or negative sentence letters.) Thus, the arguments in (17) are among those that the network could represent.

(17) a.   If A then C.
            A.
            _____
            C.

      b.   If A then C.
            Not C.
            _____
            Not A.

      c.   A or C.
            Not A.
            _____
            C.

      d.   Not both A and C.
            A.
            _____
            Not C.

The arguments in (17) are valid, but there are an equal number of invalid arguments in the full set (e.g., *If A then C; Not C; Therefore, A* is invalid). The first 8 nodes in the bottom row of the figure represent the first premise, with node 1 indicating whether the first sentence letter in the premise is positive or negative, nodes 2 and 3 indicating whether the first sentence letter is A, B, C, or D, nodes 4 and 5 indicating whether the connective is *if, not both,* or *or,* node 6 indicating whether the second sentence letter is positive or negative, and nodes 7 and 8 indicating whether the second sentence letter is A, B, C, or D. The network represents the second premise and conclusion in a similar way. For example, if we write a 1 to indicate that a node is active and a 0 to indicate that a node is inactive, then we can encode Argument (17d) using this scheme as follows:

First premise								Second premise			Conclusion		
0	0	1	1	0	0	1	1	0	0	1	1	1	1
	A	Not both			C				A	Not	C		

The top row of nodes in Figure 1 represents the logical type of the argument and its validity. The first two of these nodes distinguish whether the argument is of the *modus ponens* type as in (17a), *modus tollens* as in (17b), an *alternative syllogism* as in (17c), or a *disjunctive syllogism* as in (17d). The final node indicates whether the argument is valid or invalid.[5]

The two intermediate rows of the network in Figure 1 contain "hidden units," ten in each row. These nodes allow the network to pool information from individual nodes in the outer layers. The network contains links from each note in one layer to every node in the layer directly above. The figure shows only a few of these connections.

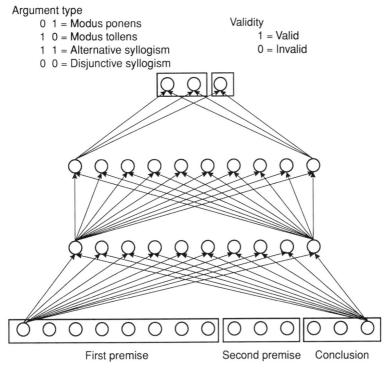

FIGURE 1 A connectionist network for recognizing the validity of some simple propositional arguments. Adapted from Bechtel and Abrahamsen (1991), Figure 5.2.

This network was supposed to learn the correct argument type (e.g., modus ponens or alternative syllogism) and validity judgment (valid or invalid) when presented with a specific argument. During training trials the network got an encoded argument in the form of an excitation pattern in the lower row of nodes. The resulting pattern of activation in its upper row of nodes was then corrected by the back propagation method until the network had achieved its performance criterion. The network was then tested by presenting it with a new set of arguments of the same basic types. Bechtel and Abrahamsen (1991) report that the network learned all of an initial set of 192 problems after training the network on 3000 presentations of each of these problems. On the transfer test, the net solved 76% of the new problems correctly. Bechtel and Abrahamsen also trained a somewhat similar network to fill in missing information on the basis of some of the facts about the argument, its type, and its validity. For example, the network might get the first premise and conclusion of Argument (17a), its type (i.e., modus ponens), and its validity (valid); it would then have to reproduce the missing second premise. In the training trials, the net achieved 98.9% correct performance after 30,000 presentations of each of 384 problems. In the transfer trials, the net was correct on 97.6% of trials that involved filling in a missing proposition, but was correct on only 46.9% of trials involving the argument type and validity.

2. Do People Reason Connectionistically?

It is not easy to assess simulations such as Bechtel and Abrahamsen's (1991) as theories of human reasoning. Although there is a large body of data concerning people's ability to recognize modus ponens and modus tollens arguments of the sort that the network learned (e.g., Marcus & Rips, 1979; Taplin & Staudenmayer, 1973), it is not clear how relevant the data are for evaluating the network. The experiments tend to show, for example, that people are faster and more accurate in judging the validity of modus ponens than that of modus tollens, and it might therefore be interesting to know whether the network in Figure 1 showed the same tendency. However, Bechtel and Abrahamsen did not intend their network as a simulation of human performance on a specific deduction task and do not report the results on an argument-by-argument basis. Instead the network is supposed to be an existence proof—a demonstration that it is possible for networks to learn logical principles in a humanlike way. The same uncertainty affects other points of comparison between the network and people. For example, the network requires a large number of trials to attain accurate performance and exhibits a modest transfer rate relative to what we would expect from human subjects. As Bechtel and Abrahamsen note, people surely do not require 576,000 trials to learn to classify a handful of argument types. They caution, however, that people come to deduction problems with a considerable advantage, having experience with both the sentence structures and the connectives that the network had to learn afresh.

The main claim for the network of Figure 1, then, is that it demonstrates the possibility of deduction along connectionist lines. If networks can learn to identify logical principles, then it is possible that humans do so in the same way—specifically, without resorting to logical rules. We noted earlier (as Bechtel and Abrahamsen also do) that both connectionist systems and rules systems engage in pattern processing, since rule systems typically determine when to apply a rule by matching its conditions to patterns in working memory. This lessens the distinctiveness of the network approach to some extent, since both rules and nets can handle much of the evidence that supports pattern recognition in logical processing. For example, the fact that people recognize elementary entailments quickly and automatically does not clearly distinguish these viewpoints. A more central difference between the connectionist approach and the rule-based approach appears to lie in the fact that a network such as Figure 1 uses the same data structures (i.e., nodes and links) for all principles, and this may introduce dependencies in the rates with which people learn or employ them. We will look at possible advantages of this interdependence in discussing empirical results below.

The claim that the network in Figure 1 can learn to identify argument types such as modus ponens is weakened, however, by restrictions on the complexity of the arguments it can handle. What the net learned to classify were items such as those in (17) where the letters *A* and *C* are atomic (i.e., not further decomposable into simpler sentences). But modus ponens and the other argument types also include cases where *A* and *C* are complex. For example, Argument (18) is a perfectly good example of modus ponens.

(18)   If (A and B), then (C or D).
         A and B.
         _____

         C or D.

The network in Figure 1 is unable to recognize (18) as an instance of modus ponens because the input nodes in the lower row cannot encode the premises and conclusion. Of course, additional nodes could be added to the row to allow the model to accommodate longer sentences, but the problem here is a general one. There are no limits on the complexity of the sentences that can appear in a modus ponens argument. However, a network encodes the premises and conclusion with a fixed set of nodes, and this imposes seemingly arbitrary limitations on what counts as members of the argument type. Figure 1 uses a local encoding scheme in which each sentence (and sentence part) is assigned to separate pools of nodes. But even a distributed encoding, which represents the argument as a global pattern of activation over a single node pool, will also run against arbitrary upper limits on the complexity of instances in an argument type. This problem is closely related to the objection that connectionist networks have no way to account for systematic relations among the sentences that humans can entertain (Fodor & McLaughlin, 1990; Fodor & Pylyshyn, 1988). In the present case, what Figure 1 leaves unexplained is why humans who can recognize (17a) as logically correct can typically also recognize (18) (and conversely).

Connectionist systems for drawing deductive inferences sometimes take a different approach to recognizing elementary entailments. For example, Ajjanagadde and Shastri (1989) have proposed an inference network that encodes conditional sentences [e.g., *(For all x) (if x is a triangle, then x has three sides)*] and atomic sentences (e.g., *ABC is a triangle*) as separate sets of nodes. Inferences are made by passing activation from a potential conclusion or query sentence (*Does ABC have three sides?*) to determine whether there are any premise sentences in the network that entail it. Unlike the network of Figure 1, this system does not learn new inference principles. It has only a single, fixed inference procedure (roughly speaking, modus ponens) that is built into the network operation. Other elementary entailments, such as the one from *Clare brought a salad and Allan brought a torte* to *Clare brought a salad,* are not recognized directly, and accommodating them would require redesigning the network or encoding them indirectly to conform to the network's restrictions. Building entailments into the network's operating principles has many advantages, of course, in terms of the efficiency and the uniformity of the system. It may be true that human inference making is also due to innate mental capacities, as we noted earlier. However, this solution to the problem of elementary entailments (unlike that of the network in Figure 1) departs radically from the idea that a system acquires these entailments by solving constraints or recognizing patterns that the logical operators impose (e.g., in language learning and communication). Thus, it sacrifices what seems to be an advantage of connectionist approaches, since it is equally possible to hardwire a system with inference rules or with mental models.

3. Connectionism and Content Effects

One place where connectionist systems may have a contribution to make is in explaining the facilitating effects of drinking regulations and other permissions on the Selection task. It is possible to explain this facilitation in term of abstract rules, perhaps pragmatic schemata or rules from modal logic based on operators for obligation and permission (see Endnote 3). But another possibility is that no abstract rules are involved and that the effect derives solely from the context in which people originally learn to check the truth of conditionals. Suppose instrumentalists are right that the procedure for checking conditionals develops mainly in the course of determining whether regulations are obeyed. For example, it may be important for children to determine whether specific contingencies are covered by conditional rules such as *If you want dessert, you must finish your parsnips*. Connectionist systems could presumably learn such checking procedures in the manner of the network in Figure 1 without using rules, and the procedures would retain sensitivity to the regulation contexts. We might therefore expect better performance from the network in tasks that center on regulations than in ones that center on arbitrary material.

The difficulties with such a theory are essentially the same as the difficulties with the instrumental approach. People's ability to recognize entailments is not always impeded by the abstractness or arbitrariness of the nonlogical terms, and it is not easy to see how a connectionist theory could account for these cases (Smith et al., 1992). Moreover, there are other effects of nonlogical terms that do not seem to depend on details of the learning context. For example, Evans, Barston, and Pollard (1983) showed that subjects are more willing to endorse an argument if its conclusion coincides with their pre-existing beliefs than if the conclusion contradicts those beliefs. Evans et al. found in a pretest that subjects rated the sentence *Some addictive things are not cigarettes* as more believable than the sentence *Some cigarettes are not addictive*. Accordingly, a separate group of subjects in the main experiment judged Argument (19) as valid more often than Argument (20).

(19)   No cigarettes are inexpensive.
         Some addictive things are inexpensive.
         _____

         Some addictive things are not cigarettes.

(20)   No addictive things are inexpensive.
         Some cigarettes are inexpensive.
         _____

         Some cigarettes are not addictive.

Although one could obviously train a network to respond positively to arguments with believable conclusions, nothing about a connectionist architecture would seem to motivate this bias. Of course, the difference between (19) and (20) is equally a problem for rule-based approaches. Because (19) and (20) have the same logical form, the difference in responses is presumably not due to any logical properties of these arguments. No purely deductive rule could depend on the contingent relation between addictive things and cigarettes.

V. WHAT IS BEHIND DEDUCTION ABILITY?

Deduction seems psychologically mysterious since it is difficult to see what cognitive principles could have produced it. Theories based on inference rules can account for the mechanics of the deduction process, but they do not explain how it is that people come to have this skill. Instrumental theories (pragmatic reasoning schemata and social contracts) and connectionist theories explain deduction via ordinary learning or evolutionary principles. They are surely right that people sometimes learn inferences (in logic or math class, for example); however, contrary to what these theories predict, deduction is not always yoked to the specific goals that motivate such learning. Diagrammatic theories presuppose mechanisms for interpreting the diagrams that seem as mysterious as the logic rules they are supposed to displace. These mechanisms cannot be solely perceptual ones, since the significance of the diagrams is not apparent from their raw perceptual properties. But if neither perception nor learning can explain how people are able to draw deductive inferences, then what does?

A possible response to the question of what is responsible for deduction is that the question itself is based on an incorrect assumption. Posing the question in this way assumes that there are cognitive processes that are somehow more central than deduction and that explaining deduction is a matter of reducing it to these processes. It seems worth exploring the opposite assumption, however: Why not take deduction to be a cognitive process on the same footing as perception, learning, memory retrieval, and other abilities? When we try to explain these latter abilities, we do so by giving a detailed account of the elementary mechanisms that participate in them, but we are not tempted to wonder in the same way about how to explain these mechanisms in terms of other sorts of skills. In the case of perception, for example, we do not typically worry about trying to explain mechanisms of vision in terms of learning or memory retrieval. Although we might try to understand certain aspects of perception, such as size constancy, using principles borrowed from learning theory, we do not doubt that there are some core visual mechanisms that are simply given as part of our mental makeup. We might find out more about how people happen to have these core mechanisms by referring these questions to physiology or to evolutionary theory. Yet we do not feel that the *psychological* attempt to explain perception is faulty or incomplete if we lack answers to these cross-disciplinary queries.

The suggestion is that deductive reasoning need not be reduced to other psychological mechanisms in order to account for it. Once we know the basic deduction principles that underlie our ability to recognize entailments, then we would be in a position every bit as enviable as knowing the basic visual mechanisms that underlie our abilities to recognize scenes. Part of the reason why we are tempted to approach deduction and perception differently may be that it is harder to understand what role deduction plays in a larger cognitive context. On one hand, the utility of perception is obvious, so there is little reason to wonder what could have produced it. On the other hand, deduction seems to be a hothouse skill that is mainly confined to math class, and explaining it seems to require showing how it arises from other processes that are more immediately useful. It is beyond the scope of this chapter to locate deduction in an overall cognitive framework (see Rips, 1994, for one attempt at this). We can get a feel for why deduction might be useful, however, by noticing the similarities to production systems (e.g., Anderson, 1983; Newell, 1990). Production systems consist of a large number of conditional rules that monitor working memory for information that matches their antecedents. If such information is available, the rule executes a set of actions, usually placing new information in memory. By chaining production rules in this way, the system can carry out complex maneuvers that can account for many information-processing tasks. Thus, production rules are essentially devices that operate according to elementary deduction principles (modus ponens and instantiation of variables), together with a few operations for inserting and retrieving symbols from working memory. It is possible, in fact, to design a productionlike system with the same sorts of inference rules that we considered in Section II of this chapter.

Viewing deduction in an executive capacity may help demonstrate what it is good for and relieve the pressure to explain it away. Obviously, many legitimate questions can be raised about deduction. We would like to know why it sometimes exhibits sensitivity to nonlogical terms and sometimes does not. We would like to know how natural language is translated into a form that the deduction routines can use. We would also like to know exactly which routines humans have available. None of these questions currently have satisfactory answers. But it may aid progress on these problems to view deduction as a first-class cognitive ability constrained by the task of carrying out other higher level mental processes.

Acknowledgment

NIMH Grant MH39633 supported work on this chapter. Please send correspondence to Lance Rips, Psychology Department, Northwestern University, Evanston IL 60208.

Endnotes

1. As an alternative to abstraction, we might consider the possibility that people store instances of successful predictions and then decide about the trustworthiness of a new prediction by its degree of similarity to these old ones (Brooks, 1978; Medin & Ross, 1989). This, however, is not the usual route for instrumentalists.
2. I have cited the exact wording from these Selection experiments because further research suggests that details of phrasing may be important. For example, Jackson and Griggs (1990) report only a 15% success rate when they gave subjects these instructions;

> Your task is to decide which of the cards you need to turn over in order to find out whether or not a certain regulation is being followed. The regulation is "If one is to

take action 'A', then one must first satisfy precondition 'P.' " Turn over only those cards that you need to check to be sure.

3. Difficulties with material conditionals, however, do not imply that logic-based approaches to deduction are unable to explain content effects. There are modal logics for conditional permission and obligation that seem particularly well suited for these contexts. See Føllesdal and Hilpinen (1971) and Lewis (1974) for expositions of these systems, and Rips (1994) for discussion of their psychological relevance. Osherson (1976) sets out a psychological theory of deduction based on rules for permission and obligation.

4. Readers who are familiar with elementary logic will also notice the similarity of these mental models to truth tables (see, e.g., Bergmann, et al., 1980). Truth tables display the truth value of a complex sentence as a function of the truth values of the atomic sentences that occur within it. The truth table for a conjunction, for example, displays the fact that the conjunction (e.g., p and q) is true just in case both p is true and q is true:

Truth of p	Truth of q	Truth of p and q
True	True	True
True	False	False
False	True	False
False	False	False

The truth table for inclusive *or* shows that p or q is true if p is true or q is true or both:

Truth of p	Truth of q	Truth of p or q
True	True	True
True	False	True
False	True	True
False	False	False

Finally, the truth table for exclusive *or* (*xor*) shows that p xor q is true when p is true or q is true, but not both:

Truth of p	Truth of q	Truth of p xor q
True	True	False
True	False	True
False	True	True
False	False	False

By comparing these truth tables to the mental models in (9a), (10b), and (10c), you can see that the models correspond to those lines of the truth table in which the more complex sentence is true. For example, to get from the truth table for inclusive *or* to the mental model in (10b), delete the final line of this table, in which p or q is false, and replace the entries in which p is true by [p], the entries in which p is false by [¬p], the entries in which q is true by [q], and the entries in which q is false by [¬q]. The same modifications will work to produce all other mental models for propositional reasoning.

5. Usually, "modus ponens," "modus tollens," and so on denote only valid arguments; however, in Bechtel and Abrahamsen's scheme these terms refer to a group of related arguments, some of which are valid and some invalid. An "invalid modus ponens" argument in this terminology would be: *If A then C; C; Therefore, A.* An "invalid alternative syllogism" would be: *A or C; A; Therefore, Not C* (see Bechtel & Abrahamsen, 1991, Table 5.1).

References

Ajjanagadde, V., & Shastri, L. (1989). Efficient inference with multi-place predicates and variables in a connectionist system. *Program of the Eleventh Annual Conference of the Cognitive Science Society.* Hillsdale, NJ: Erlbaum.

Anderson, J. R. (1983). *The architecture of cognition.* Cambridge, MA: Harvard University Press.

Barwise, J. (1987). Unburdening the language of thought. *Mind and Language, 2,* 82–96.

Bechtel, W., & Abrahamsen, A. (1991). *Connectionism and the mind: An introduction to parallel processing in networks.* Oxford: Blackwell.

Bergmann, M., Moor, J., & Nelson, J. (1980). *The logic book.* New York: Random House.

Braine, M. D. S., Reiser, B. J., & Rumain, B. (1984). Some empirical justification for a theory of natural propositional logic. In G. H. Bower (Eds.), *The psychology of learning and motivation* (Vol. 18, pp. 313–371). Orlando, FL: Academic Press.

Brooks, L. (1978). Nonanalytic concept formation and memory for instances. In E. Rosch & B. B. Lloyd (Eds.), *Cognition and categorization* (pp. 169–211). Hillsdale, NJ: Erlbaum.

Cheng, P. W., & Holyoak, K. J. (1985). Pragmatic reasoning schemas. *Cognitive Psychology, 17,* 391–416.

Cheng, P. W., Holyoak, K. J., Nisbett, R. E., & Oliver, L. (1986). Pragmatic versus syntactic approaches to training deductive reasoning. *Cognitive Psychology, 18,* 293–328.

Cosmides, L. (1989). The logic of social exchange: Has natural selection shaped how humans reason? *Cognition, 31,* 187–276.

Dummett, M. (1975). The philosophical basis of intuitionistic logic. In H. E. Rose & J. Shepherdson (Eds.), *Logic colloquium '73* (pp. 5–40). Amsterdam: North-Holland Publ.

Erickson, J. R. (1974). A set analysis theory of behavior in formal syllogistic reasoning tasks. In R. L. Solso (Ed.), *Theories in cognitive psychology* (pp. 305–329). Potomac, MD: Erlbaum.

Evans, J. St. B. T. (1989). *Bias in human reasoning.* Hove, England: Erlbaum.

Evans, J. St. B. T., Barston, J. L., & Pollard, P. (1983). On the conflict between logic and belief in syllogistic reasoning. *Memory & Cognition, 11,* 295–306.

Fodor, J. (1975). *The language of thought.* New York: Crowell.

Fodor, J., & McLaughlin, B. P. (1990). Connectionism and the problem of systematicity: Why Smolensky's solution doesn't work. *Cognition, 35,* 183–204.

Fodor, J., & Pylyshyn, Z. (1988). Connectionism and cognitive architecture: A critical analysis. *Cognition, 28,* 3–71.

Føllesdal, D., & Hilpinen, R. (1971). Deontic logic: An introduction. In R. Hilpinen (Ed.), *Denotic logic: Introductory and systematic readings* (pp. 1–35). Dordrecht: Reidel.

Frege, G. (1974). *The foundations of arithmetic* (J. L. Austen, Trans.). Oxford: Blackwell. (Original work published 1884)

Gardner, M. (1958). *Logic machines and diagrams.* New York: McGraw-Hill.

Greeno, J. (1971). The process of understanding in problem solving. In N. J. Castellan, Jr., D. B. Pisoni, & G. R. Potts (Eds.), *Cognitive theory* (Vol. 2, pp. 43–83). Hillsdale, NJ: Erlbaum.

Griggs, R. A., & Cox, J. R. (1982). The elusive thematic-materials effect in Wason's selection task. *British Journal of Experimental Psychology, 73,* 407–420.

Guyote, M. J., & Sternberg, R. J. (1981). A transitive-chain theory of syllogistic reasoning. *Cognitive Psychology, 13,* 461–525.

Harman, G. (1986). *Change in view: Principles of reasoning.* Cambridge, MA: MIT Press.

Holland, J. H., Holyoak, K. J., Nisbett, R. E., & Thagard, P. R. (1986). *Induction: Processes of inference, learning, and discovery.* Cambridge, MA: MIT Press.

Jackson, S. L., & Griggs, R. A. (1990). The elusive pragmatic reasoning schema effect. *Quarterly Journal of Experimental Psychology, 42A,* 353–373.

Johnson-Laird, P. N., & Byrne, R. M. J. (1991). *Deduction*. Hillsdale, NJ: Erlbaum.

Johnson-Laird, P. N., Byrne, R. M. J., & Schaeken, W. (1992). Propositional reasoning by model. *Psychological Review, 99,* 418–439.

Lewis, D. (1974). Semantic analyses for dyadic deontic logic. In S. Stenlund (Ed.), *Logical theory and semantic analysis* (pp. 1–14). Dordrecht: Reidel.

Macnamara, J. (1986). *A border dispute: The place of logic in psychology*. Cambridge, MA: MIT Press.

Marcus, S. L., & Rips, L. J. (1979). Conditional reasoning. *Journal of Verbal Learning and Verbal Behavior, 18,* 199–224.

Medin, D. L., & Ross, B. H. (1989). The specific character of abstract thought. In R. J. Sternberg (Ed.), *Advances in the psychology of human intelligence* (Vol. 5, pp. 189–223). Hillsdale, NJ: Erlbaum.

Newell, A. (1990). *Unified theories of cognition*. Cambridge, MA: Harvard University Press.

Newell, A., Shaw, J. C., & Simon, H. A. (1957). Empirical explorations with the Logic Theory Machine: A case study in heuristics. *Proceedings of the Western Joint Computer Conference* pp. 218–239.

Osherson, D. N. (1975). *Logical abilities in children* (Vol. 3). Hillsdale, NJ: Erlbaum.

Osherson, D. N. (1976). *Logical abilities in children* (Vol. 4). Hillsdale, NJ: Erlbaum.

Pylyshyn, Z. (1984). *Computation and cognition: Toward a foundation for cognitive science*. Cambridge, MA: MIT Press.

Quine, W. V. (1972). *Methods of logic* (3rd ed.). New York: Holt, Rinehart, & Winston.

Rips, L. J. (1983). Cognitive processes in propositional reasoning. *Psychological Review, 90,* 38–71.

Rips, L. J. (1986). Mental muddles. In M. Brand & R. M. Harnish (Eds.), *The representation of knowledge and belief* (pp. 258–286). Tucson: University of Arizona Press.

Rips, L. J. (1990a). Paralogical reasoning: Evans, Johnson-Laird, and Byrne on liar and truth-teller puzzles. *Cognition, 36,* 291–314.

Rips, L. J. (1990b). Reasoning. *Annual Review of Psychology, 41,* 321–353.

Rips, L. J. (1994). *The psychology of proof: Deductive reasoning in human thinking*. Cambridge, MA: MIT Press.

Rumelhart, D. E. (1989). Toward a microstructural account of human reasoning. In S. Vosniadou & A. Ortony (Eds.), *Similarity and analogical reasoning* (pp. 298–312). New York: Cambridge University Press.

Skyrms, B. (1966). *Choice and chance: An introduction to inductive logic*. Belmont, CA: Dickerson.

Smith, E. E., Langston, C., & Nisbett, R. E. (1992). The case for rules in reasoning. *Cognitive Science, 16,* 1–40.

Taplin, J. E., & Staudenmayer, H. (1973). Reasoning with conditional sentences. *Journal of Verbal Learning and Verbal Behavior, 12,* 530–542.

van Fraassen, B. C. (1971). *Formal semantics and logic*. New York: Macmillan.

Wason, P. C. (1968). Reasoning about a rule. *Quarterly Journal of Experimental Psychology, 20,* 273–281.

Wason, P. C., & Johnson-Laird, P. N. (1972). *Psychology of reasoning*. Cambridge, MA: Harvard University Press.

Wertheimer, M. (1945). *Productive thinking*. New York: Harper.

Yule, P., & Stenning, K. (1992). The figure effect and a graphical algorithm for syllogistic reasoning. *Proceedings of the Fourteenth Annual Conference of the Cognitive Science Society*. Hillsdale, NJ: Erlbaum.

CHAPTER 6

Inductive Reasoning

Jeffrey Bisanz
Gay L. Bisanz
Connie A. Korpan

Induction is a strikingly pervasive and important function of cognition. Inductive reasoning, alone or in conjunction with other forms of thinking, is central to many types of problem solving and learning, and it has long been recognized as an important index of cognitive development (Inhelder & Piaget, 1958) and individual differences in intelligence (Spearman, 1923, 1927; Sternberg, 1977). In contemporary cognitive science, inductive processes are viewed as responsible for generating concepts and providing links between concepts and actions (Smith, 1989), as well as for combining sensory and memorial information into percepts (Rips, 1980). In a volume on thinking and problem solving, such as this one, the topic of induction is related intimately to domains described in every single chapter. Indeed, it is difficult to decide how to extricate inductive reasoning from domains such as knowledge representations, concepts and categories, problem solving, language, development, and many others described in this book.

Considering the centrality of induction to cognition, a reader new to this area might anticipate that research on induction would constitute a long, rich, and well-integrated literature. That reader may be disappointed. In a recent review, Rips (1990) commented that

> the psychology of reasoning has been something of a research backwater. . . .
> [M]ost research on inductive reasoning seems to busy itself with the way
> people learn arbitrary sets of geometric shapes, random dot patterns, or sche-

matic faces. The "long and dull history" of other areas of experimental psychology (Tulving & Madigan, 1970) appears lively and eventful by comparison. (p. 322)

Similarly, Sternberg (1986) remarked, with regret, that "The domain of reasoning has, historically, been isolated from other domains of cognitive psychology. On the present view, this isolation is a mistake: No task requires only reasoning, and few tasks require no reasoning at all" (p. 309). Holland, Holyoak, Nisbett, and Thagard (1986) asserted that understanding inductive processes is a central issue in philosophy, psychology, and artificial intelligence, yet so little progress has been made that "induction, which has been called the 'scandal of philosophy,' has become the scandal of psychology and artificial intelligence as well" (p. 1).

Because of advances originating in information processing and cognitive science over the last decade, the prognosis for the study of inductive reasoning is much more positive than its history has been. Rather than attempt to exhaustively review recent research on inductive reasoning, we focus on emerging themes and approaches that reflect promising trends in the field. First, we describe, in a general way, the domain of induction, and we note some of the characteristics of inductive reasoning that make it of special interest in cognitive science. Next, we describe two approaches to the study of induction, the *cognitive-components approach* and the *pragmatic approach*. Both of these approaches fall within the scope of information-processing metatheory and have considerable potential for linking the study of inductive reasoning with mainstream lines of research. In the cognitive-components approach, familiar methods from the information-processing toolbox are used to generate detailed descriptions of the processes and representations used to solve induction problems. In the pragmatic approach, researchers have attempted to broaden the scope of inquiry to include a wider range of phenomena than have been studied traditionally under the heading of induction, with the goal of making the study of induction a focal point of an interdisciplinary cognitive science. In describing each approach, we note how induction is defined, we describe some illustrative research, and we evaluate the potential for contributions toward establishing the study of induction as a vital topic in the domains of cognitive science. Themes that emerge from our analysis include (1) the importance of recognizing that inductive reasoning has been defined and studied in quite different ways; (2) the central role that knowledge plays in constraining inductive reasoning; and (3) the need to integrate different approaches to ensure the vitality of research on inductive processes. Readers interested in other windows on inductive reasoning are encouraged to examine recent papers on the topic (Greeno & Simon, 1988; Holyoak & Nisbett, 1988; Holyoak & Spellman, 1993; Johnson-Laird, 1988, 1993; Osherson, Smith, Wilkie, Lopez, & Shafir, 1990; Pellegrino, 1985; Rips, 1990; Smith, 1989).

I. CHARACTERISTICS OF INDUCTION

Despite considerable agreement over the centrality of inductive reasoning to human cognition and development, the domain is difficult to define precisely, in part because *induction* and *reasoning* are used in a variety of ways by cognitive scientists.[1] Examples of induction are helpful, nevertheless, for conveying some of its central properties. Consider a scenario that is common in preschools and elementary schools. Children are presented with a variety of objects and a "water table," and their task is to discover the characteristics of objects that float as distinguished from objects that do not float. A child might observe that a piece of cork floats and that a wooden cube floats. The child might then conclude that wooden things float. To summarize this sequence of events:

P1: The cork is wood and it floats.
P2: The cube is wood and it floats.
C3: Therefore, wooden things float.

P1 and P2 are called premises, and C3 is the student's conclusion. Notice that C3 is an inference about all members of the class of wooden things, and it is based on two particular instances from that class. This conclusion thus meets the typical dictionary definition of induction, specifically, that an induction is an inference of a generalized conclusion from particular instances (or reasoning from part to whole).

Notice also that the student has engaged in precisely the kind of hypothesis-generating process that characterizes scientific investigations. He or she might go further and generate an experiment to test this hypothesis by finding another wooden item and determining whether it floats.

P4: Wooden things float.
P5: The toy fish is wooden.
C6: The toy fish (should) float.

This sequence is an example of deduction, which is typically defined as an inference in which a conclusion about a particular instance (C6) follows necessarily from general statements (P4 and P5). Note that the student's inductive conclusion (C3) has become a premise (P4) for deductive inference. A student following this entire protocol could be described as combining induction and deduction (often called hypothetico-deductive reasoning) to solve the problem posed by the teacher. (Real children rarely behave so ideally. For related research, see Kuhn, Amsel, and O'Loughlin [1988] and Sodian, Zaitchik, and Carey [1991].)

Dictionary definitions of induction are not entirely inaccurate, but they do not convey explicitly the features of induction that make it interesting and perplexing to cognitive scientists. An exhaustive list of these features is beyond the scope of this chapter and, in any event, would be difficult to compile because theorists differ in what they view as the defining features of induction. Instead, we describe three core characteristics that we believe a wide range of cognitive scientists would judge to be central to induction.

First, *inductive processes produce a net increase in knowledge.* In the water table example, for instance, the child's conclusion is a proposition about the nature of the world that is new to the child and thus represents a potentially significant increase in the child's knowledge. The notion that induction increases knowledge has been elaborated in a semiformal fashion by Johnson-Laird (1988, 1993), who defined induction as "any process of thought yielding a conclusion that increases the semantic information in its initial observations or premises" (1993, p. 60). In Johnson-Laird's view, semantic information increases to the extent that some alternative possibilities are eliminated by the induced conclusion, *if* the conclusion is true. For example, if C3 is true, then it reduces the set of alternative possibilities; the child should no longer entertain the possible conclusion that wooden things do not float, or that corks float but other wooden things do not. In contrast, deduction never results in increased semantic information, although it may result in explicit statements of knowledge that are more or less implicit in the premises. (For a thorough explication of the relation between reasoning and changes in semantic information, see Johnson-Laird, 1993, chap. 2.) Recognition that inductive processes increase semantic information has helped to extend the study of induction from a rather limited set of logical puzzles and paper-and-pencil tasks to a wide variety of learning phenomena of central interest to comparative, developmental, and cognitive psychologists (e.g., Holland et al., 1986).

Second, *an induction is risky* in the sense that it may or may not be true, even if the premises are true. In our example, C3 seems like a reasonable conclusion, given the premises, but it *might* be wrong. In fact, the student might have never formulated that conclusion if the wooden cube in P2 had been made of ebony (which sinks). Induction is wonderful for generating new knowledge, but the cost of increased semantic information is the risk of being wrong. As Johnson-Laird (1993) noted, "induction should come with a government health warning" (1988, p. 438). This characteristic of induction contrasts sharply with deduction. In deduction, a valid conclusion must be true if the premises are true; if the conclusion proves to be false, then one or more of the premises must be false. In induction, a faulty conclusion does not mean that the premises are necessarily suspect. In fact, it makes more sense to discuss the *strength* of an inductive argument, that is, how compelling the conclusion is given the premises, than the *validity* of the argument (Rips, 1990). Thus inductive processes produce new but inevitably uncertain knowledge. Because knowledge typically is acquired in environments that are inherently uncertain and adaptive processes must not only deal with but capitalize on uncertainty, the study of induction provides a window on adaptive mechanisms of change (Holland et al., 1986).

Third, *inductive processes must be severely constrained if they are to produce plausible conclusions.* Philosophers and psychologists have long recognized that an infinite number of inductive conclusions, most of them irrelevant and/or trivial, can be generated from a set of premises. After observing P1 and P2, for example, what prevents our student from generating a slew of highly inappropriate conclusions, such as "everything floats" or "Piaget was wrong"? Somehow the search through the space of possibilities must be selective and constrained so that a plausible conclusion or set of conclusions can be generated. This general problem is referred to as the *issue of constraints* (e.g., Holland et al., 1986). The necessity of constraints on induction has led to the conclusion that we cannot understand induction as an independent, logical system that is largely independent of one's knowledge of the world. Indeed, such knowledge must be one important source of constraints (Johnson-Laird, 1993). This state of affairs has made induction a messy domain for many philosophers and psychologists, especially when contrasted with the relatively neat and self-contained nature of deduction. These same characteristics, however, make induction an appealing domain for researchers who seek to develop a broad theory of thinking and adaptation (Holland et al., 1986; Sternberg, 1986).

II. A COGNITIVE-COMPONENTS APPROACH

Efforts to describe and explain behavior often proceed at three different but related levels (Marr, 1982). At a *computational* level the goal is to describe *what* the mind accomplished in terms of specific functions. At this level, the enterprise is somewhat like characterizing what a computer program can do, without specifying how. At an *algorithmic* level the goal is to describe *how* the mind operates in terms of internal mechanisms and activities that serve the functions described at the computational level. Work at the algorithmic level is similar to describing the software routines and memory structures of a computer program. At an *implementational* level the goal is to describe the material nature of the system on which algorithms are implemented, much like describing particular hardware configurations of a computer. Notice that each level is related to but not entirely constrained by the others. For example, a certain computational function *could* be served by many distinctly different algorithms, and a certain algorithm *could* be implemented in many distinctly different ways. This three-level scheme provides a useful, if somewhat simplified, view of the research enterprise in cognitive science.

To this point we have described some general characteristics of *what* the mind accomplishes in induction, but we have had little to say about *how*. Many researchers who use an information-processing framework tend to focus their efforts on the algorithmic level of description in an attempt to identify the processes that underlie performance and the information on which those processes operate. When applied to performance on reasoning tasks, their goal is to identify the *cognitive components* of performance in terms of the processes and representations used to solve problems, as well as how these components are organized (Pellegrino & Glaser, 1979).

In the study of induction, researchers proceeded initially by analyzing performance on a variety of tasks that are assumed to involve inductive reasoning. Included are such tasks as analogy, series completion and classification. Simple analogies typically are of the form "A is to B as C is to D." An example is "CAT is to LION as DOG is to __?__," and the task is to generate a suitable D term (e.g., WOLF). To solve this task, a person must induce semantic relations between CAT and LION that, when applied to DOG, could serve as a basis for generating a plausible answer. In series completion (e.g., 1, 8, 27, 64, __?__), people must find a pattern in a series of stimuli and generate an answer that represents an extension to that pattern. In classification, a group of items are presented (e.g., several different vegetables), along with one or more extra items (e.g., a watermelon and a potato). The task is to induce the relations that define group membership and to decide whether the extra item(s) properly belong in the group. Notice that induction is central in each case: the problem solver has to infer a general rule or relation based on an analysis of specific items. Moreover, the number of potential rules or relations is large, and so the process of selection must be constrained and is inherently risky. Performance on problems such as these tends to correlate relatively highly across individuals, and consequently these tasks have been used for decades in tests of intelligence to measure inductive reasoning (Thurstone & Thurstone, 1941), general intelligence (Spearman, 1923), and fluid analytic ability (Cattell, 1971). Notice that rather than proceeding from an explicit and detailed computational analysis, the domain was defined initially by a collection of tasks thought to elicit inductive reasoning.

The prototypic cognitive-components approach to studying inductive reasoning is to generate hypotheses about the representations and processes people use to solve these tasks. Measures of performance such as latency data, accuracy data, and verbal self-reports are used to identify plausible models and to rule out competing hypotheses. In the majority of studies the focus is on a single task (e.g., series completion), but comparisons across tasks have been conducted to identify common processes (e.g., Sternberg & Gardner, 1983). In principle, this approach could be used to define what inductive reasoning is, in process terms, and how it differs from deductive reasoning and other forms of thinking. That is, instead of relying solely on *computational* analyses of what is accomplished by certain types of reasoning, it may be possible to make distinctions on the basis of the processes people actually use (Sternberg, 1986).

Many of the information-processing psychologists who have worked on inductive reasoning view the identification of process models as an inter-mediate step toward other goals. Much of the research has been motivated by an interest in understanding pervasive individual differences in cognition. Process analyses of performance on tasks that typically reflect individual differences, such as tasks of inductive reasoning, provide a basis for identifying the source of those differences in terms of processes and representations (e.g., Pellegrino & Glaser, 1979; Sternberg, 1977). The loci of developmental change might be specified in a similar manner (e.g., Sternberg & Rifkin, 1979). Finally, some researchers viewed this approach as having considerable potential for providing a basis for improving instruction (Pellegrino & Glaser, 1980). Specifically, process-based assessments of learning difficulties might enable the design of instruction that matches the needs of particular students, and assessments of skilled performance might provide process-based objectives for instruction. The interest in individual differences, developmental change, and instruction was formative and con-tributed to the direction of the research.[2] Because our focus is limited to the analysis of inductive reasoning, however, we will not attempt to evaluate the cognitive-components approach with respect to its impact on differential, developmental, and instructional research.

A. Identifying Processes and Representations

To illustrate application of the cognitive-components approach to the study of inductive reasoning, we have chosen to focus primarily on a few proto-typic studies that help to define the direction of research in the area. Using information-processing models and methods, Sternberg (1977) identified and measured a handful of component processes adults use to solve verbal, geometric, and pictorial analogies. According to Sternberg, subjects had to *encode* the terms of the analogy (A, B, C, and D), *infer* the relation between A and B, and *map* the relation between A and C so that he or she could then *apply* the A–B relation to C and generate an ideal D. These four processes are followed by a *justification* process if the subject needs to select the best answer from among a set of alternatives that does not contain the ideal answer. Finally, the subject *responds*. Using solution latency as the primary dependent measure, Sternberg tested a variety of models containing these processes. The best fitting model, generally, was one in which inference from A to B was serial and exhaustive, whereas application was serial and self-terminating; that is, on false or invalid analogies subjects terminated processing of C and D terms as soon as a mismatch with the A–B relation was found.

Sternberg's (1977) focus on the identification and organization of compo-nent processes dominated cognitive-components research, and little atten-tion was paid initially to discovering the information that subjects encode

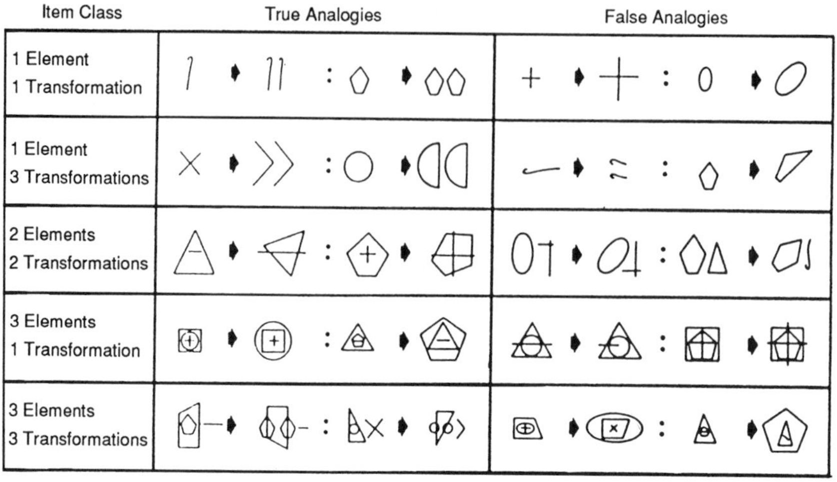

FIGURE 1 Examples of true–false analogies. From "Components of Geometric Analogy Solution" by T. M. Mulholland, J. W. Pellegrino, and R. Glaser, 1980, *Cognitive Psychology, 12,* p. 261. Copyright 1980 by Academic Press. Reprinted by permission.

and represent when solving analogies. In Sternberg's work, for example, simplifying assumptions were made about the measurement of relations between terms in verbal and geometric analogies so that questions about how individuals represented semantic or figural content could be ignored. An attempt to begin addressing questions about the interaction of content and process was made by Mulholland, Pellegrino, and Glaser (1980), who sought to identify how people solve true–false geometric analogy problems, such as those in Figure 1. (The reader is encouraged to try these problems before proceeding.)

Based on previous work in artificial intelligence (Evans, 1968), Mulholland et al. proposed that solution depends on processes required to (1) decompose complex figures into constituent elements and (2) identify specific transformations that linked pairs of figures (A and B, C and D). To solve the bottom problem in Figure 1, for example, a person presumably must decompose A into three elements and then identify the transformations applied to each of those elements to generate B. To solve the second problem from the top, subjects must identify three transformations performed on the single element in A to generate B. When the relevant transformations have been identified, the next task is to process the C and D terms so that the A → B transformation(s) can be compared with the C → D transformation(s). If a match is found, the analogy is judged to be true. If the comparison produces no match or only a partial match, then the analogy is judged to be false. If this analysis is generally correct, then problem

difficulty, as measured by solution latency and accuracy, should vary directly as a function of the number of elements and transformations in the
problems.

Using psychometric tests of reasoning to guide their construction of
stimuli, Mulholland et al. (1980) generated true–false geometric analogies
by combining six types of elements (e.g., circle, oval, cross) and six types of
transformations (e.g., rotation, reflection, increase or decrease in size). Latencies were found to increase markedly as a function of both the number of
elements and the number of transformations in a problem. Moreover, the
effects of transformations and elements were not strictly additive. For example, the best fitting function for latencies on positive trials was

$$RT = 425T + 358E + 75TE + 797$$

where RT is reaction time or solution latency in milliseconds, T is the
number of transformations, E is the number of elements, and the intercept
(797 ms) represents the time for processes that are assumed to be common
and constant for all problems (e.g., the time for a manual response). This
function accounted for 97% of the sums of squares in the latency data. The
presence of the multiplicative TE term implies a degree of curvilinearity in
the data, such that latencies increase by more than would be expected with
a simple additive model as the number of transformations and elements
grows. Mulholland et al. speculated that this curvilinearity reflects subjects'
difficulties in keeping track of the original elements, the transformations,
and the newly transformed elements as the number of transformations
grows. The suggestion is that this sort of mental bookkeeping is limited by
the capacity of working memory. This interpretation was supported by an
analysis of error rates on positive problems, which indicated that subjects
were particularly likely to make errors when multiple transformations were
applied to a single element. Based on their theoretical speculations about the
number of working-memory placekeepers that would be necessary to avoid
confusion, Mulholland et al. developed a general function for the probability of making an error on positive problems:

$$P(\text{error}) = 1 - (1 - \alpha)^T (1 - \lambda^{M-\lambda}$$

where α is the probability of incorrectly identifying or applying a transformation, T is the number of transformations, λ is the maximum amount of
information that can be held in working memory, and M is the number of
memory placekeepers required for particular problems. Notice that as M
approaches the limit λ the probability of error increases dramatically, as
would be expected if the load on working memory reaches capacity limitations. The best fitting version of this equation accounted for 93% of the
sums of squares with $\alpha = .044$ and $\lambda = 5.8$. The values of both parameters
are plausible and, as Mulholland et al. noted, "the value of λ is quite close to

the magical number 7 that is often cited as the capacity limit of short-term or working memory" (p. 268).

Mulholland et al. (1980) went on to propose a detailed, information-processing model of how geometric analogy problems are solved with encoding, decomposition, and inference processes. The critical contribution of Mulholland et al.'s work, in combination with Sternberg's previous research, was the demonstration that a pervasive form of induction—analogical reasoning—could be described in terms of a series of processes that encoded and decomposed stimuli, inferred relations, made comparisons among inferred relations, and operated within constraints imposed by working memory limitations. One shortcoming of this research stems from the fact that the kinds of knowledge required for solution of these analogies was fairly impoverished. In Mulholland et al.'s study, for example, subjects needed to have only declarative knowledge of a relatively small number of elements and transformations. To have broad applicability, models of inductive reasoning must incorporate hypotheses about how subjects use rich knowledge domains to solve problems.

Although the focus of cognitive-components research continued to be on the identification and measurement of specific processes, some research was addressed toward answering questions about representation. An early contribution was provided by Rumelhart and Abrahamson (1973), who sought to determine how the structure of semantic knowledge might affect analogical reasoning. They noted that some types of analogical reasoning are based on judgments of similarity among concepts; that is, when people solve an analogy of the form "A is to B as C is to __?__," they essentially search for an answer, D, that is similar to C in the same way that B is similar to A. Rumelhart and Abrahamson speculated that if these concepts are represented mentally in a multidimensional Euclidean space, then judgments of similarity might vary inversely with psychological distance in this space. They tested this hypothesis by presenting subjects with analogies constructed with names of mammals, such as "rat is to pig as goat is to ____," followed by four answer options. Henley (1969) had previously shown that adults' knowledge of mammals, as revealed by judgments of similarity, reflect a Euclidean space with three dimensions (size, ferocity, and humanness). If similarity judgments in this semantic space are critical for solving mammal-name analogies, then subjects' judgments about solutions should be predictable from Henley's data. Indeed, subjects rank ordered various answer alternatives in nearly perfect accordance with predictions. Rumelhart and Abrahamson recognized that not all verbal analogies could be solved in such a multidimensional space; hierarchical concepts, for example, would require a different sort of mental representation. The enduring contribution of their work is the recognition that constraints on analogical and, more generally, inductive reasoning may stem in part from the way that semantic knowledge is structured.

Sternberg and Gardner (1983, Experiments 1 and 2) incorporated assumptions about analogical processes (Mulholland et al., 1980; Sternberg, 1977) with Rumelhart and Abrahamson's (1973) insight about the role of semantic structure in a clever pair of experiments designed to test notions about aspects of inductive reasoning that are common to different kinds of tasks. First they replicated Rumelhart and Abrahamson's (1973) findings with verbal analogies and extended these results to series completion and classification tasks. For example, subjects' judgments of answers to complete the series "*squirrel, chipmunk, __?__* " was well predicted by extending a line through *squirrel* and *chipmunk* in Henley's (1969) three-dimensional space. Similarly, when subjects were asked to rank order several answer alternatives according to how well they fit in a group consisting of *zebra, giraffe, goat,* their answers were predicted from the locations of the alternatives with respect to the locations of the three instances in Henley's space. Next, Sternberg and Gardner used semantic distance among mammals in Henley's space as a basis for estimating times for specific solution components. The critical assumption here was that temporal indices of inductive processes varied as a function of psychological distance in a highly structured semantic space.

This experiment was successful in the sense that certain components appeared to be common to performance on all three induction tasks. In some respects, however, the results were disappointing. For example, the *inference* component, which most directly relates to inductive reasoning, apparently was not sufficiently reliable to be estimated across all three tasks. Thus one of the sources of commonality in inductive reasoning that presumably should have emerged did not. Nevertheless, the study represents an insightful attempt to augment a process-oriented model with constraints imposed by semantic structure.

In a recent and compelling extension of the cognitive-components approach, Carpenter, Just, and Shell (1990) developed a theory to explain how university students solve problems on the Raven Progressive Matrices Test. An example of a matrix problem is provided in Figure 2. To solve these problems, one must induce relations among figures in the rows and/or columns and use these relations to generate an answer. The Raven test is used widely in clinical and research settings, and scores on the test are generally assumed to reflect analytic reasoning ability.

Carpenter et al. (1990) developed two models. One, called FAIRAVEN, represents a theory of how moderately skilled university students solve matrices, and the second, BETTERAVEN, is an enhanced version to account for the performance of more highly skilled students. These models were implemented as computer simulations, and their outputs were found to match, to a reasonable degree, the error profiles, eye-movement data, and self-reports of moderately skilled and highly skilled subjects.

The models are far too complex to be described thoroughly in this chap-

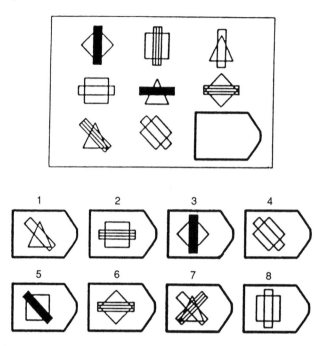

FIGURE 2   A sample matrix problem. From "What One Intelligence Test Measures: A Theoretical Account of the Processing in the Raven Progressive Matrices Test" by P. A. Carpenter, M. A. Just, and P. Shell, 1990, *Psychological Review, 97,* p. 407. Copyright 1990 by the American Psychological Association. Reprinted by permission.

ter, but some of their similarities and differences deserve mention. Both models included a number of productions to accomplish *perceptual analyses* and *conceptual analyses*. Perceptual analyses include encoding, finding correspondences between adjacent figures, and recognizing differences between adjacent figures. Because correspondences among figures are often ambiguous, both models include a small set of heuristics that help to identify possible correspondences. Conceptual analyses, performed on the outputs of perceptual analyses, include processes to induce rules that apply to an entire row of figures and processes that use these rules to generate an answer. FAIRAVEN and BETTERAVEN are similar in many respects, but they differ in two interesting ways. First, BETTERAVEN contains more knowledge about relations among figures than does FAIRAVEN. At the perceptual level BETTERAVEN has more heuristics for finding correspondences between figures, and at the conceptual level it has a larger set of rules for use in the induction process. Second, BETTERAVEN has a goal monitor that enables it to organize and execute processes in an efficient manner, whereas FAIRAVEN, with no such monitor, often suffered from failures due to working-memory limitations. Thus individual differences on matrix tasks appear to reflect differences in knowledge about relations among the stimuli and differences in memory-management processes.

Carpenter et al.'s (1990) research is an impressive demonstration of the potential power of the cognitive-components approach in generating specific models to account for performance on tasks of inductive reasoning. Of special note is that Carpenter et al. used computer simulations to test the sufficiency and plausibility of their models, and that they used a wide range of dependent measures (eye movements, errors, and comparisons of self-reports about induced rules with the rules used by the simulation). Their models are compelling, but of course they are not yet complete. For example, the computer simulations had to only recognize, rather than induce from scratch, the conceptual relations among figures. Moreover, the simulations did not have to read instructions and organize solution strategies, as human subjects must do. University students probably do not differ much in this skill on the Raven task, as Carpenter et al. noted, but induction of the constraints of a task may be critical for less savvy subjects or in situations where test instructions are ambiguous (Bisanz, Bisanz, & LeFevre, 1984).

B. An Integrative Theory

As in some of the studies described in the previous section, most studies on inductive reasoning tend to be focused on a single task (e.g., geometric analogies) and to involve models that highlight the roles of a few (of many possible) processes and/or a few (of many possible) forms of knowledge. To counteract this trend, Sternberg (1986) proposed a framework for developing a unified theory of reasoning, for providing a theoretical definition of reasoning, and for distinguishing between inductive and deductive reasoning in terms of processes. The framework includes postulates about (1) the functions served by different kinds of reasoning processes; (2) inferential rules used during reasoning; (3) mediators that influence how well specific processes make use of inferential rules; and (4) definitions of reasoning and distinctions between inductive and deductive reasoning. These postulates exceed the usually narrow confines of cognitive-components theories and constitute a statement, however wishful, about what a broad theory of reasoning needs to include. We discuss each one in turn.

1. Different Kinds of Reasoning Processes

According to Sternberg (1986), reasoning involves component processes that serve three types of functions. *Selective encoding* processes distinguish relevant from irrelevant information in the stimulus and store the selected information in working memory. *Selective comparison* processes are responsible for determining which information from long-term memory is relevant for solution and will be retrieved and stored in working memory. *Selective combination* processes analyze, manipulate, and integrate the information placed in working memory by selective encoding and comparison processes.

At this level no commitment is made about what the component processes are that constitute selective encoding, comparison, and combination, or how these components are organized; that is, these three types of functions are computational requirements rather than algorithmic specifications. In Sternberg's (1986) theory, selective encoding, selective comparison, and selective combination are best viewed as functions that are served by component processes that may vary in type and organization from task to task.

2. Inferential Rules

Reasoning involves the use of elements of knowledge that Sternberg describes as inferential rules. These rules include heuristics, mental guidelines, algorithms, procedural rules, and declarative rules. Procedural rules include specific performance components (e.g., inferring the relation between A and B in an analogy, or mapping the relation between A and C) and general strategies for combining performance components. Declarative rules also include knowledge about possible semantic bases for solving problems. The appropriateness of procedural rules varies primarily as a function of the type or form of a problem (e.g., inductive vs. deductive problems), whereas the appropriateness of declarative rules varies primarily as a function of the content of the problem (e.g., geometric analogies vs. verbal analogies).

3. Mediators

Any variable that affects the availability or the accessibility of inferential rules is called a mediator. For example, the extent to which a particular inferential rule is used to solve a problem can be influenced by other problems the person has just solved (*contextual probability*). Some inferential rules are more familiar and likely to be employed than others, even if the others are known (*entrenchment*). Problem solvers occasionally have no knowledge of some inferential rules (*prior knowledge*). Use of specific inferential rules also could be constrained by working memory capacity or by representational capacity (a person's ability to represent information, e.g., spatially as opposed to verbally).

4. Definitions and Distinctions

A number of special definitions and distinctions make Sternberg's (1986) theory unique. First, consider his distinction between a reasoning task and other tasks: "A task is a reasoning task if and only if its solution involves the mediated and controlled application of inferential rules for purposes of selective encoding, selective comparison, or selective combination" (p. 293). That is, if a person automatically retrieves a solution, the task does not involve reasoning; if a person executes controlled processes (i.e., conscious and effortful processes) that can be characterized as selective encoding, comparison, or combination, the task involves reasoning. Use of automatic and controlled processes can vary from individual to individual and from problem to problem, even on problems that have the same apparent structure (e.g., LeFevre & Bisanz, 1986). Second, the extent to which a task involves reasoning is a matter of degree: the more controlled the processes, the greater the degree of reasoning. Third, inductive and deductive reasoning are distinguished by their psychological and algorithmic properties, not only by their philosophical or computational properties. Specifically, Sternberg claims that inductive reasoning is difficult because of demands on selective encoding and selective comparison processes, both of which involve discriminating relevant from irrelevant information. Moreover, there is no logically determined set of information that must be selected. In contrast, difficulty on deductive problems arises mostly from demands on selective combination processes, and these combinations are constrained so that certain combinations are logically correct and others are not.

5. Observations

We have described Sternberg's (1986) theory primarily because it represents a radical extension of the usual, task-oriented studies that dominate the cognitive-components approach. As is often the case with a sketch of a broad theory, many of his arguments were supported with rational analyses and anecdotes rather than with empirical research. A thorough evaluation of Sternberg's framework would exceed our space limitations, but we wish to note a few special characteristics. On the negative side, we note first that some of the definitions and distinctions appear to be difficult to use unambiguously. For example, the distinction between automatic and controlled processing is pervasive in cognitive psychology, but interpretation and measurement of the difference has been hotly debated among researchers (e.g., Zbrodoff & Logan, 1986). Using such a contentious distinction for the important theoretical definition of reasoning without specifying how the distinction is to be operationalized in the context of real tasks may prove to be a difficulty.

Second, characterization of the three types of processing functions is not entirely clear, and so the process-oriented distinction between inductive and deductive reasoning is not as compelling as it might be. For example, Sternberg's (1986) distinction between inductive and deductive reasoning reflects results of laboratory studies in which subjects solve a large number of similar problems. Many difficult analogies or series completions, however, appear to call for the invention or construction of new relations based on information in working memory, as opposed to retrieval of relations stored in semantic memory. If this speculation is correct, then the source of difficulty would involve what Sternberg called selective combination (manipulations in working memory) and not, as Sternberg maintained, only selective encoding (of stimulus material) or selective comparison (obtaining relevant information from long-term memory). In fact, induction is often very constructive, such as the development of a hypothesis in scientific work or of new taxonomic categories. This observation seems to implicate the operation of a selective combination of elements in working memory rather than the selection of information from long-term memory. Thus the proposed distinction between inductive and deductive reasoning may have boundary conditions that significantly limit its applicability.

Third, although Sternberg recognized the importance of inferential rules and mediators, the elements in these categories are only sketched out in an illustrative fashion and, more important, the way in which these rules are invoked and used is vague. We return to this point in the next section.

Despite these shortcomings, some distinctive characteristics of Sternberg's (1986) theory make it an appealing source of ideas for researchers. First, Sternberg's approach is unabashedly psychological, rather than philosophical. For example, *reasoning* is defined in terms of information-processing characteristics, as are induction and deduction.

> No attempt is made to resolve any philosophical questions regarding the inductive–deductive distinction. . . . The philosophical problem of distinguishing between induction and deduction refers to the intrinsic nature of each kind of reasoning and how each differs from the other. The psychological problem, on the other hand, refers to the information processes used to solve induction and deduction problems. (p. 293)

The attempt to disassociate philosophical and information-processing goals may prove to be shortsighted because considerable potential exists for each approach to inform the other. Our impression is, however, that quasi-philosophical concerns have played a dominant, and sometimes suffocating, role in psychological research. Sternberg's approach to defining inductive reasoning is algorithmic and involves the use of necessary and sufficient features. Taken to its logical conclusion, this approach implies that there is no such thing as a "reasoning task." Whether reasoning is involved in solving a task, or the extent to which it is involved, is determined by the way in which the person solves the task, not by the nominal structure of the task itself. This view has obvious implications for the psychometric assessment of reasoning and for the study of reasoning with laboratory tasks. The costs and benefits of this approach deserve careful consideration in the cognitive science community.

Second, although Sternberg (1986) was decidedly vague about the nature of inferential rules and mediators, by incorporating them in his framework he highlighted the need to develop models that include general characteristics of human reasoning, as well as mechanisms by which general inferential rules and mediators, once identified, can influence the solution process. During a period in which theories tend to be relatively narrow in scope, Sternberg's focus on "unities of reasoning" across tasks is a welcome counterweight (cf. Siegler, 1986).

C. Summary and Evaluation

By some criteria, researchers using the cognitive-components approach have had considerable success in implementing parts of the information-processing agenda in the study of inductive reasoning. Tasks have been identified, largely with the help of the psychometric literature, that presumably involve inductive reasoning. Researchers have identified and measured specific processes and produced plausible models of how these processes are organized in the solution of these tasks. They have demonstrated how knowledge representations can influence solutions, although this part of the agenda has been somewhat less emphasized. Finally, some researchers (e.g., Sternberg, 1986) have sought to outline the elements of more comprehensive theories than are presently available. Given the relative youth of the enterprise, the cognitive-components approach has yielded useful insights about inductive thinking.

The major shortcoming of most cognitive-components research on inductive reasoning is that it contributes little toward what many people regard as the central psychological enigma relating to induction, the issue of constraints. Because induction is inherently indeterminate, a satisfactory theory must specify how the search through the space of possibilities is constrained so that plausible answers are generated. The lack of theoretical concern with this problem is striking. In Sternberg's theory, for example, the roles of *selective* encoding, *selective* comparison, and *selective* combination are central, but aside from general comments on the possible importance of inferential rules and mediators, no clues are provided about *how* processes that serve these functions manage to be selective. Pellegrino and Glaser (1980) touched on the problem of constraints when they noted the importance of *representational variability* in determining task difficulty. Representational variability refers to the fact that some analogies, because of the semantically rich domains on which they are based, are more likely than others to elicit a variety of interpretations and representations. Implicit in their writing is the recognition that the process by which an individual navigates through these alternative representations is critical, but no clues are provided about how this function is accomplished.

Insensitivity to the issue of constraints may have contributed to, and arisen from, the ways in which induction has been studied. For example, to make inductive reasoning tractable for traditional, latency-based, information-processing analyses, researchers often have found it necessary to severely limit the diversity of problems and to require subjects to solve huge numbers of problems. In Mulholland et al.'s (1980) study, for example, although some problems were quite difficult, successful solution depended on knowledge of only six transformations. Moreover, subjects accessed these six transformations repetitively over the course of 460 trials. In Experiment 3 of Sternberg and Gardner's (1983) study, subjects completed over 1400 induction problems. It seems reasonable to question whether the kinds of induction measured under these conditions bear much relation to the process of inducing characteristics of items that float, the structure of the relations among chemical elements, the mechanisms of evolution, or the principles of economic change. To the extent that aspects of performance on a large number of trials might become relatively automated, the solution process may not even qualify as reasoning (e.g., under Sternberg's constraint that automatic processes do not constitute reasoning). In an effort to study inductive reasoning with traditional information-processing methods, researchers may have wrung out many of the characteristics, such as use of a semantically rich knowledge base, that are essential for addressing the issue of constraints.[3]

More generally, the trajectory of the cognitive-components approach to inductive reasoning may reflect, in a microcosm, many of the advantages and disadvantages of using common information-processing methods. The cognitive-components approach can yield coherent and detailed theories of performance. The successes of the approach help to highlight some of its shortcomings, such as the failure to extend the theories in detailed and explicit ways to solutions involving rich semantic domains with complex and varied problem representations. The information-processing framework is not inimical to incorporating such characteristics, but methods and theories that have dominated the cognitive-components approach are not sufficient for the task of establishing the study of induction as a vital topic in cognitive science. Cognitive-components research will remain important and useful for identifying component processes that need to be incorporated in any complete theory of inductive reasoning, but it needs to be integrated with research on the "inferential rules" and "mediators," in Sternberg's (1986) terms, that is critical for solving the issue of constraints. At this point we turn to an approach that falls within the scope of information-processing meta-theory (Kail & Bisanz, 1992; Massaro & Cowan, 1993; Palmer & Kimchee, 1986) but that is designed to generate research on the issue of constraints.

III. A PRAGMATIC APPROACH

The importance of inductive reasoning and the failure of philosophers, psychologists, and computer scientists to explain induction in a satisfactory manner have led to the development of an interdisciplinary approach to the study of induction. The tenets of this approach are elaborated in a book by Holland et al. (1986) called, simply, *Induction*. The ultimate goal of this approach is a unified and comprehensive theory of induction that would use an interrelated set of theoretical concepts and computational mechanisms to account for the widest possible range of empirical phenomena. The orientation is *pragmatic* in the sense that the adaptive functions of inductive activities, as well as the contexts in which those activities occur, are regarded as central for understanding induction. This orientation contrasts sharply with *syntactic* approaches, such as the cognitive-components approach, in which the focus is on identifying the rules and/or steps that characterize induction and little if any attention is paid to adaptive functions and general contexts.

The breadth of the pragmatic approach is assured in two ways: (1) inductive processes are defined at a computational level as "all inferential processes that expand knowledge in the face of uncertainty" (Holland et al., 1986, p. 1); and (2) the goal is to develop a general theory of induction in cognitive systems from "man to mouse to microchip" (p. 2). As a consequence, and in stark contrast to the cognitive-components approach and most other orientations, the legitimate domain of induction potentially includes a vast array of phenomena, from conditioning in rats to scientific discovery in humans. Rather than defining the domain narrowly to optimize the chance of developing an explanation that fits observations, these investigators take breadth of application as an important measure of the success of their framework.

When applied to human reasoning, the tasks used by pragmatic researchers are not limited to classical "inductive" tasks, such as analogies, series completions, and classification problems as found on intelligence tests. Instead, the focus is on problem-solving situations of "the fuzzy, ill-defined sorts . . . that abound in real life" (Holland et al., 1986, p. 11). In some cases people are asked to make a generalization based on a number of observations.

> Imagine that you are an explorer who has landed on a little known island in the Southeastern Pacific. . . . Suppose you encounter a new bird, the shreeble. It is blue in color. What percentage of all shreebles on the island do you expect to be blue? (Nisbett, Krantz, Jepson, & Kunda, 1983, p. 348)

In another condition people read a story that differs only in the number of birds observed (e.g., "You see twenty such birds. They are all blue in color."). The question is whether numerical information influences the induction people make. In other tasks people are required to provide explanations for observed phenomena.

> In general the major league baseball player who wins Rookie of the Year does not perform as well in his second year. This is clear in major league baseball in the past 10 years. In the American League, 8 Rookies of the Year have done

worse in their second year; only two have done better. In the National League, the Rookie of the Year has done worse the second year 9 times out of 10. Why do you suppose the Rookie of the Year tends not to do as well his second year? (Fong, Krantz, & Nisbett, 1986, p. 279)

People also are asked to make predictions or to justify choices.

It is the first week of the winter term. Henry has signed up for five classes, but plans to take four. Three of these classes he knows he wants, so he must decide between the other two. Both are on subjects interesting to him. The student course evaluations indicate that Course A is better taught. However, he attended the first meeting of both classes and found Course B's session more enjoyable. Which course should he take and why? (Jepson, Krantz, & Nisbett, 1983, p. 501)

In each case people are required to make a conclusion in an uncertain context, and the conclusions function to reduce uncertainty. Consequently, responses to each of these scenarios involve inductive reasoning.

Pragmatic researchers recognize that a central puzzle of induction is how cognitive systems "avoid generating innumerable fruitless hypotheses in their search for useful generalizations[.] The life expectancy of a cognitive system that devoted all its processing resources to exploring misguided inductions would be brief" (Holland et al., 1986, p. 4). The tactic of these investigators in approaching this fundamental problem is to assume that a central task must be to identify "the constraints that ensure that the inferences drawn by a cognitive system will tend to be plausible and relevant to the system's goals" (p. 5). Plausibility is determined with reference to current knowledge, and current knowledge is a product of inferences made in goal-directed problem-solving situations. Thus, the paralyzing possibility of an infinity of hypotheses becomes a search for constraints, either systemic or environmental, that limit or prohibit the types of inductions a cognitive system will make as it attempts to achieve goals.

In the view of Holland et al. (1986), a complete theory of induction and its constraints would involve a program of research in which every empirical phenomenon was well documented and in which the explicitness and sufficiency of explanations for those phenomena were tested by means of implementation as a running computer program. Their work involves both the development of running computer programs and experimental research on a wide range of phenomena relevant to induction. The lines of research they have initiated are clearly "in progress" and are not yet sufficiently advanced to meet their ultimate objectives. In the following sections we describe experimental research focused on the issue of how knowledge constrains inductive reasoning. This work demonstrates how inferential rules and mediators, to use Sternberg's (1986) terms, can be explored. We illustrate their approach by focusing on research on statistical reasoning.

Research has been conducted on other types of inductive reasoning as well (for a summary, see Smith, Langston, & Nisbett, 1992), but the work on statistical reasoning is the most extensive. We close the section by evaluating the claims that Holland et al. make about this larger body of work and its importance to the vitality of research on inductive reasoning.

A. Research on Statistical Reasoning

According to the pragmatic view, inductive reasoning is constrained by inferential rules and by factors that enhance or limit the use of those rules. Inferential rules are abstract units of knowledge that apply across multiple domains and include "logical rules, rules for causal deduction dealing with necessity and sufficiency, contractual rules, including rules for permission and obligation, statistical rules such as the law of large numbers, and decision rules such as cost–benefit rules" (Smith et al., 1992, p. 5). The application of inferential rules is influenced by a number of factors, such as memory decay, encoding of features of events or features relevant to the application of an inferential rule, and the availability of relevant empirical knowledge about a situation. Constraints such as these are similar to Sternberg's (1986) notions about inferential rules and mediators, but in the pragmatic approach research on these constraints is much more central than in the cognitive-components approach.

The potential for the pragmatic approach to illuminate our understanding of rules and mediators is evident in the body of work focused on statistical reasoning. This form of reasoning involves application of a set of inferential rules or heuristics that can be derived from the law of large numbers (i.e., a family of rules including the idea that small samples are less representative of a population than large samples) and the concept of variability (i.e., that the representativeness of a sample is inversely related to its heterogeneity). Other rules related to the law of large numbers are the concept of regression to the mean and the base-rate principle. To illustrate research on rules and mediators, we briefly describe investigations on: (1) conditions that influence whether statistical reasoning is applied; (2) how knowledge about the variability of objects or events affects generalizations; and (3) how inferential rules are learned.

1. Conditions That Cue Statistical Reasoning

In one series of studies Nisbett et al. (1983) demonstrated the types of conditions that will mediate encoding in ways that enhance or inhibit statistical reasoning. Statistical reasoning occurs when one or more of three conditions hold: (1) when the sample space for a single trial is obvious and the process of sampling is clear, as with tossing a coin or dice; (2) an event is characterized by "transparent indeterminism," so that it is easy to recognize the role of chance factors, as in the bounce of a football; or (3) when there are cultural or subcultural prescriptions to reason statistically, as may be the case with sport fans or (we hope) graduate students in psychology.

To demonstrate some of these conditions, Nisbett et al. (1983, Study 3) presented university students with the problem of justifying which of two schools a student, David, should attend. The problem was similar to Henry's class selection problem (presented previously). A small set of brief, superficial personal impressions formed by David during visits to a liberal arts college and an Ivy League university was described as being in conflict with a large set of impressions formed from the experiences of friends who attended these institutions. Previous research had shown that people often ignore the impressions of others when reasoning about these situations, in part because they may not recognize the samplelike nature of their personal experiences. Nisbett et al. reasoned that if a problem could be described in a way that highlights the role of chance in small samples based on personal experience, then people might be more likely to use statistical rules and base their choice on the larger sample of other people's experience.

To examine the effect of cuing, a version of the problem was created in which David drew up a list of things he might like to see on his visits, and then he randomly selected among them to construct his schedule. Students' reasoning on this version was compared to reasoning on another version of the problem where the process for constructing the schedule was not mentioned. Of the students who did not receive the cue, many continued to base their choice on the small number of David's personal experiences. Students who received the cue, however, made more choices based on the larger sample of other people's impressions. Also, more statistical considerations regarding sample adequacy were given as the reason for this choice. These findings led to the general prediction that people are unlikely to reason statistically about whole classes of social events, even though they are capable of doing so, simply because the sample spaces for these events and the chance factors influencing them are opaque. When given an explicit, probabilistic cue, however, people do recognize the samplelike nature of the evidence about events.

In another study, Nisbett et al. (1983, Study 4) provided preliminary evidence that expertise in a problem domain is related to the application of statistical rules. Specifically, they expected that people who have greater experience with the events of a certain kind should be more inclined than people with less experience to understand the distributions underlying events and recognize the operation of chance factors. As a result, people with greater expertise should be more likely than people with less expertise to prefer statistical explanations, and less likely to prefer causal explanations. The domains were sports and acting. They obtained evidence that experience in sports facilitated recognition of regression effects in problems about sports similar to the Rookie of the Year problem presented earlier. Likewise, experience with acting facilitated recognition of regression effects in stories about acting. This study provided evidence that degree of expertise in a problem domain was related to the likelihood of encoding elements of a situation in ways that facilitated the application of statistical rules.

2. The Effects of Knowledge of Variability on Generalization

Work on statistical reasoning also provides a solution to a classic puzzle. The puzzle, long recognized by philosophers such as Hume and Mill, is that a single instance can sometimes be sufficient for a confident generalization, whereas in other occasions numerous instances are insufficient. One early study, conducted by Nisbett et al. (1983), was focused on a phenomenon often considered the prototypical case of inductive reasoning in humans—generalization from a set of instances (e.g., Holland et al., 1986; Smith & Medin, 1981). The study was designed to demonstrate that people represent variability in the world and make use of their estimates of variability when applying statistical heuristics to make inferences. The notion is that knowledge of variability provides the key to this puzzle.

In the study, university students enrolled in an introductory psychology course were presented the generalization problem (presented earlier) about the color of shreebles based on samples of either 1, 3, or 20 observations. They were also told they would encounter several animals, people, and objects. Two features of each type were mentioned. In addition to the shreeble's color, the students were told that the shreeble was encountered nesting in a eucalyptus tree. A native, called a Barratos, was described as brown in color and obese. A rare element called floridium was encountered that burned with a green flame and conducted electricity. Given the sample encountered, students were to estimate the percent of other shreebles, natives, or samples of floridium that they would expect to exhibit each feature.

Scientists presume chemical elements to be homogeneous with respect to most characteristics. At the other extreme, humans are highly heterogeneous with respect to body weight. If subjects shared these views about variability and reasoned statistically, they should have been cautious about generalizing from a single instance when heterogeneity is high, but larger samples should have increased their willingness to generalize. This pattern of results is evident in Figure 3. Furthermore, students' explanations of their estimates provided evidence of this type of reasoning. This study demonstrated that beliefs about the variability of a class of events are important mediators in the use of inferential rules related to statistics. It provides empirical evidence that inductive systems are guided by background knowledge about the variability of classes, objects, and events in the environment.

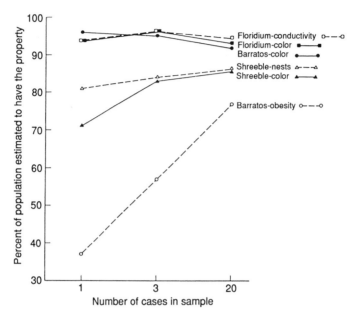

FIGURE 3 Estimates as a function of characteristics and number of cases in each sample. From "The Use of Statistical Heuristics in Everyday Inductive Reasoning" by R. E. Nisbett, D. H. Krantz, D. Jepson, and Z. Kunda, 1983, *Psychological Review, 90,* p. 349. Copyright 1983 by the American Psychological Association. Reprinted by permission.

3. Conditions That Enhance Acquisition of Inferential Rules

Perhaps the most provocative empirical effects to emerge from research on statistical reasoning are from a set of studies that have implications for higher education. These studies are focused on the effects of statistical training at the university level on the acquisition of inferential rules. In the work on conditions that cue statistical reasoning, Nisbett et al. (1983) had demonstrated some of the conditions that enhance or inhibit statistical reasoning. Evidence for the abstract, domain-independent nature of these rules, however, was not definitive.

Evidence that the statistical reasoning of individuals reflected the use of intuitive but abstract and domain-independent rules, rather than local, domain-bound rules, was provided by Fong et al. (1986). The focus of this research was on the acquisition of expertise in the rules themselves, rather than expertise in a domain of events that might mediate their application. These investigators reasoned that if statistical heuristics are abstract, "then it should be possible to improve people's everyday reasoning about everyday events by formal instruction in the rule system, without reference to any domain of everyday events" (Fong et al., 1986, p. 256). This hypothesis was supported with findings from four studies. In one of several conditions in the first study, adults and high school students were given a brief training session about concepts associated with the law of large number and then had to apply these concepts to problems in three different domains. Their performance was compared to performance of individuals in control conditions. There also were conditions in the first and second studies in which subjects were shown how to apply the law of large number to three example problems in a domain, and their ability to induce generalized rules and apply them to new problems in other domains was examined. Their performance was compared to the performance of control subjects. In a third study, the effect of academic training in statistics was examined on statistical reasoning about two versions of an everyday problem about restaurant quality. One version had a strong statistical cue regarding random selection of an item from a menu. Participants were either undergraduates with no statistics, undergraduates who had taken one introductory statistics course, graduate students in psychology who had taken one or more statistics courses, and technical staff at a research laboratory, many of whom were Ph.D. level scientists and all of whom had taken many statistics courses. In the fourth study, male undergraduate students taking a statistics course were contacted either at the beginning or the end of the semester to participate in a telephone survey on students' opinion about sports. During the survey they were required to provide explanations for problems like the Rookie of the Year problem presented at the beginning of this section. The general finding across all conditions and studies was that more instruction was associated with both greater frequency and better quality of statistical reasoning. The statistical reasoning of subjects with less statistical training was most affected by a direct statistical cue.

Finally, evidence has been provided that both undergraduate and graduate students improve on different types of reasoning tasks in ways that can be related to different rule systems taught in various disciplines. Lehman, Lepert, and Nisbett (1988) conducted research with graduate students at two different universities involving both cross-sectional and longitudinal designs. Three types of reasoning were examined. Graduate students in psychology and medicine showed improved statistical and methodological reasoning over a wide range of problems compared to graduate students in law and chemistry. Methodological reasoning involves judgments that require application of a set of rules that enhance understanding of causality in situations where confounding variables are present. It includes rules about the use of control groups, avoiding sample bias, and other problems associated with third variables that limit the conclusions one can draw from an experiment. The improved performance of students in psychology and medicine was attributed to experiences these graduate students were exposed to in how to think about variability and uncertainty in causal relations, as well as to courses they had taken in statistics.

Graduate students in psychology, medicine, and law improved in conditional reasoning relative to students in chemistry. Conditional reasoning involves reasoning on problems that could be solved by conditional and biconditional rules. The improvement for students in psychology and medicine was attributed to the thinking about causal relations that goes on in the probabilistic sciences, including procedures for evaluating evidence, rather than courses in formal logic. Similarly, improvement for students in law was attributed to instruction in thinking about contractual relations that have the form of the conditional. These differential patterns of improvement were not seen on a control measure, verbal reasoning scores.

Lehman and Nisbett (1990) asked two other questions of importance in contemporary education: Does an undergraduate education improve reasoning about problems in everyday life? Does undergraduate training in some majors improve certain types of reasoning more than others? Students who participated were majoring in either the humanities, the natural sciences, or the social sciences. They were tested during the first semester of their first year and the second semester of their fourth year of study.

Based on the study by Lehman et al. (1988) on the effects of graduate training on reasoning, it was anticipated that undergraduate training in the natural sciences and the humanities would have less effect on statistical and methodological reasoning than training in the social sciences, where the emphasis is on teaching rules for thinking about situations of uncertainty. This study provided evidence that graduate students in psychology improved in conditional reasoning. Undergraduates in the social sciences are not typically involved in intensive experimental research, and so no prediction was made concerning their improvement in conditional reasoning. Although graduate students in chemistry had not improved in conditional reasoning in the earlier study, other investigators had provided evidence that training in mathematics, which provides experience with proof by contradiction, improved the ability to solve conditional problems (Jackson & Griggs, 1988). As a result, it was anticipated that greater exposure to mathematics might improve the conditional reasoning of undergraduates in the natural sciences. There was no reason to expect greater improvement in humanities majors in any of these types of reasoning.

These differential patterns were not present at the initial testing in the first year. By the fourth year, all four groups of students had improved in statistical and methodological reasoning, although the change was quite dramatic in the social science students. Both natural science and humanities students improved dramatically in their conditional reasoning. Furthermore, there were significant correlations between improvement in statistical-methodological reasoning and the number of statistics courses taken as well as between improvement in conditional reasoning and the number of math courses taken. No explanation was offered for the improved conditional reasoning of humanities majors. These results provide preliminary evidence that an undergraduate education can improve people's ability to think about events with uncertain causes, assess the reliability of information, and solve logical problems. Furthermore, the degree of improvement in such skills depends on experiences in different disciplines.

B. Conclusions and Evaluation

When measured against the long-term objective of a complete theory of induction in which phenomena are both well documented experimentally and implemented as running computer programs, there are weaknesses in research on inferential rules and mediators that we have just described. For example, recall that pragmatic researchers have conducted preliminary research on rules other than those related to the law of large number, including rules in formal logic (e.g., modus ponens and modus tollens), as well as contractual and causal rules (see Smith, et al., 1992); Nisbett [1993a] contains a collection of many of the relevant journal articles). One clear agenda item for the future is experimental research directed toward full documentation of the latter rules and identification of other important abstract, domain-independent rules systems (Holland et al., 1986; Smith et al., 1992). Also, much of the pragmatic research on statistical reasoning is oriented toward demonstrations of effects, rather then providing a full explanation of the mechanisms by which inferential rules and mediators influence processing. More specific theories, similar in detail to the cognitive-components approach, are needed. Progress toward this goal is being made in other domains, such as analogical reasoning (e.g., Holyoak & Thagard, 1989).

Even with this unfinished business, the current body of empirical research allowed Holland et al. (1986) to make a number of claims, some of which are controversial, and all of which illustrate the potential of the pragmatic approach. One claim is that people represent variability in the environment and use it when making inferences. The evidence they present requires "that any future theories of induction must come to grips with the question of variability representation and processing" (p. 345). Thus pragmatic researchers have gone beyond the general insight that knowledge constrains induction by identifying one of the critical types of knowledge that must be characterized in theories of inductive reasoning.

A second claim, which is controversial in psychology, is that many rules and categories, such as those related to the law of large number, are of an abstract, domain-independent nature. This claim runs against a long-standing bias in North American psychology against such rules (for reviews of these views and related research, see Lehman et al., 1988; Lehman &

Nisbett, 1990; Nisbett, 1993b). For example, until the twentieth century most educators endorsed the concept of "formal discipline," in which the teaching of rules of some field (Greek, Latin, mathematics, or logic) was expected to generalize to thinking about problems outside the bounds of that field. An effective attack on this position by early psychologists like James and Thorndike undermined its credibility, an outcome that was considered one of the early victories of the new science (Lehman et al., 1988). The bias against domain-independent learning has been supported with empirical research by contemporary cognitive psychologists on the difficulty of transfer of solutions from one problem to similar problems (e.g., Gick & Holyoak, 1980) and conclusions drawn from the seminal work on judgment and decision making by Kahneman and Tversky (e.g., 1973; Tversky & Kahneman, 1971). In the latter research, it has been demonstrated that, under some conditions, people overlook statistical principles when they solve inductive reasoning problems (the nature of these conditions has been discussed by Nisbett et al., 1983, and Holyoak & Nisbett, 1988). This bias has also been reinforced by the development of alternatives to rule-based models of thinking, the most recent challenge coming from connectionist models. Although not denying the value of all this work to our understanding of human problem solving and thinking, this second claim amounts to an assertion that many psychologists have thrown the baby out with the bath water and that some version of the formal discipline view is actually tenable (Lehman & Nisbett, 1990; Nisbett et al., 1983).

A third claim is that acquisition of new knowledge must be understood in light of the knowledge a system already possesses, an idea widely accepted in psychology. Of greater interest is the form this claim takes within the context of framework outlined by Holland et al. (1986). Specifically, the abstract rules and categories we seek to teach in formal school settings are characterized as being built on, irrelevant to, or even competitive with the intuitive rules the learner already possesses. Intuitive rules, like those related to the law of large number, should (1) be relatively easy to teach, (2) be used readily in everyday reasoning once acquired, and (3) have even further impact on everyday reasoning if instructors take the trouble to directly teach the application of these rules to everyday events. Holland et al. (1986) suggest that instruction in these rules "may amount to 'swimming downstream' educationally" (p. 285), because it is vastly easier to extend a familiar rule system that may be linked to existing encoding procedures than to introduce a structurally novel one. Pragmatic researchers have provided evidence that "statistics and methodology courses have an important place in the liberal arts curriculum quite independent of any utility they have for scientific reasoning" (Holland et al., 1986, p. 286).

The complementary implication of this third claim is that teaching of nonintuitive rules, such as the abstract rules of formal logic, will not usually result in generalized use of those rules. Many syntactic rule systems that are nonintuitive do not have a major impact on everyday reasoning (see Cheng, Holyoak, Nisbett, & Oliver, 1986; Smith et al., 1992). Generalized use of these rules does not result from instruction "trying to dress up education . . . in the clothing of everyday-life examples as many teachers of logic try to do" (Holland et al., 1986, p. 285), although students may use these rules successfully within a specific domain if they are taught how to encode the domain and sets of relations in ways that the rule system can be applied. Holland et al. assert that the justification for teaching nonintuitive rules may lie in their value to special groups, such as students in philosophy and computer programming. Thus instruction in nonintuitive syntactic rule systems is likely to have little effect on everyday thinking, in contrast to instruction in intuitive rules. This assertion may prove controversial in some educational circles where classic versions of the formal discipline view are still alive and healthy.

Pragmatic research on reasoning raises the possibility of a renewed confidence among experimental psychologists that educational policy, as related to optimizing human thinking and problem solving, could be informed by experimental research rather than shaped by tradition, bias, and belief. Faith in empirical approaches to psychological phenomena is one of the constancies in psychology from its roots to its present forms. At a time when the nature and quality of education in North America is a matter of continuing public debate, widespread and renewed faith in the relevance of empirical research to the identification of educational objectives in the domain of thinking skills has the potential to contribute greatly to the vitality of the discipline. This renewed faith may be one important legacy of the work resulting from this pragmatic approach.

A foreshadowing of the legacy of the pragmatic approach at an interdisciplinary level may be evident in the types of formal and computational developments Holland et al. (1986) suggest are necessary for a complete theory of induction. Among the formal developments, they call for a mathematical theory that could work hand in hand with computer modeling. These investigators suggest that mathematics appropriate to induction would hold many elements in common with mathematics used to study other adaptive systems, such as economics and the genetics of ecologies. They also suggest that "a general mathematical theory of such adaptive systems would explain both the pervasiveness of [common] features and the relations between them" (p. 349). The computational development they suggest is most needed "concerns mechanisms that might account for the emergence of high-level cognitive processes from more elementary subcognitive ones" (p. 350). Both suggestions for development reflect a new trend in the study of thinking—an interest in biological and evolutionary contraints on cognitive theories that is often coupled with an interest in characterizing features of the environment (e.g., Anderson, 1990; Holyoak & Spellman, 1993; Reber, 1992). This trend echoes prominent themes explored at the turn of the last century when many psychologists saw their work in the context of a larger endeavor in the biological sciences (Dixon & Lerner, 1988; Siegel, Bisanz, & Bisanz, 1983).

IV. CONCLUSIONS

We close with two observations. First, one might presume that one of the most straightforward issues would be that of defining induction, yet notions about the domain of induction vary widely. Most researchers study phenomena that match, at least with loose criteria, the dictionary definitions and our general characterization of induction, but the implementation of their research betrays wide differences in their views about what is important about induction. In the cognitive-components approach, researchers generally begin with a set of tasks identified by psychometricians, largely through empirical and statistical means, as involving inductive reasoning. They then embark on a course of research designed to identify the psychological components of performance on these tasks and to use their findings to distinguish inductive reasoning from other forms of thinking. In a sense, then, they initially have a definition by extension (i.e., inductive reasoning defined in terms of the set of tasks that require inductive reasoning) and seek to establish an intentional definition in terms of critical processing features. In the pragmatic approach, researchers begin with a general computational definition in terms of the function of induction, and part of their research agenda is to identify and study phenomena that share that function. Lacking any sort of ideological commitment to either of these views, we conclude that induction, as used by cognitive scientists, is not a *nominal* or *analytic* concept. That is, induction is not something that can be defined uniquely and unambiguously (or at least uncontentiously!) in terms of necessary and sufficient features. Instead, induction may be a *natural-kinds* or a *constructive* concept.

> Analytic concepts are precise, but natural kinds and constructed entities are not, so the boundaries between their instances cannot be mapped with absolute precision. These concepts have to allow for future states of affairs. Our notions of flora, fauna, and artifacts have to anticipate entities that we have not yet encountered or that will exist only in the future. It would be a massive undertaking to specify concepts that were both precise and open to the future, and their acquisition would be likely to defeat any ordinary individual. (Johnson-Laird, 1993, pp. 95–96)

Rather than pursue defeat for ourselves or our readers, we suggest that defining induction tightly in terms of necessary and sufficient features is premature and possibly misleading. It is important for novices to the field to recognize that not all research on induction is headed in the same direction; researchers' biases about the central features of induction are reflected in radically different goals, questions, and methods.

Our final observation is that the ultimate measure of any particular approach is its utility in advancing theory, research, or application. Induction is a central characteristic of cognition and knowledge acquisition, and a thorough explanation of its intricacies should be high on the list of goals of cognitive science. The cognitive-components approach has contributed to the development of precise, process-oriented theories, but typically it is narrow in scope and has failed to address the issue of constraints seriously. The pragmatic approach has expanded the scope of exploration considerably and has helped to identify the kinds of knowledge-based and cognitive constraints that are so critical for understanding how induction operates. With the exception of some recent attempts at computer simulation (e.g., Holyoak & Thagard, 1989), however, it has been less successful at generating precise models of inductive reasoning. In practice, these two approaches seem to have been on separate trajectories: cognitive-component studies are rarely cited in the pragmatic literature, and vice versa. In principle, the two approaches are complementary and potentially synergistic. We suspect that the vitality of research on inductive reasoning will depend, in part, on how well the strengths of each approach can be integrated and on the degree to which research addresses the theoretical issues of cognitive science and the practical issues of human affairs.

Acknowledgments

Preparation of this chapter was supported in part by a grant from the Social Sciences and Humanities Research Council of Canada. We gratefully acknowledge the helpful comments of Jason Bisanz. Correspondence should be addressed to the authors at the Centre for Research in Child Development, Department of Psychology, University of Alberta, Edmonton, AB, Canada T6G 2E9.

Endnotes

1. Presumably *inductive reasoning* is a subset of *induction,* but in the literature the distinction is rarely defined. Rather than impose an arbitrary distinction that would not apply across various approaches we describe, we use the two terms interchangeably, except as noted.
2. In fact, the term *cognitive components* was used initially to describe an approach to studying individual differences in intelligence (Pellegrino & Glaser, 1979). The central feature of the approach is the use of information-processing analyses to identify the sources of differences among individuals on items that appear on intelligence tests. We use the term here in a somewhat more general sense that is not limited to the study of individual differences.
3. Research on inductive reasoning using the cognitive-components approach has waned somewhat in recent years, perhaps in part because the individual-differences aspect of the research agenda did not prove to be as immediately fruitful as anticipated initially. Recall that one motivation for the cognitive-components approach is an interest in developing

more powerful theories of individual differences in cognition, as well as more sensitive methods of assessment (Pellegrino & Glaser, 1979, 1980; Sternberg, 1977). Initial studies were encouraging, but as research accumulated, the measures of cognitive components often appeared intractable for differential research because they were unreliable, they often failed to intercorrelate in expected ways, or they showed little or no correlation with traditional (i.e., psychometric) measures. In cases where correlations were found, they were not always clearly interpretable. For example, Mulholland et al. (1980) found no significant correlations between scores on a standardized, psychometric test of analogical reasoning and the cognitive components of their task that should have been related to inductive reasoning. They did, however, find a negative correlation between psychometric scores and the *intercept* of their regression equation for latencies. The problem is that the intercept represented, theoretically, a mélange of components that were essentially un-analyzed, and so interpretation of the correlation was quite speculative. Some efforts at finding interpretable patterns of correlations were more successful (e.g., Sternberg & Gard-ner, 1983), but the nature of these analyses were highly complex and involved numerous assumptions that may have weakened the impact of the findings. These empirical problems might be addressable by improved theories. There is no strong reason to suspect, for example, that psychometric measures would be reducible necessarily to the temporal char-acteristics of a small set of information-processing measures; different people may do well on psychometric tests for different reasons. Enthusiasm for research in this area also may have been limited by the continued focus on the same sorts of tasks that psychometricians had been using for decades. As concerns for broader measures of assessment have arisen (Gardner, 1983; Sternberg, 1985), the rationale for pursuing increasingly complicated in-vestigations on experimentally purified versions of these same tasks has become less com-pelling.

Failure to elucidate individual differences does not necessarily imply that the cognitive-components approach has little value for studying commonalities in how people reason inductively (Carpenter, et al., 1990), but the effect seems to have been to deflate enthusiasm for the approach in many of its early proponents. (For commentaries on problems of information-processing approaches to the study of individual differences, see Ceci [1990], Keating [1984], and Sternberg [1991].)

References

Anderson, J. R. (1990). *The adaptive character of thought*. Hillsdale, NJ: Erlbaum.

Bisanz, J., Bisanz, G. L., & LeFevre, J. (1984). Interpretation of instructions: A source of differences in analogical reasoning. *Intelligence, 8,* 161–177.

Carpenter, P. A., Just, M. A. & Shell, P. (1990). What one intelligence test measures: A theoretical account of the processing in the Raven Progressive Matrices Test. *Psychological Review, 97,* 404–431.

Cattell, R. B. (1971). *Abilities: Their structure, growth, and action*. Boston: Houghton Mifflin.

Ceci, S. J. (1990). On the relation between microlevel processing efficiency and macrolevel measures of intelligence: Some arguments against current reductionism. *Intelligence, 14,* 141–150.

Cheng, P. W., Holyoak, K. J., Nisbett, R. E., & Oliver, L. (1986). Pragmatic versus syntactic approaches to training deductive reasoning. *Cognitive Psychology, 18,* 293–328.

Dixon, R. A. & Lerner, P. N. (1988). History of systems in developmental psychology. In M. H. Bornstein & M. E. Lamb (Eds.), *Developmental psychology: An advanced textbook* (pp. 3–50). Hillsdale, NJ: Erlbaum.

Evans, T. G. (1986). A program for the solution of geometric-analogy intelligence test questions. In M. Minsky (Ed.), *Semantic information processing* (pp. 271–353). Cambridge, MA: MIT Press.

Fong, G. T., Krantz, D. H. & Nisbett, R. E. (1986). The effects of statistical training on thinking about everyday problems. *Cognitive Psychology, 18,* 253–292.

Gardner, H. (1983). *Frames of mind: The theory of multiple intelligences.* New York: Basic Books.

Gick, M. L. & Holyoak, K. J. (1980). Analogical problem solving. *Cognitive Psychology, 12,* 306–355.

Greeno, J. G., & Simon, H. A. (1988). Problem solving and reasoning. In R. C. Atkinson, R. J. Herrnstein, G. Lindzey, & R. D. Luce (Eds.), *Stevens' handbook of experimental psychology* (2nd ed., Vol. 2, pp. 589–672). New York: Wiley.

Henley, N. M. (1969). A psychological study of the semantics of animal terms. *Journal of Verbal Learning and Verbal Behavior, 8,* 176–184.

Holland, J. H., Holyoak, K. J., Nisbett, R. E., & Thagard, P. R. (1986). *Induction: Processes of inference, learning, and discovery.* Cambridge, MA: MIT Press.

Holyoak, K. J., & Nisbett, R. E. (1988). Induction. In R. J. Sternberg & E. E. Smith (Eds.), *The psychology of human thought* (pp. 50–91). New York: Cambridge University Press.

Holyoak, K. J., & Spellman, B. A. (1993). Thinking. *Annual Review of Psychology, 44,* 265–315.

Holyoak, K. J., & Thagard, P. (1989). Analogical mapping by constraint satisfaction. *Cognitive Science, 13,* 295–355.

Inhelder, B., & Piaget, J. (1958). *The growth of logical thinking from childhood to adolescence.* New York: Basic Books.

Jackson, S. L., & Griggs, R. A. (1988). Education and the selection task. *Bulletin of the Psychonomic Society, 26,* 327–330.

Jepson, D., Krantz, D. H., & Nisbett, R. E. (1983). Inductive reasoning: Competence or skill? *Behavioral and Brain Sciences, 6,* 494–501.

Johnson-Laird, P. N. (1988). A taxonomy of thinking. In R. J. Sternberg & E. E. Smith (Eds.), *The psychology of human thought* (pp. 429–457). Cambridge: Cambridge University Press.

Johnson-Laird, P. N. (1993). *Human and machine thinking.* Hillsdale, NJ: Erlbaum.

Kahneman, D., & Tversky, A. (1973). On the psychology of prediction. *Psychological Review, 80,* 237–251.

Kail, R., & Bisanz, J. (1992). The information-processing perspective on cognitive development in childhood and adolescence. In R. J. Sternberg & C. A. Berg (Eds.), *Intellectual development* (pp. 229–260). New York: Cambridge University Press.

Keating, D. (1984). The emperor's new clothes: The "new look" in intelligence research. In R. J. Sternberg (Ed.), *Advances in the psychology of human intelligence* (Vol. 2). Hillsdale, NJ: Erlbaum.

Kuhn, D., Amsel, E., & O'Loughlin, M. (1988). *The development of scientific thinking skills.* San Diego: Academic Press.

LeFevre, J., & Bisanz, J. (1986). A cognitive analysis of number-series problems: Sources of individual differences in performance. *Memory & Cognition, 14,* 287–298.

Lehman, D. R., Lempert, R. O., & Nisbett, R. E. (1988). The effects of graduate training on reasoning: Formal discipline and thinking about everyday-life events. *American Psychologist, 43,* 431–442.

Lehman, D. R., & Nisbett, R. E. (1990). A longitudinal study of the effects of undergraduate training on reasoning. *Developmental Psychology, 26,* 952–960.

Marr, D. (1982). *Vision.* San Francisco: Freeman.

Massaro, D. W., & Cowan, N. (1993). Information processing models: Microscopes of the mind. *Annual Review of Psychology, 44,* 383–425.

Mulholland, T. M., Pellegrino, J. W., & Glaser, R. (1980). Components of geometric analogy solution. *Cognitive Psychology, 12,* 252–284.

Nisbett, R. E. (Ed.). (1993a). *Rules for reasoning.* Hillsdale, NJ: Erlbaum.

Nisbett, R. E. (1993b). Reasoning, abstraction, and the prejudices of 20th century psychology. In R. E. Nisbet (Ed.), *Rules for reasoning.* (pp. 1–12). Hillsdale, NJ: Erlbaum.

Nisbett, R. E., Krantz, D. H., Jepson, D., & Kunda, Z. (1983). The use of statistical heuristics in everyday inductive reasoning. *Psychological Review, 90,* 339–363.

Osherson, D. N., Smith, E. E., Wilkie, O., Lopez, A., & Shafir, E. (1990). Category-based induction. *Psychological Review, 97,* 185–200.

Palmer, S. E., & Kimchee, R. (1986). The information processing approach to cognition. In T. J. Knapp & L. C. Robertson (Eds.), *Approaches to cognition: Contrasts and controversies* (pp. 37–77). Hillsdale, NJ: Erlbaum.

Pellegrino, J. W. (1985). Inductive reasoning ability. In R. J. Sternberg (Ed.), *Human abilities: An information processing approach* (pp. 195–225). San Francisco: Freeman.

Pellegrino, J. W., & Glaser, R. (1979). Cognitive correlates and components in the analysis of individual differences. *Intelligence, 3,* 187–214.

Pellegrino, J. W., & Glaser, R. (1980). Components of inductive reasoning. In R. E. Snow, P.-A. Federico, & W. E. Montague (Eds.), *Aptitude, learning, and instruction: Vol. 1. Cognitive process analyses of aptitude* (pp. 176–217). Hillsdale NJ: Erlbaum.

Reber, A. S. (1992). The cognitive unconscious: An evolutionary perspective. *Consciousness and Cognition, 1,* 93–133.

Rips, L. J. (1990). Reasoning. *Annual Review of Psychology, 41,* 321–353.

Rumelhart, D. E., & Abrahamson, A. A. (1973). A model for analogical reasoning. *Cognitive Psychology, 5,* 1–28.

Siegel, A. W., Bisanz, J., & Bisanz, G. L. (1983). Developmental analysis: A strategy for the study of psychological change. In D. Kuhn & J. Meacham (Eds.), *On the development of developmental psychology* (pp. 53–80). Basel: Karger.

Siegler, R. S. (1986). Unities across domains in children's strategy choices. In M. Perlmutter (Ed.), *Minnesota Symposium on Child Development* (pp. 1–48). Hillsdale, NJ: Erlbaum.

Smith, E. E. (1989). Concepts and induction. In M. I. Posner (Ed.), *Foundations of cognitive science* (pp. 501–526). Cambridge, MA: MIT Press.

Smith, E. E., Langston, C., & Nisbett, R. E. (1992). The case for rules in reasoning. *Cognitive Science, 16,* 99–102.

Smith, E. E., & Medin, D. L. (1981). *Categories and concepts.* Cambridge, MA: Harvard University Press.

Sodian, B., Zaitchik, D., & Carey, S. (1991). Young children's differentiation of hypothetical beliefs from evidence. *Child Development, 62,* 753–766.

Spearman, C. (1923), *The nature of 'intelligence' and the principles of cognition.* London: Macmillan.

Spearman, C. (1927). *The abilities of man.* New York: Macmillan.

Sternberg, R. J. (1977). *Intelligence, information processing, and analogical reasoning: The componential analysis of human abilities.* Hillsdale, NJ: Erlbaum.

Sternberg, R. J. (1985). *Beyond IQ: A triarchic theory of human intelligence.* New York: Cambridge University Press.

Sternberg, R. J. (1986). Toward a unified theory of human reasoning. *Intelligence, 10,* 281–314.

Sternberg, R. J. (1991). Death, taxes, and bad intelligence tests. *Intelligence, 15,* 257–269.

Sternberg, R. J., & Gardner, M. K. (1983). Unities in inductive reasoning. *Journal of Experimental Psychology: General, 112,* 80–116.

Sternberg, R. J., & Rifkin, B. (1979). The development of analogical reasoning processes. *Journal of Experimental Child Psychology, 27,* 195–232.

Thurstone, L. L., & Thurstone, T.C. (1941). *Factorial studies of intelligence.* Chicago: University of Chicago Press.

Tulving, E., & Madigan, S. A. (1970). Memory and verbal learning. *Annual Review of Psychology, 21,* 437–484.

Tversky, A., & Kahneman, D. (1971). Belief in the law of small number. *Psychological Bulletin, 76,* 105–110.

Zbrodoff, N. J., & Logan, G. D. (1986). On the autonomy of mental processes: A case study of arithmetic. *Journal of Experimental Psychology: General, 115,* 118–130.

CHAPTER 7

Problem Solving

Earl Hunt

I. INTRODUCTION

Problem solving is a bit like beauty, morality, and good art. We are in favor of it, we know it when we see it, but we cannot define it. These somewhat contradictory statements do not impose much of a problem in our day-to-day activities; we muddle through. They do present a problem for the scientific study of cognition. Science depends on precise definition, coupled with accurate observation. If we want to study reasoning (or for that matter, anything at all) scientifically, we have to define it in such a way that the variables in our definition closely mirror distinctions that are made in nature. On the other hand, if we want anyone to pay attention to what we have to say about human behavior, our definitions ought to make some connection with people's intuitive, informal, and generally accurate observations about thought.

The primary purpose of this chapter is to deal with the definitional issue. A definition of problem solving will be offered. It will then be related to some of the major lines of research that have been active in the field during the late twentieth century. Since problem solving is almost the prototype of a "higher mental activity," an attempt will be made to identify constraints on human thought that stem from our biological or social nature. No attempt will be made to present a comprehensive review of all the current research on problem solving. Indeed, it could be argued that such a review would be tantamount to writing a definitive text on cognition itself. Certain key findings will be discussed, especially when they seem to address the distinction between social and biological constraints on thinking.

II. FROM INTUITIONS TO PROBLEM SPACES

While problem solving is usually considered to be a topic in human psychology, it is useful to begin with a nonhuman example, Kohler's (1927, 1959) report of problem solving in the chimpanzee (*Pan troglodytis*). One chimpanzee, the now-famous Sultan, wanted to reach a piece of fruit outside his cage. The cage contained two hollow tubes of varying diameter. Neither tube alone was long enough to reach the fruit. After some frustrating attempts, the chimpanzee retired to the far corner of the cage, looked away from the fruit, and began to play with the sticks. As he did this, he stuck the narrower one into the end of the longer one. Sultan then immediately turned back to the fruit, jammed the two sticks together, and recovered his prize.

Kohler concluded that Sultan understood the situation because he had discovered a solution without going through a sequence of exploratory motor movements. This is the essence of problem solving. In more modern terms, problem solving occurs when we understand the external world by exploring an internal mental model of that world, instead of poking around in the external world directly. This is highly advantageous, since poking around in the external world can be dangerous. On the prosaic level, we do not have to burn ourselves in order to know better than to pick up hot skillets. On a more exalted level, NASA engineers can calculate the trajectory of a satellite without actually going into space. The principles are the same, although the techniques may be different.

The skillet example represents what most of us would call informal, "inside the head" problem solving while the NASA example depends on formal problem solving, and is carried out with the help of powerful external aids, ranging from paper and pencil to computers. There are important similarities and differences between these examples. As for similarities, in both cases problem solving implies manipulation of an internal representation of external objects. We solve the problem in the internal representation, and then project its solution onto the thing being represented. This means that the thinking device, whether human or electronic, must be able to manipulate the representation. This brings us to the differences.

The sort of representation that a thinking device can manipulate depends on the nature of that device. Modern computers are designed to manipulate symbols, so symbolic and arithmetic problem representations are the natural mode of thought for computers. As for us, some million or so years of evolution have produced a highly visual ape with a capacity for language and with a working memory that lets us stitch together the immediate "here and now" perception of the current stimulus array with our memories of things just past. I shall argue that these three capacities—visual coding, language coding, and the ability to deal with situations developing over time—are crucial to human reasoning. They determine the sorts of representations we can construct, and the representations in turn determine what our problem solving capacity is.

To make this point I shall first develop a model of what problem solving is, regardless of the type of device doing the problem solving is. I shall then consider what the role of internal representation is in problem solving, and examine how human problem solving is limited by the sorts of representations that are possible to us.

III. HISTORICAL AND MODERN APPROACHES TO THE STUDY OF THOUGHT: FROM ARISTOTLE'S SYLLOGISMS TO PROGRAMS FOR THINKING

Theories of how thought ought to proceed have a long and honorable history. Aristotle's development of syllogistic reasoning is, in modern terms, a model of a perfect thinker. Following Aristotle, though, surprisingly little research on thinking grappled with fundamental issues until the development of systems of mathematical logic in the nineteenth and early twentieth centuries by Boole, Cantor, Quine, and Whitehead and Russell.

Aristotle's teachings represent an important shift from the work of his classic predecessor, Socrates. Socrates used his famous dialogues to stress how an argument was to be developed. Aristotle and his successors emphasized how the validity of an argument was to be demonstrated, once it had been developed. In today's terms, Socrates would be considered a psychologist or educator, whereas the line stretching from Aristotle to Whitehead and Russell consisted of mathematical logicians.

This is not to say that after Aristotle people lost interest in the processes of reasoning and problem solving. Numerous books were written on "how to think." The problem with this work was that it was neither systematic nor comprehensive. Psychologists tended to treat problem solving as a derivative of some more basic principle of human thought; perception in the case of the Gestaltists and learning in the case of the behaviorists (Hunt, in press). The kindest way to describe these works is to say that they provide good after-the-fact descriptions of what happens, but they fail to provide a prescription for problem solving.

Some psychologists wrote books about famous thinkers (e.g., Werthemier's [1959] account of conversations with Einstein). In other cases the books were written by the highly accomplished thinkers, especially in mathematics (e.g., Hadamard, 1945; Polya, 1954, 1957; and Einstein's numerous reflections on his own thought process). Reading these accounts leaves one impressed by the accomplishments of the person, but virtually without a clue as to how the accomplishments were achieved. For instance, Polya (1957) offers many illustrations of problems that appear difficult, but can be solved quickly after the author (Polya) shows that there is a way of looking at the problem that reveals the key underlying relationships. What Polya did not do was explain how he found an appropriate way to look at a problem *before* he knew the solution.

As an aside, the tradition of emphasizing validity checking and reveling in brilliance of an answer, rather than the process of discovering it, have had deleterious effects on the schools to this day. All too many courses in mathematics reduce to illustrations of the proof of a theorem with no concern for the process of discovery. Too many "theories" of problem solving say that the good problem solver "encodes the key elements of a problem" (or something like this) without explaining how the good problem solver knows what these elements are before the problem is solved.

A major breakthrough in the study of problem solving occurred in the mid-1950s, when Allen Newell, J. C. Shaw, and Herbert Simon proposed that computer programs be used as models for human thought (Newell, Shaw, & Simon, 1958). This work dominated the study of thought throughout the second half of the twentieth century (Newell, 1990; Newell & Simon, 1961, 1972); Newell and Simon's approach to thought rested on three ideas. They are:

1. A theory of the process of problem solving can be expressed as a program, that is, a set of rules for manipulating symbols. Indeed, if a theory is proposed that cannot be so expressed, that theory is unacceptably vague.

2. The development of an ideal problem-solving program in some field of endeavor is a goal in Artificial Intelligence.

3. A problem-solving program that, in some nontrivial sense, behaves like a human being is a descriptive theory of human problem solving.

Note that the term "computer program" was not used in the above description. In Newell and Simon's approach the world external to the problem solver is represented internally by some symbolic expression. This means that the internal representation, whatever its physical form, stands for some properties of the external world. The internal representation itself might be stated in a mathematical notation, sentences in a spoken language, or even pictures. The point is that reasoning involves manipulation of the internal representation, not the external world. Therefore the rules for manipulation must be stated in terms of the language of the representation.

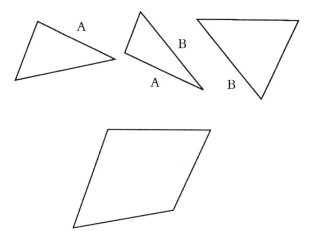

FIGURE 1 A Form Board problem. Can you slide the figures on the top row around in such a way that you construct the figure on the bottom row?

To illustrate, Figure 1 shows an example of what are known as Form Board problems. These problems are widely used in tests of visual-spatial problem solving (Pellegrino & Kail, 1982). The task is to determine whether the triangles and rectangles in the top half of the picture can be joined along the lettered lines to construct the polygon shown in the bottom half of the picture. (They can be.) People attacking form board problems have the subjective experience of "sliding" the figures together in the mind's eye. The limiting feature of problem solving seems to be the ability to manipulate pictures in a visual short-term memory, Baddeley's (1986) "visual scratch pad" component of active memory.

There are other ways of solving form board problems. Some involve comparing Fourier transforms of parts of the top and bottom figure, taken from various perspectives. Others involve locating the transformations required to establish a correspondence between angles at the intersection of nonlettered lines in the top figure and angles of the polygon in the lower figure. These different methods of problem solving do not seem to be reasonable models of human thought. On the other hand, they are quite reasonable approaches to solving form board problems using a digital computer.

This example illustrates two points. Any model of solving form board problems involves transforming the initial problem statement, that is, the top half of the figure, in order to reach the goal state, the bottom half of the figure. At this level of abstraction both human and machine problem solving can be looked on as a search for a path of transformations from the "givens" to the "to be proven" states of a problem. On the other hand, the particular transformations used depend on the sorts of representations that the problem solver can manipulate.

IV. PROBLEM SOLVING AS SEARCHING THROUGH A KNOWLEDGE SPACE

One of Newell and Simon's (1972) insights was that reasoning can be depicted as a progressive expansion of our knowledge of the problem situation, continuing until we discover the solution. This observation, alone, is hardly startling. It is simply a rewording of the definition of problem solving. What Newell and Simon added was a formalism for describing how the problem solver's efforts should be directed during the expansion. Their depiction of knowledge expansion will first be illustrated with a somewhat whimsical example, and then with some more serious ones.

Some years ago I received an invitation to attend a meeting in the Principality of Andorra.[1] This presented me with a problem: how do I get to Andorra? I started with the following pieces of information.

I am in my office in Seattle, Wa.
Andorra is in the Pyrenees mountains, on the border of France and
   Spain.

There is no direct route from Seattle to Andorra. On the other hand, a glance at a map showed me that Andorra is fairly close to Barcelona, a large city in Spain. It seemed reasonable to suppose that if I could get to Barcelona I could get to Andorra from there. I had a new problem.

(Subproblem) Find a way to get to Barcelona.

There is no direct flight from Seattle to Barcelona. However, there are direct flights from Seattle to London, and from London to Madrid. Thus a possible route is:

Drive from office to airport.
Fly from Seattle to London.
Fly from London to Barcelona.
Drive from Barcelona to Andorra.

This is only one of several alternatives. A few of the others are as shown in Figure 2.

In fact, Figure 2 shows what the Seattle-to-Andorra problem really is; a search through a (mathematical) graph, in which the nodes represent cities and the links represent permissible routes between them. Problem solving, in the travel environment, is a task of finding a feasible routing along the links, from a starting node to a goal node.

Newell and Simon's insight was that the graphic model applies to vir-

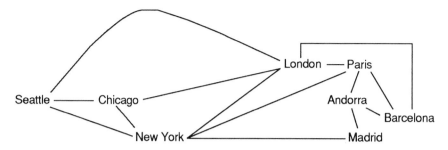

FIGURE 2   The problem of going from Seattle to Andorra. A route must be selected from the many possible routes. The travel routing problem is analogous to many other problems that can be formulated as searches for routes through a problem space.

tually all problem solving. The following two situations are quite different from traveling.

1. Chess. In chess the starting node is the board configuration at the beginning of the game. The goal node is any node in which the opponent's king is checkmated. The (large) set of all legal positions constitutes what Newell and Simon call the *problem space*. (In the travel example the set of all cities constitutes the problem space.)

2. Geometric problem solving. Consider the geometry problem shown in Figure 3. The starting node is the set of expressions in the original problem statement. Further nodes can be reached by expanding this set, one statement at a time, using the rules of inference of geometry. The goal is to reach a node where the associated statements include the statement to be proven.

According to Newell and Simon, the first step in problem solving is to determine the problem space, that is, how the nodes and links of a problem-solving graph are to be defined. The next step is to determine a strategy for moving from node to node. This is the point at which one must begin to consider the computational capacities of the particular problem solver being studied . . . in psychology's case, the human being.

To appreciate what the problem is, let us consider an impossible variety of the Andorra problem. Suppose that I had been invited to attend a fabulous conference in Shangri-La. I do not know where Shangri-La is, although I do know, from a knowledge of modern history, that Shangri-La must have an airport.[2] I can infer, therefore, that there is some city where a flight takes off for Shangri-La. In theory, I could consider all possible flights from Seattle, then all possible flights from each of these cities to each of the cities they were connected to, and so forth, until I reached a city where flights departed for Shangri-La. I would reject this problem on the grounds that it would require more computing than I could handle. "More computing,"

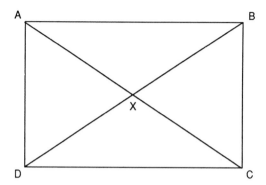

FIGURE 3 A problem in plane geometry. Prove that line AC is bisected at X. The problem solver begins with knowledge of the axioms and major theorems of geometry, and the knowledge that ABCD is a rectangle. Subsequent expansions of the problem solver's knowledge are analogous to transits from place to place in the travel problem of Figure 1.

however, is a relative term. If you were to give me enough paper and pencils, and if the conference were really that fabulous, I might be willing to try.

More seriously, if problem solving is going to be efficient, the problem solver must represent local nodes so that it is easy to find a way through the global graph. We saw this in the Andorra problem. My local representation of cities was not limited to airline connections, it also included information about geographic location. The knowledge that Andorra is between Spain and France prevented me from exploring the implications of Seattle-to-Tokyo flights. General geographic knowledge was used as a heuristic to avoid exploring fruitless paths.

Note that the sort of limitation that we have been exploring is induced by our abstract, human, information-processing capacities. More succinctly, we have been concerned with biologically produced limitations. Humans can attend to only a limited number of things at once. This constraint, which arises because of the kind of animal we are, limits the problem-solving representations that we can use at the local level. How do we manage to represent problems locally so that we produce reasonable, albeit not perfect, global problem solving?

V. PATTERN–ACTION RULES AND HUMAN PROBLEM SOLVING

Functionally, human memory can be divided into an immediate memory system containing active information, and a long-term system that contains episodic memory for prior experiences, procedural information about how to react to situations, and semantic memory about how the world is organized. The immediate memory system can further be divided into at least two "buffer" memories and a more abstract working memory. Baddeley (1986) refers to the buffer memories as a *visual scratch pad* and an *echoic buffer*. These are areas in which we visualize or "hear" information that is retained in an appropriate sensory code. Baddeley further characterizes the working memory as an abstract coding of the meaning of the current situation. We may, loosely, think of working memory as containing that information that is currently at the focus of our attention. While this is an unfortunately loose notion, it will suffice for the present purposes.

Numerous theories of problem solving (e.g., Anderson, 1983; Hunt & Lansman, 1986; Just & Carpenter, 1992; Newell, 1990; Newell & Simon, 1972) assume that the contents of the immediate memory system serve as a cue that triggers execution of pattern–action rules that, among other things, can introduce or rearrange information in the active memory system itself. The acts of solving the form board problem (Figure 1), the air travel problem (Figure 2), and the geometry problem (Figure 3) can all be treated this way. For instance, in air travel a reasonable rule is:

(1) If the goal is to arrive at a European city, AND you are at a U.S. city AND there is no flight from the U.S. city to the European city THEN search for a flight to a U.S. airline hub city east of your current location, and set a goal to fly from that city to the European city.

This rule is stated as a "forward problem-solving" rule; it tells the problem solver what to do from the place in which he or she now is. Other rules can be stated in "backward" form; what goals you should set in order to get to where you are going. An example is:

(2) If the goal is to arrive at a European city AND there is no flight between that city and a U.S. city, find a nearby larger European city and attempt to solve the problem of moving from the U.S. to the larger city.

Similar rules can be established for geometry, chess, and many other problem-solving situations. See Newell and Simon (1972) for an extensive discussion.

Problem solving is impossible if the problem solver does not have the right pattern–action rules for moving from the original state to the goal state. Problem solving is efficient to the extent that the problem solver's rules do not take he, she, or it down blind alleys. In the extreme, the problem solver knows exactly what to do. Human problem solving will be effective when the problem is represented so that (1) the representation of local situations (single nodes) does not overload the immediate memory system, and (2) the representation at each node cues pattern–action rules that move the problem solver along a correct path through the graph of the problem space.

The first of these qualifications establishes a restriction on the sorts of representations people can use. The second qualification emphasizes an important point. In human problem solving the key step is often knowing when to take a particular action, rather than knowing how to take certain actions, give that some omniscient coach has told you to take them.

VI. LIMITATIONS ON REPRESENTATIONS INTRODUCED BY IMMEDIATE MEMORY

Now let us consider another analogy between problem solving and finding a path through a graph. This time the analogy is not to air travel, but to travel on the ground. Suppose that you are lost in the woods and trying to find the right path home. You come to a branch point, where you are offered a choice between several trails. In order to pick the right one you have to examine their characteristics; the direction they seem to be going in, signs of recent travel, and so forth. Your ability to choose the correct path is going to depend on your ability to examine the alternatives. Obviously, the clearer the signs on the trail, the easier it will be to choose the correct one. (It is easier to follow a herd of buffalo than to follow the trail of a single deer.) Also, other things being equal, the more alternatives that have to be examined, the greater the likelihood that you will make a wrong choice.

Exactly the same principles apply to reasoning. At each step in reasoning a problem solver has to develop a mental construction of the logical situation, and then react to the features of that mental construction. Philip Johnson-Laird (1983; Johnson-Laird & Byrne, 1991) has referred to this as constructing a *mental model* of the situation. The complexity of the mental models we can construct are determined by the capacities of our immediate memory. Therefore, immediate memory is often the limiting feature in problem solving.

Three somewhat different lines of inquiry show how important this is. The first of these lines is based on research on categorical syllogisms, primarily by Johnson-Laird and his colleagues. Categorical syllogisms require that people reason about sets. An easy example of a syllogism is:

(3) All artists are beekeepers.
All beekeepers are chemists.

How do we know that this conclusion follows from the premises? As a matter of logic, the conclusion is true if and only if it follows under all interpretations of the premises. In this case there is only one interpretation; the set of artists is a subset of the set of beekeepers, and the set of beekeepers is a subset of the set of chemists. It follows that artists must be a subset of chemists. Only one mental model can possibly be constructed from the premises, and it is a model in which the conclusion is true.

Now compare syllogism (3) to:

(4) All of the parents are teachers.
None of the parents is a driver.

None of the teachers is a driver.

Although this conclusion is invalid, it is commonly accepted as true (Johnson-Laird, 1993, p. 35). Why? the premises in (4) support more than one model. They are consistent with the assumption that parents are subsets of teachers, and that neither parents nor teachers are drivers. On the other hand, the premises are also consistent with a model in which the set of teachers contains two disjointed proper subsets: parents and drivers who are not parents. In fact, the premises permit a third model, in which the set of teachers contains parents who are not drivers, drivers who are not parents, and nondrivers who are also not parents.

Johnson-Laird and his colleagues have shown that the difficulty of solving a syllogistic problem is closely related to the number of alternative models that have to be considered. Problems that require multiple models simply exhaust the capacities of the immediate memory system.

Johnson-Laird and his colleagues altered problem demands, assuming that immediate memory capacity was constant (or, more precisely, varied randomly across the subjects in their studies). What happens if immediate memory capacities are varied?

To answer this question, look at research on individual differences. There are substantial differences in working-memory capacity across individuals. Individuals who have high working-memory capacities have been shown to be good reasoners in a variety of situations, ranging from the analysis of electrical circuits (Kyllonen & Christal, 1990) to comprehension of text (Just & Carpenter, 1992). Furthermore, declines in working-memory capacity with advanced age seem to be closely related to declines in reasoning capacity in the elderly (Salthouse, 1991).

VII. MEANS–END ANALYSIS: BACKWARD AND FORWARD PROBLEM SOLVING

The preceeding section stressed the importance of fitting a problem representation into working memory. Now let us look at a more global aspect of problem solving—how people organize their searches through the problem space.

In their original work, Newell and Simon laid great stress on "means–

end" analysis. They argued that the good problem solver should consider his/her/its current state, compare the current state to the goal state and find some way to eliminate the differences between them. While this seems a reasonable way to proceed, observations of human problem solvers quickly showed that they do not act in this way or, more correctly, they act in this way only when they do not know, clearly, how to solve the problem.

Some of the key observations leading to this conclusion came from Larkin's (1983; Larkin, McDermott, Simon, & Simon, 1980) work on problem solving in physics. Larkin contrasted the way in which students and professional physicists attacked fairly difficult problems in physical mechanics. The students behaved somewhat like Newell and Simon's means–end strategy would suggest; they contrasted what they knew with what they needed to know to solve the problem, and then asked what operations could develop the necessary knowledge.

Experts behaved in quite a different way. First they classified the problem as being a specific example of a particular class of physics problems, for example, balance-of-force problems. They used these classifications to retrieve from memory rules for solving the general class of problems.

There is an interesting analogy here. Problem solving by experts often can be thought of as a process of dredging up from memory a set of problem-solving forms, rather like the forms one uses for computing one's income tax. Once the appropriate forms are defined, the problem solver knows just how to proceed, in a *forward-driven* manner, rather than by reasoning backward from solution to intial state.

Larkin's work was followed by the study of expert problem-solving behavior in many different fields, including physics, chess, medicine, law, and economics (see Ericsson & Smith, 1991, and Chi, Glaser & Farr, 1988, for some representative readings). The general conclusion drawn from this work is that when people are dealing with familiar material they rely to a greater extent on previously memorized solution *schemata*. While the term "schema" has never really been adequately defined, the analogy to filling out an income tax form seems apt. When a person is faced with a problem, and when he or she recognizes that it is a specific case of a general, previously encountered problem, then he or she can short-circuit the practice of poking through the problem space by simply applying previously learned rules that inevitably lead to the solution.

The fact that experienced problem solvers rely on schemata does not mean that they behave in a "knee jerk" fashion, relying solely on memorized procedures. This is far from the case. In many cases, schema application depends on abstract, sophisticated analyses of situations. In physics, for instance, the expert must realize that an elaborate problem statement involving, say, a man pushing a bobsled down an icy hill has to be stripped of its surface content and reduced to a listing of the forces impinging on the sled in the vertical and horizontal planes. Similarly, to a lawyer, a dramatic case involving hurt feelings, damaged pride, insults, crashing cars, vases, and flowerports has to be stripped down to a simpler listing of legal obligations, injuries, and liabilities. A great deal of expert reasoning depends on the expert's learning how to describe actual situations in such a way that their descriptions can be related to the abstract descriptions in the expert's memory.

The contrast between constraints on internal representations because of our limited working memories and the power of internal representations based on schematic reasoning highlights the interactions between biological and sociological effects on problem solving. We clearly have rather strict biological constraints on the number of things that we can attend to at any instant in time. Schemata, which are socially acquired ways of dealing with problems, provide an orderly way to shift attention from one aspect of a problem to another. Properly applied schemata transfer the information-processing burden from immediate memory, where the human problem solver is weak, to long-term memory, where the problem solver is strong.

VIII. SCHEMATIC REASONING AND GENERAL PROBLEM SOLVING

The results on expert problem solving leave us in a somewhat paradoxical position. If people typically solve problems by recalling previous solutions, how do we ever solve a truly new problem? Why is it possible, at all, to learn to grapple with abstract problems, as we do when we attempt mathematics and logic?

In fact, we are not particularly good at solving abstract problems. To illustrate this, consider the following problem.

Suppose that I have four cards. Each card has a number on one side and a letter on the other. I place the cards on the table, so that one side of each card is exposed. The sides that you can see show the following symbols:

A   4   K   7

I assert that the numbers and letters have been assigned according to the following rule:

"If there is a vowel on one side then there is an odd number on the other side."

Which are the fewest cards that you must turn over to determine whether or not this rule has been followed?

Logically, the rule can be rewritten as a case of logical implication;

"If there is a vowel on one side, then there is an odd number on the other."

This rule can be verified (or denied) by turning over the A, to make sure that there is an odd number on the other side, and by turning over the 4, to make sure that the other side does *not* have a vowel. Numerous studies have shown that bright college students often turn over the 7, to see if there is a vowel on the other side. In fact, this is irrelevant, since the rule does not state that the presence of an odd number implies a vowel (Wason & Johnson-Laird, 1972).

On the other hand, we can assign different cover stories to this problem to make it quite easy. here is an example:

> Inspector Hound has been assigned to enforce the state liquor laws. The Inspector knows that you can drink alcoholic beverages only if you are over twenty-one years of age. Upon entering a restaurant Inspector Hound sees the following people:
> A young man of indeterminate age with a beer.
> A high school student sipping an unknown drink.
> A young woman, in the 18- to 25-year-olds range, with a coke.
> An elderly man drinking something out of a flask.
> What should the Inspector do to see if the liquor laws are being followed?

Virtually every college student solves this problem: The Inspector should find out how old the man with the beer is, and find out what the high school student is drinking.

To a logician this is something of a paradox. In terms of formal deduction, the logic problem and the drinking problem are identical:

> If you are drinking liquor then you must be over 21.
> If there is a vowel on one side then there must be an odd number on the other side.

Why do the two problems differ in difficulty?[3]

Cheng and Holyoak (1985) claim that the drinking problem invites an interpretation as a "Permission schema," that can be worded roughly as:

> "If activity X is permitted only to people with property Y, then anyone doing X must have property Y."

The permission schema is widespread in our society, so virtually all of us are expert in determining whether or not activities are permitted. Therefore, if a problem in logical implication can be reinterpreted as an investigation into permission, we know what to do, because we can apply schematic problem solving.

The permission schema is not the only interpretation one can give to logical implication. An alternative schema is the "Causation schema":

> If causal factor A is present, then result B must occur.

An example is

If DDT is released into a river, the fish will die downstream.

Here, the relevant pieces of information are clearly "Do fish die when DDT is released?" (which is equivalent to asking "If there is an A on one side of the card is there an odd number on the other?") "Are there cases where fish do not die even though DDT is released?" (equivalent to "Is there a vowel on the unexposed side of the card with the 4 exposed?"). The causation problem is easier to solve than a logically equivalent abstract problem.[4]

The gist of Cheng and Holyoak's argument is that what appears to be everyday logical reasoning is often really a species of schematic reasoning. In one sense, this is inefficient. Instead of storing a single set of rules for manipulating logical implication problems, the human problem solver seems to memorize many localized, logically redundant rules for dealing with different interpretations of the logical relation.

But is this really redundant? What the human information processor has done is to trade off long-term memory for storing redundant rules in return for a reduction in the burden on immediate memory. Given the relative costs of long-term and immediate memory, this is a good bargain.

IX. APPLIED REASONING: THE IDEAL PROBLEM SOLVER AND HOW IT CAN BE APPROXIMATED

It would be nice if people would solve problems more accurately. What are the implications of these findings (1) for how people ought to solve problems; (2) for how they actually do solve problems; and (3) for educational programs that might improve problem solving?

To begin answering this question, we turn again to problem solving in physics. Larkin, Reif, Carbonell, and Gugliotta (1988) developed a computer program, FERMI[5], to illustrate how they thought that problem solving ought to proceed in physics and in similar domains. The basic idea behind FERMI is that problem solvers use schemata that are arranged in hierarchies, from highly specific to very general solution methods. For instance, FERMI contains rules for calculating pressure differentials between points in a medium of known density and for calculating voltage and current flow in direct current circuits. Both of these schemata are treated as special cases of linear combination rules, which are in turn treated as a special case of the problem-solving strategy of breaking a problem down into subproblems, and then combining the solutions.

FERMI attempts to solve problems at the most specific level possible, retreating to more abstract levels only when it has to. Note that this is consistent with our ideas about the use of representations that reduce the burden on working memory. Whenever possible, use problem-solving methods that are triggered by cues that are in the environment. When necessary, retreat to solving cues based on an abstract analysis of the situation, which thus imposes the burden of remembering the abstract analysis. At each stage, however, the dependence of reasoning on abstract analysis should be kept to a minimum. Because of the way that humans are built, trading off computationally intense reasoning in favor of redundant memorization is actually a good deal.

The truth of these maxims does not depend on analogies between human problem solving and problem solving by computers. They can be illustrated by observations of how people reason about the physical world.

Students who enter physics classrooms know something about the laws of physics; otherwise they simply would not be able to function. But what they know is not an orderly progression of schemata, such as that contained in FERMI. Instead, they know a somewhat motley collection of "schemata that work," without necessarily establishing a connection between them. For instance, introductory physics students know that here, on Earth, things do not keep going unless they are pushed. (Cars stop when you turn off the engine.) At the same time, most students have at least a vague idea that in space, once motion is begun, an object continues along its trajectory. What students do not seem to see is any need to resolve the contradiction between these two schemata. Instead, in DiSessa's (1983) terms, they hold "knowledge in pieces," without worrying about logical consistency. And why not? This sort of reasoning works perfectly well, so long as the students have pattern-recognition rules that tell them when to apply which of their many contradictory schemata.

X. CONCLUSION: UNDERSTANDING HUMAN PROBLEM SOLVING AND PROBLEM REPRESENTATIONS

Psychologists have offered a great many theories of human problem solving. There have been claims that humans are actually intuitive logicians, limited only by their capacity to make computations inside their heads. Other theorists have claimed that humans think "as if" they were examining Venn diagrams, or "as if" they were responding to linguistic cues in problem statements.

The contention of this chapter is that understanding human problem solving is really quite simple. All we have to remember are the following points:

1. Newell and Simon's representation of problem solving as the development of a path through a problem space provides a good way of thinking about the process of reasoning.

2. At each point in the search through a problem space the human problem solver has to respond to his or her representation of the situation at that point. Limits on working memory determine how complicated the representation of the choice problem can be.

3. In order to get around these limitations, people have memorized a variety of schemata. These are often redundant, and sometimes even contradictory, ways of organizing steps in reasoning so that when the schemata are appropriate, the answer to a problem follows from implementation of the "cookbook" approach to problem solving built into the schemata.

4. Schematic problem solving works because it moves the computational burden from immediate memory, where the human problem solver is weak, to long-term memory, where the problem solver is strong.

Endnotes

1. Unfortunately, I was unable to go, but this does not invalidate the example!
2. During World War II the first American bombing raid on Tokyo was carried out in 1942. The type of bomber used (the B-25) was land based and at the time no American air bases were within flying range of Tokyo. When President Roosevelt was asked where the bombers had come from he replied "Shangri-La," referring to a mythical city in a popular novel of the time. In fact, the bombers had taken off from an aircraft carrier.
3. The differences between performance on the card and drinking problems are so robust that the problems can be used as classroom demonstrations.
4. The case has been stated for certain causation, that is, releasing DDT always causes fish to die. Cheng and Novak (1992) have pointed out that in many extra laboratory situations causation must be inferred from statistical associations. Schematic reasoning still applies, but with slightly different schemata.
5. Larkin et al. (1988) claim that FERMI is an acronym for Flexible Extendible Reasoner for Multidomain Inferencing. Is it entirely coincidental that the famous physicist Enrico Fermi was known for his problem-solving ability?

References

Anderson, J. R. (1983), *The architecture of cognition*. Cambridge, MA: Harvard University Press.

Baddeley, A. D. (1986), *Working memory*. Oxford: Oxford University Press.

Cheng, P. W., & Holyoak, K. J. (1985), Pragmatic reasoning schemas. *Cognitive Psychology, 17*(4), 391–416.

Cheng, P. W., & Novick, L. R. (1992). Covariation in natural causal induction. *Psychological Review, 99,* 365–382.

Chi, M. T. H., Glaser, R., & Farr, M. J. (Eds.). (1988). *The nature of expertise*. Hillsdale, NJ: Erlbaum.

DiSessa, A. A. (1983). Phenomenology and the evolution of intuition. In D. Gentner & A. Stevens (Eds.), *Mental models* (pp. 15–33). Hillsdale, NJ: Erlbaum.

Ericsson, K. A., & Smith, J. (Eds.). (1991). *Towards a general theory of expertise: Prospects and limits*. Cambridge: Cambridge University Press.

Hadamard, J. (1945). *The psychology of invention in the mathematical field*. Princeton NJ: Princeton University Press.

Hunt, E. (in press). *Thoughts on thought*. Hillsdale, NJ: Erlbaum.

Hunt, E., & Lansman, M. (1986). A unified model of attention and problem solving. *Psychological Review, 93,* 446–461.

Johnson-Laird, P. N. (1983). *Mental models*. Cambridge, MA: Harvard University Press.

Johnson-Laird, P. N. (1993). *Human and machine thinking*. Hillsdale, NJ: Erlbaum.

Johnson-Laird, P. N., & Byrne, M. J. B. (1991). *Deduction*. Hillsdale, NJ: Erlbaum.

Just, M. A., & Carpenter, P. A. (1992). A capacity theory of comprehension. Individual differences in working memory. *Psychological Review, 99,* 122–149.

Kobler, W. (1959). *The mentality of apes*. London: Routledge & Kegan Paul. (Original work published by Vantage Books, 1927)

Kyllonen, P. C., & Christal, R. E. (1990). Reasoning ability is (little more than) working memory capacity?! *Intelligence, 14,* 389–433.

Larkin, J. H. (1983). Problem representation in physics. In D. Gentner & A. L. Stevens (Eds.), *Mental models*. Hillsdale, NJ: Erlbaum.

Larkin, J. H., McDermott, J., Simon, D. P., & Simon, H. A. (1980). Expert and novice performance in solving physics problems. *Science, 208,* 1335–1342.

Larkin, J. H., Reif, F., Carbonell, J., & Gugliotta, A. (1988). FERMI: A flexible expert reasoner with multi-domain inferencing. *Cognitive Science, 12*(1), 101–138.

Newell, A. (1990). *Unified theories of cognition*. Cambridge, MA: Harvard University Press.

Newell, A., Shaw, J. C., & Simon, H. A. (1958). Elements of a theory of human problem solving. *Psychological Review, 65*(3), 151–166.

Newell, A., & Simon, H. A. (1961). Computer simulation of human thinking. *Science, 134,* 2100–2017.

Newell, A., & Simon, H. A. (192). *Human problem solving*. Englewood Cliffs, NJ: Prentice-Hall.

Pellegrino, J. W., & Kail, R. (1982). Process analysis of spatial aptitude. In R. J. Sternberg (Ed.), *Advances in the psychology of human intelligence* (Vol. 1, pp. 311–365.) Hillsdale, NJ: Erlbaum.

Polya, G. (1954). *Mathematics of plausible reasoning* (Vols. 1 & 2), Princeton, NJ: Princeton University Press.

Polya, G. (1957). *How to solve it*. New York: Basic Books.

Salthouse, T. A. (1992). Why do adult adge differences increase with task complexity? *Developmental Psychology, 28,* 905–918.

Wason, P. C., & Johnson-Laird, P. N. (1972). *The psychology of reasoning: Structure and content*. Cambridge, MA: Harvard University Press.

Werthemier, M. (1959). *Productive thinking* (rev. ed.). New York: Harper.

CHAPTER 8

Language and Thought

Richard J. Gerrig
Mahzarin R. Banaji

On almost all occasions, the course of language production begins when speakers formulate the desire to convey certain thoughts. Imagine, for example, a scene in which a child has watched her father throw a ball. If the child were an English speaker, she might utter the sentence, "Daddy threw the ball." If the child spoke any other of the world's thousands of natural languages we would also expect her to be able to express the basic content of this simple English sentence. What would differ considerably, however, from language to language would be the range of grammatical markings required as obligatory addenda to the propositional content (Slobin, 1982).

The sentence "Daddy threw the ball" can serve as a starting point for a brief exploration of variation across the formal features of languages. This straightforward sentence displays much of what is formally required by English grammar (this series of cross-linguistic examples is adapted from Slobin, 1982):

DADDY	threw	the	ball
AGENT	ACTION		OBJECT
[focus]	[past]	[definite]	

Word order in English dictates that "Daddy" is the focus of the sentence. The time of the action is obligatorily marked on the verb. A determiner

Thinking and Problem Solving

indicates whether the ball in question is previously identified ("the") or newly introduced ("a").

Although German shares a strong family resemblance to English, the range of grammatical marking is quite different:

VATER	warf	den	Ball
AGENT	ACTION		OBJECT
[focus]	[past]	[definite]	
	[3rd person]	[singular]	
	[singular]	[masculine]	
		[object]	

The verb indicates not only that the action took place in the past, but also that there was a single person being referred to in the third person. The definite article "*den*" also goes far beyond the English "the" in specifying that the object of the sentence "*Ball*" is not only definite but also singular, grammatically masculine, and specifically the object of the sentence.

Consider, as a final example, the same thought rendered in Turkish:

Top- u	baba- m	at-	tı
OBJECT	AGENT	ACTION	
[definite]	[possessed	[past]	
[object]	by speaker]	[3rd person]	
		[singular]	
		[witnessed	
		by speaker]	

The basic word order of Turkish is subject–object–verb, but the child's thought is focused on her father, and Turkish uses the position immediately preceding the verb to encode focus. Therefore, "*babam*" is moved to the position just before the verb. Furthermore, the child is required by the grammar of Turkish to indicate that the father in question is her own. She must also obligatorily indicate that she is reporting an event that she experienced directly. Were the source of knowledge not direct, the child would append a different suffix to the verb.

This chapter is devoted to exploring the relationship between language and thought. This series of examples—a single thought expressed in three different languages—is intended to illustrate why the study of this relationship has so often proved compelling. We can clearly see the effect of thought on each language's rendering of the scene. In each of the languages, for example, the words for "daddy" and "ball" are kept distinct. We would be surprised, that is, if any language conflated "daddy and ball" into one lexical item (Markman & Hutchinson, 1984). In that sense, the way in which the child structures the scene in thought reflects the way the child structures the scene in language.

What is less immediately clear is whether the different formal require-ments of each language—the different obligatory aspects of grammatical marking—will have consequences for the way the child, or the child's ad-dressee, can or typically does think about the scene. Might it be the case, for example, that the German-speaking child habitually notices the genders of objects in a way that an English-speaking child would not? Might it be the case that Turkish-speaking children habitually are attuned to the directness of indirectness of their information in a way that neither English- nor German-speaking children would be? Confirmation of such speculations would constitute evidence for effects of language on thought.

In this chapter we will look at both directions of influence: thought on language and language on thought. That thought influences language has been extensively documented. We will review a representative sample of the empirical literature. The potential effect of language on thought, however, has proven to be among the more troubled areas of psychological research. In the first section of this chapter, we will review this troubled history. By the end of that section, we hope to demonstrate why a renaissance of inter-est in this topic has emerged out of a recognition of the bidirectional influ-ences of language and thought. In the latter two sections of the chapter, we take up individual topics—conceptual metaphor and language acquisition—to demonstrate the advisability of a balanced perspective on the relationship between language and thought. Although this review will at times require speculative suggestions, we believe that those speculations are justified against the background of received psychological wisdom.

I. THE SAPIR–WHORF HYPOTHESIS REVISITED

Perhaps the strongest claim relating language and thought was framed by John Watson. As part of his behaviorist program to render all aspects of psychological experience directly observable, Watson hypothesized that thought is merely subvocalized speech: "the muscular habits learned in overt speech are responsible for implicit or internal speech (thought)" (1930, p. 239). This view, however, that thought is impossible without some form of covert language has been widely discredited. Physiological aspects of Watson's hypothesis were invalidated through experiments that eliminated muscle activity without impairing cognitive processes (e.g., Smith, Brown, Toman, & Goodman, 1947): Thought remained viable in the absence of "muscular habits." Psychological aspects of Watson's hypothesis fell victim to systematic observation of the thinking skills of prelinguistic children. Well before they utter their first words, children provide abundant evidence that they are inducing structure in the world around them (for a review, see Siegler, 1986). If children begin thinking before they start speaking, we can properly wonder how pre-existing patterns of thought affect the emergence of language and, at the same time, how the emergence of language affects patterns of thought.

By offering the contrast among English, German, and Turkish renderings of "Daddy threw the ball," we wished, in fact, to create a context in which speculations about the mutual influences of language and thought would seem well motivated. Historically, theories of these interrelationships also emerged out of close analyses of the different ways in which languages convey information about the world. The scholars most associated with theory in this area, Edward Sapir and his student Benjamin Lee Whorf, began by studying just such linguistic differences. In both cases, their explorations led them to the somewhat radical conclusion that differences in language would create differences in thought:

> We see and hear and otherwise experience very largely as we do because the language habits of our community predispose certain choices of interpretation. (Sapir, 1941, 1964, p. 69)
>
> We dissect nature along the lines laid down by our native languages. The categories and types that we isolate from the world of phenomena we do not find there because they stare every observer in the face; on the contrary, the world is presented in a kaleidoscopic flux of impressions which has to be organized by our minds—and this means largely by the linguistic systems in our minds. . . . We are thus introduced to a new principle of relativity, which holds that all observers are not led by the same physical evidence to the same picture of the universe, unless their linguistic backgrounds are similar or can in some way be calibrated. (Whorf, 1956, pp. 213–214)

For Sapir and Whorf, these conclusions were not abstract ideas but emerged directly from relationships they believed to exist in their own data. Whorf, who wrote most frequently about the influence of language on thought, framed two hypotheses (see Brown, 1976):

> *Linguistic Relativity:* Structural differences between languages will generally be paralleled by nonlinguistic cognitive differences in the native speakers of the two languages.
>
> *Linguistic Determinism:* The structure of a language strongly influences or fully determines the way its native speakers perceive and reason about the world.

The burden of modern research in psychology, linguistics, and anthropology has been to create rigorous tests of these ideas (see Lucy, 1992). In this chapter, we begin by reviewing the major areas of research that have been used to argue for or against the Sapir–Whorf hypothesis. We will argue, in fact, that the influence of both thought on language and language on thought can be detected in all these areas.

A. Color Memory

When researchers first turned their attention to the Sapir–Whorf hypothesis, memory for color was considered to be an ideal domain for study (see Brown, 1976). Whorf had suggested that language users "dissect nature along the lines laid down by [their] native languages" (1956, p. 213): Color is a prototypical continuous dimension divided up in different ways across languages. Researchers set out with the initial hypothesis that differences in the quantity of color labels would bring about differences in episodic memory for those colors (e.g., Brown & Lenneberg, 1954; Lenneberg & Roberts, 1956; Stefflre, Vales, & Morley, 1966). However, two lines of research proved quite powerful in creating the opinion that the color domain provides a strong instance of "cultural universalism and linguistic insignificance" (Brown, 1976, p. 152). In the first line of research, Berlin and Kay (1969) studied the distribution of color terms cross-linguistically and discovered an orderly pattern with which languages employ from two to eleven basic color terms (see also Kay & McDaniel, 1978). Languages with only two terms will have *black* and *white* (or *dark* and *light*). If the language has a third term, it will be *red*. The next additions will be sampled from *yellow, green,* and *blue. Brown* enters next, followed by some ordering of *purple, pink, orange,* and *gray.* Thus, rather than being arbitrary in the way that Whorf might have predicted, languages choose to name different colors according to a strict hierarchy. This strictness suggests that language describes a single external reality, rather than that language divides reality in different ways.

The second line of research that argued strongly against the Sapir–Whorf hypothesis was carried out by Rosch (see Rosch, 1977, for a review) who studied the Dani tribe of New Guinea. Rosch asked members of this group as well as English speakers to try to remember color chips that were either focal or nonfocal members of the basic color categories. English speakers, who have names for all eight categories, remembered focal colors better than nonfocal colors. Dani speakers, who have only two color terms, showed the same pattern of results. Thus, although their language does not differentiate, for example, the categories red, blue, and green, the Dani responded as if their language did. Rosch's results created an indelible impression that experiences of color are unaffected by language practices.

Perhaps because the regularities revealed by Berlin and Kay and by Rosch were so impressive, subsequent research on language and color memory has only rarely penetrated from anthropology into psychology (but see Hunt & Agnoli, 1991). This later body of research, however, has done much to restore a balance toward the mutual influence of language and thought in the experience of color (e.g., Garro, 1986; Lucy & Schweder, 1979, 1988). Lucy and Schweder (1979), for example, began a series of experiments with a study that demonstrated a methodological weakness in Rosch's work. The array of color chips she had used to test both her Dani and English speakers appeared to be biased in a way that made focal colors a priori more salient than the nonfocal colors. Lucy and Shweder constructed a new test array that was not subject to this bias. With the unbiased array, they failed to replicate Rosch's original results. They demonstrated, in fact, that what mattered most for accurate recognition memory was not focality, but rather the availability of a "referentially precise basic color description" (p. 159). They concluded that "language appears to be a probable vehicle for human color memory, and the views developed by Whorf are not jeopardized by the findings of any color research to date" (p. 160).

Kay and Kempton (1984) extended this conclusion with a methodology that eliminated any possible taint from a biased array. In their initial experiment, they provided their subjects with triads of color chips all taken from the blue–green continuum. The subjects' task was to indicate which of the three hues was most different from the other two. The two groups of subjects in the study were speakers of English, a language which includes a lexical distinction between blue and green, and speakers of Tarahumara, a language that has only a single lexical item, *siyóname,* which covers both green and blue hues. Kay and Kempton argued that, if the Sapir–Whorf hypothesis is correct, "colors near the *green–blue* boundary will be subjectively pushed apart by English speakers precisely because English has the words *green* and *blue,* while Tarahumara speakers, lacking the lexical distinction, will show no comparable distortion" (p. 68). Kay and Kempton's data strongly bore out this prediction: English speakers distorted the interhue distances in line with the Sapir–Whorf hypothesis in 29 out of 30 instances; Tarahumara speakers' performance was close to the prediction of random shrinking or stretching with a 13 out of 24 split.

In a second experiment, Kay and Kempton invented a methodology that eliminated the utility of the *blue* and *green* labels for their single group of English-speaking subjects. With a special piece of equipment, Kay and Kempton displayed the triads only a pair at a time. While the experimenters showed one pair, they labeled one of the chips as *greener* than the other. While showing the second pair, they labeled a chip as *bluer.* Under these circumstances, the color boundary was transparently irrelevant to judging the distances among the three chips in the triad: the central chip was both *green* and *blue.* Under these circumstances the performance of the English speakers now nearly matched that of the Tarahumara speakers. Because of its forced irrelevance, the effect of language was eliminated. From this second experiment, Kay and Kempton argued against a "radical" form of linguistic determinism. Although language affected thought when it was relevant to the task at hand, it did not place binding constraints on performance when it became irrelevant.

Kay and Kempton's dramatic results led them to argue for a revision of received wisdom on color experience. They embraced the evidence that suggests that thought in some ways constrains the experience of color; the orderly emergence of color terms into the world's languages argues strongly toward that conclusion. However, a full review of the data also argues strongly toward an influence of language on thought. Far from being a strong case of the failure of the Sapir–Whorf hypothesis, color provides a paradigmatic instance of a domain of experience in which language and thought exert a mutual influence.

B. Counterfactual Constructions and Reasoning

During the period of time in which research on color memory seemed to argue against an influence of language on cognition, Bloom (1981) set out to provide a test of the Sapir–Whorf hypothesis that shared more of the spirit of Sapir and Whorf's original theoretical motivation. Sapir and Whorf were attuned largely to grammatical differences between languages. Bloom nominated such a difference as a possible locus for a language effect. He called attention to a difference in the grammars of English and Chinese relating to the expression of counterfactuals. Consider the English sentence, "If he were Sara's teacher, Sara would do better at school." That the speaker is reasoning contrary to fact is signaled by the subjunctive "were" and the modal "would." No competent speaker of English should mistake such a counterfactual construction for an ordinary if–then relationship. Chinese, by contrast, provides no such grammatical means for marking counterfactuals. The expression of counterfactual reasoning is constructed from ordinary implicational statements: "He is not Sara's teacher. If he is, then Sara will do better at school" (Au, 1988). Bloom hypothesized that this linguistic difference between English and Chinese might cause Chinese speakers to be less able than English speakers to recognize counterfactual arguments.

Bloom (1981) presented evidence in favor of this speculation. He gave English and Chinese speakers stories to read that contained counterfactual implications. For example, one story told of a European philosopher named Bier who would have been able to contribute to philosophy in a variety of ways had he been able to read Chinese. The two sets of subjects were asked to indicate whether Bier had actually made the contributions outlined in the story. Of the English speakers, 98% indicated that he failed to do so. The comparable figure was only 6% for native Chinese speakers. From a series of results of this sort, Bloom concluded that language could have an influence on thought: the absence of a grammatical counterfactual construction impaired the Chinese speakers' ability to perform counterfactual reasoning.

Bloom's results, however, have been widely criticized on methodological grounds (Au, 1983, 1984, 1992; Cheng, 1985; Liu, 1985; Takano, 1989). Au (1983), for example, argued that the stories read by Bloom's Chinese speakers were not written in idiomatic Chinese. Au suggested, in particular, that Bloom's rendering of "if–then" conditionals provided a different meaning to the Chinese stories than the one he had intended. When Au repaired Bloom's Chinese, all evidence for an influence of language on thought disappeared. Chinese and English speakers correctly perceived counterfactuality at near-perfect rates. Bloom (1984) complained that Au's subjects might have developed a facility with counterfactuals through experience in English, but studies with more purely Chinese monolinguals argued equally against the Sapir-Whorf hypothesis when the stories were appropriately idiomatic (Liu, 1985).

Along with an empirical invalidation of Bloom's results came a shifting of causal analysis from the influence of language on thought to the influence of thought on language. Au (1992), for example, argued persuasively that what in retrospect makes Bloom's claim seem so unlikely is that the types of life situations that give rise to the need for counterfactual reasoning are inescapable, irrespective of language. Although Bloom had argued that counterfactual reasoning is scarcely present in Chinese culture, Au (1992) observed that this type of reasoning underlies a wide variety of human functions: "If regret, frustration, sympathy, causal attribution, gratitude, and feeling vindictive permeate the everyday life of people from all cultures, counterfactual reasoning has to be fundamental and pervasive in human thinking as well" (p. 202). Consider, as one example, feelings of regret. To experience this emotion, speakers must be able to reason about alternatives to reality, for example, If I had pursued other job opportunities, I wouldn't be miserable now (see Kahneman & Miller, 1986; Kahneman & Tversky, 1982). Au's argument, therefore, is that, given the range of everyday thoughts that presuppose consideration of counterfactual states, speakers of all languages must be well practiced at this sort of reasoning. Thought drives language; speakers must find a way to express counterfactuals, whatever the resources of their languages.

Au (1992) also adduced developmental data to support the dominance of thought over language in the use of counterfactuals. Four-year-olds were placed in an experimental situation in which they were asked to pretend that common objects, such as a drinking straw, were some other object, such as a pencil. In one condition of the experiment these pretend transformations were introduced by an explicit counterfactual marker, the subjunctive: "If this were a pencil, what could you do with it?" In the other condition, children heard a simple if–then conditional: "If this is a crayon, what can you do with it?" The children were subsequently asked, "Can you really [whatever the child had said earlier one could do with a pencil] with it?" Au reasoned that if language is necessary to assist in counterfactual reasoning, the children who heard the subjunctive would be more likely than their peers to answer this last question correctly. In fact, the children in both conditions responded appropriately. Au concluded that the children's ability to reason counterfactually was not particularly reliant on the correct use of the subjunctive by their conversational partner. Here, patterns of thought are well formed independent of the contribution of language.

The difficulty with these conclusions—as well founded as they are—is that they cannot logically be extended to conclude that there is no influence of language on thought. Although the experiences undergirded by counter-factuality may be universal, the ease with which various languages allow the counterfactual to be expressed may still have a cross-linguistic impact on ease of thought. Bloom's original experiment, and also therefore those experiments that reworked his translations, took as their dependent measure the accuracy of Chinese and English speakers' reports of counterfactual statements. Error rates, however, are only one index of performance and might mask more subtle differences (Cheng, 1985; Hunt & Agnoli, 1991; Hunt & Banaji, 1988). Imagine, for example, that subjects from both lan-guage groups were asked to perform Bloom's task but that their responses were timed. There is no a priori argument that can rule out the possibility that, despite equivalent accuracy, Chinese speakers would take longer to arrive at the correct answers. If this were so—and if we consider this puta-tive result against the background of the limited cognitive resources avail-able to cope with the time pressures of day-to-day conversation—we could imagine it to be the case that Chinese speakers would be less likely, all other things being equal, to undertake counterfactual thought. If this were true, language would be considered to have a clear influence on thought.

We intend this line of speculation to make the Sapir–Whorf hypothesis seem less monolithic than it sometimes has seemed. Sapir and Whorf have often been caricatured as suggesting that the two possible directions of influence between language and thought are mutually exclusive. This is clearly incorrect. We believe it is essential to acknowledge that thought influences language with respect to counterfactuals while still allowing the possibility that language could affect thought. Language may have exactly the type of small but consistent influence on thought that dominates theory building in psychology (Glucksberg, 1988; Hardin & Banaji, 1993; Hunt & Agnoli, 1991; Hunt & Banaji, 1988).

We believe, further, that it is critical to free the study of the Sapir–Whorf hypothesis from any overtones of immorality. The claim that Chinese speakers cannot perform counterfactual reasoning is clearly insulting. To refine the claim by imagining, for example, that this flaw may exist only at the level of response time does little to remove the sting of that insult. A renaissance of interest in both directions of influence between language and thought should, however, reveal the possibility of a diverse set of advantages and disadvantages for each individual language (something Whorf himself emphasized). It seems quite likely that some functions of thought will be so critical that no language will have evolved that would "force" its speakers to perform that function slowly or poorly. It seems equally likely that some languages will have evolved such that some, perhaps more peripheral, functions will suffer indelible influence. Researchers should be open to both possibilities.

Our review of research on counterfactuals has been intended to argue in favor of theoretical balance. Early research favored an influence of language on thought. Later research corrected methodological weaknesses and suggested, instead, that thought influences language. While embracing that conclusion, we have nonetheless emphasized that the expectation of all-or-none direction of influence is unwarranted. Although Bloom's (1981) research was flawed in method, it was solid in theory (Cheng, 1985; Hunt & Agnoli, 1991). There is ample reason to study the influence of language on thought even against the background of a universal cognitive function. We turn now to an area of research that has provided less controversial instances of language affecting thought.

C. Concept Labels and Cognition

Perhaps the greatest myth on the subject of language and thought concerns the number of words that Eskimos have to refer to snow. Although Whorf mentions the example only in passing (1956, p. 216), and claims only that "Eskimo" contains three different snow words (p. 210), the example has been taken up into scholarly and popular culture and exaggerated to as many as one or two hundred different words (Martin, 1986). Whorf introduced this example, among a set of others, to document the different levels of precision with which languages carve up the world. Whorf believed that those linguistic differences would bring about differences in thought. It seems more likely, however, that thought precedes language in establishing such differences: speakers typically find ways to talk about the things that are most important to them (for a review, see Clark & Clark, 1977). This can be seen even within languages, because speakers vary in their expertise. Surgeons and car mechanics, for example, both have ranges of vocabulary that fall outside the competence of most users of English. In fact, once those specialized vocabularies are in place, they may help call attention to distinctions that would be overlooked by the uninitiated and they might contribute to efficient problem solving. Expertise, thus, can provide circumstances in which language, at least, facilitates thought.

The availability of labels has most thoroughly been shown to influence thought when information must be committed to memory. In a classic demonstration, Carmichael, Hogan, and Walter (1932) showed that the label applied to ambiguous figures could influence subjects' ability to reproduce those figures. Subjects, for example, were shown a drawing that consisted of a pair of circles connected by a short line segment. Half were given the label "eyeglasses" to go with the drawing. Half were given "dumbbells." When later asked to reproduce the figure, subjects' drawings tended to err in the direction of the label. No claim can be made that the application of the label changed the original perception of the figure, but language nonetheless affected the way in which the figure was reconstructed from memory.

Verbal labels can also affect other judgments that rely on reconstructions from memory. Consider an experiment by Loftus and Palmer (1974) in which subjects watched a film depicting a traffic accident. Each subject was required to provide a general description of what had happened and then answer a series of questions. One critical question had the form, "How fast were the cars going when they _____ each other?" For each subject, the blank was filled with a verb ranging from *contacted* through *hit, bumped,* and *collided,* to *smashed.* Subjects who read the question with *contacted* estimated the cars' speeds to have been 31.8 mph. With *smashed,* the estimates rose to 40.8 mph—and, in a subsequent question, subjects were more likely to report that they had seen broken glass in the original film. Here again, language had an effect on what subjects believed they had experienced.

In each of these earlier studies, the experimenters manipulated the verbal labels that were given to the subjects. Schooler and Engstler-Schooler (1990) have examined circumstances in which memory is impaired when the subjects themselves have been responsible for generating the verbal information. In one experiment, for example, subjects were asked to watch a 30-second videotape of a bank robbery. Twenty minutes later, half of the subjects spent five minutes writing a detailed description of the robber's face. The other half of the subjects were in a control group that performed an unrelated task. Schooler and Engstler-Schooler found that 64% of the control subjects were able to recognize the robber's face correctly among an array of eight faces—but only 38% of the subjects who verbalized about the face. In another experiment, subjects were presented with color chips and were asked to write about the color or to perform a control activity. Recognition performance was, once again, much impaired by verbalization: 73% versus 33% accuracy for the control and verbalization groups, respectively.

Schooler and Engstler-Schooler designed a further experiment that enabled them to focus in on the causal mechanism for this decrement in performance. Subjects in this experiment viewed black and white photographs from a university yearbook. As in the previous studies, half of the subjects were asked to write descriptions of the faces in the photographs and half were in a control group. In this experiment, however, half of the subjects from each of these two groups were asked to make their recognition judgments within five seconds whereas the other half were given as much time as they wanted. With unlimited time, subjects again suffered a performance decrement from verbalization: 80% versus 50%. However, with limited time, there was no such decrement: performance was 76% correct for the control group and 73% correct for the verbalization group.

Schooler and Engstler-Schooler argue that this pattern arises as a consequence of *recoding interference*. Subjects, they believe, tend "to rely on a verbally biased recoding at the expense of the original visual memory" (p. 37). With limited time to make their recognition judgments, subjects relied more heavily on their accurate visual memory. With unlimited time, however, the inaccurate verbal information overwhelmed the original visual information. These results are compelling not just because they demonstrate an effect of verbal information on subsequent judgments. Beyond that, they show that subjects defer to the language information even when access to memories for the original information allows more accurate performance.

Hoffman, Lau, and Johnson (1986) moved the study of the effects of labels on memory to comparisons between speakers of different languages. These authors created descriptions of four individuals, two of whom could easily be labeled by personality type terms in English, but not in Chinese, and two of whom could easily be labeled in Chinese, but not in English. Consider the term *shì gù*. In Chinese, this term succinctly captures an individual who is "worldly, experienced, socially skillful, devoted to his or her family, and somewhat reserved" (p. 1098). In English, no single term or phrase unifies these diverse traits. Hoffman et al. suggested that the availability or unavailability of succinct labels in each language would have a direct influence on the way in which speakers of the two languages made judgments about the characters. To make as dramatic a comparison as possible, Hoffman et al. used as subjects Chinese–English bilinguals. By random division, half of these subjects were asked to read character descriptions in Chinese and half in English. This methodology allowed Hoffman et al. to make claims about the impact of language differences independent of cultural differences.

Predictions for the study arose from the belief that the availability of a succinct label would cause subjects to reason in a fashion guided by their stereotypes. That is, if the bilinguals read the description of the *shì gù* individual in Chinese, Hoffman et al. expected to see evidence that they had reasoned with recourse to the *shì gù* stereotype. If comparable bilinguals read the description in English, they expected to see little evidence of stereotype-based reasoning. This expectation was borne out. The impressions subjects wrote down for each character were considerably more congruent with a stereotype when the language of processing matched the language in which a succinct label was available. The subjects' ability to recognize statements from the original stories and their ratings of the likelihood that other statements would be true of each character were similarly contingent on the match between the processing language and the label language. Hoffman *et al.* acknowledged that their procedure was abstracted away from ordinary circumstances of "person cognition." Nonetheless, their data provide a compelling example of circumstances in which the language in which readers encountered an identical body of information had a substantial impact on their later performance with respect to that information. The study demonstrated, as the authors put it, "that a language's repertory of labeled categories (its lexicon) affects the categorizing behavior of its speakers" (p. 1105).

Having reviewed a selection of past research on language and thought, we will now turn our attention to two areas that augur the future. Researchers on both *conceptual metaphor* and *language acquisition* have provided avenues for speculation, and alluring data, with respect to the impact of both thought on language and language on thought.

II. CONCEPTUAL METAPHORS

Shortly before the Gulf War erupted, George Lakoff (1991) circulated over computer networks an essay entitled "Metaphor and war: The metaphor system used to justify war in the gulf." The essay began in a striking fashion: "Metaphors can kill." Lakoff filled out this claim by identifying a series of metaphorical systems that he believed to underlie discourse about the actions of Saddam Hussein and the United States' possible responses. These metaphors could kill, Lakoff argued, because they allowed details of reality to be ignored in a potentially harmful way. Consider a metaphorical schema that Lakoff refers to as "The Fairy Tale of the Just War." This schema requires a cast of characters, a villain, a victim, and a hero, for which there were easy matches in the Gulf. Kuwait was the innocent victim, invaded by the villainous Saddam Hussein at the helm of Iraq. At the time Lakoff wrote his essay, the United States and its allies were impatient to fill the role of the hero. The difficulty with this metaphor is that it makes it all too easy to ignore finer aspects of the real-life situation. Even as the consensus toward war was emerging, for example, Kuwait's innocence was regularly called into question. The United Nations formally acknowledged, for example, that Kuwait had stolen oil from Iraq. Meanwhile, the narrow focus on Saddam Hussein as villain made it possible to forget that many other Iraqis would be adversely affected by war (and, as it turned out, Saddam survived the war intact while thousands of innocent Iraqis were killed). Lakoff's general claim, thus, was that the metaphors that were used to rouse public sentiment in favor of the Gulf War shaped the public's perception of the world. This is a straightforward assertion that language affected thought. In this section, we examine both this possibility that metaphors can structure thought as well as the possibility that thought structures metaphors.

A broad spectrum of life experiences are, in fact, communicated almost entirely by virtue of metaphor (Gibbs, 1994; Lakoff, 1987; Lakoff & Johnson, 1980). Consider this series of utterances that might be spoken retrospectively about an argument (Lakoff & Johnson, 1980, p. 4):

He *attacked every weak point* in my argument.
His criticisms were *right on target*.
I *demolished* his argument.
If you use that *strategy,* he'll *wipe you out.*
He *shot down* all of my arguments.

What unifies this series of statements is the conceptual metaphor ARGUMENT IS WAR. If none of the statements seem particularly metaphorical it is because speakers of English have grown so accustomed to using war expressions to characterize argument that those uses have lost their novelty. It is almost impossible to talk about arguments without making tacit reference to this metaphor. This need not, however, be the case. We could imagine, for example, that English might be governed by the metaphor ARGUMENT IS A GAME OF CHANCE in which case we would say things like, "I was lucky to think of that point" or "I probably won't win the next time around." Or English might use the metaphor ARGUMENT IS A THEATRICAL PRODUCTION, which might lead to "I performed my side of the argument brilliantly" or "I think he took his curtain call too soon."

Against this example, we can frame the question of the influence of both thought on language and language on thought. One reason that English characterizes argument as war might be that the way that people think about argument makes the metaphorical extension of the war lexicon particularly apt. If this is true, we could look for evidence across languages that argument is often characterized as war. At the same time, we can wonder what effects the characterization of argument as war might have on the way that English speakers think about arguments. We can wonder whether the use of the metaphor ARGUMENT IS WAR rather than ARGUMENT IS A GAME OF CHANCE or ARGUMENT IS A THEATRICAL PRODUCTION might change the types of thoughts English speakers can have about their life experiences.

A. The Influence of Thought on Metaphorical Language

We begin with instances in which universal patterns of thought appear to dictate the emergence of highly similar metaphors cross-culturally. Asch

(1955) began one early demonstration of cross-cultural equivalence with the observation that the same terms, for example, *warm, cold, hard, bitter,* and *bright,* are often applied both to physical sensations and to people. He wondered if the extension of those terms from the physical to the psychological domain was governed purely by conventional associations or if there was a systematicity that would establish a deeper consonance.

To answer this question, Asch turned to a comparison across languages. He sought to see, first, whether all of the languages he consulted used these words for dual functions and then, second, whether the use of the words remained consistent across languages. Asch chose for his explorations a group of languages "belonging to different families and as far as possible separated in time and space" (p. 31): Old Testament Hebrew, Homeric Greek, Chinese, Thai, Malayalam (a language spoken in southwestern India), and Hausa (a language spoken in western Africa). Asch found that each of these languages did, in fact, include physical terms that had been extended to the psychological domain, although the number of such extensions differed among languages. Furthermore, some of the terms were extended in strikingly similar ways across this diverse sample. Asch concluded, for example, that "the morpheme for 'straight' (which may also denote 'right' or 'vertical') designates well-nigh universally honesty, righteousness, and correct understanding. Correspondingly, the [morpheme] for 'crooked' stands equally clearly for dishonesty and wile" (p. 33). Given the great differences among the cultures in which Asch's sample of languages were spoken, it seems safe to conclude that overlapping perceptual experiences gave rise to the consistency of these metaphors—thought influenced language.

For a second example of the way that thought may influence metaphorical language, we can look to metaphors that relate different sensory modalities. Consider these lines of poetry, each of which unites the visual and auditory domains (from Marks, 1982a):

The murmur of the gray twilight (Poe)
The quiet-colored end of evening (Robert Browning)
A soft yet glowing light, like lulled music (Shelley)

Marks (1982a) asked subjects to read each of a set of fifteen such metaphorical phrases and adjust a light stimulus and sound stimulus such that the intensities of each stimulus matched those implied by the line of poetry. Marks found that there was a nearly perfect correlation between the levels set in each domain. Furthermore, subjects' performance on this task very nearly mimicked the results of more traditional experiments that have examined equivalences between perceptual domains, independent of language. Marks (1982b) suggested that the equivalence of direct perceptual experience and perceptual experience mediated through language may well arise from some "fundamental, phenomenological property of the makeup of sensory experience" (p. 192). If that is true, we would expect to find universal consistency in the way that languages map relations between sensory modalities.

On the whole, there are a broad range of physical experiences that are shared regardless of culture and language, experiences that may give rise to equally shared metaphors. Table 1 presents five examples of conceptual metaphors that are used in English and that also might be universal because they arise from experiences in the physical world (see also Johnson, 1987). These conceptual metaphors are potentially universal in two senses. First, some languages might choose not to use the potential mapping between these target domains and the up–down dimension. That is, we would not expect to find that every language uses these conventional expressions. Second, there is always the possibility that some language might violate

TABLE 1   Potentially Universal Conceptual Metaphors[a]

1. HAPPY IS UP; SAD IS DOWN
Linguistic instantiations: I'm feeling *up*. That *boosted* my spirits. He's really *low* these days. I *fell* into a depression.
Physical basis: Drooping posture typically goes along with sadness and depression, erect posture with a positive emotional state.

2. CONSCIOUS IS UP; UNCONSCIOUS IS DOWN
Linguistic instantiations: Get *up*. He *rises* early in the morning. He *dropped* off to sleep. He *sank* into a coma.
Physical basis: Humans and most other mammals sleep lying down and stand up when they awaken.

3. HAVING CONTROL or FORCE IS UP; BEING SUBJECT TO CONTROL or FORCE IS DOWN
Linguistic instantiations: I have control *over* her. I am *on top of* the situation. He *fell* from power. He is my social *inferior*.
Physical basis: Physical size typically correlates with physical strength, and the victor in a fight is typically on top.

4. MORE IS UP; LESS IS DOWN
Linguistic instantiations: The number of books printed each year keeps going *up*. My income *rose* last year. The number of errors he made is incredibly *low*. His income *fell* last year.
Physical basis: If you add more of a substance or of physical objects to a container or pile, the level goes up.

5. FORESEEABLE FUTURE EVENTS ARE UP (and AHEAD)
Linguistic instantiations: All *up*coming events are listed in the paper. I'm afraid of what's *up ahead* of us.
Physical basis: Normally our eyes look in the direction in which we typically move (ahead, forward). As an object approaches a person (or the person approaches the object), the object appears larger. Since the ground is perceived as being fixed, the top of the object appears to be moving upward in the person's field of vision.

[a] Adapted from Lakoff and Johnson (1980, pp. 15–16).

these mappings and, for example, associate "happy" with "down." The safest prediction, therefore, would be that, to the extent that the claims about the physical bases of these metaphors are accurate, the vast majority of languages that make these mappings would align the dimensions identically. We would interpret all of these cross-linguistic parallels as instances in which thought constrained the type of language structures that can emerge.

B. The Influence of Metaphorical Language on Thought

Even if many conceptual metaphors arise from universal experiences, there are still a variety of circumstances in which different metaphors apply within the same domain. We can wonder, in those cases, whether the use of one metaphor rather than another can have an impact on thought. Consider an experiment by Gentner and Gentner (1983), which provides direct evidence that a particular metaphorical characterization of a domain can influence success at reasoning in that domain. These authors began by observing that analogies are quite often used in science, and wondered to what extent the use of these analogies influences thought in those domains. To address this question, they proposed a test of the Generative Analogy hypothesis: "that conceptual inferences in the target [domain] follow predictably from the use of a given base domain as an analogical model" (p. 100).

Gentner and Gentner chose electricity as their domain of inquiry and outlined two contrasting metaphors that help to explain the behavior of electricity in circuits. The first metaphor, the water-flow model, likens electricity flowing through a wire to water flowing through a pipe. Along these lines, batteries can be conceived of as pumps or reservoirs and resistors as narrow pipes. The second metaphor, the moving-crowd model, characterizes electric current as crowds of objects moving through passageways. Batteries can be thought of as a force that encourages the crowds to move and resistors as gates along the passageways.

Gentner and Gentner found that different individuals from a group that had been screened to be "fairly naive about physical science" (1983, p. 117), spontaneously used these two different metaphorical mappings. Furthermore, the use of one or the other model predicted success on different types of electricity problems. The water-flow model allows problem solvers to have easy access to prior knowledge about pumps and reservoirs, which facilitated performance on problems about configurations of batteries. The moving-crowd model allows easy access to prior knowledge about the way in which gates regulate the flow of movement, which facilitated performance on problems about configurations of resistors.

Consider a contrast between circuits containing one versus two resistors. With respect to the moving-crowd model it is easy to understand that two parallel gates would allow more of the crowd to pass than one gate would, and thus two resistors allow more current to pass than a single resistor allows. The water-flow model, on the other hand, provides a contrast between one and two narrow pipes. The intuition is not nearly so clear—and, accordingly, subjects' performance suffered. With respect to the domain of electricity, thus, the success of reasoning is genuinely influenced by the metaphorical mapping of choice. Because the metaphorical mapping is mediated through language, this result constitutes an influence of language on speakers' ability to formulate certain thoughts efficiently. Research like Gentner and Gentner's may provide a cautionary note to teachers: Some metaphorical mappings may make aspects of a subject area less rather than more accessible to easy cognition. We now look to instances where language might influence thought well outside the classroom.

Consider an important domain of human experience for which there are a great number of overlapping conceptual metaphors, the domain of romantic love (see Kovecses, 1988, 1990; Lakoff & Johnson, 1980). Kovecses (1988) estimated that there are about three hundred conventional expressions about love in English, many of which can be subsumed within a variety of productive conceptual metaphors. Consider these instantiations of the metaphor LOVE IS A NUTRIENT (pp. 13–14):

> She's *starved for* affection.
> I *need* love.
> I *can't live without* love.

Or these instantiations of LOVE IS A JOURNEY (p. 15):

> Look *how far we've come.*
> We'll just have *to go our separate ways.*
> We've gotten *off the track.*

We can wonder, in each case, whether the expressions that individuals use to talk about love will influence the way in which they think about their relationships. We can make, along these lines, a variety of speculations. It might be the case, for example, that someone who talks of love as a nutrient might experience more distress by being without a partner than someone whose language is not dominated by this image. Such a person might also be more likely to stay in a bad relationship. We might also predict that those individuals whose language is dominated by the metaphor of love as a journey would have a different sense of how a relationship should unfold over time than would other individuals who chose other metaphors. Finally, we can wonder whether individuals who primarily express themselves about love via contrasting metaphors might find themselves to be strangely incompatible. Note that it could very well be the case that different life experiences would give rise to the preference for different metaphors. What we are suggesting is that once those preferences are in place, there could be consequences for subsequent behavior. Such predictions are well within the range of psychological experimentation.

For a final example, we turn to a case in which a single conceptual metaphor characterizes a domain, but that metaphor alone might prevent successful reasoning. Consider this series of statements (Reddy, 1979, p. 286):

> Try to *get* your *thoughts across* better.
> None of Mary's *feelings came through* to *me* with any clarity.
> You still haven't *given me* any *idea* of what you mean.

Reddy (1979) provided a series of examples like these to argue that talk about language is dominated by "The Conduit Metaphor." This metaphor has three components (Lakoff & Johnson, 1980, p. 10):

IDEAS (or MEANINGS) ARE OBJECTS.
LINGUISTIC EXPRESSIONS ARE CONTAINERS.
COMMUNICATION IS SENDING.

It is virtually impossible to talk about communication in English without partaking of this metaphor—and that, Reddy explicitly argued, has undesirable consequences. To make this case, Reddy focused on the way that the conduit metaphor trivializes the real difficulties of communication: "In terms of the conduit metaphor . . . success [at communication] appears to be automatic" (p. 295). But in real-life circumstances, "partial miscommunication, or divergence of readings from a single text, are not aberrations. They are tendencies inherent in the system, which can only be counteracted by continuous effort and by large amounts of verbal interaction" (p. 295).

Reddy suggests that the conduit metaphor has ill effects at both the personal and societal level. At a personal level, the conduit metaphor encourages speakers, in particular, to attribute miscommunication to their own ineptness rather than to the inherent difficulty of encoding and decoding ideas. At a societal level, the conduit metaphor encourages communities to believe that culture can be preserved independent of human cognition. But, as Reddy points out, "we do not preserve ideas by building libraries and recording voices. The only way to preserve culture is to train people to rebuild it, to 'regrow' it, as the word 'culture' itself suggests, in the only place it can grow—within themselves" (p. 310). Reddy acknowledged that English speakers are capable of thinking about the true complexity of language: the conduit metaphor does not make such thoughts impossible (as required, perhaps, by the strongest version of the Sapir–Whorf hypothesis). Even so, because this metaphor so permeates everyday discourse, Reddy argues that it is the habitual basis for our reasoning about meaning—so that language consistently leads us astray. This strong prediction of an effect of language on thought warrants empirical scrutiny.

In this section on conceptual metaphor we have suggested that each of language and thought influences the other. Many metaphorical mappings seem to arise out of universal aspects of human experience. In those cases, thought has a major impact on language. Other metaphorical mappings seem to be relatively less constrained by experience itself. In those cases, there is room to speculate that language constrains thought.

III. LANGUAGE ACQUISITION

At the beginning of the chapter, we gave renderings of the same idea in three different languages, English, German, and Turkish, and observed that each language requires the child to make a different range of formal distinctions. In this section, we will first consider how the universal unfolding of children's cognitive capacities constrains the time course with which they can acquire these formal distinctions. We then provide some examples of circumstances in which the formal structure of a language may have an impact on children's cognitive development.

A. The Influence of Cognitive Development on Language Acquisition

The proposition that the course of language acquisition is constrained in some ways by the cognitive preparedness of the child is widely accepted (see papers collected in Gelman & Byrnes, 1991; Slobin, 1985a, 1985b, 1992). Because some of the distinctions languages require are beyond children's understanding at the chronological moment at which they begin to acquire language, language development must often wait on cognitive development. All other things being equal, the order in which children acquire the formal devices of their language will be highly correlated with the complexity of the concepts those devices encode. Consider a classic study, in which Brown (1973) examined the time course with which children acquired fourteen suffixes and function words in English. Brown was able to order this set of grammatical morphemes in terms of their relative semantic and syntactic complexity. To master the plural -s, for example, English-acquiring children must understand the concept of number. To use the uncontractible copula *be* correctly, they must understand both number and time ("*Is* he your father?" "*Was* that an airplane?"). To use the uncontractible auxiliary *be* correctly, they must understand as well the third concept of the ongoingness of a process ("*Is* that your ball?" "*Was* that your bus?"). Brown demonstrated that children acquired these three devices, and with few exceptions the entire set of morphemes, in order of increasing complexity (see also de Villiers & de Villiers, 1973). These data show strong evidence that cognitive attainments most often precede linguistic attainments.

Given that children of all cultures will likely experience the same unfolding of cognitive potential, we would have the strong expectation that children would acquire the same semantic distinctions in the same order (if, that is, their language makes formal notice of a particular distinction). To the extent, for example, that children must discover the concept of plural, we might expect children the world over to acquire mastery of the plural at the same chronological moment. What moves actual performance away from this idealization is the complexity of the means by which each individual language achieves the same semantic distinctions. For example, because of the complexity of the system, German children acquire mastery of plural forms relatively later than their English counterparts (Mills, 1985). On the other hand, to form a tag question speakers of German add a set word or phrase (e.g., "Peter kauft Brötchen, *oder?*"), whereas speakers of English must, in general, know the right verb and reverse the polarity of the main clause (e.g., "Peter is buying rolls, *isn't he?*"). Consequently, German children master tag questions before English children (Mills, 1985). Cognitive development, thus, most often provides a window of opportunity for children to acquire particular formal devices.

Because the influence of cognitive development on language acquisition has been so widely documented (e.g., Slobin, 1985a, 1985b, 1992), we have kept this discussion quite brief. We turn now to the less widely discussed possibility that formal features of certain languages might prompt language-specific advances in cognitive development.

B. The Influence of Language Acquisition on Cognitive Development

A major grammatical feature of the Turkish example that began this chapter was the verb suffix that marked the child's utterance as a product of direct experience. In Turkish, each past tense expression must be obligatorily marked as the product of direct experience, with the suffix *-di* or one of its phonological variants (e.g., it is realized as *-ti* in our example), or of indirect experience, with the suffix *-miş* or one of its variants (see Slobin & Aksu, 1982). The situations that are properly marked by *-di* versus *-miş* are often only subtly different:

> For example, . . . *Kemal gelmiş* 'Kemal came,' is appropriate in the context of encountering Kemal's coat, but not in the context of hearing the approach of

> Kemal's car. In both cases, the speaker has not SEEN Kemal or his arrival, but in the latter case the auditory sensory experience is part of the process of Kemal's arrival, and thus the speaker's consciousness was involved in the process before its actualization. (Slobin & Aksu, 1982, p. 192)

Slobin and Aksu, in fact, argue that the distinction encoded within this suffix system counts as an "implicit theor[y] of conscious experience": "The distinction between the two past tense forms [encodes] . . . the degree to which the speaker's mind has been prepared to assimilate the event in question prior to forming an utterance about that event" (p. 198). Children who learn Turkish must come into possession of this implicit theory. They begin by using -di and then, with full mastery arriving at about age five, they begin to separate out circumstances in which -miş is appropriate (Aksu-Koç, 1986; Aksu-Koç & Slobin, 1985). In their review of the acquisition of this distinction, Aksu-Koç and Slobin (1985) suggest that "an intriguing research task would be to investigate the possibility that marking of the distinction between direct experience and inference/hearsay might make Turkish children more sensitive at an early age to issues of evidence, point of view, and source of information" (p. 865). We would reinforce that suggestion by recommending the same program of research for adult speakers. A strong claim that speakers, say, of English or German cannot ever be sensitive to the source of information is clearly untenable. Nonetheless, we believe alongside Aksu-Koç and Slobin that speakers of Turkish may have more immediate facility with such analysis—and such a claim may be borne out through data collection. If the experience of language acquisition focuses obligatory attention on a distinction that might otherwise be only voluntarily visited, we might fruitfully explore the possibility of lingering effects on cognition.

Studies of the acquisition of Japanese provide similar instances in which formal characteristics of the language might lead to cognitive precocity. Clancy (1985), for example, reviewed the time course with which Japanese children acquire the ability to make the social distinctions required of them by their language. She suggested that "Japanese children are exposed to linguistic differences correlated with social variables from a very early age, and are probably more sensitive to the social factors which trigger linguistic differences in Japanese, such as relative age, sex, and status of speaker and hearer, than are American children of comparable age" (p. 478). The putative influence, thus, is from language to social cognition. Clancy notes, as well, that personal reference in Japanese is also conditioned on the addressee. Although in English, *I* is used by both men and women, regardless of their addressee, male and female Japanese speakers use different pronouns at different times. For children, the term expected of girls, *(w)atashi,* is more formal than the terms expected for boys, *boku* or *ore*. Clancy reports a conversation in which a 3½-year-old girl tried to refer to herself with *boku* while her mother struggled to correct her. The girl "seemed to be rebelling rather violently against the social behavior characteristic of *atashi,* preferring to identify herself as *boku,* and allowed to engage in the loud, active behavior which kindergarten boys enjoy" (pp. 480–481). This one young girl, thus, treated the name with which she could call herself as constitutive of her behavior. More generally, Clancy suggested that the "acquisition of this [first person] system will probably affect the child's developing sense of identity, especially in the area of social and sexual roles" (p. 479). As much as all children come to acquire sex roles, Japanese children might experience them all the more vividly since the little boy's *I* is not the little girl's *I.*

For a final pair of examples, we turn to Hebrew. In Hebrew, there is reason to speculate that formal features of the language might heighten awareness of gender identity. Berman (1985) observed that Hebrew requires the gender of the subject of a sentence to be marked explicitly on the verb. In English, for example, the same verb phrase *is going* would be used for either Ron or Rina. In Hebrew, the two sentences would be rendered *Ron holech* and *Rina holechet.* Berman suggests that the "formal encoding of sex difference as heard, and subsequently produced, by Israeli children . . . may compel them to make these cognitive distinctions earlier than, say, their English-speaking counterparts" (p. 335). She also cites cross-cultural data that show, in fact, that Hebrew-speaking children's gender identities are fixed somewhat in advance of their English-speaking peers. Berman identifies a handful of other potential loci in Hebrew for language development leading cognitive development. As our final example, consider sentence forms that translate to "She's crying, the girl" or "Don't take it, my ball" (p. 336). In Hebrew, such right-dislocation is used quite frequently by even 2- to 3-year-olds to mark the focus of the utterance. English speakers must learn relatively more complicated passive and cleft constructions to perform the same functions. Accordingly, Hebrew children might get some early help from their language in recognizing "such notions as 'That's what I'm talking about,' or 'What matters to me isn't who or what did something, but who or what it happened to'" (p. 336).

It is likely that cognitive development has a more profound impact on language development than the other way around. Even so, we have provided a series of examples from reasonably dissimilar languages, Turkish, Japanese, and Hebrew, all of which provide instances in which formal aspects of a language may prompt young speakers of those languages to acquire conceptual distinctions in advance of some of their peers. In each case, cross-linguistic data collection could confirm these differences for children and search out perhaps small but consistent differences in their parents.

C. Bilingualism

Our discussion of language acquisition has been focused so far on circumstances in which an individual is learning a first language. Many individuals, however, become to some extent proficient in more than one language. The achievement of bilingualism has, in fact, often become an explicit goal of higher education. The Yale College Programs of Study, for example, dictates that "students should be able to understand, speak, read, and write a language other than their own, and should be acquainted with the literature of that language in the original. Such abilities increase subtlety of mind and sharpen sensitivity to use of one's own language" (1992, p. 15). What Yale College asserts confidently—that bilingualism increases "subtlety of mind"— has often been the source of empirical and even political controversy.

In fact, much of the earliest research on bilingualism focused directly on the question of whether the possession of two languages had good or bad consequences for general cognitive performance (for reviews, see Hakuta, 1986; Hoffmann, 1991; Reynolds, 1991). Initially, this research reported that bilingualism was associated with decrements in performance. These early studies, however, most often compared immigrant bilinguals with native monolinguals, permitting no conclusions to be drawn about the effects of bilingualism independent of the consequences of social and economic disadvantage.

More recent research has reached cautious conclusions more in line with Yale College's assertion that bilingualism is advantageous. Mohanty and Babu (1983), for example, compared monolingual and bilingual members of the Kond tribal society in India. They suggested that experience with two languages would enable bilinguals to reason more effectively about abstract properties of languages. They found, in fact, that even with nonverbal intelligence taken into consideration the bilinguals showed superior meta-linguistic ability. Okuh (1980) reasoned that two languages would provide bilingual children with "two windows or corridors through which to view the world" (p. 164), yielding the potential for greater creativity among bilinguals. In studies with both Nigerian and Welsh children, Okuh demonstrated exactly such enhanced creativity for bilinguals with respect to monolinguals, beyond differences in intelligence.

Studies of this sort, with monolingual and bilingual children drawn from the same cultures, provide compelling evidence in favor of the hypothesis that bilingualism covaries with facilitation in certain types of thought. Even so, these studies suffer from the inevitable methodological flaw that monolinguals and bilinguals have not been randomly assigned to the two groups (and random assignment is, of course, virtually prohibited) (Hakuta, 1986; Reynolds, 1991). Without such random assignment, establishing causality in this domain remains somewhat murky. There remains the possibility that the same cultural circumstances that encourage bilingualism will also encourage, for example, creativity.

To make a less ambiguous argument that bilingualism has a facilitative effect on thought, researchers have begun to study educational settings in which children acquire a second language. Diaz (1985) and Hakuta (1987), for example, report data from a longitudinal study of bilingual education in the New Haven, Connecticut school system. Children in this program were native speakers of Spanish who began to receive training in English in elementary school (the goal of the program was to move the children into monolingual English classrooms). Both Diaz and Hakuta found a positive relationship between the degree of bilingualism and the children's cognitive abilities, but this relationship was strongest for students who were least proficient in their second language. For example, within the group of children who on average had low English proficiency, degree of bilingualism predicted "a substantial amount of cognitive variability" (Diaz, 1985, p. 1382) with respect, for example, to metalinguistic ability. Diaz concluded that "the positive effects of bilingualism are probably related to the initial efforts required to understand and produce a second language rather than to increasingly higher levels of bilingual proficiency" (p. 1387).

Opponents of bilingual education have often claimed that such programs hinder the educational development of minority students (for discussions, see Hakuta & Garcia, 1989; Padilla et al., 1991). Results of the type obtained by Diaz and Hakuta suggest instead that early bilingual training can expand children's cognitive capabilities. In this context, experience with more than one language has genuine potential to enhance the quality of thought. A second important conclusion is that the second language should not be acquired at the expense of the first. The greatest relative advantage almost certainly accrues to children who are able to retain, for example, their native Spanish while acquiring English (see Hakuta, 1986, 1987).

Although there are few methodologically pure data to support the specific claim that bilingualism can "increase subtlety of mind and sharpen sensitivity to the use of one's own language," a general conclusion from this tradition of research is that one's habits of thought can be improved through the acquisition of at least a second language. In a sense, therefore, proponents of nationalistic monolingualism (e.g., English First) risk impoverishing the mental lives of their compatriots (Hakuta, 1986; Lambert, 1992). Future research should confirm that the most thoughtful public policy is to promote widespread multilingualism.

IV. CONCLUSIONS

This chapter has been intended to give a balanced account of the effects of thought on language and language on thought. In almost every instance, the impact of thought on language has been supported by abundant data. Language's impact on thought has consistently required more speculation. Although we suspect that some of these speculations will prove false, we hope to have demonstrated that the ideas originated by Sapir and Whorf warrant much more systematic exploration than they traditionally have been afforded.

Acknowledgments

We wish to thank Curtis Hardin and Letitia Naigles for their many helpful comments on earlier drafts of this chapter. We also thank Robert Crowder for calling our attention to Yale College's stance on bilingualism.

References

Aksu-Koç, A. (1986). The acquisition of past reference in Turkish. In D. I. Slobin & K. Zimmer (Eds.), *Studies in Turkish linguistics* (pp. 247–264). Amsterdam: John Benjamins Publishing Company.

Aksu-Koç, A., & Slobin, D. I. (1985). The acquisition of Turkish. In D. I. Slobin (Ed.), *The crosslinguistic study of language acquisition: Vol. 1. The data* (pp. 839–878). Hillsdale, NJ: Erlbaum.

Asch, S. E. (1955). On the use of metaphors in the description of persons. In H. Werner (Ed.), *On expressive language* (pp. 29–38). Worcester, MA: Clark University Press.

Au, T. K. (1983). Chinese and English counterfactuals: The Sapir-Whorf hypothesis revisited. *Cognition, 15,* 155–187.

Au, T. K. (1984). Counterfactuals: In reply to Alfred Bloom. *Cognition, 17,* 289–302.

Au, T. K. (1988). Language and cognition. In R. L. Schiefelbusch & L. L. Lloyd (Eds.), *Language perspectives: Acquisition, retardation, and intervention* (2nd ed., pp. 125–146). Austin, TX: Pro-ed.

Au, T. K. (1992). Counterfactual reasoning. In G. Semin & K. Fiedler (Eds.), *Language, interaction, and social cognition* (pp. 194–213). London: Sage.

Berlin, B., & Kay, P. (1969). *Basic color terms: Their universality and evolution.* Berkeley: University of California Press.

Berman, R. A. (1985). The acquisition of Hebrew. In D. I. Slobin, *The crosslinguistic study of language acquisition: Vol. 1. The data* (pp. 255–371). Hillsdale, NJ: Erlbaum.

Bloom, A. H. (1981). *The linguistic shaping of thought: A study in the impact of language on thinking in China and the West.* Hillsdale, NJ: Erlbaum.

Bloom, A. H. (1984). Caution—the words you use may affect what you say: A response to Au. *Cognition, 17,* 275–287.

Brown, R. (1973). *A first language: The early stages.* Cambridge, MA: Harvard University Press.

Brown, R. (1976). Reference: In memorial tribute to Eric Lenneberg. *Cognition, 4,* 125–153.

Brown, R., & Lenneberg, E. (1954). A study in language and cognition. *Journal of Abnormal and Social Psychology, 49,* 545–462.

Carmichael, L., Hogan, H. P., & Walter, A. A. (1932). An experimental study of the effect of language on the reproduction of visually perceived form. *Journal of Experimental Psychology, 15,* 73–86.

Cheng, P. W. (1985). Pictures of ghosts: A critique of Alfred Bloom's *The linguistic shaping of thought. American Anthropologist, 87,* 917–922.

Clancy, P. M. (1985). The acquisition of Japanese. In D. I. Slobin, *The crosslinguistic study of language acquisition: Vol. 1. The data* (pp. 373–524). Hillsdale, NJ: Erlbaum.

Clark, H. H., & Clark, E. V. (1977). *Psychology and language*. New York: Harcourt Brace Jovanovich.

de Villiers, J. G., & de Villiers, P. A. (1973). A cross-sectional study of the acquisition of grammatical morphemes in child speech. *Journal of Psycholinguistic Research, 2,* 267–278.

Diaz, R. (1985). Bilingual cognitive development: Addressing three gaps in current research. *Child Development, 56,* 1376–1388.

Garro, L. C. (1986). Language, memory, and focality: A reexamination. *American Anthropologist, 88,* 128–136.

Gelman, S. A., & Byrnes, J. P. (1991). *Perspectives on language and thought: Interrelations in development.* Cambridge: Cambridge University Press.

Gentner, D., & Gentner, D. R. (1983). Flowing waters or teeming crowds: Mental models of electricity. In D. Gentner & A. L. Stevens (Eds.), *Mental models* (pp. 99–129). Hillsdale, NJ: Erlbaum.

Gibbs, R. W. (1994). *The poetics of mind.* Cambridge: Cambridge University Press.

Glucksberg, S. (1988). Language and thought. In R. J. Sternberg & E. E. Smith (Eds.), *The psychology of human thought* (pp. 214–241). Cambridge: Cambridge University Press.

Hakuta, K. (1986). *Mirror of language: The debate on bilingualism.* New York: Basic Books.

Hakuta, K. (1987). Degree of bilingualism and cognitive ability in mainland Puerto Rican children. *Child Development, 58,* 1372–1388.

Hakuta, K., & Garcia, E. E. (1989). Bilingualism and education. *American Psychologist, 44,* 374–379.

Hardin, C., & Banaji, M. R. (1993). The influence of language on thought. *Social Cognition, 11,* 277–308.

Hoffman, C., Lau, I., & Johnson, D. R. (1986). The linguistic relativity of person cognition: An English-Chinese comparison. *Journal of Personality and Social Psychology, 51,* 1097–1105.

Hoffmann, C. (1991). *An introduction to bilingualism.* London: Longman.

Hunt, E., & Agnoli, F. (1991). The Whorfian hypothesis: A cognitive psychology perspective. *Psychological Review, 92,* 377–389.

Hunt, E., & Banaji, M. R. (1988). The Whorfian hypothesis revisited: A cognitive science view of linguistic and cultural effects on thought. In J. W. Berry, S. H. Irvine, & E. B. Hunt (Eds.), *Indigenous cognition: Functioning in cultural context* (pp. 57–84). Dordrecht, The Netherlands: Martinus Nijhoff.

Johnson, M. (1987). *The body in the mind.* Chicago: University of Chicago Press.

Kahneman, D., & Miller, D. T. (1986). Norm theory: Comparing reality to its alternatives. *Psychological Review, 93,* 136–153.

Kahneman, D., & Tversky, A. (1982). The simulation heuristic. In D. Kahneman, P. Slovic, & A. Tversky (Eds.), *Judgment under uncertainty: Heuristics and biases* (pp. 201–208). New York: Cambridge University Press.

Kay, P., & Kempton, W. (1984). What is the Sapir-Whorf hypothesis? *American Anthropologist, 86,* 65–79.

Kay, P., & McDaniel, C. K. (1978). The linguistic significance of the meanings of basic color terms. *Language, 54,* 610–646.

Kovecses, Z. (1988). *The language of love.* Lewisburg, PA: Bucknell University Press.

Kovecses, Z. (1990). *Emotion concepts.* New York: Springer-Verlag.

Lakoff, G. (1987). *Women, fire, and dangerous things.* Chicago: University of Chicago Press.

Lakoff, G. (1991). Metaphor and war: The metaphor system used to justify war in the gulf. *Postmodern Culture.* PMC @ NCSUVM.

Lakoff, G., & Johnson, M. (1980). *Metaphors we live by.* Chicago: University of Chicago Press.

Lambert, W. E. (1992). Challenging established views on social issues. *American Psychologist,* *47,* 533–542.

Lenneberg, E., & Roberts, M. R. (1956). The language of experience: A study in methodology. *International Journal of American Linguistics, Memoir,* No. 13.

Liu, L. G. (1985). Reasoning counterfactually in Chinese: Are there obstacles? *Cognition, 21,* 239–270.

Loftus, E. F., & Palmer, J. C. (1974). Reconstruction of automobile destruction: An example of the interaction between language and memory. *Journal of Verbal Learning and Verbal Memory, 13,* 585–589.

Lucy, J. A. (1992). *Grammatical categories and cognition.* Cambridge: Cambridge University Press.

Lucy, J. A., & Shweder, R. A. (1979). Whorf and his critics: Linguistic and nonlinguistic influences on color memory. *American Anthropologist, 81,* 581–615.

Lucy, J. A., & Shweder, R. A. (1988). The effect of incidental conversation on memory for focal colors. *American Anthropologist, 90,* 923–931.

Markman, E. M., & Hutchinson, J. E. (1984). Children's sensitivity to constraints on word meaning: Taxonomic versus thematic relations. *Cognitive Psychology, 16,* 1–27.

Marks, L. E. (1982a). Synesthetic perception and poetic metaphor. *Journal of Experimental Psychology: Human Perception and Performance, 8,* 15–23.

Marks, L. E. (1982b). Bright sneezes and dark coughs, loud sunlight and soft moonlight. *Journal of Experimental Psychology: Human Perception and Performance, 8,* 177–193.

Martin, L. (1986). "Eskimo words for snow": A case study in the genesis and decay of an anthropological example. *American Anthropologist, 88,* 418–423.

Mills, A. E. (1985). The acquisition of German. In D. I. Slobin, *The crosslinguistic study of language acquisition: Vol. 1. The data* (pp. 141–254). Hillsdale, NJ: Erlbaum.

Mohanty, A. K., & Babu, N. (1983). Bilingualism and metalinguistic ability among Kond tribals in Orissa, India. *Journal of Social Psychology, 121,* 15–22.

Okuh, N. (1980). Bilingualism and divergent thinking among Nigerian and Welsh school children. *Journal of Social Psychology, 110,* 163–170.

Padilla, A. M., Lindholm, K. J., Chen, A., Durán, R., Hakuta, K., Lambert, W., & Tucker, G. R. (1991). The English-Only Movement. *American Psychologist, 46,* 120–130.

Reddy, M. J. (1979). The conduit metaphor—A case of frame conflict in our language about language. In A. Ortony (Ed.), *Metaphor and thought* (pp. 284–327). Cambridge: Cambridge University Press.

Reynolds, A. G. (1991). The cognitive consequences of bilingualism. In A. G. Reynolds (Ed.), *Bilingualism, multiculturalism, and second language learning* (pp. 145–182). Hillsdale, NJ: Erlbaum.

Rosch, E. (1977). Linguistic relativity. In P. N. Johnson-Laird & P. C. Wason (Eds.), *Thinking: Readings in cognitive science* (pp. 501–519). Cambridge: Cambridge University Press.

Sapir, E. (1964). *Culture, language, and personality.* Berkeley: University of California Press. (Original work published 1941).

Schooler, J. W., & Engstler-Schooler, T. Y. (1990). Verbal overshadowing of visual memories: Some things are better left unsaid. *Cognitive Psychology, 22,* 36–71.

Siegler, R. S. (1986). *Children's thinking.* Englewood Cliffs, NJ: Prentice-Hall.

Slobin, D. I. (1982). Universal and particular in the acquisition of language. In E. Wanner & L. Gleitman (Eds.), *Language acquisition: the state of the art* (pp. 128–170). Cambridge: Cambridge University Press.

Slobin, D. I. (Ed.). (1985a). *The crosslinguistic study of language acquisition: Vol. 1. The data.* Hillsdale, NJ: Erlbaum.

Slobin, D. I. (Ed.). (1985b). *The crosslinguistic study of language acquisition: Vol. 2. Theoretical issues.* Hillsdale, NJ: Erlbaum.

Slobin, D. I. (Ed.). (1992). *The crosslinguistic study of language acquisition* (Vol. 3). Hillsdale, NJ: Erlbaum.

Slobin, D. I., & Aksu, A. (1982). Tense, aspect, and modality in the use of the Turkish evidential. In P. J. Hopper (Ed.), *Tense-aspect: Between semantics & pragmatics* (pp. 185–200). Amsterdam: John Benjamins Publishing Company.

Smith, S. M., Brown, H. O., Toman, J. E. P., & Goodman, L. S. (1947). The lack of cerebral effects of *d*-tubocurarine. *Anesthesiology, 8,* 1–14.

Stefflre, V., Vales, V. C., & Morley, L. (1966). Language and cognition in Yucatan: A cross-cultural replication. *Journal of Personality and Social Psychology, 4,* 112–115.

Takano, Y. (1989). Methodological problems in cross-cultural studies of linguistic relativity. *Cognition, 31,* 141–162.

Watson, J. B. (1930). *Behaviorism.* New York: Norton.

Whorf, B. L. (1956). In J. B. Carroll (Ed.), *Language, thought and reality: Selected writings of Benjamin Lee Whorf.* Cambridge, MA: MIT Press.

Yale College programs of study. (1992). New Haven, CT: Yale University Printing Service.

CHAPTER 9

Intelligence

Robert J. Sternberg

Few constructs are asked to serve as many functions in psychology as is the construct of human intelligence. The main thesis of this chapter is that the way in which intelligence is conceived depends in a major way on the function that intelligence is viewed as serving. People who are interested in intelligence as a biological construct, for example, are likely to construe it differently from those who are interested in it as a construct created in part by context. Consider four of the main functions addressed in theory and research on intelligence, and how they differ from one another.

1. Biological. This type of account looks at biological processes. To qualify as a useful biological construct, intelligence should be a biochemical or biophysical process or at least somehow a resultant of biochemical or biophysical processes.

2. Cognitive approaches. This type of account looks at molar cognitive representations and processes. To qualify as a useful mental construct, intelligence should be specifiable as a set of mental representations and processes that are identifiable through experimental, mathematical, or computational means.

3. Contextual approaches. To qualify as a useful contextual construct, intelligence should be a source of individual differences in accomplishments

Thinking and Problem Solving
Copyright © 1994 by Academic Press, Inc. All rights of reproduction in any form reserved.

in "real-world" performances. It is not enough just to account for performance in the laboratory. On the contextual view, what a person does in the lab may not even remotely resemble what the person would do outside it. Moreover, different cultures may have different conceptions of intelligence, which affect what would count as intelligent in one cultural context versus another.

4. Systems approaches. Systems approaches attempt to understand intelligence through the interaction of cognition with context. They attempt to establish a link between the two levels of analysis, and to analyze what forms this link takes.

It is tempting to argue that there is a "right" point of view about intelligence. For example, a biologically oriented scientist might argue that what really matters is that intelligence should be understood biologically, and that attempts to understand the construct from the point of view of cognition or context are beside the point. The problem is that people adopting any one point of view can equally well say the same for the other points of view. Intelligence has multiple loci that can be understood from diverse perspectives.

Thus, the old saw, "Seek and thou shalt find," holds especially true for intelligence. Investigators are likely to find intelligence almost without regard to where they look. But where they look will determine what they find. Investigators who look inside the head will find a biological or mental construct, depending on their aims (which largely determine their methods), because without doubt, there is an aspect of intelligence that is biological, which in turn affects mental processing. Those who look to the cultural context in which people live will find intelligence there, because what is considered intelligent in one culture may differ radically from what is considered intelligent in another cultural context.

Because the volume in which this chapter appears is oriented toward cognition, I shall consider in this chapter primarily approaches that interface in one way or another with cognitive processing. However, I would be remiss if I did not point out the origins of contemporary thinking about intelligence in psychometric approaches to the construct.

The psychometric approach dates back to Galton (1883), who tried to understand intelligence in terms of basic psychophysical processes. He measured the various psychophysical processes, such as strength of hand grip and visual acuity, and interrelated them to one another. Later research by Wissler (1901) suggested that the approach of Galton was probably not well guided. Psychophysical tasks did not correlate well with each other, nor with performance in college. But although the Galtonian approach went into remission for a number of years, it reappeared later in another guise in the work of cognitive psychologists looking at basic information processing as a cornerstone of intelligence (e.g., Hunt, 1980).

An alternative approach, proposed by Binet and Simon (1905, 1916), proved to be more successful in many respects. This approach generated a test of intelligence, a form of which is still in widespread use today. And it also generated later cognitive research that looked at intelligence as a higher rather than as a lower cognitive process (e.g., R. J. Sternberg, 1977).

Neither the approach of Galton nor that of Binet was strongly grounded in theory. Charles Spearman (1904, 1927) tried to change things by creating a method, factor analysis, that could be used quantitatively to test, as well as actually to generate, theories of intelligence. The method involved statistical analysis of test intercorrelations to try to determine the mental structures (or factors) underlying test performance. Spearman concluded that intelligence comprised a general factor, *g,* which pervaded performance on all tests, and a set of specific factors, *s,* which were limited to single tests.

A rival theorist, Louis Thurstone (1938), suggested that Spearman was mistaken in his belief that intelligence was best understood in terms of just a single general factor and relatively uninteresting specific factors. Thurstone suggested instead that intelligence was best understood in terms of a set of correlated "primary mental abilities," namely, verbal comprehension, number, memory, inductive reasoning, perceptual speed, verbal fluency, and spatial visualization. Thurstone's theory received widespread acceptance in the United States, whereas Spearman's theory was generally preferred in Great Britain. It was probably no coincidence that the theories were each most widely accepted in their own countries of origin.

J. P. Guilford (1967) tried further to elaborate Thurstone's theory by proposing 120 different factors of intelligence generated by combining various processes, contents, and products. The theory met with a great deal of interest in the 1960s and early 1970s, but work by Horn and Knapp (1973) suggested that at least some of the empirical support that Guilford had generated for his theory was a statistical artifact of the way Guilford rotated his factors. The theory also was too unparsimonious to be practical for some purposes, such as testing.

Other theorists went beyond Thurstone, not in suggesting more factors, but in suggesting a different organization of factors. Cattell (1971) and P. E. Vernon (1971) both suggested hierarchical organizations of abilities, and more recently Gustafsson (1984) has suggested a hierarchical model that integrates aspects of several past ones. An even more elaborate psychometric theory has been proposed by Guttman (1954, 1965), who views intelligence as a radix, meaning that abilities are located in terms of polar rather than Cartesian coordinates.

In the 1960s and 1970s, many investigators became disillusioned with the psychometric approach. In concentrating on individual differences, the approach did not seem to say enough about what people had in common. And the approach had little to say about the biology, processes, or cultural contexts relating to human abilities. The approaches considered in this chapter have attempted to deal with these issues.

I. BIOLOGICAL APPROACHES TO INTELLIGENCE

Those looking for intelligence within the person may turn to a biological approach to intelligence. Their goal is to find the internal locus of abilities, whether in terms of current functioning (the brain and central nervous system) or of the transmission of functioning (the genes). There are several distinct subapproaches within the overall biological approach, which differ in their methodologies and assumptions.

A. Global Theories of Brain and Intelligence

Earlier theories relating brain to intelligence tended to be global in nature, although not necessarily backed by strong empirical evidence. Four such theories are those of Halstead, Konorski, Hebb, and Luria.

Halstead (1951) suggested that there are four biologically based abilities, which he called (1) the integrative field factor, (2) the abstraction factor, (3) the power factor, and (4) the directional factor. Halstead attributed all four of these abilities primarily to the cortex of the frontal lobes. Although Halstead's theory has been somewhat influential in neuropsychology and especially in neuropsychological testing, it has not had much impact on mainstream cognitive-psychological theorizing.

Konorski (1967) suggested that information in long-term memory is represented as an associative network of elements, which he referred to as "gnostic units." Konorski viewed short-term memory as that portion of the memory elements that was in a temporary state of excitation at a given time. Although Konoroski was ignored for many years, his work experienced something of a revival lately (e.g., Dickinson & Boakes, 1979).

More influential than either Halstead or Konorski in current thinking about intelligence was Donald Hebb (1949), who distinguished between two basic types of intelligence, Intelligence A and Intelligence B. According to Hebb, Intelligence A is innate potential; Intelligence B is the functioning of the brain in which development has occurred. These two basic types of intelligence should be distinguished from Intelligence C, or intelligence as measured by tests of intelligence. Although today some take this point for granted, when Hebb was writing, it was not at all obvious that there could be a major difference between intelligence, per se, and intelligence as tested. Hebb proposed a theory of Intelligence A whereby the repeated stimulation of specific receptors slowly would lead to the formation of what Hebb called "cell assemblies," or modules of thinking and learning. The idea of the cell assembly was prescient with respect to the kind of modular theorizing that is popular today, as discussed below.

Luria (1973, 1980) suggested that the brain comprises three main units with respect to intelligence: (1) a unit of arousal in the brain stem and midbrain structures, (2) a sensory-input unit in the temporal, parietal, and occipital lobes, and (3) an organization and planning unit in the frontal cortex. Luria's theory has been adapted by some modern-day psychologists interested in the assessment of abilities, such as Das and his colleagues (e.g., Das Kirby, & Jarman, 1979) and Kaufman and Kaufman (1983).

B. Nerve Conduction Velocity

It has not escaped the notice of theorists of intelligence that smart people seem to do things faster. Indeed, they have to, given the way we measure intelligence in our society; virtually all group tests of intelligence are timed, so that those who do not work quickly are automatically pegged as less intelligent. But the idea that intelligent people are more rapid learners or thinkers is not limited to the purveyors of intelligence tests—it is a part of the implicit theory of intelligence that pervades our society (R. J. Sternberg, Conway, Ketron, & Bernstein, 1981).

Some investigators believe that the apparently greater speed of thought or behavior witnessed in intelligent people derives from a more fundamental kind of speed, namely, speed of conduction of nerve impulses. On this view, the greater speed of functioning of smart people has a strictly biological origin: smart people act and think faster because information is transmitted in the body more rapidly than in less intelligent people.

1. Response-Time Paradigms

This view was originally supported by evidence that represented a large leap from data to theory, namely, results from molar response-time studies.

In one paradigm, the *reaction-time/movement-time paradigm* (e.g., Jensen, 1982), the subject places his or her preferred index finger on a so-called "home" button. A beep indicates a trial is about to begin, and then, after a random interval of from 1 to 4 seconds, one of two or more green lights flashes. The subject's task is to extinguish the light as quickly as possible by touching a button immediately adjacent to the light. This paradigm enables the investigator to make two direct measurements, including reaction time (the time from the flashing of the green light until the subject takes his or her finger off the home button) and movement time (the time from when the subject takes his or her finger off the home button until he or she pushes the button that extinguishes the light). Over many such trials, varying in the number of lights (often from as few as 2 to as many as 8), it is possible to compute a number of derived statistics, including both means and standard deviations of reaction and movement times.

Such studies generally reveal a small to moderate negative correlation between reaction time, and to a lesser extent, movement time, and scores on tests of cognitive abilities (Jensen, 1982). Often, the standard deviation of the times, representing variability in response rate, proves to be a better predictor than the mean, with higher variability associated with lower performance. Most derived scores, moreover, are highly reliable across trials, and are relatively immune from practice effects. Although the actual correlations with ability tests vary from one study to another, depending on variability of abilities within the sample as well as the nature of various experimental procedures, correlations are typically in the range of −.3 to −.5 with typical samples, such as secondary and tertiary school students (Jensen, 1979; Jensen & Munro, 1979). Correlations are higher with retarded samples (P. E. Vernon, 1971).

Jensen, Vernon, and others have interpreted these correlations as proxy indicators of a correlation between speed of conduction in the nervous system and intelligence. Longstreth (1984) has criticized both the methodology and the interpretation of results, and indeed, there seems to be quite a gap between response-time studies and conclusions about velocities of conduction along nerves. For this reason, Jensen, Vernon, and others have turned to directly measuring such conduction velocities. These studies will be described below after a description of another related paradigm.

2. The Inspection-Time Paradigm

This paradigm, introduced by Nettlebeck (1973, 1982), typically involves tachistoscopic or computer presentation of two adjacent vertical lines followed by a visual mask (to destroy the image in visual iconic memory). The two lines differ in length by varying amounts, as do the lengths of time for which the two lines are presented. The subject's task is to say which line is longer. But instead of using raw response time as the dependent variable, investigators typically use measures derived from a psychophysical function estimated after many trials. For example, the measure might be the duration of a single inspection trial at which 50% accuracy is achieved.

Initial reports of correlations between inspection time and measured intelligence suggested that the correlation was quite high (Brand & Deary, 1982; Nettlebeck & Lally, 1976) if the range of levels of intelligence in the sample was large and, preferably, if the sample was small. Correlations go down to the more typical .3 to .5 levels if more typical samples are used (Nettlebeck, 1987). Moreover, these correlations can be achieved even with the use of an auditory inspection-time measure (Deary, 1988; Raz & Willerman, 1985). Although values of the correlation vary, the existence of a correlation seems to be beyond dispute.

3. Direct Measurement of Nerve-Conduction Velocities

Because inferences from these data to psychological theory are so indirect, investigators have turned as well to procedures that measure nerve-conduction velocities directly. Two procedures measure conduction velocities, either centrally (in the brain) or peripherally (e.g., in the arm).

Reed and Jensen (1992) tested brain nerve conduction velocities via two medium-latency potentials, N70 and P100, which were evoked by pattern-reversal stimulation. Subjects saw a black and white checkerboard pattern in which the black squares would change to white and the white squares to black. Over many trials, responses to these changes were analyzed via electrodes attached to the scalp in four places. Correlations of derived latency measures with IQ were small (generally in the .1 to .2 range of absolute value), but were significant in some cases, suggesting at least a modest relation between the two kinds of measures.

P. A. Vernon and Mori (1992) reported on two studies investigating the relation between nerve-conduction velocity in the arm and IQ. In both studies, nerve-conduction velocity was measured in the median nerve of the arm by attaching electrodes to the arm. In the second study, conduction velocity from the wrist to the tip of the finger was also measured. Vernon and Mori found significant correlations with IQ in the .4 range, as well as somewhat smaller correlations (around −.2) with response-time measures. They interpreted their results as supporting the hypothesis of a relation between speed of information transmission in the peripheral nerves and intelligence. However, these results must be interpreted cautiously, as P. A. Vernon (personal communication, September, 1992) has indicated that he has been unable to replicate these results.

C. Hemispheric Specialization

Theories of the relation between hemispheric specialization and intelligence go back to Marc Dax, an obscure country doctor in France who, in 1836, noted that his patients who had suffered a loss of speech (aphasia) all had brain damage in the left hemisphere of the brain, a repeated pattern that seemed to defy explanation as a coincidence. Paul Broca, by 1864, later expanded upon and elaborated this claim.

More recently, Sperry (1961) suggested that each hemisphere behaves in many respects like a separate brain. For example, Sperry, Myers, and Schrier (1960) showed that visual information presented to one hemisphere of a cat with its corpus callosum severed was not available to the other hemisphere. Localization applies to humans as well. Gazzaniga (1970) observed a patient who, angry at his wife, reached for her with his left hand while his right hand tried to stop his left one.

One of the most active debates in the field has been over whether language is completely localized in the left hemisphere, a claim going back to Dax and Broca. Zaidel (1975, 1978) has argued for at least some right-hemisphere processing of language, whereas Gazzaniga (1985) has argued that right-hempisheric processing of language is extremely rare and nonexistent in normal people.

Some have suggested that the two hemispheres have different styles of processing information. For example, Jerre Levy (1974) has argued that the left hemisphere tends to process information analytically, whereas the right tends to process it holistically.

Gazzaniga (1985) has staked out a different position, arguing that the brain is organized modularly. His view, in the spirit of Fodor (1983) as well as much present-day connectionist modeling (e.g., McClelland, Rumelhart, & PDP Research Group, 1986), is that there exist many discrete units of the mind, each operating relatively independent of the others. Moreover, these modules operate at a level that is not conscious. The left hemisphere tries to assign interpretations to the processing of these modules. Thus, instead of understanding preceding the thoughts we have about things, understanding may be our attempt to make sense of the thoughts we have.

D. Brain Size

Some investigators have attempted to assess the relation between brain size or cranial capacity and intelligence. Jerison (1982) concluded that brain size (or to be more precise, encephalization) is correlated with intellectual level across but not within species. Although few have accepted the argument that there is any within-species relation between brain size and intelligence, the argument keeps reappearing. For example, Rushton (1990, 1992) has advanced such a claim, which others have rebutted (Cain & Vanderwolf, 1990). At present, what relation there is, if any, between brain size and intelligence within species is unclear.

E. Brain Activity

Probably the most popular biological approach has been one that seeks to relate brain activity to intelligence. Early work of this type used electroencephalographic (EEG) measurement. For example, Galin and Ornstein (1972) showed a link between amount of EEG activity in each of the hemispheres and the type of task performance. In particular, they found that the ratio of right- to left-hemisphere alpha processing was greater in verbal than in spatial tasks. EEG measurement is highly problematic because it is a has recording, and hence more recent work has tended to use evoked potentials (EPs), which are measured by averaging wave forms on successive presentations of a stimulus obtained from EEG recordings.

One line of work, by Emanuel Donchin (e.g., Donchin, 1979; McCarthy & Donchin, 1981) and others, has looked at a particular wave form, P300. The label P300 refers to a positive component of evoked potentials that has a latency anywhere from 300 to 900 ms after presentation of a stimulus. The amplitude of P300 seems to reflect the allocation of cognitive resources to a given task. Ertl and his colleagues (e.g., Chalke & Ertl, 1965; Ertl, 1966; Ertl & Schafer, 1969) found consistent correlations between averaged evoked potentials and IQ, although their results did not always replicate. Schafer (1982) has suggested that the tendency to show a large P300 response to surprising stimuli may be an individual-differences variable, whereby more intelligent individuals should show a smaller P300 to expected stimuli than would less intelligent individuals (because the more intelligent would not need to devote much in the way of attentional resources to familiar stimuli). In fact, Schafer reported a correlation of .82 between an individual-differences measure of P300 and IQ. The size of the correlation seems a bit large, given the reliabilities of the measures involved.

Hendrickson and Hendrickson (1980) have suggested that errors can occur in the passage of information through the cerebral cortex, and that these errors, which probably occur at synapses, are responsible for variability in evoked potentials. On this view, individuals with low IQs will have noisy, error-phone channels of information processing in the nervous system, with the result that when evoked potentials are averaged out, they will have a smoother appearance than those produced by individuals with consistent and less noisy channels. Hendrickson (1982) and Hendrickson and Hendrickson (1980) presented data in support of this hypothesis, as did Blinkhorn and Hendrickson (1982) and Barrett and Eysenck (1992), among others. Obviously, the empirical result is conceptually rather distant from the theory, and thus may hold whether or not the theory is correct.

Some of the most interesting current biological work is being done by Richard Haier and his colleagues. For example, Haier et al. (1988) showed that cortical glucose metabolic rates as revealed by PET scan analysis of subjects solving Raven Matrix problems were lower for more intelligent than for less intelligent subjects, suggesting that the more intelligent subjects needed to expend less effort than the less intelligent ones in order to solve the reasoning problems. A later study (Haier, Siegel, Tang, Abel, & Buchsbaum, 1992) showed a similar result when more and less intelligent subjects played the computer game of Tetris. In other words, smart people do not have to work as hard as less smart people at a given problem. What remains to be shown, however, is the causal direction of this finding. One could more sensibly argue that the smart people expend less glucose (as a proxy for effort) because they are smart, rather than that people are smart because they expend less glucose. In other words, we should not always assume that the biological event is a cause (in the reductionistic sense). It may be, instead, an effect.

To summarize, biological approaches to intelligence are yielding exciting but still puzzling findings regarding the relationship of the brain and nervous systems to intelligence. Cognitive approaches, discussed next, also attempt to look at this relation, but from a more molar standpoint.

II. COGNITIVE APPROACHES

Cognitive approaches to intelligence complement rather than contradict biological ones. The idea is that the two approaches look at different levels at which intelligence can be analyzed. Levels are not better or worse than each other, just different. We learn different things about a phenomenon by studying it at different levels.

A reductionist might question this point of view. But the review of biological approaches above should make clear that one can interpret biological results in cognitive terms as easily as one can interpret cognitive results in biological terms. For example, evoked-potential studies can be viewed as providing us with a biological dependent variable for studying cognitive processing. The pattern of evoked potentials, or of glucose metabolism, for that matter, reflects cognitive processing, rather than the other way around. Thus, if a person finds a problem (cognitively) easy, he or she does not need to put much effort into it, resulting in lower glucose metabolism. It is the cognition that controls the biological process, rather than the other way around. Of course, there are also biological constraints on cognition, resulting in a continual interaction between the two levels of processing.

A. Historical Approaches

Strange as it may seem, the cognitive approach to intelligence has its roots in the same theorist who is often seen as the father of the psychometric approach, Charles Spearman. Spearman (1923) proposed what he believed to be three fundamental qualitative principles of cognition. *Apprehension of experience* is essentially what we today call "encoding": the perception of a stimulus and the relation of it to the contents of long-term memory. *Eduction of relations* is what we today call "inference": the interrelation of two stimuli so as to understand their similarities and differences. And *eduction of correlates* is what we today call "application": the applying of an inferred relation to a new domain (see R. J. Sternberg, 1977). Spearman (1923) suggested the analogy as an ideal test problem for studying these processes, because in an analogy, such as LAWYER is to CLIENT as DOCTOR is to _____?_____, a subject has to encode each term of the analogy, infer the relation between LAWYER and CLIENT, and apply the inferred relation to DOCTOR to generate the completion, PATIENT.

Although Spearman proposed a cognitive approach, this approach to intelligence lay fallow until Cronbach (1957) called for the unification of the two disciplines of scientific psychology—namely, correlational psychology and experimental psychology. In the 1960s, there were some tentative efforts to achieve such unification, which were perhaps best represented in a book edited by Gagné (1968). But if there was a real milestone, it was in a book edited by Resnick (1976), in which various contributors again suggested that we take seriously a cognitive approach to intelligence. Carroll (1976), in particular, proposed that psychometric tests be understood as cognitive tasks. Carroll's own work in this regard was to reach a culmination almost twenty years later, when he published a massive review of the entire factor-analytic literature on intelligence (Carroll, 1993). Although his own review was factor analytic, he attempted to understand the factors of the mind from the cognitive perspective he had proposed much earlier. But back in the 1970s, the new wave of intelligence research was getting under way. Although this first wave culminated in the book edited by Resnick, it started somewhat earlier.

Royer (1971) was probably the first to take a psychometric test, the digit-symbol substitution task found on the *Wechsler Adult Intelligence Scale,* and do an information-processing analysis of it. For whatever reason, the paper fell into undeserved obscurity. People instead were attracted to work published just slightly later that used what has come to be called the cognitive-correlates approach to understanding intelligence, discussed below.

B. The Cognitive-Correlates Approach

The impetus for the cognitive-correlates approach came with the publication of a seminal paper by Hunt, Frost, and Lunneborg (1973), three years before the publication of the Resnick book. In this paper, Hunt and his colleagues showed that tasks that had formerly been studied by cognitive psychologists as vehicles for understanding human cognition could also be used as vehicles for understanding human intelligence. In retrospect, that claim seems quite natural, because certainly we could not fully understand human intelligence without an understanding of human cognition. But because research on intelligence had been so strongly associated with the psychometric approach (at least in the United States, whereas the Piagetian approach was dominant in Europe), the claims of Hunt were novel at the time.

Even more influential in the long run was probably the article by Hunt, Lunneborg, and Lewis (1975), which sought an understanding of verbal ability. Hunt and his colleagues suggested that verbal ability could be understood in large part in terms of speed of access to lexical information stored in long-term memory, and they used a task earlier proposed by Posner and Mitchell (1967) as a basis for testing their claim.

Hunt and his colleagues used the letter-comparison task as the main task for staking their claim. They had subjects do both physical and name comparisons of pairs of letters, such as "A A," "A a," and "A b." In the physical-match condition, subjects simply had to say whether two letters were identical to each other in appearance. In the name-match condition, subjects had to say whether the two letters were identical in letter name. By taking the difference between the two average response times, Hunt and his colleagues computed what they believed to be the amount of time it took to access lexical information in long-term memory.

Why was the approach of Hunt and his colleagues called the cognitive-correlates approach? Because in this and later work (e.g., Hunt, 1978), Hunt correlated parameters of information-processing models (such as the name-match vs. physical-match difference score) with scores on psychometric tests of abilities. Hunt and his colleagues found correlations roughly at the level of about $-.3$ (with the correlations being negative because a response time was being correlated with a proportion or number correct score). Although this correlation is not particularly strong, it is strong enough to suggest at least some relation between two constructs. Of course, the nature of the relation was and still is open to debate. One could as easily say that high verbal ability leads to quick cognitive access as one could say the converse. The advantage of the Hunt approach seemed to be in the explanation of psychometric factors in terms of cognitive processes, rather than the other way around.

Not all cognitive-correlates research used the Posner–Mitchell task, or followed the theorizing of Hunt, which was based on his distributed-memory model (see Hunt, 1980). Some theorists believed that intelligence would be better understood through the study of simpler processes. For example, Jensen (1979, 1982), although physiological in his theorizing, used simple and choice-reaction time procedures to study intelligence.

C. The Cognitive-Components Approach

An alternative approach had its roots in the information-processing work of Donders (1868) in the nineteenth century. Donders argued that if you timed a person doing one task, and also timed him doing a second task that differed from the first task only in requiring one more mental operation in order to complete it, then the difference in response time between the second task and the first would be a measure of the time it took to execute the single process.

This approach was brought into twentieth-century cognitive psychology by S. Sternberg (1969) in his work on memory scanning, and indeed, the memory-scanning task later became one of the tasks studied under the cognitive-correlates approach (e.g., Chiang & Atkinson, 1976). The approach was used by other cognitive psychologists with success (e.g., Clark & Chase, 1972; Shepard & Metzler, 1971), and seemed to provide as well an entrée for studying cognitive bases of intelligence.

R. J. Sternberg (1977) proposed a method for studying intelligence, which he referred to as componential analysis. The basic method had two parts. The first, internal validation, involved isolating the information-processing components and strategy involved in the solution of a cognitive task hypothesized to relate to intelligence. The second part, external validation, involved correlating component scores with psychometric reference tests hypothesized both to correlate (convergent validation) and not to correlate (discriminant validation) with the target cognitive process.

The method was initiated by taking a cognitive task and setting up timed experimental conditions that could be used jointly to isolate the information-processing components of the kind identified by Newell and Simon (1972). Consider, for example, the analogies task. Subjects would be timed as they solved analogies under several different experimental conditions. In one condition, subjects were timed for solving the whole analogy, A is to B as C is to D (where D might be represented either as a set of multiple-choice answers options or as a single option to be identified as true or false). In a second condition, subjects would be given as long as they wanted to solve A is to B as C is to (where D was not visible on the screen), and then would be timed as they viewed and solved the last part, D. In yet another condition, subjects would see A is to B, and then would be timed separately for solving C is to D. And in a fourth condition, subjects would see just A in the first part of the trial, and would be timed separately for solving B as C is to D. By varying the difficulty of the multiple items constituting the various experimental conditions, it was possible to use multiple regression to estimate component latencies and difficulties. Alternative models of information processing would be compared for their fit to the latency data. Then, individual parameter estimates for the best fitting model would be correlated with the psychometric-ability test scores.

The cognitive-components approach was applied by a number of investigators to different kinds of information-processing problems (e.g., Pellegrino & Glaser, 1979, 1980; Snow, 1979; R. J. Sternberg, 1983). It proved to be useful in elucidating cognitive processes, and is still used today. But it ran into some difficulties that resulted in the approach having somewhat less success than originally had been hoped for. One difficulty was that truly complex tasks just do not lend themselves well to subtractive decomposition because subjects do not solve the problems in a linear way. For another thing, when component scores were correlated with ability-test scores, in some instances, the highest correlations were with the unanalyzed regression constant (e.g., R. J. Sternberg, 1977). Moreover, some investigators believed that even the kinds of problems found on intelligence tests were too simple truly to grasp the essence of human intelligence.

D. Artificial-Intelligence Approaches

One could write a whole book, or even several volumes, on the various artificial-intelligence (AI) approaches that have been used in efforts to elucidate the nature of human intelligence. All of these approaches have in common the use of the computer metaphor, and usually the computer, for understanding intelligence. I will briefly highlight some of the major efforts here, although of course many other important efforts will not be covered.

This approach has its origins in the work of Newell, Shaw, and Simon (1958) on the Logical Theorist (LT). This program was written to prove theorems in plane geometry, using the heuristic of working backward. Working backward is actually a strategy used in solving a variety of problems, although used more by novices than by experts (Simon & Simon, 1978). The Logical Theorist soon gave way to a much more general program, General Problem Solver (GPS) (Newell & Simon, 1972), which could solve a variety of MOVE-type problems in which the path to solution consists of a series of well-defined steps through an easily specifiable problem space. This program used a different heuristic, means–ends analysis, to accomplish its goals. It would do an operation, and then compute the difference between the actual state and the desired state. The next move would be chosen so as to maximize the distance covered between the actual and the desired states.

At the same time that Newell, Simon, and other colleagues at Carnegie–Mellon were developing programs specializing in relatively domain-general heuristics that could be used for a number of different types of logically based problems, other investigators in other sites were taking different approaches. Work at the Massachusetts Institute of Technology under the direction of Marvin Minsky tended to concentrate on the development of programs for semantic information processing (Minsky, 1968), although some of the work looked at more structured problems, such as nonverbal analogies. Indeed, Evans (1968) wrote a program that could solve even fairly difficult geometric analogies. This program was a precursor to a later one by Hunt (1974), which could solve some items from the Raven Progressive Matrices, and even a much later one by Carpenter and Just (1975), which would be able to solve even the most complex abstract reasoning items from the Raven Progressive Matrices. A next-generation descendant of the Minsky tradition was to be found in the work of Terry Winograd (1972), who wrote a program that was far more sophisticated in its processing of language and could actually control a robot arm that could manipulate a world of geometric blocks.

Roger Schank and his colleagues followed in the Minsky tradition of investigating semantic information processing, but their programs, like Winograd's, tended to be much more sophisticated in their approach to language (Schank, 1972, 1975, 1980). Schank (1972) proposed a model of what he referred to as "conceptual dependency" to serve as a basis for understanding how concepts could be related to one another. These ideas formed the basis for script theory (Schank & Abelson, 1977), which attempted to account for how we know what to do when we go to, say, a restaurant or a doctor's office. A script is basically a schema consisting of a set of actions that we typically follow in a given type of situation, and as it turned out, much of human behavior proves to be scriptlike in nature.

Although many other approaches have been taken to artificial intelligence, perhaps the most influential has been that of the construction of expert systems. Early systems such as MYCIN (Shortliffe, 1976), which did medical diagnosis, and DENDRAL (Feigenbaum, Buchanan, & Lederberg, 1971), which identified structures of organic molecules, gave rise to later expert systems in a large variety of fields of endeavor. Although the expert systems differ widely in the domains to which they are applied and in the ways in which they work, the expert systems tend to have certain common characteristics (Hayes-Roth, Waterman, & Lenat, 1983): a language processor facilitating communication between user and system, a knowledge base that is subdivided into knowledge of facts and rules, an interpreter that applies these rules, a scheduler that controls the sequence of application, a consistency enforcer that modifies conclusions when new data contradict old data, and a justifier that can explain the system's line of reasoning.

The expert-system approach, and most of the other approaches described above as well, make little effort to stimulate human cognitive processing. Rather, the goal is to create programs that operate as effectively and as efficiently as possible. Nowhere is this better seen than in chess-expert systems, which almost always use advanced methods evaluating millions of possible moves per round to beat chess masters. No one claims that chess masters do anything like what the programs do. On the contrary, chess masters consider only a few moves per round, but these moves are far superior to the overwhelming majority of moves that the computer would consider. The programs can be quite good because they are so fast in evaluating moves, and can beat some chess masters through sheer brute force of calculation.

Other theorists, however, have tried to create programs that simulate human intelligence, and in some cases they have combined programming with experimental tests of their models. One of the best examples of such work is that of John Anderson (1983, 1986), whose ACT model simulates many aspects of human cognition. Anderson is not the only theorist from Carnegie–Mellon to relate computer data to human data. As early as 1963, Simon and Kotovsky wrote a computer program to solve letter-series problems, and then compared the performance of that program with human data.

The various cognitive approaches have been successful in elucidating many relations between mental processes and representations, on one hand, and human abilities, on the other. The review above, of course, covers only a fraction of the work in the field, and more detailed reviews can be found in R. J. Sternberg (1982b, 1990, 1994). But some theorists have believed that these approaches all leave certain questions unanswered, and, in particular, it has been suggested that all of the cognitive approaches may be too narrow to capture the broad essence of intelligence.

III. CONTEXTUAL APPROACHES TO INTELLIGENCE

The basic idea underlying contextual approaches goes back at least to Ferguson (1954), who stated that "cultural factors prescribe what shall be learned and at what age; consequently different cultural environments lead to the development of different patterns of ability" (p. 121). Contextualists have in common the belief that because intelligence cannot be understood outside a cultural context, no psychometric or cognitive approach could possibly do justice to the construct.

The most extreme contextualist position is that of radical cultural relativism (Berry, 1974), according to which cultural universals are soundly repudiated. On this view, one has to study intelligence in each culture emically, meaning that intelligence must be understood from within the system of meaning created by the culture. Simply taking a standardized test of intelligence and translating it, as has so often been done, is a far cry from what this approach calls for.

One way of understanding emic concepts of intelligence is to ask people what they mean by the term "intelligence," or otherwise to try to elucidate concepts from the inside. For example, Berry (1984) reviewed many studies attempting to understand intelligence in this way, and concluded that cultural conceptions of intelligence can be quite different across cultures. In a recent study, for example, Berry and Bennet (1990) found that Cree conceptions of intelligence come closer to our own conventional notions of wisdom than they do to our conventional notions of intelligence.

Neisser (1979) proposed applying such methodologies to our own, common-cultural conceptions of intelligence, and R. J. Sternberg, Conway, Ketron, and Bernstein (1981) did just that. In a series of studies, they found that laypeople have views of intelligence that encompass attributes of practical problem solving, verbal ability, and social competence. Although the first two of these attributes are measured by standard tests of intelligence, the last almost never is.

Other positions are less extreme in that they do not require studying intelligence in a wholly endemic or endogenous way. The Laboratory of Comparative Human Cognition (1982) has proposed a kind of conditional comparativism, according to which comparisons between cultures are possible so long as tasks are made equivalent for the members of the different cultures. If they are not made equivalent, the results will be nonsense. Thus, when Luria (1976) asked his subjects: "From Shakhimardan to Vuadil it is three hours on foot, while to Fergana it is six hours. How much time does it take to go on foot from Vuadil to Fergana?" he found his Russian peasant subjects giving answers like "You're wrong . . . it's far and you wouldn't get there in three hours" (p. 129). The point is simply that using local place names does not constitute making tasks equivalent. A more interesting kind of equivalence was obtained by Wagner (1978), who found, as have others, that subjects from other cultures can do better than subjects from our own culture on memory tasks if they are given stimuli to remember that are familiar to them and not to us, rather than the other way around as is typical in conventional intelligence tests devised in our own culture.

Other contextualists have also rejected strict cognitivism, although the forms of contextualism they have proposed have been milder than those proposed by Berry or Cole. For example, Keating (1984) pointed out the need to take into account context, and yet has been a leading contributor to the understanding of cognitive functioning. Baltes and his colleagues (e.g., Baltes, Dittmann-Kohli, & Dixon, 1984) have also studied cognitive processes in a contextual framework.

Contextualists have been criticized for not being clear as to what they mean by "context," but in fact, Berry and Irvine (1986) have proposed a four-level model of context that specifies at least part of what context means. At the highest level is ecological context, which comprises all of the permanent or almost permanent characteristics that provide the backdrop for human action. It is the natural cultural habitat in which a person lives. The second level of context is the experiential level of context, or the pattern of recurrent experiences within the ecological context that provides a basis for learning and development. The third kind of context is the performance context, comprising the limited set of environmental circumstances that account for particular behaviors at specific points in space and time. And finally there is the experimental context, nested under the others, which is what we study when we do research in the laboratory, or when we give intelligence tests.

On this view, the context in which a task is administered could strongly affect the outcomes on that task. But does it? Apparently so. There is now strong evidence to suggest context effects on human performance that are not accounted for by strictly cognitive models.

In one study, Ceci and Bronfenbrenner (1985) studied children's performance on a time-estimation task either in a home environment or in the laboratory. They found that the patterns of results shown by the children were completely different under the two circumstances. Not only do people show different patterns of performance in different contexts, but different levels of performance as well. Ceci and Liker (1986) found that expert bettors at horse-race tracks who consistently performed above chance and whose performance could be simulated only by highly complex regressions had an average IQ of just 97. Lave (1988) found that housewives who could not perform fairly elementary mathematical operations on an arithmetic test had no problem performing them in an actual supermarket food-buying situation. And Nuñes, Schliemann, and Carraher (1993) found that Brazilian street children who would fail school mathematics could quite adequately do the math required of them in their roles as street vendors.

The same principles that apply in more everyday kinds of situations, such as supermarkets and street vending, apply in more complex situations as well. R. J. Sternberg and Wagner (1986, 1993) studied the practical intelligence of business executives, and found that tests of practical intelligence that predicted executive success were uncorrelated with standard measures of intelligence. Similar results emerged in studies of other occupations as diverse as salesperson and college professor.

As is true with other approaches, much more could be said about contextual ones, and for other references, we recommend Rogoff and Lave (1984) or R. J. Sternberg and Wagner (1986). Although contextual approaches have a definite edge on cognitive models in specifying the importance of context as an influence on cognitive performance, they tend to be weak in the specification of cognitive processing. Ideally, perhaps, a theory would take fully into account both cognition and context. That is what exponents of the last approach we will consider, a systems approach, have tried to do.

IV. THE SYSTEMS APPROACH

I refer to as "systems approaches" ones that try to look at the interaction of cognition and context as a system. Although several efforts of this kind have been made, I shall describe here only two of the more well-known ones, those of Gardner (1983, 1993) and of R. J. Sternberg (1985, 1988).

A. The Theory of Multiple Intelligences

According to Howard Gardner (1983), intelligence is not a unitary construct at all, but rather a multiple construct. According to Gardner, there is not one intelligence, but seven "multiple intelligences." These multiple intelligences are (1) linguistic intelligence, used in reading, writing, speaking, and listening; (2) logical-mathematical intelligence, used in thinking logically and in solving mathematics problems; (3) spatial intelligence, used in negotiating the physical environment; (4) musical intelligence, used in singing and in appreciating music; (5) bodily-kinesthetic intelligence, used in athletics and in dancing; (6) interpersonal intelligence, used in relating to other people; and (7) intrapersonal intelligence, used in understanding ourselves. These intelligences are relatively independent, although they may be linked by higher order modules. If one accepts this theory, then conventional intelligence tests would be seen as being quite limited, concentrating as they do on linguistic, logical-mathematical, and spatial intelligences, but measuring little or nothing of the other four intelligences.

Gardner tested his theory not by collecting experimental evidence in support of the theory, but rather by reviewing various literatures relating to human abilities and finding results that are consistent with his theoretical proposal. For example, he believes that the literatures on brain functioning, idiots savants, and cognitive development are supportive of the kinds of claims he is making. When it comes to matters of definition, as of the term "intelligence," it is not clear that there is really any empirical operation that can specify the correctness or incorrectness of a proposal, but there is certainly evidence to suggest the existence of the abilities of which Gardner speaks. Whether they are all intelligences, and whether they are really as distinct as Gardner claims, is a matter for debate.

B. The Triarchic Theory of Human Intelligence

R. J. Sternberg's (1985, 1988) triarchic theory of human intelligence takes a somewhat different tack from that taken by Gardner. The theory attempts to link cognition to context through three parts or subtheories—hence the name "triarchic."

First, according to this theory, intelligence serves three functions in real-world contexts. The first, adaptation to the environment, refers to people's changing of themselves in order to suit the environments in which they live. The second, shaping of environments, refers to people's changing of their environments to suit themselves. And the third, selection of environments, refers to people's choosing new environments when they are unable to make their environment work for them either through adaptation or shaping.

Second, according to the triarchic theory, environments and the tasks we confront within them vary in terms of their familiarity. At one extreme, we have tasks within environments that are extremely novel and that we have never before encountered. At the other extreme we have tasks that are so familiar that we accomplish them almost without thinking. According to the triarchic theory, the two levels of experience that are most relevant for assessing intelligence are the zones of relative novelty and of automatization.

Other investigators, too, have suggested the importance of relatively (but not extremely) novel tasks for measuring intelligence (e.g., Cattell, 1971; Piaget, 1972; Raaheim, 1974). The idea is that a task that is totally novel—calculus problems for a five-year-old, for example—is not a good measure of intelligence because we have no cognitive structures to bring to bear upon it. Automatization, such as we require in learning to read or to speak a foreign language, is also important for efficient functioning in everyday life. Without it, we could not adequately accomplish even the most common tasks, such as walking or driving.

Third, we apply certain cognitive processes to tasks as various levels of experience in order to adapt to, shape, and select environments. The triarchic theory distinguishes among three types of information-processing components—metacomponents, performance components, and knowledge-acquisition components. Metacomponents are used to decide what to do, to monitor it while it is being done, and to evaluate what one has done after it is completed. Performance components are used in the actual execution of a task. And knowledge-acquisition components are used to learn how to perform a task in the first place. Metacomponents activate performance and knowledge-acquisition components, which in turn provide feedback to the metacomponents.

To summarize, the systems theories attempt in different ways to integrate cognition and context. The theories might be seen as having as an advantage their breadth and their scope. But some might argue that they have taken the notion of intelligence too far, and have included within their scope abilities or attributes that go beyond intelligence. Moreover, the theories are so broad that it is unclear just what operations might be used adequately to falsify them.

V. CONCLUSION

In this chapter, I have reviewed four different approaches to the understanding of intelligence—the psychometric, the cognitive, the contextual, and the systems approaches. There are other approaches as well that have not been discussed here (see Baron, 1985; Brody, 1992; Ceci, 1990; R. J. Sternberg, 1982b, 1990; for other approaches). But I have covered some of the major approaches that have influenced contemporary thinking about human intelligence.

Although each approach is different, and proponents of each approach try to highlight the advantages of their own approach over others, it turns out that the different approaches often address somewhat different questions, and thus are not mutually contradictory. The psychometric approach tries to "map" the mind. The biological approach attempts to find intelligence in the brain. The cognitive approach tries to specify the mental representations and processes that underlie intelligence. The contextual approach tries to specify how context affects intelligence, thought, and action. And the systems approach tries to provide some integration of the cognitive and contextual approaches. At times, it is frustrating to contemplate on how little we know about human intelligence. Yet, if we consider that the scientific analysis of human intelligence did not get under way until the twentieth century, whereas the scientific analysis of, say, light had an edge of several centuries, then we realize not only how much we do not know, but how far we have come.

Acknowledgments

Research for this paper was supported under the Javits Act Program (Grant No. R206R00001) as administered by the Office of Educational Research and Improvement (OERI), U.S. Department of Education. Grantees undertaking such projects are encouraged to express freely their professional judgment. This paper, therefore, does not necessarily represent positions or policies of the Government, and no official endorsement should be inferred.

I would like to thank the Office of Educational Research and Improvement for supporting my work and research on human intelligence.

References

Anderson, J. R. (1983). *The architecture of cognition.* Cambridge, MA: Harvard University Press.

Anderson, J. R. (1986). Knowledge compilation: The general learning mechanism. In R. S. Michalski, J. G. Carbonell, & T. M. Mitchell (Eds.), *Machine learning: An artificial intelligence approach* (Vol. 2, pp. 289–310). Los Altos, CA: Kaufmann.

Baltes, P. B., Dittmann-Kohli, F., & Dixon, R. A. (1984). New perspectives on the development of intelligence in adulthood: Toward a dual-process conception and a model of selective optimization with compensation. In P. B. Baltes & O. G. Brim, Jr. (Eds.), *Life-span development and behavior* (Vol. 6, pp. 33–76). New York: Academic Press.

Baron, J. (1985). *Rationality and intelligence.* Cambridge: Cambridge University Press.

Barrett, P. T., & Eysenck, H. J. (1992). Brain evoked potentials and intelligence: The Hendrickson Paradigm. *Intelligence, 16,* 361–381.

Berry, J. W. (1974). Radical cultural relativism and the concept of intellectual development during adulthood. In J. W. Berry & P. R. Dasen (Eds.), *Culture and cognition: Readings in cross-cultural psychology* (pp. 225–229). London: Methuen.

Berry, J. W. (1984). Towards a universal psychology of cognitive competence. In P. S. Fry (Ed.), *Changing conceptions of intelligence and intellectual functioning* (pp. 35–61). Amsterdam: North-Holland Publ.

Berry, J. W., & Bennet, J. A. (1990, February). *Cree conceptions of cognitive competence.* Report to Advisory Research Committee, Queens University, Ontario.

Berry, J. W., & Irvine, S. H. (1986). Bricolage: Savages do it daily. In R. J. Sternberg & R. K. Wagner (Eds.), *Practical intelligence: Nature and origins of competence in the everyday world.* New York: Cambridge University Press.

Binet, A., & Simon, T. (1916). *The development of intelligence in children.* Baltimore, MD: Williams & Wilkins. (Original work published 1905)

Blinkhorn, S. F., & Hendrickson, D. E. (1982). Averaged evoked responses and psychometric intelligence. *Nature (London), 295,* 596–597.

Brand, C. R., & Deary, I. J. (1982). Intelligence and "inspection time." In H. J. Eysenck (Ed.), *A model for intelligence.* Berlin: Springer-Verlag.

Brody, N. (1992). *Intelligence.* San Diego: Academic Press.

Cain, D. P., & Vanderwolf, C. H. (1990). A critique of Rushton on race, brain size, and intelligence. *Personality and Individual Differences, 11,* 777–784.

Carpenter, P. A., & Just, M. A. (1975). Sentence comprehension: A psycholinguistic processing model of verification. *Psychological Review, 82,* 45–73.

Carroll, J. B. (1976). Psychometric tests as cognitive tasks: A new "structure of intellect." In L. B. Resnick (Ed.), *The nature of intelligence.* Hillsdale, NJ: Erlbaum.

Carroll, J. B. (1993). *Human cognitive abilities: A survey of factor-analysic studies.* New York: Cambridge University Press.

Cattell, R. B. (1971). *Abilities: Their structure, growth, and action.* Boston: Houghton Mifflin.

Ceci, S. J. (1990). *On intelligence . . . more or less.* Englewood Cliffs, NJ: Prentice-Hall.

Ceci, S. J., & Bronfenbrenner, U. (1985). "Don't forget to take the cupcakes out of the oven.": Prospective memory, strategic time-monitoring, and context. *Child Development, 56,* 152–164.

Ceci, S. J., & Liker, J. (1986). Academic and nonacademic intelligence: An experimental separation. In R. J. Sternberg & R. K. Wagner (Eds.), *Practical intelligence: Nature and origins of competence in the everyday world* (pp. 119–142). New York: Cambridge University Press.

Chalke, F., & Ertl, J. (1965). Evoked potentials and intelligence. *Life Sciences, 4,* 1319–1322.

Chiang, A., & Atkinson, R. C. (1976). Individual differences and interrelationships among a select set of cognitive skills. *Memory & Cognition, 4,* 661–672.

Clark, H. H., & Chase, W. G. (1972). On the process of comparing sentences against pictures. *Cognitive Psychology, 3,* 472–517.

Cronbach, L. J. (1957). The two disciplines of scientific psychology. *American Psychologist, 12,* 671–684.

Das, J. P., Kirby, J., & Jarman, R. F. (1979). *Simultaneous and successive cognitive processes.* New York: Academic Press.

Deary, I. J. (1982). Intelligence and "inspection time." In H. J. Eysenck (Ed.), *A model for intelligence.* Berlin: Springer-Verlag.

Dickinson, A., & Boakes, R. A. (Eds.). (1979). *Mechanisms of learning and memory.* Hillsdale, NJ: Erlbaum.

Donchin, E. (1979). Event-related brain potentials: A tool in the study of human information processing. In H. Begleiter (Ed.), *Evoked potentials and behavior* (pp. 13–75). New York: Plenum.

Donders, F. C. (1868). Over de snelheid van psychische processen. *Onderzoekingen gedaan in het Physiologisch Labororium der Utrechtsche Hoogeschool, Tweede Reeks, 2,* 92–120.

Ertl, J. (1966). Evoked potentials and intelligence. *Revue de l'Université d'Ottawa, 30,* 599–607.

Ertl, J., & Schafer, E. (1969). Brain response correlates of psychometric intelligence. *Nature (London), 233*, 421–422.

Evans, T. G. (1968). Program for the solution of a class of geometric-analogy intelligence-test questions. In M. Minsky (Ed.), *Semantic information processing*. Cambridge, MA: MIT Press.

Feigenbaum, E. A., Buchanan, B. G., & Lederberg, J. (1971). On generality and problem solving: A case study using the DENDRAL program. In B. Meltzer & D. Michie (Eds.), *Machine intelligence 6*. Edinburgh: Edinburgh University Press.

Ferguson, G. A. (1954). On learning and human ability. *Canadian Journal of Psychology, 8*, 95–112.

Fodor, J. A. (1983). *The modularity of mind*. Cambridge, MA: MIT Press.

Gagné, R. M. (1968). Contributions of learning to human development. *Psychological Review, 75*, 177–191.

Galin, D., & Ornstein, R. (1972). Lateral specialization of cognitive mode: An EEG study. *Psychophysiology, 9*, 412–418.

Galton, F. (1883). *Inquiry into human faculty and its development*. London: Macmillan.

Gardner, H. (1983). *Frames of mind: The theory of multiple intelligences*. New York: Basic Books.

Gardner, H. (1993). *Multiple intelligences: The theory in practice*. New York: Basic Books.

Gazzaniga, M. S. (1970). *The bisected brain: Discovering the networks of the mind*. New York: Plenum.

Gazzaniga, M. S. (1985). *The social brain: Discovering the networks of the mind*. New York: Basic Books.

Guilford, J. P. (1967). *The nature of human intelligence*. New York: McGraw-Hill.

Gustafsson, J. E. (1984). A unifying model for the structure of intellectual abilities. *Intelligence, 8*, 179–203.

Guttman, L. (1954). A new approach to factor analysis: The radex. In P. E. Lazarsfeld, (Ed.), *Mathematical thinking in the social sciences*. Glenmore, IL: Free Press.

Guttman, L. (1965). A faceted definition of intelligence. In R. R. Eiferman (Ed.), *Scripta Hierosolymitana* (Vol. 14). Jerusalem: Magnes Press.

Haier, R. J., Nuechterlein, K. H., Hazlett, E., Wu, J. C., Paek, J., Browning, H. L., & Buchsbaum, M. S. (1988). Cortical glucose metabolic rate correlates of abstract reasoning and attention studied with positron emission tomography. *Intelligence, 12*, 199–217.

Haier, R. J., Siegel, B., Tang, C., Abel, L., & Buchsbaum, M. S. (1992). Intelligence and changes in regional cerebral glucose metabolic rate following learning. *Intelligence, 16*, 415–426.

Halstead, W. C. (1951). Biological intelligence. *Journal of Personality, 20*, 118–130.

Hayes-Roth, F., Waterman, D. A., & Lenat, D. B. (1983). An overview of an expert system. In F. Hayes-Roth, D. A. Watterman, & D. B. Lenat (Eds.), *Building expert systems* (pp. 3–29). Reading, MA: Addison-Wesley.

Hebb, D. O. (1949). *The organization of behavior*. New York: Wiley.

Hendrickson, A. E. (1982). The biological basis of intelligence: Part I. Theory. In H. J. Eysenck (Ed.), *A model for intelligence* (pp. 151–96). Berlin: Springer-Verlag.

Hendrickson, A. E., & Hendrickson, D. E. (1980). The biological basis for individual differences in intelligence. *Personality & Individual Differences, 1*, 3–33.

Horn, J. L., & Knapp, J. R. (1973). On the subjective character of the empirical base of Guilford's structure-of-intellect model. *Psychological Bulletin, 80*, 33–43.

Hunt, E. B. (1974). Quote the raven? Nevermore! In L. W. Gregg (Ed.), *Knowledge and cognition* (pp. 129–157). Hillsdale, NJ: Erlbaum.

Hunt, E. B. (1978). Mechanics of verbal ability. *Psychological Review, 85*, 109–130.

Hunt, E. B. (1980). Intelligence as an information-processing concept. *British Journal of Psychology, 71*, 449–474.

Hunt, E. B., Frost, N., & Lunneborg, C. (1973). Individual differences in cognition: A new approach to intelligence. In G. Bower (Ed.), *The psychology of learning and motivation* (Vol. 8). New York: Academic Press.

Hunt, E. B., Lunneborg, C., & Lewis, J. (1975). What does it mean to be high verbal? *Cognitive Psychology, 7,* 194–227.

Jensen, A. R. (1979). g: Outmoded theory or unconquered frontier? *Creative Science and Technology, 2,* 16–29.

Jensen, A. R. (1982). Reaction time and psychometric g. In H. J. Eysenck (Ed.), *A model for intelligence.* Berlin: Springer-Verlag.

Jensen, A. R., & Munro, E. (1979). Reaction time, movement time, and intelligence. *Intelligence, 3,* 121–126.

Jerison, H. J. (1982). The evolution of biological intelligence. In R. J. Sternberg (Ed.), *Handbook of human intelligence* (pp. 723–91). Cambridge: Cambridge University Press.

Kaufman, A. S., & Kaufman, N. L. (1983). *Kaufman assessment battery for children (KABC).* Circle Pines, MN: American Guidance Service.

Keating, D. P. (1984). The emperor's new clothes: The "new look" in intelligence research. In R. J. Sternberg (Ed.), *Advances in the psychology of human intelligence* (Vol. 2, pp. 1–46). Hillsdale, NJ: Earlbaum.

Konorski, J. (1967). *Integrative activity of the brain: An interdisciplinary approach.* Chicago: University of Chicago Press.

Laboratory of Comparative Human Cognition (1982). Culture and Intelligence. In R. J. Sternberg, (Ed.), *Handbook of human intelligence* (pp. 642–719). New York: Cambridge University Press.

Lave, J. (1988). *Cognition in practice.* Cambridge: Cambridge University Press.

Levy, J. (1974). Psychobiological implications of bilateral asymmetry. In S. Dimond & S. Beaumont (Eds.), *Hemispheric function in the human brain* (pp. 121–183). New York: Halstead.

Longstreth, L. E. (1984). Jensen's reaction-time investigations of intelligence: A critique. *Intelligence, 8,* 139–160.

Luria, A. R. (1973). *The working brain.* New York: Basic Books.

Luria, A. R. (1976). *Cognitive development: Its cultural and social foundations.* Cambridge, MA: Harvard University Press.

Luria, A. R. (1980). *Higher cortical functions in man* (2nd ed., rev. & expanded). New York: Basic Books.

McCarthy, G., & Donchin, E. (1981). A metric for thought: A comparison of P300 latency and reaction time. *Science, 211,* 77–79.

McClelland, J. L., Rumelhart, D. E., & the PDP Research Group. (1986). *Parallel distributed processing. Explorations in the microstructure of cognition: Vol. 2. Psychological and biological models.* Cambridge, MA: MIT Press.

Minsky, M. (Ed.). (1968). *Semantic information processing.* Cambridge, MA: MIT Press.

Neisser, U. (1979). The concept of intelligence. In R. J. Sternberg & D. K. Detterman (Eds.), *Human intelligence: Perspectives on its theory and measurement* (pp. 179–90). Norwood, NJ: Ablex.

Nettlebeck, T. (1973). Individual differences in noise and associated perceptual indices of performance. *Perception, 2,* 11–21.

Nettlebeck, T. (1982). Inspection time: An index for intelligence? *Quarterly Journal of Experimental Psychology, 34A,* 299–312.

Nettlebeck, T. (1987). Inspection time and intelligence. In P. A. Vernon (Ed.), *Speed of information processing and intelligence.* Norwood, NJ: Ablex.

Nettlebeck, T., & Lally, M. (1976). Inspection time and measured intelligence. *British Journal of Psychology, 67,* 17–22.

Newell, A., Shaw, J. C., & Simon, H. A. (1958). Elements of a theory of human problem solving. *Psychological Review, 65,* 151–166.

Newell, A., & Simon, H. A. (1972). *Human problem solving.* Englewood Cliffs, NJ: Prentice-Hall.

Nuñes, T., Schliemann, A. D., & Carraher, D. W. (1993). *Street mathematics and school mathematics.* New York: Cambridge University Press.

Pellegrino, J. W., & Galser, R. (1979). Cognitive correlates and components in the analysis of individual differences. In R. J. Sternberg & D. K. Detterman (Eds.), *Human intelligence: Perspectives on its theory and measurement.* Norwood, NJ: Ablex.

Pellegrino, J. W., & Glaser, R. (1980). Components of inductive reasoning. In R. E. Snow, P.-A. Federico, & W. E. Montague (Eds.), *Aptitude, learning, and instruction: Vol. 1. Cognitive process analyses of aptitude.* Hillsdale, NJ: Erlbaum.

Piaget, J. (1972). *The psychology of intelligence.* Totowa, NJ: Littlefield, Adams.

Posner, M. I., & Mitchell, R. F. (1967). Chronometric analysis of classification. *Psychological Review, 74,* 392–409.

Raaheim, K. (1974). *Problem solving and intelligence.* Oslo: Universitesforlaget.

Raz, N., & Willerman, L. (1985). Aptitude-related differences in auditory information processing: Effects of selective attention and tone duration. *Personality and Individual Differences, 6,* 299–304.

Reed, T. E., & Jensen, A. R. (1992). Conduction velocity in a brain nerve pathway of normal adults correlates with intelligence level. *Intelligence, 16,* 259–272.

Resnick, L. B. (Ed.). (1976). *The nature of intelligence.* Hillsdale, NJ: Erlbaum.

Rogoff, B., & Lave, J. (1984). *Everyday cognition, its development in social context.* Cambridge: MA: Harvard University Press.

Royer, F. L. (1971). Information processing of visual figures in the digit symbol substitution task. *Journal of Experimental Psychology, 87,* 335–342.

Rushton, J. R. (1990). Race, brain size, and intelligence: A rejoinder to Cain and Vanderwolf. *Personality and Individual Differences, 11,* 785–794.

Rushton, J. R. (1992). Cranial capacity related to sex, rank, and race in a stratified random sample of 6,325 U.S. military personnel. *Intelligence, 16,* 401–413.

Schafer, E. W. P. (1982). Neural adaptability: A biological determinant of behavioral intelligence. *International Journal of Neuroscience, 17,* 183–191.

Schank, R. C. (1972). Conceptual dependency: A theory of natural language understanding. *Cognitive Psychology, 3,* 552–631.

Schank, R. C. (1975). *Conceptual information processing.* Amsterdam: North-Holland Publ.

Schank, R. C. (1980). How much intelligence is there in artificial intelligence? *Intelligence, 4,* 1–14.

Schank, R. C., & Abelson, R. P. (1977). *Scripts, plans, goals, and understanding.* Hillsdale, NJ: Erlbaum.

Shepard, R. N., & Metzler, J. (1971). Mental rotation of three-dimensional objects. *Science, 171,* 701–703.

Shortliffe, E. H. (1976). *Computer-based medical consultations: MYCIN.* New York: American Elsevier.

Simon, H. A., & Kotovsky, K. (1963). Human acquisition of concepts for sequential patterns. *Psychological Review, 70,* 534–546.

Simon, D. P., & Simon, H. A. (1978). Individual differences in solving physics problems. In R. Siegler (Ed.), *Children's thinking: What develops?* (pp. 325–343). Hillsdale, NJ: Erlbaum.

Snow, R. E. (1979). Theory and method for research on aptitude processes. In R. J. Sternberg & D. K. Detterman (Eds.), *Human intelligence: Perspectives on its theory and measurement.* New York: Cambridge University Press.

Spearman, C. (1904). General intelligence, objectively determined and measured. *American Journal of Psychology, 15,* 201–293.

Spearman, C. (1923). *The nature of 'intelligence' and the principles of cognition.* London: Macmillan.

Spearman, C. (1927). *The abilities of man.* New York: Macmillan.

Sperry, R. W. (1961). Cerebral organization and behavior. *Science, 133,* 1749–1757.

Sperry, R. W., Myers, R. E., & Schrier, A. M. (1960). Perceptual capacity of the isolated visual cortex in the cat. *Quarterly Journal of Experimental Psychology, 12,* 65–71.

Sternberg, R. J. (1977). *Intelligence, information processing, and analogical reasoning: The componential analysis of human abilities.* Hillsdale, NJ: Erlbaum.

Sternberg, R. J. (1982a). *Advances in the psychology of human intelligence,* Vol. 1. Hillsdale, NJ: Erlbaum.

Sternberg, R. J. (Ed.). (1982b). *Handbook of human intelligence.* New York: Cambridge University Press.

Sternberg, R. J. (1983). Components of human intelligence. *Cognition, 15,* 1–48.

Sternberg, R. J. (Ed.). (1984). *Advances in the psychology of human intelligence,* Vol. 2. Hillsdale, NJ: Erlbaum.

Sternberg, R. J. (1985). *Beyond IQ: A triarchic theory of human intelligence.* New York: Cambridge University Press.

Sternberg, R. J. (1988). *The triarchic mind: A new theory of human intelligence.* New York: Viking.

Sternberg, R. J. (1990). *Metaphors of mind: Conceptions of the nature of intelligence.* New York: Cambridge University Press.

Sternberg, R. J. (Ed.) (1994). *Handbook of perception and cognition: Vol. 12. Thinking and problem solving.* San Diego: Academic Press.

Sternberg, R. J., Conway, B. E., Ketron, J. L., & Bernstein, M. (1981). People's conceptions of intelligence. *Journal of Personality and Social Psychology, 41,* 37–55.

Sternberg, R. J., & Wagner, R. K. (Eds.). (1986). *Practical intelligence: Nature and origins of competence in the everyday world.* New York: Cambridge University Press.

Sternberg, R. J., & Wagner, R. K. (1993). The *g*-ocentric view of intelligence and job performance is wrong. *Current Directions in Psychological Science, 2*(1), 1–4.

Sternberg, S. (1969). The discovery of processing stages: Extensions of Donders' method. *Acta Psychologica, 30,* 276–315.

Thurstone, L. L. (1938). *Primary mental abilities.* Chicago: University of Chicago Press.

Vernon, P. A., & Mori, M. (1992). Intelligence, reaction times, and peripheral nerve conduction velocity. *Intelligence, 8,* 273–288.

Vernon, P. E. (1971). *The structure of human abilities.* London: Methuen.

Wagner, D. A. (1978). Memories of Morocco: The influence of age, schooling and environment on memory. *Cognitive Psychology, 10,* 1–28.

Winograd, T. (1972). *Understanding natural language.* New York: Academic Press.

Wissler, C. (1901). The correlation of mental and physical tests. *Psychological Review, Monograph Supplement, 3*(6).

Zaidel, E. (1975). A technique for presenting lateralized visual input with prolonged exposure. *Vision Research, 15,* 283–289.

Zaidel, E. (1978). Auditory language comprehension in the right hemisphere following cerebral commissurotomy and hemispherectomy: A comparison with child language aphasia. In A. Caramazza & E. Zurif (Eds.), *Language acquisition and language breakdown.* Baltimore, MD: Johns Hopkins University Press.

CHAPTER 10

Creativity

Todd I. Lubart

Have you ever noticed that some people can come up with new, useful solutions to a problem when everyone else is stuck? Did you ever wonder how those new ideas came to be? Or were you ever curious about who invents new gadgets or cooks up new theories and why they do it but others don't?

Questions about creativity are being asked more and more frequently as the rate of change in our world increases, the problems become more complex and less routine, and people increasingly seek a competitive edge. Creativity is important at both the individual and societal levels. At an individual level, creativity is relevant on the job and in daily life. At a societal level, creativity can lead to new scientific findings, new movements in art, new inventions, and new social programs.

This chapter addresses four fundamental questions about creativity. The first question is: What is creativity? Creativity is defined and issues of its distribution in the population and domain generality are discussed. The second question is: What enables a person to be creative? A number of diverse theories are described. Drawing on these theories and research findings, a survey of cognitive, personality-motivational, and environmental components of creativity is presented. Then, a third issue is raised: Is there a special working process that leads to creative products? There are several

Thinking and Problem Solving

possible views on the creative process. These proposals involve a variety of special steps or thinking patterns that distinguish between creative and routine problem solving. Finally, there is the pragmatic question of measuring creativity. Positive and negative features of different measurement techniques are examined.

I. THE BASIC PHENOMENON: DESCRIPTIVE ISSUES

A solid definition of creativity provides the base from which the source of creativity, the creative process, and the measurement of creativity can be examined. In addition to the definition, the distribution and domain specificity of creativity are discussed to provide an overview of the phenomenon.

A. Definition of Creativity

1. Central Features

Creativity is the ability to produce work that is both novel and appropriate (Barron, 1988; Jackson & Messick, 1967; MacKinnon, 1962; Ochse, 1990). A novel product is one that is original and not predicted. A novel product stands apart from the work that the individual and other people have already produced. A novel product provokes surprise in the viewer because it is more than the logical next step.

There are different degrees to which a product can be novel. Some novel products involve a minor deviation from prior work, whereas other novel products involve a major leap. The highest levels of creativity involve a large step from preceding work. The perceived novelty of a product also depends on an audience's prior experiences (Boden, 1992). For example, often a product is novel for the person who made it but already known to others. This is a case of re-invention. Sometimes, a product is novel for the producer and for a limited set of people who see the product. However, the product exists elsewhere in the broader society. Finally, the product can be novel at an individual level, at a local level, and at a societal or worldwide level. This third level of novelty is characteristic of the most creative work (Young, 1985).

An appropriate product satisfies problem constraints; the product fulfills a need, is sensible, and is useful. Of course, there is a range of appropriateness from minimally satisfactory to an extremely good fulfillment of problem constraints (Besemer & Treffinger, 1981). It is important to note that something that is novel but does not at all fit the problem's constraints is not creative—it is just a strange, irrelevant response.

2. Peripheral Features

In addition to novelty and appropriateness, which are the central features of creativity, there are several peripheral features. These peripheral features can enhance or diminish the basic creativity of a product. Consider three such features: quality, importance, and production history.

A high-quality product is one that shows a high level of technical skill. It is well executed. If a novel and appropriate concept is not skillfully turned into a full-fledged product, then the work may be viewed as less creative because the audience does not fully appreciate or see its novelty and appropriateness (Bailin, 1988).

The importance of a product can also serve to enhance or diminish judgments of creativity. Sometimes a creative product satisfies a particular but limited need. For example, perhaps someone has devised a new alarm system for automobiles that eliminates false alarms due to weather or animals disturbing the car. In contrast, other creative products fulfill a pressing need of one's audience. For example, perhaps someone has designed a new way to capture energy from the sun and use it to power automobiles. This energy-capture idea would be considered more creative than the alarm system by most people, because the energy idea fulfills a more important need. Also part of the importance of a product, and relevant to creativity judgments, is the extent to which a product has a wide scope of application and leads the producer or other people to even further ideas (Besemer & Treffinger, 1981). When a product serves as a base from which further ideas can be generated, then the perceived creativity of the initial product is enhanced.

Finally, the production history of a work can affect the ultimate judgment of creativity (Boden, 1992; Brogden & Sprecher, 1964). For example, if people know that a novel, appropriate product came about purely by chance or by following a set of prescribed rules, then the perceived creativity of the product dramatically decreases (Amabile, 1983; Johnson-Laird, 1988; Weisberg, 1993). In contrast, if people hear that a creator had to work hard and had many ups and downs on the route to a final product, then the creativity of the outcome is enhanced.

Several additional features of products may also be considered relevant to creativity judgments. These include the extent to which a product pulls together disparate ideas (Jackson & Messick, 1967), the marketability of a product (Finke, Ward, & Smith, 1992), and the evocative power of a product to stir emotions in the audience.

3. Social Consensus

Judgments of creativity (and the implicit judgments of novelty, appropriateness, quality, importance, and production history) involve social consensus

(Amabile, 1983). There is no absolute standard for creativity. An individual judge, a panel of people, or a society as a whole evaluates products and determines how creative one product is compared to others or how creative one person is compared to others.

Creativity judgments can vary across different audiences and across time as preferences change (Csikszentmihalyi, 1988b). It may seem odd that the same product (or person) could be judged to be highly creative by one group of people (e.g., laypeople) but average or low on creativity by another group (e.g., experts in a field). However, there are at least two main reasons why discrepancies can occur.

First, judges have different background experiences against which they compare a new product. For example, a teacher who has seen hundreds of students' drawings has a broader basis for judging the creativity of a particular student's work than a parent who has seen only a handful of children's drawings. Both the teacher and the parent may be looking for novel, appropriate work but they are not using the same set of work against which to judge a new product. Differences in the background against which a product is judged are especially apparent when judges come from different cultures or different age generations.

Second, judges may give different weights to novelty, appropriateness, and other implicit criteria when they make their judgments of creativity. For example, one judge may implicitly weigh novelty 70 percent and appropriateness 30 percent when evaluating creativity. Another judge may weigh these two criteria equally. Differences in the weights given to the separate criteria for creativity may also vary, in general, across domains of work. For example, engineers may weigh the appropriateness criterion more heavily than artists (Finke et al., 1992).

4. Nuances of Terminology

Before leaving the definition of creativity, it is useful to note the differences between creative performance, the creative person, and creative potential. Creative performance is a demonstration of the ability to produce novel, appropriate work. Creative performance is marked by observable creative products; these products may be tangible (e.g., a painting) or intangible (e.g., an idea or new manufacturing process). A creative person is one who produces creative work. Typically, people are called "creative" when they have creative ideas on a regular basis. Creative potential is a latent, unobserved capacity for creative work that may occur in the future. Creative potential can be estimated by either extrapolating a person's previous creative performance record into the future or by measuring a person on the cognitive, personality-motivational, and environmental components that are needed for creativity (these components are described later).

B. Distribution of Creativity

There are two fundamental issues concerning the distribution of creativity. First, are highly eminent creators such as Michelangelo, da Vinci, or Einstein exhibiting the same phenomenon as everyday people who show creativity? It is most parsimonious to assume that eminent creativity stems from the same basic sources as does everyday creativity (Guilford, 1950). As discussed later, there are multiple components that contribute to creativity. If all the components coincide in an ideal way, then it is quite plausible that eminent levels of creativity can result (Eysenck, 1993). However, if someone wanted to argue that eminent creativity is not part of the same phenomenon as everyday levels of creativity, then distinct theories for each level of creativity would be needed. At present, there is only scant evidence to support such a distinction (see Nicholls, 1972).

The second question is whether the distribution of creative products is normal (a bell curve) or skewed. When the full range of creative products is considered, evidence suggests the distribution has a positive skew. Examples of highly creative products in any domain are salient but rare. Performance for a typical domain or task may be characterized as follows: There is often a group of products that lack creativity altogether, a large group of products showing low levels of creativity, fewer products with moderate levels, and a handful of products that show high, eminent levels of creativity. The median of the distribution falls toward the low end and the upper (high creativity) tail of the distribution extends quite far. This pattern is supported by analyses of artistic and scientific achievements (Dennis, 1955; Simonton, 1984, 1988c). Consistent with the earlier hypothesis of a common set of sources for all levels of creativity, a skewed distribution can result when multiple abilities or traits, each with a normal distribution, interactively combine to yield observed products (Eysenck, 1993).

C. Domain Specificity

Creative work can occur in virtually any domain including visual arts, music, dance, writing, advertising, science, mathematics, social problem solving, business, teaching, and everyday life. Is creativity, however, a general ability that a person will show across domains, or is creativity domain specific? For example, will a person who is creative when making a drawing show a similar level of creativity when writing a story? Some have even questioned whether creativity is consistent across tasks within a single domain, such as poem writing and storywriting (Baer, 1991). Research suggests that creativity is moderately but not completely domain specific. Studies have had children and adults describe their creative achievements or complete creativity tasks in a variety of domains (Baer, 1991; Lubart &

Sternberg, in press; Runco, 1987). The interdomain correlations of creativity show a large amount of variability, ranging from approximately zero to .60. Typical correlations are between .20 and .30, indicating only a weak relationship across domains. Studies of task-specific creativity, keeping the domain constant, have been less frequent but also show, at best, moderate intertask correlations. With eminent creators, specificity is also observed. In one study, Gray (1966) reported on 2400 historically significant creators. Only 17% of the total sample were noted for work in two or more domains and only 2% of the sample showed creative accomplishments in disparate domains (e.g., painting and writing).

The specificity can be explained through the cognitive, personality-motivational, and environmental components of creative performance (discussed in detail later). Several components, such as knowledge and risk taking, tend to be specific. However, other components, such as intellectual abilities, might be fairly general. The combination of components can explain why weak interdomain or intertask correlations do exist. Another factor that can contribute to relatively weak interdomain correlations is the natural fluctuations in a person's creative performance that occur on a daily basis. These fluctuations mean that performance on identical tasks two days in a row will not correlate perfectly.

II. THE SOURCE OF CREATIVITY

To find the source of creativity has been a central goal of theory and research. This section has two parts. First, the main alternative conceptions of the source of creativity are described. I characterize these as the mystical, psychodynamic, cognitive, social-psychological, and confluence approaches. Second, consistent with the confluence approach, six components that lead to creativity are described in detail. These components are intellectual abilities, knowledge, thinking styles, personality, motivation, and environment. Special attention is given to the intellectual abilities and knowledge components.

Before turning to the survey of alternate approaches, it is important to note two points. The description of the approaches and components of creativity seeks to be representative rather than comprehensive. Also, there are alternative ways in which the different theories and research findings could have been organized.

A. An Overview of Alternate Conceptions

1. The Mystical Approach

Perhaps the earliest accounts of creativity relied on divine intervention. The creative person was seen as an empty vessel that a divine being would fill with inspiration. The individual would then pour out the inspired ideas, forming an "unearthly" product. In this vein, Plato argued that a poet is able to create only that which the Muse dictates. For one person it may be choral songs and for another it may be epic poems (Rothenberg & Hausman, 1976). Often, mystical sources have been suggested in creators' introspective reports (Ghiselin, 1985). For example, Rudyard Kipling referred to the "Daemon" that lives in the writer's pen: "My Daemon was with me in the Jungle Books, *Kim,* and both Puck books, and good care I took to walk delicately, lest he should withdraw . . . When your Daemon is in charge, do not think consciously. Drift, wait, and obey" (Kipling, 1937/1985, p. 162).

Some people today still subscribe to a supernatural source for creativity. Psychology, however, has traditionally sought naturalistic, person-, or environment-centered explanations for creativity.

2. The Psychodynamic Approach

One of the earliest psychological perspectives on creativity, the psychodynamic approach, suggests that creativity arises from the tension between conscious reality and unconscious drives. Freud (1908/1959) proposed that writers and artists produce creative work as a way to express their unconscious wishes in a publicly acceptable fashion. These unconscious wishes may concern power, riches, fame, honor, or love (Vernon, 1970). Case studies of eminent creators, such as Leonardo da Vinci (Freud, 1910/1964), have been used to support these ideas.

Kris (1952) developed the psychoanalytic approach with the concepts of adaptive regression and elaboration. Adaptive regression, the primary process, refers to the intrusion of unmodulated thoughts in consciousness. Unmodulated thoughts can occur during active problem solving but often occur during sleep, intoxication from drugs, fantasies or daydreams, or psychoses. Elaboration, the secondary process, refers to the reworking and transformation of primary-process material through reality-oriented, ego-controlled thinking. Kubie (1958) emphasized that the preconscious, which falls between conscious reality and the encrypted unconscious, is the true source of creativity because thoughts are loose and vague but interpretable. In contrast to Freud, Kubie claimed that unconscious conflicts actually have a negative effect on creativity because they lead to fixated, repetitive thoughts. Recent work seems to have been influenced by cognitive psychology; primary and secondary processes are viewed as equally valid modes of thinking that are both needed for creativity (Noy, 1969; Rothenberg, 1979; Suler, 1980; Werner & Kaplan, 1963).

3. The Cognitive Approach

The cognitive tradition focuses on thinking abilities and knowledge as the basis of creative work. The cognitive approach can be traced to the early

1900s, when Binet and others started to explore imaginational skills as part of their research on intelligence (Binet & Henri, 1896; K. A. Brown, 1988). Guilford (1950) brought this line of work to the forefront with his address on creativity to the American Psychological Association. It is probably fair to say that the cognitive approach has dominated ideas about the source of creativity since that point.

According to Guilford (1956, 1977), creativity especially involves the divergent-thinking facet of mental abilities. Divergent thinking refers to the ability to generate many different ideas in response to a problem (see R. T. Brown, 1989; Runco, 1991). Divergent thinking is part of Guilford's (1967) broader structure-of-intellect model. Divergent thinking was originally conceived as a set of abilities that were differentiated by the content of the productions (e.g., figural, verbal) and the level or type of production (e.g., idea unit, class, system). Guilford and his colleagues developed several tests to measure divergent thinking. One of these was the Unusual Uses Test, in which an examinee thinks of as many uses for a common object (such as a brick) as possible. The tests were a convenient way of comparing people on a standard "creativity" scale. Accordingly, Guilford-style tests are often called the "psychometric approach" to creativity. Today, this line of cognitive work continues with the *Torrance Tests of Creative Thinking,* described in detail later (Torrance, 1974). Runco (1991), Baer (1991), Milgram (1990), and others have also been actively extending research on divergent-thinking skills.

Work on divergent thinking, however, represents only part of the cognitive approach to creativity. Other cognitive theorists have emphasized a wide range of abilities, which will also be examined later in detail. Examples of these abilities are perceptual processes (Schachtel, 1976; Smith & Carlsson, 1990), problem-definition skills (Getzels & Csikszentmihalyi, 1976), insight skills (Finke et al., 1992; Sternberg & Davidson, in press-a), and induction skills (Holland, Holyoak, Nisbett, & Thagard, 1986; Langley, Simon, Bradshaw, & Zytkow, 1987). A great deal of work has focused on the ability to form analogies, unusual associations, or combinations of diverse knowledge elements (Boden, 1992; Finke et al., 1992; Koestler, 1964; Mednick, 1962; Ochse, 1990; Rothenberg, 1979; Spearman, 1931). A subgroup of "association" theorists give a role to chance, or semirandom processes, as the source of associations (Boden, 1992; Campbell, 1960; Findlay & Lumsden, 1988; Simonton, 1988a). Introducing a role for chance typically leads to an emphasis on idea-evaluation skill and certain association-fostering attributes of the knowledge base. These attributes, as described later, may involve the quantity of knowledge and the organization of an individual's knowledge (Boden, 1992; Mednick, 1962; Simonton, 1988a).

Recent cognitive work has used a variety of methodologies that include laboratory experiments, computer simulations, and case studies. Finke et al.

(1992) exemplify the experimental approach in which people work under a range of controlled, instructional conditions to uncover creativity-relevant abilities, processes, and mental representations. For example, studies have examined the fixating effects when examples are provided before task performance. Subjects may work under instructions with no examples or examples that range in the type of product features emphasized. The products are examined for evidence of biases.

Boden (1992) reviews research using computer simulation techniques. Langley et al. (1987), for example, have developed a set of programs that rediscover basic scientific laws. These computational models rely on heuristics—problem-solving guidelines—for searching a data set or conceptual space and finding hidden relationships between input variables. The initial program, named BACON, uses heuristics such as "if the value of two numerical terms increase together, consider their ratio" to search data for patterns. One of BACON's accomplishments has been to examine observational data on the orbits of planets and rediscover Kepler's third law of planetary motion (Langley et al., 1987). Further programs have extended the search heuristics, the ability to transform data sets, and the ability to reason with qualitative data and scientific concepts. In a related line of work, Schank (1988a, 1988b) has proposed computational mechanisms for accessing and modifying old explanation patterns to provide a creative angle on a new problem. An explanation pattern is a stereotyped causal description for an event. Explanation patterns for a situation might be modified by "tweaking heuristics" such as reversing the actors and objects, changing the focus to a peripheral element of an established explanation, or substituting a new object for one in the explanation already.

Pursuing a computationally oriented approach to creativity in an artistic domain, Johnson-Laird (1988) has developed a jazz improvization program. This program features a representational system for jazz and generative rules for combining notes. Basic chord sequences are generated "off-line" and then used "on-line" during an improvisational composition. Novel deviations from the basic chord sequence are guided by harmonic constraints (or tacit principles of jazz) and random choice when several allowable directions for the improvisation exist.

In addition to computational models and laboratory experiments, case studies of artists, scientists, and inventors have also been used to support the importance of cognitive variables (Sternberg & Davidson, in press-a; Wallace & Gruber, 1989; Weber & Perkins, 1992; Weisberg, 1993). For example, the Wright brothers, who invented the first airplane, achieved their creative accomplishment, in part, through a representational ability to visualize physical forces and translate these forces into mechanical models (Crouch, 1992). One of the themes of case studies by Weisberg (1993) is that creativity has a strong basis in and continuity with previously existing knowledge; the generation of creative ideas on a topic often involves "near analogies" and small steps from prior attempts at a problem.

Returning to the survey of cognitive approaches to creativity, researchers, finally, have pursued biological bases of creativity. Several have emphasized either the right hemisphere of the brain because of its integrative, holistic processing, the role of hemispheric specialization, or the density of neural connections between the hemispheres (Katz, 1983; Martindale, Hines, Mitchell, & Covello, 1984). Prentky (1989) and others who examine the link between psychopathology and creativity may also be considered within the cognitive-biological group. Prentky (1989), for example, suggests that there is a continuum of input-information processing from extreme constriction of the inputs to extreme expansion of the input array. Normals tend to fall near the middle of the distribution. Creative people deviate from the middle and the mentally ill fall at one of the extreme ends of the spectrum. In general, research suggests that schizophrenia, manic-depressive psychosis, unipolar depression, and mild forms of these psychopathologies can be related to creativity through the basic idea that creativity involves some biologically based deviations (e.g., neurotransmitters) from normal cognition, but large deviations will result in psychopathology (Eysenck, 1993; Richards, Kinney, Lunde, Benet, & Merzel, 1988; Rothenberg, 1990). It should be noted that there is also a large literature on the connection between creativity and psychopathology that falls outside of the cognitive approach. Some of this research, focusing on personality or motivational variables, fits within the social-psychological approach, which is described next (Prentky, 1989; Richards, 1993; Rothenberg, 1990).

4. The Social-Psychological Approach

Developing in parallel with the cognitive approach, work in the social-psychological tradition has focused on personality variables, motivational variables, and the sociocultural environment as sources of creativity. Briefly consider each of these areas, which will be examined in detail later.

Researchers such as Amabile (1983), Barron (1968, 1969), Dudek and Hall (1991), Eysenck (1993), Gough (1979), MacKinnon (1965), Martindale (1989), Roe (1952), and others have noted that certain personality traits often characterize creative people. Through correlational studies and research contrasting high-creative and low-creative samples (at both eminent and everyday levels), a large set of potentially relevant traits has been identified (Barron & Harrington, 1981). These traits include independence of judgment, self-confidence, attraction to complexity, aesthetic orientation, and risk taking.

Proposals regarding self-actualization and creativity can also be considered within the personality tradition. According to Maslow (1968), boldness, courage, freedom, spontaneity, self-acceptance, and other traits lead a person to realize his or her full potential. Creativity is one benefit of a self-actualized state. Rogers (1954) anticipated other aspects of the social-psychological approach to creativity. He described the tendency toward self-actualization as having motivational force and being promoted by a supportive, evaluation-free environment.

Focusing on motivation for creativity, a number of theorists have hypothesized the relevance of intrinsic motivation (Amabile, 1983; Crutchfield, 1962; Golann, 1962), need for order (Barron, 1963), need for achievement (McClelland, Atkinson, Clark, & Lowell, 1953), and other motives. Amabile (1983) and her colleagues have conducted seminal research on intrinsic and extrinsic motivation. Studies using motivational training and other techniques have manipulated these motivations and observed effects on creative performance tasks, such as poem writing and collage making.

The relevance of the social environment to creativity has also been an active research area. At the societal level, Simonton (1984, 1988c) has conducted numerous studies in which eminent creativity over large spans of time in diverse cultures has been statistically linked to environmental variables; features of the environment that are relevant include cultural diversity, war, availability of role models, availability of resources (such as financial support), and number of competitors in a domain. Cross-cultural comparisons (Lubart, 1990) and anthropological case studies (Maduro, 1976; Silver, 1981) demonstrate cultural variability in the expression of creativity. At the field and domain levels, Csikszentmihalyi (1988b) describes several important environmental elements, including "gatekeepers," such as art critics and gallery owners, who are key people that control a field and evaluate creativity. At the task level, the effects of situational variables such as home environment, external evaluation, surveillance while working, and task choice have been examined (Amabile, 1983; Harrington, Block, & Block, 1987; Rogers, 1954; Torrance, 1965). Finally, within the environmental approach, a number of researchers have looked at how people judge creativity (Amabile, 1983; Lubart & Sternberg, in press; B. B. Rossman & Gollob, 1975).

5. The Confluence Approach

Many recent theories and studies of creativity, in a partial synthesis of earlier work, hypothesize that multiple components must converge for creativity to occur (Amabile, 1983; Csikszentmihalyi, 1988a, 1988b; Gardner, 1993; Gruber, 1989; Mumford & Gustafson, 1988; Perkins, 1981; Simonton, 1988a; Sternberg, 1985; Sternberg & Lubart, 1991b; Weisberg, 1993; Woodman & Schoenfeldt, 1989). Sternberg (1985), for example, examined laypersons' and experts' modern conceptions of the creative person. People's "implicit theories" contained a combination of cognitive and personality elements (e.g., connects ideas, sees similarities and differences, has flexibility, has aesthetic taste, is unorthodox, is motivated, is inquisitive, questions societal norms).

In terms of explicit theories, Amabile (1983) describes creativity as the result of intrinsic motivation, domain-relevant knowledge and abilities, and creativity-relevant skills. Creativity-relevant skills consist of (1) a cognitive style that involves coping with complexities and breaking one's mental set during problem solving, (2) knowledge of heuristics for generating novel ideas, such as trying a counterintuitive approach, and (3) a work style characterized by concentrated effort, an ability to set aside problems, and high energy (Amabile, 1983). Different levels on these three components, when combined, lead to the range of creativity that can be observed.

In contrast to Amabile's model, Gruber and his colleagues, through case studies of eminent creators, have proposed a developmental evolving-systems approach (Gruber, 1974/1981, 1989; Gruber & Davis, 1988). A person's knowledge, purpose, and affect grow over time, amplify deviations that an individual encounters, and lead to creative products. Developmental changes in the knowledge system have been documented in cases such as Charles Darwin's thoughts on evolution. Purpose refers to a set of interrelated goals, which also develop and guide an individual's behavior. Finally, the affect or mood system notes the influence of joy or frustration over the projects undertaken.

Csikszentmihalyi (1988b) has taken a different "systems" approach to creativity. He highlights the role of the individual, the field, and the domain. The individual draws upon information in a domain and transforms or extends it via cognitive processes, personality traits, and motivation. The field, consisting of people who control or influence a domain, evaluates and selects valuable new ideas produced by individuals. The domain, a culturally defined symbol system, preserves and transmits creative products to other individuals and future generations. These three systems jointly yield the phenomenon of creativity. Gardner (1993) has conducted case studies that draw upon this systems view and employ a developmental perspective. Gardner's studies suggest that the development of creative projects may stem from an anomaly within a system (e.g., tension between competing critics in a field) or moderate asynchronies between the individual, domain, and field (e.g., unusual individual talent for a domain). Gardner further finds evidence of a matrix of intellectual and personal support at the time of creative breakthroughs, a trend toward "Faustian bargains" in which personal life is sacrificed for creative work, and a tendency to retain a connection with childhood in adult creative work.

A final confluence theory considered here is Sternberg and Lubart's (1991b) investment approach, which specifies aspects of intelligence, knowledge, thinking styles, personality, motivation, and the environment for creativity. These components lead to a pattern of "buying low, and selling high" in the realm of ideas (see also Rubenson & Runco, 1992). Buying low means pursuing ideas that are unknown and out of favor but that have growth potential. Selling high involves presenting one's work and moving on to new projects when an idea or product becomes valued and yields a significant return. Preliminary research within the investment framework supports the value of a confluence of components when accounting for creative performance (Lubart & Sternberg, in press). This framework will serve as the basis for organizing the following discussion on the components of creativity.

B. Components of Creativity

1. Intellectual Abilities

Intellectual abilities are, arguably, the most important component of creativity. Extensive theoretical and empirical work has pointed to a set of high-level and basic-level creativity-relevant abilities (Barron & Harrington, 1981; Perkins, 1981; Sternberg & Lubart, 1991b). These abilities may exist in domain-general forms or in domain- and task-specific forms. The abilities are described below and then the relationship between creativity and general intelligence is discussed.

Problem finding is one of the important high-level abilities (Isaksen & Parnes, 1985; Mackworth, 1965; Ochse, 1990; Schank, 1988a). Problem finding means detecting a gap in the current state of knowledge, a need for a new product, or a deficiency with current procedures in a domain. Sometimes problems are presented (as in schools or laboratory settings). However, many of the most important problems are not obvious or are actively ignored by most people (K. A. Brown, 1988). Problem finding opens the door to creativity because if no problem exists, then no creative solution is possible. The ability to find problems can be manifested through question asking or by considering how things could ideally be and then comparing this ideal to the present situation. Some preliminary research has linked question asking to creativity, as measured by the Torrance tests (Artley, Van Horn, Friedrich, & Carroll, 1980; Glover, 1979; Lembright & Yamamoto, 1965).

Once a problem has been noticed or presented, the ability to define (and redefine) the problem becomes important. John Dewey is credited with the maxim: A problem well put is half solved. Many problems that offer the possibility of a creative solution are ill defined. The problem may have a vague, underspecified goal or an ill-specified goal that would not resolve the true problem (Hayes, 1978). Supporting the importance of problem definition, Getzels and Csikszentmihalyi (1976) presented art students with the task of making a still-life drawing using some or all of a set of objects that was provided. The task was ill defined because the artistic problem that the composition should resolve was unspecified. The art students who produced the most original still-life drawings spent more time formulating their compositions than did their less creative peers. In particular, they explored the still-life objects in greater detail, examined a greater number of objects, and redefined the scene as they worked on it (see also Okuda, Runco, & Berger, 1991; Runco & Okuda, 1988).

Closely tied to problem definition is the ability to choose a useful problem representation. Kotovsky, Hayes, and Simon (1985), for example, found that solution time for the Tower of Hanoi problem could be altered by a factor of eight if the problem were rephrased in terms of monsters who had to move globes rather than the traditional problem of moving disks between pegs. The representation of a problem can affect memory load, the extent to which everyday knowledge can be linked to the problem, and the ease with which rules are learned and applied. In regard to problem representations for creativity, there are numerous reports that visual imagery facilitates creative problem solving (Ghiselin, 1985; Shepard, 1978; Weber & Perkins, 1992). For example, Einstein developed the special theory of relativity partially through a visualization of traveling along a beam of light (Shepard, 1978). Experimental studies on creative invention support the use of visual mental representations for combining parts (e.g., handles, wheels) to make useful, new objects, such as toys (Finke, 1990; Finke et al., 1992). Visual thinking may be particularly useful for creativity because images are easily altered, can represent multiple aspects of a problem, can be manipulated rapidly, and often do not have the well-defined boundaries of verbal representations (John-Steiner, 1987; Kim, 1990).

Another relevant high-level ability is strategy selection. There are a variety of possible problem-solving strategies that can be used to guide problem-solving efforts. Research based on simulations of the scientific-discovery process, described earlier, and case studies of inventors suggests that the ability to employ heuristic search is a beneficial strategy for creativity (Langley et al., 1987; McGuire, 1983; Qin & Simon, 1990; Weber & Perkins, 1992). Heuristic search (as opposed to exhaustive search) allows the problem solver to focus on potential solution paths and to ignore the wide array of fruitless options. Theorists (Baer, 1991; Mumford, Mobley, Uhlman, Reiter-Palmon, & Doares, 1991; Sternberg & Lubart, 1993) have also suggested that knowing when to use divergent or convergent thinking is strategically important. Divergent thinking, generating many possible options, means that choices will be available. People often seem to "satisfice" when working on a problem, accepting the first idea that comes to their mind (Simon, 1976). Convergent thinking, attempting to home in on the one best response, narrows the range of possible next steps so that problem-solving efforts do not get sidetracked. Alternating between these modes of thinking may be an optimal strategy for creativity (Isaksen & Parnes, 1985; Merrifield, Guilford, Christensen, & Frick, 1962).

A final high-level skill for creativity is the ability to evaluate effectively (Lubart, 1994; Runco, 1992). Poincaré (1921), in his introspective account, claimed to use aesthetic criteria unconsciously as a "delicate sieve" to separate creative ideas from the mass of generated possibilities. Only those ideas deemed "harmonious" would receive further attention. James (1980) and Campbell (1960), in their theoretical writings, also emphasized this ability to select among competing ideas in order to develop potentially valuable ideas more fully. Furthermore, examination of eminent creators' work, such as poets' rough drafts, shows multiple points where evaluation and revision occurred, sometimes so numerous that the original text is illegible (Weisberg, 1993). Evaluative ability keeps progress on a problem in accord with the desire for a novel, appropriate, high-quality solution.

Distinct from high-level abilities are insight abilities and divergent thinking skills. These are widely regarded as basic-level abilities for creative performance.

Numerous investigations have examined insight abilities (see Sternberg & Davidson, in press-a). Sternberg and Davidson (in press-b), in a summary of current work, propose that insight is a "cognitive transition" that involves restructuring the nature of a problem or the elements that contribute to a problem's solution. Subjectively, insights seem to occur suddenly and to evoke a feeling of "eureka." Insight abilities, specifically, may consist of noticing relevant new information, comparing disparate information and finding relevant connections, and combining information in a problem-relevant fashion (Davidson, in press). Consider each of these abilities.

Often key information to solve a problem already exists or becomes available, but people do not see its value (Schachtel, 1976). For example, at least 28 scientists before Alexander Flemming had reported a mold (*Penicillium*) killing bacteria colonies, but this result was seen by the early scientists as an unfortunate experimental error rather than as a potential source of medicine (Rosenman, 1988). At an everyday level, studies have clearly demonstrated that people often do not notice hints for solving a problem even when the hints are quite blatant (Gick & Holyoak, 1980; Perfetto, Bransford, & Franks, 1983; Weisberg, DiCamillo, & Phillips, 1978). Seifert, Meyer, Davidson, Patalano, and Yaniv (in press) propose that the key to "encoding insights" is the tendency to store in long-term memory two pieces of information: the state of a problem when an impasse is reached and a failure index marking the difficulty encountered. Storing this information primes the person to find problem-relevant information when new information is processed through regular cognitive channels (see also Langley & Jones, 1988).

Another route to insightful ideas is by directly comparing disparate ideas—using analogies or metaphors to see connections (or points of dissimilarity). This ability can involve accessing potentially related cases for a problem at hand, mapping similar features between the analogue and problem base, and then transferring further parts of the accessed idea to illuminate the unsolved problem (Holyoak & Thagard, 1989a, 1989b; Johnson-Laird, 1989; Vosniadou & Ortony, 1989). There are numerous cases of analogies leading to creative insights (Dreistadt, 1968; Ochse, 1990). Examples include Keuklé using the image of a snake biting its tail to discover the molecular ring structure of benzene; Johannes Kepler using the workings of a clock to understand movement of celestial bodies (Rutherford, Holton, & Watson, 1975); Alexander Graham Bell conceiving of the telephone through selective analogy to the human ear (Barron, 1969; Carlson & Gorman, 1992); and William James using metaphors to conceptualize, psychological functions (e.g., thought is a "stream") (Gruber & Davis, 1988). Empirically, Barron (1988) reports significant correlations between scores on a test of metaphor generation (the *Symbolic Equivalence Test*) and creative accomplishments in samples of writers, architects, artists, and entrepreneurs.

The third insight ability on which creativity theorists have focused is combination of information. Along these lines, Mednick (1962) highlighted the ability to join *remotely associated* knowledge elements and form new combinations. Koestler (1964) viewed creativity as an act of "bisociation"—the fusing of two or more thought matrices that habitually have been seen as incompatible or unrelated. Routine thinking involves perceiving an idea through only a single frame of reference. One example of bisociation is Gutenberg's joining of three lines of thinking to arrive at the movable-type printing press: (1) multiple images can be printed with woodcuts that are inked and applied to paper; (2) coins with different features are manufactured by pressing the stamp into soft metal; (3) a wine press exerts uniform pressure over a wide area. Boden (1992) uses computational models to clarify how different matrices of thought (conceptual spaces) might be represented and joined, as with connectionist networks (see Baer, 1991). Connectionist networks are composed of many simple processing units. Weighted links join the units together and allow active units to stimulate other units and lead the system to a new state. The representation of an idea is often distributed across many units. This computational architecture automatically leads to tendencies for pattern completion, pattern matching, multiple constraint satisfaction, and conceptual blending (Rumelhart, McClelland, & the PDP Research Group, 1986).

Rothenberg (1979) has distinguished aspects of combination called "homospatial thinking" and "janusian thinking." Homospatial thinking involves the conception of two or more distinct thoughts as occupying the same space and yielding a new entity. In one study, students of writing saw picture slides displayed side by side or superimposed visually. Metaphors created under the superimposed-presentation condition were more creative than those produced under the side-by-side condition (Rothenberg & Sobel, 1980). Janusian thinking refers to the simultaneous conception of opposite or antithetical thoughts. Case studies in art, science, music, and literature, as well as experiments, indicate a link between janusian thinking and creativity (Rothenberg, 1979).

Divergent thinking, also a basic-level ability, was mentioned above as part of a creativity-relevant problem-solving strategy. As a strategy, people may vary on whether they choose to engage in divergent thinking or not. People can also vary on the ability itself. Some people can generate multiple, disparate, uncommon ideas in response to a problem, whereas others can only squeeze out a few, related, common ideas. The mechanism by which divergent thinking operates may involve multiple memory searches in which the problem probe (given topic) is modified each time (see Schank, 1988b). For example, one feature of the probe may be dropped so that the probe activates a greater number of related memory items.

Numerous studies, including longitudinal ones, have examined correlations between divergent-thinking ability and creative achievement (Baer, 1991; Barron & Harrington, 1981; R. T. Brown, 1989; Harrington, Block, & Block, 1983; B. B. Rossman & Horn, 1972; Runco, 1991; Torrance, 1988). These studies often show relatively low correlations, typically in the .2 to .3 range (Guilford, 1967; Torrance, 1974, 1988). The strength of these correlations is reasonable if divergent thinking is seen as only part of a larger set of intellectual abilities for creativity. However, there is debate over the "true" correlation between divergent thinking and creativity. Critics have noted flaws in many studies, including the use of weak criteria for creative achievement and a failure to address domain or task specificity in divergent thinking (Baer, 1991; R. T. Brown, 1989; Runco, 1991). Thus, the *relative* importance of divergent-thinking ability for creativity, as with the other abilities described, remains an open issue.

Distinct from high-level abilities and basic-level abilities, the relationship between *general intelligence and creativity* has been the subject of extensive investigation and speculation (Barron & Harrington, 1981; Cox, 1926; Glover, Ronning, & Reynolds, 1989; Haensly & Reynolds, 1989; Runco & Albert, 1986; Simonton, 1976). Tests of general intelligence tend to measure a wide variety of information-processing abilities as well as general world knowledge. General intelligence is often reported in terms of IQ (intelligence quotient) scores, which represent a standardized metric for comparing people. The population average IQ is defined as 100 with scores typically ranging between 70 (low intelligence) and 130 (high intelligence).

There are three basic findings concerning general intelligence and creativity. First, creative individuals tend to be above average on general intelligence, often with IQs above 120 (Barron & Harrington, 1981; Hayes, 1989; Simonton, 1976). Second, the correlation between intelligence and creativity is quite variable across studies. The correlations tend to range considerably, from indicating a slightly negative or zero correlation to a moderately strong relationship (e.g., $r = .50$) (Barron, 1963; Barron & Harrington, 1981; Lubart & Sternberg, in press; MacKinnon, 1978; Meer & Stein, 1955). The significance levels (p values) of observed correlations also vary but depend, in part, on the sample size used in each study. Third, typical correlations tend to be weak (Barron & Harrington, 1981). Surveying research findings, I estimate the median correlation to be roughly $r = .20$.

There are several alternative explanations for this pattern of results. These explanations are not mutually exclusive. One explanation is a "diminishing returns" hypothesis: A minimum level of general intelligence (IQ = 120) is required for creativity, but beyond the "threshold" there are rapidly diminishing returns for increasingly high ability levels. In other words, beyond an above-average level, general intelligence is essentially superfluous (Hayes, 1989; Schubert, 1973). It is possible, however, that a few highly relevant cognitive abilities (such as the ones described above) continue to enhance creativity. A second explanation is the "certification" hypothesis: Above-average general intelligence facilitates entry (e.g., completing an advanced degree) into fields that offer the most opportunities and rewards for creativity (Hayes, 1989). The actual relevance of general intelligence to creative work, once a person is in the field, is minimal, however. Third, there is the "additional-components" hypothesis: General intelligence, at every level, contributes to creativity, but for high levels of creativity, other components (e.g., personality traits and motivation) are also important (Barron, 1963; McNemar, 1964). Thus, there is a large amount of variability in creativity at high levels that cannot be accounted for by intelligence. For each of the first three hypotheses, the range of correlations observed across studies can be explained; research samples vary on the extent to which they fall in the high end of the intelligence distribution and therefore vary on the magnitude of correlations between general intelligence and creative performance.

A fourth hypothesis concerns "measurement": intelligence tests vary on the specific abilities that are measured. Sometimes highly relevant abilities (as specified earlier) are emphasized on a test, leading to high correlations between the test and creative performance. Other times less relevant abilities are emphasized and, therefore, correlations are low. In general, intelligence tests measure at least some creativity-relevant abilities, leading creative people to show elevated average test scores. Also, there can be variability across studies on the measurement of creativity, which can contribute to a range of observed correlations (see the last section of this chapter).

Fifth, there is the "restriction-of-range" hypothesis: Research samples vary on the extent to which an adequate range of intelligence and/or creativity is exhibited (Haensly & Reynolds, 1989). Restriction in the range of these variables affects the observed correlation between general intelligence and creativity. Further research is needed before any of these competing hypotheses can be eliminated.

2. Knowledge

Knowledge, a second component, is necessary to make an informed, creative contribution to any field (Mednick, 1962; Simonton, 1988a; Weisberg, 1986, 1993). Knowledge can be both formal, such as facts that can be found in books, and informal, such as heuristics, or knowing who are the important players in a field. Hayes (1989) has found that several years of knowledge acquisition are necessary before creative masterworks tend to be produced. For over 500 notable musical compositions, produced by 76 "great" composers, only three pieces were composed before the tenth year of the composers' careers. A similar pattern was found with 131 painters, although six years was the average preparatory period (see also Gardner, 1993).

How is knowledge important for creativity? First, without knowledge it is difficult to recognize problems or to understand the nature of these problems. Second, knowledge prevents a person from simply rediscovering old ideas. Third, knowledge also helps a person to be contrarian—to know where the current thinking is, to move away from these ideas, and to introduce novelty. Fourth, knowledge helps a person to produce high-quality work, which is important for conveying an idea effectively. Fifth, knowledge helps a person to notice and make use of chance occurrences as a source of ideas (Rosenman, 1988). As Louis Pasteur said, "Chance favors only the prepared mind" (Rosenman, 1988). Sixth, and finally, knowledge helps a person to concentrate his or her cognitive resources on the processing of new ideas because the basics of a task are already known.

Given these benefits of knowledge, it is important to realize that knowledge can also have a cost. Knowledge comes at the expense of flexibility in thinking about new problems (Schank, 1988a). For example, there are numerous studies with insight problems that show conceptual fixedness; people learn to use an object for a particular purpose and then do not see how the object can be used in a different way to solve a new problem (see Sternberg & Davidson, in press-a; Weisberg, 1986). Demonstrating how experts can become entrenched in their thinking, Frensch and Sternberg (1989) found that knowledgeable bridge players were more impaired than were novice players when basic rules of the game were altered. And Simonton (1984) found that 192 eminent creators showed an inverted-U relationship between years of formal education and creativity—too much education can stifle new ideas, but the exact turning point probably depends on the domain.

A final aspect of knowledge, which may have beneficial or detrimental effects, is the organization of the knowledge base. Mednick (1962) contrasts steep "knowledge hierarchies" with flat ones. People with a steep hierarchy of associations will have strong bonds between highly related terms but will find it difficult to move beyond the normal associates of a term. People with a flat hierarchy have relatively weak associations and find it easier to access links between diverse terms, leading to remote associations and creativity. In a related proposal, Simonton (1988a) hypothesized that a knowledge base with multiple kinds of associations between elements (behavioral, attentional, cognitive, and habit-based associations) will be more conducive to creativity than will be a knowledge base with mainly habit-based associations.

3. Thinking Styles

Thinking styles exist at the interface between cognition and personality traits. Thinking styles are preferred ways of applying one's intellectual abilities and knowledge to a problem. Two people may have equal levels of intelligence but differ on how they focus their abilities on a task. Research indicates that some thinking styles promote creativity, whereas others diminish it.

For example, Jung (1923; Myers & Myers, 1980) distinguishes between sensing and intuitive styles. People who show the sensing style like to approach a problem through their five senses. They rely heavily on externally available information, and focus their cognitive abilities on the realities of a situation, working with what is given. Intuitive stylists, in contrast, rely on their hunches, feelings, and internal sources of knowledge. Empirically, creative samples of mathematicians, scientists, writers, students, and others show a strong tendency for the intuitive style (Myers & McCaulley, 1985). In one study by Hall and MacKinnon (1969), all 40 architects whom peers rated as highly creative showed a preference for the intuitive type of thinking. In a matched control group of architects, only 61 percent preferred the intuitive style over the sensing style.

From another perspective, Kirton (1976) has proposed the creativity-relevant adaptor–innovator styles. Adaptors seek problem solutions that involve small adjustments or incremental modifications. They prefer to maintain the initial structure or paradigm and work with established procedures or constraints. Innovators, in contrast, prefer to restructure a problem by approaching it from a new angle. Research studies show moderate correlations between a preference for the innovative style and divergent-thinking tests of creativity (Isaksen & Puccio, 1988; Masten & Caldwell-Colbert, 1987; Mulligan & Martin, 1980; Torrance & Horng, 1980).

Several other thinking styles have been hypothesized as important for creativity. One of these styles is the global–local style dimension (Sternberg & Lubart, 1991b). Local stylists like to work on the narrow, detailed aspects of a problem. Global stylists prefer to work on the broad, general level of a problem. Creative solutions often involve seeing the big picture first, and hence a global style is hypothesized to be important. However, in some of the later phases of creative work, attention to detail becomes necessary for completing a task. Thus, some balance between the global and local styles may be optimal.

4. Personality

Personality traits may facilitate the effective use of the cognitive components and help to turn fleeting ideas into real products (Mumford & Gustafson, 1988). There have been numerous studies of the personality attributes needed for creativity (Barron & Harrington, 1981; Dellas & Gaier, 1970). A constellation of five attributes seems to co-occur across these studies (Sternberg & Lubart, 1991b).

The first attribute is tolerance of ambiguity (Barron & Harrington, 1981; Golann, 1963). There are often periods of uncertainty when the pieces of the problem being solved do not fit together. During these times a person may feel some anxiety and pressure to pursue an available but nonoptimal solution (Simon, 1976). Tolerating ambiguity provides time for difficult aspects of a problem to be resolved.

The second attribute is perseverance (Csikszentmihalyi, 1988a; Golann, 1963; Roe, 1952). Biographies of creative people virtually always show them to have confronted obstacles during their work (K. A. Brown, 1988; Ghiselin, 1952/1985; Roe, 1952). These obstacles must be faced and conquered for creative products to occur. In a survey of 710 inventors, J. Rossman (1931) found that perseverance was, in fact, the most frequently mentioned characteristic for success.

The third attribute is openness to new experiences. Openness means a willingness to try out new ideas, to explore, to be curious about one's inner ideas and the world we live in (Costa & McCrae, 1985). Rogers (1954) saw openness as one of the key aspects of creativity. He contrasted open individuals with psychologically defensive ones who protected themselves from potentially disruptive new experiences. McCrae's (1987) research shows moderate correlations ($r = .40$) between openness and divergent-thinking test performance.

Connected with openness is the desire to grow beyond one's current position (Sternberg & Lubart, 1991b). If a person has a creative idea and is rewarded for the idea, then it may be difficult to leave the success for uncharted territory. However, creativity over prolonged periods involves continually moving on to new projects.

The fourth attribute is willingness to take risks (McClelland, 1956; Sternberg & Lubart, 1991b). Creative work involves deviating from the crowd. When a person chooses the novel route there is the potential for gain (internal and external rewards) or loss (time, energy, criticism), and the outcome is uncertain. Studies have found positive relationships between risk-taking behavior in contests or hypothetical scenarios and divergent-thinking scores (Eisenman, 1987; Glover & Sautter, 1977). In one study, a risk-oriented state of mind was experimentally induced. People showed heightened originality and flexibility on the *Torrance Tests of Creative Thinking* (Glover, 1977).

To the detriment of creativity, most people are relatively risk averse. They prefer ideas that are already fairly well accepted. This risk aversion may ultimately be due to a low tolerance for failure. Clifford (1988) showed that tolerance for failure declines as children progress through school. Clifford presented 4th, 5th, and 6th graders with math, spelling, and vocabulary problems that were marked as varying in difficulty from a 2nd-grade level to a 9th-grade level. Fourth graders, on average, chose problems rated as six to eight months below their ability level; 5th graders chose problems one year below their ability level; and 6th graders chose problems rated one and a half years below their ability level.

Finally, there is the courage of one's convictions and belief in oneself (Amabile, 1983; Barron & Harrington, 1981; Dellas & Gaier, 1970; Golann, 1963; MacKinnon, 1962, 1965; Ochse, 1990; Sternberg & Lubart, 1991b). There are times when a creator may begin to doubt his or her ideas. Teachers, employers, or peers may criticize or ridicule these ideas. Independence of judgment and self-esteem are needed to maintain unpopular ideas. Supporting this hypothesis, experiments on group conformity show that subjects rated higher on creativity have less tendency to yield their individual opinion to the group's opinion (Crutchfield, 1962). Other studies with architects, chemists, writers, and psychologists show links between creativity and self-assertiveness, self-sufficiency, dominance, and independence (Barron, 1963; Chambers, 1964; MacKinnon, 1962).

5. Motivation

Motivation provides the driving force to use the cognitive components for creative purposes. Traditionally, intrinsic motivators have been viewed as beneficial for creativity and extrinsic motivators have been considered detrimental (Amabile, 1983, 1985; Hill, 1990; MacKinnon, 1962). Intrinsic motivators are internally generated drives or desires that are satisfied by task completion. For example, task performance may serve to satisfy a person's curiosity, need for novelty, or desire to realize his or her own potential (Golann, 1962; Maddi, 1965; Rogers, 1954). People who are intrinsically motivated often say they engage in a task because they "enjoy" it or find it "interesting." Extrinsic motivators, in contrast, are rewards that the environment offers. Examples of extrinsic motivators are money, job advancement, recognition (praise from a superior, awards, fame), and power. Studies show that people who perform a task for a reward are less creative than those who receive no reward or a reward that is not linked to the task (Amabile, 1982a; Amabile, Hennessey, & Grossman, 1986; Kruglanski, Friedman, & Zeevi, 1971).

The simple picture of intrinsic motivation as good for creativity and extrinsic motivation as bad has received some modifications. First, the strictly beneficial effect of intrinsic motivation has been questioned. Crutchfield (1962), for example, points out that intrinsic motivators such as the desire for self-expression can be detrimental to creativity if the desire becomes too explicit and too consciously apparent.

Second, the negative effect of extrinsic motivators has been questioned (Hill, 1990; Ochse, 1990). There are cases, such as Crick and Watson's discovery of the double helix constituting the structure of DNA, in which extrinsic rewards appear to have had a positive effect. Extrinsic motivation may be beneficial if a person does not become distracted by the "carrot at the end of the stick" (Sternberg & Lubart, 1991b). Extrinsic motivation may serve as a helpful, additional incentive if sufficient intrinsic motivation already exists (Hennessey, Amabile, & Martinage, 1989). Finally, extrinsic motivation may be useful during tedious portions of creative work, such as working out the details of an invention (Amabile, 1988).

Third, some motivators relevant to creativity seem to lie at the interface between the intrinsic and extrinsic types of motivation. Perhaps the best example is achievement motivation—a desire to succeed at a high standard of excellence (Maddi, 1965; McClelland et al., 1953). The desire to succeed may come from within but satisfaction of the goal involves external recognition. Studies report links between need for achievement and creative performance, choosing challenging problems, and moderate risk taking (McClelland, 1962; McClelland & Watson, 1973; Touhey & Villemez, 1975).

Based on these discrepancies, Sternberg and Lubart (1991b, 1993) suggest that the crucial aspect of motivation for creativity is actually the way the motivator affects a person's attention toward a task rather than the intrinsic–extrinsic nature of the motivator. A task-focusing motivator is one that energizes a person to work and keeps the person's attention on the task. In contrast, a goal-focusing motivator leads a person to focus attention on the reward to the detriment of the task itself. Intrinsic motivators tend to be task focusing because the goal (e.g., personal fulfillment) is integrated with the task itself. Extrinsic motivators tend to be goal focusing because the rewards are salient and distinct from the task. People are hypothesized to vary, however, on the extent to which motivational goals can distract them from their task (explaining the potential benefits of extrinsic motivators or negative effects of intrinsic motivators). Also, motivators are believed to show a curvilinear relationship to creativity because low levels give insufficient drive, intermediate levels are most task focusing, and high levels are too goal focusing (Lubart & Sternberg, in press).

6. Environment

The final component of creativity is environmental context. Environments can provide physical or social conditions that help new ideas to form and develop; environments can trigger the use of creativity-relevant cognitive abilities (Amabile, 1983; Lubart, 1990; Rubenson & Runco, 1992; Simonton, 1984). For example, Ward (1969) found that children who take a divergent-thinking test in a room full of objects generate more ideas than those tested in a bare room. Developmentally, creative people often grow up in intellectually stimulating home environments (Ochse, 1990). These formative environments may include home libraries, magazine subscriptions, or a variety of hobbies available in the home (Simonton, 1988a).

Another developmental influence of the environment comes through role models. Studies of historical trends in European and Chinese creativity show that the availability of eminent creative role models in one generation positively affects observed creativity in the next generation (Simonton, 1975, 1984, 1988b). Zuckerman's (1977) research on Nobel Prize-winning scientists indicates that role models convey cognitive benefits such as the ability to recognize important problems, useful ways of thinking about problems, evaluative standards, and informal knowledge about the way the scientific community operates.

In the workplace, environmental conditions such as freedom over one's work, sufficient time to think, collaboration across divisions, and sufficient resources to develop ideas have been found to be facilitative for creativity (Amabile, 1988). At a societal level, conditions such as cultural diversity, which can be indexed by political fragmentation or physical proximity to large cultural centers, show a positive influence on creativity (Csikszentmihalyi, 1988b; Simonton, 1975, 1984).

Given these positive environmental influences, it is important to note that environments also can put up cognitive barriers to creativity. Traditional schools, for example, have been criticized as having a number of features that inhibit creativity (Sternberg & Lubart, 1991a, 1991b). For example, knowledge is often presented in discrete, isolated units, which makes integrative associations difficult. Tests typically emphasize factual recall and rote learning. Test questions often have one "correct" answer, which limits a student's need for divergent thinking and creative thought. Assignments tend be short, well-defined tasks that do not promote tolerance of ambiguity or perseverance. The reward system in schools discourages risk taking and relies on extrinsic, goal-focusing motivators. Finally, many teachers view the ideal student as one who sits at a desk quietly, follows instructions, and does not ask questions or otherwise disrupt the teacher's lesson plan. In general, some environments value conformity more than others (Mann, 1980; Torrance, 1964).

Beyond strictly positive or negative effects, the environment places constraints on creative work. Anthropological research offers clear evidence of this environmental effect. For example, the Ashanti, a West African culture, encourage creativity in the carving of secular objects but discourage creativity in religious objects (Silver, 1981). The Yoruba, another group, impose more precise limitations on creativity: The ear and face of carved figures must be treated in a standardized fashion but variation is allowed in the hand of the figure, the ritual item, the costume, and arrangement of figures (Bascom, 1969).

Constraints can be stifling if they are severe, creating mental gridlock (Finke, 1990). However, at least some constraints are necessary because they lead to the appropriateness component of creativity judgments. Without constraints, creative work would degenerate into productions that were simply novel.

Some theorists argue that constraints are also useful because they give the individual something to struggle against (Finke, 1990; May, 1975); constraints may force the individual to move beyond the early, mundane ideas that readily come to mind. Finke (1990; Finke et al., 1992) conducted a series of studies in which people created inventions from parts of objects. Across the studies, restrictions were introduced in various ways (e.g., restrictions on parts used, general type of invention, or specific function of invention). The results support the idea that some constraints lead to increased creativity but other constraints can be too stringent and stifle creativity.

In a final role, the social environment serves to evaluate subjectively a product's creativity or an individual's creative performance (Amabile, 1983; Csikszentmihalyi & Robinson, 1986; Reis & Renzulli, 1991). The same idea that is perceived as creative in one setting may be perceived as dull elsewhere. Earlier, in the section on the definition of creativity, the important dimensions that judges use were described. Part of being creative is finding an environment in which the kind of product that an individual has to offer is valued. Another part of being creative is internalizing the environment's criteria for creativity so that they become part of the individual's own evaluative processes. For example, a person may internalize domain-specific standards for what is considered original and appropriate.

7. The Confluence of Components

There is growing evidence that the cognitive, personality-motivational, and environmental components must co-occur for creativity to exist (Gruber, 1974/1981; Lubart & Sternberg, in press; Mumford & Gustafson, 1988; B. B. Rossman & Horn, 1972). However, creativity is not simply the result of adding up a person's level on each component. If a person is near zero on any particular component, then the chance of being creative at all is low. For example, someone who knows absolutely nothing about nuclear physics has basically no chance of being creative in that field even if all of the other creativity components are at optimal levels. Partial compensation can occur, however, for weak components that meet a minimally acceptable level. For example, a high level of perseverance may compensate somewhat for an environment that is lukewarm toward novel ideas.

Finally, there is the possibility that components may interact with each other to enhance creativity (Meehl, 1965; Sternberg & Lubart, 1991b). The co-occurence of high levels on two components, such as intelligence and motivation, may contribute an extra boost to creativity that exceeds the simple effect of these components. The confluence and interaction of components needs to be specified in greater detail in future research.

III. THE CREATIVE PROCESS

The creative process refers to the sequence of thoughts and actions that lead to a creative product. A theory of the creative process needs to show how the creative process differs from a routine problem-solving process. I propose that there are four distinct ways (Type I to Type IV) in which the creative process could be different. After considering each position, a widely held process model is described and examined as a case study.

A. Different Theoretical Positions on the Creative Process

1. Type I

The first possibility retains the closest connection between routine and creative problem solving (see Weisberg, 1993). Let us assume that all problem solving involves certain fundamental steps: Defining a problem-solving goal, accessing relevant information, building a solution from this information, and then evaluating and refining the proposed solution. The creative problem-solving process is marked by doing one or more of the basic steps more effectively than average. For example, when linking prior knowledge to aspects of the problem, most people will find simple, mundane connections. The creative problem solver, however, may find complex, novel connections. As another example, consider the evaluation of a potential solution to a problem. The creative problem solver may have more developed and comprehensive criteria for evaluating an idea than does the average problem solver. Thus the main difference between creative and routine problem solving is the *quality* with which each step is performed. The fundamental steps, however, are the same (leading some people to claim there really is no distinct creative *process*).

2. Type II

A second position on the creative process also proposes that the same basic activities are involved in creative and routine problem solving. The difference lies in the *amount of time* devoted to each step or in the *number of times* that each activity is performed. For example, consider the problem-definition phase. Many problems are initially ill defined; it is unclear exactly what the problem is or what the features of a good solution would be. The creative process may involve spending more time on problem definition than in routine problem solving. As described earlier, one study found that art students who produced highly original still-life drawings spent more time formulating their compositions than low-originality students (Getzels & Csikszentmihalyi, 1976). Creative artists also distinguished their working process by the number of times that they engaged in certain activities, such as manipulating and exploring objects. To take another example, suppose that most people use analogies once or twice when solving a problem. The creative process may involve multiple uses of analogies. The analogical process is the same but it is used more often in the creative process.

3. Type III

A third theoretical position on the creative process centers on the need for a special *sequence* of problem-solving activities. A skill, such as evaluation of one's own ideas, must occur at a particular point or be concentrated during a particular portion of the problem-solving process (Lubart, 1994). If evaluation occurs at a nonoptimal time, then the problem solution will be less creative. Theorists such as Osborn (1953) and Parnes (1962), for example, suggest that it is best to engage in unconstrained thinking at first and to evaluate only after several ideas have accumulated. On this view, early evaluation can stifle innovative thinking about a topic by constraining idea generation too severely. An alternative hypothesis argues for a different time sequence; early evaluation is best because it keeps people from being satisfied with the first minimally acceptable solution that comes to mind.

4. Type IV

Finally, there is a fourth position on the creative process, which maximizes the difference from the normal problem-solving process. On this view, the creative process involves a *special activity* or stage of processing that is not found in mundane problem solving. For example, Koestler (1964) proposed that bisociation is part of the creative process but not the routine thinking process. Several other theorists have proposed similar "special" activities, such as Rothenberg's (1979) work on janusian thinking—the simultaneous integration of antithetical thoughts. Alternatively, divergent thinking could be the special activity that is included in the creative process but absent from routine problem solving. And psychoanalytic theorists have proposed that regression to primary-process material (unmodulated thought) is a central feature of the creative process that the routine problem-solving process does not involve.

B. The Four-Stage Creative Process Model: A Case Study

The four positions on the creative process described above provide a framework for examining specific models. Sometimes several types of special-process features are possible in the same model. As a case study, consider the popular four-stage creative process model. This model stems from proposals by Hadamard (1945), Poincaré (1921), Ribot (1906), J. Rossman (1931), and Wallas (1926).

Creative problem solving involves four stages: Preparation, incubation, illumination, and verification. The first activity, preparation, consists of preliminary analysis of a problem, gathering information and materials, and initial conscious work on the task. Preparation can also include the acquisition of skills and knowledge through general education before the specific task is encountered.

After preparation has progressed, incubation begins. Unconsciously, progress is made and possible solutions emerge. Incubation may involve: (1) active processing similar to conscious work; (2) slow, automatic spreading of memory activation; (3) passive forgetting of superficial details or previous attempts at the problem; or (4) associative play between problem elements. The creative problem solver may cycle between incubation and preparation as further information becomes necessary. One part of a large problem might be in the preparation stage while another part is in the incubation stage.

Regarding incubation, Hadamard (1945) emphasized that incubation is more than a rest period that lets the individual face the problem with new strength (although some hold this view). Poincaré (1921), a French mathematician, introspectively described incubation as a phase when ideas "rose in crowds" and randomly bounced off each other like molecules of gas until "pairs interlocked."

Illumination occurs when a promising idea suddenly becomes consciously available. Illumination is often metaphorically described as a light bulb coming on. Ideas may break into consciousness because they satisfy some unconscious "aesthetic sensibility" or cohere as stable cognitive patterns (Campbell, 1960; Poincaré, 1921; Simonton, 1988a).

The creative idea must then be evaluated, developed, and refined during a stage called verification. If verification shows an idea to be unworkable, then there will be a return to incubation, or even to preparation. Eventually, the creative product is formalized for public view.

Since the early theorists, there have been several proposals to change or enhance the basic model (see Mumford et al., 1991). For example, Osborn (1953) emphasized the need for a separate problem-construction phase. Campbell (1960) and Simonton (1988a) developed the hypothesis that the creative process involves the combination of ideas in random or semirandom ways. Mansfield and Busse (1980) proposed a process model that included stages of setting constraints on a solution and then modifying these constraints.

Somewhat larger departures from the historic model have recently been suggested. For example, Mumford et al. (1991) specified a set of detailed stages consisting of problem construction, information encoding, category search to access information, specification of best fitting categories, combination and reorganization of category information, idea evaluation, implementation, and monitoring. Finally, Finke et al. (1992) proposed the "geneplore" model, which involves generative and exploratory phases. The generative phase involves the construction of loosely formulated ideas called preinventive forms. The generative phase can be seen as similar to the traditional preparation and incubation activities. Generative processes include knowledge retrieval, idea association, synthesis, transformation, and analogical transfer. The exploratory phase is similar to the verification activity. Exploratory processes include interpretation of pre-inventive forms, examining potential contexts and functions for the forms, hypothesis testing, and searching for limitations. The geneplore model allows for a cyclic movement between the phases, although sometimes a single generation–exploration sequence is sufficient.

The basic four-stage model and its variants can distinguish between creative and normal problem-solving outcomes through several of the logical positions (Type I to Type IV) described earlier. A Type I explanation would focus on the skill with which a stage is performed. Some people may be better at preparation or verification, for example, which leads to more creative outcomes. A Type II explanation would propose that some activities have more time devoted to them or are used more frequently (by returning to early stages). Perhaps a longer incubation period would increase the likelihood of creative products. A frequency explanation, centering on the number of generation–exploration cycles, fits well with the Finke et al. (1992) model. A Type III explanation would require that the order of the stages differ between routine problem solving and creative problem solving. This is a difficult position to hold with the four-stage model. Each stage seems to depend on outputs from the previous stage; it makes no sense to engage in verification if there is no idea yet. Also, most theorists allow for returns to earlier stages of processing as needed by the problem solver. This flexibility in the model limits the possibility of strong Type III explanations. Finally, a Type IV explanation is possible. Certain stages, such as incubation or information combination and reorganization (according to Mumford et al., 1991), may be present for creative work but absent from routine problem solving.

Theorists who endorse the four-stage model may emphasize one type of explanation or a combination of explanations when distinguishing the creative process from routine problem solving. Often the particular type of explanation that a theorist favors has not been explicitly stated. Work on the creative process may advance through attention to this issue.

IV. TECHNIQUES FOR MEASURING CREATIVITY

One of the most important practical questions about creativity is how it can be measured effectively and efficiently. It may be desirable to assess creativity for educational selection purposes, for recognition in contests, for job recruitment, or for job performance evaluation. It is also useful to be cognizant of measurement issues when designing and evaluating research on creativity.

Drawing on the theoretical and empirical treatments of creativity described earlier in this chapter, eight major methods have been devised to measure creativity (Hocevar & Bachelor, 1989). These are: (1) cognitive ability tests; (2) personality inventories; (3) biographical inventories; (4) attitude and interest surveys; (5) person-centered ratings by teachers, peers, or supervisors; (6) eminence; (7) self-reports of achievements; and (8) judgments of work samples. Consider the basic characteristics and the positive and negative features of each type. None of the measurement methods is perfect. However, some methods are stronger than others, in general, and some may be more useful in a particular situation than others.

A. Cognitive Ability Tests

Cognitive tests seek to engage and measure the basic thinking processes that lead to creative products. These tests measure the ability to think in a particular way when requested but do not assess the extent to which a person will spontaneously use this ability in nontest situations. Guilford's divergent-thinking tests and the more recent *Torrance Tests of Creative Thinking* have been the dominant measures (Torrance & Presbury, 1984). Consider the Torrance tests in some detail.

The Torrance tests consist of relatively simple verbal and figural tasks that involve divergent thinking plus other problem-solving skills. Some samples of subtests from the Torrance battery are described below:

1. Asking questions: The examinee writes out all the questions he or she can think of, based on a drawing of a scene.
2. Product improvement: The examinee lists ways to change a toy monkey so that children will have more fun playing with it.

3. Unusual uses of tin cans: The examinee lists interesting and unusual uses of tin cans.
4. Circles: The examinee expands empty circles into different drawings and titles them.

The subtests can be scored for fluency (total number of relevant responses), flexibility (number of different categories of responses), originality (unusualness of responses), and elaboration (amount of detail in the responses). The exact way that responses are scored depends on the subtest. Using the Unusual Uses test as an example, an examinee might give five different uses for a tin can (*fluency*). These responses could show *flexibility* by spanning the categories of furniture (can as a foot stool), eating utensils (can as a drinking cup), and containers (can as a garbage receptacle). Some uses for a can are more *original* than others. For example, "garbage can" is a common response but "foot stool" is an uncommon response. Originality is operationally defined as statistical rarity and the scoring manual provides response norms. Finally, *elaboration* can be seen in responses like "put holes in the sides of the can and run a wire through to make a pail," versus "use can as a pail." Recent work has proposed tasks with more real-world content and new scoring methods that, for example, look at a person's divergent responses to a problem as a set (Runco, 1991).

In addition to tests involving divergent thinking, several other cognitive tests have been used as measures of creativity. For example, there have been insight tests (Sternberg & Davidson, in press-a), word- or object-combination tests (Dougan, Schiff, & Welsh, 1949; Welch, 1946), and tests of metaphor generation (Barron, 1988). One of the most widely used tests has been Mednick and Mednick's (1967) *Remote Associates Test* (RAT). According to Mednick's (1962) theory, mentioned earlier, creativity stems from an ability to see associations and form new combinations between diverse knowledge elements. Each item on the RAT consists of three stimulus words that are indirectly related to each other. The test taker must supply a fourth word that relates to each of the original three. For example, "blue," "rat," and "cottage" are given. The answer would be "cheese."

The RAT has been criticized on several points and illustrates the difficulties of constructing a cognitive test of creativity (Buros, 1972). The RAT has been criticized because: (1) it often shows weak correlations with creative accomplishments and product ratings (poor convergent validity); (2) it measures verbal ability and academic intelligence to a large extent (poor discriminant validity); (3) it measures a limited ability, given the range of cognitive abilities relevant to creativity (poor content validity); and (4) it does not operationalize Mednick's theory properly (poor construct validity). For example, each item's answer is a common associate shared by the three words, rather than a remote associate (Ochse, 1990).

In general, cognitive tests of creativity have been subject to criticisms that they measure only part of creativity, are too closely linked to intelligence, and involve trivial levels of creativity. The Torrance tests, in particular, have been criticized because they are relatively knowledge free, distort the meaning of creativity by using fluency, flexibility, and elaboration, and inappropriately use the same originality-response norms for many different samples (R. T. Brown, 1989; Hennessey & Amabile, 1988; Mitchell, 1985). Cognitive tests, however, have been the most popular mode of creativity assessment; these tests seem to tap relevant skills. They are brief, easy to administer and score, and provide "objective," numerical creativity scores for comparing people.

B. Personality Inventories

Another way to identify creative people is through their personality traits. Via a standard personality test, responses to selected items are scored in terms of a "creative-personality" profile (e.g., Gough & Heilbrun, 1983). Items for the profile may be selected because they look relevant to creativity ("I consider myself a risk taker") or because they statistically distinguish high- and low-creative people (criterion groups are selected by other methods). Omnibus personality tests with creativity subscales are useful but limited, like cognitive tests, because they tap only some of the components of creativity. Some specialized personality tests have also been developed to measure only creativity-relevant characteristics. Although briefer tests, the purpose of these focused inventories is often obvious to test takers, which can lead to response biases. People may wish to appear creative and respond accordingly.

C. Biographical Inventories

Biographical inventories work on the assumption that certain common background experiences lead people to creativity. For example, research indicates that creative people often grow up in a home environment that has a wide variety of reading materials available (Ochse, 1990). Items on a biographical inventory may ask about one's home environment (including a home library), educational experiences, family history, hobbies, social clubs, or interests (e.g., Schaefer, 1970). Items can be selected through research findings on creativity or by statistically choosing items that distinguish between high- and low-creative samples (deemed creative by other methods) (Hocevar & Bachelor, 1989). The positive and negative features of biographical inventories are both tied to the relative obscurity of the item content as a measure of creativity. It would be relatively difficult to fake creativity because many of the items do not bear an obvious relation to creativity. However, the down side is that responses on the inventory are still one or more steps removed from creative performance and the measurement of creativity is therefore weaker.

D. Attitude and Interest Surveys

These instruments measure the extent to which people like, dislike, or are interested in a variety of activities that foster or involve creative work (Hocevar & Bachelor, 1989). For example, people may be asked if they like to write stories, daydream about unsolved problems, invent things, or if they would enjoy being a sculptor if they had artistic skills. An attitudinal item might measure if a person prefers to follow textbook examples or learn on their own. A major problem with these measures is the scattered item content that tends to touch on many domains of creative activity without adequately measuring any of them.

E. Person-Centered Ratings by Teachers, Peers, and Supervisors

In daily life, teachers, peers, and supervisors are often making judgments about creativity (see Hocevar & Bachelor, 1989). These judgments tend to be global, assessing the person as a whole. On the positive side, the judge can take into account all of the situations and products over a long period during which an individual has been observed. On the negative side, these kinds of judgments are often based on a single judge's opinion, which highlights the subjective nature of creativity. Further, these person–centered creativity judgments are subject to halo effects, correlating highly with other positively valued ratings by the same judge. Finally, it is nearly impossible to make creativity comparisons across people who do not share the same teacher, supervisor, or peer.

F. Eminence

Eminence ratings are an extension of the concept of ratings by peers or supervisors. Eminence ratings represent a field's or society's judgment of a person's accomplishments as a whole. To assess eminence, researchers have measured the amount of space devoted to a person in biographical dictionaries or used membership in elite professional societies, citation counts, expert ratings, and awards (such as the Nobel Prize) (Hocevar & Bachelor, 1989). Eminence is particularly useful for studying creativity over large time frames and obtaining relative rankings of historical cases of creativity (Simonton, 1984). However, on the negative side, eminence ratings tend to take into account more than just creativity and are often unstable or unavailable for contemporary creators.

G. Self-Reports of Achievements

The most straightforward way to measure creativity is to ask an individual what his or her creative achievements have been. To facilitate reporting on personal creative activities, several checklists have been developed that cover activities in art, science, literature, music, performing arts, and other domains (Hocevar & Bachelor, 1989). Also, Richards, Kinney, Benet, and Merzel (1988) have developed the *Lifetime Creativity Scales,* which use a structured interview to gather information on vocational and avocational creative accomplishments.

Self-reports of creative performance are a useful indicator because they cover long periods of time and they show creative behavior that occurred naturally (rather than in response to a laboratory task). In general, past behavior is a good predictor of future behavior. Self-reports are subjects to serious reporting biases, however. For example, the individual may be modest or boastful in general, may inadvertently forget some accomplishments, or may not regard an accomplishment as creative when others would, and vice versa.

H. Judgments of Work Samples

Perhaps the most central measure of creativity is examination of a person's work, the "creative" product. A creative product can be a short story, a drawing, a scientific problem solution, a poem, an invention, a musical composition, a recipe, a new woodworking process, or any other idea that can be expressed in an observable form. Amabile (1982b, 1983) has conducted extensive research on judging products for creativity with consensus techniques. Several judges view a set of products and rate them for creativity using numerical scales, such as a 1 (low) to 7 (high) system. Each judge works alone. The judges' individual ratings for each piece of work are averaged together and the composite score is used. In general, the judges can be peers or experts. They can use their own personal definition of creativity to guide their ratings or use specific guidelines from the researchers.

Judges' ratings are affected by both the relative quality of the products in the set and by the judges' absolute standards for creativity. Judges make distinctions on creativity within a set and further may rate a whole set of work as somewhat low or high on creativity. When all of the products are responses to the same problem task (e.g., writing a short poem), then comparing the products against each other is easier, and finer distinctions can be made.

Judgments of work samples are perhaps the most useful indicators of creativity (Hocevar & Bachelor, 1989). Creative products are central to the definition of creativity. The judgments are based on tangible work that is subject to scrutiny by independent observers. When multiple judges are used, the combined product ratings show high reliability (Amabile, 1982b, 1983; Lubart & Sternberg, in press). The main problem with judged products is that they represent a limited behavioral sample of the individual. Furthermore, the products are often produced because a test or research project requests them. Thus, the products indicate the ability to be creative on demand. These concerns can be alleviated if it is possible to examine a portfolio of naturally produced work from each individual.

V. SUMMARY AND CONCLUSIONS

This chapter has addressed basic questions about the definition, source, process, and measurement of creativity. The definition of creativity involves primarily novelty and appropriateness but is influenced by the quality, importance, and production history of a piece of work. In future research, the behavior of judges could be examined further to refine the definition of creativity. The source of creativity involves intelligence, knowledge, thinking styles, personality attributes, motivation, and the environment. These components work together to yield creative performance. Each component deserves further study and the interaction of components especially needs to be explored. With regard to the creative process, the theoretical range of process models was described. The examination of the four-stage process model points to the need for more specification and development of creative process models in general. In particular, differences between the creative and routine problem-solving process need to be determined and the use of intellectual abilities, knowledge, and other components of creativity need to be linked to the process in more detailed ways. Finally, creativity assessment methods have been examined. Each method has positive features, negative features, and room for improvement. If creativity can be measured well, then it can be better studied and promoted.

References

Amabile, T. M. (1982a). Children's artistic creativity: Detrimental effects of competition in a field setting. *Personality and Social Psychology Bulletin, 8,* 573–578.
Amabile, T. M. (1982b). Social psychology of creativity: A consensual assessment technique. *Journal of Personality and Social Psychology, 43*(5), 997–1013.
Amabile, T. M. (1983). *The social psychology of creativity.* New York: Springer-Verlag.
Amabile, T. M. (1985). Motivation and creativity: Effects of motivational orientation on creative writers. *Journal of Personality and Social Psychology, 48*(2), 393–399.
Amabile, T. M. (1988). A model of creativity and innovation in organizations. *Research in Organizational Behavior, 10,* 123–167.
Amabile, T. M., Hennessey, B. A., & Grossman, B. S. (1986). Social influence on creativity: The effects of contracted-for reward. *Journal of Personality and Social Psychology, 50,* 14–23.
Artley, N. L., Van Horn, R., Friedrich, D. D., & Carroll, J. L. (1980). The relationship

between problem finding, creativity and cognitive style. *Creative Child and Adult Quarterly, 5*(1), 20–26.

Baer, J. (1991). *Creativity and divergent thinking: A task-specific approach.* Hillsdale, NJ: Erlbaum.

Bailin, S. (1988). *Achieving extraordinary ends: An essay on creativity.* Boston: Kluwer Academic Publishers.

Barron, F. (1963). The need for order and for disorder as motivation in creative activity. In C. W. Taylor & F. Barron (Eds.), *Scientific creativity: Its recognition and development* (pp. 153–160). New York: Wiley.

Barron, F. (1968). *Creativity and personal freedom.* New York: Van Nostrand.

Barron, F. (1969). *Creative person and creative process.* New York: Holt, Rinehart, & Winston.

Barron, F. (1988). Putting creativity to work. In R. J. Sternberg (Ed.), *The nature of creativity: Contemporary psychological perspectives* (pp. 76–98). New York: Cambridge University Press.

Barron, F., & Harrington, D. M. (1981). Creativity, intelligence, and personality. *Annual Review of Psychology, 32,* 439–476.

Bascom, W. (1969). Creativity and style in African art. In D. P. Biebuyck (Ed.), *Tradition and creativity in tribal art.* Berkeley: University of California Press.

Besemer, S., & Treffinger, D. J. (1981). Analysis of creative products: Review and synthesis. *Journal of Creative Behavior, 15*(3), 158–178.

Binet, A., & Henri, V. (1896). La psychologie individuelle. *Année Psychologique, 2,* 411–465.

Boden, M. (1992). *The creative mind: Myths and mechanisms.* New York: Basic Books.

Brogden, H. E., & Sprecher, T. B. (1964). Criteria of creativity. In C. W. Taylor (Ed.), *Creativity: Progress and potential* (pp. 156–176). New York: McGraw-Hill.

Brown, K. A. (1988). *Inventors at work: Interviews with 16 notable American inventors.* Redmond, WA: Microsoft Press.

Brown, R. T. (1989). Creativity: What are we to measure? In J. A. Glover, R. R. Ronning, & C. R. Reynolds (Eds.), *Handbook of creativity* (pp. 3–32). New York: Plenum.

Buros, O. K. (Ed.). (1972). *The seventh mental measurements yearbook* (Vol. 1). Highland Park, NJ: Gryphon Press.

Campbell, D. T. (1960). Blind variation and selective retention in creative thought as in other knowledge processes. *Psychological Review, 67*(6), 380–400.

Carlson, W. B., & Gorman, M. E. (1992). A cognitive framework to understand technological creativity: Bell, Edison, and the telephone. In R. J. Weber & D. N. Perkins (Eds.), *Inventive minds: Creativity in technology* (pp. 48–79). New York: Oxford University Press.

Chambers, J. A. (1964). Relating personality and biographical factors to scientific creativity. *Psychological Monographs, 78*(7, Whole No. 584).

Clifford, M. M. (1988). Failure tolerance and academic risk taking in ten- to twelve-year-old students. *British Journal of Educational Psychology, 58*(1), 15–27.

Costa, P. T., Jr., & McCrae, R. R. (1985). *The NEO personality inventory manual.* Odessa, FL: Psychological Assessment Resources.

Cox, C. (1926). *The early mental traits of three hundred geniuses.* Stanford, CA: Stanford University Press.

Crouch, T. D. (1992). Why Wilbur and Orville? Some thoughts on the Wright brothers and the process of invention. In R. J. Weber & D. N. Perkins (Eds.), *Inventive minds: Creativity in technology* (pp. 80–92). New York: Oxford University Press.

Crutchfield, R. S. (1962). Conformity and creative thinking. In H. E. Gruber, G. Terrell, & M. Wertheimer (Eds.), *Contemporary approaches to creative thinking* (pp. 120–140). New York: Prentice-Hall.

Csikszentmihalyi, M. (1988a). Motivation and creativity: Towards a synthesis of structural and energetic approaches. *New Ideas in Psychology, 6*(2), 159–176.

Csikszentmihalyi, M. (1988b). Society, culture, and person: A systems view of creativity. In R. J. Sternberg (Ed.), *The nature of creativity: Contemporary psychological perspectives* (pp. 325–339). New York: Cambridge University Press.

Csikszentmihalyi, M., & Robinson, R. E. (1986). Culture, time, and the development of talent. In R. J. Sternberg & J. E. Davidson (Eds.), *Conceptions of giftedness* (pp. 264–284). New York: Cambridge University Press.

Davidson, J. E. (in press). Searching for insight. In R. J. Sternberg & J. E. Davidson (Eds.), *The nature of insight*. Cambridge, MA: MIT Press.

Dellas, M., & Gaier, E. L. (1970). Identification of creativity: The individual. *Psychological Bulletin, 73,* 55–73.

Dennis, W. (1955). Variations in productivity among creative workers. *Scientific Monthly, 80,* 277–278.

Dougan, C. P., Schiff, E., & Welsh, L. (1949). Originality ratings of department store display department personnel. *Journal of Applied Psychology, 33,* 31–35.

Dreistadt, R. (1968). An analysis of the use of analogies and metaphors in science. *Journal of Psychology, 68,* 97–116.

Dudek, S. Z., & Hall, W. B. (1991). Personality consistency: Eminent architects 25 years later. *Creativity Research Journal, 4*(3), 213–231.

Eisenman, R. (1987). Creativity, birth order, and risk taking. *Bulletin of the Psychonomic Society, 25,* 87–88.

Eysenck, H. J. (1993). Creativity and personality: Suggestions for a theory. *Psychological Inquiry, 4*(3), 147–178.

Findlay, C. S., & Lumsden, C. J. (1988). The creative mind: Toward an evolutionary theory of discovery and innovation. *Journal of Social and Biological Structures, 11,* 3–55.

Finke, R. A. (1990). *Creative imagery: Discoveries and inventions in visualization.* Hillsdale, NJ: Erlbaum.

Finke, R. A., Ward, T. B., & Smith, S. M. (1992). *Creative cognition: Theory, research, and applications.* Cambridge, MA: MIT Press.

Frensch, P. A., & Sternberg, R. J. (1989). Expertise and intelligent thinking: When is it worse to know better? In R. J. Sternberg (Ed.), *Advances in the psychology of human intelligence* (Vol. 5, pp. 157–188). Hillsdale, NJ: Erlbaum.

Freud, S. (1959). Creative writers and day-dreaming. In J. Strachey (Ed.), *Standard edition of the complete psychological works of Sigmund Freud* (Vol. 9, pp. 143–153). London: Hogarth Press. (Original work published 1908)

Freud, S. (1964). *Leonardo da Vinci and a memory of his childhood.* New York: Norton. (Original work published 1910).

Gardner, H. (1993). *Creating minds.* New York: Basic Books.

Getzels, J., & Csikszentmihalyi, M. (1976). *The creative vision: A longitudinal study of problem-finding in art.* New York: Wiley (Interscience).

Ghiselin, B. (Ed.). (1985). *The creative process: A symposium.* Berkeley: University of California Press. (Original work published 1952)

Gick, M. L., & Holyoak, K. J. (1980). Analogical problem solving. *Cognitive Psychology, 12,* 306–355.

Glover, J. A. (1977). Risky shift and creativity. *Social Behavior and Personality, 5,* 317–320.

Glover, J. A. (1979). Levels of questions asked in interview and reading sessions by creative and relatively non-creative college students. *Journal of Genetic Psychology, 135,* 103–108.

Glover, J. A., Ronning, R. R., & Reynolds, C. R. (Eds.). (1989). *Handbook of creativity.* New York: Plenum.

Glover, J. A., & Sautter, F. (1977). Relation of four components of creativity to risk-taking preferences. *Psychological Reports, 41,* 227–230.

Golann, S. E. (1962). The creativity motive. *Journal of Personality, 30,* 588–600.

Golann, S. E. (1963). Psychological study of creativity. *Psychological Bulletin, 60,* 548–565.

Gough, H. G. (1979). A creative personality scale for the adjective check list. *Journal of Personality and Social Psychology, 37*(8), 1398–1405.

Gough, H. G., & Heilbrun, A. B. (1983). *The adjective check list manual.* Palo Alto, CA: Consulting Psychologists Press.

Gray, C. E. (1966). A measurement of creativity in western civilization. *American Anthropologist, 68,* 1384–1417.

Gruber, H. E. (1981). *Darwin on man: A psychological study of scientific creativity* (2nd ed.). Chicago: University of Chicago Press. (Original work published 1974)

Gruber, H. E. (1989). The evolving systems approach to creative work. In D. B. Wallace & H. E. Gruber (Eds.), *Creative people at work: Twelve cognitive case studies* (pp. 3–24). New York: Oxford University Press.

Gruber, H. E., & Davis, S. N. (1988). Inching our way up Mount Olympus: The evolving-systems approach to creative thinking. In R. J. Sternberg (Ed.), *The nature of creativity: Contemporary psychological perspectives* (pp. 243–270). New York: Cambridge University Press.

Guilford, J. P. (1950). Creativity. *American Psychologist, 5,* 444–454.

Guilford, J. P. (1956), The structure of the intellect. *Psychological Bulletin, 53,* 267–293.

Guilford, J. P. (1967). *The nature of human intelligence.* New York: McGraw-Hill.

Guilford, J. P. (1977). *Way beyond the IQ.* Buffalo. NY: Creative Education Foundation.

Hadamard, J. S. (1945). *The psychology of invention in the mathematical field.* Princeton, NJ: Princeton University Press.

Haensly, P. A., & Reynolds, C. R. (1989). Creativity and intelligence. In J. A. Glover, R. R. Ronning, & C. R. Reynolds (Eds.), *Handbook of creativity* (pp. 111–132). New York: Plenum.

Hall, W. B., & MacKinnon, D. W. (1969). Personality inventory correlates of creativity among architects. *Journal of Applied Psychology, 53,* 322–326.

Harrington, D. M., Block, J., & Block, J. H. (1983). Predicting creativity in preadolescence from divergent thinking in early childhood. *Journal of Personality and Social Psychology, 45,* 609–623.

Harrington, D. M., Block, J. H., & Block, J. (1987). Testing aspects of Carl Roger's theory of creative environments: Child-rearing antecedents of creative potential in young adolescents. *Journal of Personality and Social Psychology, 52*(4), 851–856.

Hayes, J. R. (1978). *Cognitive psychology: Thinking and creating.* Homewood, IL: Dorsey Press.

Hayes, J. R. (1989). Cognitive processes in creativity. In J. A. Glover, R. R. Ronning, & C. R. Reynolds (Eds.), *Handbook of creativity* (pp. 135–146). New York: Plenum.

Hennessey, B. A,. & Amabile, T. M. (1988). The role of environment in creativity. In R. J. Sternberg (Ed.), *The nature of creativity: Contemporary psychological perspectives* (pp. 11–38). New York: Cambridge University Press.

Hennessey, B. A., Amabile, T. M., & Martinage, M. (1989). Immunizing children against the negative effects of reward. *Contemporary Educational Psychology, 14,* 212–227.

Hill, K. (1990). *An ecological approach to creativity and motivation: Trait and environment influences in the college classroom.* Unpublished doctoral dissertation, Brandeis University, Waltham, MA.

Hocevar, D., & Bachelor, P. (1989). A taxonomy and critique of measurement used in the study of creativity. In J. A. Glover, R. R. Ronning, & C. R. Reynolds (Eds.), *Handbook of creativity* (pp. 53–76). New York: Plenum.

Holland, J. H., Holyoak, K. J., Nisbett, R. E., & Thagard, P. R. (1986). *Induction: Processes of inference, learning, and discovery.* Cambridge, MA: MIT Press.

Holyoak, K. J., & Thagard, P. (1989a). Analogical mapping by constraint satisfaction. *Cognitive Science, 13,* 295–356.

Holyoak, K. J., & Thagard, P. (1989b). A computational model of analogical problem solving. In S. Vosniadou & A. Ortony (Eds.), *Similarity and analogical reasoning* (pp. 242–266). New York: Cambridge University Press.

Isaksen, S. G., & Parnes, S. J. (1985). Curriculum planning for creative thinking and problem solving. *Journal of Creative Behavior, 19,* 1–29.

Isaksen, S. G., & Puccio, G. J. (1988). Adaption-innovation and the Torrance tests of creative thinking: The level-style issue revisited. *Psychological Reports, 63,* 659–670.

Jackson, P. W., & Messick, S. (1967). The person, the product, and the response: Conceptual problems in the assessment of creativity. In J. Kagan (Ed.), *Creativity and learning* (pp. 1–19). Boston: Houghton Mifflin.

James, W. (1880). Great men, great thoughts, and the environment. *Atlantic Monthly, 46,* 441–459.

Johnson-Laird, P. N. (1988). Freedom and constraint in creativity. In R. J. Sternberg (Ed.), *The nature of creativity: Contemporary psychological perspectives* (pp. 202–219). New York: Cambridge University Press.

Johnson-Laird, P. N. (1989). Analogy and the exercise of creativity. In S. Vosniadou & A. Ortony (Eds.), *Similarity and analogical reasoning* (pp. 313–331). New York: Cambridge University Press.

John-Steiner, V. (1987). *Notebooks of the mind: Explorations of thinking.* New York: Harper & Row.

Jung, C. (1923). *Psychological types.* New York: Harcourt, Brace.

Katz, A. (1983). Creativity and individual differences in asymmetric cerebral hemispheric functioning. *Empirical Studies of the Arts, 1*(1), 3–16.

Kim, S. H. (1990). *Essence of creativity: A guide to tackling difficult problems.* New York: Oxford University Press.

Kipling, R. (1985). Working-tools. In B. Ghiselin (Ed.), *The creative process: A symposium* (pp. 161–163). Berkeley: University of California Press. (Original work published 1937)

Kirton, M. J. (1976). Adaptors and innovators: A description and measure. *Journal of Applied Psychology, 61,* 622–629.

Koestler, A. (1964). *The act of creation.* New York: Macmillan.

Kotovsky, K., Hayes, J. R., & Simon, H. A. (1985). Why are some problems hard? Evidence from tower of Hanoi. *Cognitive Psychology, 17,* 248–294.

Kris, E. (1952). *Psychoanalytic exploration in art.* New York: International Universities Press.

Kruglanski, A. W., Friedman, I., & Zeevi, G. (1971). The effects of extrinsic incentives on some qualitative aspects of task performance. *Journal of Personality, 39,* 608–617.

Kubie, L. S. (1958). *Neurotic distortion of the creative process.* Lawrence: University of Kansas Press.

Langley, P., & Jones, R. (1988). A computational model of scientific insight. In R. J. Sternberg (Ed.), *The nature of creativity: Contemporary psychological perspectives* (pp. 177–201). New York: Cambridge University Press.

Langley, P., Simon, H., Bradshaw, G. L., & Zytkow, J. M. (1987). *Scientific discovery: Computational explorations of the creative process.* Cambridge, MA: MIT Press.

Lembright, M. L., & Yamamoto, K. (1965). Subcultures and creative thinking: An exploratory comparison between Amish and urban American school children. *Merrill Palmer Quarterly, 11,* 49–64.

Lubart, T. I. (1990). Creativity and cross-cultural variation. *International Journal of Psychology, 25,* 39–59.

Lubart, T. I. (1994). *Product-centered self-evaluation and the creative process.* Doctoral dissertation, Yale University, New Haven, CT.

Lubart, T. I., & Sternberg, R. J. (in press). An investment approach to creativity: Theory and data. In S. M. Smith, T. B. Ward, & R. A. Finke (Eds.), *Creative cognition approach.* Cambridge, MA: MIT Press.

MacKinnon, D. W. (1962). The nature and nurture of creative talent. *American Psychologist, 17,* 484–495.

MacKinnon, D. W. (1965). Personality and the realization of creative potential. *American Psychologist, 29,* 273–281.

MacKinnon, D. W. (1978). *In search of human effectiveness.* New York: Creative Education Foundation.

Mackworth, N. H. (1965). Originality. *American Psychologist, 20,* 51–66.

Maddi, S. R. (1965). Motivational aspects of creativity. *Journal of Personality, 33,* 330–347.

Maduro, R. (1976). *Artistic creativity in a Brahmin painter community* (Research Monograph No. 14). Berkeley: University of California, Center for South and Southeast Asia Studies.

Mann, L. (1980). Cross-cultural studies of small groups. In H. C. Triandis & R. W. Brislin (Eds.), *Handbook of cross-cultural psychology: Vol. 5. Social psychology* (pp. 155–210). Boston, MA: Allyn & Bacon.

Mansfield, R., & Busse, T. (1980). Theories of the creative process: A review and a perspective. *Journal of Creative Behavior, 14*(2), 91–132.

Martindale, C. (1989). Personality, situation, and creativity. In J. A. Glover, R. R. Ronning, & C. R. Reynolds (Eds.), *Handbook of creativity* (pp. 211–232). New York: Plenum.

Martindale, C., Hines, D., Mitchell, L., & Covello, E. (1984). EEG alpha asymmetry and creativity. *Personality and Individual Differences, 5*(1), 77–86.

Maslow, A. (1968). *Toward a psychology of being.* New York: Van Nostrand.

Masten, W. G., & Caldwell-Colbert, A. T. (1987). Relationship of originality to Kirton's scale for innovators and adaptors. *Psychological Reports, 61,* 411–416.

May, R. (1975). *The courage to create.* New York: Norton.

McClelland, D. C. (1956). The calculated risk: An aspect of scientific performance. In C. W. Taylor (Ed.), *The 1955 University of Utah research conference on the identification of creative scientific talent* (pp. 96–110). Salt Lake City: University of Utah Press.

McClelland, D. C. (1962). On the psychodynamics of creative physical scientists. In H. E. Gruber, G. Terrell, & M. Wertheimer (Eds.), *Contemporary approaches to creative thinking* (pp. 141–174). New York: Atherton Press.

McClelland, D. C., Atkinson, J. W., Clark, R. W., & Lowell, E. L. (1953). *The achievement motive.* New York: Appleton-Century-Crofts.

McClelland, D. C., & Watson, R. I., Jr. (1973). Power motivation and risk-taking behavior. In D. C. McClelland & R. S. Steele (Eds.), *Human motivation: A book of readings* (pp. 164–180). Morristown, NJ: General Learning Press.

McCrae, R. R. (1987). Creativity, divergent thinking, and openness to experience. *Journal of Personality and Social Psychology, 52,* 1258–1265.

McGuire, W. J. (1983). A contextualist theory of knowledge: Its implications for innovation and reform in psychological research. In L. Berkowitz (Ed.), *Advances in experimental social psychology* (Vol. 16) (pp. 1–47). New York: Academic Press.

McNemar, Q. (1964). Lost: Our intelligence. Why? *American Psychologist, 19,* 871–882.

Mednick, S. A. (1962). The associative basis of the creative process. *Psychological Review, 69,* 220–232.

Mednick, S. A., & Mednick, M. T. (1967). *Examiner's manual: Remote associations test.* Boston, MA: Houghton Mifflin.

Meehl, P. E. (1965). The creative individual: Why it is hard to identify him. In G. A. Steiner (Ed.), *The creative organization* (pp. 25–34). Chicago: University of Chicago Press.

Meer, B., & Stein, M. I. (1955). Measures of intelligence and creativity. *Journal of Psychology, 39,* 117–126.

Merrifield, P. R., Guilford, J. P., Christensen, P. R., & Frick, J. W. (1962). The role of intellectual factors in problem solving. *Psychological Monographs, 76,* 1–21.

Milgram, R. M. (1990). Creativity: An idea whose time has come and gone? In M. A. Runco & R. S. Albert (Eds.), *Theories of creativity* (pp. 215–233). Newbury Park, CA: Sage.

Mitchell, J. V. (Ed.). (1985). *The ninth mental measurements yearbook* (Vol. 2). Lincoln: University of Nebraska Press.

Mullligan, G., & Martin, W. (1980). Adaptors, innovators and the Kirton adaption-innovation inventory. *Psychological Reports, 46,* 883–892.

Mumford, M. D., & Gustafson, S. B. (1988). Creativity syndrome: Integration, application, and innovation. *Psychological Bulletin, 103,* 27–43.

Mumford, M. D., Mobley, M. I., Uhlman, C. E., Reiter-Palmon, R., & Doares, L. M. (1991). Process analytic models of creative capacities. *Creativity Research Journal, 4*(2), 91–122.

Myers, I. B., & McCaulley, M. H. (1985). *Manual: A guide to use of the Myers-Briggs Type Indicator.* Palo Alto, CA: Consulting Psychologists Press.

Myers, I. B., & Myers, P. B. (1980). *Gifts differing.* Palo Alto, CA: Consulting Psychologists Press.

Nicholls, J. G. (1972). Creativity in the person who will never produce anything original and useful: The concept of creativity as a normally distributed trait. *American Psychologist, 27,* 717–727.

Noy, P. (1969). A revision of the psychoanalytic theory of the primary process. *International Journal of Psychoanalysis, 50,* 155–178.

Ochse, R. (1990). *Before the gates of excellence: The determinants of creative genius.* New York: Cambridge University Press.

Okuda, S. M., Runco, M. A., & Berger, D. E. (1991). Creativity and the finding and solving of real-world problems. *Journal of Psychoeducational Assessment, 9,* 45–53.

Osborn, A. F. (1953). *Applied imagination.* New York: Scribner's.

Parnes, S. J. (1962). Do you really understand brainstorming? In S. J. Parnes & H. F. Harding (Eds.), *A source book for creative thinking* (pp. 284–290). New York: Scribner's.

Perfetto, G. A., Bransford, J. D., & Franks, J. J. (1983). Constraints on access in a problem-solving context. *Memory & Cognition, 11,* 24–31.

Perkins, D. N. (1981). *The mind's best work.* Cambridge, MA: Harvard University Press.

Poincaré, H. (1921). *The foundations of science.* New York: Science Press.

Prentky, R. (1989). Creativity and psychopathology: Gamboling at the seat of madness. In J. A. Glover, R. R. Ronning, & C. R. Reynolds (Eds.), *Handbook of creativity* (pp. 243–270). New York: Plenum.

Qin, Y., & Simon, H. (1990). Laboratory replication of scientific discovery processes. *Cognitive Science, 14,* 281–312.

Reis, S. M., & Renzulli, J. S. (1991). The assessment of creative products in programs for gifted and talented students. *Gifted Child Quarterly, 35,* 128–134.

Ribot, T. A. (1906). *Essay on the creative imagination.* Chicago: Opencourt.

Richards, R. (1993). Everyday creativity, eminent creativity, and psychopathology. *Psychological Inquiry, 4*(3), 212–217.

Richards, R., Kinney, D. K., Benet, M., & Merzel, A. P. C. (1988). Assessing everyday creativity: Characteristics of the Lifetime Creativity Scales and validation with three large samples. *Journal of Personality and Social Psychology, 54,* 476–485.

Richards, R., Kinney, D. K., Lunde, I., Benet, M., & Merzel, A. P. C. (1988). Creativity in manic-depressives, cyclothymes, their normal relatives, and control subjects. *Journal of Abnormal Psychology, 97,* 281–288.

Roe, A. (1952). *The making of a scientist.* New York: Dodd, Mead.

Rogers, C. R. (1954). Toward a theory of creativity. *ETC: A Review of General Semantics, 11,* 249–260.

Rosenman, M. F. (1988). Serendipity and scientific discovery. *Journal of Creative Behavior, 22,* 132–138.

Rossman, B. B., & Gollob, H. F. (1975). Comparison of social judgments of creativity and intelligence. *Journal of Personality and Social Psychology, 31*(2), 271–281.

Rossman, B. B., & Horn, J. (1972). Cognitive, motivational and tempermental indicants of creativity and intelligence. *Journal of Educational Measurement, 9*(4), 265–286.

Rossman, J. (1931). *The psychology of the inventor.* Washington, DC: Inventors Publishing Company.

Rothenberg, A. (1979). *The emerging goddess: The creative process in art, science, and other fields.* Chicago: University of Chicago Press.

Rothenberg, A. (1990). *Creativity and madness: New findings and old stereotypes.* Baltimore, MD: Johns Hopkins University Press.

Rothenberg, A., & Hausman, C. R. (Eds.). (1976). *The creativity question.* Durham, NC: Duke University Press.

Rothenberg, A., & Sobel, R. S. (1980). Creation of literary metaphors as stimulated by superimposed versus separated visual images. *Journal of Mental Imagery, 4,* 77–91.

Rubenson, D. L., & Runco, M. A. (1992). The psychoeconomic approach to creativity. *New Ideas in Psychology, 10*(2), 131–147.

Rumelhart, D. E., McClelland, J. L., & the PDP Research Group. (1986). *Parallel distributed processing: Explorations in the microstructure of cognition* (Vol. I). Cambridge, MA: MIT Press.

Runco, M. A. (1987). The generality of creative performance in gifted and nongifted children. *Gifted Child Quarterly, 31,* 121–125.

Runco, M. A. (1991). *Divergent thinking.* Norwood, NJ: Ablex.

Runco, M. A. (1992). The evaluative, valuative, and divergent thinking of children. *Journal of Creative Behavior, 25,* 311–319.

Runco, M. A., & Albert, R. S. (1986). The threshold theory regarding creativity and intelligence: An empirical test with gifted and nongifted children. *Creative Child and Adult Quarterly, 11,* 212–218.

Runco, M. A., & Okuda, S. M. (1988). Problem discovery, divergent thinking, and the creative process. *Journal of Youth and Adolescence, 17,* 211–220.

Rutherford, F. J., Holton, G., & Watson, F. G. (1975). *Project physics.* New York: Holt, Rinehart, & Winston.

Schachtel, E. G. (1976). Perceptual modes and creation. In A. Rothenberg & C. R. Hausman (Eds.), *The creativity question* (pp. 153–161). Durham, NC: Duke University Press.

Schaefer, C. (1970). *Manual for the biographical inventory creativity (BIC).* San Diego, CA: Educational and Industrial Testing Service.

Schank, R. C. (1988a). *The creative attitude.* New York: Macmillan.

Schank, R. C. (1988b). Creativity as a mechanical process. In R. J. Sternberg (Ed.), *The nature of creativity: Contemporary psychological perspectives* (pp. 220–238). New York: Cambridge University Press.

Schubert, D. S. (1973). Intelligence as necessary but not sufficient for creativity. *Journal of Genetic Psychology, 122,* 45–47.

Seifert, C. M., Meyer, D. E., Davidson, N., Patalano, A. J., & Yaniv, I. (in press). Demystification of cognitive insight: Opportunistic assimilation and the prepared mind perspective. In R. J. Sternberg & J. E. Davidson (Eds.), *The nature of insight.* Cambridge, MA: MIT Press.

Shepard, R. N. (1978). Externalization of mental images and the act of creation. In B. S. Randhawa & W. E. Coffman (Eds.), *Visual learning, thinking, and communication* (pp. 133–189). New York: Academic Press.

Silver, H. R. (1981). Calculating risks: The socioeconomic foundations of aesthetic innovation in an Ashanti carving community. *Ethnology, 20,* 101–114.

Simon, H. A. (1976). *Administrative behavior* (3rd ed.). New York: Free Press, Macmillan.

Simonton, D. K. (1975). Sociocultural context of individual creativity: A transhistorical time-series analysis. *Journal of Personality and Social Psychology, 32*(6), 1119–1133.

Simonton, D. K. (1976). Biographical determinants of achieved eminence: A multivariate approach to the Cox data. *Journal of Personality and Social Psychology, 33*(2), 218–226.

Simonton, D. K. (1984). *Genius, creativity, and leadership.* Cambridge, MA: Harvard University Press.

Simonton, D. K. (1988a). Creativity, leadership, and chance. In R. J. Sternberg (Ed.), *The nature of creativity: Contemporary psychological perspectives* (pp. 386–426). New York: Cambridge University Press.

Simonton, D. K. (1988b). Galtonian genius, Kroeberian configurations, and emulation: A generational time-series analysis of Chinese civilization. *Journal of Personality and Social Psychology, 55,* 230–238.

Simonton, D. K. (1988c). *Scientific genius: A psychology of science.* New York: Cambridge University Press.

Smith, G. J., & Carlsson, I. M. (1990). *The creative process: A functional model based on empirical studies from early childhood to middle age.* Madison, CT: International Universities Press.

Spearman, C. (1931). *The creative mind.* New York: Appleton.

Sternberg, R. J. (1985). Implicit theories of intelligence, creativity, and wisdom. *Journal of Personality and Social Psychology, 49,* 607–627.

Sternberg, R. J., & Davidson, J. E. (Eds.). (in press-a). *The nature of insight.* Cambridge, MA: MIT Press.

Sternberg, R. J., & Davidson, J. E. (in press-b). What is insight? In R. J. Sternberg & J. E. Davidson (Eds.), *The Nature of insight.* Cambridge, MA: MIT Press.

Sternberg, R. J., & Lubart, T. I. (1991a, April). Creating creative minds. *Phi Delta Kappan,* pp. 608–614.

Sternberg, R. J., & Lubart, T. I. (1991b). An investment theory of creativity and its development. *Human Development, 34,* 1–31.

Sternberg, R. J., & Lubart, T. I. (1993). Creative giftedness: A multivariate investment approach. *Gifted Child Quarterly, 37*(1), 7–15.

Suler, J. R. (1980). Primary process thinking and creativity. *Psychological Bulletin, 88*(1), 144–165.

Torrance, E. P. (1964). *Role of evaluation in creative thinking.* Minneapolis: University of Minnesota, Bureau of Educational Research.

Torrance, E. P. (1965). *Rewarding creative behavior: Experiments in classroom creativity.* Englewood Cliffs, NJ: Prentice-Hall.

Torrance, E. P. (1974). *The Torrance tests of creative thinking: Technical-norms manual.* Bensenville, IL: Scholastic Testing Services.

Torrance, E. P. (1988). The nature of creativity as manifest in its testing. In R. J. Sternberg (Ed.), *The nature of creativity: Contemporary psychological perspectives* (pp. 43–75). New York: Cambridge University Press.

Torrance, E. P., & Horng, R. Y. (1980). Creativity and style of learning and thinking characteristics of adaptors and innovators. *Creative Child and Adult Quarterly, 5,* 80–85.

Torrance, E. P., & Presbury, J. (1984). The criteria of success used in 242 recent experimental studies of creativity. *Creative Child and Adult Quarterly, 9*(4), 238–242.

Touhey, J. C., & Villemez, W. J. (1975). Need achievement and risk-taking preference: A clarification. *Journal of Personality and Social Psychology, 32*(4), 713–719.

Vernon, P. E. (Ed.). (1970). *Creativity: Selected readings.* Middlesex, England: Penguin Books.

Vosniadou, S., & Ortony, A. (Eds.). (1989). *Similarity and analogical reasoning.* New York: Cambridge University Press.

Wallace, D. B., & Gruber, H. E. (Eds.). (1989). *Creative people at work: Twelve cognitive case studies.* New York: Oxford University Press.

Wallas, G. (1926). *The art of thought.* New York: Harcourt, Brace.

Ward, W. C. (1969). Creativity and environmental cues in nursery school children. *Developmental Psychology, 1,* 543–547.

Weber, R. J., & Perkins, D. N. (1992). *Inventive minds: Creativity in technology.* New York: Oxford University Press.

Weisberg, R. W. (1986). *Creativity, genius and other myths.* New York: Freeman.

Weisberg, R. W. (1993). *Creativity: Beyond the myth of genius.* New York: Freeman.

Weisberg, R. W., DiCamillo, M., & Phillips, D. (1978). Transferring old associations to new situations: A nonautomatic process. *Journal of Verbal Learning and Verbal Behavior, 17,* 219–228.

Welch, L. (1946). Recombination of ideas in creative thinking. *Journal of Applied Psychology, 30,* 638–643.

Werner, H., & Kaplan, B. (1963). *Symbol formation.* Hillsdale, NJ: Erlbaum.

Woodman, R. W., & Schoenfeldt, L. F. (1989). Individual differences in creativity: An interactionist perspective. In J. A. Glover, R. R. Ronning, & C. R. Reynolds (Eds.), *Handbook of creativity* (pp. 77–92). New York: Plenum.

Young, J. G. (1985). What is creativity? *Journal of Creative Behavior, 19*(2), 77–87.

Zuckerman, H. (1977). *Scientific elite: Nobel laureates in the United States.* New York: Free Press.

CHAPTER 11

Development of Problem Solving

Shari Ellis
Robert S. Siegler

Georgie (a 2-year-old) wants to throw rocks out the kitchen window. The lawnmower is outside. Dad says that Georgie can't throw rocks out the window because he'll break the lawnmower with the rocks. Georgie says "I got an idea." He goes outside, brings in some green peaches that he had been playing with, and says: "They won't break the lawnmower."

(Waters, 1989, p. 7)

This example illustrates the essence of problem solving: a goal, an obstacle, and a strategy for circumventing the obstacle and reaching the goal. Georgie's goal was to throw objects out the window; the obstacle was his father's command not to throw rocks; his solution was to throw peaches, not rocks. Children's lives are filled with problems like these. Most often, the problems involve other people—sometimes, as the previous example illustrated, as obstacles to attaining a goal, other times, as the following conversation illustrates, as components of solution strategies:

Scene: 6-year-old and father in yard. Child's playmate appears on bike:
Child: Daddy, would you unlock the basement door?
Daddy: Why?
Child: 'Cause I want to ride my bike.
Daddy: Your bike is in the garage.
Child: But my socks are in the dryer.

(Klahr, 1978, pp. 181–182)

In recent years, cognitive psychologists have become increasingly interested in problem solving in social contexts (Levine, Resnick, & Higgins, 1993). This trend has been manifested in increasing research on how children think about other people's reasoning (Feinman, 1992; Siegler, 1993; Wellman, 1990), on how children solve problems collaboratively (J. S. Brown, Collins, & Duguid, 1989; Resnick, Levine, & Teasley, 1991), and on how social relationships impact on cognitive development (Azmitia & Perlmutter, 1989; Rogoff, 1990).

Given the importance accorded social influences in recent thinking about the development of problem solving, and given our enthusiastic approval of this trend, we decided to use this chapter to integrate findings from traditional studies that have not focused on social influences with findings from newer ones that have. The selection of domains and skills discussed in the chapter reflects this emphasis. The areas on which we focus are not only inherently important for understanding the development of problem solving but also have been the subject of high-quality research within both individual-based and social-constructivist approaches to problem solving.

Specifically, we focus on three aspects of the development of problem solving—formation of strategies, representation, and self-regulation. These phenomena vary considerably in the ages at which they become prominent, with strategies seeming to play an important role from infancy (birth to 12 months); use of varied representations such as language, maps, and models becoming prominent during toddlerhood (one through three years); and cognitive self-regulation becoming increasingly critical during the preschool period (three to five years), as children have more varied strategies and representations from which to choose and greater cognitive resources to devote to planning, self-monitoring, and other regulatory processes. For this reason, and because we wish to convey a flavor of the types of research on the development of problem solving being conducted with children of different ages, we will focus in each of the three initial discussions on the age range in which the phenomena first seems especially prominent. We later return to each topic and examine its development in later childhood, when developments in all three areas have provided a platform for more advanced developments in problem solving.

I. THE EARLY DEVELOPMENT OF PROBLEM SOLVING

A. Strategic Development

Problem solving strategies are procedures that overcome obstacles and meet goals. The capacity to devise such strategies appears to be present at birth (Butterworth & Hopkins, 1988; Willats, 1990). Even young babies communicate their desires to bring caregivers closer in order to obtain comfort and food. Although it is clear that young babies obtain such goals, it is often difficult to tell, in the absence of language or other straightforward behavioral criteria, whether their actions reflect intention to achieve goals or whether the actions have this effect without necessarily reflecting intent. However, some relatively straightforward criteria for inferring intent have been identified: persistently seeking the goal in the face of obstacles, failures, and interruptions; reversing actions that make goal attainment more difficult; and ending activity when the goal is obtained (Willats, 1990).

Underlying the view that infants use strategies is the assumption that they can represent goals. Perhaps the most compelling evidence for such representation of goals in the first six months of life comes from studies of contingency learning. Rovee-Collier and her colleagues have conducted a variety of studies using a paradigm in which a mobile is placed above an infant's crib and a string attached to the mobile and to one of the infant's ankles. Infants soon learn that kicking makes the mobile move in interesting ways. Varying the characteristics of the mobile, the setting in which the mobile is presented, and the amount of time between sessions provide means for assessing infants' cognitive capacities (see Rovee-Collier, 1987, for a review).

In one study (Mast, Fagan, Rovee-Collier, & Sullivan, 1980), 3-month-olds were presented a mobile that had either six or ten components. The mobile with the larger number of parts made more varied and interesting movements and jingling sounds. Over the course of their exposure to the mobile, babies in both groups increased their rate of kicking. A day later, some of the babies were presented the same mobile, while others were presented a mobile with only two component parts that made considerably less interesting motions and noises. All of the babies at first responded to the reduction in the number of parts (and to the mobile's less interesting actions) by increasing their rate of kicking. Those who underwent the smaller decrease persisted in this activity, but those who made the shift from the ten to the two component mobile quickly gave up and started crying. These findings suggest that infants as young as three months not only maintain a representation of a reinforcement contingency for up to 24 hours, but that they become emotionally distressed when they can only achieve a poor approximation of their original goal.

This early goal directedness characterizes problem solving in social situations as well. Relevant evidence comes from studies where maternal behavior is experimentally manipulated in ways that prevent infants from engaging in reciprocal interaction. For example, in an experiment described in Tronick (1989), mothers were asked either to remain still-faced while looking at their infants or to behave in a disruptive fashion (i.e., to interact in an emotionally flat or withdrawn fashion). Three-month-olds confronted with the problem of how to change this disturbing behavior initially signaled to their mothers with facial expressions, vocalizations, and gestures. When this failed to obtain the desired changes, they expressed negative emotions and engaged in self-comforting strategies such as looking away or thumbsucking (Tronick, 1989). In contrast, infants of depressed mothers, whose behaviors are less responsive to their children's activities than those of most mothers, did not engage in these behaviors as much. The difference supported Tronick's interpretation that the infants' behaviors are a kind of problem solving strategy, and that the degree to which they engage in them reflect how successful they are likely to be.

How do infants acquire strategies? One way is from observing the actions of other people. Their imitation is not automatic, but instead seems to depend on their understanding the relation between means and ends embodied in the strategy. In one study that illustrated this point, Case (1985) presented infants a balance scale with a bell beneath one end; pushing down on that end made the bell ring. Infants of age 4 to 8 months who saw an experimenter produce the ringing sound by pushing one end of the arm down on the bell responded by reaching to strike or touch that end themselves. However, they would not imitate the experimenter's solution to a harder problem: depressing one end of the arm so that the other end would go up and ring a bell above it. Not until 12 to 18 months would many infants imitate this solution. The fact that the solution to both problems was motorically identical, but infants below one year would imitate only the action with the simpler relation between means and ends, suggests that ability to represent how an action meets a goal influences acquisition of new strategies, even when there is a model to imitate and the actions are within the infants' behavioral repertoires.

Given the extensive evidence that very young infants can elicit desired responses from caregivers, one might expect equally extensive documentation of their use of other people as aids for solving problems. There is little research on this topic, however. Observers of joint action among infants and adults often marvel at the fine-tuned nature of early interactions and tend not to focus on infant problem solving efforts per se (Papousek & Papousek, 1987). The responsiveness of adults—typically mothers—even to subtle cues from their infants generally precludes analysis of infants' strategies for using other people as tools for solving problems; the mothers react too quickly for the infants' strategies to be revealed in any detail. However, one unusual investigation did make it possible to observe such use of other people as problem-solving tools. Rogoff, Mistry, Radziszewska, and Germond (1992) observed two infants engage in dyadic interactions with 21 different adults (most of them graduate students) every 2 or 3 weeks over a period of 11 months. Because most of the adults were not familiar with the babies, and most were not parents themselves, they were less likely than the babies' regular caregivers to respond in ways the babies found satisfying. Hence, the infants had greater opportunity (and need) to display their strategies for getting the adults to do what they wanted. By their first birthday, the babies were clearly using the adults as tools to help them reach desired goals. The most frequent goal was getting adults to manipulate objects in ways that would have been impossible for the infants themselves to accomplish, but that they wished to see.

Ability to use simple forms of means–ends analysis also is evident in the second half of the first year. Willats (1989) presented 9-month-olds with a foam rubber barrier, behind which was a cloth. For some of the babies, a small toy rested on the far end of the cloth. Other babies encountered the same arrangement, except that the toy was beside, rather than on top of, the cloth. Babies who had seen the toy on the cloth were much more likely to push the barrier aside and pull the cloth to them than were babies who had seen the toy next to the cloth. Pushing the barrier aside would have been more likely among babies in the one group only if it was a means within an overall strategy for getting the toy, since any rewarding quality of removing the barrier per se would have been identical in the two conditions.

B. Representational Development in the Toddler Period

Much of the progress in children's problem solving after the first year comes from improving ability to internally represent goals, actions, objects, and events. For example, increasing ability to form detailed and accessible representations allows toddlers, unlike infants, to find toys hidden days earlier. The improving representational skills also allow toddlers to utilize a broader range of the resources of the social world. They form more enduring representations of the ways they have seen other people solve problems, and use those methods themselves at later times. Improved linguistic competence, both expressive and receptive, also makes large contributions to development of problem solving in this age range. Infants can make known to caretakers some of the problems they wish to solve, but toddlers' language skills allow them to more precisely indicate what they want to accomplish and why they are unable to accomplish it themselves. Yet another way in which increasing ability to utilize the resources of the social world helps young children solve problems involves understanding and use of artifacts that are part of the culture, such as scale models. Below we examine some of the varied ways in which enhanced representational abilities contribute to improvements in problem solving in this age range.

1. Representing Past Occurrences

During the second year of life, children grow increasingly adept at representing goals and the actions used to attain them after a delay and/or in contexts different than the original situation. One way in which this skill manifests itself is in young children's skill at finding toys hidden from view in naturalistic settings. Near their first birthday, children become able to walk or crawl to rooms they cannot see at the beginning of the trip, in order to get toys they also cannot see from where they started (Benson, Arehart, Jennings, Boley, & Kearns, 1989). To do this, they must represent the existence of the objects and rooms, the objects' locations within the rooms, and the actions needed to obtain the objects.

By 18 months, children begin to take steps that help them maintain representations that otherwise might become inaccessible. In one study (DeLoache, Cassidy, & Brown, 1985), 18- to 24-month-olds saw a Big Bird doll hidden in natural locations, such as under a pillow, in a familiar room. The toddlers were made to wait three or four minutes before they could retrieve Big Bird. During the waiting period, they looked at the hiding place, pointed to it, and named the hidden toy. Having performed these activities, the toddlers retrieved more than 80% of objects without error after the delay (DeLoache, 1989). They did not exhibit such behaviors during the intervening period when Big Bird was placed under transparent objects, that is, when the external environment made maintenance of the internal representation less crucial. Thus, the behaviors seemed to be aimed specifically at maintaining the internal representation.

Part of how increasing representational skill contributes to the development of problem solving is in allowing toddlers to remember goal-directed actions modeled by adults or peers (Hannah & Meltzoff, 1993; Meltzoff, 1985). In one study, experimenters trained a 14-month-old to perform five different actions, for example, inserting a finger through an opening in a box to operate a buzzer. This 14-month-old then demonstrated the routines for a number of same-age peers in a daycare setting. Two days later, an experimenter visited the homes of the peers who had witnessed the acts. They were able to reproduce more than 70% of the target acts that the 14-month-old "expert" had performed.

Increasingly specific and durable representations also allow toddlers to pursue specific goals within an activity, rather than focusing on the activity as a whole. In one study that illustrates this developmental trend particularly clearly, Bullock and Lutkenhaus (1988) asked 15- to 35-month-olds to pursue a series of specific goals, such as building a house that looked like a model that the experimenter provided. Even 17-month-olds engaged in activities appropriate to the general task (e.g., building with the blocks), but pursuit of the specific goal (e.g., building the particular house) was not apparent until 26 months. Illustrative of this trend, 26-month-olds were more likely than younger toddlers to stop the activity when they had built an approximation of the model; the younger children tended to simply continue playing with the blocks. Efforts to monitor their own actions also increased with age. All of the 35-month-olds, but only half of the 17-month-olds, corrected their block constructions to make them look more like the model. Positive affective reactions to completion of the tasks (e.g., smiles, abrupt movements of hands and arms) also increased with age. It seems, then, that part of development of problem solving between one and three years involves representing specific goals more prominently in memory, and pursuing the goals more single mindedly.

1. Language and Problem Solving

What types of representational capacities underlie the early development of problem solving? One representational medium whose contribution can hardly be overestimated is language. As children become able to represent linguistically an increasing range of situations and events, their problem solving shows corresponding gains. Language ability seems especially important for transferring lessons learned on previously encountered problems to new ones. Some of the gains come from toddlers' increasing ability to understand what other people tell them. Children as young as two years of age can transfer strategies to a new problem when the new problem is perceptually similar to the old and children are told the problems are the same (Crisafi & Brown, 1986).

Young children show considerably more transfer, however, when they themselves generate a verbal explanation for a phenomenon than when someone else tells them the explanation. This was demonstrated in another study of analogical problem solving (A. L. Brown & Kane, 1988). Four-year-olds were presented a series of stories involving pairs of animals that rely on the same defense mechanism, mimicry, even though the realization of the mechanism and the animals that use it are quite distinct. For example, the children were told that certain types of caterpillars looked like snakes, and were asked, "Why would a furry caterpillar want to look like a snake?" and, "What could the furry caterpillar do to stop the big birds from eating him?" Other children were read the same story, and then were told by the experimenter that certain types of caterpillars mimic snakes so that they will not be eaten. When later presented problems that required conceptually similar solutions, the children who had earlier been asked to generate the explanation for themselves succeeded more often than those who had been told the explanation by the experimenter. Presumably, the need to generate an explanation for the phenomenon led children to elaborate their representations in ways that helped them transfer the principle to new situations.

What motivates children to generate such explanations? One important motive may be to understand the reasoning of other people. The beneficial effects of such efforts to explain the thinking of others were evident in a recent study of acquisition of number conservation (Siegler, 1993). Five-year-olds who were given feedback on the correctness of their responses and then asked by the experimenter, "How do you think I knew that?" learned much more than children who were just given the feedback or children who were given the feedback and asked to explain their own reasoning. The invitation to explain the experimenter's reasoning appeared to lead the children to generate more elaborated representations of the logic that underlay the experimenter's conclusion and subsequently to more frequently adopt the other person's logic as their own.

3. External Representations

Toddlers show increasing ability to use not just internal but also external representations as tools for solving problems. In a particularly impressive demonstration, DeLoache (1987) provided 2½- and 3-year-olds with a scale model of a room. After familiarizing the children with both the room itself and the model of it, the experimenter hid a "Baby Snoopy" in the scale model and asked the children to use it to find a Big Snoopy that had been hidden in the room.

Both groups of children located the original object easily. However, despite the small (7-month) difference in average age of children in the two groups, they differed greatly in their ability to use the scale model. The 3-year-olds found the hidden object without error on more than 70% of the trials; the 2½-year-olds found it without error on fewer than 20%. Examination of children in the interval between 2½ and 3 years indicated that most children first could use the model at between 33 and 35 months, and that as soon as they did so, they usually did so perfectly or almost perfectly (DeLoache, 1989).

Why did the 2½-year-olds have such difficulty translating between the model and the room? One possibility was that they did not understand how any type of representation could be used as a tool to solve this type of problem. To test this interpretation, DeLoache (1987) showed 2½-year-olds either line drawings or photographs of the larger room. The same children who could not use the scale model to find hidden objects were able to use line drawings and photographs to do so. Thus, they could use some representations as tools for solving problems, just not the scale model.

The source of young children's difficulty with the scale model may be difficulty in simultaneously viewing it as an object in itself and as a representation of another object. Photographs and line drawings may be easier to use as tools than the scale model because they are interesting only as representations of another object. Consistent with this explanation, 3-year-olds who were allowed to play with the same model, which would encourage them to think of the model more as an object in itself, were less successful when later asked to use the model to find objects. Conversely, eliminating any potential interaction with the model—by putting it in a glass case, so that the children could see but not play with it—facilitated its usefulness as a tool for finding hidden objects later (DeLoache, 1989). Thus, toddlers can use scale models as tools for solving problems, but have a tendency to confuse the representation as an object in its own right with its role as symbol of another situation.

C. Self-Regulation in Preschoolers' Problem Solving

As children acquire increasing numbers of strategies and increasing representational capacities, their ability to effectively regulate their cognitive activities becomes increasingly central to their problem solving. Among the self-regulative activities that show substantial development in early childhood are planning and self-directed speech.

1. Planning

Planning is a key self-regulatory process, because in many situations it can be used to avoid potentially costly errors. Several of the examples used in the preceding sections to illustrate developmental changes in use of strategies and representations have involved planning. For example, ability to retrieve a toy from another room involves planning the series of actions necessary to meet the goal of getting from here to there. These early plans tend to be made close in time to the actions they are guiding, to incorporate only one or a few actions (thought they may be executed repetitively), and to be aimed directly at meeting the main goal. Only later in development do children begin to form plans that are further removed in time from the actions they will guide, that include more diverse actions, and that incorporate hierarchically organized subgoals, especially ones that involve actions whose immediate impact is to take the problem solver further from the overall goal.

The types of plans that begin to be made toward the end of the preschool period can be observed on the Tower of Hanoi task. A typical Tower of Hanoi problem begins with a series of disks stacked on a peg in ascending size from the largest disk on the bottom to the smallest disk on the top. Two other pegs are empty. The goal is to duplicate the original configuration of disks on a new peg in the fewest moves possible without violating two rules: Move only one disk at a time, and never place a larger disk on top of a smaller one. The property that makes the Tower of Hanoi task interesting for those interested in planning is that making the correct first move is essential for successful problem solving. If it is not made, the only possible solution often involves undoing all subsequent moves and returning to the original configuration. Knowing which first move is correct, however, demands working through the problem from beginning to end. Thus, consistently solving such problems demands planning the entire sequence of moves before making any of them.

Even 3- and 4-year-olds are able to solve Tower of Hanoi problems when the subgoal structure is simple and when the task is modified in ways that diminish memory requirements and encourage adequate representation of the problem. Klahr (1978) created a version of the Tower of Hanoi that included a cover story (copycat monkey families jumping from tree to tree), materials that supported the rules (small cans that could not fit over large cans), and an externalized final goal state (an identical set of materials illustrating the goal the children were trying to reach). The children were asked to describe what they would do before they made any moves, thus separating the planning from the problem-solving actions it regulated.

Most 3-year-olds generated plans that would solve problems requiring two moves to progress from the initial arrangement to the goal; most 4-year-olds generated plans that would solve four-move problems; and most 5- and 6-year-olds generated plans that would solve five- or six-move problems (Klahr & Robinson, 1981). More interesting than these changes in the length of problems children could solve were changes in the specific plans the children made. The 3-year-olds' plans were limited to direct attempts to reach the main goal. When they could not move a can to its goal because another can was on top of it, they often simply planned to break the rules and put the can there anyway. The 5- and 6-year-olds reacted to such situations by establishing subgoals that moved them in promising directions for fulfilling the original goals, though not always ones that worked out. Even at age 6, formulating subgoals that would move the configuration further from the final goal was only sometimes possible.

Much of the problem solving that children perform in their everyday lives occurs jointly with adults, rather than in isolation. In these situations, adults often structure the activities in ways that relieve children of the burden of planning but allow them to realize its benefits. The term *scaffolding* (Wood, Bruner, & Ross, 1976) is often used to describe such adult activities. Scaffolding involves use of specific strategies aimed at simultaneously allowing children to participate, maintaining their interest, and increasing their competence. When involved in such episodes, adults often at first take responsibility for the most difficult parts of tasks—for example, dividing the task into subgoals, constructing plans for meeting them, and monitoring the success of different strategies—while allowing children to perform the parts of the task they can accomplish successfully (Wertsch, 1978). As the child demonstrates increasing skill on the task, the adult gradually relinquishes control until the child is performing independently both the actions and the self-regulatory aspects of the task.

Interest in whether adults' scaffolding facilitates the development of children's self-regulative skills is especially relevant to the preschool years. Children of this age can understand and use language quite well and are capable of sustained attention to a particular task, but have limited skill in planning and regulating their own problem-solving efforts.

Several studies have shown that scaffolding is both a pervasive activity in the everyday environment and that it helps children learn planning and other self-regulative skills. Adults often provide preschoolers with scaffolded instruction and adjust the kind of instruction offered to the competence of the learner (Gauvain, 1992; Rogoff, Ellis, & Gardner, 1984; Wertsch, McNamee, McLane, & Budwig, 1980). When adult experimenters follow scripts based on a model of ideal scaffolding, the interactions enhance the later performance of children solving problems individually, relative to the performance of children who had been shown or told what to do more directly (Pacifici & Bearison, 1991; Wood et al., 1976; Wood, Wood, & Middleton, 1978). These benefits of scaffolding also are evident in naturally occurring interactions. For example, Freund (1990) compared the performance of 3- and 5-year-olds who earlier had worked with their mothers on a classification task to that of peers who earlier had solved the problem alone, receiving only corrective feedback from the experimenter. The preschoolers who earlier had worked with their mothers did better when later working alone. Both the 3- and 5-year-olds with the highest performance had mothers characterized as providing instruction that resembled the scaffolding described by Wood, Bruner, and colleagues. Thus, scaffolding seems to be an important means through which adults help preschoolers (and children of other ages) acquire self-regulatory skills.

2. Private speech

Language plays a critical role in regulating cognitive activity. It is used not only to communicate to others but also to direct children's own problem solving. This regulative function of self-directed speech can be seen in the following statements of a 4-year-old playing by himself with a set of tinkertoys:

> The wheels go here, the wheels go here. Oh, we need to start it all over again. We need to close it up. See, it closes up. We're starting it all over again. Do you know why we wanted to do that? Because I needed it to go a different way. Isn't it going to be pretty clever, don't you think? But we have to cover up the motor just like a real car.
>
> *(Kohlberg, Yaeger, & Hjertholm, 1968, p. 695)*

Spontaneous self-directed speech emerges in children's problem solving around age 4 or 5; prior to this age, children sometimes talk to themselves (even babies in their cribs do so), but the self-directed speech is not coordinated with their problem-solving behavior (Luria, 1961). Older children also use self-directed language to regulate their cognitive activity, but theirs, unlike that of preschoolers, is rarely audible (Berk, 1986; Bivens & Berk, 1990; Frauenglass & Diaz, 1985; Kohlberg et al., 1968). Most contemporary investigations of private speech are based on Vygotsky's (1934/1962) proposal that private speech originates from speech that has a communicative function. As linguistic competence increases, speech becomes directed toward the self as well as toward other people, and gradually becomes internalized. Vygotsky posited that at some points in development, specifically, early on when the border between social and private speech is fuzzy, frequency of private and communicative speech would be influenced by the same variables. His own research supported this prediction. Children of preschool age generated less private speech in situations inhospitable to conversation—noisy settings or settings in which children who spoke different languages were in the same room—than they did in situations that would have made conversation easier.

Numerous other factors have been found to influence the frequency with which children talk to themselves while solving problems. Such speech occurs most often on tasks that are challenging but not impossibly difficult (Behrend, Rosengren, & Perlmutter, 1989; Berk & Garvin; 1984; Kohlberg et al., 1968). It is more common on problems that benefit from verbal mediation such as picture sequencing, than on problems where such benefits are less likely, such as puzzles (Berk & Landau, 1993; Frauenglass & Diaz, 1985). It is seen most among children who experience the greatest difficulty solving that type of problem (Berk & Landau, 1993). Within a given child, it occurs more often following failure to solve a problem than following success (Goodman, 1981).

Self-directed speech plays an especially interesting role in situations in which the child's problem is to resist tempting but nonoptimal courses of action. Many problems are problematic not because it is difficult to abstractly identify what ought to be done but because it is hard to prevent oneself from taking a less desirable alternative path. Representative of such problems is a task in which children can either have a small candy bar now or a larger candy bar later. Even young children know that the larger reward would be preferable, but restraining oneself from taking the smaller, immediate reward poses a real problem.

Self-directed speech can help preschoolers resist the temptation. Four-year-olds who are taught such strategies as telling themselves, "I am not going to play with that" or making statements that direct their attention elsewhere more often succeed in obtaining the larger reward than do other children (Mischel & Patterson, 1978). Similar instruction in self-directed speech has helped 5-year-olds labeled "impulsive" succeed more often on problems that demand careful attention (Meichenbaum & Goodman, 1971).

There are a number of reasons why self-directed speech may facilitate problem solving: it can slow down actions and thus prevent unthinking errors, help the child keep the goal in mind, facilitate planning and the establishment of subgoals, and facilitate the encoding of subtle but critical features of the problem. All of these are important contributors to the kind of self-regulation needed for effective problem solving.

II. DEVELOPMENT OF PROBLEM SOLVING IN LATER CHILDHOOD

The problem-solving abilities of 5-year-olds and adolescents differ profoundly. The change, however, is not typically from young children being absolutely unable to execute a process to older children being able to do so consistently. Instead, most changes seem to be in the range of situations in which children successfully execute the problem-solving processes. These changes in large part result from specific experiences faced by children as they go to school, interact with a broader range of people, and have greater demands placed on them. Schooling influences: (1) the problems children encounter (e.g., problems involving reading, writing, mathematics, science, and social studies); (2) the general-purpose tools children have available for solving problems (e.g., reading and writing, mathematics, scientific experimentation); and (3) specifically relevant knowledge in particular domains that children can apply to solving novel problems in those domains. Below we examine how such changes influence the strategies, representations, and self-regulative devices through which children apply their enhanced capabilities to the challenges of abstract and demanding problems.

A. Strategic Development

Development of problem-solving strategies follows markedly different courses when children have extensive experience with a task than when they do not. In particular, on tasks in which children have little experience, individuals often consistently use a single strategy to solve problems. In contrast, on tasks in which children have considerable experience, individuals often know and use multiple strategies. In this section, we consider strategic development on problems in which children have little experience; the more complex course of development of problem solving on heavily practiced tasks is considered later in the chapter.

Because it is applicable from infancy to adulthood, the balance scale offers a particularly useful task on which to obtain a sense of the types of changes that characterize development of problem solving on unfamiliar tasks. The type of balance scale that has most often been used (e.g., in Siegler, 1976) has a fulcrum in the middle from which is suspended an arm that extends in both directions. The arm can tip left or right or remain level, depending on how weights (metal disks with holes in their centers) are placed on pegs. The pegs are spaced at regular intervals along the arm. The child's task is to examine the arrangement of weights on pegs and to predict which (if either) side would go down if a lever, which holds the arm motionless, were released.

As noted previously, Case (1985) demonstrated that infants have some rudimentary understanding regarding balance scales. He showed that 12- to 18-month-olds imitated a strategy that seemed to require an understanding of the motions that balance scales can make and their effects on other objects. However, it did not demand an understanding of the effects of quantitative variations in weight and distance on the balance scale's activities. These types of understanding are acquired in childhood and adolescence.

Movement toward systematic, rule-governed solutions for balance scale problems begin in the preschool period. When asked to predict which side of a balance scale will go down, the majority of 3-year-olds do not use any systematic rule; they appear to guess or switch frequently among alternative approaches (Siegler, 1978, 1981). A few 3-year-olds, and more 4-year-olds, use a partially systematic approach, which Richards and Siegler (1981) labeled Rule I'. These children consistently predict that the side with more weight will go down when one side has more weight. However, their approach is not yet entirely systematic; if the two sides have equal weight, they guess or respond arbitrarily. More advanced 4-year-olds, and the large majority of 5-year-olds, use a consistently systematic approach, Rule I. They predict that whichever side has more weight will go down, and that when the weights are equal, the scale will balance. They follow this rule regularly; for example, in Siegler (1976), 90% of 5-year-olds generated performance that conformed to it on at least 20 of 24 problems.

By age 8 or 9, most children adopt more sophisticated rules that take into account not just the amount of weight on each side but also the distance of the weight from the fulcrum (Siegler, 1976). Some children adopt a rule in which they only consider distance when the amount of weight is equal (Rule II); others adopt a more sophisticated approach in which they always consider both weight and distance, regardless of whether the weight on the two sides is equal (Rule III). However, even children who use Rule III do not know how to solve problems on which one side has more weight and the other has its weight farther from the fulcrum (for example, 3 weights on the fourth peg to the left of the fulcrum versus 6 weights on the second peg to the right of the fulcrum). They therefore muddle through or guess. Consistent solutions to these problems do not come until children understand that relative torques on the two sides are what determines which side will go down (Rule IV). Only a minority of college students (typically around 20%) know this last rule and can apply it to making predictions. For example, on the problem described above, these students know that the torques are equal and that the two sides will balance ($3 \times 4 = 6 \times 2$). Similar sequences of rules have been found on problems involving shadows projection, inclined planes, sweetness, temperature, causal reasoning, happiness, fairness, and a host of other tasks (see Case, 1992, and Siegler, 1991, for reviews).

The balance scale also has proved to be a useful task for investigating the effects of social interaction on problem solving. After assessing 5- to 9-year-olds' initial balance scale rules, Tudge (1992) assigned them to work alone, to work with a partner who initially used the same rule, or to work with a partner who initially used a different rule. The children working in pairs took turns making predictions and explaining their reasoning before they decided on one, mutually agreed-upon prediction. They did not receive any feedback on their predictions, either from the experimenter or from observing the balance scale's movements in response to specific configurations of weights on pegs.

The benefits of social interaction were limited to partners with quite specific combinations of initial knowledge. The only dyads that showed unqualified improvement were those in which the more advanced child used a rule that produced a determinate prediction on each problem and the less advanced child used a rule that led to indeterminate predictions on at least some problems. For example, a child who used Siegler's Rule II would predict that if the weights are equal, the side with the greater distance will go down. A child who used Rule I' would make inconsistent predictions when the weights are equal. When a child using Rule I' was paired with a child using Rule II, the Rule I' child generally advanced and the Rule II child did not regress. This may have reflected the more advanced child making consistently correct predictions on such problems and the less advanced one not being strongly committed to an incorrect approach.

Tudge's work with the balance scale illustrates several findings common to the studies of collaborative problem solving: (1) in the absence of feedback, pairs of novices do not generally move to a more advanced rule; (2) in the absence of feedback, the only children who make progress are novices paired with relative experts; (3) when one partner is more expert than another, the highest rule attained is that of the more advanced partner (Mackie, 1983; S. A. Miller & Brownel, 1975; Mugny & Doise, 1978; Radziszewska, 1993; Russell, Mills, & Reiff-Musgrove, 1990).

Like Tudge's investigation, most studies of collaborative problem solving have not provided children with feedback concerning the correct answer. Providing such feedback complicates the task of determining the contribution of the social interaction per se. However, not providing it may entail a worse problem—systematically, underestimating the beneficial effects of collaboration. Feedback provides a basis for choosing among alternative perspectives and also provides a graceful way for children to adopt an approach without seeming to "give in" to the child or children who generated it.

The beneficial effects of collaboration in combination with feedback were evident in a recent study that focused on children's comparisons of the relative sizes of decimal fractions (Ellis, Siegler, & Klahr, 1993). Children learning decimal fractions often misapply mathematical rules acquired in the course of learning about whole numbers or common fractions (Resnick et al., 1989). Many 10- and 11-year-olds adopt an incorrect rule based on prior knowledge of whole numbers (the Whole Number Rule); they reason that the more digits there are to the right of the decimal point, the larger the number (e.g., $0.37 > 0.4$). A smaller percentage of children of this age adhere to the Fraction Rule. They reason that the fewer digits to the right of the decimal points, the larger the number ($0.7 > .094$); to explain their reasoning on this problem, they sometimes say that one number is tenths and the other is hundredths, that tenths are bigger than hundredths, and therefore that the number in tenths is bigger.

Ellis et al. initially identified fifth graders who, on a pretest, used either the Whole Number Rule or the Fraction Rule. These children were assigned to work either alone, with a partner who used the same rule, or with a partner who used a different rule. They then received a series of 12 practice problems. Some children who worked alone and some dyads received feedback on each practice problem concerning which answer was correct; others did not. After completing the practice problems, the children individually performed a posttest.

Slightly more than half of the children who worked with a partner and received feedback performed consistently correctly on the posttest. Less than a quarter of those who worked alone and received feedback did similarly well, and none of the children who did not receive feedback did. The differences in outcomes appeared attributable to several specific differences in the learning process. One difference was the frequency of generation of the correct rule for comparing decimal fractions. The correct rule for solving decimal fraction problems was generated at some time during the practice session by a large majority of children working with a partner and receiving feedback, a substantial minority of children working alone and receiving feedback, and almost no children not receiving feedback, whether they worked alone or with a partner. Thus, both working with a partner and receiving feedback made more likely generation of rules consistent with the feedback. Feedback also influenced children's likelihood of adopting the correct rule once it was generated. Of those who ever generated the correct rule, a large majority of those in a dyad and who received feedback used that rule on the posttest, a smaller majority of those working alone who received feedback did, and none of those who did not receive feedback did. Thus, feedback may be critical both to generation of good ideas and to their adoption.

Feedback may have proven critical in this study because none of the children knew how to solve decimal comparison problems at the beginning of the session and hence would be expected to be relatively inarticulate in describing and defending the correct approach even when they generated it. In a second experiment, Ellis et al. (1993) examined whether the consistency across sessions with which one partner used the correct rule influenced the likelihood of their partner adopting that rule. In this second experiment, a fifth grader who used the Whole Number Rule was paired either with a peer who used the correct rule on two different days or with a peer who used an incorrect rule on the first day but the correct rule on the second.

Children who worked with a partner who used the correct rule on both occasions were much more likely themselves to adopt the correct rule on the posttest than those whose partner used the correct rule only on the later occasion (67% vs. 15%). This appeared to be due to the partners who used the correct rule on both occasions making more convincing arguments for it; the children who used the correct rule only on the later occasion also argued in favor of it, but appeared less articulate and persuasive in motivating the less expert partner to adopt it. These findings suggest that feedback is not absolutely necessary for novices to adopt a new, superior approach to solving mathematical problems. The evidence also suggests, however, that good ideas do not automatically win out over bad. Either external evidence of the validity of the better approach, such as that provided by feedback, or convincing arguments, such as those made by the children who used the correct rule on both occasions, seem essential for good strategies to consistently win out.

B. Representational Development

1. Mental Models

Much of development of problem solving in childhood and beyond is due to children building increasingly veridical and encompassing mental models of the problems they are trying to solve. Halford (1993) noted several central characteristics of such mental models. The most important is that the model accurately represent the structure of the problem. Relations among components of the mental model should parallel the essential structural relations in the problem. These relations include not only static features but also dynamic ones, such as possible moves and operations. Thus, mental models constrain the problem-solving process by ruling out many imaginable solution paths. Creating such models also involves stripping away incidental features of problems, thus facilitating generalization to new problems with different particulars.

A key determinant of the   of mental models is whether the critical
structural features of proble.   ncoded. This can be seen quite dramatically in situations in which n.   models do not include critical information. One such case involves 4   11-year-olds' representations of the trajectory of a ball that has been dropped from the bottom of a moving electric
train car. Many of the children represented the ball as moving horizontally
at first, and then suddenly dropping vertically (as in a Roadrunner cartoon).
Even some college students who had taken physics courses perceived this
path of motion. Their mental model of falling objects was sufficiently
strong that it outweighed both the abstract knowledge they had acquired in
their physics course(s) and what transpired before their eyes.

Encoding all of the critical structural information about problems within
mental models seems to play an especially crucial role in analogical reasoning. Children, like adults, strive to form analogies in which the system of
relations within the target domain resembles the system of relations within
the base. The objects within each domain need not have any particular
resemblance. Instead, the key to a good analogy is the similarity of the
corresponding relations in the two situations. Thus, the mental model for
the classic analogy "Heat flow is like water flow" emphasizes the parallels
between the structural relations among variables that influence the two
types of flows (Gentner, 1989).

Children, like adults, represent information about both objects and relations within analogies. A critical source of development, however, is in
ability to detect the analogical relation in situations in which objects are
dissimilar. Gentner and Toupin (1986) found that 4- to 6-year-olds required
similarities among objects to detect analogies, whereas 8- to 10-year-olds
detected the same analogies even when the objects were dissimilar. Gentner
(1988) reported a similar developmental trend in understanding of metaphors; again, older children understood metaphors in which only relations
were parallel, whereas younger ones required similarities among the objects
to understand the metaphors. Thus, while preschoolers can form and recognize analogies, ability to penetrate beneath surface differences increases
greatly during the course of development.

As in many other problem-solving situations, increasing ability to encode the critical information contributes greatly to developmental changes
in analogical reasoning. Adults actually spend more time than 7-year-olds in
encoding the relations within analogical reasoning problems; however, their
overall problem solving is faster, because the superior encoding allows them
to proceed with the rest of problem solving much more rapidly (Sternberg
& Rifkin, 1979). Similarly, high-IQ children spend more time on encoding
the relations within analogical reasoning problems than do low-IQ peers
(Marr & Sternberg, 1986). Superior encoding also appears to be a critical
source of development in ability to solve insight problems (Davidson &

Sternberg, 1984), balance scale problems (Siegler, 1976), and a host of other problems (e.g., Halford, 1993).

2. Specialized Representations

Although children begin during the first two years of life to acquire the most widely used representations, such as language, mental imagery, and spatial representations, they do not acquire many more specialized representations until considerably later. Acquisition of these specialized representations tends to be less universal and more variable in timing than acquisition of the broadly useful ones. The interaction of biological maturation and general experience leads to almost all children acquiring speech, mental imagery, and spatial representations early in life. In contrast, whether and when a given child learns to write, to draw maps and diagrams, to understand graphs and number lines, to use conventional measures and measurement devices, and to perform controlled scientific experiments depend on the child's particular experience.

One specialized but frequently useful type of representation involves maps. Maps are often thought of solely as ways of representing the locations and boundaries of political entities such as cities, states, and nations, or as ways of describing road systems. However, they also can serve far more varied purposes, ranging from indicating the relative amount of hydrocarbons spewed into the atmosphere from different factories to reflecting a 5-year-old's impression of her neighborhood. The essential property of maps is that they allow representation of unperceivable aspects of the world in perceivable form (Liben & Downs, 1989).

Maps are probably used most often within a problem-solving context as a means for getting another person to understand how to get from here to there. By age 5, the larger majority of children are able to comprehend simple maps drawn by other people, and to use them as tools for finding objects (Bluestein & Acredolo, 1979; Uttal & Wellman, 1989). Ability to draw informative maps develops over a considerably longer period, however. Children between 5 and 10 grow progressively better at including not only particular landmarks but also the appropriate topological relations among the landmarks, and at adopting a consistent perspective within a given map (Feldman, 1980; Perry & Wolf, 1986). Accurate depiction of distance as well as maintenance of topological relations and adoption of a consistent perspective come even later (Piaget & Inhelder, 1956).

Producing optimal maps for communicating how to get from here to there demands good decisions concerning what to leave out as well as what to put in. Including too much information can be just as confusing as not including enough. Karmiloff-Smith's (1979) observations of map drawing document the difficulties that 7- to 11-year-olds have in making such decisions. The children played the part of ambulance drivers who needed to transport a sick patient to the hospital. The patient's home was represented by a picture at one end of a long roll of paper; the hospital was represented by a picture at the other end; in between were a large number of choice points. Children were told to make the trip once without the patient so that they could find the fastest route, and were encouraged to mark up the paper to help them remember which route to take later.

Within the one-hour session, children often changed the types of marks they made, even when the original marks were optimally informative. Many children started with a simple, informative system for indicating which route to take, then started including redundant information that cluttered up the map without adding any information that seemed useful, and then went back to the original system. Karmiloff-Smith suggested that the changes reflected children's efforts to understand their own notational system; the redundancy in the middle of the experimental session arose because children did not understand that their original notations communicated all necessary information.

Older children also gain increasing sophistication in using other types of specialized representations such as measurement procedures. Rulers, scales, clocks, calendars, and other cultural artifacts allow children to solve many problems. Like other problem-solving devices, however, they are two-edged swords. Used appropriately, they enhance problem-solving capabilities; used inappropriately, they can lead to serious errors.

Children's main difficulty with measurement devices tends not to be in using them per se but in knowing when to use them. One version of this problem was evident in children's paying of a game in which the aim was to give two turtles identical amounts of food. Several potentially useful measurement devices were available, and children were told they might want to use them. However, most 5- and 7-year-olds used a measurement system that did not fit the situation—distributive counting, in which they divided the food by giving one piece to one turtle, the next piece to the other turtle, and so on. This resulted in an equal division of the number of pieces of food, but often not in equal amounts of food, since the pieces varied in size. Belief in counting as an appropriate measurement tool was sufficiently strong that when one turtle had one more piece of food than the other, some children simply tore in two a piece from the turtle that had one less, and then said that now both turtles had the same amount. Not until age 9 did most children divide the food into equal amounts.

In general, an important part of mastering the use of specialized representational tools is knowing when they are and are not useful. K. F. Miller (1989) quoted a statement of the philosopher Ludwig Wittgenstein that particularly well conveyed the relation between children's understanding and the representational tools that cultures make available to them: "a curious analogy could be based on the fact that even the hugest telescope has to have an eye-piece no larger than the human eye" (Wittgenstein, 1980, p. 17).

Measurement tools and other specialized representations greatly enhance children's potential for solving problems, but their usefulness inherently depends on the child's understanding.

3. Goal-Oriented Representations

As discussed earlier, ability to represent goals is present early in life. When children go to school, however, they often encounter major problems in connecting procedures that they learn with the goals those procedures are designed to meet. Seen from another perspective, an important difference between school and "real-world" problems is the frequent difficulty in school of identifying what the problem is (J. S. Brown et al., 1989). Consider the following example, a typical algebra problem:

> Write an equation using the variables C and S to represent the following statement. "At Mindy's restaurant, for every four people who order cheesecake, there are five people who order strudel." Let C represent the number of cheesecakes and S represent the number of strudels ordered.
> *(Clement, Lochhead, & Soloway, 1979, p. 46)*

Most high school students answer this problem by writing "4C = 5S". In so doing, they show that they are not connecting the goal of writing an equation—to represent in symbolic form a semantic relation of equality—with the equation they are actually writing. After all, the story indicates that more people order strudel; how can multiplying two bigger numbers (5 and the number of people who order strudel) yield a product equal to that obtained by multiplying two smaller numbers (4 and the number of people who order cheesecake)? The commonly written equation bears a superficial resemblance to the semantic relations in the story, and also looks like a plausible algebraic equation, but indicates a total failure to connect the goal of writing an equation with the equation that was actually written.

In response to such difficulties in representing the goals of school-related tasks, children often reinterpret problems in ways that make sense to them, rather than solving the problem as originally presented. For example, when 3rd graders were presented a potential hypothesis about how a "mystery key" on a programmable robot worked, they reacted quite differently depending on the initial plausibility of the hypothesis (Klahr, Fay, & Dunbar, 1993). When presented a hypothesis that seemed intuitively unlikely, they circumvented the suggestion that they test the hypothesis and instead generated a more intuitively likely hypothesis and concentrated on collecting confirmatory evidence for it. In contrast, adults tested the hypothesis that was suggested, regardless of its initial plausibility, and usually discovered that the unlikely seeming hypothesis was in fact correct. Thus, part of development of problem solving among older children involves accepting goals set by the social environment when the task calls for it.

When children do accurately represent the goals that procedures must meet, their generation of new procedures can benefit in interesting ways. This was evident in a study in which 4- and 5-year-olds who could add by counting from one, but did not know how to add by counting from the larger number (e.g., solving 3 + 6 by counting, "6, 7, 8, 9" or "7, 8, 9") were given roughly 30 sessions of experience solving addition problems (Siegler & Jenkins, 1989). The children's strategy use was assessed on each trial, so as to allow identification of the trial on which they first used the strategy of counting from the larger addend.

A surprising aspect of the findings was that the children were able to discover the new strategy without ever having attempted any illegal strategy, such as counting the first addend twice. In other words, they made the discovery without any trial and error. To explain the results, Siegler and Jenkins advanced the *goal sketch hypothesis,* which proposes that when children understand the goals that legitimate strategies in a domain must meet, they use their understanding both to reject potential strategies that do not meet those goals and to channel their search for new strategies toward procedures that do meet the goals. For example, the goal sketch in addition would involve the knowledge that a legitimate addition strategy must represent each of the addends and must generate a single number to represent their combined quantity.

Siegler and Crowley (in press) tested the goal sketch hypothesis by posing a hypothetical problem to children who could add by counting from one but who did not yet know the strategy of counting from the larger addend. The children were asked to evaluate the smartness of three approaches that hypothetical other children were said to have used: their usual approach of counting from one, the novel approach of counting from the larger addend, and the equally novel but illegal approach of counting the first addend twice. The children judged counting from the larger addend, the more advanced approach they did not use, to be just as smart as counting from one, the approach they did employ, and judged both to be considerably smarter than the illegal approach. Thus, they appeared to understand the goals that legitimate addition strategies must meet sufficiently well to discriminate desirable novel approaches from undesirable novel approaches. In general, understanding the goals that legitimate strategies in a domain must meet seems critical to minimizing or avoiding altogether trial and error in the course of problem solving.

C. Self-Regulation

1. Strategy Choice

As noted earlier, in domains in which children have experience solving particular problems, they often acquire multiple strategies for solving the class of problems. Domains in which such diverse strategy use have been noted include many academic areas: addition, subtraction, multiplication, word identification, spelling, time telling, writing, and physics problem solving among them (Siegler, in press). For example, in solving simple addition problems, 4- to 8-year-olds use such strategies as counting from one, counting from the larger addend, decomposing a single difficult problem into two simpler ones (e.g., when presented $9 + 4$, thinking $10 + 4 = 14$, $14 - 1 = 13$; $9 + 4 = 13$), and retrieving the answer from memory.

This variability in strategy use has obvious adaptive value—it makes it possible for children to choose strategies that are particularly well suited to the characteristics of a given problem. It also raises a critical question: how do children choose which of their several strategies to use to solve a given problem? One explanation that was frequently advanced when this question first received serious attention was that children use conscious, explicit, metacognitive knowledge about the problems they are presented, available strategies, and their own cognitive capacities to choose which strategy to use (e.g., Flavell & Wellman, 1977). However, such explicit metacognitive knowledge has proved less predictive of strategy choices than had initially been expected (e.g., Flavell, Miller, & Miller, 1993).

If not through rational consideration of problem difficulty and characteristics of available strategies, how do children choose which strategy to use? The basic answer appears to be that basic associative knowledge, together with relatively simple algorithms for choosing most often those strategies that have in the past worked best, can yield adaptive strategy choices comparable to those generated by children. A recent computer simulation illustrated the mechanisms that could give rise to such adaptive strategy choices (Siegler & Shipley, in press). This simulation did not possess explicit metacognitive knowledge of strategies and problems, but did possess basic mechanisms that made learning possible. In particular, the simulation possessed several strategies for solving arithmetic problems, the capacity to keep records of how effective these strategies were, a simple algorithm for choosing strategies based on the records of their previous effectiveness, and the capacity to associate problems with particular answers.

The behavior of the simulation resembled that of children in numerous, quite specific, ways (Siegler & Shipley, in press). Like children, the simulation used the more time-consuming and effortful strategies primarily on the most difficult problems, chose strategies that work particularly well on certain problems disproportionately often on those problems, and used multiple strategies within as well as between problems for a prolonged period of time. The simulation's pattern of learning also resembled that of children. With experience, it became faster and more accurate and used the more advanced strategies increasingly often. Its relative success in solving different problems, and the types of strategies it used most often to solve them, also correlated highly with children's patterns of performance. Beyond this, empirical tests of predictions generated by the simulation, regarding the relation between early and later tendencies to use particular strategies most often, and also regarding individual differences in performance, have been borne out (Kerkman & Siegler, 1993). Thus, at least with frequently encountered problems, conscious, explicit metacognitive knowledge is not the only route to adaptive strategy choices, and may not be the main one. Effective choices among strategies also can grow out of simple learning mechanisms operating on basic associative knowledge.

2. Planning

Effective planning requires the ability to formulate actions in advance, as well as skill at monitoring and modifying plans as circumstances and goals require. As illustrated by the earlier description of infants crawling into another room to retrieve a toy they could not initially see, some ability to plan is evident as early as 12 months of age. With age, however, children become increasingly skilled at monitoring their plans and adjusting them to circumstances.

A study of children's planning on paper-and-pencil mazes illustrates this growing sensitivity to task demands (Gardner & Rogoff, 1990). Children ranging in age from 4 to 10 years were presented a series of mazes and given instructions that emphasized either speed and accuracy or accuracy alone. When only accuracy mattered, 7- to 10-year-olds planned the entire route before they began and, as a result, made few wrong turns. When both speed and accuracy mattered, these children planned some of the route in advance and the rest as they came to choice points. In contrast, the 4-year-olds did not adjust their plans to the different instructions. Under both conditions, they planned some of the route in advance and the rest later. The older children realized the benefits of planing when time spent planning was unimportant, and avoided the time cost of planning when speed was important.

Despite these advances, children often fail to plan in circumstances where it would be helpful. The failure of school age children to plan has been observed on a myriad of tasks including writing (Bereiter & Scardamalia, 1987), route planning (Gauvain & Rogoff, 1989), instructing other children (Ellis & Rogoff, 1986), and referential communication (Cosgrove & Patterson, 1977).

Why do children fail to plan in so many situations in which it would be useful to do so? The above-described ideas about strategy choice suggests an explanation (Ellis & Siegler, in press). Planning can be viewed as one among a number of competing strategies that might be followed in a given situation. Whether a child will in fact plan is a function of both the value of planning for the child in that situation and the value of alternative courses of action other than planning. Planning has the advantage of making accurate and direct solutions possible in many situations, but also has several disadvantages. It is often time consuming and tedious, does not directly bring goal attainment, and can be subjectively unpleasant if it is taken to imply lack of competence. In contrast, unplanned problem solving can be fun in its own right, and many children may value more highly the immediate attainment of goals than their delayed attainment. Further, many children may underestimate the likelihood of task success with planning, and/or overestimate its likelihood without planning, and therefore underestimate its potential benefits. Considering all of these potential reasons not to choose to plan, it is impressive that children plan as often as they do.

Interactions with adults seem to be prominent among the influences that lead to children sometimes planning. Children are more likely to plan when they solve problems in collaboration with adults than when they solve problems alone (Hudson & Fivush, 1991). The experience of planning with adults also leads to more sophisticated planning when they later solve problems by themselves (Gauvain, 1992; Radziszewska & Rogoff, 1988). Experience with peers and with older children also can be somewhat helpful, but does not in general seem to be as helpful as experience with adults. In several studies, adults have proven to be more effective than 9-year-olds in helping 5-, 7-, and 9-year-olds learn to plan, even when the 9-year-olds were trained to ensure that they understood the task as well as adults (Radziszewska & Rogoff, 1991). Adults' superiority in facilitating the development of planning skills seems attributable to their discussing the strategies more with the younger children, reminding them more often about the goals of the task, and monitoring their progress more closely. Adults also appear more sensitive in adjusting the kind of help they provide, depending on the needs of the child (Gauvain, 1992; Rogoff et al., 1984).

3. Joint Decision Making

Regulation of cognitive activities is often accomplished through the interaction of people working together, rather than through the efforts of a lone individual. Such beneficial effects do not flow automatically from working with others, however; they depend on the nature of the interaction. To the extent that partners work in parallel, or one partner dominates the interaction, collaborations often do not yield more successful problem solving than that of individuals working alone. This was illustrated in a study in which 11-year-olds played a computer adventure game alone or with a partner (Blaye, Light, Joiner, & Sheldon, 1991). The computer game resembled the well-known missionaries and cannibals problem. The goal was to retrieve a king's crown from an island, but there were multiple constraints on the means by which the crown could be retrieved. To solve the problem, several, nonobvious subgoals had to be established and met; hence the solution was less direct than it first appeared.

Pairs of 11-year-olds were more likely to solve the problem than peers working alone, and performed better on an individual posttest as well. The extent to which individual performance benefited from the interaction was linked to the extent to which decisions were made jointly. Pairs that engaged in joint decision making were more likely than were children working alone to realize that they needed to divide the problem into subgoals, thus channeling their cognitive activity in useful directions. Another study showed that children's performance on the Tower of Hanoi problem was facilitated by working with a partner, but only when the partners were required to decide jointly which moves to make (Glachan & Light, 1982).

At first impression, the importance of joint decision making to the success of collaborative efforts might suggest that interactions between children would be more successful than collaborations between children and adults, since the children's cognitive levels would tend to be more similar. In fact, children below school age rarely collaborate successfully (Azmitia & Perlmutter, 1989; Perlmutter, Behrend, Kuo, & Muller, 1989), though they at times can do so in simple situations in which both the need for cooperation and the division of labor are readily apparent (Azmitia, 1988; Brownell & Carriger, 1991). Preschoolers' general difficulty in collaborating effectively may be due to their difficulty in thinking analytically about another person's reasoning (Tomasello, Kruger, & Ratner, in press).

Even when children are of school age, the effects of collaboration between young children who are novices and older children who are more expert tend to benefit the novices less than when they solved the problem with an adult. This appears due in large part to the reluctance of the older, more expert children to relinquish control of the task to the younger, less expert one (Azmitia & Hesser, 1993; Duran & Gauvain, 1993; Ellis & Rogoff, 1986). Observations of problem-solving interactions among triads of children—each triad including a 7-year-old, the child's 9-year-old sibling, and a friend of the 9-year-old sibling—illustrated a major course of the difficulty. Even older children who were relatively skilled at monitoring the younger child's problem solving would not turn over control of the task, which seemed to be a barrier to the younger children acquiring independent problem-solving skills. The following exchange between a 7- and a 9-year-old whose task was to build a model from geometric shapes and connectors is illustrative:

> Teacher: *Now a little tube.*
> Learner: *Where does it go?*
> Teacher: *Here you gotta look.*
> Learner: *OK, let me try. Another little tube . . .*
> Teacher: *I'm supposed to tell you what to do.*
> Learner: *But I'm looking. Let me.*
> Teacher: *No.* She [the experimenter] *put me in charge.*
> Learner: *You think you know everything.*

Teacher: *I do cause I did this before. Get a little tube.*
Learner: (Complies).

(Azmitia & Hesser, 1993, p. 438)

The reluctance of older children to cede power to younger children during joint problem solving is not inevitable. A comparison of collaborative problem solving among 7- and 9-year-old Navajo and Euro-American children revealed that the 9-year-old Navajo children were less likely to intervene in the problem-solving attempts of their younger partners than were 9-year-old Euro-American children (Ellis & Siegler, in press). By waiting longer before offering assistance, the older Navajo children allowed the younger ones to formulate their own plans and attempt to solve the problems independently. This may have been what led to the younger Navajo children making fewer errors during the session. Interaction patterns reflect both the cognitive and social abilities of participants, and their cultural values and practices. In the Navajo culture, the right of individuals to make their own decisions is highly respected (Chisolm, 1983). This emphasis on autonomy helps shape the kinds of problem-solving interactions that are observed, whether the participants are adults or children.

4. Self-Monitoring

Skilled problem solvers spontaneously engage in a great many self-monitoring activities, such as questioning and elaborating their own knowledge, assessing their degree of understanding, and thinking of counterexamples and possible generalizations (Palincsar & Brown, 1984). In many ways, these activities resemble what might be hoped for in a good discussion or debate with another person. This resemblance has been among the influences that has suggested that one way to inculcate such useful self-monitoring skills is through collaborative problem solving and learning. Studies of the way in which collaborative interactions actually occur, however, suggest that such idealized interactions are the exception rather than the rule. For this reason, a number of educational interventions have been aimed at training teachers and children how to interact in ways that are likely to facilitate the acquisition of self-monitoring skills.

A particularly successful example of this kind of intervention is known as *reciprocal teaching* (A. L. Brown & Palincsar, 1989; Palincsar & Brown, 1984). It emphasizes four strategic activities: summarizing, clarifying, questioning, and anticipating future questions. These activities are embedded in group discussions, led alternately by the teacher and students. At first, the teacher structures the discussion, but over time, students assume increasing responsibility for it.

Reciprocal teaching was originally applied to improving the reading comprehension of 7th graders from disadvantaged backgrounds. It showed extremely impressive effects, leading to marked improvement not only in classroom and standardized tests of reading comprehension but also in tests of other areas where reading comprehension is critical, such as science and social studies (Palincsar & Brown, 1984).

The basic principles of reciprocal teaching have since been applied to a number of other areas, including general problem-solving skills. For example, King (1991) examined the benefits of instructing pairs of 5th graders in how to engage in strategic monitoring during joint problem solving. Children in the guided questioning group were taught via a "think aloud" procedure to ask each other a set of questions designed to focus attention on formulating problems, generating alternative strategies, monitoring goals, and evaluating progress toward a solution. They were given a list of the questions and practiced asking them and applying the procedure over five sessions. Students in the unguided questioning condition also worked in pairs, and saw the same scripted sequence of questions modeled by the teacher. However, they did not receive the list of specific questions nor practice in asking them, only general encouragement to ask their partners questions during problem solving and to respond to their partner's questions. A control condition was composed of dyads who received no training, modeling, or instructions regarding questioning. Children in the guided, peer questioning condition outperformed the other groups on new tests of problem solving that differed from the instructed ones in many ways but that also would benefit from the types of planning, self-monitoring, and self-evaluation that the children learned in the original situation.

The reasons why reciprocal teaching has proven more effective than many previous attempts to inculcate general learning and problem-solving skills are not obscure. A. L. Brown and Palincsar (1989) noted that much of what is intended as strategy instruction in schools is actually stripped down, decontextualized methods that are difficult to transfer to new problems. In contrast, the self-monitoring and planning strategies emphasized in reciprocal instruction are practiced in context, in response to diverse specific problems. Learning is accomplished jointly by group members, with novices contributing what they can when they are able; such conditions are motivating, allow active participation from early in the learning process, encourage deep rather than superficial processing, and enable skills to be practiced in sufficiently diverse domains for their general applicability to become apparent. The overlap of these reasons with the apparent reasons for the effectiveness of scaffolding and self-explanations is probably not coincidental.

III. CONCLUSIONS

Human problem solving is an inherently social activity. In all periods of development, it directly involves other people; they function as goals to be attained, as tools for attaining other goals, as obstacles blocking attainment of yet other goals, and as resources capable of conveying useful skills and knowledge. The social world also profoundly influences acquisition of cognitive processes involved in problem solving. Goals, strategies, modes of representation, and self-regulatory devices all are often acquired in social interactions. Recognizing the extent to which the social world permeates the development of problem solving broadens understanding of the range of problems that children must learn to solve, the range of cognitive and social processes that are part of problem solving, and the range of experiences that, together with biological maturation, determine the types of problems that children can solve at different ages.

Thinking about the development of problem solving chronologically reveals how profoundly it is intertwined with the social world at all points in development. The competence of infants and young children is often most striking when solving problems involving other people. Infants as young as 4 to 8 months can solve problems by imitating adults' solutions. By 14 months, children can replicate actions of peers that they saw a full day earlier, in a different context. Also by the end of the first year, infants obtain goals and learn more about the world by using others as tools to allow them to achieve objectives they could not achieve on their own. In turn, adults facilitate the acquisition of problem-solving strategies by making clear their own problem-solving procedures, by structuring interactions so that infants can participate to the degree of their capabilities, and by providing infants and toddlers opportunities to explore objects.

In the period immediately after infancy, the contribution of the social world is particularly evident in the acquisition of widely applicable representational abilities, such as language. Among other benefits, language facilitates joint problem solving between children and older individuals. Toddlers learn problem-solving procedures from other people describing them, and increasingly strive to reach specific goals that other people set for them. Language also enables young children to communicate well enough for scaffolding to allow them to learn many other problem-solving skills. During this age range, children also gain competence in using nonlinguistic representational systems that are part of their culture, such as scale models. Increasing linguistic capabilities help children not only in solving problems jointly with other people but also in solving problems individually. Talking to one's self while solving a problem, especially in ways resembling the speech used by adults when engaged in joint problem solving with children, facilitates 4- and 5-year-olds' performance. Trying to verbally explain a more advanced problem solver's reasoning also facilitates preschoolers' problem solving. The increasing linguistic competence is among the factors that allow children to benefit from formal schooling and thus to be exposed to the great variety of problem-solving techniques taught in that context.

Schooling influences problem solving in myriad ways. It adds to the broadly applicable problem-solving skills that children have at their disposal, to the content knowledge that they can use to solve problems in particular domains, and to the range of problems with which they have experience. Formal and informal lessons from teachers and peers, and exposure to cultural artifacts such as books, calculators, computers, measurement systems, and maps, are prominent contributors to the development of problem solving during childhood and adolescence. School-based problems also present special types of difficulty, however; much of children's problem solving in school is geared toward figuring out what the goal of a problem is, and how to work within seemingly arbitrary constraints set by others.

Although preschoolers can, under especially favorable circumstances, coordinate efforts with peers, collaborative problem solving generally is of limited benefit until children are of school age. Among school age children, effective collaborations can aid acquisition of problem-solving skills; lead to better decision making; facilitate the construction of plans, strategies, and monitoring of task performance; expose children to alternative perspectives; and force them to articulate their own ideas more clearly. Joint decision making seems to be a particularly important determinant of whether collaborations have such beneficial effects. Even when decisions are reached jointly between or among older children, however, successful problem solving is not guaranteed; feedback from the physical or social environment and articulate explanations also can be essential to the success of collaborative problem solving.

In this chapter, we have described a number of studies by investigators who approached problem solving from a social-constructivist perspective. Social influences on problem solving, however, are not limited by the theoretical framework of the investigator who does the research. They permeate all problem-solving activity. The two illustrations of children's problem solving provided on the first page of the chapter illustrate the point. Neither Klahr nor Waters works within the social-constructivist framework, and neither sets out to examine social influences on problem solving. Both, however, chose unambiguously social situations as their prototypic examples of children's problem solving. Many researchers interested in the development of problem solving never mention social influences, yet they examine children's growing ability to solve problems whose goals are defined by experimenters, employing strategies, representations, and self-regulatory processes that the children have learned from others, and using culturally derived artifacts to enhance their problem-solving capabilities. In other words, it is not the fact that social phenomena are being investigated that is new in the study of children's problem solving. What is new is the increasingly widespread realization of how deeply the social world is implicated in the development of problem solving, a broadened vision of what the development of problem solving entails, and a growing commitment to explicating the mechanisms through which cognitive and social processes jointly contribute to children's developing ability to solve problems.

Acknowledgments

The research was supported by grants from the Spencer Foundation, the McDonnell Foundation, the Mellon Foundation, and the National Institutes of Health (Grant HD19011), as well as by a National Institute of Mental Health postdoctoral fellowship.

References

Azmitia, M. (1988). Peer interaction and problem solving: When are two heads better than one? *Child Development, 59,* 87–96.

Azmitia, M., & Hesser, J. (1993). Why siblings are important agents of cognitive development: A comparison of siblings and peers. *Child Development, 64,* 430–444.

Azmitia, M., & Perlmutter, M. (1989). Social influences on children's cognition: State of the art and future directions. In H. Reese (Ed.), *Advances in child development and behavior* (Vol. 22, pp. 89–144). San Diego: Academic Press.

Behrend, D. A., Rosengren, K. S., & Perlmutter, M. (1989). A new look at children's private speech: The effects of age, task difficulty, and parental presence. *International Journal of Behavioral Development, 12,* 305–320.

Benson, J. B., Arehart, D. M., Jennings, T., Boley, S., & Kearns, L. (1989, April). *Infant crawling: Expectations, action-plans, and goals.* Paper presented at the biennial meeting of the Society for Research in Child Development, Kansas City, MO.

Bereiter, C., & Scardamalia, M. (1987). *The psychology of written composition.* Hillsdale, NJ: Erlbaum.

Berk, L. E. (1986). Relationship of elementary school children's private speech to behavioral accompaniment to task, attention, and task performance. *Developmental Psychology, 22,* 671–680.

Berk, L. E., & Garvin, R. A. (1984). Development of private speech among low-income Appalachian children. *Developmental Psychology, 20,* 271–286.

Berk, L. E., & Landau, S. (1993). Private speech of learning disabled and normally achieving children in classroom academic and laboratory contexts. *Child Development, 64,* 556–571.

Bivens, J. A., & Berk, L. E. (1990). A longitudinal study of the development of children's private speech. *Merrill-Palmer Quarterly, 36,* 443–463.

Blaye, A., Light, P., Joiner, R., & Sheldon, S. (1991). Collaboration as a facilitator of planning and problem solving on a computer based task. *British Journal of Developmental Psychology, 9,* 471–483.

Bluestone, N., & Acredolo, L. (1979). Developmental changes in map-reading skills. *Child Development, 50,* 691–697.

Brown, A. L., & Kane, M. J. (1988). Preschool children can learn to transfer: Learning to learn and learning from example. *Cognitive Psychology, 20,* 493–523.

Brown, A. L., & Palinscar, A. S. (1989). Guided, cooperative learning and individual knowledge acquisition. In L. B. Resnick (Ed.), *Knowing, learning, and instruction: Essays in honor of Robert Glaser* (pp. 393–451). Hillsdale, NJ: Erlbaum.

Brown, J. S., Collins, A., & Duguid, P. (1989). Situated cognition and the culture of learning. *Educational Researcher, 18,* 32–42.

Brownell, C. A., & Carriger, M. S. (1991). Collaborations among toddler peers: Individual contributions to social contexts. In L. B. Resnick, J. M. Levine, & S. D. Teasley (Eds.),

Perspectives on socially shared cognition (pp. 365–383). Washington, DC: American Psychological Association.

Bullock, M., & Lutkenhaus, P. (1988). The development of volitional behavior in the toddler years. *Child Development, 59,* 664–674.

Butterworth, G., & Hopkins, B. (1988). Hand-mouth coordination in the newborn baby. *British Journal of Developmental Psychology, 6,* 303–314.

Case, R. (1985). *Intellectual development: A systematic reinterpretation.* Orlando, FL: Academic Press.

Case, R. (1992). *The mind's staircase: Exploring the conceptual underpinnings of children's thought and knowledge.* Hillsdale, NJ: Erlbaum.

Chisolm, J. S. (1983). *Navajo infancy: An ethnological study of child development.* New York: Aldine.

Clement J., Lochhead, J., & Soloway, E. (1979, March). *Translation between symbol systems: Isolating a common difficulty in solving algebra word problems* (COINS Techn. Rep. No. 79-19). Amherst: University of Massachusetts, Department of Computer and Information Sciences.

Cosgrove, J. M., & Patterson, C. J. (1977). Plans and the development of listener skills. *Developmental Psychology, 13,* 557–564.

Crisafi, M. A., & Brown, A. L. (1986). Analogical transfer in very young children: Combining two separately learned solutions to reach a goal. *Child Development, 57,* 953–968.

Davidson, J. E., & Sternberg, R. J. (1984). The role of insight in intellectual giftedness. *Gifted Child Quarterly, 28,* 58–64.

DeLoache, J. S. (1987). Rapid change in the symbolic functioning of young children. *Science, 238,* 1556–1557.

DeLoache, J. S. (1989). The development of representation in young children. In H. W. Reese (Ed.), *Advances in child development* (Vol. 22, pp. 1–39). San Diego: Academic Press.

DeLoache, J. S., Cassidy, D. J., & Brown, A. L. (1985). Precursors of mnemonic strategies in very young children's memory. *Child Development, 56,* 125–137.

Duran, R., & Gauvain, M. (1993). The role of age versus expertise in peer collaboration during joint planning. *Journal of Experimental Child Psychology, 55,* 227–242.

Ellis, S., & Rogoff, B. (1986). Problem solving in children's management of instruction. In E. Mueller & C. Cooper (Eds.), *Process and outcome in peer relationships* (pp. 301–325). Orlando, FL: Academic Press.

Ellis, S., & Siegler, R. (in press). Planning and strategy choice, or why don't children plan when they should? In S. L. Friedman & E. K. Scholnick (Eds.), *Why, how, and when do we plan: The developmental psychology of planning.* Hillsdale, NJ: Erlbaum.

Ellis, S., Siegler, R. S., & Klahr, D. (1993). *Effects of feedback and collaboration on changes in children's use of mathematical rules.* Manuscript in progress.

Feinman, S. (1992). *Social referencing and the social construction of reality in infancy.* New York: Plenum.

Feldman, H. D. (1980). *Beyond universals in cognitive development.* Norwood, NJ: Ablex.

Flavell, J. H., Miller, P. H., & Miller, S. A. (1993). *Cognitive development.* Englewood Cliffs, NJ: Prentice-Hall.

Flavell, J. H., & Wellman, H. (1977). Metamemory. In R. V. Kail & J. W. Hagen (Eds.), *Perspectives on the development of memory and cognition* (pp. 3–33). Hillsdale, NJ: Erlbaum.

Frauenglass, M. H., & Diaz, R. M. (1985). Self-regulatory functions of children's private speech: A critical analysis of recent challenges to Vygotsky's theory. *Developmental Psychology, 21,* 357–364.

Freund, L. S. (1990). Maternal regulation of children's problem solving behavior and its impact on children's performance. *Child Development, 61,* 113–126.

Gardner, W., & Rogoff, B. (1990). Children's deliberateness of planning according to task circumstances. *Developmental Psychology, 26,* 480–487.

Gauvain, M. (1992). Social influences on the development of planning in advance and during action. *International Journal of Behavioral Development, 15,* 377–398.

Gauvain, M., & Rogoff, B. (1989). Collaborative problem solving and children's planning skills. *Developmental Psychology, 25,* 139–151.

Gentner, D. (1988). Metaphor as structure mapping: The relational shift. *Child Development, 59,* 47–59.

Gentner, D. (1989). The mechanisms of analogical transfer. In S. Vosniadou & A. Ortony (Eds.), *Similarity and analogical reasoning.* New York: Cambridge University Press.

Gentner, D., & Toupin, C. (1986). Systematicity and similarity in the development of an analogy. *Cognitive Science, 10,* 277–300.

Glachan, M., & Light, P. (1982). Peer interaction and learning: Can two wrongs make a right? In G. Butterworth & P. Light (Eds.), *Social cognition: Studies of the development of understanding* (pp. 238–262). Chicago: University of Chicago Press.

Goodman, S. (1981). The integration of verbal and motor behavior in preschool children. *Child Development, 52,* 280–289.

Halford, G. (1993). *Children's understanding: The development of mental models.* Hillsdale, NJ: Erlbaum.

Hannah, E., & Meltzoff, A. N. (1993). Peer imitation by toddlers in laboratory, home, and day-care contexts: Implications for social learning and memory. *Developmental Psychology, 29,* 701–710.

Hudson, J. A., & Fivush, R. (1991). Planning in the preschool years: The emergence of plans from general event knowledge. *Cognitive Development, 6,* 393–415.

Karmiloff-Smith, A. (1979). Micro- and macro-developmental changes in language acquisition and other representational systems. *Cognitive Science, 3,* 91–118.

Kerkman, D. D., & Siegler, R. S. (1993). Individual differences and adaptive flexibility in lower-income children's strategy choices. *Learning and Individual Differences, 5,* 113–136.

King, A. (1991). Effects of training in strategic questioning on children's problem-solving performance. *Journal of Educational Psychology, 83,* 307–317.

Klahr, D. (1978). Goal formation, planning, and learning by preschool problem solvers or: "My socks are in the dryer." In R. S. Siegler (Ed.), *Children's thinking: What develops?* (pp. 181–212). Hillsdale, NJ: Erlbaum.

Klahr, D., Fay, A., & Dunbar, K. (1993). Heuristics for scientific experimentation: A developmental study. *Cognitive Psychology, 5,* 111–146.

Klahr, D., & Robinson, M. (1981). Formal assessment of problem solving and planning processes in children. *Cognitive Psychology, 13,* 113–148.

Kohlberg, L., Yaeger, J., & Hjertholm, E. (1968). Private speech: Four studies and a review of theories. *Child Development, 39,* 691–736.

Levine, J. M., Resnick, L. B., & Higgins, E. T. (1993). Social foundations of cognition. *Annual Review of Psychology, 44,* 585–612.

Liben, L. S., & Downs, R. M. (1989). Understanding maps as symbols: The development of map concepts in children. In H. W. Reese (Ed.), *Advances in child development and behavior* (Vol. 22, pp. 145–201). San Diego: Academic Press.

Luria, A. R. (1961). *The role of speech in the regulation of normal and abnormal behavior.* London: Pergamon.

Mackie, D. (1983). The effects of social interaction on conservation of spatial relations. *Journal of Cross-Cultural Psychology, 14,* 131–151.

Marr, D. B., & Sternberg, R. J. (1986). Analogical reasoning with novel concepts: Differential attention of intellectually gifted and nongifted children to relevant and irrelevant novel stimuli. *Cognitive Development, 1,* 53–72.

Mast, V. K., Fagan, J. W., Rovee-Collier, C. K., & Sullivan, M. W. (1980). Immediate and long-term memory for reinforcement contexts: The development of learned expectancies in early infancy. *Child Development, 51,* 700–707.

Meichenbaum, D. H., & Goodman, J. (1971). Training impulsive children to talk to themselves: A means of development self-control. *Journal of Personality and Social Psychology, 34,* 942–950.

Meltzoff, A. N. (1985). Immediate and deferred imitation in fourteen and twenty-four-month-old infants. *Child Development, 56,* 62–72.

Miller, K. F. (1989). Measurement as a tool for thought: The role of measuring procedures in children's understanding of quantitative invariance. *Developmental Psychology, 25,* 589–600.

Miller, S. A., & Brownell, C. (1975). Peers, persuasion, and Piaget: Dyadic interaction between conservers and nonconservers. *Child Development, 46,* 972–997.

Mischel, H. N., & Patterson, C. J. (1978). Effective plans for self-control in children. In W. A. Collins (Ed.), *Minnesota Symposium on Child Psychology* (Vol. 11, pp. 199–230). Hillsdale, NJ: Erlbaum.

Mugny, G., & Doise, W. (1978). Socio-cognitive conflict and structure of individual and collective performances. *European Journal of Social Psychology, 8,* 181–192.

Pacifici, S., & Bearison, D. (1991). Development of children's self-regulations in idealized and mother–child interaction. *Cognitive Development, 6,* 261–278.

Palincsar, A. M., & Brown, A. L. (1984). Reciprocal teaching of comprehension-monitoring activities. *Cognition and Instruction, 1,* 117–175.

Papousek, H., & Papousek, M. (1987). Intuitive parenting: A didactic counterpart to the infant's precocity in integrative capacities. In J. Osofsky (Ed.), *Handbook of infant development* (2nd ed., pp. 669–720). New York: Wiley.

Perlmutter, M., Behrend, S. D., Kuo, F., & Muller, A. (1989). Social influences on children's problem solving. *Developmental Psychology, 25,* 744–754.

Perry, M. D., & Wolf, D. P. (1986). *Mapping symbolic development.* Paper presented at the sixteenth annual symposium of the Jean Piaget Society, Philadelphia.

Piaget, J., & Inhelder, B. (1956). *The child's conception of space* (F. J. Langdon & J. L. Lunzer, Trans.). New York: Norton.

Radziszewska, B. (1993, March). *Sociocognitive processes in adult–child and peer collaboration on area and volume tasks.* Paper presented at the meetings of the Society for Research on Child Development, New Orleans, LA.

Radziszewska, B., & Rogoff, B. (1988). Influence of adult and peer collaborators on children's planning skills. *Developmental Psychology, 24,* 840–848.

Radziszewska, B., & Rogoff, B. (1991). Children's guided participation in planning imaginary errands with skilled adult or peer partners. *Developmental Psychology, 27,* 381–389.

Resnick, L. B., Levine, H. M., & Teasley, D. S. (Eds.) (1991). *Perspectives on socially shared cognition.* Washington, DC: American Psychological Association.

Resnick, L. B., Nesher, P., Leonard, F., Magone, M., Omanson, S., & Peled, I. (1989). Conceptual bases of arithmetic errors: The case of decimal fractions. *Journal of Research in Mathematics Education, 20,* 8–27.

Richards, D. D., & Siegler, R. (1981). Very young children's acquisition of systematic problem-solving strategies. *Child Development, 52,* 1318–1321.

Rogoff, B. (1990). *Apprenticeship in thinking: Cognitive development in social context.* New York: Oxford University Press.

Rogoff, B., Ellis, S., & Gardner, W. P. (1984). Adjustment of adult–child instruction according to child's age and task. *Child Development, 20,* 193–199.

Rogoff, B., Mistry, J., Radzisewska, B., & Germond, J. (1992). Infants' instrumental social interaction with adults. In S. Feinman (Ed.), *Social referencing and the social construction of reality in infancy* (pp. 323–348). New York: Plenum.

Rovee-Collier, C. (1987). Learning and memory in infancy. In J. Osofsky (Ed.), *Handbook of infant development.* New York: Wiley.

Russell, J., Mills, I., & Reiff-Musgrove, P. (1990). The role of symmetrical and asymmetrical social conflict in cognitive change. *Journal of Experimental Child Psychology, 49,* 58–78.

Siegler, R. S. (1976). Three aspects of cognitive development. *Cognitive Psychology, 8,* 481–520.

Siegler, R. S. (1978). The origins of scientific reasoning. In R. S. Siegler (Ed.), *Children's thinking: What develops?* Hillsdale, NJ: Erlbaum.

Siegler, R. S. (1981). Developmental sequences within and between concepts. *Society for Research in Child Development Monograph, 46* (Serial No. 189).

Siegler, R. S. (1991). *Children's thinking* (2nd ed.). Englewood Cliffs, NJ: Prentice-Hall.

Siegler, R. S. (1994). *A microgenetic study of number conservation.* Manuscript submitted for review.

Siegler, R. S. (1994). Cognitive variability: A key to understanding cognitive development. *Current Directions in Psychological Science, 3,* 1–5.

Siegler, R. S., & Jenkins, E. A. (1989). *How children discover new strategies.* Hillsdale, NJ: Erlbaum.

Siegler, R. S., & Crowley, K. (In press). Constraints on learning in non-privileged domains. *Cognition Psychology.*

Siegler, R. S., & Shipley, C. (in press). Variation, selection, and cognitive change. In G. Halford & T. Simon (Eds.), *Developing cognitive competence: New approaches to process modeling.* Hillsdale, NJ: Erlbaum.

Sternberg, R., & Rifkin, B. (1979). The development of analogical reasoning processes. *Journal of Experimental Child Psychology, 27,* 195–232.

Tomasello, M., Kruger, A., & Ratner, H. (1993). Cultural learning. *Behavioral and Brain Sciences, 16,* 495–552.

Tronick, E. Z. (1989). Emotions and emotional communication in infants. *American Psychologist, 44,* 112–119.

Tudge, J. R. H. (1992). Processes and consequences of peer collaboration: A Vygotskian analysis. *Child Development, 63,* 1364–1379.

Uttal, D., & Wellman, H. M. (1989). Young children's representation of spatial information acquired from maps. *Developmental Psychology, 25,* 128–138.

Vygotsky, L. A. (1962). *Thought and language.* Cambridge, MA: MIT Press. (Original work published 1934)

Waters, H. S. (1989, April). *Problem solving at two: A year-long naturalistic study of two children.* Paper presented at the meetings of the Society for Research in Child Development, Kansas City, MO.

Wellman, H. M. (1990). *The child's theory of mind.* Cambridge, MA: MIT Press.

Wertsch, J. V. (1978). Adult-child interaction and the roots of metacognition. *Quarterly Newsletter of the Laboratory of Comparative Human Cognition, 2,* 15–18.

Wertsch, J. V., McNamee, G. D., McLane, J. B., & Budwig, N. A. (1980). The adult-child dyad as a problem-solving system. *Child Development, 51,* 1215–1221.

Willats, P. (1989). Development of problem solving in infancy. In A. Slater & J. G. Bremner (Eds.), *Infant development* (pp. 143–182). Hillsdale, NJ: Erlbaum.

Willats, P. (1990). Development of problem solving strategies in infancy. In D. Bjorklund (Ed.), *Children's strategies: Contemporary views of cognitive development* (pp. 23–66). New York: Erlbaum.

Wittgenstein, L. (1980). *Culture and value.* Chicago: University of Chicago Press.

Wood, D., Bruner, J., & Ross, G. (1976). The role of tutoring in problem solving. *Journal of Child Psychology and Psychiatry, 17,* 89–100.

Wood, D., Wood, H., & Middleton, D. (1978). An experimental evaluation of four face to face teaching strategies. *International Journal of Behavioral Development, 1,* 131–147.

CHAPTER 12

Cultural Dimensions of Cognition: A Multiplex, Dynamic System of Constraints and Possibilities

Robert Serpell
A. Wade Boykin

I. INTRODUCTION

Why does a chapter about culture belong in a handbook on perception and cognition? We would distinguish three main lines of argument. First is the argument from intentionality. Thought is always an adjunct to the formulation or planning of action. Thus theoretical models of thinking are most appropriately considered "as models of ways in which individuals interact cognitively with objects and structures of situations" (Greeno, 1989, p. 136). As Bruner (1990) has noted, one of the motivating themes of the "cognitive revolution" at its inception in the late 1950s was the desire to restore to scientific psychology an acknowledgment of humans as purposive actors. These purposes, as the sister disciplines of anthropology and sociology have long been wont to emphasize, arise in large part from social interaction with other intentional agents to whom we like to present our actions as intelligible and appropriate. And it is the sharing of culture that makes this possible.

Second is the argument from communication. Representation is central to the analysis of thinking and problem solving. As a cognitive act, it draws on a repertoire of symbols that acquire meaning by virtue of their currency within a system of communication among a section of the world's population. "[To] understand man you must understand how his experiences and his acts are shaped by his intentional states, and . . . the form of these intentional states is realized only through participation in the symbolic systems of the culture" (Bruner, 1990, p. 33). The notion of culture is an abstraction of a system of shared meanings that both reflect and inform other socially shared phenomena such as practices, institutions, and technology.

In addition to acknowledging the cultural context of the participants, any theoretical account of cognition a scientist may generate needs to take account of the system of meanings at the disposal of the intended audience. Many of the criteria for judging the adequacy of a theory are grounded in a particular cultural perspective, a fact that acquires particular significance in the case of theories that pertain to the functioning of the very minds to whom they are addressed as an audience (Serpell, 1990).

Third is the argument from child development. Evidently, adult cognition is partly a function of prior experience, and a great deal of attention has been devoted in the elaboration of cognitive theory to its developmental genesis. The eco-cultural niche within which any given child grows up is structured by culture in at least three ways: physical and social settings; child-rearing customs; and ethnotheoretical beliefs about children (Super & Harkness, 1986). Each of these parameters reflects wider aspects of the society's culture, which collectively tend to prioritize certain fundamental philosophical themes. The criteria by which child development may be considered adaptive, leading us to regard certain forms of behavior as "more mature" than others, are thus grounded in a multiplex cultural framework. Since behavior that is adaptive in one such niche may not be so in another niche, cognitive development can only be intelligibly assessed with reference to the demands and opportunities of a particular culture.

For instance, Piaget's genetic epistemology gave rise to a burst of cross-cultural studies in the 1960s and 1970s designed to assess the degree to which the theory has universal applicability (Dasen, 1972, 1977a; Segall, Dasen, Berry, & Poortinga, 1990). Many researchers observed that the cultural context constrains the range of effective ways of eliciting evidence of a child's competence (Greenfield, 1966; Okonji, 1971). Some concluded that cultural variations in experience influence the rate at which children progress through the various stages delineated by Piaget, either in particular domains (Price-Williams, Gordon, & Ramirez, 1974; Dasen, 1977b) or more generally (Piaget, 1966). Yet others believe that the theory is fundamentally inappropriate for characterizing the directions in which children's thinking develops in cultures unaffected by modern technology (Buck-Morss, 1975; Preiswerk, 1976). While opinions differ as to the key factors contributing to the variable outcomes of these studies, it is widely agreed that the full range of inferences to be drawn from a child's performance on one of Piaget's tasks requires the interpreter to take account of the child's cultural context.

We cite Piaget's theory here because it is well known to have been subjected to a great deal of cross-cultural research. Although many other theories pertaining to cognitive development have been less intensively discussed in the cross-cultural literature, broadly similar arguments have been advanced with the support of empirical evidence to the effect that information-processing models of cognition can make accurate predictions of how people will perform on a given cognitive task only by taking account of cultural variables (e.g., Cole, Gay, Glick, & Sharp, 1971; Nunes, Schliemann, & Carraher, 1993); Saxe & Posner, 1983; Wagner, 1978).

Our task in this chapter is to explain the various ways in which culture and cognition interact. Cultural factors impinge on several aspects of the cognitive processes that an individual deploys in thinking and problem solving: knowledge base, structural organization, hierarchy of values, and pragmatic focus. We discuss this taxonomy further in Section II. Furthermore, culture itself can be analyzed in several different ways relevant to such influences on cognition. It can be construed as a system of social relationships, as an organized collection of practices that give rise to recurrent activities, and as a system of meanings that inform the interpretation of those relationships and practices. We discuss in Section III how these various conceptualizations interlock and complement one another.

In order to provide a coherent account of how these two sets of parameters interact, we believe it is essential to include both the ontogenetic processes of individual development in context, and also the historical processes of societal change. On the other hand, a notable shift of emphasis in accounts of culture and cognition over the past twenty years has been from a preoccupation with explaining differences between groups, and toward a search for understanding of the interface between any given cultural context and the psychological processes to which it gives rise. The central point of cultural (as distinct from cross-cultural) psychology is that cognition arises as an adjunct to the formulation of action plans, which in turn are embedded in a social system in which communication is essential. The development of individual cognition can be construed as a process of appropriating the resources of the culture for the purpose of socially meaningful action.

Seeking to clarify the notion of cultural integrity leads us to a consideration of the historical process through which cultures evolve. The sociohistorical school of cultural psychology provides a powerful framework for situating ontogenesis within a context of historically evolving cultural practices. We argue, however, that it needs to be enriched with a reflexive awareness of the cultural and historical situatedness of theorists and their theories, as well as policy makers and practitioners of applied psychology.

In reflecting on the impact of cross-cultural studies on the mainstream of contemporary American psychology, we have been struck by a tendency for their implications to be more widely accepted with respect to international variations than with respect to cultural variations within the United States. A striking example has been the much greater readiness to take seriously the possibility that school and preschool education may need to be designed differently for children of culturally different homes when this idea is raised with reference to a distant society than within the context of the United States (cf. Stevenson & Stigler, 1992; Tobin, Wu, & Davidson, 1989). In Section IV, we consider a number of reasons for the apparent blind spot that prevents some American scholars from transferring the cross-cultural analysis to their own society.

When we speak of *a culture,* the prototypical referent is a group of people who share a distinctive common history, language, and social institutions that set them apart from other social groups. In the late twentieth century, however, monocultural, homogeneous social groups exist less as a tangible reality than as an idealized pure form in the imagination of theorists. While we recognize that this idealization has served some useful expository purposes in the past, we have decided in the present chapter to eschew the simplification that it entails, and to focus on ways in which various cultural resources are deployed in the cognitive activity of people who live at the interface between more than one cultural tradition. In Sections V and VI, we consider two particular examples of children enrolled in a formal system of schooling at two widely separated geographic locations: low-income African-American communities in the United States, and a rural neighborhood of Zambia in central Africa.

In both cases, an important feature of the schoolchild's experience is a sharp disjunction between the cultural premises of the school curriculum and those of the child's socialization at home. The origins of this disjunction are historical, and its contemporary manifestation is sustained by political forces in the societal macrosystem. At the level of the individual's experience, the cognitive challenge posed by the disjunction can be addressed in a number of ways, each of which has specifiable implications for the understanding of the child's thinking and problem solving. We trace these implications in some detail both through an interpretive analysis and by presenting a selection of results obtained by means of systematic empirical research.

Our decision to focus on groups living at the interface between two contrasting cultural traditions requires us to deal explicitly with certain issues that have often been ignored in the theoretical and empirical literatures of both cultural and cross-cultural psychology. In Section VII, we discuss the significance for psychological functioning of the mutual perspectives of interacting cultural systems on one another; of the range of depth and integration characterizing an individual's pattern of participation in each of two juxtaposed cultural systems; and of alternative forms of interpenetration among coexisting cultural traditions both at the level of society and within a single individual's cognitive repertoire.

Finally, because we believe that the science of psychology, especially those subfields concerned with cognition and development, has an enduring obligation to remain accountable to the recipients and practitioners of education, in Section VIII we consider the implications of our analysis for the design of schooling and the training of teachers. Like many others, we believe there are clear logical connections between the goals of research on cognitive development and those of professional practice in education. And the cultural contextualization of theory in the former field has implications for how those connections are realized in practice (cf. Forman, Minick, & Stone, 1993; Moll, 1990).

II. DIMENSIONS OF COGNITION AMENABLE TO CULTURAL INFLUENCE

Cultural factors impinge on several aspects of the cognitive processes that an individual deploys in thinking and problem solving. In this section we shall discuss these factors under the headings of knowledge base, structural organization, hierarchy of values, and pragmatic focus. We recognize, however, that the borders between these categories are not clear-cut, reflecting the absence of a fully articulated, integrative theoretical framework for understanding their interconnections.

A. Knowledge Base

This cultural source of variation in cognitive behavior is widely recognized: living in a given eco-cultural niche affords distinctive opportunities for acquiring culture-specific knowledge and skills. An experimental study designed to examine the consequences of this phenomenon for performance on structured tasks was conducted in 1971 by Serpell in the cities of Lusaka, Zambia, and Manchester, England (Serpell, 1979). Schoolchildren were asked to reproduce the same patterns (some geometrical, others more concretely meaningful) in each of three media: pencil drawing, clay modeling, and modeling with strips of wire. As predicted from an analysis of the children's everyday play activities, the Zambians excelled at pattern reproduction in the medium of wire, and the English with paper and pencil, whereas both groups performed equally well with clay.

This "cross-over" research design helps to eliminate alternative explanations of group differences in performance in terms of broader cognitive characteristics such as "practical intelligence" (Vernon, 1969) or "field-dependency" (Witkin & Berry, 1975). Although the results do not specify in detail the cognitive and motivational processes responsible for the group differences, they make it clear that those differences arise from relatively specific aspects of experience with these particular performance media.

Similar results have been obtained in several comparative cross-cultural studies examining the impact of the respondent's culturally specific knowledge base on the skilled performance of structured cognitive tasks (Hall, Cole, Reder, & Dowley, 1977; Irwin, Schaefer, & Feiden, 1974; LCHC, 1983; Okonji, 1971; Weiss, 1987). The implications of such findings for an understanding of cultural bias in standardized cognitive testing have been the subject of extensive speculation and some empirical research. One conclusion, which commands quite a wide consensus, is that they invalidate the notion of "culture-free" or "culture-fair" tests of cognitive functioning.

The logic of the reasoning that leads to this conclusion has, however, been somewhat variable. Whether certain test items adequately differentiate between groups identified by culture remains ambiguous at best (Helms, 1992). Sattler (1988, p. 594) concludes from a review of empirical studies of standardized testing in the United States that "there is little if any evidence to support the position that intelligence tests are culturally biased," preferring the formulation that bias exists in the society's distribution of economic and educational resources among different cultural groups. The studies that he reviews were designed to assess test bias by various standard psychometric criteria of validity (predictive, construct, content, etc.). While such studies are useful in clarifying what does *not* constitute test bias, they adopt a narrow focus, and pay insufficient attention to the complex relations among the constructs inferred from test performance, the developmental opportunities afforded by a given eco-cultural niche, and the educational and occupational opportunities to which access is formally governed by test scores.

For instance, Vernon (1969), Durojaiye (1984), and others have argued from the predictive correlations found in Africa between scores on Western aptitude tests and various educational outcomes that these tests are psychologically valid and socioeconomically appropriate. Yet, the mediating construct of spatial ability that is used by psychometricians to explain such correlations may arguably be less relevant than such factors as gender and social class (S. H. Irvine, 1969; Serpell, 1993b). Extrapolating from the experimental study cited above, for instance, we might consider that in Zambia, scores on a paper-and-pencil test of pattern reproduction would predict performance on a school-leaving science examination and on supervisor ratings of engineering trainees because males and children of privileged families have a social advantage in all three domains; but a better estimate of the construct of spatial ability would be a test based on pattern reproduction in the medium of wire or clay. Multivariate studies adequately designed to evaluate such complex hypotheses have not to our knowledge been conducted either in Africa or in the United States.

B. Structural Organization

This aspect of cognition concerns the organization of form, sometimes termed cognitive architecture. The metaphor of architecture evokes an image of cognitive elements as a rather concrete set of building blocks, whereas more often than not these elements are more appropriately construed as processes, in which case the nature of their formal organization may be more aptly likened to orchestration. The kind of structuralization that we have in mind here is more domain specific and more closely tied to institutionalized practices than the better known concept of a culturally specific cognitive style. Cognitive-style accounts of cultural variations (e.g., Witkin & Berry, 1975) have been plagued with connotations of stereotypy, connected with the limitations of certain ways of characterizing cultural traditions and world views that we discuss below in Section III (cf. LCHC, 1983; Serpell, 1976).

The metaphor of architecture has been used by various neural and information scientists to characterize the constraints that they identify as universal for the human species (Estes, 1991; Hubel & Wiesel, 1965; Newell, 1990). In a certain, limited sense we agree that the structure of cognition may be biologically constrained by the anatomy and physiology of the human nervous system, with its specialized distribution of functions. Examples abound in the literature: basic coding of, for example, color and shape in multisynaptic sensory pathways; subcortical activation of perceptual processing; limbic system consolidation of recent memory; hemispherically lateralized verbal processes, and so on. Moreover, many types of environmental information have a logic of their own such that it makes sense to postulate a single, best algorithm for all people to determine the relative distance of two objects in the range of their vision (Gibson, 1966), to decide which end of a balance beam will go down depending on the distribution of weights (Siegler, 1976), or to locate a destination on a road map (cf. Feldman, 1980). When experimental psychologists isolate such problems in laboratory tasks, the cognitive operations they observe, such as encoding, rehearsal, or deduction, may appear quite similar in respondents sampled from widely differing cultural populations, leading some theorists to argue for their universality (e.g., Van de Vijver & Poortinga, 1982).

However, many of the more challenging problems in everyday life call for a deployment of cognitive resources in ways that go beyond such universal constraints. In such cases it is often a particular cultural practice that provides, through the system of meanings that informs it, a set of organizational constraints within which the thinker is invited to operate. For instance, a competent participant in a culture is conversant with a number of "routines," subsets of behavioral regularities acknowledged within that culture as having a participant structure, a set of appropriate contexts, rules of adequate performance, emotional and social connotations, and so on.

Bilingual participants in Anglo-French conferences often remark on the relative directness of the English cultural style as compared with a greater preference for elaborate courtesies and philosophical circumlocutions in French. In many ethnographic accounts of everyday discourse in African societies, adults are described as inclined to invoke a proverb to suggest an idea, whereas in many Western cultures, a more explicit didactic expository form would be more likely to be used (e.g., Ngugi, 1982; Read, 1959). In the expressive domain of narrative, a number of studies have suggested that cultural traditions vary in their preferred style and sequence for organizing the presentation of events, facts, and comments (Heath, 1983; Hicks, 1990; Michaels, 1981). Another distinctive interactional routine has been described by several researchers as constituting a recurrent structure for the expression of both cognition and affect in African-American, urban working-class culture. Known variously as, for example, "sounding," "joaning," or "playing the dozens," it consists of a sequence of elaborate insults, countered with repartees that escalate the level of disparagement, while also invoking an element of verbal artistry (Labov, 1972; Mitchell-Kernan, 1971; Smitherman, 1977, 1991).

For a cultural outsider observing such interactions, it can be difficult to grasp the indigenous criteria for evaluating the performance. Familiarity with the form is acquired as part of the process of indigenous enculturation. Peters and Boggs (1986) extrapolate from several ethnographic studies of language socialization three criteria for identifying an "interactional routine" as characteristic of a given cultural system: (1) predictability of the next step by a cultural insider; (2) consistency of children's responses to particular cues; and (3) the extent to which indigenous participant adults are able to verbalize what is going on.

The interconnections among different social functions in the overall character of cultural routines are what give them the feel of uniqueness. Thus Blacking's (1988) account of dance and music in the cognitive development of South African Venda children in the 1950s evokes a cultural ambience that accords much greater salience to the medium of music for the everyday exercise of skill and expression of affect than is regarded as normal in most Western cultural groups. Polyrhythmic interactive drumming and interactive rhythmic movement were encouraged from infancy, and construed as indispensable steps "on the path to understanding the human predicament" (p. 108). Since these activities are linked to a social medium, a Venda proverb holds that "a person [can] only become a person through social interactions with other persons" (p. 101).

C. Hierarchy of Values

Cultural values also infuse cognitive activities. This infusion can be conceptualized in two different ways. From a functional standpoint, it can refer to the valuing of certain activities over others that serve important instrumental or technological purposes relevant to the productive capabilities of a given culture. Some cultures place a premium on text-based literacy; some may place more value on weaving (Rogoff, 1990) or tailoring (Lave, 1988). In any of these cases, practice at and instruction pertinent to the activities in question promote the exercise and application of thinking and problem solving that is appropriate to the task demands of each setting and a family of relevant contexts. On the other hand, we can also conceive of values in a more philosophically fundamental way and speak of core values that manifest a given culture's belief system or world view that underlies how reality is to be codified. Certain cultures, for instance, may place a greater premium on rugged competitive individualistic achievement (Spence, 1985), while others lean more heavily toward communally based, mutual interdependence, and socially synergistic activity (Boykin, 1983; Nobles, 1991). Related to this is the possibility of fundamental cultural divergences in the very definition of self. Several authors have advanced the position that the "individualized" self prominent in many Western societies may not be a universal expression. For example, in Hindu culture, personal identity may be elaborated in a more socially embedded, relational manner, resulting in limited applicability of certain Western formulations of individual rights as distinct from social roles (Markus & Kitayama, 1991; J. G. Miller, 1994).

In contemporary Western culture, reality tends to be conceived primarily in materialistic terms. In such a conceptual scheme, the objects of reality feature as essential elements, so that thinking about objects and the manipulation of objects and the thinker's relationship to the world of objects become major preoccupations (Dixon, 1976; Okagaki & Sternberg, 1991). In other cultures, however, reality may be construed principally in nonmaterialistic terms. In such a scheme, more focus would be on nonmaterial characteristics, such as the spiritual qualities that constitute the essence of all things, so that true understanding of a phenomenon cannot be reached without apprehending such an essence. Awareness of spiritual forces operating in one's life would be a major cognitive consideration, and thinking and problem-solving activities would likely be bound up in communicating with, or in acknowledging such forces. Indeed, a major aspect of life's challenges would be bound up in negotiating with such forces, or in negotiating in general in the light of such spiritual presences or realities (Nobles, 1991).

Such different cultural renditions, with their different emphases, have direct implications for thinking and problem solving. The different value orientations are surely linked to different metaphors that are typically used for representation of events and behaviors. They are surely linked to different frequency of engagement in particular concrete activities. They underlie what is salient, what is familiar, what is liked, preferred, esteemed, and encouraged. As such they relate to what gets thought about, and to the delineation of what problems are to be solved and the "proper" manner in which solution is expected to transpire. More abstractly, they provide the lenses through which one's experiences literally get interpreted. Indeed, as such, they help frame what Greeno (1989) has referred to as "personal epistemologies," which contribute greatly to individuals' ". . . beliefs and understandings of what knowledge and learning are" (p. 136).

D. Pragmatic Focus

Collectively, the culturally informed knowledge base, structural organization of cognition, and hierarchy of values serve to direct the individual's sense of what to accomplish in a given context. This pragmatic focusing of thought can be conceptualized from two complementary perspectives: the detection and utilization of contextual cues, and the motivation of transcendant integrative themes.

The detection and utilization of cues to guide performance in a structured context can be facilitated in a number of different ways:

1. Perceptual differentiation: Because of familiarity with such contexts and experiences in the past, more cues are discernible or available to trigger appropriate, effective cognitive processes and effective solutions.

2. Functional hierarchy of attentional salience: Because of greater familiarity with the specific dimensions of relevant information and with functionally consequential patterns of information, the central aspects of the task to be accomplished are easier to discern.

3. Integrative meaning as a source of intrinsic motivation: Since the situation has salience and meaningfulness for the individual, it will be taken more seriously and valued more highly.

4. Socioemotional affect and confidence: The motivational potency of the setting is enhanced, leading to greater enjoyment, attentional focus, effort, and persistence.

The motivation of transcendent integrative themes is a more contentious idea, linked to the notions of cultural authenticity and integrity. We will discuss its rationale in Section III below.

III. CONCEPTUALIZATIONS OF CULTURAL CONTEXT

A. Relationships, Practices, and Meanings

Introductory discussions of culture often allude to the diversity of ways in which it has been defined by anthropologists (Kroeber & Kluckhohn, 1952). In this section, we distinguish three broad types of emphasis that appear to us to be of equal and complementary relevance to the understanding of human cognition. Culture can be construed as a system of social relationships, as an organized collection of practices with an associated technology, and as a system of meanings (cf. Serpell, 1993c).

Bronfenbrenner's (1979) influential formulation of the ecology of human development conceptualizes the context as an incorporating system of social activity. The interaction between the child and her context is construed as a process of socialization, whose developmental outcome is some form of integration into the social system. The structure of the context according to such theories comprises sociocultural routines, practices, and institutions. The developing child may be said to interact with this contextual structure through the process of guided participation (Rogoff, 1990), resulting in a gradual expansion of her behavioral repertoire.

An illuminating account of one sociocultural routine has been provided by P. Miller and Sperry (1987) in their account of "the socialization of anger and aggression" in a white, working-class community of inner-city Baltimore. The behavioral and situational contexts for a child's expression of anger are sharply differentiated by the caregiver in terms of her beliefs, values, and child-rearing goals, which include raising a child to be (in terms of the indigenous lexicon) neither "sissy" (unwilling to defend oneself against aggression by others) nor "spoiled" (tending to respond angrily or aggressively without reason). The recurrent interactional routine of "teasing" infants as young as two years old is construed as a socialization practice designed to generate tension combined with a playful attitude, affording the child an opportunity to rehearse semiotic moves in a sequence of turns. The same defiant words and gestures that are greeted with laughter and verbal encouragement in this teasing context are severely punished if they occur in a different context such as receiving a disciplinary reprimand.

At a somewhat larger scale of analysis, and often more immediately accessible to an indigenous informant, a social system is structured in terms of culturally specific practices[1], in which the developing child participates in

---

[1] Still more conspicuous as a cultural source of structuration for cognition are political, religious, and educational institutions. The institution of schooling, which takes a variety of forms across different societies and legitimates particular practices and routines for the promotion and direction of learning, is discussed in Sections VI and VIII below.

ways that are both legitimate and yet peripheral (Lave & Wenger, 1991). One way in which the changing form of participation can be construed as developmental has been termed "apprenticeship" (Rogoff, 1990). Cultural practices that have been analyzed in this way as contexts for cognitive socialization include cooking, storybook reading, and supermarket shopping. This theoretical perspective focuses less on the elaboration of the child's cognitive repertoire than on her changing social role, along such dimensions as legitimation and centralization.

The adult caregivers who manage this social-incorporation process not only act on children and on their environment but also actively interpret the child's behavior, development, and interaction with others (Super & Harkness, 1986). Underlying this interpretive activity a system of cultural meanings relating to child development can be inferred, which is shared among the participants in a sociocultural system.

The idea that culture is best understood as a meaning system has been elaborated in a variety of forms (D'Andrade, 1984; Quinn & Holland, 1987). One of the consequences is that the structure of the context of child development includes the symbolism distinctive to a particular culture. In Shweder's (1990) radical statement of direction for the field of cultural psychology, all human action is construed as informed by intentions and directed at mental representations. These representations constitute the forms of life in which humans participate, and through their participation both they as agents and the forms of life are constantly undergoing change. Representations are also embodied in various, relatively enduring elements of culture that are passed on from one generation to the next (institutions, practices, artifacts, technologies, art forms, texts, and modes of discourse).

Theoretical analyses of the interface between culture and cognition all tend to treat the relationship as a form of contextual embeddedness. But there are several senses in which this metaphor can be explained (Serpell, 1993a):

1. The individual is embedded in a niche;

2. Dyads (such as a mother and her infant) constitute microsystems, which are embedded in larger scale mesosystems (such as a family or a neighborhood), which in turn are embedded in an overarching macrosystem (such as a cultural group or a nation-state);

3. Individuals, dyads, and other social groups participate in activities (such as literacy), which are embedded in activity settings, which in turn are "shaped and sustained by ecological and cultural features of the family niche." Facing inward, "children's activity settings are the architecture of their daily life"; facing outward, they are "a perceptible instantiation of the social system" (Gallimore & Goldenberg, 1993); or

4. Cognition is embedded in social activities, mediated by a cultural meaning system.

The first two of these conceptions tend to formulate the cultural embeddedness of cognition in terms of location, timing, and the social organization of participation, whereas the latter two emphasize regulation, accountability, and membership or ownership. The interaction of the developing child with a cultural system of meanings can be conceptualized as internalization (Vygotsky, 1978) eventuating in competence, or more actively as negotiation (Ochs, 1990), or co-construction (Valsiner, 1991), leading to a participatory form of enculturation in which the child transforms and appropriates cultural resources.

B. Appropriation of Cultural Resources

The process of appropriation, or "taking on cognitive authority" (Wertsch, Tulviste, & Hagström, 1993), imparts to the developing individual not only confidence in her competence to act autonomously, but also a sense of membership in the group and corresponding ownership of its cultural resources. The authority of the claim, "this is my language, my culture, my community" is simultaneously based in a sense of belonging (of being owned and accepted by the group) and in a sense of control (of owning the medium and hence having the power to use it skillfully and innovatively). The shared web of meanings informs (rather than determines) the interpretations placed by each participant on the other's provisional moves, and as interaction proceeds a consensual definition of the task demands and script evolves through negotiation (Serpell, 1977b).

In the case of mathematics, the process through which this appropriation of an inherited technology is achieved has been described by Saxe (1991) as the emergence of goals in the course of participation in practices and the construction of strategies for attaining those goals, involving the adaptation of pre-existing form-function relationships. To the extent that the child perceives the goals of a given task as factitious and/or imposed by others, rather than as emerging from her own spontaneous activity, the educational process may be regarded as inauthentic and unlikely to engage intrinsic motivation. This argument lies at the root of a growing movement in educational circles to ground education in activities that resonate with the cultural meaning system of the child's home environment (Nunes et al., 1993; Tharp, 1989).

C. The Nature of Cultural Integrity

The concept of a cultural meaning system shares with the anthropological term "collective representation" (ably expounded for a psychological audience by Jahoda, 1989), and the more conventional expressions "world view," and "cultural tradition," a certain quality of "fuzziness" that calls for some further explanation. As we conceptualize it, there is some kind of functional autonomy to the symbolic aspects of a cultural meaning system. In other words, the variance in behavior and cognition explained by this notion is partially independent of the variance explicable by skill based on experience with cultural artifacts, and by responsiveness to the social organization of the immediate behavioral context.

A cultural meaning system is not a personal representation of the world encoded in a single mind ("in someone's head"), but rather a representation of the world encoded in the cultural milieu inhabited by a set of people, and thus shared by all the participants of that milieu. Thus, when we contrast two cultural groups, we would not be inclined to state that people in culture A think in linear terms (or taxonomically, or in affective-expressive ways); rather we would state that culture A is preoccupied with linear (or taxonomic, or affective) issues, and that the culture's preoccupation with certain topics gives rise to certain distinctive and appropriate forms of discourse and associated practice, that are more likely to be invoked by knowledgeable participants (sometimes known as members or owners) of that culture than by those of another culture that privileges different topics and forms of discourse.

A cultural practice, or recurrent activity, is psychologically lifeless until we acknowledge its connection with a system of values. It is to the characterization of the value hierarchy of a cultural meaning system that Boykin's (1993) notion of cultural deep structure is addressed. The depth that this designation is intended to connote is not along a dimension of the individual mind (as in the psychoanalytic conception of the unconscious). It refers to the fact that certain aspects of a cultural system of beliefs and practices serve a more profound organizing function than others, and may thus be considered philosophically fundamental. For instance, the principle of communal interdependence is presented below as a fundamental theme of both the indigenous perspective of rural Chewa society in central Africa, and the Afro-cultural domain of African-American culture. This type of transcendent integrative theme provides a complementary way of understanding the significance of culture in the pragmatic focusing of thought in context.

The very notion that culture is structurally organized implies some degree of internal consistency or coherence, and claims of authenticity or integrity for a cultural tradition generally rest part of their argument on evidence of such coherence. Yet coincidental events can also have a major impact on the course of a society's history. Moreover, awareness of the original stimulus for a cultural innovation is often lost over the course of history, while the practice itself remains firmly embedded within the cultural tradition. Nevertheless, all human societies construct narrative accounts of their history as an interpretive resource on which successive generations can draw for articulating a sense of collective ownership/membership of a dynamically changing system of meanings. It seems essential, therefore, to include a historical dimension in the cultural psychology of cognition.

D. The Significance of History

The sociohistorical school of thought that has emerged from a renewed interest in the writings of Vygotsky (1978) has articulated one account of the relations among ontogenesis, enculturation, and cultural change over the course of social history (Forman et al., 1993; LCHC, 1983; Moll, 1990; Rogoff, 1990; Wertsch, 1985). While we see much to commend this perspective, we also detect two major areas of difficulty. First, the explicit parallels drawn between diachronic change at multiple levels invite the drawing of potentially misleading analogies between evolution, history, and ontogenesis. Children develop from immaturity toward maturity and in some domains, at least, generally achieve a modicum of progress. But it does not follow that societies generally develop in the same progressive sense.

As Scribner (1985) has argued, it is necessary at the very least to acknowledge that the histories of particular societies constitute a separate level of analysis from the broader changes in human culture over the period from stone-age to iron-age technology, which in turn is best considered as discontinuous from the period of prehominid evolution. The temptation to search for examples in the contemporary world of "residual," stone-age cultures that can be treated as a "zero-point" on some continuum of cultural evolution (Konner, 1981) reflects the endurance of mythological themes in Western social scientific theorizing (LCHC, 1983; Wilmsen, 1990).

What is needed is a theoretical framework that acknowledges the possibility of "progress" within culturally structured contexts, without ordering those contexts along a continuum of progress. While the international interdependence of the modern world makes a radical cultural relativism untenable for many widely valued purposes, we nevertheless consider that understanding a less privileged and prestigious sociocultural system in its own terms is an essential starting point or bridgehead (Horton, 1982) for constructive international communication among different cultural groups, and (as we shall explain in more detail in Section VIII) for unleashing the competencies of individuals socialized in a "minority" culture when they are called upon to operate within a relatively culturally alien, "mainstream" context.

In our view, the transcendent organizing themes that characterize a given cultural system arise from a complex interplay among the patterns of historically accumulated semiotic resources, technological practices, and systems of social organization (Serpell, in press). Ong's (1958) account of the web of consequences of the proliferation of printed texts, Merchant's (1980) account of the Renaissance scientific program of control over nature, Weber's (1958) account of the Protestant Ethic, and Berlin's (1956) account of the Enlightenment philosophy, each illustrate the complexity of these relations for a salient dimension of European cultural tradition that has exerted a powerful influence on the contemporary Euro-American culture.

Although there is a good deal of diversity among African philosophers, many of them have commented on the contrast between some of these themes in European culture and the ontological, epistemological, and axiological perspectives indigenous to African cultures (Abraham, 1962; Mbiti, 1970; Wiredu, 1980). Boykin (1983) has identified several major lines of convergence among the works of social historians, anthropologists, educators, and philosophers, which have been taken up within the framework of Black Psychology (Jones, 1979; Nobles, 1976) as a basis for articulating the distinctive character of an Afro-cultural ethos, within which he distinguishes nine salient dimensions: spirituality, harmony, movement, verve, affect, communalism, expressive individualism, orality, and social time perspective.

This profile stands in contrast to the profiles of other cultures not in terms of the absolute presence or absence of a given feature, but as a total configuration with a particular hierarchy of values. Unlike the more ecologically determined accounts of cultural practices favored by other cross-cultural theorists (e.g., Berry, 1971; Levine, 1990; Segall et al., 1990; Whiting, 1963), Boykin's conceptual approach emphasizes value-laden meaning systems, and derives its validation in part from philosophical, metatheoretical considerations. Further, the specific contents of the nine dimensions constitute distilled interpretations derived from a diverse and wide-ranging literature, yet may be subject to refinement or more substantial modification in the future in light of empirical data or other forms of evidence.

The second difficulty that we see with the neo-Vygotskian account of the interface between culture and cognition is a tendency to emphasize human actions in the physical world and economic activities. Like the concept of social progress, technological mastery over the physical world was a salient cultural theme in the society to which Vygotsky's theorizing was addressed. But this may not adequately reflect the hierarchy of values that informs other societies' perspectives on child development.

It is probably no accident that many of the cross-cultural studies grounded in the sociohistorical school have focused on activities related to distinctive features of each society's material culture, such as, for example, pottery, weaving, and cooking. So long as these activities are presented as merely illustrative of the influence of a culturally informed knowledge base on cognitive performance, there is no reason to give greater attention to one than to another. But when extrapolating to the wider domain of public policy, there is a danger in assuming that the focus is itself free of cultural bias. Interpretations of history can no more reasonably aspire to present an Olympian perspective (Berrien, 1967), or a "view from nowhere" (Nagel, 1986), than can cross-cultural theories of psychology (Serpell, 1990). Spiritual values and social processes are just as integral to the understanding of human history as technological efficiency, and a less progressivist ideology than that which informs much of Western public policy would likely pay more attention to the connections between socialization practices and education on one hand and the quality of children's social and spiritual development on the other.

It is not only theorists and policy makers whose cultural preoccupations tend to narrow their understanding of cultural dimensions of cognition. In the field of applied psychology, there is also a tendency to overlook the influence of culture on the practitioner's technical activities. Sternberg (1984) argues cogently for the necessity of complementing his "two-process" and "componential" sub-theories of intelligence with a third, "contextual" sub-theory. But his account focuses only on context as the socializing environment of the person whose intelligence is to be assessed. An additional dimension of context surrounds the activity of assessment—a context that implicates not only the subject of assessment but also the author. The very agenda of assessment, as well as the agenda of measurement and the agenda of theorizing are all culturally informed agendas. They would have no meaning to an audience that is situated in a radically different cultural system (e.g., that of a relatively isolated village with a close-knit, kinship-based community, a small-scale, subsistence economy, and no system of formal schooling).

This culturally contextualized account of the process of assessment meshes with Sternberg's (1984) relativistic treatment of the socializing environment of the person whose intelligence is to be assessed as follows. Not only does the assessor need to know about where the subject is coming from and the directions in which her/his developmental niche is steering her development in order to know what to measure, but the assessor also needs to pose the reflexive questions, "What is the cultural meaning of the activity in which I am engaged? How can my assessment serve as a guide to action in the life of this individual? How does my perspective on this individual's behavior relate to that of the subject and to that of the various audiences that I am in a position to address (the parents, the teachers, the state's various social service agencies, etc.)?"

IV. A BLIND SPOT IN AMERICAN PSYCHOLOGY

The field of academic research known as cross-cultural psychology first came into sharp focus in the 1960s and 1970s (Berry & Dasen, 1974; Cole &

Scribner, 1974; Price-Williams, 1969; Serpell, 1976; Whiting, 1963). Yet, despite the widespread articulation of its fundamental relevance to theories of human cognition and development and the accumulation of a good deal of empirical research, its status has remained somewhat marginal to mainstream Western psychology. Levine (1989) has offered a thoughtful analysis of the reasons for this phenomenon with respect to human development. He suggests three reasons for its occurrence: the *optimality assumption* (which tends ethnocentrically to construe non-Western cultural forms as deviant and deficient); the *assumption of endogenous development* (which tends to prioritize biological over social factors in the explanation of development, and thus construes cultural variations as marginal); and the *assumption of methodological rigor* (which tends to discount accounts of development that are grounded in naturalistic, ethnographic, or interpretive study methods in favor of those that are documented through the methods of standardized testing and/or experimentation).

The optimality assumption treats the particular cultural practices favored by middle-class, formally educated Anglo-Americans with respect to various psychological domains (cognitive functioning, interpersonal relationships, parenting, etc.) as a normative standard against which to rate all human development. As participants, if not trend setters, in the mainstream of contemporary Western culture, American psychologists share a preoccupation with certain cultural themes, including such core values as the competitive individualism and materialism discussed in Section IIC above, as well as more concrete, overt societal goals such as technological and bureaucratic efficiency (Berger, Berger, & Kellner, 1973). Their theories and models are selected not only because they capture some of the variance in observed behavior but also because that portion of the variance appears especially illuminating and empowering from the perspective of an actor or set of actors engaged in an ongoing flow of socially organized activities (Serpell, 1990). Taking for granted the structuration of a contemporary Western industrialized society prioritizes certain types of data and intervention strategies over others, for example, test-based assessments of competency, school-based presentation of information, financially remunerative forms of cognitive achievement, and employment-based opportunities for economic productivity.

In recent years, the ideological supposition that cultural traits such as the cultivation of a need for achievement have contributed in a substantive way to the international economic and political ascendancy of Western societies (cf. McClelland, 1961) has received critical attention. It is, for instance, very hard to reconcile this supposition with the extraordinary rate of economic progress achieved by Japan without any marked diminution in the local culture's traditional valuation of *amae,* a relationship of passive dependency between the young child and his or her mother (Azuma, 1984; Spence,

1985). There remains, however, a resilient assumption that, at least under local conditions ("on its own turf"), the psychological orientation of mainstream, middle-class Western culture is ideally suited to the attainment of generally desirable outcomes.

The possibility that things might be otherwise for people in Japan, Africa, or some other, far-off land seems to be less disconcerting for many Americans than the challenge that arises from the postulation of significant alternative forms of psychological adaptation within their own society. If this seems paradoxical in a society with such a salient history of immigration from many lands, it should be recalled that the ideological theme of a common national identity forged by people from many lands has had to compete with the residual prejudices of a society founded on radical political inequalities among the indigenous peoples, the European settlers and their slaves. Thus, within American society, cultural differences have most often been construed as evidence of deviance, inferiority, or deficiency, variously attributed to genetic weaknesses or environmental deprivation, which in turn lead to inadequate psychological functioning (Cole & Bruner, 1971; Howard & Scott, 1981).

On the other hand, the notion of "color-blind" egalitarianism that came into favor in liberal circles in the context of the civil rights movement of the 1950s and 1960s has come to be regarded as philosophically inadequate to deal with the persistence of discriminatory practices. Rather than hoping to make differences disappear by insisting that they are of no ethical importance, we would favor seeking to create a "culturally visioned" society (Boykin, 1993), in which individuals are encouraged to define their unique identity with explicit reference to various cultural themes, and to negotiate their relations with others on the basis of their behavior rather than of superficial appearances. In this respect, we regard the connection between ethnicity and culture in a similar fashion to that proposed between sex and voice in the work of Gilligan (1982). Just as the "different voice" that she has articulated is gendered but not restrictively accessible only to people of female sex, so also the cultural values attributed by Boykin (1983) and others to the Afro-cultural domain[2] are intrinsically linked, but not exclusively restricted, to African-origin ethnic group membership.

One reason for resisting the overt acknowledgment of cultural diversity as an inherent characteristic of American society may be a fear that it could lead to a political fragmentation of the nation. This fear may derive some unwarranted sustenance from the tendency for cross-cultural researchers to select for comparison two or more societies that are completely isolated from one another. Yet "pure form," monocultural, homogeneous societies, untouched by some other cultural system, are surely quite scarce in the

---

[2] The Afro-cultural tradition is discussed further in Section V below.

contemporary world. It may be important to study these rare instances for reasons of explanatory parsimony, to discern "untarnished" non-Western cultural forms, or to provide a rigorous test of universal principles. But explanatory appraisals based on such contrastive analyses are inherently limited in relevance to the kaleidoscopic, multicultural configurations of many countries of the world today, including the United States. The studies reviewed in Sections V, VI, and VII below attempt to address some of the cognitive complexities of life in such multicultural societies.

One of the salient features of interaction among cultural systems that coexist in a single society is the tendency for their resources to become stratified along dimensions of prestige. The historical origins of such asymmetries are political in nature, and confronting them can be a socially uncomfortable process. Many American psychologists express a preference for keeping the domains of political analysis and scientific research sharply separated. As a result, they tend to treat differences in social status as if they were static phenomena, and/or direct consequences of individual characteristics rather than the dynamic constructions of social relations. Resistance to the inclusion in a psychological analysis of the uncomfortable topic of political oppression may thus be a further factor contributing to the blind spot that we have identified. For, from our perspective, a cultural account of cognitive development in minority groups of the United States cannot dispense with such an explicit political dimension.

A more specific factor that seems to militate against the type of cultural analysis we wish to advance of cognitive development among African-Americans is a strikingly powerful popular disbelief in any cultural continuity with Africa. There may be several dimensions to this phenomenon. One is a relatively unsophisticated insistence on the authenticity of a pan-American insider's cultural intuition: Americans (whatever their ethnicity) are wont to express a strong sense of cultural identity as Americans. Another reason is the absence of some salient manifestations of culture such as language, mode of production, or formal institutions to serve as ostensible indicators of continuity: given that slaves from Africa did not pass on their indigenous languages and the like to their descendants, many Americans find it implausible to suppose that they could have preserved any other cultural characteristics.

We would argue, however, that cultural themes such as those represented in Boykin's nine dimensions may be susceptible to tacit intergenerational transmission without the mediation of language or explicit institutional processes. Early communicative socialization, for instance, is grounded in microlevel patterns of behavioral coordination that establish and expand the scope of intersubjectivity even before the advent of speech (Trevarthen & Hubley, 1978), and sensory thresholds may be profoundly influenced by early patterns of ambient stimulation. Even as abstract a disposition as spirituality may arise in part from the cumulative elaboration of intuitive interpersonal interactions.

Finally, there is the generally negative stigma with which Africa has been marked in Western culture. Related to this are two defensive concerns commonly expressed by African-American critics of the thesis of Afro-cultural continuity. Some argue that identification of African-Americans as a group associated with Africa will tend to bring into ridicule a group already burdened with oppressive barriers against upward social mobility, and thus "play into the hands of racists." Others argue, in a more general vein, that the specification of any psychological characteristics as intrinsically linked to African ethnicity tends toward the promotion of ethnic stereotypes, and thus runs contrary to their (pan-American) ideological commitment to individualism.

The relations among such political concerns and the responsibilities of theorists and practitioners of cognitive and developmental science will be taken up again in Sections VII and VIII. Meanwhile, in concluding this section, we would reiterate that there does not appear to us to exist any sound, logical reason for separating the insight of cross-cultural psychology, namely, that different societies tend to structure the eco-cultural niche of child development in systematically different ways with identifiable consequences for the pattern of cognitive development, from the likelihood that cultural variations among ethnic groups in the United States give rise to identifiable differences in child socialization and cognitive development. Given the remarkable cultural diversity that characterizes contemporary American society, we contend, therefore, that the study of thinking and problem solving in mainstream American psychology stands to gain considerably in theoretical power by the inclusion of cultural processes as an essential dimension of analysis.

V. COGNITION AND SCHOOLING IN LOW-INCOME AFRICAN-AMERICAN COMMUNITIES: EMPIRICAL STUDIES

It is commonplace when studying immigrant minority groups in North America to acknowledge that they bring with them elements of a coherent alternative cultural tradition, including language, values, and practices. On this view, while different from the culture of the host society, that foreign culture has its own integrity (cf. Ogbu, 1990). But when it comes to domestic minority groups within the United States, until recently little attention has focused on illuminating integrity-based cultural factors that may be nonisomorphic to mainstream American cultural ethos. However, in more recent times, such acknowledgment is beginning to be shown (Tharp, 1989).

Many scholars have pointed to cultural manifestations among African-

Americans, especially of low-income backgrounds, that are postulated to be continuations of traditional African cultural legacy (Ladson-Billings, 1992; Nobles, 1991; Thompson, 1983). Boykin (1983, 1986) has argued that such cultural manifestations help comprise one of three distinct but interlocking realms of social experience in which African-Americans participate. Beyond this Afro-cultural realm, there is also the Minority realm and the Mainstream realm. The Minority realm speaks to experiences bound up in, for example, racial oppression, low status, and social marginalization. The Mainstream realm involves experiences attendant to the dominant cultural mores and institutions in American society. In Section VII, we shall discuss the nature of the triple quandary (Boykin, 1986) that arises for African-Americans growing up at the nexus of these three contrasting experiential realms.

At this juncture, we would argue that the Afro-cultural realm deserves special attention for several reasons. It has been the most distorted, least understood, and least acknowledged aspect of the overall African-American experience. It also is postulated to have a certain developmental primacy for many African-Americans and thus comes to frame participation in and orientation toward other realms (Boykin & Ellison, in press). Consequently, it helps shape the approaches that many African-American children take when they interact with the mainstream dominated institutions of formal schooling (Boateng, 1990; Gay, 1988; Irvine, 1990). The disjunction between this cultural orientation and what is currently available in most schools provide part of the explanation for the dynamics of the schooling process and the consequent academic successes and failures for many African-American children.

Specific aspects of this Afro-cultural ethos have been identified. They include movement expressiveness or a premium placed on the interwoven mosaic of movement, dance, music, percussion, syncopated rhythm; communalism, which denotes a commitment to the fundamental interdependence of people and to social bonds and group responsibility; affect, which implies a focus on emotional expressiveness linked to the co-importance and intertwining of thoughts and feelings; and verve, which involves an especial receptiveness to high levels of intensity and variability in physical stimulation.

In the terms of our analysis in Sections II and III above, the existence of such distinctive themes in the Afro-cultural repertoire would imply that certain ways of structuring the context in which tasks are presented would tend to be particularly effective in guiding the cognitive performance of African-American children because of perceptual differentiation, functional hierarchy of attentional salience, integrative meaning as a source of intrinsic motivation, and socioemotional affect and confidence. Following from this, in recent years Boykin and his colleagues have attempted to forge a research program aimed at discerning the potential value of proactively infusing Afro-cultural expression into cognitive-performance contexts. By means of experimental manipulation, they have constructed various contexts and conditions for task performance and learning, in order to determine prescriptions, if justified, for eventual incorporation into formal educational settings. In pursuing this tack, possibly fruitful academic methods can be put in the service of many African-American children who are placed at educational risk.

In this work, Boykin and his associates have generated learning and performance contexts that provide an opportunity for rhythmic-movement expression (Allen & Boykin, 1991; Boykin & Allen, 1988); responsiveness to stimulation variability (Boykin, 1982; Boykin & Allen, in press; Tuck & Boykin, 1989); and cooperative/communal expression (Albury, 1993; Ellison & Boykin, 1994; Jagers, 1987). They have examined the impact of such contexts, relative to more "traditional" ones on learning and performance outcomes and processes, and on motivation. Among the more salient findings have been that the providing of rhythmic music and the opportunity for movement expression significantly enhanced learning for low-income, African-American children but proved detrimental to low-income, Euro-American children's learning (Allen & Boykin, 1991). The reverse effects on learning obtained when the test materials were presented to these 1st and 2d graders in a movement—restrained, no—music condition. The tested African-American children also expressed overwhelming preference for learning under the rhythmic-movement condition as opposed to the more stationary one.

Elsewhere, Tuck and Boykin (1989) found that low-income, African-American children (4th and 6th graders) performed substantially better on a set of four different types of problem-solving tasks when the tasks were presented in a random order, regardless of type, as opposed to when they were presented blocked by type. This format manipulation represented an operationalization of the verve dimension. The enhanced performance under the former, more varying, format was directly related to the perceived level of physical stimulation present in a child's home environment. Yet the level of home stimulation was inversely related to teacher perceptions of an African-American child's academic performance and motivation levels. A corresponding sample of low-income, Euro-American children also performed better under the more varied format than under the unvaried presentation format, but the difference for the African-American children was significantly more pronounced. Moreover, the Euro-American children's performance did not relate systematically to teacher perceptions and home stimulation.

An investigation by Albury (1993) is also worthy of note. When comparing four different learning conditions for 4th and 5th graders, she found that low-income, Euro-American children's learning gains were at their highest and low-income, African-American children's gains were at their lowest under an individual learning condition where children worked individually and were individually rewarded for their learning outcomes. However, learning gains were at their highest for African-American children and at their lowest for Euro-American children who were placed in a communal learning condition where three children had to work together simply to help each other out without any external reward inducement. In this study, it was further revealed that in the communal condition, African-American children reported utilizing more sophisticated group-process learning strategies than did their Euro-American counterparts.

Taken together, the results of these experimental studies are consistent with the cultural-process argument advanced in this chapter. When contexts offer African-American children the opportunity for Afro-cultural expression, competencies are revealed and performance and motivation are enhanced.

VI. THE SIGNIFICANCE OF SCHOOLING IN A RURAL AFRICAN NEIGHBORHOOD: A CASE STUDY

One line of evidence about the system of cultural meanings within which cognitive development is interpreted comes from the analysis of indigenous terminology. The initial goal of Serpell's (1993b) study in the rural Chewa neighborhood of Kondwelani in eastern Zambia was to arrive at an understanding of what is meant by intelligence in a rural African community. The question was approached in a somewhat indirect manner for methodological reasons that have been discussed elsewhere (Serpell, 1977a). Adults who were familiar with a group of children of the same gender and age range living in a single small village were asked to select one among them for each of a series of imaginary tasks—tasks which could be regarded as high in "ecological validity" (Brunswik, 1956), but which contained a sufficient element of novelty to demand more from the child than mere repetition of a well-established routine. After the respondent had selected a child, she or he was asked to justify the choice and a record was made of the precise terminology used in these replies. None of these tasks had any connection with the activities of schooling, and very few of the children in question were yet enrolled in school.

Among the set of words describing children's intellectual dispositions deployed by our respondents in these structured conversations there emerged a family of characteristics that may be globally designated as qualities of *nzelu* (broadly corresponding to intelligence), within which we can discern three main groups of terms, one of which can be further subdivided into two subgroups. The dimensions of meaning that this lexicon articulates can be characterized as follows: (1) *nzelu,* in addition to its function as an over-arching term, specifies a dimension of wisdom whose primary thrust is the notion of the complete person, who has all that it takes to be truly *wa-nzelu;* (2) the *-chenjela* dimension, which corresponds quite closely to the English notion of cleverness and intellectual alacrity. This is a component part of *nzelu* so that the term *nzelu* is sometimes used to connote just this sub-dimension, whereas the term *-chenjela* is more precisely attuned to this dimension; (3) the *-tumikila* dimension, which is perhaps best expressed in English by responsibility. This includes two subdimensions: (3a) the *-mvela* subdimension, which comprises the domains of listening, hearing, under-standing, and obeying; and (3b) the *-khulupilika* subdimension, which com-prises the notion of trustworthiness. For the kind of responsibility connoted by *-tumikila,* both of these complementary characteristics are required: a cooperative responsiveness to others, and a commitment to honesty and truthfulness. These together make up a person who is known as *-tumikila,* a person who can be sent, who can be entrusted with responsibility.

A tension between the *-chenjela* and *-tumikila* dimensions arises from the possibility that the intellectual alacrity of the *-chenjela* dimension is poten-tially either creative or destructive. It is capable of being deployed in a socially productive way, in which case it is indeed part of what is required of a true *nzelu.* On the other hand, it can also be deployed in a selfish, self-advancing manner that is socially counterproductive and results in the indi-vidual being perceived as lacking in true *nzelu.* One well-known illustration of this tension is the character from African folklore known as *Kalulu* in Chi-Chewa, who is a hare. This character is known to the English-speaking culture of the United States through an oral tradition imported from Africa, and eventually welcomed into the annals of English literature under the name of Brer Rabbit. The character of *Kalulu* is primarily endowed with the *-chenjela* dimension of *nzelu.* He is a clever fellow whose mischievous, ma-nipulating attitude is by and large socially counterproductive. Both the humor and the moral implications of his various pranks hinge on a recogni-tion by the audience of the essentially self-interested nature of his brand of intelligence.

The etymology of the term *-tumikila,* literally a person who is fit to be sent (*-tuma*), illustrates how the system of meanings indigenous to a culture both reflects and sustains the culture's traditional practices. In rural Chewa society, and indeed quite widely across African societies, sending a person on an errand is a pervasive practice, beginning with asking a toddler to fetch you something you cannot reach without standing up, and extending to commissioning a friend to make a purchase for you while away on a journey out of the neighborhood. To be "sent" on such an errand is a sign of recognition as a responsible person and as a comrade. The appearance of strictness that many traditional African parents project to Western eyes arises in part from the frequency with which such assignments are given to children at an early age. But in a society where obedience (-mvela) is regarded as a sign of responsibility (ku-tumikila) rather than of weakness or lack of imagination, errands are more of an opportunity for displaying competence than an infringement of freedom.

Echoes of this taxonomy can be found in the vocabulary of evaluative discourse about intellectual functioning and development in several other African cultures. Key terms corresponding to at least two of the three dimensions of nzelu delineated above were identified in studies independently conducted among the Ba-Bemba in northern Zambia, the Ba-Ganda in Uganda, the Tale in Ghana, the Djerma-Songhai in Niger, the Kipsigis in Kenya, and the Baoule in Ivory Coast. Only the last two of these studies were conducted with any knowledge of findings among the Chewa. Yet many of them underline the importance of the social-responsibility dimension represented by the Chewa concept of -tumilikila.

Because of the intimate linkage evoked above between social cooperation and intelligence in Chewa culture, it may be tempting for some readers to conclude that intellectual ability and maturity are not really valued traits among Chewa adults. For instance, Ammar's account of indigenous education in a village of southern Egypt (Ammar, 1954) describes parental socialization as focused on imparting to children the quality of adab, defined as discipline, politeness, and conformity with adult expectations. Nzelu is a much more explicitly intellectual quality than this, and other words exist in Chi-Chewa that are closer in meaning to adab: for instance, ulemu (respectfulness) and manyazai (shame, including the observance of taboo). When members of the same Zambian study cohort were interviewed as young adults, they were requested to place in rank order of desirability a set of ten characteristics, including several of the key terms within the nzelu family discussed above, as well as ulemu and some other, nonintellectual characteristics. For most of these young people, respectfulness and compassion were considered even more important than trustworthiness, cooperativeness, or intelligence.

In conjunction with this analysis of the indigenous Chewa lexicon, observations of established cultural practices and the developmental opportunities they afford yielded the following summary of the principal characteristics of the indigenous Chewa point of view for conceptualizing children's intellectual development. "Its main dimensions are:

1. Nzelu, an overarching, superordinate concept which encompasses both the notion of cognitive alacrity (-chenjela) and the notion of social responsibility and cooperativeness (-tumikila, which requires both -khulupilika and -mvela);

2. an awareness that *-chenjela* in the absence of *-tumuikila* is a negative social force which would certainly not be part of the objectives of the indigenous educational philosophy;

3. shared responsibility among adult members of the community for the socialization of children;

4. a set of assumptions, largely implicit, about the psychological processes in children's minds stimulated or enabled by various types of adult intervention and their likely, desirable outcomes over various periods of time, which collectively constitute a way of building an educational function into the everyday interactions of adults with children;

5. a range of elaborately structured, unsupervised play activities through which various cognitive skills and social dispositions are practiced and elaborated by children, over and above those acquired in the context of their various domestic and economic chores." (Serpell, 1993, pp. 73–74)

Despite the rarity with which its dimensions are explicitly articulated or affirmed in public discourse, and despite its low prestige in the arena of national and international debate about education, this system of constructs and practices encoded in Chewa culture constitutes a coherent alternative to those represented by the system of formal schooling. Moreover, the point of view represented by this indigenous system derives great strength from the facts of its familiarity and its continuity with many other aspects of contemporary life in the community. These subjectively experienced features of its social reality, perhaps more than any explicit commitment to a historical tradition, underlie its informal legitimacy and its capacity to pose a real challenge on the local stage to the might of the establishment view represented by the primary school.

The philosophy underpinning Zambia's system of schooling differs from the indigenous Chewa perspective on children's intellectual and moral development with respect to each of the characteristics highlighted above. Its theories of pedagogy and instruction are much more explicit; cognitive functions are conceptually segregated much more sharply from the conative and emotional aspects of human thought; technological mastery over the environment is construed as an intrinsically desirable feature of mental function and perhaps the preeminent goal of human development. Moreover, the responsibility for children's socialization is highly differentiated, with a clear division of tasks between the home and the school (as well as more individualized control over decision making by the nuclear family relative to the wider community), and a consequent professionalization of pedagogy complete with a mystique of what constitutes education (Serpell, 1993b, Chap. 3). The spatial, temporal, and social coordinates of the school

are classified into a compartmentalized, taxonomically ordered set of elements, susceptible to efficient management, and conceptualized as reflecting
a rational analysis of the school's pedagogical agenda of promoting the
intellectual development of the students it "processes."

As a result of this evolution, we find in contemporary Western societies,
and in the ideals propagated by modern, African school systems, a set of
assumptions that collectively stand in contrast to the ethnotheories of child
development and socialization endogenous to rural African communities.
The normal state of childhood is no longer defined in terms of immaturity
and peripheral participation in the life of the community. Instead, it has
become characterized by incompleteness and exclusion from the social domain of adult activities. Child development is no longer likened to organic
growth that will benefit from cultivation. Rather, it is conceived as the
product of an accumulation of information. The role of teacher, instead of
guiding an apprenticed, peripheral participant, has been specified as the
modular transmission of information. And the central goal of education,
rather than *nzelu,* an integrated blend of understanding and responsibility,
has been defined as technological expertise independent of moral accountability.

VII. PROCESSES OF BICULTURAL MEDIATION

Beliefs and practices that appear to "belong" to two contrasting cultural
systems often coexist within the cognitive and behavioral repertoire of a
single, multicultural individual. Not only can different cultural perspectives
coexist within a multicultural community, but they are also amenable to
various forms of psychological integration within a single person.

Primary school teachers in Zambia and in other independent African
countries occupy a strategically important, but also culturally ambiguous
position in the scenario described in Section VI. On one hand, their professional training commits them to the rationale and practices of the school
curriculum; on the other hand, their personal identities are often rooted in
indigenous norms of socialization. A preliminary analysis has been developed elsewhere of the ways in which teachers mediate the interface between
these different cultural systems of meanings and values (Serpell, 1993b,
chap. 4). The stimulus for this mediation comes from several directions.
Their professional role mandates intensive interaction with other people's
children (cf. Delpit, 1988), and most of the parents whose children they are
expected to educate have little or no experience of schooling themselves.
They need, therefore, to have "a position" on the differences and commonalities among the two cultural perspectives when interacting with parents.
Moreover, as parents themselves, they are subject to the pressures of social
comparison, and often have to decide between culturally contrastive alter-

natives on their children's behalf. Often the existence of points of conflict are communicated to teachers indirectly by the behavior of their students as they commute between the worlds of home and school. The teachers are then called on to take a position on the conflict when interacting with their pupils. Finally, it is arguable that within their own personal identities, teachers have to find ways of integrating the different themes of the two cultures that have contributed to their own development.

Yet, in some important respects the potential of this biculturation seems to be underrealized. The challenge for teachers as bicultural mediators is to identify (or build) bridges between the cultures of home and school. Such bridges can most readily be constructed through a process of dialogue and negotiation. But teachers tend to regard the school culture as privileged territory, on which parents should not be encouraged to trespass. Furthermore, in the rural African community that hosted Serpell's study, most parents seemed to conspire with teachers to perpetuate their own exclusion from the kind of discourse that would be most productive, by insisting on discussing school success only in terms of its external facets as a mode of access to secondary school, which in turn is construed instrumentally as a route for obtaining credentials to deploy in the formal sector labor market. This elitist view excludes from consideration any of the young people who do not proceed to secondary school, who constitute the great majority of all those who enter primary school.

Teachers in rural African primary schools are faced with an extraordinarily difficult version of the challenge confronting all teachers everywhere: to interpret the world for other people's children in ways that will expand their horizons and enrich their understanding without alienating them from the culture of their home community. Arguably, their own biculturation equips them uniquely well to address this challenge as mediators between the two cultures they straddle. This optimistic view presupposes that the perspectives of those two cultures, although quite different, are not irredeemably closed to one another. In practice, however, the challenge of coordinating or integrating culturally different perspectives seems to be evaded rather than confronted in the rural Chewa community that hosted Serpell's longitudinal study of schooling. Teachers, parents, and students unselfconsciously conspire to compartmentalize the domains of school and home socialization, and to align them counterproductively with a series of contrasts between masculine and feminine roles, literate and oral communication, English and Chi-Chewa language, modern and traditional values, high- and low-prestige occupations, urban and rural residence. The challenge posed by this analysis for educational policy and practice in African societies is discussed in Section VIII.

In the United States, African-American children, as we noted in Section V, are confronted with three disparate cultural realms: the Afro-cultural realm with its distinctive, yet subtly articulated and seldom formally ac-knowledged themes; the mainstream realm, which not only displays a con-trastive hierarchy of values and structural organization informing cognition, but also directly contradicts some of the core values of the Afro-cultural tradition and stigmatizes that culture as "crude" and "deficient;" and the minority-cultural realm, which derives its knowledge base and values from the experience of racial and economic oppression. The demands of this minority realm can undermine commitment to both the other realms, by placing a premium on reactive coping mechanisms for immediate survival, and on counteracting disempowerment and marginalization through what-ever devices are politically or personally expedient. In this configuration of circumstances, the developing individual is caught in a poignant, triple quandary (Boykin, 1986; Boykin & Ellison, in press) that makes success in addressing the demands and priorities of one of these realms quite easily count as failure within one of the other realms.

The impact of this triple quandary is particularly acute for children from low-income African-American communities as they enter school. In the years prior to formal schooling, these children are often cut off from mainstream-cultural practices, and in turn have relatively greater access to Afro-cultural forms (Boykin & Toms, 1985). They are, therefore, likely to bring a meaning system heavily infused with such forms into their inaugural encounter with the mainstream-dominated institution of formal schooling. Several possible consequences may arise, including the following: Children may try to shed their Afro-cultural ways generally in an effort to acquiesce to the mainstream dictates of the classroom. Conversely, they may cling tenaciously to their Afro-cultural frame of reference as a protective shield against what they experience as affronts to their personal integrity. They may adopt a minority empowerment posture, become alienated from the schooling process, and help turn classrooms into "us versus them" power contests with school personnel. They may come to differentiate among situations in which mainstream and Afro-cultural manifestations are most proper. Or they may find a way to appropriate certain mainstream cultural forms, incorporating them as extensions of their existing cultural frame of reference, and generating an integrative approach that can be applied across a greater range of contexts.

Teachers can play an important role in determining which of these vari-ous scenarios is played out. Their own biases are likely to contribute to channeling their students in one direction rather than another. By signaling what kinds of compromise they expect of their students, they can help to avert or contribute to classroom power contests, they can provide various cognitive outlets for Afro-cultural expression, and they can seek to foster various modes of compartmentalization or integration of cultural forms. The nature of this educational challenge will be further discussed in Section VIII.

There are clearly some similarities between the situations we have evoked for African-American children and for rural Chewa children. In both settings people live at the interface between two or more partially dissonant cultural meaning systems. In both cases, one of the systems is super-posed politically above the other in a hierarchy of prestige, although the lower-status system seems to exercise a complementary privileged influence on certain domains of interpersonal functioning, especially those connected with emotional relationships, domestic activities, and spiritual aspects of experience.

There are also, however, some significant differences. In rural Chewa society, the indigenous cultural system of meanings is encoded in ostensible cultural forms such as the vocabulary of everyday discourse, recurrent activities acknowledged as part of the local community's collective way of life, and rituals performed (albeit often in somewhat syncretic fusion with exogenous cultural symbolism) on the occurrence of important public occasions such as the celebration of developmental, social, or ecological transitions. In African-American communities, on the other hand, there is little consensus as to what constitute authentic expressions of the Afro-cultural tradition, and the legitimacy of displaying such potential forms is constantly open to challenge not only from cultural outsiders representing the hegomonistic agenda of the Mainstream culture but also from fellow African-Americans.

Limitations of space preclude a full analysis here of how the actors on these two social stages invoke or deploy the multiple cultural resources at their disposal to deal with the particular challenges that arise in various thinking and problem-solving tasks. But we would note that several layers of interaction can be distinguished:

1. The mutual perspective of juxtaposed meaning systems on one another, including the relative level of awareness, depth of knowledge, and tone of evaluation of each system held by owner/member insiders of the other;

2. the patterns of participation by an individual in each system, including the relative depth and breadth of that participation, the individual's level of competence or fluency in signature activities of each system, and the participation patterns of significant influential others in her social network;

3. the interpenetration of the systems, including the degree to which they are understood as mutually compatible, the extent to which they are in practice integrated, and the degree to which they are perceived as susceptible to meaningful and legitimate integration by significant influential others.

Such considerations bear on cognitive operations at the levels of knowledge base, structural organization, and hierarchy of values. Their influence on the pragmatic focus of thinking and problem solving is partly determined by the contexts prevailing in the individual's life. But these are not passively experienced. As Gumperz (1982) and others have shown in the case of code switching among bilinguals, contexts are co-constructed through processes of negotiation, in which the connotations of a particular cultural (or linguistic) form are subtly modulated in the light of an elaborate repertoire of knowledge about social structure and cultural practices shared by the interacting participants.

VIII. IMPLICATIONS FOR EDUCATIONAL PRACTICE

The analysis we have presented in this chapter construes cognition as an adjunct to intentional action, and cognitive development as involving a process of appropriation of cultural resources. Culture informs the knowledge base and the structural organization of cognition, as well as the individual's hierarchy of values. These various dimensions of cultural influence combine to focus thought by prioritizing the detection and utilization of cues relevant to performance of a given task in context. The cultural organization of context includes systematic patterns of social relationships, of recurrent activities, and of meanings. Over the course of their socialization, children gradually appropriate this complex system, becoming part of it, and by the same token coming to regard it as their own. The distinctiveness of cultures can be explained in part through a historical analysis of their evolution, including ecological, technological, and philosophical dimensions. Each cultural tradition tends to combine many such features and also organizes them into a coherent interpretive scheme, which variously informs the discourse and associated practices of everyday life, of social theory, of public policy, and of professional activities.

We have discussed the application of this theoretical perspective in relation to three topics: The treatment of cultural variation within American psychology; cognition and schooling in low-income African-American communities; and the significance of schooling in a rural African neighborhood. In Section VII, we have argued that many children grow up on the interface among two or more distinct systems of cultural meanings, and that the success with which they learn to act purposefully and intelligibly in such a society will depend on processes of mediation between these juxtaposed alternative systems of meaning. In our view, these mediational processes constitute a major challenge for education. To the extent that children are expected in schools to think and solve problems within a cultural framework that is disjoined from the system of meanings that informs their everyday lives, these tasks are less likely to engage their cognition and motivation in ways that are conducive to personal development and social integration.

The educational establishment in most societies has tended to define the curriculum in terms of a rather static and homogeneous culture. By contrast, the account of culture that we have proposed here is of a dynamic and multiplex system in which many different strands are interacting dialectically, and which the aspiring student may expect to transform in the very process of appropriation.

The crisis in American education is widely acknowledged, from the much publicized overviews of low average levels of literacy to the recurrent episodes of anguish over violence and absenteeism in inner-city schools. Perhaps the most notorious flaws in the system are the gross tax-based inequalities in the distribution of resources to public education across different residential communities, and the extraordinary persistence of ethnic and class differences in academic attainment. A similar crisis is occurring in Africa and many other parts of the third world, but it is masked by the elitist selection system, which ensures that only a very small proportion of students enrolled in the early grades will have any opportunity to complete the more advanced grades of the educational curriculum. As a result, many students can leave the schools with little or no benefit without the issue being construed as relevant to policy, since there will always be enough students "succeeding" by the system's internal criteria to fill the small percentage of places available at the next step on the ladder.

Since schools as institutions are generally construed by adult members of society as legitimate representatives of the cultural "mainstream" or "establishment," encounters between schooling and children of groups placed at risk for educational failure tend to be construed as opportunities for cultural enrichment. If, however, the form in which these opportunities are presented is insufficiently attuned to allow the student to detect and utilize cues effectively to guide his or her performance, the result of the encounter is more likely to be frustration and alienation; hence, the importance that we attach to grounding education in activities that resonate with the cultural meaning system of the child's home environment. We believe the culturally informed perspective on cognition described in this chapter should be helpful to teachers in their attempts to create: (1) outlets and developmental opportunities for existing or emerging skills and competencies; (2) increased access to pertinent information; (3) enhanced personal meaningfulness of learning experiences; and (4) heightened motivational potency of educational situations leading to greater preference, effort, persistence, and attentional focus. As we noted in Section III, this concern is shared by the adherents of a growing movement in American educational circles (Ladson-Billings, 1992; Lee, 1992; Tharp, 1989).

With respect to the particular needs of African-American children, Allen and Boykin (1992) have articulated the case for grounding a prescriptive pedagogy in a systematic analysis of cultural characteristics of their home environment that are typically neglected or even directly opposed by the traditional pedagogical practices of mainstream schooling. In order to cultivate "cultural integrity," they argue that particular attention should be paid by educators to the affirmation of psychological themes centrally valued within the Afro-cultural realm of experience. This is because, as we have noted above, many forces in society tend to divert the child's attention from these valued themes, and in some cases actively to counteract them.

We also believe that teachers should be oriented toward the process of bridging the worlds of children's home culture with the resources of the mainstream. In addition to facilitating the student's initial engagement with the learning opportunities afforded by the curriculum, teachers in their role as broker can foster approximation of mainstream cultural forms by ethnic minority students, and counter any pre-existing disposition toward alienation, to the extent that they make it clear that their educational agenda is not predicated on undermining the child's existing cultural allegiances. Rather than adopting mainstream cultural forms as symbolic appendages, or as radical alternatives that require one to shed one's existing authentic cultural self, culturally sensitive teachers can encourage students to appropriate such forms through a transformation that makes them functional for and integrative with their real-life circumstances.

The strategy of comparmentalization between the domains of home and school described in Section VII, while respecting the distinctiveness of different cultural forms, is an inadequate response to the challenges facing public education, since it fails to explore the potential for cross-cultural communication, and hence tends to fragment the society's cultural resources. The increasingly interdependent world in which we live demands that culturally contrasting perspectives enter into dialogue and attempt to negotiate a fusion of horizons (Gadamer, 1970; Serpell, 1994). Thus, teachers have a special responsibility as "intercultural brokers," who will either bridge or widen the cultural gaps that occur in classroom life (Beckum & Zimney, 1991). While the balance of importance between introduction to a "new world" and building continuity between the worlds of home and school may be variable across national settings (Tobin et al., 1989), every teacher must be concerned with the "goodness of fit" between school-based education and home-based socialization.

The social relations between teachers and their students and the larger scale relations between the school and the community it purports to serve are integral to the process of education. Education cannot be reduced analytically to microlevel instructional processes on the supposition that these are the "real" or core aspects of education, whereas the rest of the social process is somehow external or incidental. Sociocultural interaction and cultural mediation are an intrinsic part of the educational enterprise of recruiting the younger generation to a transformative participation in the wider society.

References

Abraham, W. (1962). *The mind of Africa.* Chicago: University of Chicago Press.

Albury, A. (1993). *Social orientations, learning conditions and learning outcomes among low-income Black and White grade school children.* Unpublished doctoral dissertation, Howard University, Washington, DC.

Allen, B., & Boykin, A. W. (1991). The influence of contextual factors on Afro-American and Euro-American children's performance: Effects of movement opportunity and music. *International Journal of Psychology, 26,* 373–387.

Allen, B. A., & Boykin, A. W. (1992). African-American children and the educational process: Alleviating cultural discontinuity through prescriptive pedagogy. *School Psychology Review, 21*(4), 486–596.

Ammar, H. M. (1954). *Growing up in an Egyptian village.* London: Kegan Paul.

Azuma, H. (1984). Psychology in a non-Western country. *International Journal of Psychology, 19,* 45–55.

Beckum, L., & Zimney, A. (1991). School culture in multicultural settings. *In* N. B. Wyner (Ed.), *Current perspectives in the culture of schools.* Brookline, MA: Brookline Books.

Berger, P. L., Berger, B., & Kellner, H. (1973). *The homeless mind.* New York: Random House.

Berlin, I. (1956). Introduction. In I. Berlin (Ed.), *The age of enlightenment.* New York: Mentor.

Berrien, F. K. (1967). Methodological and related problems in cross-cultural research. *International Journal of Psychology, 2,* 33–44.

Berry, J. W. (1971). Ecological and cultural factors in spatial perceptual development. *Canadian Journal of Behavioral Science, 3,* 324–36.

Berry, J. W., & Dasen, P. R. (1974). *Culture and cognition: Readings in cross-cultural psychology.* London: Methuen.

Blacking, J. (1988). Dance and music in Venda children. In G. Jahoda & I. Lewis (Eds.), *Acquiring culture: Cross-cultural studies in child development.* London: Croom Helm.

Boateng, F. (1990). Combating deculturalization of the African American child in the public school system: A multicultural approach. In K. Lomotey (Ed.), *Going to school: The African American experience* (pp. 73–84). Albany: SUNY Albany Press.

Boykin, A. W. (1982). Task variability and the performance of Black and white schoolchildren: Vervistic explorations. *Journal of Black Studies, 12,* 469–485.

Boykin, A. W. (1983). The academic performance of Afro-American children. In J. Spence (Ed.), *Achievement and achievement motives.* San Francisco: Freeman.

Boykin, A. W. (1986). The triple quandary and the schooling of Afro-American children. In U. Neisser (Ed.), *The school achievement of minority children.* Hillsdale, NJ: Erlbaum.

Boykin, A. W. (1993). *Cultural deep structure analysis of the schooling of African American children: Conceptual, empirical and practical considerations.* Unpublished manuscript, Howard University, Washington, DC.

Boykin, A. W. (1994). Harvesting talent and culture: African American children and educational reform. In R. Rossi (Ed.), *Schools and students at risk: Context and framework for positive change* (pp. 116–138). New York: Teachers College Press.

Boykin, A. W., & Allen, B. (1988). Rhythmic-movement facilitated learning in working-class Afro-American children. *Journal of Genetic Psychology, 149,* 335–347.

Boykin, A. W., & Allen B. (in press). Heuristic investigations into Afrocultural ethos: The development of the verve and movement expressive paradigms. In R. Jones (Ed.), *Advances in black psychology.* Hampton, VA: Cobb & Henry.

Boykin, A. W., & Ellison, C. (in press). The multiple ecologies of Black youth socialization: An Afrographic analysis. In R. Taylor (Ed.), *African American Youth: Their social and economic status in the United States.* Westport, CT: Greenwood.

Boykin, A. W., & Toms, F. (1985). Black child socialization: A conceptual framework. In H. McAdoo & J. McAdoo (Eds.), *Black children*. Beverly Hills, CA: Sage.

Bronfenbrenner, J. (1979). *The ecology of human development*. Cambridge, MA: Harvard University Press.

Bruner, J. S. (1990). *Acts of meaning*. Cambridge, MA: Harvard University Press.

Brunswik, E. (1956). *Perception and the representative design of psychological experiments*. Berkeley: University of California Press.

Buck-Morss, J. (1975). Socio-economic bias in Piaget's theory and its implications for cross-cultural studies. *Human Development, 18*, 35–49.

Cole, M., & Bruner, J. S. (1971). Cultural differences and inferences about psychological processes. *American Psychology, 26*, 867–876.

Cole, M., Gay, J., Glick, J. A., & Sharp, D. W. (1971). *The cultural context of learning and thinking*. New York: Basic Books.

Cole, M., & Scribner, S. (1974). *Culture and thought*. New York: Wiley.

D'Andrade, R. G. (1984). Cultural meaning systems. In R. A. Shweder & R. A. Levine (Eds.), *Culture theory: Essays on mind, self and emotion* (pp. 88–119). Cambridge: Cambridge University Press.

Dasen, P. R. (1972). Cross-cultural Piagetian research: A summary. *Journal of Cross-Cultural Psychology, 3*, 23–40.

Dasen, P. R. (Ed.). (1977a). *Piagetian psychology: Cross-cultural contributions*. New York: Gardner.

Dasen, P. R. (1977b). Are cognitive processes universal? *In* N. Warren (Ed.), *Studies in cross-cultural psychology*. London: Academic Press.

Delpit, L. (1988). The silenced dialogue: Power and pedagogy in educating other people's children. *Harvard Educational Review, 58*, 280–298.

Dixon, V. (1976). World views and research methodology. *In* L. King, V. Dixon, & W. Nobles (Eds.), *African philosophy: Assumptions and paradigms for research on Black persons*. Los Angeles: Fanon Center.

Durojaiye, M. O. (1984). The impact of psychological testing on educational and personnel selection in Africa. *International Journal of Psychology, 19*, 135–144.

Ellison, C., & Boykin, A. W. (1994). Comparing the outcomes from differential cooperative and individualistic learning methods. *Social Behavior and Personality, 22*, 91–103.

Estes, W. K. (1991). Cognitive architectures from the standpoint of an experimental psychologist. *Annual Review of Psychology, 42*, 1–28.

Feldman, D. H. (1980). *Beyond universals in cognitive development*. Norwood, NJ: Ablex.

Forman, E., Minick, N., & Stone, C. A. (Eds.). (1991). *Contexts for learning: Sociocultural dynamics in children's development*. New York: Oxford University Press.

Gadamer, H.-G. (1975). *Truth and Method*. London: Sheed & Ward.

Gallimore, R., & Goldenberg, C. (1993). Activity settings of early literacy: Home and school factors in children's emergent literacy. In E. Forman, N. Minick, & A. Stone (Eds.), *Contexts for learning: Sociocultural dynamics in children's development*. New York: Oxford University Press.

Gay, G. (1988). Designing relevant curricula for diverse learners. *Education and Urban Society, 20*, 322–340.

Gibson, J. J. (1966). *The senses considered as perceptual systems*. Boston: Houghton Mifflin.

Gilligan, C. (1982). *In a different voice*. Cambridge, MA: Harvard University Press.

Greenfield, P. M. (1966). On culture and conservation. In J. S. Bruner, R. R. Olver, & P. M. Greenfield (Eds.), *Studies in cognitive growth*. New York: Wiley.

Greeno, J. G. (1989). A perspective on thinking. *American Psychologist, 44*(2), 134–141.

Gumperz, J. J. (1982). *Discourse strategies*. Cambridge: Cambridge University Press.

Hall, W., Cole, M., Reder, S., & Dowley, P. (1977). Variations in young children's use of language: Some effects of setting and dialect. In *R. O. Freedle (Ed.), Discourse production and comprehension*. Hillsdale, NJ: Erlbaum.

Heath, S. B. (1983). *Ways with words*. Cambridge: Cambridge University Press.

Helms, J. (1992). Why is there no study of cultural equivalence in standardized cognitive ability testing? *American Psychologist, 47,* 1083–1101.

Hicks, D. (1991). Kinds of narrative. Genre skills among first graders from two communities. In A. McCabe & C. Peterson (Eds.), *Developing narrative structure*. Hillsdale, NJ: Erlbaum.

Horton, R. (1982). Tradition and modernity revisited. In M. Hollis & S. Lukes (Eds.)., *Rationality and relativism*. Oxford: Blackwell.

Howard, A., & Scott, R. A. (1981). The study of minority groups in complex societies. In R. H. Munroe, R. L. Munroe, & B. Whiting (Eds.), *Handbook of cross-cultural human development* (pp. 113–152). New York: Garland STPM Press.

Hubel, D. H., & Wiesel, T. N. (1965). Receptive fields, binocular interaction, and functional architecture in the cat's visual cortex. *Journal of Physiology (London), 180,* 106–154.

Irvine, J. (1990). *Black children and school failure: Policies, practices and prescriptions*. New York: Greenwood Press.

Irvine, S. H. (1969). Factor analysis of African abilities and attainments: Constructs across cultures. *Psychological Bulletin, 71,* 20–32.

Irwin, M. H., Schaefer, G., & Feiden, C. P. (1974). Emic and unfamiliar category sorting of Mano farmers and U.S. undergraduates. *Journal of Cross-Cultural Psychology, 5,* 407–423.

Jagers, R. (1987). *Communal orientation and cooperative learning among Afro-American college students*. Unpublished doctoral dissertation, Howard University, Washington, DC.

Jahoda, G. (1989). *Psychology and anthropology*. London: Academic Press.

Jones, J. (1979). Conceptual and strategic issues in the relationship of Black psychology to American social science. In A. W. Boykin, A. J. Franklin, & J. F. Yates (Eds.), *Research directions of Black psychologists*. New York: Russell Sage.

Konner, M. J. (1981). Evolution of human behavior development. *In* R. H. Munroe, R. L. Munroe, & B. B. Whiting (Eds.), *Handbook of cross-cultural human development*. New York: Garland STPM Press.

Kroeber, A. L., & Kluckhohn, C. (1952). *Culture: A critical review of concepts and definitions*. New York: Vintage/Peabody Museum of American Archaeology & Ethnology, Harvard University, Cambridge, MA.

Labov, W. (1972). *Sociolinguistic patterns*. Philadelphia: University of Pennsylvania Press.

Ladson-Billings, G. (1992). Culturally relevant teaching: The key to making multicultural education work. In C. Grant (Ed.), *Research and multicultural education: From the margins to the mainstream*. Washington: Falmer.

Lave, J. (1988). *Cognition in practice: Mind, mathematics and culture in everyday life*. Cambridge: Cambridge University Press.

Lave, J., & Wenger, E. (1991). *Participation in practices*. Cambridge: Cambridge University Press.

LCHC. (1983). Culture and cognitive development. In P. H. Mussen (Ed.), *Handbook of child psychology: Vol. 1. History, theory and methods* (W. Kessen, Ed.), New York: Wiley, pp. 295–356.

Lee, C. (1992). Literacy, cultural diversity, and instruction. *Education and Urban Society, 24,* 279–291.

Levine, R. A. (1989). In W. Damon (Ed.), *Child development: Today and tomorrow*. San Francisco: Jossey-Bass.

Levine, R. A. (1990). Infant environments in psychoanalysis: A cross-cultural view. In J. W. Stigler, R. A. Shweder, & G. Herdt (Eds.), *Cultural psychology*. Cambridge, MA: Harvard University Press.

Markus, H., & Kitayama, S. (1991). Culture and the self: Implications for cognition, emotion, and motivation. *Psychological Review, 98*(2), 224–253.

Mbiti, J. S. (1970). *African religions and philosophy.* Garden City, NY: Anchor Books.

McClelland, D. C. (1961). *The achieving society.* Princeton, NJ: Van Nostrand.

Merchant, C. (1980). *The death of nature: Women, ecology, and the scientific revolution.* San Francisco: Harper Row.

Michaels, S. (1981). "Sharing time": Children's narrative style and differential access to literacy. *Language in Society, 10,* 423–442.

Miller, J. G. (1994). Cultural diversity in the morality of caring: Individually-oriented versus duty-based interpersonal moral codes. *Cross-Cultural Research, 28,* 3–39.

Miller, P., & Sperry, L. L. (1987). The socialization of anger and aggression. *Merrill-Palmer Quarterly, 33,* 1–31.

Mitchell-Kernan, C. M. (1971). Language behavior in a black urban community. *Monographs of the Language Behavior Research Laboratory* (No. 2). Berkeley: University of California.

Moll, L. C. (Ed.). (1990). *Vygotsky and education: instructional implications and applications of sociohistorical psychology.* Cambridge: Cambridge University Press.

Nagel, T. (1986). *The view from nowhere.* Oxford: Oxford University Press.

Newell, A. (1990). *Unified theories of cognition.* Cambridge, MA: Harvard University Press.

Ngugi Wa Thiongo (1982). *Devil on the cross.* London: Heinemann.

Nobles, W. (1976). *A formulative and empirical study of Black families* (Final Report #90-C-255). U.S. Department of Health, Education and Welfare, Office of Child Development. Washington, DC:

Nobles, W. (1991). African philosophy: Foundations for a Black psychology. In R. Jones (Ed.), *Black psychology* (3rd ed.). Hampton, VA: Cobb & Henry.

Nunes, T., Schliemann, A. D., & Carraher, D. W. (1993). *Street mathematics and school mathematics.* New York: Cambridge University Press.

Ochs, E. (1990). Indexicality and socialization. In J. W. Stigler, R. A. Shweder, & G. Herdt (Eds.), *Cultural psychology.* Cambridge, MA: Harvard University Press.

Ogbu, J. (1990). Cultural models, identity and literacy. In J. W. Stigler, R. A. Shweder, & G. Herdt (Eds.), *Cultural psychology.* Cambridge, MA: Harvard University Press.

Okagaki, L., & Sternberg, R. J. (1991). Cultural and parental influences on cognitive development. In L. Okagaki & R. J. Sternberg (Eds.), *Directors of development: Influences on the development of children's thinking.* Hillsdale, NJ: Erlbaum.

Okonji, M. O. (1971). A cross-cultural study of the effects of familiarity on classificatory behavior. *Journal of Cross-Cultural Psychology, 2,* 39–50.

Ong, W. J. (1958). *Ramus: Method, and the decay of dialogue.* Cambridge, MA: Harvard University Press.

Peters, A. M., & Boggs, S. T. (1986). Interactional routines as cultural influences upon language acquisition. In B. B. Schieffelin & E. Ochs (Eds.), *Language socialization across cultures.* Cambridge: Cambridge University Press.

Piaget, J. (1966). Need and significance of cross-cultural studies in genetic psychology. *International Journal of Psychology, 1*(1), 3–13.

Preiswerk, R. (1976). Jean Piaget et l'étude des relations interculturelles. *Revue Europeene des Sciences Sociales, 14,* 495–511.

Price-Williams, D. R. (Ed.). (1969). *Cross-cultural studies.* Harmondsworth, UK: Penguin.

Price-Williams, D. R., Gordon, W., & Ramirez, M. III (1974). Skill and conservation: A study of pottery-making children. *Developmental Psychology, 1,* 769.

Quinn, N., & Holland, D. (19887). Culture and cognition. In D. Holland & N. Quinn (Eds.), *Cultural models in language and thought* (pp. 3–40). Cambridge: Cambridge University Press.

Read, M. (1959). *Children of their fathers.* London: Methuen.

Rogoff, B. (1990). *Apprenticeship in thinking: Cognitive development in social context*. New York: Oxford University Press.

Sattler, J. M. (1988). *Assessment of children* (3rd ed.). San Diego: J. M. Sattler.

Saxe, G. B. (1991). *Culture and cognitive development: Studies in mathematical understanding*. Hillsdale, NJ: Erlbaum.

Saxe, G. B., & Posner, J. (1983). The development of numerical cognition: Cross-cultural perspectives. In H. P. Ginsburg (Ed.), *The development of mathematical thinking*. New York: Academic Press.

Scribner, S. (1985). Vygotsky's uses of history. In J. V. Wertsch (Ed.), *Culture, communication, and cognition: Vygotskian perspectives*. Cambridge: Cambridge University Press.

Segall, M. H., Dasen, P. R., Berry, J. W., & Poortinga, Y. H. (1990). *Human behavior in cross-cultural perspective: An introduction to cross-cultural psychology*. New York: Pergamon.

Serpell, R. (1976). *Culture's influence on behavior*. London: Methuen.

Serpell, R. (1977a). Strategies for investigating intelligence in its cultural context. *Quarterly Newsletter of the Institute for Comparative Human Development, 1*(3), 11–15.

Serpell, R. (1977b). Context and connotation: The negotiation of meaning in a multiple speech repertoire. *Quarterly Newsletter of the Institute for Comparative Human Development, 1*(4), 10–15.

Serpell, R. (1979). How specific are perceptual skills? A cross-cultural study of pattern reproduction. *British Journal of Psychology, 70*, 365–380.

Serpell, R. (1990). Audience, culture and psychological explanation: A reformulation of the emic-etic problem in cultural psychology. *Quarterly Newsletter of the Laboratory Comparative Human Cognition, 12*(3), 99–132.

Serpell, R. (1993a). Interface between sociocultural and psychological aspects of cognition. In E. Forman, N. Minick, & A. Stone (Eds.), *Contexts for learning: Sociocultural dynamics in children's development* (pp. 357–368). New York: Oxford University Press.

Serpell, R. (1993b). *The significance of schooling: Life-journeys in an African society*. Cambridge: Cambridge University Press.

Serpell, R. (1993c). Interaction of context with development: Theoretical constructs for the design of early childhood education programs. In L. Eldering & P. Leserman (Eds.), *Early intervention and culture*. Paris: UNESCO.

Serpell, R. (1994). Negotiating a fusion of horizons: A process view of cultural validation in developmental psychology. *Mind, Culture and Activity, 1*, 43–68.

Serpell, R. (in press). Situated theory as a bridge between experimental research and political analysis. In L. Martin, K. Nelson, & E. Tobach (Eds.), *Cultural psychology and activity theory*. New York: Cambridge University Press.

Shweder, R. A. (1990). Cultural psychology—what is it? In J. W. Stigler, R. A. Shweder, & G. Herdt (Eds.), *Cultural psychology*. Cambridge, MA: Harvard University Press.

Siegler, R. S. (1976). Three aspects of cognitive development. *Cognitive Psychology, 8*, 481–520.

Smitherman, G. (1977). *Talkin' and testifyin': The language of Black America*. Boston: Houghton Mifflin.

Smitherman, G. (1991). Talkin and testifyin: Black English and the Black experience. In A. Jones (Ed.), *Black psychology* (3rd ed.). Hampton, VA: Cobb & Henry.

Spence, J. T. (1985). Achievement American style: The rewards and costs of individualism. *American Psychologist, 40*, 1285–1295.

Sternberg, R. J. (1984). Toward a triarchic theory of human intelligence. *Behavioral and Brain Sciences, 7*, 269–315.

Stevenson, H. W., & Stigler, J. W. (1992). *The learning gap*. New York: Summit.

Super, C. M., & Harkness, S. (1986). The developmental niche: A conceptualization at the interface of child and culture. *International Journal of Behavioral Development, 9*, 545–569.

Tharp, R. G. (1989). Psychocultural variables and constraints: Effects on teaching and learning in schools. *American Psychologist, 44,* 349–359.

Thompson, R. (1983). *Flash of the spirit: African and Afro-American art and Philosophy.* New York: Random House.

Tobin, J. J., Wu, D. Y. H., & Davidson, D. H. (1989). *Preschool in three cultures: Japan, China and the United States.* New Haven, CT: Yale University Press.

Trevarthen, C., & Hubley, P. (1978). Secondary intersubjectivity: Confidence, confiding and acts of meaning in the first year. In A. Lock (Ed.), *Action, gesture and symbol: The emergence of language.* London: Academic Press.

Tuck, K., and Boykin, A. W. (1989). Task performance and receptiveness to variability in Black and white low-income children. In A. Harrison (Ed.), *The Eleventh Conference on Empirical Research in Black Psychology.* Washington, DC: NIMH Publications.

Valsiner, J. (1991). Social co-construction of psychological development from a comparative-cultural perspective. In J. Valsiner (Ed.), *Child development within culturally structured environments* (Vol. 3). Norwood, NJ: Ablex.

Van de Vijver, F. J. R., & Poortinga, Y. H. (1982). Cross-cultural generalizability and universality. *Journal of Cross-cultural Psychology, 13,* 387–408.

Vernon, P. E. (1969). *Intelligence and cultural environment.* London: Methuen.

Vygotsky, L. S. (1978). *Mind in society: The development of higher psychological processes.* M. Cole, V. John-Steiner, S. Scribner, & E. Sonberman (Eds.), Cambridge, MA: Harvard University Press.

Wagner, D. A. (1978). Memories of Morocco: The influence of age, schooling and environment on memory. *Cognitive Psychology, 10,* 1–28.

Weber, M. (1958). *The Protestant ethic and the spirit of capitalism.* New York: Scribner's.

Weiss, J. (1987). Its time to examine the examiners. *Negro Educational Review, 38,* 107–124.

Wertsch, J. V. (1985). *Vygotsky and the social formation of mind.* Cambridge, MA: Harvard University Press.

Wertsch, J. V., Tulviste, P., & Hagström, F. (1993). A socio-cultural approach to agency. In E. Forman, N. Minick, & A. Stone (Eds.), *Contexts for learning: Sociocultural dynamics in children's development.* New York: Oxford University Press.

Whiting, B. B. (Ed.). (1963). *Six cultures: Studies of child-rearing.* New York: Wiley.

Wilmsen, E. N. (1990). *Land filled with flies: A political economy of the Kalahari.* Chicago: University of Chicago Press.

Wiredu, K. (1980). *Philosophy and an African culture.* Cambridge: Cambridge University Press.

Witkin, H. A., & Berry, J. W. (1975). Psychological differentiation in cross-cultural perspective. *Journal of Cross-Cultural Psychology, 6,* 4–87.

CHAPTER 13

The Teaching of Thinking and Problem Solving

Raymond S. Nickerson

I. INTRODUCTION

The conjunction of *thinking* and *problem solving* in the title of this chapter suggests that, at least for present purposes, these terms are not considered synonymous. Both are used in a variety of ways in the literature, and some of their connotations are synonymous, but others are not. Thinking may be done for the express purpose of finding the solution to a problem; but one may also think deeply about a subject without having any particular problem in mind. One may reflect, for example, on the structure of crystals with no other purpose than to appreciate their simple beauty. Similarly, problem solving sometimes, but not always, requires intense cognitive effort; the problem of finding one's way without tripping over the furniture in a dark room is solved by flicking on the light. Reflecting on crystalline structure can be described in problem-solving terms—the problem being addressed is that of satisfying one's desire to see beauty in one's world—and one might argue that even the simple act of flicking on a light requires some minimal thought. But this would seem to be stretching the connotations of thinking and problem solving beyond their usual bounds, at least as these terms are typically used in the psychological literature.

Here, thinking and problem solving are treated as closely related but not identical concepts. Much of the discussion will focus on thinking in the context of problem solving, or, conversely, problem solving that typically requires effortful thinking. Some attention will also be given, however, to thinking for purposes other than problem solving, but none to problem solving, like that involved in switching on the light, that involves minimal thought; although it is noted that some of the teaching aimed at improving problem solving focuses on techniques the purpose of which is to reduce the amount of thinking required.

There are several other terms that are closely related to thinking and problem solving, as they are used in the psychological literature. At the most general level are *reasoning* and *decision making*. Extensive literatures exist on both of these subjects. At a slightly less general level are distinctions within these domains, such as that between formal and informal reasoning and that between decision making under certainty and decision making under uncertainty. At a still less general level are such terms as *imagining, inferring, inventing, deliberating, reflecting, . . .* and numerous others.

I shall not try to define any of these terms precisely here. I raise the topic of terminology to make two points. (1) Interest in the teaching of thinking and problem solving extends to essentially all of the topics that can be encompassed by thinking and problem solving, very broadly conceived, and this includes much of what is typically discussed under reasoning and decision making. (2) Not everyone who is interested in the teaching of thinking or problem solving is focusing on the same aspect(s) of these multifaceted activities.

II. THE NEED TO TEACH THINKING AND PROBLEM SOLVING

There are some things that people seldom, if ever, learn to do unless they are given explicit instruction in how to do them. Playing the violin, solving differential equations, flying an airplane, and performing surgery are examples of such activities. The skills on which primary education has traditionally focused—reading, writing, arithmetic—are probably in this category, at least for most people.

Thinking and problem solving are not of this kind. Everyone thinks, and everyone engages in problem solving, with or without the benefit of formal education. This is not to suggest, of course, that people think effectively about subjects of which they have no knowledge, or that all of us can, without instruction, solve the kinds of problems one finds, say, in mathematics or physics textbooks. But people who lack any formal schooling or training abstract, categorize, generalize, make inferences, assign effects to causes and causes to effects, form hypotheses about how things work, imagine the consequences of possible courses of action, plan, strategize, scheme, and so on. All of us must do these things in order to cope with the challenges of daily life, and doing them is as natural as breathing. It is hard to imagine how one could stop doing them if one tried, and the consequences, were it possible to do so, would be dire indeed.

The fact that we think and engage in problem solving naturally and spontaneously does not mean that we invariably do these things especially well or that there is no reason to attempt to learn to be better at them than we typically are. Researchers and educators have expressed concern, especially in recent years, that many students at all levels of formal education are unable to do the kind of thinking and problem solving that their schoolwork requires (Lapointe, Mead, & Phillips, 1989; McKinnon & Renner, 1971; National Assessment of Educational Progress [NAEP], 1981, 1983; National Commission on Excellence in Education, 1983).

The 1981 NAEP study led to the conclusion that only about half of the country's 17-year-olds could write a wholly satisfactory piece of explanatory prose and only about 15% could defend a point of view effectively with a persuasive argument. McKinnon and Renner (1971) concluded, on the basis of Piagetian measures of thinking ability, that not more than half of freshmen college students could think effectively at an abstract level. Psychologists have documented numerous ways in which the thinking of many, if not most, of us appears frequently to go astray (R. F. Nisbett & Ross, 1980; Tversky & Kahneman, 1974; Wason, 1966).

Concern about the educational situation is reflected in the objective set by the U.S. Department of Education's National Educational Goals Panel (1991) of a substantial improvement in the critical thinking and problem solving abilities of college graduates by the year 2000. There is a collateral concern also for the need to develop an effective process for assessing the thinking ability of adults on a national scale (Halpern, 1992).

III. INTEREST IN THE TEACHING OF THINKING AND PROBLEM SOLVING

Interest in the teaching of thinking and problem solving in the classroom is not new. There have always been educators who see the cultivation of the thinking ability of their students as one of their most important objectives. The inclusion of logic in many curricula reflects an explicit interest in the teaching of specific tools of thought; and courses in mathematics and the sciences have traditionally given much attention to the teaching of techniques for solving problems in these domains.

Even the idea that the enhancement of thinking ability should be a special focus of education is an old one. Largely due to the influence of John Dewey (1910/1991) considerable energy was devoted during the 1920s and 1930s to making the development of reasoning ability a fundamental goal of education, at both primary and secondary levels, in the United States. Among numerous innovations directed at this objective at that time was a highly visible Eight-Year Study initiated in 1933 by the Progressive Education Association that was intended to make the cultivation of critical thinking a major focus of instruction. But educational practice did not change much as a result of these efforts, or at least did not do so for long (Cuban, 1984). Several people published books or articles on the importance of teaching thinking in the schools during the 1940s (Preisseisen, 1986). These include Gage (1940), Gans (1940), E. M. Glaser (1941), Wilson (1942), W. S. Howell (1943), and Murray (1944). As in the case of the earlier efforts, however, these appear to have produced little in the way of significant lasting change.

Thus, one might say that history is repeating itself in the current interest that is being shown among researchers and educators in the teaching of thinking and problem solving. Are there reasons to expect that the efforts that are now being made in this regard are likely to be more successful than those of previous years? Perhaps the current interest is nothing more than the latest manifestation of a recurring phenomenon that can be expected to cause a little stir from time to time, but never to make a real difference in what, or the way in which, teachers teach and students learn.

Although this possibility cannot be ruled out, there are reasons to believe that dissatisfaction with the results that primary, secondary, and higher educational institutions are producing is deeper and more widespread than it has been in the past and the need for change is more strongly felt. In particular, interest in greater emphasis on the teaching of thinking and problem solving in public schools appears to be at an all-time high. Several states have mandated the incorporation of items designed to assess thinking ability in their educational testing programs. Conferences on the teaching of thinking are being held frequently and in numerous places. Professional organizations of teachers, school administrators and educational researchers are sponsoring in-service training programs, workshops, and symposia on the subject. Teacher training organizations have acknowledged the need for more emphasis on the teaching of thinking in teacher college curricula.

Considerable research is being directed at questions relating to the teaching of thinking and problem solving, and several programs have been developed that are intended to support specific aspects of this goal at various educational levels (Chance, 1986; Nickerson, Perkins, & Smith, 1985; Resnick, 1987). Overviews of specific research and demonstration programs are contained in several edited volumes, including those compiled by Chipman, Segal, and Glaser (1985), Costa (1985), J. B. Baron and Sternberg (1986), Schwebel and Maher (1986), Presseisen (1988), and Mulcahy, Short, and Andrews (1991). Books that provide extensive information on individual programs include *Instrument Enrichment* (Feuerstein, Rand, Hoffman, & Miller, 1980), *Philosophy in the Classroom* (Lipman, Sharp, & Oscanyan, 1980), and *Intelligence Applied* (Sternberg, 1986a).

Published sets of program materials intended for classroom use include

Basics (Ehrenberg & Ehrenberg, 1982), *Odyssey* (M. J. Adams, 1986), and *Tactics for Thinking* (Marzano & Arredondo, 1986). Several books have appeared during the past couple of decades that could serve as texts or resource books for high school- or college-level courses on thinking or problem solving or that could be used to improve one's own thinking and problem-solving skills (J. L. Adams, 1974; Bransford & Stein, 1984; Halpern, 1989; Hayes, 1981; Kahane, 1992; Nickerson, 1986; Rubenstein, 1975; Ruggiero, 1984; Schoenfeld, 1985; Wickelgren, 1974).

IV. WHY THE INTEREST IN TEACHING THINKING AND PROBLEM SOLVING?

Several arguments can be, and have been, made for teaching thinking and problem solving. Some writers have stressed the importance of high-level cognitive functioning as a requirement of many job opportunities of the future (Bartel, Lichtenberg, & Vaughan, 1989; Cyert & Mowery, 1989; W. C. Howell & Cooke, 1989; U.S. Department of Labor, 1987). The ability to acquire new skills quickly, to adapt to rapidly changing workplace conditions, and to exercise judgment and intellectual initiative will be increasingly valued in the work force, it is claimed. Moreover, the robustness of economies of the future, it is argued, will depend on the availability of a workforce that is more capable of independent thinking and problem solving than those of the past (Jones & Idol, 1990; Kasarda, 1988; Reich, 1983; The Secretary's Commission on Achieving Necessary Skills, 1992).

A thinking citizenry is seen by many as essential to preservation of a democratic way of life. The reason given for making critical judgment an educational objective in the National Education Association's *The Purposes of Education in American Democracy,* published in 1938, was the need for citizens to be able to defend themselves against propaganda (Metcalf, DeBoer, & Kaulfers, 1966). Similar views have been expressed by Paul (1984), E. M. Glaser (1985), Postman (1985), and Morse (1989). Lipman (1991) also has recently characterized the role of critical thinking as primarily a defensive one: "to protect us from being coerced or brainwashed into believing what others want to compel us to believe without our having an opportunity to inquire for ourselves" (p. 144). Skepticism is healthy for a democratic society, Lipman contends, because it protects us against forces that would subvert individual rights to the special interests of powerful groups.

Some writers have argued that the problems facing society at all levels, from neighborhoods and towns to countries and the world community as a whole, are increasingly complex, and that the best hope of solving them lies in substantially improving the quality of thinking and problem solving of people on a broad scale (Botkin, Elmandjra, & Malitza, 1979). "Solutions to the significant problems facing modern society demand a widespread, qualitative improvement in thinking and understanding . . . We need a breakthrough in the *quality* of thinking employed both by decision makers at all levels of society and by each of us in our daily affairs" (Ornstein, quoted in McTighe & Schollenberger, 1985, p. 4).

It can also be argued that people who think well are better equipped to manage their lives and to adjust effectively to the realities of existence than those who do not. Many of the problems with which people are confronted in daily life are personal in nature, and how effectively they can deal with them should be a major determinant of the level of happiness they achieve.

All of these arguments can be challenged (Nickerson, 1987); which is not to suggest that they are without merit, or that they are nullified by the counterarguments that can be made against them. They have in common the fact that they justify the teaching of thinking and problem solving on the basis of the practical consequences that such teaching, assuming it is successful, is expected to have. The persuasiveness of the arguments is weakened if the expected consequences are put in doubt. For example, the belief that jobs of the future will require less in the way of thinking and problem-solving ability than those of the past, which some observers consider to be a possibility at this point (Kraft, 1987; Kraut, 1987), would weaken the first of the arguments mentioned above.

To me the most compelling reason for teaching thinking and problem solving is not the practical consequences of doing so, although I believe them to be important; it has to do with what it means to be human. The potential to reason with which each of us is born distinguishes us, at least as much as anything else, as a species. Failure to develop this potential can be viewed as a failure to find the full expression of one's humanity, and that is personal tragedy, independently of other important implications it may have.

V. FOCI OF EFFORTS TO TEACH THINKING AND PROBLEM SOLVING

Thinking and problem solving encompass a broad range of cognitive activities including logical inferencing, reflecting, inventing, imagining, planning, estimating, predicting, and numerous others. Different approaches to the improvement of cognitive ability and performance focus on different aspects of this complex of activities. There are many ways in which these approaches might be classified. Here, I shall borrow a scheme from an earlier publication (Nickerson, 1988–1989); it is somewhat arbitrary, but no more so perhaps than others that might be used.

A. Basic Operations or Processes

Some approaches to the teaching of thinking and problem solving could be described as "componential" in that they identify certain operations or processes as basic constituents of thinking and concentrate on the teaching of them. Science—a Process Approach (SAPA) focuses on observing, using space/time relationships, using numbers, measuring, classifying, communicating, predicting, and inferring, which its developers consider to be the basic cognitive processes of science (Gagne, 1967; Klausmeier, 1980). Other structured programs that emphasize basic operations or processes—which are sometimes referred to as skills, abilities or functions—include Instrumental Enrichment (Feuerstein et al., 1980), the Structure of Intellect Program (Meeker, 1969), Basics (Ehrenberg & Ehrenberg, 1982), the McREL Thinking Skills program/Tactics for Thinking (Marzano & Arrendondo, 1986), and at least the first lesson series of Project Intelligence/Odyssey (M. J. Adams, 1986; Herrnstein, Nickerson, Sanchez, & Swets, 1986).

B. Domain-Specific Knowledge

There can be no doubt of the importance of domain-specific knowledge to thinking and problem solving within a specific domain. One cannot think deeply about chemical processes or solve problems of a chemical nature unless one knows something about chemistry; the ability to observe, classify, and predict, or even an abstract knowledge of problem-solving heuristics, will not suffice.

The issue is not whether teaching should be focused on domain-specific knowledge *or* on thinking; the importance of both is generally acknowledged. Some investigators have urged, however, that domain knowledge be given a more prominent role in the teaching of thinking and problem solving than it often receives (Gagne, 1980; R. Glaser, 1984). Considerable evidence shows that the performance of experts working on problems in their domains of expertise differs in several ways from that of nonexperts working on problems in the same domains; this has been attributed to the greater domain-specific knowledge that the experts possess (R. Glaser, 1990), although it has also been argued that thinking skills are themselves domain specific (McPeck, 1981).

A question that has caused some debate is whether it is reasonable to try to teach thinking and problem solving in separate courses focused on this objective, as opposed to integrating the teaching of thinking and problem solving with the teaching of traditional content (Bransford, Sherwood, Vye, & Rieser, 1986; Bransford, Vye, Kinzer, & Risko, 1990; R. Glaser, 1984; Joyce, 1985; Sternberg, 1985; Swartz, 1987, 1991). Whatever position one takes on this issue, the results of numerous educational assessments make it clear that neither the development of thoughtful attitudes nor enhancement of the ability to think is a necessary consequence of the teaching of content; whether done in separate courses or within the traditional curriculum, improving the quality of the thinking and problem solving that students do appears to require, at least, an effort aimed explicitly at that objective.

Numerous attempts have been made to revamp courses in traditional subjects such as mathematics (Fawcett, 1983; Schoenfeld, 1985), physics (Arons, 1976; Minstrell, 1982), English (Gans, 1940; E. M. Glaser, 1941), history (O'Reilly, 1983–1985; Patterson & Jamieson, 1991), social studies (Giroux, 1978; Newmann, 1970) and others (Fuller et al., 1980) so that students will not only acquire factual information about the subjects but will learn also to think more critically and creatively about them. (SAPA fits this description, although I have put it in the class that emphasizes basic processes, which illustrates the limitations of my classification scheme.) Efforts have also been made to embed the teaching of thinking in specific contexts other than those that comprise the standard curriculum, such as jury trials (Waller, 1988) and professional decision making (Wales, Nardi,& Stager, 1986). Perhaps the best-known attempt to teach thinking in the context of a traditional subject, albeit one not usually offered at the grade school or even high school level, is the Philosophy for Children Program (Lipman et al., 1980).

C. Knowledge of Normative Principles of Reasoning

Probably the most time-honored approach to the teaching of thinking has focused on principles of sound reasoning as incorporated since the days of classical Greece in logic and rhetoric and, more recently, in the rules of statistical inference. John Stuart Mill believed the benefit to be gained from training in logic to be great; more specifically, he believed such training to be essential to reasoners who would minimize their vulnerability to the numerous opportunities that any reasoning situation provides to deviate from the strictures of logic.

Mill's emphasis on the preventive value of training in logic gains some credence from research that has shown that the logical errors that people commonly make on syllogistic reasoning tasks are not random but that specific premise combinations tend to yield certain dominant error types (Dickstein, 1978; Erickson, 1978; Roberge, 1970). Failure to recognize the fallaciousness of denying the antecedent, or affirming the consequent, in a conditional syllogism is an example of a common problem. There are many others. To the extent that specific inference forms can be identified that consistently give people trouble, it seems reasonable to expect that training with respect to these forms should help improve their thinking. More generally, the results of research support the idea that we tend to be insufficiently critical in our evaluations of formal arguments, and this tendency, too, is something one might reasonably expect to be correctable, to some degree, through training.

Some investigators have argued that many, if not most, apparent errors of reasoning are really errors of language interpretation and use (Erickson, 1978; Geis & Zwicky, 1971; Henle, 1962; Revlis, 1975). Misinterpretations of the statement "All A are B" as "All B are A," for example, would cause some of the kinds of errors that are often seen in the evaluation of syllogisms, as would misinterpretation of "If A then B" as "If, and only if, A then B." Evidence that such linguistic confusions occur is compelling. To the extent that what appear to be errors of reasoning are the consequences of such confusions, training in the more careful and precise use of language should help reduce the frequency of their occurrence.

Despite these expectations, at least since the time of Thorndike (1913) psychologists have questioned, and some have denied, the effectiveness of training in any formal disciplines, including logic, as a means of improving the quality of the thinking people do in their daily lives. Much evidence has been presented that indicates that most of us are prone to make certain errors in reasoning that a knowledge of logic and statistics ought to preclude (R. F. Nisbett & Ross, 1980; Tversky & Kahneman, 1974). Some of this research suggests that people who have had formal training in these disciplines are not much less prone to make these types of errors than those who have not had such training. The argument has also been made that formal logic has little relevance to the thinking and problem solving required to meet most of the challenges of everyday life.

It is difficult to believe that a familiarity with logic and related disciplines has no beneficial effect on everyday thinking and problem solving, and I confess to being unconvinced that this is the case. To be sure, there is some evidence that completion of a full-year course in formal logic may not decrease by much the likelihood of committing logical errors of affirming the consequent or denying the antecedant in solving conditional reasoning problems (Cheng, Holyoak, Nisbett, & Oliver, 1986), but this could be a consequence of teaching methods that do not attempt to get students to understand common reasoning errors or that fail to make a sufficiently clear connection between the principles that are being taught in class and their application in other contexts. Moreover, some of the experimental evidence of purportedly illogical behavior in experimental situations has been challenged (Berkeley & Humphreys, 1982; L. J. Cohen, 1979, 1981; Macdonald, 1986). It is not time to give up on logic, but there is a need to make more explicit its applicability to the reasoning problems of daily life.

The results of a series of studies conducted over a 10-year period, and recently brought together in one volume (R. E. Nisbett, 1993), show that not only do people who are untrained in probability and statistics display some appreciation for statistical constraints, such as those implied by the law of large numbers, in everyday reasoning, but that the quality of their thinking about statistical and probabilistic processes is improved by training in these disciplines. Evidence has also been presented that training in certain "pragmatic reasoning schemas," such as permission and obligation schemas, can improve performance on deductive reasoning tasks (Cheng & Holyoak, 1985; Cheng et al., 1986). Cheng and colleagues advocate the policy of training people to use more effectively reasoning schemas that appear to be already in their repertoire. Permission and obligation schemas are in this category, in their view, as is some form of the law of large numbers.

D. Knowledge of Informal Principles and Tools of Thought

Computer scientists make a sharp distinction between an algorithm and a heuristic strategy. An algorithm is a step-by-step procedure—a prescription, or recipe—for accomplishing a specific goal that, if followed precisely, will invariably produce the intended result. The procedure that we learn for doing long division in grade school is an algorithm. It always works; when we sometimes get an incorrect answer on a division problem, it is because we have made an error at one or more steps in following the procedure as prescribed.

A heuristic strategy, or simply "heuristic" as it is often called, is also a procedure for accomplishing a goal, but unlike an algorithm, it is not guaranteed to produce the desired result. It is a "rule of thumb" that often works, but not always. What makes it of value is that it gives one a better chance of realizing one's goal than would a trial-and-error approach, in some cases by a considerable amount. Obviously, if one were to purchase either an algorithm or a heuristic to apply to a particular problem, the algorithm would be preferred, if both could be acquired and applied at the same cost.

Heuristics are of interest to computer scientists for at least two reasons. First, many of the problems to which computers might be applied are such that no one knows how to design algorithms that will solve them. In some of these cases it is possible to specify heuristic procedures that will yield acceptable solutions with sufficiently high probability to make them well worthwhile. Second, algorithms tend to be applicable only in relatively precisely defined situations, whereas a given heuristic can be applicable over a wide assortment of problem types. These same considerations make heuristics also of interest in the context of teaching thinking and problem solving. It is not possible to specify algorithmic approaches to most of the problems that people face in everyday life, but heuristics can be described that often are helpful. And some of the heuristics that can be taught are applicable to a broad range of problem types.

Some of the heuristics on which developers of programs to teach thinking and problem solving have focused have been identified in studies of how the performance of expert problem solvers differs from that of novices (Anderson, 1990; Chi, Feltovich, & Glaser, 1981; Larkin, 1979; Larkin, McDermott, Simon, & Simon, 1980a; Lesgold, 1984; Van Lehn, 1989). Such studies have shown that experts make frequent use of certain heuristic strategies—making qualitative representations of problems, considering problems that are analogous to the ones they are trying to solve, analyzing problems into manageable components—whereas novices are much less likely to do so.

More will be said about specific heuristics strategies in a subsequent section of this chapter. Here, I wish only to note that such strategies have been at least one of the foci of some efforts to teach thinking and problem solving (M. J. Adams, 1986; Covington, Crutchfield, Davies, & Olton, 1974; Wheeler & Dember, 1979) and of books aimed at helping individuals improve their own problem-solving abilities (J. L. Adams, 1974; Bransford & Stein, 1984; Halpern, 1989; Hayes, 1981; Polya, 1945/1957; Whimbey & Lochhead, 1982; Wickelgren, 1974).

E. Metacognitive Knowledge

Metacognitive knowledge is knowledge about cognition—knowledge about thought processes in general and about one's own cognitive strengths and weaknesses in particular. It includes knowledge about how to monitor, control, and evaluate one's performance on cognitively demanding tasks. Metacognition is a relatively new focus of researchers and educators; the studies that first gave prominence to this idea occurred in the 1970s (Brown, 1978; Flavell, 1978, 1979; Flavell & Wellman, 1977). Most approaches to the teaching of thinking and problem solving now put some emphasis on metacognition in one or another way; Presseisen (1987) sees this fact as a major difference between current efforts and earlier ones.

Much of the metacognitive training that is done is aimed at helping people manage their cognitive resources more effectively. The need for such training is seen in evidence that people sometimes fail to apply knowledge they have that is relevant to problems they are attempting to solve. This can happen either because they are unaware of the relevance of the knowledge they have—say of the applicability of a specific strategy to a given problem —or they simply fail to access that knowledge when it is needed. Some writers have stressed the importance of explicitly teaching, along with problem-solving strategies, the conditions under which those strategies are likely to be helpful (Baker & Brown, 1984; H. A. Simon, 1980).

F. Attitudes, Dispositions, Values, and Styles

The importance of such cognitive-ability factors as knowledge, skills, and strategies to the quality of thinking is widely recognized. Several investigators have stressed also the importance of other types of factors, such as attitudes, dispositions, values, and styles (J. Baron, 1985; Ennis, 1969, 1985, 1987; Newmann, 1991; Paul, 1992; Resnick, 1987; Schrag, 1987). Some see the cultivation of thoughtfulness or reflectiveness, as a pervasive cognitive style, to be more important than the teaching of specific skills or strategies. Impulsiveness, the opposite of reflectiveness, has been emphasized as a disposition or style that is especially antithetical to good thinking (Ault, 1973; J. Baron, Badgio, & Gaskins, 1986; Kagan, 1966; Kurtz & Borkowski, 1987).

Ennis (e.g., 1987) lists several dispositions that he considers to be important to critical thinking. These include the dispositions to "seek a clear statement of the thesis or question," to "look for alternatives," and to "deal in an orderly manner with the parts of a complex whole" (p. 12). The reader will note considerable similarity between these dispositions and some of the problem-solving strategies discussed below. What Ennis means by a disposition, I believe, is an inclination or tendency to behave habitually in a certain way. It is one thing to understand the potential utility of taking a certain approach to a cognitive challenge, and quite another to be disposed to take that approach as a matter of personal inclination.

A strong motivation to think well is also seen to be essential, inasmuch as doing so can be hard work and is sometimes unsettling or even painful, as when it involves the critical examination of one's own beliefs (Newmann, 1991; Paul, 1992; Peters, 1973). In distinguishing between "weak-sense" and "strong-sense" critical thinking, Paul (1984) points out the difference between being able to construct strong arguments in support of one's own point of view and being able to critique one's own thinking effectively, given due weight to points of view differing from one's own. A similar distinction is that between building a case and weighing evidence impartially (Nickerson, 1986, 1991). The concept of fairness in the treatment of evidence is fundamental to these distinctions (J. Baron, 1985, 1988) and how one's behavior relates to this concept is at least as much a matter of attitudes and motivation as of knowledge.

G. Beliefs

Beliefs are relevant to the teaching of thinking and problem solving in a variety of ways. Some beliefs—for example, that thinking ability is genetically determined and not subject to change through learning, or that the major function of teachers is to dispense knowledge—can inhibit the teaching of thinking by undercutting the rationale and motivation for doing so. The belief that one's intelligence is unchangeable may also demotivate students from making an effort to learn, whereas the contrary belief that one's cognitive capabilities can be enhanced through learning can motivate effort (Dweck & Eliot, 1983; Torgeson & Licht, 1983; Stevenson, Chen, & Lee, 1993). Beliefs about the usefulness, or uselessness, of what is being studied (Lampert, 1986; Schoenfeld, 1983), beliefs about the causes of success and failure on cognitively demanding tasks (Andrews & Debus, 1978; Deci & Ryan, 1985; Dweck, 1975; Reid, 1987), and beliefs about the effectiveness of thinking (J. Baron, 1991) have been seen as important determinants of the quality of thinking and of the effort that people are willing to put into improving it.

H. Interdependence of Factors

Although different approaches to the teaching of thinking and problem solving emphasize the factors mentioned above to different degrees, none of them focuses on a single one to the total exclusion of all the others. Given the complex and multifaceted nature of thinking, it probably would be impossible to focus on any one of them with complete disregard for the rest. If it were possible, it would not be advisable, inasmuch as all are important and any attempt to enhance thinking and problem solving ability in a general way can ill afford to ignore any of them. This is not to suggest that all are *equally* important. Our knowledge of thinking and problem solving, and how they are best enhanced, is too limited to justify that assertion. A major need is for continuing research aimed at extending this knowledge and at determining more precisely the various ways in which thinking and problem solving can be improved.

What is clear is that the factors that have been discussed interact in complex ways. Borkowski and colleagues have stressed, for example, the two-way causal relationship between attributional beliefs and metacognitive knowledge (Borkowski, Carr, Rellinger, & Pressley, 1990; Borkowski, Johnston, & Reid, 1987). Some beliefs about the relationship between effort and success or failure—that intelligence is unmodifiable or that success and failure are strictly matters of luck—can inhibit the acquisition of metacognitive knowledge; other beliefs—that cognitive ability can be enhanced or that success and failure depend largely on effort—can motivate its acquisition. Conversely, the acquisition of metacognitive knowledge can help shape the attributional beliefs one holds.

Given the multifaceted nature of thinking, it would be surprising if there were only one way to improve it, or even if everyone had the same idea of what it means to think well. One risk of approaches that are narrowly focused and that fail to take many of the aspects of thinking into account is the possibility of improving thinking in one way, while impairing it in others. People can be taught to do a better job of defending their own points of view on controversial topics, for example, without becoming more sensitive to the importance of attempting to see the merits of opposing views. It is conceivable that attempts to improve people's ability to defend their own positions, unless balanced with some attention to our natural tendency to interpret evidence in accordance with existing beliefs, can have the effect of making people more effective thinkers in a close-minded way. It is certainly possible to give people tools that will make them better problem solvers without making them better able to decide what problems are worth solving.

VI. THEORIES, MODELS, AND CONCEPTUAL FRAMEWORKS

"Schools that are planning to teach critical thinking are surrounded by what seems to be a bewildering variety of programs. It would be helpful to have a theory of critical thinking that would allow educators to assess the theoretical soundness and effectiveness of such programs" (Glatthorn & Baron, 1985). It would indeed be useful to have such a theory, not only of critical thinking but of whatever other types of thinking there are as well.

Some attempts to develop approaches to the teaching of thinking and problem solving have been guided by one or another theory, model, or conceptual framework of thinking, or some aspect thereof; others have been relatively theory free. The Structure of Intellect program, for example, is based on the theory of intelligence put forward by Guilford (1967; Guilford & Hoepfner, 1971); the Instrumental Enrichment program finds its rationale in Feuerstein's own model of intelligence and intellectual development (Feuerstein, Rand, & Hoffman, 1979; Feuerstein et al., 1980); several of the remedial programs that have been designed for use at the undergraduate college level have taken their lead from Piagetian ideas about stages of cognitive development (Fuller et al., 1980).

None of the approaches to the teaching of thinking and problem solving that has yet been developed is firmly based on a well-articulated theory of cognition that is universally recognized as valid by scientists who work in this area. This observation is a safe one, because such a theory does not yet exist. This fact helps account for the wide range of opinions that exist regarding how best to teach thinking and problem solving and it points up the most fundamental impediment to faster progress in the field. Until thinking and problem solving are much better understood—until more precise, more predictive, more comprehensive, more testable theories of cognition are developed and successfully put to the test—attempts to enhance these abilities will, of necessity, retain the character of trial-and-error processes, to some degree.

J. Baron (1985, 1988), who has pointed out the need for better theorizing in the field, has proposed a conceptual model of good thinking that emphasizes search and fair-mindedness. (The importance of search in thinking and problem solving has also been emphasized by Newell and Simon [1972] and by Johnson-Laird [1982, 1983].) According to this model, good thinking involves searching effectively for goals, for possible ways to attain goals, and for evidence (facts, arguments, analogies) that can be used to evaluate possibilities. Poor thinking, again according to this conceptualization, often has its roots either in premature termination of search (being too readily satisfied with the initial results of a search process) or the operation of bias in searching or in evaluating what a search turns up (searching only for evidence that supports a preferred view or giving such evidence more weight than it deserves). While this conceptualization needs considerable elaboration if it is to become a theory that can make precise testable predictions, it is, to the writer at least, an attractive beginning and a useful way of thinking about what it means to think well.

Sternberg (1983, 1985, 1986a, 1986b) has also worked on theory development and has used the results of this work to guide the design of methods and materials for teaching thinking and problem solving. His triarchic theory (1) distinguishes three components of intelligence; (2) specifies the role of intelligence, especially as shown in the ability to deal with novelty and to automatize certain mental processes in the handling of specific tasks; and (3) characterizes intelligent behavior in the everyday world in terms of adaptation, selection, and environmental shaping. The three components of intelligence—three types of mental processes that are essential to intelligent performance—identified by Sternberg are as follows. *Performance components* (of which there are assumed to be many) are the processes used in the performance of cognitively demanding tasks. *Metacomponents* are higher order or executive processes that are involved in managing (planning, monitoring, evaluating) one's cognitive performance. *Knowledge-acquisition components* are those processes used in learning.

A variety of taxonomies of thinking skills and processes have been proposed by other investigators. The intended purpose of such taxonomies is the identification of objectives for training; if a particular skill or process is believed to be essential to high-level cognitive performance, then its development or strengthening is assumed to be a reasonable objective of a program to enhance thinking. Among the more visible of such taxonomies is one that identifies 21 skills—relatively low-level cognitive operations—and eight processes—higher level and more complex operations that draw upon these skills (Marzano et al., 1988). I have expressed reservations about this conceptualization of thinking elsewhere (Nickerson, 1990) and will not repeat them here, beyond making the point that taxonomies often are taken to be more precise representations of reality than their original proponents intended. Given our still limited understanding of thinking, it is important to be sensitive to the risk of reification.

VII. STEPWISE CONCEPTIONS OF PROBLEM SOLVING

Many writers have conceptualized problem solving as a stepwise process. Sometimes the conceptualization has been meant to characterize the way problem solving is typically done. Sometimes it has been offered as prescriptive of the way it should be done. Perhaps the first and best known of these conceptualizations is the one proposed by Polya (1945/1957) nearly 50 years ago. Polya distinguished four steps, which he intended to be seen as prescriptive of how the problem solver should proceed:

1. Understanding the problem
2. Devising a plan
3. Carrying out the plan
4. Looking back

Hayes (1981) expanded this conceptualization by including an explicit reference to representation and by breaking "looking back" into two components, one focused on evaluating the immediate problem-solving effort and the other on learning something that would be useful in the future:

1. Finding the problem
2. Representing the problem
3. Planning the solution
4. Carrying out the plan
5. Evaluating the solution
6. Consolidating gains

A similar conceptualization has been made to fit the easily remembered acronym IDEAL by Bransford and Stein (1984):

I = Identify the problem
D = Define and represent the problem
E = Explore possible strategies
A = Act on the strategies
L = Look back and evaluate the effects of your activities

Many other writers have proposed similar stepwise conceptualizations of the problem-solving process. Most can be viewed as variations on, or elaborations of, Polya's initial scheme. Perhaps the most significant extension of what Polya originally proposed has been the addition, in many cases, of an explicit step involving finding a representation of the problem. Problem representation has been an important topic in the literature on problem solving; we will return to this topic presently.

VIII. PROBLEM-SOLVING METHODS AND STRATEGIES

Much of the theoretical debate about thinking and problem solving has centered on the question of whether there are aspects of thinking or problem solving that are independent of the content domain in which the thinking or problem solving occurs. With regard to problem-solving methods and strategies, this question becomes: are there methods and strategies that are effective across different contexts of application? Can one hope to teach or learn something about problem solving that will be useful in a variety of domains, or are the techniques that work well in a given domain likely to be unique to that domain?

The evidence seems to indicate that there are many methods and strategies that are relatively specific to particular domains, but that there are also some that can be effective across domains as well. Generally speaking, there appears to be a trade-off between range of applicability and power. The more widely applicable—the less domain dependent—a method or strategy is, the less powerful it is likely to be in any particular application. If one wishes to do serious work in a particular domain, one must learn the approaches that have been developed for that domain. But one cannot be an expert in everything, so it is useful also to know of strategies that can be used to some advantage across domains.

As already noted, some generally useful strategies have been identified by computer scientists in their efforts to give computers the ability to solve problems in a variety of domains. Others have been identified by researchers in their study of human problem solving, sometimes by novices, sometimes by experts working within their domains of expertise, and sometimes by experts trying to solve problems outside those domains. The following are some of the heuristic methods that these efforts have brought to light. Further discussion of these strategies and many examples of their use can be found in Newell and Simon (1972), Wickelgren (1974), Hayes (1981), Bransford and Stein (1984), and elsewhere.

A. Problem Decomposition or Subgoaling

Sometimes it is possible to break a complex problem down into a set of sequence of simpler problems and to solve the complex problem by combining the solutions to the simpler subproblems. Computer programmers use this strategy to great advantage. Complex programs can invariably be thought of as collections of simpler programs. The simpler programs typically are collections of simpler programs still; the process of decomposition can be carried to many levels.

A major objective of the planning phase of problem solving spoken of by Polya (1945/1957) and Hayes (1981), among others, is the identification of the subproblems into which a problem can be broken. The process of analysis that is required to realize this objective may result in the identification of a promising solution path, but even when it does not do that, the effort can help one better understand the problem. A risk in this strategy is that of changing the nature of the problem, perhaps by eliminating a critical aspect of it, either in the process of breaking it down or in that of combining the subproblem solutions.

B. Working Backwards

Many investigators have found it useful to characterize problems in terms of a journey metaphor: one begins at point A (the initial state) and tries to reach point B (the goal), the challenge being to find a path that will bring one from the former to the latter. Sometimes, when one finds it difficult to make much progress from A to B, it can be helpful to try working from B backward toward A. If, for example, one's problem is literally to find a route from one geographical location to another, it may, in some cases, be easier to work from the destination back toward the point of departure than the reverse.

One can work backward not only from a final goal state but from intermediate goal states, if these can be identified. But the strategy can be used only when a goal state (final or intermediate) can be specified in fairly concrete terms. Many of the types of problems that one sees in books on problem solving—The Tower of Hanoi problem and its analogues, numbered tile rearranging problems, water jug problems—are this type. Others are not. The goal states of many problems in mathematics and logic, for example, can be expressed only in abstract terms before the problems are solved.

C. Hill Climbing

A variation on the journey metaphor likens the process of problem solving to that of climbing a hill. If one's purpose is to get to the top of a hill and there is not a clearly marked path to follow, a strategy that can be used is to walk in such a way that one is always going up; so if one finds oneself descending, one turns around and goes the other way. Applied to problem solving, this means that one takes only steps that bring one closer to one's goal.

The major weakness of the hill-climbing rule is apparent; one can get stuck on the top of a small hill in the vicinity, or even on the slope, of the large hill that one wishes to climb. Just as it is sometimes necessary in hill climbing to take a few steps downhill in order to reach a desired peak, so in problem solving one sometimes must take steps that seem directly away from the goal in order to attain the goal in the end. This seems often to be a difficult thing for people to do (Anderson, 1990).

D. Means–End Analysis

Means–end analysis is similar in some respects to hill climbing but more flexible and adaptable to the specifics of different problem situations. It has been discussed in detail by Newell and Simon (1972) and used extensively by them and others in the development of problem-solving computer programs. This approach begins with the identification of a goal state and a detailed listing of the differences between it and the current state. The journey metaphor is applicable again; the current state is where one is and the goal state is where one wants eventually to be.

One proceeds by trying to take some action that will reduce the disparity (shorten the list of differences) between the goal state and the current state. This can be done either by taking a step that will make the current state more similar to the goal state or by taking one that (working backward) will bring the goal state closer to the current state. Means–end analysis, like hill climbing, can get one stuck if one adheres too compulsively to the rule of never taking a step that increases the difference between the current and goal states.

Anderson (1993) sees means–end problem-solving methods as an innate part of the cognitive machinery not only of humans but of other primates as well. He cites the problem-solving activities of chimpanzees observed by Köhler during the 1920s as evidence of the use of such methods by nonhuman species. It does not follow, of course, nor does Anderson suggest it does, that there is nothing to be gained by trying to learn to use means–end methods more effectively than one might use them spontaneously.

E. Forward Chaining

In forward chaining, one begins with the givens and works directly toward the goal. Use of this strategy appears to depend on having a sufficiently deep understanding of a problem to be able to construct a correct concrete representation of it from the problem statement (D. P. Simon & Simon, 1978). This being so, experts are more likely to use this strategy than novices, who are more likely to use such strategies as means–end analysis and working backward (Larkin et al., 1980a, 1980b). It is the experts' ability to classify problems in terms of basic principles and their knowledge of approaches that work for specific problem types that make this possible. Sweller, Mawer, and Ward (1983) found that, when given extended practice with problems of a specific type, subjects tended to switch spontaneously from a means–end strategy that they employed to a forward-chaining strategy.

F. Considering Analogous Problems

Sometimes one can solve a problem by finding a solution to an analogous, but easier, problem. The analogous problem may be intrinsically easier, or easier just because the problem solver happens to know what its solution is, perhaps from having solved it before. Consider the following problem, adapted from Poundstone (1990).

> Six people are in an elevator. Can you demonstrate that it must be the case that *either* at least three of them are mutual acquaintances *or* at least three are complete strangers to one another?

Poundstone points out that, while the demonstration that is called for is logically difficult, the problem has a readily understood graphical analogue. Let the six people in the elevator be represented by six dots on a piece of paper. (The dots can be positioned in any way, except that no three should be on the same line.) Let a solid line between any two dots represent acquaintance between the people represented by those dots, and let a dashed line indicate that the people are strangers. With this scheme, a solid triangle represents three mutual acquaintances and a dashed triangle a trio of mutual strangers. Now the question is, using either a solid line or a dashed line between any given pair of dots, is it possible to connect every dot with every other dot in such a way that no solid triangles and no dashed triangles appear in the result?

It should be clear that this problem is indeed analogous to the original elevator problem and that the solution to one will reveal the solution to the other. As it happens, the dot-connecting problem is much easier to solve than the original elevator problem, which is what makes the former a useful analogue of the latter. The risk in using this strategy is that of identifying as an analogue to the problem one wishes to solve a problem that appears to be analogous in the right way(s) but actually is not.

G. Specialization and Generalization

Mason, Burton, and Stacey (1985) emphasize the importance of the interplay between specialization and generalization, especially in mathematical problem solving. Specialization means considering a concrete example of an abstract problem. If one is trying to solve a problem that has to do with the properties of parallelograms, say, one may find it useful to begin by considering a particular parallelogram, or several particular parallelograms.

By working with specific cases, one may find a solution that is generalizable or get the insights that are necessary to formulate a general solution. One way in which this can happen is that one may see in the solutions to several specific cases of the problem of interest a pattern that is suggestive of some principle that, if made explicit, would be recognized as the general solution that is sought.

H. Considering Extreme Cases

A heuristic that is often used to advantage, especially, but not exclusively, in mathematical problem solving, is that of considering extreme cases. This trick, which is an instance of specialization, is nicely illustrated by Polya (1954), who strongly advocated its use.

> Two men are seated at a table of usual rectangular shape. One places a penny on the table, then the other does the same, and so on, alternatively. It is understood that each penny lies flat on the table, and not on any penny previously placed. The player who puts the last coin on the table takes the money. Which player should win, provided that each plays the best possible game? (p. 23)

Polya reports having watched a mathematician to whom this puzzle was posed respond with, "Suppose that the table is so small it is covered by one penny. Then obviously the first player must win." Of course, if this were the situation, the first player would win only his own penny and the game would not be interesting, but considering this extreme case provides the clue needed to see the solution to the problem as originally stated. Imagine the size of the table being gradually increased. If the first player places the first penny precisely in the center, as soon as the table is large enough to hold a penny beside the first penny on any side, it will be large enough to hold another penny on the opposite side as well.

By generalizing this argument, we can see that, irrespective of the size of the table, if the first player puts his first penny in the middle and after that always precisely matches what the second player does, but on the opposite side of the table, he will invariably win. It is not essential to imagine the extreme case to solve this problem; an argument could be made from symmetry straightaway. A similar point could be made with respect to most instances of the use of the extreme-cases heuristic, but its use can be effective in helping one see a solution that may otherwise be obscure.

I. Mixing Strategies

The strategies mentioned here are not the only ones that have been advocated by people who study problem solving, but they are among those that have received the greatest amount of attention. Although different writers have stressed specific strategies to different degrees, no one suggests that any is adequate to ensure effective problem solving by itself. They can be used to advantage in many combinations. Working backward, for example, can be done within the context of means–end analysis. The strategy of breaking a complex problem into simpler problems can be combined with essentially any other strategy; one simply treats any of the subproblems into which the original problem is decomposed as a problem in its own right and applies the desired strategies—including further decomposition—to it. Use of a particular strategy seldom precludes the use also of others.

IX. REPRESENTATION

If there is a single aspect of problem solving that has been stressed above all others it is problem representation. Researchers who have studied the performance of expert problem solvers and attempted to specify how it differs from the performance of novices have often stressed the role that representations—especially qualitative representations—play in the experts' performance (Chi et al., 1981; Larkin, 1983; Larkin et al., 1980). Nearly everyone who has written prescriptively about problem solving has emphasized the importance of finding an effective way of representing a problem as a first step in working toward a solution; and advice that is commonly given for getting "unstuck" when one finds oneself unable to make progress on a problem is to find a new way to represent it (J. L. Adams, 1974; Bransford & Stein, 1984; Greeno, 1980;. Hayes, 1981; Novak, 1977; Wickelgren, 1974). The production of inadequate representations has been seen as a major limitation of children's problem-solving capabilities (Klahr, 1978).

But it is one thing to understand that an effective representation of a problem can put one well on the way to the solution and quite another to be able to produce such a representation. What can be taught that will help problem solvers produce better representations than they otherwise would? It does not suffice to say that novices should be taught to produce the kind of representations that experts produce; so much is obvious. The question is how this can be done. Are expert problem solvers expert because they produce better problem representations than do novices, or do experts produce better representations than novices because they are experts? If the former is the case, we would expect to increase the expertise of novices by teaching them to produce better representatives; if the latter, it would seem that the way to teach people to construct better representations is first to turn them into experts.

This is more than a play on words, and the truth, I suspect, lies somewhere between the extremes as stated. Something can be taught about problem representation that can be helpful to the problem solver who is not an expert in a given domain, but it seems unreasonable to expect that, all else equal, a person who is not an expert in a domain will ever be as facile as the expert at producing representations that are effective in that domain. There is more to turning novices into experts than teaching them about representations, but that is a significant part of the process.

One answer to the question of what can be taught about problem representation is that people who are to do serious problem solving in specific domains have to know about the representational systems that are generally used in those domains. Chemists must know how to represent molecular structures with chemical formulas and atomic bonding diagrams; physicists must be familiar with the particle-state notation developed by Niels Bohr and with Feynman diagrams; logicians must know about truth tables, Euler and Venn diagrams, and a variety of notational schemes. Indeed, one must learn these representational systems in order to comprehend much of what has been written in these domains, even if one does not engage in problem solving in them.

Mathematics has a number of representational systems, and anyone who would do much mathematical problem solving must learn one or more of these systems. Sometimes mathematics is treated as a subject-specific domain, like physics, chemistry, or music, and with some justification. It is a discipline, or perhaps a constellation of disciplines, that can be studied in its own right and for its own sake. But it is also a collection of tools that can be applied to great advantage to the solution of problems in a wide variety of domains. This being the case, when one learns how to represent problems mathematically, one presumably learns something that will prove to be useful in many contexts.

Unfortunately, the evidence seems to indicate that many students learn how to solve mathematical problems that have already been represented mathematically but fail to acquire much skill in representing verbally described problems in mathematical form (Carpenter, Corbitt, Kepner, Lindquist, & Reys, 1980; Clement, 1982; Clement, Lochhead, & Monk, 1981; Rosnick & Clement, 1980). This suggests that what is being learned is the rote application of algorithmic procedures without a deep understanding of how or why they work. It points up the importance of teaching students not only how to manipulate mathematical symbols by applying operators to equations, but the rationale behind the representations and how to apply it to situations that have not yet been represented in mathematical form.

Is there anything that can be taught about problem representation beyond the symbol systems and notational schemes that have been developed for use in specific domains and the generally useful systems of mathematics? There are certain types of representations that are commonly used in a variety of different domains. Contingency tables are a case in point. The following identity problem from Mind Benders (Midwest Publications, 1981) is representative of many problems found in books of puzzles and logical or mathematical diversions.

A cat, a small dog, a goat, and a horse are named Angel, Beauty, King, and Rover. From the clues below, find each animal's name.
King is smaller than either the dog or Rover.
The horse is younger than Angel.
Beauty is the oldest and is a good friend of the dog.

This problem is quite simple and the reader may feel that a representation of it beyond the verbal description is unnecessary, but it serves to illustrate a tabular representation, which is useful also with much more difficult problems. One begins by setting up a table in which the rows represent one of the variables mentioned in the problem and the columns represent the other.

	Angel	Beauty	King	Rover
cat				
dog				
goat				
horse				

One then proceeds to fill in the cells of the table so as to represent the information that is contained explicitly in, or can be inferred from, the assertions that are contained in the problem statement. One learns something from filling in some of the table's cells that has implications for the contents of the reamining cells. If one does this in the present case, using O to indicate an animal–name pairing that has been ruled out and X to indicate a pairing that has been identified (often, as it happens, by elimination), one will eventually arrive at the following solution:

	A	B	K	R
c	O	O	X	O
d	X	O	O	O
g	O	X	O	O
h	O	O	O	X

Tabular representations are especially well suited for identity problems that involve only two variables, as does the example. They can be used also when there are more variables than two, but they become awkward when there are more than three or four, especially if each variable has many values or states.

Another generally useful representation for problem solving is that of a tree, which is a collection of nodes linked in such a way that there is always a unique path from any specified point to any other specified point. When looked at from one direction (as from the bottom of a natural tree), the branches of a tree diverge, with two or more points emerging from a single point; when looked at from the opposite direction, the paths in a tree converge, those emanating from two or more points leading to a common point. The fact that any two points in a tree are connected by a unique path distinguishes this representation from that of a network, in which there may be many paths connecting two nodes. Trees, which are sometimes referred to as "family trees," "decision trees," or "fault trees," depending on the context of their use, are often applied to diagnostic or trouble-shooting problems, and in domains as widely disparate as medicine and automotive repair.

There are other representations that can be useful as problem-solving aids in a variety of contexts. These include function graphs (representing functional relationships between variables); flow charts (representing stepwise details of a procedure or process); and maps, blueprints, scale drawings (representing precise spatial and structural relationships), and their rough-sketch analogues. Familiarity with these and other generally useful representational schemes is one reasonable objective of teaching aimed at improving problem solving in a broad way.

Whether the ability of people to invent new representational schemes that will be useful aids to problem solving in particular instances can be improved by training is a question that has not, to my knowledge, received much attention from researchers. It is an important question and one that could benefit from some insightful research. More generally, the question of what can be taught about representations and their construction that will enhance thinking and problem solving deserves much more research than it has yet received.

X. EVALUATION

We would like to know whether the various approaches to the teaching of thinking or problem solving that have been advocated work. We would like to know what can be expected to be accomplished with specific methods and materials and under what conditions. This is the issue of evaluation. A discussion of it will be aided by a distinction between studies aimed at answering questions about specific aspects of teaching thinking and problem solving and efforts to evaluate programs as such.

Numerous studies have been done to provide data on the effects of specific variables on certain aspects of cognitive performance. Studies aimed at testing the effectiveness of training specific skills or processes have, in some instances, obtained evidence of modest improvements as indicated by performance on standardized or specially designed tests (Vye, Delclos, Burns, & Bransford, 1988). Some success has been reported in attempts to train children to approach cognitive tasks more attentively and reflectively—less impulsively—and to improve their task performance in this way (Parish & Ericksen, 1981). A literature review by Belmont, Butterfield, and Ferretti (1982) led these investigators to the conclusion that the teaching of executive control strategies—strategies to guide one's own thinking and learning— can be effective. Nisbett and his colleagues have presented evidence that training in statistics and probability improves performance in situations where statistical or probabilistic thinking is required (Fong, Krantz, & Nisbett, 1986; Lehman, Lempert, & Nisbett, 1988; R. E. Nisbett, Fong, Lehman, & Cheng, 1987).

Efforts have also been made to evaluate programs designed to teach thinking or problem solving. Programs involved in these efforts include the Structure of Intellect Program (Jacobs & Vandeventer, 1971, 1972), the Productive Thinking Program (Covington et al., 1974), the Practicum in Thinking (Wheeler & Dember, 1979), Science—a Process Approach (Klausmeier, 1980), Instrumental Enrichment (Savell, Twohig, & Rachford, 1986), Project Intelligence (Hernstein et al., 1986), the McREL thinking skills program (Marzano, 1986), and the Cognitive Curriculum for Young Children (Haywood, Brooks, & Burns, 1986; Price, 1991).

The data obtained in these and similar evaluation studies, although not entirely unequivocal, provide a basis for guarded optimism that enough is now known about thinking and problem solving that serious attempts to teach them in classrooms well informed by this knowledge can be expected to produce at least modestly positive results. They also demonstrate, however, that we are still a long way from knowing how to teach all aspects of thinking and problem solving as effectively as we would like. Moreover, the attempts at evaluation that have been made notwithstanding, it must be said that the claims and hopes of the developers and proponents of some programs have sometimes gotten ahead of the objective evidence of their justification.

There are several reasons that reliable evaluative data are not more abundant. The first that must be mentioned is an unpleasant one to note, but real. Some developers of materials and programs have had little concern about the problem of evaluation. They have seized the opportunity that the widespread interest in the teaching of thinking and problem solving provides to promote their own ideas about how to accomplish the teaching, and have not been reluctant to claim effectiveness for the approaches they advocate, despite the lack of adequate empirical or theoretical justification for that claim.

I do not wish to speculate here on what motivates people to behave in this way, beyond making two brief observations. First, education is big business. The potential market for material that appears to meet a widely recognized educational need is huge. This fact invites selling and promotionalism. Second, I suspect that most people who make inadequately justified claims for specific approaches to the teaching of thinking and problem solving are convinced of the legitimacy of those claims. In some cases the claims may be correct, but it is important for the educational community, as a whole, to withhold judgment until evidence more compelling than personal conviction is obtained.

Although promotionalism undoubtedly contributes to the paucity of evaluative data, it is only one of several factors that do so and it may be a minor one; my sense is that most developers of methods and materials for the teaching of thinking and problem solving are deeply concerned about the issue of evaluation and frustrated by the difficulty of getting unambiguous data on the matter. The fact that evaluations must typically be done in situations that are affected by numerous uncontrolled and uncontrollable variables is one source of frustration. Another is the vested interests—of teachers, administrators, school boards, textbook publishers, and parents—that are not always mutually consistent and supportive of educational research. Evaluation efforts are also constrained, as they should be, by ethical considerations; researchers cannot let the conducting of a scientifically valid evaluation take precedence over the best educational interests of the students involved.

All of this points up the need for some innovative work on the question of how best to evaluate educational innovations. There are countless ways to do it wrong—to ask the wrong questions; to confound variables; to obtain uninterpretable, or easily misinterpreted, results; to have unwanted side effects on the education of participating students. The difficulty of empirical evaluation in educational settings also reinforces the need for a better theoretical understanding of thinking and problem solving and of the ways in which cognitive abilities—as well as noncognitive determinants of cognitive performance—can be enhanced. Theories of cognition developed and refined in the research laboratory must ultimately be predictive of cognitive performance in the classroom and other contexts if they are to survive, but much can be learned in the laboratory that can be used to guide the development of classroom teaching and learning techniques.

XI. THE QUESTION OF TRANSFER

The evidence indicates that at least some aspects of thinking and problem solving can be taught—that people can learn to be better thinkers and problem solvers in certain respects (Halpern, in press; Nickerson et al., 1985). But does what is learned transfer to contexts other than those in which it was learned? When people learn how to analyze verbal arguments and to identify the kinds of logical errors that are frequently made, do they thereby become less prone to make invalid inferences in daily life? Do people who become adept at solving inference puzzles of the kind encountered in books on problem solving also become better able to deal with the reasoning problems that present themselves elsewhere? Are the principles, skills, and strategies that people learn in courses on thinking or problem solving applied effectively outside the classroom?

Most of the research on thinking and problem solving has been done in college classrooms and in psychological laboratories and relatively little is known about cognitive performance in everyday life. The methodological difficulties involved in studying thinking and problem solving in everyday situations are formidable (Galotti, 1989). Despite these difficulties, however, some investigators have been studying thinking and problem solving in a variety of real-world situations (e.g., Ceci & Liker, 1986; Perkins, Faraday, & Bushey, 1991; Scribner, 1986; Voss, 1991).

One conclusion that has been drawn from such investigations is that the types of cognitively demanding tasks that are encountered in the day-to-day world tend to differ in important ways from those that traditionally have been used to study thinking and problem solving in the classroom and psychological laboratory. In particular, problems studied in the laboratory have typically been well defined, with all the information needed to solve them being provided, whereas those encountered in the day-to-day world are more likely to be ill defined, to be lacking required information, and in many cases to not have a known correct or best solution (Frederiksen, 1986; Glass, Holyoak, & Santa, 1979).

The difference has been considered by some investigators to be sufficiently great to warrant a distinction between academic and practical intelligence (Sternberg & Wagner, 1986). Although I am not convinced this distinction is justified (Nickerson, 1988), the findings that motivate it demonstrate the inadvisability of assuming that performance on the kinds of cognitively demanding tasks typically used to study thinking and problem solving in academic settings is a reliable predictor of how individuals will perform the cognitively demanding tasks they will encounter in everyday life.

There is a need for much more research focused on the kinds of thinking and problem solving challenges that people face, and on the thinking and problem solving that people do, outside academic contexts. We need a better understanding than we now have of the kinds of thinking and problem-solving challenges that people face in everyday life. Hayes (1981) has made the important point that sophisticated problem solvers recognize a variety of problem types: "distance–rate–time problems, age problems, river-crossing problems, and so on" (p. 5). This is important because problems in the same category may be approachable in more or less the same way; so if one knows an approach that works for a given category, recognizing a problem as belonging to that category can put one well on the way to its solution.

The categories used by Hayes to make the point are illustrative of the kinds of problems typically found in books on mathematics or problem solving. The question arises as to whether the problems that people typically encounter in everyday life are sortable into readily distinguishable categories and whether the problems in a given category can be solved in the same way. I am not aware of any attempts to develop a taxonomy of real-life-problem types. It is interesting to speculate on what such a taxonomy might be like. Where would dealing with a medical emergency fit within it, or finding a job, resolving a family dispute, planning a project or vacation, accessing some hard-to-locate information, managing personal or household expenses, evaluating the credibility of what one hears or reads, deciding how large a family to have, evaluating the merits of a political agenda, selecting which of several makes of a particular product to buy?

There is a need not only for a better understanding of the thinking and problem-solving challenges of life outside academic contexts, but also for research aimed at determining how what is taught in the classroom affects people's ability to meet those challenges. We need a clearer indication, too, of whether the efforts to enhance thinking and problem-solving ability of the type that are currently being made are likely to have any appreciable impact on society's ability to deal with the larger problems—poverty, crime, economic stagnation, environmental spoliation, malaise, famine, war, and the like—that beset municipalities, nations, and the globe. And whatever research might reveal on these questions, there can be little doubt of the continuing need to search for ways to do a better job of teaching thinking and problem solving than has been done in the past.

One generalization about transfer that is particularly important, in my view, is that it deserves explicit focus in any approach to the teaching of thinking and problem solving. Whether thinking skills or problem-solving strategies are taught in the context of conventional subjects or in stand-alone courses, students need to be made aware of the applicability of what they are learning to contexts other than that in which they are learning it. When students are taught principles and procedures in the abstract, they need to learn from examples something of the range of situations in which those principles and procedures are potentially applicable. Conversely, when they learn how to solve a particular problem, they need to be able to abstract the approach they are taking and see how it can be applied in other contexts as well. It is not safe to assume that transfer will occur spontaneously; the teacher who wants it to occur should make that an explicit goal toward which to work.

XII. PRACTICALITIES OF TEACHING THINKING AND PROBLEM SOLVING

Education, as an institution, has many layers of organization and serves numerous interests in addition to that of educating young people. In part for these reasons, educational process is notoriously resistant to change (D. K. Cohen, 1988; Cuban, 1984; Saranson, 1971). Students, too, at least in the higher grades, may come to the classroom with expectations that are not necessarily conducive to new approaches and may be difficult to change (Sternberg & Davidson, 1987). The common fate of innovations, even those that cause some initial excitement and seem to show promise of real change, is to fade, after their novelty has worn off, into the status quo of the established classroom routine.

Educational reform that is to make a lasting difference must occur at several levels. It must involve what happens in the classroom, how teachers are trained, the perspectives and objectives of school administrators, the attitudes and expectations of parents, and the educational standards demanded by the community and society as a whole. An isolated intervention aimed at enhancing the thinking and problem-solving abilities of the students in a particular class may have beneficial effects on the students involved, but if those students do not find an environment that values and nurtures what they are learning, beyond the class in which they are learning it, the effects are unlikely to be built upon, or perhaps even to persist. Satisfaction with the status quo in education and failure of parents to see the need for improvement are believed by some investigators to be major impediments to educational advance (Stevenson, 1992; Stevenson et al., 1993).

No attempt to improve the teaching of thinking and problem solving in the schools on a large scale can succeed without some careful attention to the issue of teacher training. The teacher is the critical variable in any effort to change what happens in the classroom, and the assumption that any approach to the enhancement of the thinking of students can be effective independently of the competence of the teachers involved in its application is naïve in the extreme. For this reason, the passage in February, 1989, of a resolution by the American Association of Colleges for Teacher Education to encourage its membership, "as a high priority, to implement within teacher preparation programs: (a) course work that requires those future teachers to enhance their own higher-order thinking skills, and (b) courses in pedagogy in which future teachers become proficient in applying strategies that will enable learners to acquire higher-order thinking skills of their own," is heartening. The resolution calls also for the National Council for Accreditation of Teacher Education to incorporate the concept of higher order thinking in its assessment standards for teacher-education institutions. Researchers working in this area will find it easy to endorse these resolves; the challenge will be to figure out how best to implement and follow through on them.

XIII. COGNITIVE RESEARCH AND THE PRACTICE OF TEACHING

If this chapter were being written twenty years ago, I would, at this point, bemoan the lack of communication between people who are doing research on human learning and other aspects of cognition and those who are engaged in classroom teaching. In 1993 the gulf between these two worlds is not quite as wide as it once was; numerous efforts—with conferences, symposia, and books—have been made to increase the communication between researchers and practitioners. This is an encouraging fact and one can only hope that it marks the beginning of a trend that will continue indefinitely.

It is still the case, however, that the coupling between research and practice is not as strong as it should be. For understandable reasons, researchers usually publish their results in research journals, which are not the journals that practitioners typically read. And practitioners tend to contribute to publications that are read primarily by other practitioners. Thus both researchers and practitioners communicate primarily with other members of their respective professional groups. This is natural and hardly surprising. But it means that explicit efforts will be required if communication across the groups is to be maintained at a level that will substantively affect the thinking of each group. Such efforts are most likely to come, as they have in the past, primarily from the not-numerous people who have a foot in both worlds, which is to say the rare individuals who have training or experience in both research and teaching.

Much of the research that is done in the psychology laboratory is of questionable relevance to the problem of classroom teaching. However, one of the most noteworthy trends in psychological research during the recent past has been an increasing emphasis on questions that are motivated by an interest in what one might call real-world cognition; learning as it occurs in natural settings, and thinking and problem solving in daily life. It would be surprising if this focus did not yield some knowledge that could be applied to the teaching of thinking and problem solving in the classroom, and in fact such knowledge has been forthcoming.

Research has revealed, for example, that domain-specific knowledge is a necessary but not sufficient condition for deep thinking about a domain (R. Glaser, 1984). Specific differences have been discovered between the approaches that experts typically take in problem solving and those typically adopted by novices (Chi et al., 1981; Larkin et al., 1980a). The importance of dispositions, attitudes, and beliefs as causal factors in thinking is becoming better understood (J. Baron, 1985; Dweck & Eliot, 1983; Ennis, 1987). The role that metacognitive factors—knowledge about cognition, self-monitoring and -managing techniques—can play as determinants of cognitive performance has been noted (Flavell, 1979, 1981). Much is being learned about how people reason and solve problems in everyday life (R. E. Nisbett, 1993; Saxe, 1990; Sternberg & Wagner, 1986). And evidences of successful attempts to improve specific aspects of thinking through instruction are being obtained (Halpern, in press; Nickerson et al., 1985).

XIV. CONCLUDING COMMENT

Helping students to become better thinkers and problem solvers is an old quest in education. The current interest in finding ways to pursue this objective more effectively appears to be widespread and fairly intense. In the aggregate, the results of numerous efforts to enhance thinking and problem solving through classroom instruction, and findings from the last few decades of research on cognition and learning, provide a basis for optimism that progress is being made. They also make it clear, however, that designing an educational process that will develop competent thinkers and problem solvers is ambitious and something we do not yet know how to do as well as we would like. More research focused on questions that have clear relevance to thinking and problem solving in everyday life and the teaching and learning thereof is needed, as is greater two-way communication between the worlds of educational research and educational practice.

There is also a continuing need for reflection on, and discussion of, what it means to think well and what the specific objectives of efforts to enhance thinking ability should be. Teaching problem solving, or skillful thinking toward given ends, important as it is, is surely not enough. It does not suffice to be able to bring effective strategies to bear on problems as given; one should be able also to make reasonable judgments about which problems are worth solving and which are not. Similarly, it is not enough to be able to think logically and insightfully about given topics; rationality, in the most general sense, must include not only an ability to think but a willingness to give some thought to what to think about.

Acknowledgments

I am grateful to Jonathan Baron, Robert Glaser, Diane Halpern, and Fred Newmann for helpful comments on a draft of this chapter.

References

Adams, J. L. (1974). *Conceptual blockbusting: A guide to better ideas.* San Francisco: Freeman.

Adams, M. J. (Coord.). (1986). *Odyssey: A curriculum for thinking.* Watertown, MA: Mastery Education Corporation.

Anderson, J. R. (1990). *Cognitive psychology and its implications* (3rd ed.). New York: Freeman.

Anderson, J. R. (1993). Problem solving and learning. *American Psychologist, 48,* 35–44.

Andrews, G. R., & Debus, R. I. (1978). Persistence and the causal perception of failure: Modifying cognitive attributions. *Journal of Educational Psychology, 70,* 154–166.

Arons, A. B. (1976). Cultivating the capacity of formal reasoning: Objectives and procedures in an introductory physical science course. *American Journal of Physics, 44,* 834–838.

Ault, R. L. (1973). Problem-solving strategies of reflective, impulsive, fast-accurate, and slow-inaccurate children. *Development Psychology, 1,* 717–725.

Baker, L., & Brown, A. L. (1984). Metacognitive skills and reading. In P. D. Pearson, M. Kamil, R. Barr, & P. Mosenthal (Eds.), *Handbook of reading research.* New York: Longman.

Baron, J. (1985). *Rationality and intelligence.* New York: Cambridge University Press.

Baron, J. (1988). *Thinking and deciding.* New York: Cambridge University Press.

Baron, J. (1991). Beliefs about thinking. In J. F. Voss, D. N. Perkins, & J. W. Segal (Eds.), *Informal reasoning and education* (pp. 169–186). Hillsdale, NJ: Erlbaum.

Baron, J., Badgio, P. C., & Gaskins, I. W. (1986). In R. J. Sternberg (Ed.), *Advances in the psychology of human intelligence* (Vol. 3). Hillsdale, NJ: Erlbaum.

Baron, J. B., & Sternberg, R. J. (Eds.), (1987). *Teaching thinking skills: Theory and practice.* New York: Freeman.

Bartel, A. P., Lichtenberg, F. R., & Vaughan, R. (1989). Technological change, trade, and the need for educated employees: Implications for economic policy. *National Center on Education and Employment NCEE Brief, 5,* 1–4.

Belmont, J. M., Butterfield, E. C., & Ferretti, R. P. (1982). To secure transfer of training instruct self-management skills. In D. K. Detterman & R. J. Sternberg (Eds.), *How and how much can intelligence be increased.* Norwood, NJ: Ablex.

Berkeley, D., & Humphreys, P. (1982). Structuring decision problems and the "bias" heuristic. *Acta Psychologica, 50,* 201–252.

Borkowski, J. G., Carr, M., Rellinger, E., & Pressley, M. (1990). Self-regulated cognition: Interdependence of metacognition, attributions, and self-esteem. In B. F. Jones & L. Idol (Eds.), *Dimensions of thinking and cognitive instruction* (pp. 53–92). Hillsdale, NJ: Erlbaum.

Borkowski, J. G., Johnston, M. B., & Reid, M. K. (1987). Metacognition, motivation and controlled performance. In S. Ceci (Ed.), *Handbook of cognitive, social, and neurological aspects of learning disabilities* (Vol. 2). Hillsdale, NJ: Erlbaum.

Botkin, J. W., Elmandjra, M., & Malitza, M. (1979). *No limits to learning: Bridging the human gap.* London: Pergamon.

Bransford, J. D., Sherwood, R., Vye, N., & Rieser, J. (1986). Teaching thinking and problem solving. *American Psychologist, 41,* 1078–1089.

Bransford, J. D., & Stein, B. S. (1984). *The ideal problem solver: A guider for improving thinking, learning, and creativity.* New York: Freeman.

Bransford, J. D., Vye, N., Kinzer, C., & Risko, V. (1990). Teaching thinking and content knowledge: Toward an integrated approach. In B. F. Jones & L. Idol (Eds.), *Dimensions of thinking and cognitive instruction* (pp. 381–413). Hillsdale, NJ: Erlbaum.

Brown, A. L. (1978). Knowing when, where, and how to remember: A problem in metacognition. In R. Glaser (Ed.), *Advances in instructional psychology.* Hillsdale, NJ: Erlbaum.

Carpenter, T. P., Corbitt, M. K., Kepner, H., Lindquist, M., & Reys, R. (1980). Problem solving in mathematics: National assessment results. *Educational Leadership, 37,* 562–563.

Ceci, S. J., & Liker, J. (1986). Academic and nonacademic intelligence: An experimental separation. In R. J. Sternberg & R. K. Wagner (Eds.), *Practical intelligence: Nature and origins of competence in the everyday world* (pp. 119–142). New York: Cambridge University Press.

Chance, P. (1986). *Thinking in the classroom.* New York: Teachers College Press.

Cheng, P. W., & Holyoak, K. J. (1985). Pragmatic reasoning schemas. *Cognitive Psychology, 17,* 391–416.

Cheng, P. W., Holyoak, K. J., Nisbett, R. E., & Oliver, L. (1986). Pragmatic versus syntactic approaches to training deductive reasoning. *Cognitive Psychology, 18,* 293–328.

Chi, M. T. H., Feltovich, P. J., & Glaser, R. (1981). Categorization and representation of physics problems by experts and novices. *Cognitive Science, 5,* 121–152.

Chipman, S. F., Segal, J. W., & Glaser, R. (Eds.). (1985). *Thinking and learning skills: Vol. 2. Research and open questions.* Hillsdale, NJ: Erlbaum.

Clement, J. (1982). Students' preconceptions in introductory mechanics. *American Journal of Physics, 50,* 66–71.

Clement, J., Lochhead, J., & Monk, G. S. (1981). Translation difficulties in learning mathematics. *American Mathematical Monthly, 88*(4), 286–290.

Cohen, D. K. (1988). Educational technology and school organization. In R. S. Nickerson & P. P. Zodhiates (Eds.), *Technology in education: Looking toward 2020* (pp. 231–264). Hillsdale, NJ: Erlbaum.

Cohen, L. J. (1979). On the psychology of prediction: Whose is the fallacy? *Cognition, 7,* 385–407.

Cohen, L. J. (1981). Can human irrationality be demonstrated? *Behavior and Brain Sciences, 4,* 317–370.

Costa, A. L. (Ed.). (1985). *Developing minds: A resource for teaching thinking.* Alexandria, VA: Association for Supervision and Curriculum Development.

Covington, M. V., Crutchfield, R. S., Davies, L., & Olton, R. M. (1974). *The productive thinking program: A course in learning to think.* Columbus, OH: Merrill.

Cuban, L. (1984). Policy and research dilemmas in the teaching of reasoning: Unplanned designs. *Review of Educational Research, 54,* 655–681.

Cyert, R. M., & Mowery, D. C. (1989). Technology, employment and U.S. competitiveness. *Scientific American, 260*(5), 54–62.

Deci, E. L., & Ryan, R. M. (1985). *Intrinsic motivation and self-determination in human behavior.* New York: Plenum.

Dewey, J. (1991). *How we think.* Buffalo, NY: Prometheus Books. (Original work published 1910)

Dickstein, L. S. (1978). Error processes in syllogistic reasoning. *Memory & Cognition, 6,* 537–543.

Dweck, C. S. (1975). The role of expectations and attributions in the alleviation of learned helplessness. *Journal of Personality and Social Psychology, 45,* 165–171.

Dweck, C. S., & Eliot, E. S. (1983). Achievement motivation. In P. H. Mussen (Ed.), *Handbook of child psychology* (Vol. 4). New York: Wiley.

Ehrenberg, S. D., & Ehrenberg, L. M. (1982). *BASICS: Building and applying strategies for intellectual competencies in students.* Coshocton, OH: Institute for Curriculum and Instruction.

Ennis, R. H. (1969). *Logic in teaching.* Englewood Cliffs, NJ: Prentice-Hall.

Ennis, R. H. (1985). Critical thinking and the curriculum. *National Forum, 65,* 28–31.

Ennis, R. H. (1987). A taxonomy of critical thinking dispositions and abilities. In J. B. Baron & R. J. Sternberg (Eds.), *Teaching thinking skills: Theory and practice.* New York: Freeman.

Erickson, J. R. (1978). Research on syllogistic reasoning. In R. Revlin & R. E. Mayer (Eds.), *Human reasoning.* New York: Holt, Rinehart & Winston.

Fawcett, H. P. (1983). *The nature of proof (1983 yearbook of the National Council of Teachers of Mathematics).* New York: Columbia University Teachers College.

Feuerstein, R., Rand, Y., & Hoffman, M. B. (1979). *The dynamic assessment of retarded performers: The learning potential assessment device, theory, instruments, techniques.* Baltimore, MD: University Park Press.

Feuerstein, R., Rand, Y., Hoffman, M. B., & Miller, R. (1980). *Instrumental enrichment.* Baltimore, MD: University Park Press.

Flavell, J. H. (1978). Metacognitive development. In J. M. Scandura & C. J. Brainerd (Eds.), *Structural/process theories of complex human behavior.* The Netherlands: Sijthoff & Noordoff.

Flavell, J. H. (1979). Metacognition and cognitive monitoring: A new area of psychological inquiry. *American Psychologist, 34,* 906–911.

Flavell, J. H. (1981). Cognitive monitoring. In W. P. Dickson (Ed.), *Children's oral communication skills.* New York: Academic Press.

Flavell, J. H., & Wellman, H. M. (1977). Metamemory. In R. V. Kail & J. W. Hagen (Eds.), *Perspectives on the development of memory and cognition.* Hillsdale, NJ: Erlbaum.

Fong, G. T., Krantz, D. H., & Nisbett, R. E. (1986). The effects of statistical training on thinking about everyday problems. *Cognitive Psychology, 18,* 235–292.

Frederiksen, N. (1986). Toward a broader conception of human intelligence. In R. J. Sternberg & R. K. Wagner (Eds.), *Practical intelligence: Nature and origins of competence in the everyday world* (pp. 84–116). New York: Cambridge University Press.

Fuller, R. G., Bergström, R. F., Carpenter, E. T., Corzine, H. J., McShane, J. A., Miller, D. W., Moshman, D. S., Narveson, R. D., Petr, J. L., Thornton, M. C., & Williams, V. G. (Eds.). (1980). *Piagetian programs in higher education.* Lincoln, NE: ADAPT Program.

Gage, F. A. (1940). A unit of propaganda analysis. *Social Education, 6,* 483–488.

Gagne, R. (1967). *Science—a process approach: Purposes, accomplishments, expectations.* Washington, DC: American Association for the Advancement of Science, Commission on Science Education.

Gagne, R. (1980). Learnable aspects of problem solving. *Educational Psychologist, 15,* 84–92.

Galotti, K. M. (1989). Approaches to studying formal and everyday reasoning. *Psychological Bulletin, 105,* 331–351.

Gans, R. (1940). *Critical reading comprehension in the intermediate grades.* New York: Columbia University Teachers College.

Geis, M. C., & Zwicky, A. M. (1971). On invited inferences. *Linguistic Inquiry, 2,* 561–566.

Giroux, H. (1978). Writing and critical thinking in the social studies. *Curriculum Inquiry, 8,* 291–310.

Glaser, E. M. (1941). *An experiment in the development of critical thinking.* New York: Columbia University Teachers College.

Glaser, E. M. (1985). Critical thinking: Education for responsible citizenship in a democracy. *National Forum, 65,* 24–27.

Glaser, R. (1984). Education and thinking: The role of knowledge. *American Psychologist, 39,* 93–104.

Glaser, R. (1990). Expertise. In M. W. Eysenck, A. Ellis, & E. Hunt (Eds.), *The Blackwell dictionary of cognitive psychology* (pp. 139–142). Oxford: Basil/Blackwell.

Glass, A. L., Holyoak, A. J., & Santa, J. L. (1979). *Cognition.* Reading, MA: Addison-Wesley.

Glatthorn, A. A., & Baron, J. (1985). In A. L. Costa (Ed.), *Developing minds: A resource book for teaching thinking.* Alexandria, VA: Association for Supervision and Curriculum Development.

Greeno, J. G. (1980). Trends in the theory of knowledge for problem solving. In D. T. Tuma & F. Reif (Eds.), *Problem solving and education: Issues in teaching and research* (pp. 9–23). Hillsdale, NJ: Erlbaum.

Guilford, J. P. (1967). *The nature of human intelligence.* New York: McGraw-Hill.

Guilford, J. P., & Hoepfner, R. (1971). *The analysis of intelligence.* New York: McGraw-Hill.

Halpern, D. F. (1989). *Thought and knowledge: An introduction to critical thinking* (2nd ed.). Hillsdale, NJ: Erlbaum.

Halpern, D. F. (1992). *A national assessment of critical thinking skills in adults: Taking steps toward the goal.* Paper commissioned by the U.S. Department of Education, Office of Educational Research and Improvement, Washington, DC.

Halpern, D. F. (in press). Assessing the effectiveness of critical thinking instruction. *Journal of General Education.*

Hayes, J. R. (1981). *The complete problem solver.* Philadelphia: Franklin Institute Press.

Haywood, H. C., Brooks, P. H., & Burns, S. (1986). *Stimulating cognitive development at developmental level: A tested, nonremedial preschool curriculum for preschoolers and older children.* Watertown, MA: Charlesbridge.

Henle, M. (1962). On the relation between logic and thinking. *Psychological Review, 69,* 366–378.

Herrnstein, R. J., Nickerson, R. S., de Sánchez, M., & Swets, J. A. (1986). Teaching thinking skills. *American Psychologist, 41,* 1279–1289.

Howell, W. C., & Cooke, M. J. (1989). Training the human information process: A look at cognitive models. In I. E. Goldstein (Ed.), *Training and development in work organizations: Frontiers of industrial and organizational psychology* (pp. 121–182). San Francisco: Jossey-Bass.

Howell, W. S. (1943). The effects of high school debating on critical thinking. *Speech Monographs, 10,* 96–113.

Jacobs, P. I., & Vandeventer, M. (1971). The learning and transfer of double-classification skills: A replication and extension. *Journal of Experimental Child Psychology, 12,* 240–257.

Jacobs, P. I. & Vandeventer, M. (1972). Evaluating the teaching of intelligence. *Educational and Psychological Measurement, 32,* 235–248.

Johnson-Laird, P. N. (1982). Thinking as a skill. *Quarterly Journal of Experimental Psychology, 34A,* 1–29.

Johnson-Laird, P. N. (1983). *Mental models.* Cambridge, MA: Harvard University Press.

Jones, B. F., & Idol, L. (1990). *Dimensions of thinking and cognitive instruction.* Hillsdale, NJ: Erlbaum.

Joyce, B. (1985). Models for teaching thinking. *Educational Leadership, 42,* 4–7.

Kagan, J. (1966). Reflection-impulsivity: The generality and dynamics of conceptual tempo. *Journal of Abnormal Psychology, 71,* 17–24.

Kahane, H. (1992). *Logic and contemporary rhetoric: The use of reason in everyday life* (6th ed.) Belmont, CA: Wadsworth.

Kasarda, J. D. (1988). Population and employment change in the United States: Past, present, and future. In *A look ahead: Year 2020* (Special Report No. 220). Washington, DC: National Research Council, Transportation Research Board.

Klahr, D. (1978). Goal formation, planning, and learning by pre-school problem solvers, or: My socks are in the dryer. In R. S. Siegler (Ed.), *Children's thinking: What develops?* (pp. 181–212). Hillsdale, NJ: Erlbaum.

Klausmeier, H. J., with the assistance of Sipple, T. S. (1980). *Learning and teaching concepts—a strategy for testing applications of theory.* New York: Academic Press.

Kraft, P. (1987). Computers and the automation of work. In R. E. Kraut (Ed.), *Technology and the transformation of white collar work* (pp. 99–111). Hillsdale, NJ: Erlbaum.

Kraut, R. E. (1987). Social issues and white-collar technology: An overview. In R. E. Kraut (Ed.), *Technology and the transformation of white-collar work* (pp. 1–21). Hillsdale, NJ: Erlbaum.

Kurtz, B. E., & Borkowski, J. G. (1987). Development of strategic skill in impulsive and reflective children: A longitudinal study of metacognition. *Journal of Experimental Child Psychology, 43,* 129–148.

Lampert, M. (1986). Teaching multiplication. *Journal of Mathematical Behavior, 5,* 241–280.

Lapointe, A., Mead, N., & Phillips, G. (1989). *A world of differences.* Princeton, NJ: Educational Testing Service.

Larkin, J. H. (1979). Information processing models and science instruction. In J. Lochhead & J. Clement (Eds.), *Cognitive process instruction: Research on teaching thinking skills.* Philadelphia: Franklin Institute Press.

Larkin, J. H. (1983). Mechanisms of effective problem representation in physics. *C.I.P. 434,* Pittsburgh: Carnegie Mellon University.

Larkin, J. H., McDermott, J., Simon, D. P., & Simon, H. A. (1980a). Expert and novice performance in solving physics problems. *Science, 208,* 1335–1342.

Larkin, J. H., McDermott, J., Simon, D. P., & Simon, H. A. (1980b). Modes of competence in solving physics problems. *Cognitive Science, 4,* 317–345.

Lehman, D. R., Lempert, R. R., & Nisbett, R. E. (1988). The effects of graduate training on reasoning: Formal discipline and thinking about everyday events. *American Psychologist, 43,* 431–443.

Lesgold, A. M. (1984). Acquiring expertise. In J. R. Anderson & S. M. Kosslyn (Eds.), *Tutorials in learning and memory.* San Francisco: Freeman.

Lipman, M. (1991). *Thinking in education.* New York: Cambridge University Press.

Lipman, M., Sharp, A. M., & Oscanyan, F. (1980). *Philosophy in the classroom.* Philadelphia: Temple University Press.

Macdonald, R. R. (1986). Credible conceptions and implausible probabilities. *British Journal of Mathematical and Statistical Psychology, 39,* 15–27.

Marzano, R. J. (1986). *An evaluation of the McREL thinking skills programs.* Aurora, CO: Mid-continental Regional Educational Laboratory.

Marzano, R. J., & Arredondo, D. E. (1986). *Tactics for thinking.* Auroa, CO: Mideast Regional Educational Laboratory.

Marzano, R. J., Brandt, R. S., Huges, C. S., Jones, B. F., Preisseisen, B. Z., Rankin, S. C., & Suhor, C. (1988). *Dimensions of thinking: A framework for curriculum and instruction.* Alexandria, VA: Association for Supervision and Curriculum Development.

Mason, J., Burton, L., & Stacey, K. (1985). *Thinking mathematically* (rev. ed.). Reading, MA: Addison-Wesley.

McKinnon, J. W., & Renner, J. W. (1971). Are colleges concerned with intellectual development? *American Journal of Psychology, 39,* 1047–1052.

McPeck, J. (1981). *Critical thinking and education.* Oxford: Martin Robinson.

McTighe, J., & Schollengberger, J. (1985). Why teach thinking: A statement of rationale. In A. L. Costa (Ed.), *Developing minds: A resource book for teaching thinking* (pp. 3–6). Alexandria, VA: Association for Supervision and Curriculum Development.

Meeker, M. N. (1969). *The structure of intellect: Its interpretation and uses.* Columbus, OH: Charles E. Merrill.

Metcalf, L. E., DeBoer, J. J., & Kaulfers, W. V. (Eds.). (1966). *Secondary education: A textbook of readings.* Boston: Allyn & Bacon.

Midwest Publications (1981). *Mind benders.* Pacific Grove, CA: Midwest Publications.

Minstrell, J. (1982). Conceptual development research in the natural setting of the classroom. In M. B. Rowe (Ed.), *Education in the 80s—Science.* Washington, DC: National Education Association.

Morse, S. W. (1989). *Renewing civic capacity: Preparing college students for service and citizenship.* 1989 ASHE-ERIC Higher Education Reports.

Mulcahy, R. F., Short, R. H., & Andrews, J. (Eds.). (1991). *Enhancing learning and thinking.* New York: Praeger.

Murray, E. (1944). Conflicting assumptions. *Mathematics Teacher, 37,* 57–63.

National Assessment of Educational Progress (NAEP). (1981). *Reading, thinking, and writing: Results from the 1979–1980 national assessment of reading and literature* (Report No. 11-L-01). Denver, CO: Education Commission of the States.

National Assessment of Educational Progress (NAEP). (1983). *The third national mathematics assessment: Results, trends, and issues* (Report No. 13-MA-01). Denver, CO: Education Commission of the States.

National Commission on Excellence in Education. (1983). *A nation at risk: The imperative for educational reform.* Washington, DC: U.S. Government Printing Office.

National Education Association. (1938). *The purpose of education in American democracy.* Washington, DC: U.S. Government Printing Office.

National Educational Goals Panel. (1991). *The national educational goals report.* Washington, DC: U.S. Government Printing Office.

Newell, A., & Simon, H. A. (1972). *Human problem solving.* Englewood Cliffs, NJ: Prentice-Hall.

Newmann, F. M. (1970). *Clarifying public controversy.* Boston: Little, Brown.

Newmann, F. M. (1991). Higher order thinking in the teaching of social studies: Connections between theory and practice. In J. F. Voss, D. N. Perkins, & J. W. Segal (Eds.), *Informal reasoning and education* (pp. 381–400). Hillsdale, NJ: Erlbaum.

Nickerson, R. S. (1986). *Reflections on reasoning.* Hillsdale, NJ: Erlbaum.

Nickerson, R. S. (1987). Why teach thinking? In J. B. Baron & R. J. Sternberg (Eds.), *Teaching thinking skills: Theory and practice* (pp. 27–38). New York: Freeman.

Nickerson, R. S. (1988). Practical intelligence. *American Journal of Psychology, 101,* 293–302. [Review of R. J. Sternberg & R. K. Wagner (Eds.). (1986). *Practical intelligence.* New York: Cambridge University Press.]

Nickerson, R. S. (1988–1989). On improving thinking through instruction. In E. Z. Rothkopf (Ed.), *Review of research in education* (Vol. 15, pp. 3–58). Washington, DC: American Educational Research Association.

Nickerson, R. S. (1990). Dimensions of thinking: A critique. In B. F. Jones & L. Idol. (Eds.), *Dimensions of thinking and cognitive instruction* (pp. 495–509). Hillsdale, NJ: Erlbaum.

Nickerson, R. S. (1991). Modes and models of informal reasoning: A commentary. In J. F. Voss, D. N. Perkins, & J. W. Segal (Eds.), *Informal reasoning and education* (pp. 291–309). Hillsdale, NJ: Erlbaum.

Nickerson, R. S., Perkins, D. N., & Smith, E. E. (1985). *The teaching of thinking.* Hillsdale, NJ: Erlbaum.

Nisbett, R. E. (Ed.). (1993). *Rules for reasoning.* Hillsdale, NJ: Erlbaum.

Nisbett, R. E., Fong, G. T., Lehman, D. R., & Cheng, P. W. (1987). Teaching reasoning. *Science, 238,* 625–631.

Nisbett, R. E., & Ross, I. (1980). *Human inference: Strategies and shortcomings of social judgment.* Englewood Cliffs, NJ: Prentice-Hall.

Novak, G. (1977). Representations of knowledge in a program for solving physics problems. *International Joint Conference on Artificial Intelligence, 5*, 286–291.

O'Reilly, K. (1983–1985). *Critical thinking in American history* (Vols. 1–4). Pacific Grove, CA: Midwest Publications.

Parish, J. M., & Ericksen, M. T. A. (1981). A comparison of cognitive strategies in modifying the cognitive style of impulsive third-grade children. *Cognitive Therapy and Research, 5,* 71–78.

Patterson, R. S., & Jamieson, S. I. (1991). Exploring the teaching of thinking skills in history. In R. F. Mulcahy, R. H. Short, & J. Andrews (Eds.), *Enhancing learning and thinking* (pp. 123–136). New York: Praeger.

Paul, R. (1984). Critical thinking: Fundamental to education for a free society. *Educational Leadership, 42,* 4–14.

Paul, R. (1992). *Critical thinking: What every person needs to know in a rapidly changing world.* Sonoma, CA: Foundation for Critical Thinking.

Perkins, D. N., Farady, M., & Bushey, B. (1991). Everyday reasoning and the roots of intelligence. In J. F. Voss, D. N. Perkins, & J. W. Segal (Eds.), *Informal reasoning and education* (pp. 83–106). Hillsdale, NJ: Erlbaum.

Peters, R. S. (1973). *Reason and compassion.* London: Routledge & Kegan Paul.

Polya, G. (1954). *Mathematics and plausible reasoning: Vol. 1. Induction and analogy in mathematics.* Princeton, NJ: Princeton University Press.

Polya, G. (1957). *How to solve it: A new aspect of mathematical method.* Garden City, NY: Doubleday. (Original work published 1945)

Postman, N. (1985). Critical thinking in the electronic era. *National Forum, 65,* 4–8.

Poundstone, W. (1990). *Labyrinths of reason.* New York: Doubleday.

Presseisen, B. Z. (1986). *Critical thinking and thinking skills: State of the art definitions and practice in public schools.* Philadelphia: Research for Better Schools.

Presseisen, B. Z. (1987). *Thinking skills throughout the curriculum: A conceptual design.* Bloomington, IN: Pi Lamda Theta.

Presseisen, B. Z. (Ed.). (1988). *At-risk students and thinking: Perspectives from research.* Washington, DC: National Education Association.

Price, M. A. (1991). Teaching thinking to preschoolers. In R. F. Mulcahy, R. H. Short, & J. Andrews (Eds.), *Enhancing learning and thinking* (pp. 53–65). New York: Praeger.

Reich, R. B. (1983). *The next American frontier.* New York: Times Books.

Reid, W. A. (1987). Institutions and practices: Professional education reports and the language of reform. *Educational Researcher, 16*(8), 10–15.

Resnick, L. B. (1987). *Education and learning to think.* Washington, DC: National Academy Press.

Revlis, R. (1975). Syllogistic reasoning: Logical decisions from a complex data base. In R. Falmagne (Ed.), *Reasoning: Representation and process.* Hillsdale, NJ: Erlbaum.

Roberge, J. J. (1970). A study of children's abilities to reason with basic principles of deductive reasoning. *American Educational Research Journal, 7,* 583–596.

Rosnick, P., & Clement, J. (1980). Learning without understanding: The effect of tutoring strategies on algebra misconceptions. *Journal of Mathematical Behavior, 3,* 3–27.

Rubenstein, M. F. (1975). *Patterns of problem solving.* Englewood Cliffs, NJ: Prentice-Hall.

Ruggiero, V. R. (1984). *The art of thinking: A guide to critical and creative thought.* New York: Harper & Row.

Saranson, S. B. (1971). *The culture of the school and the problem of change.* Boston: Allyn & Bacon.

Savell, J. M., Twohig, P. T., & Rachford, D. L. (1986). Empirical status of Feuerstein's "Instrumental Enrichment" (FIE) technique as a method of teaching thinking skills. *Review of Educational Research, 56,* 389–409.

Saxe, J. (1990). *Culture and cognitive development: Studies in mathematical understanding.* Hillsdale, NJ: Erlbaum.

Schrag, F. (1987). Thoughtfulness: Is high school the place for thinking? *Newsletter, National Center on Effective Secondary Schools, 2*, 2–4.

Schoenfeld, A. (1983). Episodes and executive decisions in mathematical problem solving instruction. In H. P. Ginsberg (Ed.), *The development of mathematical thinking*. New York: Academic Press.

Schoenfeld, A. (1985). *Mathematical problem solving*. New York: Academic Press.

Schwebel, M., & Maher, C. A. (Eds.). (1986). *Facilitating cognitive development: International perspectives, programs, and practices*. New York: Haworth Press.

Scribner, S. (1986). Thinking in action: Some characteristics of practical thought. In R. J. Sternberg & R. K. Wagner (Eds.), *Practical intelligence: Nature and origins of competence in the everyday world*. (pp. 13–30). New York: Cambridge University Press.

Secretary's Commission on Achieving Necessary Skills. (1992, April). *Learning a living: A blueprint for high performance*. Washington, DC: U.S. Department of Labor.

Simon, D. P., & Simon, H. A. (1978). Individual differences in solving problems. In R. S. Siegler (Ed.), *Children's thinking: What develops?* Hillsdale, NJ: Erlbaum.

Simon, H. A. (1980). Problem solving and education. In D. T. Tuma & R. Reif (Eds.), *Problem solving and education: Issues in teaching and research*. Hillsdale, NJ: Erlbaum.

Sternberg, R. J. (1983). Components of human intelligence. *Cognition, 15*, 1–48.

Sternberg, R. J. (1985). Instrumental and componential approaches to the nature and training of intelligence. In S. F. Chipman, J. W. Segal, & R. Glaser (Eds.), *Thinking and learning skills: Vol. 2. Research and open questions*. Hillsdale, NJ: Erlbaum.

Sternberg, R. J. (1986a). *Intelligence applied: Understanding and increasing your intellectual skills*. New York: Harcourt Brace Jovanovich.

Sternberg, R. J. (1986b). Toward a unified theory of human reasoning. *Intelligence, 10*, 281–314.

Sternberg, R. J., & Davidson, J. E. (1987). Teaching thinking to college students: Some lessons learned from experience. *Teaching Thinking and Problem Solving, 9*(1–2), 10–11.

Sternberg, R. J., & Wagner, R. K. (Eds.). (1986). *Practical intelligence: Nature and origins of competence in the everyday world*. New York: Cambridge University Press.

Stevenson, H. W. (1992). Learning from Asian schools. *Scientific American, 267*(6), 70–76.

Stevenson, H. W., Chen, C., & Lee, S.-Y. (1993). Mathematics achievement of Chinese, Japanese, and American children: Ten years later. *Science, 259*, 53–58.

Swartz, R. J. (1987). Teaching for thinking: A developmental model for the infusion of thinking skills into mainstream instruction. In J. B. Baron & R. J. Sternberg (Eds.), *Teaching thinking skills: Theory and practice* (pp. 106–126). New York: Freeman.

Swartz, R. J. (1991). Structure teaching for critical thinking and reasoning in standard subject area instruction. In J. F. Voss, D. N. Perkins, & J. W. Segal (Eds.), *Informal reasoning and education* (pp. 415–450). Hillsdale, NJ: Erlbaum.

Sweller, J., Mawer, R. F., & Ward, M. R. (1983). Development of expertise in mathematical problem solving. *Journal of Experimental Psychology: General, 122*, 639–661.

Thorndike, E. L. (1913). *The psychology of learning*. New York: Mason-Henry.

Torgeson, J. K., & Licht, B. G. (1983). The LD child as an interactive learner: Retrospects and prospects. In K. D. Gadow & I. Bialer (Eds.), *Advances in learning and behavioral disabilities*. Greenwich, CT: JAI Press.

Tversky, A., & Kahneman, D. (1974). Judgment and uncertainty: Heuristics and biases. *Science, 185*, 1124–1131.

U.S. Department of Labor. (1987). Apprenticeship 2000. *Federal Register, 52*(231), 45905–45908.

Van Lehn, K. (1989). Problem solving and cognitive skill acquisition. In M. I. Posner (Ed.), *Foundations of cognitive science* (pp. 527–580). Cambridge, MA: MIT Press.

Voss, J. F. (1991). Informal reasoning and international relations. In J. F. Voss, D. N. Perkins, & J. W. Segal (Eds.), *Informal reasoning and education* (pp. 37–58). Hillsdale, NJ: Erlbaum.

Vye, N. J., Delclos, V. R., Burns, S., & Bransford, J. D. (1988). In R. J. Sternberg & E. E. Smith (Eds.), *The psychology of thought* (pp. 337–365). New York: Cambridge University Press.

Wales, C. E., Nardi, A. H., & Stager, R. A. (1986). *Professional decision-making*. Morgantown, WV: Center for Guided Design.

Waller, B. N. (1988). *Critical thinking: Consider the verdict*. Englewood Cliffs, NJ: Prentice Hall.

Wason, P. C. (1966). Reasoning. In B. M. Foss (Ed.), *New Horizons in psychology I*. Harmondsworth, UK: Penguin.

Wheeler, D. D., & Dember, W. N. (Eds.). (1979). *A practicum in thinking*. Cincinnati, OH: University of Cincinnati.

Whimbey, A., & Lochhead, J. (1982). *Problem solving and comprehension* (3rd ed.). Philadelphia: Franklin Institute Press.

Wickelgren, W. A. (1974). *How to solve problems*. San Francisco: Freeman.

Wilson, H. E. (1942). Developing skill in critical thinking through participation in school and community life. In H. R. Anderson (Ed.), *Teaching critical thinking in the social studies* (13th yearbook). Washington, DC: National Council for the Social Studies.

Index

Wechsler Adult Intelligence Scale, 273
Wertheimer, Max, 16
Whole Number Rule, 348
Working backwards, in problem solving, 426
Working memory, 21

Work samples, judgments, 322–323
Wundt, Wilhelm, 5–7, 9, 41–43

Y

Yerkes, R. M., 24